News
Reporting
and Writing

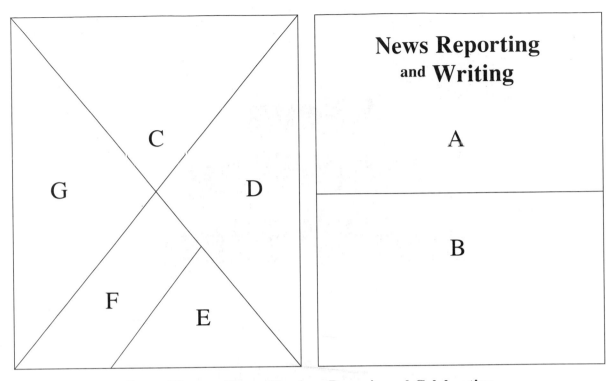

News Reporting and Writing

Cover Photos: Hope, Tension, Despair and Celebration

The photographs on the front and back covers of the seventh edition of *News Reporting and Writing* illustrate the scope and variety of the journalist's work.

(A) Enrique Valentin of *The Miami Herald* took this photograph of young men fleeing Cuba on their makeshift raft. One rafter prays for their rescue.

(B) This is the moment of decision for these young football players as their team captain ponders whether to try for the first down or to play it safe and punt. Ray Saint Germain took this photograph for the *Daily Ledger Dispatch* of Antioch, Calif.

Journalism is the story of how we live now, and these portraits on the back cover capture the events journalists cover in their wide-ranging reporting:

(C) A somber Haitian holds a commemorative flower as his country charts the difficult transition to democracy in this photo by Patrick Farrell of *The Miami Herald*.

(D) To celebrate their fifteenth birthday, Mexican-American young women are honored by the Quinceañera. Betty Tichich of the *Houston Chronicle* photographed this happy birthday celebrant.

(E) The horror of Rwanda is captured in this photograph of a dying child. Given the name Eric by hospital workers, the child was one of tens of thousands of innocents caught in the murderous tribal warfare. Pim Van Hemmen took the photograph for *The Star-Ledger* of Newark, N.J.

(F) Mike Roemer's photograph of a Lakota Sioux youngster dancing at a tribal ceremony was taken for the *Argus Leader* of Sioux Falls, S.D.

(G) Tony Miceli snapped this photograph of an Alpha Sigma Alpha member and her sorority's mascot during the annual Greek Sing on the Northwest Missouri State University campus. The picture appeared in the school yearbook, the *Tower*.

McGraw-Hill

A Division of The McGraw-Hill Companies

Book Team

Executive Publisher   *Edgar J. Laube*
Project Editor   *Kassi Radomski*
Publishing Services Coordinator   *Peggy Selle*
Proofreading Coordinator   *Carrie Barker*
Art Editor   *Miriam Hoffman*
Production Manager   *Beth Kundert*
Production/Imaging and Media Development Manager   *Linda Meehan Avenarius*
Production/Costing Manager   *Sherry Padden*
Visuals/Design Freelance Specialist   *Mary L. Christianson*
Marketing Manager   *Amy Halloran*
Copywriter   *Sandy Hyde*

Basal Text   *10/12 Times Roman*
Display Type   *Futura*
Typesetting System   *Macintosh™*
          QuarkXPress™
Paper Stock   *45# Bulkton*
Production Services   *Impressions*
          Book and Journal Services, Inc.

Executive Vice President and General Manager   *Bob McLaughlin*
Vice President, Business Manager   *Russ Domeyer*
Vice President of Production and New Media Development   *Victoria Putman*
National Sales Manager   *Phil Rudder*
National Telesales Director   *John Finn*

The credits section for this book begins on page 685 and is considered an extension of the copyright page.

Cover design by Lesiak/Crampton Design, Inc.

Photo research by Shirley Lanners

Copyedited by Sarah Lane

Proofread by Ann M. Kelly

Library of Congress Catalog Card Number: 95–83695

ISBN 0–697–28901–X

Printed in the United States of America

10   9   8   7   6   5   4   3

News
Reporting
and Writing

Seventh Edition

Melvin Mencher
Columbia University

Boston, Massachusetts   Burr Ridge, Illinois   Dubuque, Iowa
Madison, Wisconsin   New York, New York   San Francisco, California   St. Louis, Missouri

Contents

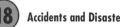

Preface

News Reporting and Writing, Seventh Edition, proposes to teach the beginner how to become a practicing journalist. Learning to report accurately and to write precisely and vigorously are no simple tasks. The young man or woman who would join the ranks of journalists must learn and then put into practice principles and concepts that have been developed over the years by practitioners who understand first, that truth is elusive and second, that its pursuit and capture on paper require mastery of a demanding discipline.

To explain and illustrate these principles, we will spend a lot of time with truth seekers—another way to describe good journalists—on newspapers and at broadcast stations as they go about their work. We will accompany a young reporter as he conducts his first interview, and we will watch an experienced reporter cover a racial confrontation. We will overhear another reporter's thinking as she works out the lead to her story about a city council meeting.

We will sit in the press box with reporters covering high school football and major league baseball games. We will join a police reporter as she makes her rounds and races to a triple murder.

We will watch a reporter labor over his story until "little beads of blood form on his forehead," as Red Smith described the agony of the journalist's search for the words that will accurately portray the event. And we will share in the reporter's joy when the story is finished and is given a byline and placed on the front page.

In other words, we will be concerned with the processes of reporting and writing—how reporters gather information from sources and from their observations, how they verify the material, and how they put it together in stories.

The journalists we will be watching work for small newspapers in Iowa, South Dakota and Oregon, and they are on the staffs of metropolitan dailies in Chicago and Los Angeles. One reporter writes for a network television station in New York; another covers local events for a television station in San Francisco. We will see how general assignment reporters and the men and women assigned to cover politics, sports, business, the police, city hall, education and other beats do their jobs.

Covering a Rotary Club luncheon speech or the president's State of the Union address, the journalist follows the same basic processes. The general assignment reporter in a town of 25,000 and the AP's White House correspondent share a way of thinking, a set of techniques and an approach to journalism.

We will see that these journalists also share an ethic that directs and gives meaning to their work. The literary critic Northrop Frye could have been describing journalistic morality: "The persistence of keeping the mind in a state of disciplined sanity, the courage of facing results that may deny or contradict everything that one had hoped to achieve—these are obviously moral qualities, if the phrase means anything at all."

Mary McGrory, the Washington columnist, described another aspect of the journalist's approach to his or her work in comments she made after interviewing 45 journalists who had applied for Nieman Fellowships at Harvard. She said she found these journalists to have a "great deal of commitment and compassion." Most had a trait in common, she said: "They knew a great deal about what they were doing. They did not think it enough."

In our journey to look at the work of journalists, we will pause for the photographs of Donna Ferrato. As she became increasingly alarmed at the growing abuse of women and children, she found that some material had been written on the topic but there was almost no photographic documentation. She was determined to show domestic abuse, although editors told her that "domestic violence wasn't important," she says.

"The more I saw, the more I knew that I had to get their stories out so that people would care about them," Ferrato says.

She took photographs of the victims, and, slowly, gradually, editors used them. And people cared. Her work helped to place domestic abuse on the public agenda. As a result of her photojournalism, an enlightened public insisted on stricter laws and their enforcement.

The journalists I know—my former colleagues and students, from whom I have shamelessly taken time and borrowed ideas—would shrink at being described as moralists. Yet they consider their work to have a large moral component. Most of them worry about the abuse of power.

Although adversary journalism is often criticized and sometimes ignored, it is as old as the Republic. In our third century as a nation, we must remember that today's journalists are descended from a press described by the historian Robert A. Ruthland as "obstreperous newspapers (that) signalled the rise of a new kind of journalism in America that would not truckle long to any officialdom."

The journalist knows that democracy is healthiest when the public is informed about the activities of captains of industry and chieftains in public office. Only with adequate information can people check those in power. Repression and ignorance are the consequences of unbridled power. Walt Whitman, journalist and poet, described the fragility of democracy and its source of strength this way: "There is no week nor day nor hour when tyranny may not enter upon this country, if the people lose their supreme confidence in themselves—and lose their roughness and spirit of defiance."

Confident, rough and defiant. An apt description of the journalist—but also characteristics that have aroused public animosity. In its role as watchdog for the public, the press has been attacked by those it has relentlessly scrutinized.

Power of Knowing. "Knowledge will govern ignorance, and a people who mean to be their own governors must arm themselves with the power knowledge gives. A popular government without popular information or the means of acquiring it is but a prologue to a farce or a tragedy or perhaps both."—James Madison

Journalists know that the path of the truth teller is not always smooth, that people are sometimes disturbed by what they do not want to hear. Journalists also know that many in their audience prefer entertainment to information.

Over the past 25 years, the number of daily newspapers has declined from 1,748 to 1,585. Readership has dropped among those ages 21 to 35, the young men and women considered society's big spenders, thus attractive to advertisers, the lifeblood of the mass media.

The consequence has been alarm and retreat. Journalists are urged to look to what have been regarded as the peripheral areas of journalism: graphics, short features, color, layout and design.

As this seventh edition moves into classrooms and newsrooms, students and practitioners are being counseled to provide "reader-friendly news"—stories about food, fitness, investing, dieting. Celebrity stories abound. Television news-magazine shows—sexy blends of fiction and fact—are big on television. Christopher Lasch, a cultural historian, says, "Much of the press, in its eagerness to inform the public, has become a conduit for the equivalent of junk mail."

Despite the fear-driven urge to seek the lowest common denominator, newspapers and television programs that offer their readers and viewers telling insights into contemporary society remain in sound financial condition. We will visit the newsrooms of these newspapers and drop in on Ted Koppel's "Nightline," whose executive producer tells us, "People turn on 'Nightline' to find out if there's something they need to know. . . . They aren't interested in being entertained. 'Nightline' has its largest audiences when there is real news," says Tom Bettag.

"At a time when television has gone more and more down the tabloid road, 'Nightline' has differentiated itself by refusing to take that route." The result: "It is a big commercial success for ABC," Bettag says.

The newspapers and stations and magazines that do not skimp on hiring a full and competent local staff, that do not flinch from taking on powerful adversaries—whether in a corporate boardroom or city hall—are healthy despite the uncertainties of the economy.

This seventh edition is offered to students with a commitment to and a belief in the traditional role of the press as the means of enabling people to improve their lot and to govern themselves intelligently through robust debate on relevant issues. It takes seriously the comment in the Book of Proverbs: "The instruments of both life and death are contained within the power of the tongue."

The kind of journalism that animates this textbook can be described as public-service journalism. It has a long and glorious history that was expressed well by Charles Dickens in his crusading newspaper *Household Words*. Week after week, Dickens poured into his newspaper his indignation at the indecencies visited on the young, the poor and the powerless.

Dickens' biographer, Edgar Johnson, described the novelist-journalist-editor as practicing an "uncompromising humanitarian radicalism." Dickens visited orphanages, saw for himself the conditions of homeless women. He urged schooling for the young born into poverty.

Dickens said his ambition as an editor was that his newspaper "be admitted into many homes with confidence and affection," and it was. Johnson says the result of Dickens' crusades was a "huge and steadily growing audience ranging in both directions from the middle and upper middle classes."

One of the premises of this book is that journalists do not write writing; they write reporting. The vitality of democracy depends on a press that is able to grasp the complexities of modern society and communicate them intelligibly to the public, on a press that puts important issues on the public agenda.

Consequently, I have resisted advice to delete some of the more difficult subject areas and replace them with more writing tips, and I have declined suggestions that I jazz up the appearance of this edition. *News Reporting and Writing* will have to stand on the merits—or the inadequacies—of its content as a guide to serious journalism.

Journalism has always had its down periods, and there has been no shortage of nostrums offered for a quick cure. Its survival, however, has rested on the bedrock of its tradition. Albert Camus, the French journalist and author, was sustained by that sense of his calling during the Nazi occupation of France when he wrote from the underground. Accepting the Nobel Prize for literature in 1957, Camus said, "Whatever our personal frailties may be, the nobility of our calling will always be rooted in two commitments difficult to observe: refusal to lie about what we know and resistance to oppression."

In much of what the journalist does, there is an awareness of the relevance of his or her work to human needs and purposes, for the reporter knows that news represents reality to most people. The reporter is interested in ideas but avoids the sin of making the concrete abstract.

Journalism "is something more than a craft, something other than an industry, something between an art and a ministry," says Wickham Steed, an editor of *The Times* of London. "Journalists proper are unofficial public servants whose purpose is to serve the community."

My model for this amalgam of artist, sentry, public servant and town crier is Ralph M. Blagden, who taught a generation of journalists their duty and introduced them to the power and splendor of their native language. Ralph's classrooms were the newsrooms of newspapers from New Hampshire to California, where he worked as reporter and editor.

Ralph was my competitor as a state capitol correspondent, and never was there such a mismatch. As a beginning reporter, I reported what people said and did and stopped there. Ralph generously took the youngster in tow and showed him that a good reporter never settles for the surface of the news, that the compelling commandment of the journalist is to dig out the truth. He refused to make reporting divisible: All good reporting is investigative reporting, he insisted.

Long before investigative reporting became the fashion, Ralph was digging out documents and records to disclose truths. His journalism was in the tradition of Joseph Pulitzer and that publisher's crusading editor, O.K. Bovard. Those of us who were fortunate to work with Ralph feel ourselves to be members of a journalistic family whose roots are embedded in a noble tradition.

Benjamin C. Bradlee of *The Washington Post* says of Blagden:

> Ralph taught me to be dissatisfied with answers and to be exhaustive in questions. He taught me to stand up against powers that be. He taught me to spot bullies and resist them. He taught me about patience and round-the-clock work. He taught me about ideas and freedom and rights—all of this with his own mixture of wit and sarcasm and articulate grace. He could also throw a stone farther than I could, which annoys me to this day.

Bradlee, who directed the *Post*'s coverage of the Watergate story that earned his newspaper a Pulitzer Prize for meritorious public service, recalls his first story for Blagden when he was a young reporter.

"It had to do with the post-war housing mess, and he made me rewrite it 16 times. I've never done that to a reporter, but I suspect I should have. He had a great dollop of righteous indignation, which I learned to admire enormously.

"And of course he wrote with style and punch and clarity."

I recall the first story I covered with Ralph. He had heard that patients in a state hospital for the mentally ill were being mistreated. Some had mysteriously died. We interviewed doctors, nurses, attendants and former patients, and we walked through the wards and corridors of the institution. I learned that second-hand accounts are just a starting point, that direct observation and other techniques of verification are essential, and when we wrote the story I learned the power of the simple declarative sentence. I also learned that journalists can be useful members of society, for after the story appeared and both of us had moved on, the state built a modern hospital to replace that aging snake pit.

Acknowledgments

News Reporting and Writing was written in the belief that journalism is a moral enterprise and that this gives meaning to its practice. The morality of journalism can be taught, as it was by Ralph L. Crosman, Zell Mabee and A. Gayle Waldrop at the University of Colorado. Theirs was a journalism of commitment, compassion and conscience. Those of us who studied with them are forever in their debt.

I am also indebted to my former newsroom colleagues and to my students. They all have contributed to this book, some indirectly, like George Baldwin, my first city editor at *The Albuquerque Tribune,* and some directly, like Berkley Hudson, one of my former students, whose work is included here. I learned from the young woman who stormed out of my classroom when I said I would not assign her to a certain story because I worried about her safety, and I learned from the copy editor many years ago who had worn down a pencil putting black lines through my copy. "Just show us what the guy did," he told me. "Let the reader draw the conclusions."

For this seventh edition, I had the help of many colleagues. Elizabeth Brennan, the Columbia University Journalism Librarian, and Steve Toth of the university library tracked down clippings and citations with the enthusiasm and generosity that I have experienced from librarians everywhere. Sheila Thalhimer prepared the index. Wendy P. Shilton saved me from prolixity and grammatical blunders with her careful copy editing.

Special thanks to Bill and Diane Biggs, proprietors of the French River Trading Post, who generously allowed me the use of their office facilities.

The following colleagues made useful suggestions for this edition:

Warren Barnard
Indiana State University

Ben Burns
Wayne State University

James Crook
University of Tennessee

DeAnn Evans
University of Utah

Phil Ward
Louisiana State University

The following list acknowledges some of those who shared in the preparation of *News Reporting and Writing*. Only I bear responsibility for the contents.

Marjorie Arnold
The Fresno (Calif.) *Bee*

Brian Barrett
Office of the New York County
District Attorney

Frank Barrows
The Charlotte (N.C.) *Observer*

Barbara Belford
Columbia University

Tom Bettag
"Nightline"

Joan Bieder
Columbia University

Mervin Block
Broadcast writing coach

Art Carey
Bucks County (Pa.) *Courier Times*
Philadelphia Inquirer

Marcia Chambers
The New York Times

Kenneth Conboy
Coordinator of the New York City Criminal
Justice System

Claude Cookman
The Miami Herald

Robert A. Dubill
Executive Director,
Gannett News Service

Jack Dvorak
Indiana University

Julie Ellis
Freelance writer,
Photo researcher

Fred Endres
Kent State University

Heidi Evans
Daily News, New York City

Ellen Fleysher
WCBS-TV, New York City

Joseph Galloway
UPI

Mary Ann Giordano
Daily News, New York City

Joel M. Gora
American Civil Liberties Union

Sara Grimes
University of Massachusetts, Amherst

Susan Hands
The Charlotte Observer

Donna Hanover
WTVN-TV, Columbus, Ohio

Michael Hiltzik
Courier-Express, Buffalo, N.Y., and
Los Angeles Times

Louis E. Ingelhart
Ball State University

Thomas H. Jones
Chicago Sun-Times

E.W. Kenworthy
The New York Times

Jeff Klinkenberg
St. Petersburg Times

Eric Lawlor
The Houston Chronicle

Lynn Ludlow
San Francisco Examiner

Jack Marsh
Argus Leader, Sioux Falls, S.D.

Tony Mauro
Gannett News Service

John McCormally
The Hawk Eye, Burlington, Iowa

Frank McCulloch
The Sacramento Bee

Bill Mertens
The Hawk Eye, Burlington, Iowa

Alan Miller
University of Maine at Orono

John D. Mitchell
Syracuse University

Ellen Perlman
City & State

Merrill Perlman
The New York Times

L.D. Pinkham
University of Massachusetts at Amherst

Lew Powell
The Charlotte Observer

Ron Rapoport
Los Angeles Times, Chicago Sun-Times and
Los Angeles *Daily News*

Elizabeth Rhodes
The Charlotte (N.C.) *Observer* and
Seattle Times

Ronald Robinson
Augustana College, Sioux Falls, S.D.

Sam Roe
The Blade, Toledo, Ohio

Mort Saltzman
The Sacramento Bee

Sydney Schanberg
The New York Times

John Schultz
Columbia University

Wendy Shilton
University of Southern Maine, Portland

Allan M. Siegal
The New York Times

Eleanor Singer
Public Opinion Quarterly

Herbert Strentz
Drake University

Diana K. Sugg
The Sacramento Bee

Lena H. Sun
The Washington Post

Mike Sweet
The Hawk Eye, Burlington, Iowa

Jeffrey A. Tannenbaum
The Wall Street Journal

Bob Thayer
The Providence Journal

Jim Toland
San Francisco Chronicle

Carolyn Tuft
Belleville (Ill.) *News-Democrat*

Mary Voboril
The Miami Herald

Howard Weinberg
Executive producer, "Bill Moyers' Journal"

Jan Wong
The Globe and Mail, Toronto

Emerald Yeh
KRON-TV, San Francisco

The affiliations of the contributors are given as of the time of their assistance.

A Personal Word

Some of you may be thinking about the future, the kind of journalism you want to do, the station or newspaper that is the best place to launch a career in journalism.

Years ago, a reporter who had worked on several newspapers around the country advised a journalism student: "Find a small newspaper or station where you can keep learning, where you will be assigned to everything—schools, local politics, the courthouse, police, the city council and the Kiwanis Club."

Such advice is still given, and it's still sound. Why a small newspaper or station? Let Eugene Roberts, managing editor of *The New York Times,* answer the question. Roberts, who has his pick of job applicants, says he has a prejudice "in favor of the reporter who cut his professional teeth doing everything under the sun on a small newspaper.

"If you're on a paper of, say, less than 20,000 circulation, during the run of the year you're probably going to cover every conceivable type of story—trials and floods and politics and crime and breaking news and nonbreaking news and features."

Not every small newspaper or station is worth your time. Some are understaffed and do little more than slap at the news. But there are many good ones, and it isn't difficult to find out which they are.

These are the newspapers and stations that win awards for their reporting. The duPont-Columbia and George Foster Peabody Awards honor broadcast journalists; the Pulitzer Prizes and the Associated Press Managing Editors awards are for newspaper journalists. Many honors exist for both print and broadcast journalists, such as the George Polk Awards and the Sigma Delta Chi Awards of the Society of Professional Journalists.

Reading through professional publications such as *Broadcasting* and *Editor & Publisher,* you will come across pieces about the good work being done by smaller staffs. Ever hear of *The Winter Haven News Chief,* circulation 15,000? Probably not. This small central Florida daily newspaper was the subject of a long article in *Editor & Publisher. The News Chief* revealed that inadequate background checks were made of Florida teachers and, as a result, more than 35 convicted child molesters, rapists, drug sellers and other criminals were teaching children. After the stories appeared, a state law was adopted requiring more extensive background checks of applicants. Newspapers over the country followed the lead of the small Florida daily.

Opportunities ►

There are plenty of newspapers like *The News Chief* that beginners can look into. It is not difficult to find newspapers and stations that take pride in public service journalism.

Such newspapers and stations are the first step on the ladder. The next jump is to a medium-sized newspaper or station, and then, if you are interested in metropolitan journalism or foreign correspondence, the big stations and newspapers.

Some newspapers regularly figure in lists of the country's best newspapers. At the head of the list, invariably, is *The New York Times,* the nation's newspaper of record. It has a large Washington and foreign staff, and its national correspondents span the continent. Right behind are *The Washington Post* and *Los Angeles Times,* both likely to do more investigative reporting than *The New York Times. The Wall Street Journal* is considered the best written newspaper of all. Much more than a daily chronicle of business, the *Journal* offers excellent Washington coverage and has an enterprising staff of digging reporters. *The Miami Herald* is considered to offer the best coverage of Latin America. It is one of the crown jewels in a string of excellent newspapers operated by the Knight-Ridder newspaper chain.

The Philadelphia Inquirer, another Knight-Ridder newspaper, has stressed investigative journalism and has won many Pulitzer Prizes. *The Boston Globe, Newsday, Chicago Tribune, The Milwaukee Journal, The Courier-Journal* (Louisville, Ky.) and *St. Petersburg Times* are also among the nation's best.

Here are the call letters of some of the radio and television stations that have won prizes for outstanding reporting over the past few years:

KVUE-TV, Austin, Tex. WJZ-TV, Baltimore. WBRZ-TV, Baton Rouge, La. WGBH-TV, WCVB-TV, Boston. KGAN-TV, Cedar Rapids, Iowa. WBBM-TV, WMAQ-TV, WTTW-TV, Chicago. WVXU-FM, Cincinnati. WFFA-TV, KRLD-AM, Dallas. KBDI, Denver. KTVS-TV, Detroit. KSEE-TV, Fresno, Calif. KPRC-TV, KTRH-AM, Houston. WJXT-TV, Jacksonville, Fla. KAIT-TV, Jonesboro, Ark. KNX-AM, KNXT-TV, Los Angeles. WHAS, Louisville. WPLG-TV, Miami.

WCCO-TV, WTCN, Minneapolis. WSMV-TV, Nashville. WWL-AM, WWL-TV, New Orleans. WMTV-TV, Omaha. KWY, KWY-TV, WCAU-TV, Philadelphia. WRAL-TV, Raleigh. KSBW-TV, Salinas, Calif. KSL-TV, Salt Lake City. KCST-TV, San Diego. KGO-AM, KGO-TV, KRON-TV, KPIX-TV, San Francisco. KCTS-TV, KING-TV, Seattle. KMOX, KMOV, St. Louis. KGUN-TV, Tucson. KTUL-TV, Tulsa. WDVM-TV, WRC-TV, Washington, D.C. KWWL-TV, Waterloo, Iowa.

Race and sex are no longer barriers to media jobs. Most newspapers are committed to finding and hiring men and women of all races. In fact, women make up almost half of the new hires, and each year the percentage of minorities employed rises.

In the not-too distant past, women were confined to the so-called society section, and a black or Hispanic in the newsroom was a rarity. Some years ago, Nan Robertson applied for a transfer from *The New York Times* local staff to its Washington bureau. During her visit to Washington, Russell Baker turned to the bureau chief, James Reston, and asked, "Do I encourage her or discourage her,

Scotty?" Reston replied, "Discourage her." Robertson threatened to quit the paper, and the managing editor persuaded Reston to give Robertson a chance.

Much has changed. Today, a third of all journalists are female; the majority of reporters on small newspapers are female.

Minority journalists now constitute almost 11 percent of newsroom workers. About one-fourth of new hires are black, Hispanic, Native American or Asian American.

A study of newspapers with circulations under 25,000 showed that 90 percent hire graduates of journalism programs with no professional experience. The survey by Michael Shelly of Illinois State University found the editors looked for graduates with experience in desktop publishing and the computer, an internship experience and an academic grounding in history, political science, economics and English. Shelly says he found, "Most editors want plenty of hands-on experience and a good knowledge of language and of government."

◀ **Beginners**

Newspaper salaries for beginners on small papers average $300 to $400 a week. Those who start with medium-sized papers make $50 to $100 a week more, and those who start on a larger newspaper may make around $600 a week. Beginners in radio and television can expect to be offered about $300 a week.

◀ **Salaries**

With experience, salaries can climb sharply. Large newspapers pay good reporters $1–2,000 a week, and television anchors are in the six-figure bracket. Here are median salaries in various media areas in the late 1990s:

News magazines—$75,000
Television—$30,000
Wire services—$47,500
Daily newspapers—$40,000
Radio—$23,500
Weekly newspapers—$23,500

Money is important, but no one enters journalism to get rich. The rewards are elsewhere. As Ben Bradlee of *The Washington Post* puts it, "You can have tremendous impact. You can do things. You can get someone out of jail; you can put someone in jail; you can pass something; you cannot pass something . . . it's the way to make a difference."

Good Luck.

Part Opener Photos

Part One

"Make sure you get it down right," a nursing home resident tells a reporter for the *Duluth News-Tribune*.

Photo by Jack Rendulich, *Duluth News Tribune*.

Part Two

The flow from Mexico is unending. This woman is crossing the Rio Grande so that her child can be born in the United States.

Photo by Carlos Antonio Rios, *Houston Chronicle*.

Part Three

Mary Van Beusekom, the police reporter for the *Argus Leader* in Sioux Falls, S.D., races her deadline to finish a story about an arrest.

Photo by Greg Latza, *Argus Leader.*

Part Four

These exhausted runners console each other at the end of a race at the annual Montana high school meet.

Photo by Bob Zellar, *The Billings* (Mont.) *Gazette.*

Part Five

Firefighters attend to one of their own who was overcome in battling a blaze.

Photo by Dave Kline, *Eagle–Gazette,* Lancaster, Ohio.

Part Six

When *The Bakersfield Californian* published this photograph of a grieving family whose son had just drowned, the response was vigorously negative. Readers said the picture violated the family's privacy. The photographer replied it provided a powerful message for water safety.

Photo by John Harte, *The Bakersfield Californian*.

News
Reporting
and Writing

On the Job

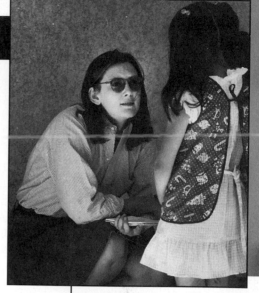

Chris Hardy,
San Francisco *Examiner*

Reporters seek out those affected by events.

Preview

Watching reporters at work, we see that they are:

- Hard working
- Enterprising
- Curious
- Dependable despite pressure
- Knowledgeable
- Compassionate
- Courageous

Reporters are tenacious in their search for facts that will give their readers and viewers information about events. They work quickly and efficiently against deadlines. They have a passion for accuracy and a determination to dig out all aspects of the story.

0461 OKOK (09:12AM)
BC-OK—APNewsAlert
Explosion hits federal courthouse in downtown Oklahoma City

Freeport Parent-Teacher Association discusses raising teacher salaries $2,000 a year.

The State Board of Education decides to ask the Planned Parenthood Federation to help it develop a program to educate high school students about AIDS.

A candidate for the city council says he opposes a proposed city park and recreation bond issue.

Five governors argue about water rights at an interstate water compact commission meeting.

A0522
URGENT
NAPLES, Italy (AP)—A NATO plane went down today in Bosnia, and a U.N. source said it was shot down over the Serb stronghold of Banja Luka.

Few people witness these events. But everyone will be able to read, see or hear about them this evening or tomorrow morning because a reporter is covering the news as it develops. The reporter is the link between the event and the reader, viewer or listener. The public sees the PTA debate through a reporter's eyes, hears the candidate's speech through a reporter's ears.

Even when people witness events, they want to savor the experience again and to have details they may have missed. The news story also provides interpretations and explanations. Readers want to know how the proposed salary scale for teachers will affect the property tax, whether the mayor opposes the bond issue, whether the AIDS program will involve distribution of condoms in the schools.

A tacit agreement exists between the reporter and the public:

1. **The reporter** does his or her best to give the listener, reader and viewer a complete and accurate account of the event. When the Oklahoma City federal courthouse was blown up, the entire Associated Press staff in Oklahoma City was mobilized, and additional reporters were flown in to cover the worst act of terrorism in the history of the United States.

With the first report of the downing of a NATO plane, reporters knew that people everywhere would want to know the country and the identity of the pilot. They pressed their sources for the complete identification, and two minutes after the URGENT had signed off, this appeared on AP wires:

> APNewsAlert.
> NATO says plane shot down in Bosnia was a U.S. F-16.

And then, within minutes, this lead moved:

> BULLETIN
> NAPLES, Italy (AP)—An American plane went down today in Bosnia, and a U.N. source said it was shot down over the Serb stronghold of Banja Luka.

2. **The public** presumes that the reporter's account is honestly and fully reported and written.

This agreement is important, for people act on what they read and hear:

A legal secretary in Utah, worried by the Oklahoma City terrorism, faxes one of her senators to switch his stand against stringent gun control legislation.

The last paragraph of the story on the Freeport Parent-Teacher Association meeting states that parents are invited to a dinner meeting Thursday at the local high school where teacher salaries will be discussed. A Freeport couple decides to attend.

A local parents' organization drafts a petition that opposes AIDS education in the high schools.

A mother of three small children, angered by the candidate's position on the park and recreation program, calls friends and tells them to vote against him.

Texas cattle ranchers wire their governor urging him to turn down the Colorado governor's proposal for water allotments.

Concerned about the fate of the downed U.S. airman, a California accountant starts a letter to his local newspaper in which he opposes the deployment in combat areas of U.S. personnel by the United Nations.

Reporters stay with these stories. Knowing the public's interest in these events, the men and women covering them keep readers, listeners and viewers informed.

Story after story went out from Oklahoma City as the death toll mounted and the hunt for the perpetrators widened. Photos of the scene also gave an account of developments until, finally, the government completed what a car-bomb attack had begun—the building was demolished.

Freeport reporters continued their coverage of the proposed teacher-salary increase that the PTA approved. They watched the local school board discuss the issue, and one reporter wrote a story comparing local teacher salaries with those of teachers in other cities in the state. She found local teachers were among the lowest paid.

Local reporters also looked into the State Board of Education proposal for AIDS education in the high schools. How representative of local sentiment was the organization actively opposing the proposal? The city editor asked a reporter to find out.

The Associated Press stayed with the downed-pilot story, first reporting that faint radio signals from him had been heard, then describing a dramatic

◀ **Follow-Up Stories**

Associated Press.

Rescued Pilot

Air Force Capt. Scott O'Grady returns to Andrews Air Force Base in Maryland after his rescue following six days of hiding in the Bosnian countryside.

Final Chapter

The Alfred P. Murrah Federal Building in downtown Oklahoma City falls in a cloud of dust as it is demolished by explosives. The building was partially destroyed five weeks earlier by a car bomb that took 169 lives.

Associated Press.

rescue mission and, finally, covering his triumphant return home after six days of hiding in the countryside of Bosnia.

Now, let's get to know the men and women who gather and write news stories. We'll visit them in their newsrooms and on their beats.

An Announcement ▶
and a Fire

We are in the newsroom of a midwestern newspaper with a circulation of 25,000. The telephone on the city editor's desk rings and, after listening for a moment, the city editor calls out to a young reporter, "Bob, the publicity director of the Lions Club has a story."

The caller tells the reporter his club intends to donate some equipment to a city playground next Saturday at 10 a.m. at a ceremony the governor will attend.

The reporter calls the governor's press secretary to check the governor's itinerary in case he is making other local stops. In 15 minutes, he has written a short piece, putting the governor in the lead. He again checks the date, time and location of the ceremony against his notes.

A few minutes later, he is told to cover a fire with a photographer.

An hour later, Bob returns to the newsroom.

"It was a small fire, about $7,500 in damages, but there's some good human interest in it," he tells the city editor.

"Don't tell me you've got three columns on a three-paragraph fire, Bob," the city editor replies. "What's it about?"

Without looking at his notes, he answers, "The story isn't the fire but the background. I found out the family bought the house a few months ago. They had just remodeled it, and this week the wife went to work to help pay for it. She leaves their 10-year-old boy home with his 12-year-old brother for a few hours every day.

"Well, the 12-year-old wanted to make some money cutting grass. He knows they're short of money. He was filling the lawn mower with gasoline in the garage when the tank tipped over against the water heater. Woosh. Lucky he wasn't hurt."

The city editor thinks a moment.

"Got any good quotes from the older boy?" he asks.

"Yes."

"Well, it sounds as though it's worth more than a couple of paragraphs. But don't make it a chapter in the book, Bob."

At his desk, Bob pauses before writing. He can start his story like most accounts of fires he has read:

A fire of accidental origin caused $7,500 in damages to a dwelling at 1315 New Hampshire St. today.

No one was injured in the blaze that started in the garage when the 12-year-old son of the owners, Mr. and Mrs. Earl Ruman . . .

He has put a direct news lead on the story, which he knows his newspaper prefers for stories of this sort. But he is unhappy with this start. This is not the way he described the fire to the editor, he recalls. Then he remembers advice he was given by a reporter: "Every story demands to be told a certain way. Don't impose a form or style on it. The way you write it has to flow from the nature of the event."

The nature of his story was the youngster's good intentions gone awry. So he starts again:

Two months ago, Mr. and Mrs. Earl Ruman moved into a three bedroom house at 1315 New Hampshire St. It was their dream house.
After years of skimping and saving . . .

At this rate, he will write the book his editor warned him against, he thinks. Although he wants a dramatic story—one that will build to a climax—he cannot take forever to develop the point. Readers will drift away.

His editor has been telling his reporters to try for feature-type leads when the event makes it possible. Perhaps this is one of those events. The youngster is the heart of the story, he reasons, and the boy must go into the lead. He tries again:

Teddy Ruman knew his father and mother had skimped and saved to put aside enough money to buy their dream house at 1315 New Hampshire St.
This morning, he decided to help, too. But his well-intentioned efforts turned to tragedy.
The 12-year-old . . .

That seems to be more like it. In 40 minutes, he has the story in good shape, he thinks.

The city editor reads through the copy.

"Yes, it's a sad story," he tells his cub reporter. "It's hardly a tragedy, but it would be sadder if they didn't have insurance to cover their loss."

Bob makes for the telephone on his desk. He remembers another bit of advice: "Don't leave unanswered any questions the reader may have. Don't leave any holes in your story."

Raymond R. Coffey has been sent to cover a student riot on the University of Mississippi campus. Coffey can hear the shouts of the students, but police have closed off the campus. The reporters try one entrance, then another, five in all, and each is blocked.

There is a story behind those walls, and Coffey intends to dig it out.

"Back in my hotel room, I took off my suit," he said later, "put on khaki pants, rolled up the sleeves of my blue shirt, and left the collar open. I left my notebook with other reporters and stuffed a few pieces of paper and a pencil into a pocket."

Resembling a student, he slipped into the campus and gathered material for his story.

◀ Student Riot

TV Covers a Fire ▶

It is Christmas day in the newsroom of a television station. A teletype clicks off a story about a fire in a small town in New Jersey. The AP reports that, while a family was asleep, a fire broke out and flames raced through their house. Four died. Only two boys escaped.

The news editor calls to a reporter, "Elaine, take this one on."

On the way to the fire, Elaine thinks of questions to ask and the locations in which to shoot the story.

"When I go out on an assignment I am conscious of the need for pictures," she said later. "I look for things that have an immediate impact, because I have a short time to tell the story—maybe two-and-a-half minutes.

"So I look for the strongest statement in a talk, the most emotionally appealing part of a running story. When I arrive at a story, I want to be the first one to interview the eyewitness, so that the person is still experiencing the event. The emotional facts have to tell the story."

On the scene, Elaine learns from the fire chief that the surviving youngsters had run to a neighbor's house during the fire. As crews from competing stations arrive, she and her crew approach the neighbor's house through the backyard to avoid being spotted.

"When I spoke to the woman next door, I asked her what happened when the boys burst into her home. She became tense and distraught as she described one boy's face, burned and blackened by the fire," Elaine recalled.

"On a breaking story, a broadcast journalist usually asks fewer questions than the print journalist. On this story all I needed to ask the neighbor was two or three questions and let her tell the story."

On the return drive, Elaine structures the script in her mind. She has pictures of the fire scenes and interviews of the neighbor and the fire chief. She works the script around these, the most dramatic shots.

A Child's Death ▶

It was a drive-by shooting. The victim: 2-year-old Heather Brown. The family had been to church and stopped on the way home at McDonald's for ice cream. At home, Heather was fidgety and wouldn't go to sleep, so her father took her into the living room and began to rock her to sleep on the couch.

Suddenly, 60 high-caliber slugs tore into the house. One struck Heather in the head and she died in her father's arms.

For Diane Sugg of *The Sacramento Bee* the story was not so much the shooting death and injury but the story of a lovable little girl. She found that story by driving out to the Valley Christian Church and waiting for its pastor, A.D. Olivan. He was close to Heather's parents and had spoken to them since the shooting.

Sugg tried to reach the minister but he didn't want to talk, so she drove to the church and waited. One hour. Two. After three hours, he arrived and Sugg persuaded him to talk to her about the child who used to run around the church singing to herself and hugging everyone she saw. There was something special about Heather, and everyone knew it.

"I would never have gotten Heather's story if I hadn't waited in a dark parking lot for three hours, hoping the family's pastor would come back to the church," Sugg says. "He did, and he could see I was sincere."

"The message on my answering machine was straightforward: 'I have a story that may be of interest to you.'

"Although reporters often get calls like this, many of which lead nowhere, I was intrigued, given the source, someone I had interviewed from time to time during the three years I covered the health, hospital and AIDS beat for the New York *Daily News . . .* someone who had never called me before . . . someone who sounded troubled."

Heidi Evans returned the call. The caller told her that the city health department had quietly stopped giving Pap smear tests to thousands of low-income women who depended on its clinics for free gynecological care.

"Since many of the clients of these clinics fit the profile of women most at risk of developing cervical cancer—sexually active women who have had several partners and little access to medical care—I knew I had the start of an important story.

"I didn't know how important, however."

In Chapter 3, we will pick up Evans' coverage of what turned out to be a major investigation that led to a shake-up in the city health department.

◀ A Tip and an Exposé

In their search for news, journalists can run into trouble. As they move close to the scene, journalists sometimes are the targets of frustration and anger as well as accidental victims.

When Hindu fundamentalists planned to demolish a Muslim mosque because, they said, it had been built on one of their holy sites, journalists were on the scene. Tens of thousands of Muslims and Hindus had been killed in religious strife in India, and the Hindu call for action foretold trouble.

As the screaming mob of thousands began to tear down the mosque, reporters moved closer. Suddenly the mob turned on the journalists. Edward A. Gargan, there for *The New York Times,* describes what followed:

◀ **Dangerous Assignments**

I saw a group of young men begin to harass Bob Drogin of *The Los Angeles Times.* I shouted at them to leave him alone, and then I was clubbed from behind.

I tried to hold myself up, but fell to the ground. Outraged Hindus were screaming at me, kicking and punching me. One grabbed my notebook; another punched me in the head, sending my glasses flying. . . .

As I tried to orient myself, I saw Peter Heinlein, the New Delhi correspondent for the Voice of America, being half-carried into the courtyard, his gray T-shirt soaked in blood, his head and face streaked with blood. He told me that he had been clubbed unconscious by one of the militants as he tried to enter the mosque.

Sometimes the pressure on journalists is a smothering surveillance in a country uncomfortable with inquisitive reporters. Journalists are confined to specific areas for their coverage. Officials are protected by cadres of security officers and so-called information specialists. Reporters are followed on their assignments.

Correspondents in China are accustomed to working under these difficult circumstances. When a reporter goes on an assignment, says Nicholas D. Kristof, who was *The New York Times* correspondent in Beijing, "three carloads of security

◀ Behind the Bamboo Curtain

agents can miraculously appear at 10 on a rainy Saturday night to pursue a foreign reporter." Every time Kristof left his residence he was trailed, he says.

When Lena H. Sun, Beijing bureau chief for *The Washington Post* in China, was relaxing at home with her husband and 2-year-old son one Sunday, her doorbell rang. Sun opened her door and four men and a woman in civilian clothes shouldered their way inside.

"We are from the Beijing State Security Ministry," one of the men said in Chinese. "We would like to talk to you."

This began what Sun later described in the story she wrote for the *Post* as a "three-hour ordeal that included breaking open a locked drawer in my office safe, confiscation of personal papers and two notebooks related to stories I had written, interrogation about my relationship with a Chinese friend and virtual house arrest for my husband and 2-year-old son."

The police accused the young journalist of violating the laws of China and of engaging in activities "incompatible" with her status as a foreign journalist. They never specified the laws she had broken or the activities the government objected to.

While Sun was being interviewed in her office, her husband and son were being guarded in their apartment. When her husband called her, Sun's guards would not let them speak.

They asked Sun about a former classmate at Beijing University who, they told her, had been arrested. When she asked if he had been charged with a crime, the officer snapped, "You don't need to know such things. Your attitude has some problems. You have not been cooperative enough."

Later, Chinese authorities reported that they had confiscated "secret documents" in Sun's office and arrested a former Foreign Ministry employee on charges of giving Sun publications about the Chinese economy, politics and social issues.

"None of the materials would be considered secret by western standards," Sun later wrote, "but in China these came from publications allowed to circulate only at certain levels within the ruling Communist Party. The materials were the sort that foreign correspondents in any country normally get."

A colleague of Sun, Jan Wong of *The Globe and Mail* of Toronto, was also targeted by Chinese security officers.

As she was walking down a street, three men grabbed Wong and tried to force her into their car. She screamed, kicked and broke free. Looking back, she is angry—at herself for reacting instinctively. "If I'd been smart, I would have let them kidnap me. Then, I'd have had a real story."

A few weeks after Cammy Wilson took a reporting job with the *Minneapolis Tribune,* her city editor gave her a feature assignment: Spend a day with a woman in a wheelchair to see how handicapped people get around in the city. Wilson accompanied the woman as she went about her chores, shopped and had lunch. At the end of the day, the woman remarked to Wilson, "Isn't it awful how much we have to pay to be taken to the doctor?" How much? Wilson asked. "Forty to fifty dollars," she replied.

Interrogated

Lena H. Sun later learned what had happened to the man she interviewed.

After a secret trial, he was sentenced to 10 years in prison, his wife to six years. Sun described Chinese justice for *Post* readers: "Every day, individuals are arrested and sentenced for political crimes, and may even be tortured, in total obscurity."

Investigative Reporting ▶

Wilson sensed a story of greater impact than the feature she was assigned to write. Wilson asked the woman if she had a receipt for a trip to the doctor. The woman did.

By the time she finished her reporting, Wilson had a major scandal laid out: The transportation of the disabled was a multimillion-dollar operation in which the poor, the elderly and the handicapped were being billed $40 to $120 for a round-trip to a medical facility. Companies were billing at an individual rate even when they took groups from a nursing home or a senior citizen center to a clinic.

Her stories interested the Health, Education and Welfare Department in Washington D.C., and, since Medicaid money was involved, HEW investigated. The Minnesota legislature held hearings and enacted several laws to regulate the transportation firms.

A couple of weeks later, Wilson was house hunting. In one house, she noticed that every item was for sale. From worn-out washcloths to underwear, everything had a price tag. "Has the owner died?" she asked the realtor. "No," he said, "the owner is in a nursing home." "Why is he selling?" "He's not selling it. The conservator is," the realtor replied.

Once again, Wilson had a story. She learned that the owner, Ludvig Hagen, 86, suffered a fall and was taken to a nursing home to recover. While there, the church that he had named in his will marked the house and all of Hagen's possessions for sale. Wilson began her story this way:

> "4415 17th Ave. S."
> "4415 17th Ave. S."
> The old man in his wheelchair repeated the address, tears beginning to well.
> "I don't have to sell my house. It's paid for."
> But his house is for sale. It and all his possessions are part of an estate valued at $140,000. . . .

As a result of the story, the county attorney launched an investigation.

Wilson then looked at probate, the handling of wills and estates by the courts. She learned that the county probate court had appointed a management firm to handle the estates of various people and that the firm had sold their homes for well under the market price to the same buyer, who within six months resold the houses for 50 to 100 percent more than the purchase price.

"I doubt if there is any other place in the world where so many people who write for a living used the phrase 'words cannot describe'. . . ." This was how Mark Fritz, AP's West Africa correspondent, described his tour in Rwanda. He continued:

◀ **Horror Everywhere**

> You can describe how 15 women were forced to lie down in a circle outside of a maternity clinic and then, one by one, were brained with cudgels.

> You can report precisely and evocatively how families hugged each other in terrified resignation as they were sliced with machetes between the pews of a Roman Catholic Church.

Fritz said he went to one village "where everybody was dead." The ethnic conflagration was so massive, so vast, Fritz said, that it reached what he described as "a saturation point, where meting out pain and death reaches the apex of pointlessness. That level, I think, was reached in Rwanda."

Fritz was awarded the 1995 Pulitzer Prize for his reporting from Rwanda. The AP has won almost 40 Pulitzer Prizes for reporting and photography.

The AP ▶

The AP is the oldest and largest news-gathering organization in the world and supplies more then 1,700 newspapers and 6,000 television and radio stations in the U.S. with national and international news. It is a not-for-profit news cooperative, owned by its thousands of members.

AP's news originates in its vast network of 230 bureaus around the world in which 3,000 staff members produce an average of 20 million words a day. Most stories begin on state or regional news wires. If a story is seen to have more than regional interest, it is sent to AP's New York headquarters where the story is edited and placed on the major DataStream report.

Members of the AP also contribute news stories to the AP via their local bureaus.

The wire service supplies photographs and graphics to members, and the AP Network News is a full-service radio network.

A Press Release That Needs Backgrounding ▶

In the newsroom of a daily newspaper in Maryland, the editor calls the education reporter over to his desk. "Dick, here's something pretty important. Overnight took these notes from a fellow who said he is the publicity chairman of an organization called the Black Parents Association. See if the outfit amounts to anything and, if it does, let's have some comments. Write it down the middle. It's a touchy issue."

The notes read as follows:

> The association has just sent a complaint to the state board of education. We are disturbed by the use of certain books our children are being given in the city's schools and school libraries.
>
> Some of this reading gives the children—black or white—a stereotyped view of minority people. At a time when we are in danger of becoming two societies, every effort must be made to understand each other. Some of the books our children are being asked to read do not accomplish this. They portray black people as ignorant, lacking in culture, childlike, sexually loose, etc.
>
> We are asking that certain books be removed from the library and the classroom—Huck Finn, Manchild in the Promised Land and Down These Mean Streets. We intend to add to the list.

"The picture of Jim in the Twain book is that of the stereotyped black man of slave days," says James Alberts, association president. "Impressionable children are led to think of black people as senseless, head-scratching, comic figures. We object to that portrayal of Nigger Jim."

Alberts said that in 1957 the Finn book was banned from elementary and junior high schools in New York City by the city board at the request of the NAACP. Later, he said, black students at Brandeis University picketed a school near the university that used the book. In recent years, some cities have removed the book from reading lists. In Waukegan, Ill., it was removed on the ground that it was offensive to blacks. Dr. John H. Wallace, an educator on the Chicago School Board, calls it "the most grotesque example of racist trash ever written."

"If it is to be read, it should be read at home under the direction of their parents," Alberts said.

The group met in Freedom Hall of the Mt. Zion Baptist Church tonight.

Dick checks his newspaper's morgue (library) to see if there are any stories about the association. He finds that the association was formed in 1955, one year after the U.S. Supreme Court ruling on school desegregation, and has been active in local school affairs.

He telephones the president of the association to ask if any particular incident provoked the action. The president tells him a parent brought up the issue at a meeting last month. Dick asks for the name of the parent, but the president has forgotten it.

For reaction from the schools, he looks up the telephone numbers of the city school superintendent, some high school principals and the head of the board of education. He calls for their comments. If he has time, he thinks he will try to go over to a high school. It would be appropriate to interview black students, he decides. But that may have to wait for a folo (follow-up story).

He rereads the release. Many readers will know *Huckleberry Finn,* but what about the other books? He will have to find out something about them.

He remembers that, when he took a course in American literature, one of his textbooks described *Huckleberry Finn* as the greatest of all American novels. Maybe he will work that in to give the story some balance. He read the book for the course and remembers Jim as a man of dignity. But his reactions certainly are not those a black high school student might have, he concedes. Yes, he will have to talk to students and to their parents as well. He also will have to guard against putting his opinions into the story.

Dick looks under *Twain* in the encyclopedia and, to his surprise, he finds that the book is properly titled, *The Adventures of Huckleberry Finn.* He had better check the other titles.

Dick admits to himself he does not like what the association is doing. It is too close to censorship, he thinks. After all, Mark Twain is a great writer. And people are always objecting that some authors are dangerous reading for the young—Hemingway, Salinger, Vonnegut, Steinbeck. But Mark Twain?

Can a great writer be prejudiced? There's a running debate about Shakespeare's The Merchant of Venice and Dickens' *Oliver Twist*. He recalls reading a wire story from a city in Canada about some parents asking that The Merchant of Venice be restricted to high school seniors on the ground that younger students are vulnerable to the anti-Semitic stereotypes in the play.

He also recalls reading that, when Twain was a young reporter in San Francisco, he wrote an account of an attack by a gang of young whites on a Chinese man. Several policemen stood by and watched, Twain had written. Twain's story, a straightforward account of the incident, never ran in the newspaper. Even so, it's possible Twain could have been a racist by today's definition.

Dick has a vague recollection of reading a story about Twain helping a black student at Yale. Better look into that, too.

He will need time to check out all these recollections, he decides. He will not trust his memory. Also, he will need to look into the whole issue of book censorship, which has been in the news for some time. He knows that battles are being waged across the country over appropriate material for the school curriculum. He takes out of his desk a story he kept about a national organization, Citizens for Excellence in Education, which advised parents to remove "the evil influences children are subjected to in public schools." The article recommends that parents take "control of schools by electing fundamentalist Christians to local school boards." Some local people were forming a chapter of the national group.

Dick decides to consult the on-line information service his newspaper uses, Lexis®-Nexis®, to find material about Twain and about book censorship. A colleague in the newsroom has told Dick that she recalls reading about Twain's black butler as the inspiration for the character of Jim, the runaway slave in *Huckleberry Finn*.

He locates a 1994 story datelined Hartford that describes Twain's relationship with George Griffin, Twain's butler for 18 years. The home in which Twain and Griffin lived in Hartford has been made into a museum, the Mark Twain Memorial. Museum officials say Griffin, whom Twain said came "one day to wash the windows and stayed for 18 years," became Twain's close friend, confidant, adviser on legal and literary matters and playmate for Twain's children.

Twain wrote of Griffin as "shrewd, wise, polite, always good-natured, cheerful to gaiety, honest, religious, a cautious truth-speaker, devoted friend to the family," the story relates. The story also contains the reaction Twain and Griffin experienced when they walked into the Century Building in New York:

> A white man and a negro walking together was a new spectacle to them. The glance embarrassed George but not me, for the companionship was proper; in some ways, he was my equal, in some others my superior; and besides deep down in my interior I know that the difference

between any two of those poor, transient things called beings was but microscopic, trivial, a mere difference between worms.

Dick also notes that the story includes a comment about *Huckleberry Finn* by the actor Hal Holbrook, who has portrayed Twain on stage for more than 30 years. Holbrook says that many people misread *Huckleberry Finn* as racist, but that it actually satirizes prejudice.

Dick decides to search the database for book censorship. Dozens of articles come up on the screen. As he scans the summaries, he sees that his story is national as well as local. Many communities are facing demands by parents and religious groups to remove books from libraries and school reading lists.

He tells his editor that making a full check will take time. No great rush, his editor tells him. "Just make sure to get all sides." They agree he will write a story for the next day's newspaper on the association's complaint and then do an extensive takeout as soon as he can gather background and conduct interviews, possibly for this Sunday's paper.

He sets to work on the story before him. He wants to include as much background as possible in this first piece rather than simply rewrite the organization's press release.

Dick locates a *New York Times* story about the discovery of a letter that Twain wrote in 1865 to the dean of Yale Law School. In it, Twain offered to provide financial help to one of the school's first black students.

"I do not believe I would very cheerfully help a white student who would ask benevolence of a stranger," Twain wrote, "but I do not feel so bad about the other color. We have ground the manhood out of them, & the shame is ours, not theirs; & we should pay for it." Twain subsidized the student until he graduated in 1867.

Another story quotes the American Library Association's finding that more than a thousand attempts had been made to ban or restrict book usage in public schools in the 1980s. School book censors were even more active in the 1990s. Dick reads a story that, in the past year, there were 376 incidents in 44 states in which attacks were made on schools and libraries because of the books they had on their reading lists and on their shelves.

The censors, he learns, were successful 41 percent of the time in removing or restricting the materials they challenged.

Canada, Dick discovers, is not exempt from the censorship forces. In his trek through the database material and other references, he finds that a union representing loggers asked that a book, *Maxine's Tree,* with an ecological theme be banned from school libraries because, the union said, the book presents the logging industry negatively. In St. John, New Brunswick, a group called Pride of Race, Unity and Dignity Through Education asked the school district to remove *Huckleberry Finn* and *To Kill a Mockingbird* from reading lists because the group (PRUDE) felt the books portrayed minority groups in a bad light.

A study at the University of Alberta found that a challenge was made daily to some Canadian library's right to carry a book on its shelves.

◀ **Book Censorship**

Censored Books. "Cumulative findings since 1982 show that the most frequently attacked books are American classics. The top three targets since we began our monitoring have been John Steinbeck's *Of Mice and Men,* J.D. Salinger's *The Catcher in the Rye* and Mark Twain's *The Adventures of Huckleberry Finn.*"—People for the American Way, a constitutional liberties group.

◀ **Mark Twain's Generosity**

◀ **Canada, Too**

Book Banning Unconstitutional ▶

He finds a U.S. Supreme Court decision in a Long Island, N.Y., book banning. The Court upheld an appeal against book banning. Dick calls up the story from the database. The school board of the Island Trees Union Free School District removed nine books from the shelves of junior and senior high schools on the grounds they were "anti-American, anti-Christian, anti-Semitic and just plain filthy." *Down These Mean Streets* was one of the banned books.

Writing the Story ▶

He has an hour before his first deadline and decides he had better start writing:

> A local school group, the Black Parents Association, has asked the city school system to remove three books from high school libraries because they allegedly present a stereotyped view of blacks.

Too long, he thinks. Dull. Maybe he should try a more dramatic lead:

> Huckleberry Finn should be banned from high school libraries, a local black parents organization urged today.

Too sensational for this kind of story, he decides, and discards this lead. Another couple of tries, and he hits on something he likes:

> A local black parents organization has charged that the city school system uses books that debase blacks and other minorities.
> The organization, the Black Parents Association, asked that the State Board of Education order three books removed from Freeport school libraries and classrooms. The group charged that the books present a "stereotyped view of minority people."
> The books are "The Adventures of Huckleberry Finn" by Mark Twain, "Manchild in the Promised Land" by Claude Brown and "Down These Mean Streets" by Piri Thomas.
> The association, which took the action at a meeting last night in the Mt. Zion Baptist Church, said it intends to add other books to the three it named.

Dick realizes he will need to put the reaction of educators up high and that he must quote extensively from the association statement so that readers have the full flavor of the group's anger.

"Too bad," he says to himself, "we didn't have a reporter there." Then he would have something to work with—the sense of outrage, rebuttals. He puts aside the luxury of speculation and settles down to more writing.

Interviewing Students ▶

After he has written his story, Dick decides to drive to a luncheonette near the high school where students hang out. He sits at the counter and orders a pizza and a soft drink. Around him, students are talking about a basketball game. Gradually, Dick eases into the conversation. He remarks that the team will have its work cut out for it next week. The students agree.

In a short time, he is chatting easily with three boys. He slowly turns the conversation from sports to school work and asks them about the books they read for English classes. He asks if any one has been assigned *Huckleberry Finn*. One student says he has read the book on his own.

Dick decides that this is the time to identify himself. He asks the student for his reaction to the book and then tells him about the association's action. One of the boys calls over some other students in a booth nearby, and soon several students, both black and white, are chatting with Dick. He lets them talk. He does not take out his notebook. He wants them to speak freely. He trusts his memory for this part of the discussion.

One student says, "Maybe there are some bad things in those books. But maybe censorship is worse." The others agree. Dick takes out his pad.

"That's interesting," he says. "Mind if I jot that down here?"

They go on talking, and Dick quickly writes down what he has stored in his memory as he tries to keep up with the running conversation.

He asks some students for their names. He would like to use them in his piece, he says. He knows that readers distrust the vague attribution to "a student."

Back in the newsroom, Dick tells his editor about his chat with the students. The editor suggests Dick use the material as the basis for his Sunday interpretative piece. He and Dick discuss other people to interview.

"Maybe you'd better talk to some of the people over at the university," the editor suggests. "They can tell us about efforts to condemn or censor important works."

In the Time & Life Building on New York City's Avenue of the Americas, editors are looking at a story that has come over the news wires: Abimael Guzmán Reynoso, the elusive head of the Peruvian guerrilla movement, the Sendero Luminoso or Shining Path, has been captured in a raid on a house in a middle class Lima suburb.

◀ **Inside** *Time*

Presidente Gonzalo, as Guzmán calls himself, has led his followers in a civil war that has all but destroyed Peru's economic and political structure. He was Latin America's most wanted man for a decade, and he is now behind bars.

Over the next few days, reporters, researchers and the main writer for the story, Michael S. Serrill, an associate editor, will whip the material into shape. The Latin American bureau chief, Laura Lopez, who is based in Mexico City, flies to Lima to join *Time*'s stringer in Peru. The senior editor in New York, George Russell, asks for background from other Latin American capitals and from think-tank experts in Washington.

A decision is made on how the story will be played: a six-page cover story for the Latin America edition; a story of the same length for the other international editions; a three-page story for the domestic *Time*.

"To do a proper job on a story of this kind," says Serrill, "you need a thorough grounding in Latin American politics, economics and the history of the region's many, multifaceted guerrilla movements." Serrill, who speaks fluent Spanish, is a student of Hispanic and Iberian politics and culture and has done many stories about the area for *Time*.

A mountain of material confronts Serrill as he begins to write. *Time* cover stories used to run 700 to 800 lines. Now, he knows, he will be lucky to be given

500 lines. An editor passes by and informs him he has a bit more than 400. At six words to a line, he has around 2,400 words, and he wonders how he will blend the history of Sendero, the background of the social, political and economic institutions in Peru and the violence and counterviolence with the good anecdotes and other color that the reporters have gathered.

Since *Time* has a news digest at the front, he need not bother with the details of last week's news. He can select a theme, a point of view, and exploit this in his piece.

Newsmagazine work is team driven, and Serrill has to run his work past editors whose perceptions of Peru and the Sendero differ from those of the reporters. Serrill knows that, while some at the magazine see the president of Peru as anti-democratic, others give the president credit for strengthening the economy, reforming the judiciary and devising workable—although undemocratic—strategies for going after Sendero.

So Serrill not only has to cope with space limitations, he must steer his piece through journalists whose perceptions differ from his. He knows that he will write more than the editors want, but he is accustomed to cutting his copy—"greening" it, as the editing process is known at the magazine because editing was done with a green pencil before the age of the computer. He also knows he will be making some calls himself to close holes in the story, to provide information that the magazine's many reporters and researchers did not turn up.

He also knows that he is writing for readers who have had a week's news about the capture. His story must provide perspective and details. He begins:

> In a way, the police raid on the house at 459 First Street in the Lima suburb of Surquillo had been 12 years in the making—ever since Abimael Guzmán Reynoso and his fanatical followers in the Shining Path faction of the Community Party of Peru declared war on the state. . . .

Other Stories ▶

Unmarried—with Son

We will be looking at other reporters as they cover stories for their newspapers, magazines and broadcast stations. We will follow Carolyn Tuft of *The Belleville* (Mo.) *News-Democrat* as she reveals the existence of a special police squad whose job it was to harass black motorists to keep them out of the city's affluent west end.

We will go along with Sam Roe of *The Blade* in Toledo as he gathers material for his series on single-parent families. One out of every two babies born in Toledo, he learns, is born to a single mother.

We will watch the development of the television documentary "Sports for Sale" as it moves from the idea stage to finished product. Howard Weinberg, the producer and director, will take us from his first outline for Bill Moyers which began:

> America is a society obsessed with winning.
> Many American universities have made a business of winning.

And then take us to the beginning of the program.

BILL MOYERS, Host: (voice-over) The name of the game is winning, to be number one, to sell the university's image and gain the money to do it all again, especially by getting on television. It's mass entertainment and America's colleges are providing more of it than ever before. The top 100 big-time sports universities, the ones you see on TV, now take in total revenues of more than a billion dollars a year.

Different as these journalists may appear at first glance, they share certain characteristics, and there are many similarities in the way they handle their assignments.

◀ **The Qualities of a Reporter**

One characteristic we notice is the reporter's attitude. He or she is curious. The reporter wants to know what is happening—firsthand. Coffey would not accept the version of officials about the demonstrations on the campus. He had to go in and see for himself, and he did.

The journalist knows how important persistence is in getting to the truth. "Let me tell you the secret that has led me to my goal," said Louis Pasteur, the French chemist whose studies of bacteria led to the pasteurization process. "My only strength lies in tenacity."

◀ Persistence

Persistence allowed Lisa Newman to tell the story of how a Chicago police officer was transferred as punishment for giving the daughter of the police superintendent a traffic ticket. Newman heard about the incident from an officer, but when she talked to the officer who issued the ticket he refused to confirm her tip.

GOYA/KOD

When *The Washington Post* was digging up exclusives in its Watergate coverage, the national editor of *The Los Angeles Times* was disturbed by the failure of the *Times'* Washington bureau to match the coverage. The *Times'* reporters were trying to cover the scandal by telephone, the editor learned.

"Tell them to get off their asses and knock on doors," the editor shouted to the Washington news editor. The advice went out with increasing frequency and ferocity, until the Washington editor decided to post a sign in the office:

GOYA/KOD
Get Off Your Asses
and
Knock On Doors

Newman, a reporter for *The Daily Calumet and Pointer,* gradually lessened the policeman's resistance, and he finally gave her the details. She also learned that the ticket was dismissed in traffic court.

With the information, Newman wrote several stories that led to an investigation of the department and traffic court.

The reporter has an eye for detail. Journalism can be defined as the practice of the art of the specific. Journalism is also marked by innovation. Reporters and their editors are always alert to new ideas for stories, new types of beats.

Knowing It All ▶

Stanley Walker, one of the great city editors, was once asked, "What makes a good reporter?"

"The answer is easy," he replied, with a show of a smile around his eyes. "He knows everything. He is aware not only of what goes on in the world today, but his brain is a repository of the accumulated wisdom of the ages." Walker, who helped make *The New York Herald Tribune* into a writer's newspaper, continued: "He hates lies and meanness and sham, but keeps his temper. He is loyal to his paper and to what he looks upon as his profession; whether it is a profession, or merely a craft, he resents attempts to debase it."

Enterprise ▶

When Chinese troops shot down hundreds of students demonstrating in Tiananmen Square for democratic reforms, reporters were prevented from entering the area. Officials denied that any of the young men and women were killed. Jan Wong realized she could learn about casualities by going to local hospitals. She found the front doors were barred to outsiders.

"But no one guards the back door," and she went in. "Dozens of corpses, mostly unrefrigerated, decompose on the fifth day after Chinese troops slaughtered unarmed demonstrators near Tiananmen Square," she wrote for her newspaper, *The Globe and Mail* of Toronto.

A week later, the authorities decided Wong was finding out too much. As she was walking down a street, a car with no license plate and a motorbike cut her off, secret servicemen grabbed her and they tried to shove her in the car.

Courage ▶

Some might say that journalists are courageous in pursuit of the news, although many reporters would shrug off this description. It was obviously courageous for Ellen Whitford of *The Norfolk Virginian-Pilot* to go into an abortion clinic and allow herself to be examined and prepared for an abortion. Whitford wanted to prove what she had learned secondhand, that abortions were being performed on women who were not pregnant.

Reporters and photographers have died covering wars and disasters, and every journalist is familiar with harassment. A reporter needs courage to refuse the official version and to ask questions that seem to challenge an official's probity. Reporters question authority, and those in command dislike being questioned.

The reporter needs courage to face facts, especially those that contradict his or her beliefs. The reporter who covered the Black Parents Association's condemnation of *Huckleberry Finn* had to question his assumptions about discrimination and censorship.

The journalist has a commitment to accuracy that encompasses the correct spelling of a name and the refusal to accept unproven assertions no matter how prestigious the authority or expert who makes them.

◀ **Christmas Fund**

When Cailin Brown took over the Christmas Fund stories for the *Times Union* in Albany, N.Y., the newspaper had been running brief pieces taken from material submitted by local social service agencies. Fictitious names were used for the people briefly profiled. The reporters handling the Fund drive never interviewed those whose stories they told.

Brown decided to change everything. She felt that the "same tenets of journalism" that work for other stories should be applied to the fund-raising drive.

"After countless meetings and some heated disagreements, the newspaper, social service workers and I came to terms on my plan," she says. She would interview the elderly the newspaper profiled and the paper would run their photographs. The pictures, Brown says, "made sense to me because newspaper readers are drawn to illustrated stories."

The stories, which appear on page one of the *Times Union,* are tales of courage and despair, devotion and loneliness. Brown, a general assignment reporter during the year, says that the people she interviews "are usually forgotten by their families, something unthinkable to our readers.

"I have covered my share of crime, both violent and white collar. I have written the story of a vibrant 3-year-old waiting for the death knell of leukemia. Yet never in 13 years as a reporter have I been so moved by the human condition as I have been listening to these people talk about getting old."

Downed, but Still Feisty

Stella Jabonaski makes her point emphatically to reporter Cailin Brown, who each Christmas covers the fund drive of the *Times Union* that helps the needy elderly in the Albany, N.Y., area. During the holiday season, Brown profiles 26 men and women for front-page stories of courage and hope in the face of debilitating physical condition and, too often, forgetful families. Brown's stories have led to a steady increase in donations.

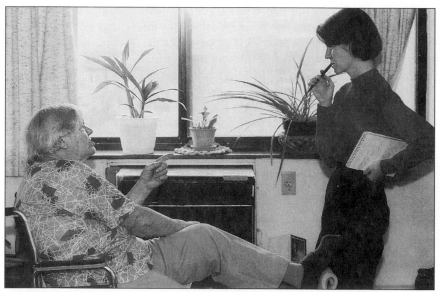

John Carl D'Annabile, *Times Union.*

Helen Robbins' story is one of devotion to her family, despite her own problems. Her son was paralyzed in a farm accident and could no longer work the farm that was in the family for five generations. It was sold at a tax sale. The Robbins story begins this way:

> The heart attack Helen Robbins suffered six months ago was just the latest in a long list of setbacks she and her family have been through recently.
>
> But she doesn't have time to take care of herself because she is busy taking care of her grandchildren since their father, her son, was hospitalized months ago.

In the Newsroom: ▶ The News Flow

Before we dig into the business of reporting and writing, let us see how the reporter fits into the newsroom operation. We will learn that decisions about what is covered are made by editors, that what is published is based on balancing the relative importance of the stories against the space and the time available.

We could visit any one of thousands of newsrooms as decisions are being made about the stories that will be used for that day's newspapers and the major broadcast newscasts.

ABC's 'Nightline' ▶

First, let's drop in on Tom Bettag, the executive producer of "Nightline." It's 10 a.m. and Bettag is making a conference call to all the ABC News bureau chiefs around the world. The program won't air until 11:35 p.m., more than 13 hours later, but Bettag has been thinking about the news for that day from the moment he awoke.

In Moscow, Russia's president has been taken to the hospital with a serious heart condition. In Burma, Aung San Suu Kyi, the champion of the country's democratic movement, who had been under house arrest for six years, was suddenly released. Bettag asks his correspondents what these developments mean.

He takes a breather from the task of laying out the day's news agenda. "Our job is to illuminate the major issues of our time," he tells a visitor. He makes no apologies for the seriousness of the "Nightline" program. "People turn on 'Nightline' to find out if there's something they need to know, if there's something people are going to be talking about in the morning.

© Capital Cities/ABC, Inc.
Ted Koppel

"They aren't interested in being entertained. 'Nightline' has its largest audience when there is real news." The program's high ratings attest to the public's appetite for serious news.

Argus Leader ▶

Next, we journey west some 1,300 miles to look in on the 50,000-circulation *Argus Leader* in Sioux Falls, S.D. We're in time for another preliminary news conference, this one at 10:30 a.m., for which several of the paper's editors have gathered to get a sense of the news that could make tomorrow morning's newspaper.

Sioux Falls is a fast-growing commercial center that always makes the lists of the country's most livable cities. Its circulation area covers parts of Minnesota

News Conference

Editors of the *Argus Leader* discuss stories and art for tomorrow's newspaper. Graphics editor Lynn Schiefelbein, left, jots down the go-ahead from Executive Editor Jack Marsh, to her left, to use a large photo to illustrate a feature about the growing health industry in Sioux Falls. Features Editor Jon Walker describes the copy, and Managing Editor Peter Ellis keeps tabs of front-page possibilities.

and Iowa as well as much of the eastern half of South Dakota. Many of the *Argus Leader*'s readers are engaged in agriculture.

This has been an unusually wet spring, so wet that the corn and soybean growers have been unable to plant their crops. Today, it turns out, is the last day farmers will be eligible for full federal crop insurance for their corn. The longer planting is delayed, the less coverage will be guaranteed, and this has the farmers worried. It makes for a good story, probably on page one.

"Do you think you can get a photo of a farmer in his unplanted field?" asks Jack Marsh, the executive editor. He is assured that the reporter, Kevin Woster, is considering a picture.

Woster, a veteran staffer, covers agriculture and has been on top of the delayed planting story for weeks. Like other reporters we will be watching, Woster develops his own story ideas. By keeping abreast of developments on his beat— such as the wet spring—he does not have to rely on his editors for assignments.

Another continuing news event comes up: The trial of O.J. Simpson, the former football player who is being tried for the murder of his ex-wife and her friend. The AP is carrying a story about the dismissal of still another juror. The editors agree, some with reluctant grunts, that the story should be considered for page one. Simpson's trial, which has been going on for months now, has been given enormous coverage, some editors describing it as "the trial of the century." Clearly, the intense coverage has dulled the story's novelty for some of the editors. Just as clearly, the public cannot be given enough.

◀ **Front Page**

Page One

Five hours later, the editors gather again for the final planning session. The late planting and Simpson trial are scheduled for page one. Mary Kueter, the city editor, says she has a good piece on the impact of the health-care industry on the Sioux Falls economy. Almost $800 million is pumped into the community by what is emerging as a major regional medical center.

Marsh is told that there is a good photo to go with this major story, and it and the headline will be played above the *fold* (the vertical midpoint of the page). No photo will be used with Woster's late-planting piece, it turns out.

Inside Pages ▶

The editors turn to the inside pages and section fronts. The city council meets tonight, but there seems little of importance on the agenda, the city editor says. The business writer has a piece on new flights out of Sioux Falls to Denver, and the education reporter is tracking attempts by the state's universities to cope with tight budgets by limiting out-of-state enrollment.

A nearby town, Tyndall, is to vote on whether to spend $5,000 to add a heating unit to the community pool. The *Argus Leader* has established a relationship with this rural community and has been covering developments in the town of 1,200. "This is the first crisis in the town," says Peter Ellis, the managing editor. (Despite a spirited campaign in favor, the vote, it turns out, goes against spending $5,000 to make the pool usable all year.)

A Metro Daily ▶

Next, we're back in the east to visit the newsroom of the *Daily News* in New York City. We are at the city desk and the telephone is ringing. An assistant editor takes the call and turns to the city editor.

"This fellow says the governor's daughter is going to get a marriage license at 2:30. Maybe we ought to get a picture," he suggests.

The city editor is not enthusiastic.

"We had her announcement a few weeks ago," he says. But he decides they may as well take it. Nothing better may turn up for inside pages. (Nothing does, and the picture will run on page three.)

A courthouse reporter calls about a suit he thinks will make a good story. A 21-year-old woman on welfare has won $925,000 from a car-rental company. The reporter is given the go-ahead and is told to slug the story "Suit." (The slug is important, for this is the story's identifying mark.) Usually, the desk will tell a reporter how long the piece should run, but the city editor knows that his courthouse man, an experienced reporter, will hold it to 450 to 500 words.

Early in the day, the city desk had made up a schedule of stories the local staff would work on. (See Figure 1.1 on the opposite page.) One of these, a murder, had broken the day before in the *New York Post*. The *Post* story began:

> A 22-year-old American Airlines employee was slain by one of three holdup men in her Bronx apartment early today while her husband, bound hand and foot, lay helplessly in another room.

```
CAREY—Names Joe Hynes and Morris Abrams as special
     nursing home prosecutor and Moreland Commissioner,
     respectively.
PROFILES—of Hynes and Abrams.
NURSE—Nearly half of the 175 nursing homes in city
     could face cutoff of federal funds, according to
     list made available to us.
BERGMAN—files libel suit against Times, Stein et al
     for $1 million.
SLAY—Robbers invade home, slay wife, bind hubby and
     escape with car.
SUIT—Good reader on young woman, blinded and severely
     hurt in car crash in France, living off welfare's
     $154 Month, wins $925,000.
JOBS—On deadline, city submits proposal for $46.7M in
     fed job funds.
UN—Ralph Bunche Institute report finds incompetence,
     cronyism and nepotism in the folks who work for
     our world body.
ABORT—Morgy OK's abortion for woman in her 28th week,
     2 weeks late.
AUDIT—Levitt report says city isn't even close to
     coping with fraud in the welfare department,
     citing huge jump in fraudulent checks.
CIVIL—Service News column.
BRIEFS—Etc.
```

City Desk Schedule. This list of stories is made up early in the day by the city editor and is submitted to the managing editor at the early-afternoon news conference at which the various editors discuss the stories in hand and anticipated. This discussion gives the managing editor the information needed to decide on major play in the morning newspaper.

Figure 1.1

A reporter in the Bronx was told to dig into the story, which was slugged "Slay." The reporter learns that the victim was a flight attendant, which gives the slaying what journalists describe as "class." The death of someone with a glamorous or out-of-the-ordinary job is assumed to perk up reader interest.

The *News* picks up a few other facts the *Post* did not have. The police report that the gunmen had asked for $25,000 and that the woman was slain with a shot from a pistol that was placed against her head. The rewriteman double-checks the names, and he learns that the victim's name was Gwendolyn Clarke, not Gwendolin Clark. Also, she was 27, not 22.

The rewriteman, Arthur Mulligan, asks if there are any pictures of the victim. There is nothing available yet, he is told.

"I have a theory on this one," he says. A copy editor looks up. "Take it easy," she tells Mulligan. "Remember your theory on the Rainslayer?" (After three holdup victims were murdered during nighttime rainstorms several months before, Mulligan had theorized the killer was the "Roving Rainstorm Robber," who preyed on people when their heads were bent under umbrellas. Nope.)

Mulligan says, "My theory is that it was narcotics. Must be. Who has $25,000 sitting around the house? The guy has no job and drives a new Lincoln Continental. She'd just come in from a run, too."

It makes sense, the city editor agrees and calls his Manhattan police headquarters man to check out the narcotics possibility.

It is 3:40 p.m. and "Slay" has not yet taken shape. The reporters have not called in. At the news conference, the city editor had suggested that "Slay" might be page-one material, and the managing editor gave the story the green light. (Murders are given good play in the *News*. The day before, a knifeslaying in New Jersey was displayed on page one of the *News*. *The New York Times*—the *News'* morning competition—played the story on page 39.)

It is now 4 p.m.—an hour before the copy should be off the city desk—and the activity in the newsroom picks up. Reporters are writing faster, copy is moving to the various desks in greater volume, and the tension increases. Copy should be in the hands of the news editor by 5 p.m., but on big stories the paper can hold until 6:00 for the first edition.

At 4:30 p.m., the police reporter in Manhattan headquarters calls in with additional information on "Slay." He reports that the narcotics bureau is looking

Newspaper Newsroom. The newsroom is organized to process stories quickly and efficiently. Local stories and copy from the newspaper's bureaus are filed by reporters. Some reporters—known as general assignment reporters—are based in the newsroom. Others, called beat reporters, are based at the police station, city hall, the courthouse and other locations where news is likely to be found. Their copy is read by the city editor and then assigned to a copy editor for detailed editing. Length of the story, size of type and headline are determined by editors.

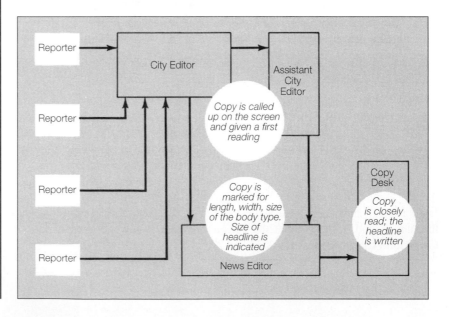

Figure 1.2

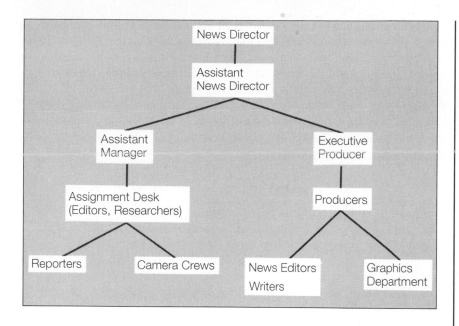

Figure 1.3

into the possibility that drugs were involved. Mulligan has enough information to go to work on the story.

Ten minutes later, the picture editor relays information from the police radio, which has been crackling with calls all day. "The police think they've spotted a suspect in that bank holdup where the cop was killed," he says. "They're stopping the subways around 42nd Street and Eighth Avenue."

This could be a good story—a chase for a cop killer through the New York subway system during the rush hour. But the desk takes the information calmly. Rather than send someone out, an editor calls the Manhattan police reporter—a busy man today—and asks him to pinpoint the search area. He had already started to do so.

At 4:58, Mulligan has the first two takes of "Slay" on the city desk. The city editor changes a couple of words, deletes others. It now reads:

> Bronx homicide police were puzzled yesterday by circumstances surrounding the murder of a 27-year-old American Airlines flight attendant who was shot in the head by one of three men who burst in on her and her husband shortly after midnight in the couple's apartment.

After describing the demands of the three men and the details of the slaying, giving the address of the victim and explaining how the men got away, the story refers to "speculation by the police that the shooting involved narcotics. . . ."

At 5:01, the police radio carries the information that a man has been picked up in the subway for questioning. Later, he is released. No one is ruffled by the collapse of the story about the search for a cop killer.

At 5:07, the third take of "Slay" is on the desk. At 5:15, the Manhattan police reporter calls Mulligan and says that the police think there may be a link between the murder of the flight attendant and the slayings of two men whose bodies were discovered in the Bronx. One of the victims was stuffed into a steamer trunk and the other was put into a wooden box. An insert is written for "Slay," and a short piece that had been written about the bodies and slugged "Trunk," is killed.

The next day, a general assignment reporter, Daniel O'Grady, is assigned to check out the narcotics angle. Police confirm Mulligan's theory about narcotics, and the lead in Sunday's newspaper reads:

> A gangland war for control of the lucrative narcotics trade in Harlem and the Bronx reportedly has left six dead in the last two months, including an American Airlines flight attendant who, police believe, may have smuggled drugs from the Caribbean for one faction of the mob.

Story Types ▶

You may have noticed that the stories described in this chapter fall into two categories:

1. **Breaking news events** such as the Oklahoma City courthouse bombing, the two fires, the student riot and the drive-by shooting early in the chapter. In our newsroom visits, we saw many such stories—the sudden illness of the Russian president, the release of a popular leader from house arrest, a crop insurance deadline, a juror's dismissal in the trial of O.J. Simpson, a community's vote on heating a swimming pool, a suit against a car-rental company and the murder of an airline stewardess.

2. **Enterprise stories** such as the revelation of the termination of Pap smear tests; the ripoff of the poor, elderly and handicapped by transportation companies; Dick's decision to take the action of a local group beyond the news release to the general area of book censorship; punishment of an honest police officer. We mentioned stories we will discuss later: the harassment of black motorists, single-parent families, the commercialization of collegiate sports.

Developing Story Ideas ▶

The second type of story may seem beyond your grasp at this time. Relax. As you familiarize yourself with the ways in which journalists work, and as you develop an interest in the subjects that journalists cover, ideas for stories will begin to flow. In fact, your only problem will be how to find time to handle all the ideas you come up with along with covering breaking news events.

A Useful Tactic ▶

One tactic some journalists use to develop story ideas is to remember that all events have a cause and a consequence. By going back to causes and ahead to consequences, we can produce interesting and newsworthy ideas.

Take the earliest story we looked at in this chapter, the garage fire.

Cause: Filling the lawn mower with gasoline in a closed area. Usually, such machines have warnings about filling their fuel tanks. Did the mower? Do other such home-use machines? Or, more generally, how about making a survey of home accidents, fires and other mishaps for the last six months or year? The home is said to be the most dangerous place for humans, not the highways or sports fields. Now that we've started thinking about this, what's the most dangerous *room* in the home? Bathroom? Kitchen? Or adjoining rooms—garage, workroom?

Consequence: Look at the Christmas fire that took four lives. It suggests that smoke alarms could have saved those four. Are smoke alarms a good idea to require for all households? Is anyone thinking of introducing such an ordinance for the city? Interview the chief of the fire department, city council members, insurance firms.

We might list under *consequences* the journalist's conscience. That is, journalists make news out of situations and events they find intolerable, that need the spotlight of public attention so that remedies can be put in place. We've seen Heidi Evans and Cammy Wilson make journalism out of situations they considered immoral.

Major changes in society have resulted from the focus of media attention on such subjects as domestic abuse, the treatment of gays and lesbians, racism and environmental degradation.

◄ Read, Look and Listen

Journalists develop story ideas by being alert to what interests people as well as by consulting their consciences. Go where people congregate—a lunch counter, the laundromat, a hotel lobby. Listen in. Read the popular magazines . . . and the not so popular.

An article in a sociology journal says that more and more young women, girls really, are taking diet pills. This conclusion is from a study made by several college sociologists. It has the makings of a good local story. The enterprising reporter will talk to physicians, school counselors, parents and, of course, the young women themselves.

Patrick Fagan,
Keller Crescent Co.

How Come?

Why is an order of nuns advertising? How did this start, and how effective has it been?

Advertisements are a good source of story ideas. What's the latest fashion in men's shoes and youth apparel? Has the price of a foodstuff suddenly gone up? Is there some new electronic game that has captured the youth market?

There is no end to the ideas available to the alert and the inquisitive, which takes us back to our description of the journalist that begins on page 19. Fully functioning journalists know how to handle breaking news stories and the assignments their editors make. They also are fountains of story ideas that will interest and entertain their readers and viewers.

◄ **Summing Up**

Journalists live in a world of confusion and complexity. Nevertheless, they manage through enterprise, wit, energy and intelligence to move close to the truth of the event and to shape their understanding into language and a form that can be understood by all. The task ahead of us in this book is to help you develop the journalist's craft and to find a personal credo to work by. A reporter who worked her way from small newspapers in New Mexico, Pennsylvania and New Jersey to the AP and then to *The New York Times* says her motto is "Keep cool but care."

This philosophy seems to describe the reporters we will be following in the rest of this book.

Journalists make mistakes. It is important to learn from mistakes and not to be discouraged. Although mistakes can be embarrassing and humiliating, they are unavoidable. Look at the Corrections box on page three of any issue of *The New York Times,* which is staffed by some of the best journalists in the business. Day after day, two to five admissions of error are published—wrong names, wrong addresses, wrong figures. Don't live in fear of making a mistake; that will cut down your range. Do the best you can. That's all that anyone can ask of you.

Further Reading ▶

At the end of each chapter, suggested supplementary reading is listed. The listed books have been recommended by journalists and by authorities in the fields discussed in the chapter.

This list includes, for example, the autobiography of a major figure in American journalism, Lincoln Steffens. It also includes Vincent Sheean's recollections of his life as a foreign correspondent, a book that persuaded many young men and women that journalism is for them. Also listed is a biography of Edward R. Murrow, the eminent broadcast journalist, and a study of the country's most influential newspaper, *The New York Times.* One book describes the women journalists who broke through barriers at the *Times.* Finally, no journalism bibliography would be complete without the book that describes how two young reporters, Bob Woodward and Carl Bernstein, toppled a president.

Kendrick, Alexander. *Prime Time: The Life of Edward Murrow.* Boston: Little, Brown & Co., 1969.

Kroeger, Brooke. *Nellie Bly: Daredevil, Reporter, Feminist.* New York: Times Books, 1994.

Robertson, Nan. *The Girls in the Balcony: Women, Men, and The New York Times.* New York: Random House, 1992.

Sheean, Vincent. *Personal History.* Boston: Houghton Mifflin Co., 1969.

Steffens, Lincoln. *The Autobiography of Lincoln Steffens.* New York: Harcourt, Brace and Co., Inc., 1931.

Talese, Gay. *The Kingdom and the Power.* New York: World Publishing Co., 1969.

Waldron, Ann. *Hodding Carter: The Reconstruction of a Racist.* Chapel Hill, N.C.: Algonquin Books of Chapel Hill, 1993.

Woodward, Bob, and Carl Bernstein. *All the President's Men.* New York: Simon & Schuster Inc., 1974.

2 Components of the Story

Steve Apps, *The Post-Crescent,*
Appleton, Wis.

**On the scene at a stadium
stampede.**

Preview

News stories must be:

- **Accurate.** All information is verified before it is used.
- **Properly attributed.** The reporter identifies his or her sources of information.
- **Balanced and fair.** All sides in a controversy are given.
- **Objective.** The news writer does not inject his or her feelings or opinions.
- **Brief and Focused.** The news story gets to the point quickly.
- **Well written.** Stories are clear, direct, interesting.

Direct observation is the surest way to obtain accurate information. With secondhand and thirdhand accounts, the reporter tries to verify the material by seeking out documents and records. When only human sources are available for verification, reporters check the source's reliability.

If we were to generalize from the work of the reporters we have been watching, we might conclude that the reporter:

1. Attempts to report accurately the truth or reality of the event through:
   A. Direct observation.
   B. The use of (a) authoritative, knowledgeable and reliable human sources and (b) relevant and reliable physical sources.
2. Tries to write an interesting, timely and clearly written story. Quotations, anecdotes, examples and human interest enliven the story.

If journalism needs rules, these points would be their bases.

Underlying and directing the application of these rules or guidelines is the reporter's imperative: The story must be accurate. Whether news story or feature, conveyer of fact or entertainment, accuracy is essential.

The highest praise A.J. Liebling, a master reporter for newspapers and *The New Yorker* magazine, could pay a colleague was, "He is a careful reporter," by which Liebling meant that the reporter took great care to be accurate. Although the reporter works under severe space and time limitations, he or she makes every effort to check the accuracy of information through verification and documentation.

◀ **Accuracy**

33

Misspelled Name

Joseph Pulitzer, a towering figure in U.S. journalism, had a cardinal rule for his staff: "Accuracy, accuracy, accuracy." There may be arguments in newsrooms about writing style, about the best way to interview a reluctant source, but there is no debate about errors. A journalist may be tolerated if his or her writing does not sparkle, but reporters won't last the week if they are error prone.

When the news editor of *The New York Times* spotted a line in a story that described the Canadian city of Sudbury as a "suburb of Toronto," he checked an atlas. Sudbury, he found, is 250 miles north of Toronto. The reporter blamed the source, an FBI agent, but the editor found that to be no excuse. "It should have been second nature to check," he said.

Mistakes occur when the writer fails to check an assumption. A headline writer put the famous mountain peak El Capitan in Yellowstone National Park. He was wrong. Where is it?

When the deadline looms and the reporter is tempted by a story that requires time-consuming verification, temptation sometimes wins. The supermarket tabloid *GLOBE* had a tempting tip: ABC-TV's Joan Lunden of "Good Morning America" was having an extramarital affair. As soon as the story was published, Lunden's lawyer was in touch with the newspaper, and the *GLOBE* retreated. It published a lengthy retraction under the four-column headline:

SORRY, JOAN, WE WERE WRONG

When newspapers make mistakes, corrections are published as soon as possible. Here's one:

CORRECTION

In last week's edition of the Michigan Chronicle, the story "Fauntroy stirs breakfast crowd," Congressman Walter Fauntroy's grandmother was misidentified. The matriarch was known to Fauntroy family members as "Big Ma," not "Big Mouth" as reported.

Accuracy also applies to the use of language. The writer who settles for the imprecise rather than the exact word lives dangerously, teetering on the brink of being misunderstood or misleading readers and listeners.

Costly Difference. The recipe in *Gourmet* magazine called for a dash of wintergreen *oil.* While the magazine was on the press, someone discovered that wintergreen *extract* was called for. Wintergreen oil is poisonous. Oops. The magazine printed the proper ingredients on a sticker and put it on the 750,000 copies of the magazine.

Firsthand Observation ▶

The reporter knows that a story based on the reporter's firsthand observation is superior in accuracy and reader interest to one based on secondhand information.

As Bertrand Russell, the British philosopher, advised students:

Make the observation yourself. Aristotle could have avoided the mistake of thinking that women have fewer teeth than men by the simple device of asking Mrs. Aristotle to keep her mouth open while he counted. Thinking you know, when in fact you don't, is a fatal mistake to which we are all prone.

During the Vietnam War, a wire service reporter wrote a graphic account of a battle from a government press release, a secondhand account. Homer Bigart, one of the great war correspondents, was working for *The New York Times* and was appalled to find the young reporter's story on page one of the *Times*. Bigart had been to the front and knew the release made exaggerated claims.

Bigart took the reporter to the scene. "See," he told the reporter, "it isn't there."

Peter Arnett, another much-respected war reporter, says his motto is "to write only what I saw myself."

Despite the air of certainty in the tone of news stories, a close reading reveals that many are not based on the reporter's direct observation. The reporter rarely sees the burglar breaking in, the policy being drafted, the automobile hitting the telephone pole. The reporter obtains information about these events from authoritative sources such as documents and records (police files for the burglary and the accident) and from reliable individuals (policy makers and participants and witnesses).

When the reporter bases his or her story on direct observation, the story is a firsthand account. But when the reporter is not on the scene and information is obtained from those who were present, the reporter's story is a secondhand account. It has been filtered through the source.

Some stories are based on accounts that have been filtered twice before reaching the reporter. For example, an official agency holds a meeting at which the participants are sworn to secrecy. The reporter learns that one of those attending the meeting described it to a member of his staff, who happens to be a good source of news for the reporter. The reporter manages to obtain the staff member's account of the executive's account of what occurred.

Here are examples of stories based on direct observation and on secondary sources:

Kevin Hann, *The Toronto Sun*.

Breath of Life

Kevin Hann caught this drama by being on the scene when the paramedic was handed a baby girl who seemed lifeless. Hann interviewed a passerby who told him: "The woman was screaming, 'My baby. My baby.'"

◀ News Filters

By Elaine Silvestrini and Sherry Figdore

Press Staff Writers

SHREWSBURY—About 250 anti-abortion demonstrators were arrested yesterday and charged with trespassing and violating a court order after they blocked the doors to the Planned Parenthood clinic for several hours.

The protesters, who prayed and sang as they were dragged and carried to police vans and a rented bus, were part of a new national group, called Operation Rescue, which has targeted abortion clinics. The group takes its name from a Bible passage in the Book of Proverbs: "Rescue those who are being drawn away to death."

Firsthand Account. Elaine Silvestrini and Sherry Figdore saw the protest and watched the protesters being dragged into the waiting police vans.

How the News Is Filtered

News Filters

Firsthand Account

The story is based on direct observation of the event by the reporter.

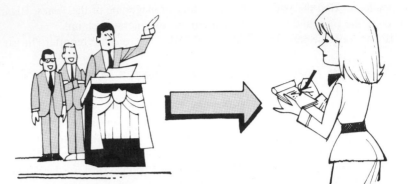

Secondhand Account

The story is based on the account passed on by a participant or witness.

Thirdhand Account

The story is based on information supplied by a source who was informed by a participant.

WASHINGTON (UPI)—Two U.S. aircraft carrier battle groups left Italian ports Wednesday and steamed south toward the central Mediterranean for an expected third round of flight operations off Libya, U.S. officials said.

Secondhand Account. The reporter was told about the naval operation by officials.

FBI agents have established that the Watergate bugging incident stemmed from a massive campaign of political spying and sabotage conducted on behalf of President Nixon's re-election and directed by officials of the White House and the Committee for the Re-election of the President.

The activities, according to information in FBI and Department of Justice files, were aimed at all the major Democratic presidential contenders and—since 1971—represented a basic strategy of the Nixon re-election effort.

During their Watergate investigation federal agents established that hundreds of thousands of dollars in Nixon campaign contributions had been set aside to pay for an extensive undercover campaign aimed at discrediting individual and Democratic presidential candidates and disrupting their campaigns. . . .

—*The Washington Post*

Thirdhand Account. Carl Bernstein and Bob Woodward based their story "on strains of evidence, statements from numerous sources, deduction, a partial understanding of what the White House was doing, the reporters' familiarity with the 'switchblade mentality' of the President's men and disparate pieces of information the reporters had been accumulating for months"

◀ **Covering a Riot**

Reporters want to be on the scene, to let the reader see the event through their eyes, hear the sounds of conflict through their ears. When Miami's black section erupted in violence following the police shooting of an unarmed motorcyclist, Will Lester of the Associated Press went to police headquarters to obtain police reaction.

He spotted a city commissioner leaving the headquarters. She told him she was on her way to Overtown, which had been torched by rioters. "Mind if a reporter comes along?" Lester asked. No, the commissioner replied, and with police permission they left the closed-off area. They rode in an unmarked car, through barricades, past police officers on every corner. When they sped down one darkened street, Lester said, "policemen at the end of the street ducked behind closed car doors and leveled pistols at our heads." They heard gunfire as they sped on. Flames leaped from shops. Snipers' bullets whizzed by.

The commissioner talked to a group of young people. "The police are too quick to use their guns," one told her. "The Cubans take our jobs." Lester jotted it down. He noted that, as the rioters spoke, they grew angrier. A rock flew into the street near them. Police officers leveled their rifles. The crowd grew ugly, and police fired tear gas to back people away from the street.

"One of the young men standing by the street gave me a look of desperation," Lester said. "You put it in the paper. Tell them how we feel," the man told Lester. Lester said he understood, but the young man countered, "You can't understand."

But Lester wrote his story, describing what he had seen and heard, hoping that his readers would understand.

◀ **Attribution**

The farther the reporter is from direct observation, the more concerned he or she is about the accuracy of the report. Accurate and comprehensive direct observation is difficult enough. After the information has been filtered once or twice, only the most foolhardy journalist would stake his or her reputation on the accuracy of the report. To make clear to the reader that secondhand and thirdhand accounts are not based on the reporter's direct observation of the event, the reporter attributes the information about the event to a source.

Here are the first two paragraphs from a story in *The Detroit News:*

> For six minutes, a Detroit police operator listened on the telephone as 24 bullets were fired into the bodies of an East Side couple.
> But, according to the police, the civilian mistook the shots for "someone hammering or building something" and dispatched the call as a routine burglary.

The lead may give the reader the impression the reporter was at the phone operator's elbow. But the second paragraph attributes the information to the police.

Attribution actually refers to two concepts:

1. **Statements** are attributed to the person making them.
2. **Information** about the events not witnessed by the reporter is usually attributed to the source of the information.

Here is a story that contains both types of attribution:

(**1**) Mayor Stanley Kretchmer said yesterday the city probably could balance its budget this year and next without laying off any workers.

(**1**) The decision, he said, "depends on a number of factors—the passage of a new tax package, the cooperation of municipal labor unions, general prosperity that keeps revenues high."

(**2**) At a meeting last week, the mayor told department heads they should consider the possibility of layoffs of about 10 percent of their work force, according to city officials who attended the meeting.

(**2**) Police and fire department personnel would be exempt from the cuts, sources reported.

Generally, we attribute what we do not observe or know to be factual. Although the reporter may take the information from a police record, the document does not necessarily attest to the truth of the information, only that some source—the police, a victim, the suspect, a witness—said that such-and-such occurred. The reporter attributes the information to this source.

Some news organizations such as the AP demand rigid adherence to the following policy: Always attribute what you do not see unless it is common knowledge.

Let us examine three stories to see how this policy is carried out. Under each story is the speculation of an experienced reporter about the reasons attribution was or was not used. (Her direct quotes follow each story.)

YMCA ▶

(**1**)   NEW YORK AP—Dr. Jesse L. Steinfeld, former Surgeon General of the U.S. Public Health Service, has been appointed chairman of the National YMCA Health and Physical Education Advisory Council.

(**2**)   Steinfeld is professor of medicine at the University of California at Irvine, Calif., and chief of medical services

for the Veterans Hospital in Long Beach, Calif.

(**3**)   The advisory council will play an important role in the setting of future directions of the Y's nationwide programs, national board chairman Stanley Enlund said today in announcing Steinfeld's appointment to the nonsalaried post.

Doug Carroll,
The Norfolk Daily News.

Attribution?

Not really necessary here. No member of *The Norfolk Daily News* staff was on hand when this stolen car plowed into a home at 3 a.m. But the evidence speaks for itself.

(1) There is no need for attribution of the appointment because the action is obviously on the record.

(2) Steinfeld's background is taken from records and needs no attribution.

(3) The role of the council is an opinion offered by the chairman of the board and must be attributed to him.

◀ HOTEL FIRE

(1) BRANFORD, Conn. AP—The Waverly Hotel, popular earlier in the century, was destroyed by a two-alarm fire today.

(2) The roof collapsed into the heart of the building. At daylight the burned-out hotel was still smouldering.

(3) Myrtle Braxton, 73, who lived alone in the massive three-story building, was reported in fair condition at Yale-New Haven Hospital suffering from smoke inhalation.

(4) Officials said the fire was reported by Mrs. Braxton at 3:41 a.m. They said it apparently started in the kitchen area where Mrs. Braxton was living after having closed off most of the rest of the building. She was living there without central heating or electricity, officials said.

(5) A neighbor said that a large number of antiques on the third floor were destroyed. Also lost was a huge ship's wheel from a sailing ship, a centerpiece in the dining room.

(6) The bank that holds the mortgage said the land and hotel were worth $40,000 to $50,000.

(1)(2) The condition of the hotel is a physical fact about which the reporter has no doubt.

(3) The attribution is implied as coming from the hospital.

(4) "Officials," presumably fire department officials, are cited as the authority because only they could have known this. In the second sentence, the cause is attributed. (Always attribute the cause of a fire.)

(5)(6) Attribution gives the information credibility.

◀ CBC

(1) The Citizen's Budget Commission, a private taxpayer's organization, said today that the proposed city budget of $185 million is more than the city can afford.

(2) The budget was submitted two weeks ago. Mayor Sam Parnass described it as an austerity budget.

(3) The Commission said it concluded after studying the budget that "significant cuts can be made."

(4) The $185 million spending plan is up 12 percent from the current year.

(5) When he submitted the budget, Mayor Parnass said anticipated revenues would cover the increase. The Commission is supported by the city's business community.

(1) A charge, allegation or opinion is always attributed, usually at the beginning of the lead. Here, the Commission is immediately identified as the source of the allegation.

(2) Background need not be attributed since it is part of the record.

(3) Attribution to the source of the material.

(4) Background needing no attribution.

(5) Attribute the mayor's statement. (The last sentence is the reporter's attempt to give the reader the why of the Commission's opposition—it's a taxpayer's group that likes austerity budgets because it means lower taxes. Nice touch.)

"You identify the source of the information in your story," a reporter commented after going through the three stories, "so that if it isn't true then the paper isn't blamed for the mistake, unless your reporting is bad and you misquoted someone, or didn't read the record carefully.

"If you don't identify the source, the reader is going to assume that we stand behind the statements because we know they are true."

Types of Attribution ▶

Four Types. *On the Record:* All statements are directly quotable and attributable, by name and title, to the person who is making the statement.

On Background: All statements are directly quotable, but they cannot be attributed by name or specific title to the person commenting. The type of attribution to be used should be spelled out in advance: "A White House official," "an Administration spokesman."

On Deep Background: Anything that is said in the interview is usable but not in direct quotation and not for attribution. The reporter writes it on his or her own.

Off the Record: Information is for the reporter's knowledge only and is not to be printed or made public in any way. The information also is not to be taken to another source in hopes of getting official confirmation.

When the source of information for a story says nothing about being quoted, the reporter can presume that the information is on the record, that the source can be named.

A source may ask to go on background, usually so that the source can provide the reporter with information that will clarify an event or situation. The source cannot be named but may be described as a "city hall official" or a "state legislator" or by some other general term. To some sources, *background* means no direct quotes; others permit direct quotes. The reporter must be clear about the terms of the agreement with the source.

Sometimes, a source asks to go off the record, and it is up to the reporter to decide whether to accept information on this basis.

Some reporters refuse to accept material if there is a condition that it may not be used in any form. They may bargain with the source, asking if they can go to another source to obtain confirmation. Or they may ask if the material can be used without using the source's name.

Caution: Many editors refuse to accept copy that contains charges or accusations with no named source. They will not accept attribution to "an official in city hall," "a company spokesperson."

Background and off-the-record information pose problems for conscientious reporters because they know that backgrounders can be used to float *trial balloons.* These stories are designed by the source to test public reaction without subjecting the source to responsibility for the material. Reporters, eager to obtain news of importance and sometimes motivated by the desire for exclusives, may become the conduits for misleading or self-serving information.

When a reporter attributes assertions to a source, the reader can assess the accuracy and truth of the information on the basis of the general reliability of the source and his or her stake in the information.

The lesson for reporters is clear: Avoid commitments not to use names of sources.

Anonymous Sources ▶

Journalists are careful about using sources who refuse to be identified. Some newspapers insist that all material be attributed to a named source, but others will use nonattributed information if the reporter is certain the material is reliable.

Special care must be exercised when an anonymous source makes a charge of wrongdoing. *The New York Times* told its staff:

> We do not want to let unidentified sources (like "law enforcement officials") use us to circulate charges against identifiable people when they provide no named complainants or other verifiable evidence.

Here is the policy of the Associated Press:

> We do not routinely accede to requests for anonymity. We want information on the record. When a news source insists that he or she not be identified by name, we say so. If we accept the condition of anonymity, we keep our word. But within the rule set by the newsmaker, we do everything possible to tell readers the source's connections, motivations and viewpoints.

Attributing secondhand and thirdhand accounts to their sources does not absolve reporters of responsibility for libelous statements in their stories. A reporter for a Florida newspaper reported that a county employee smoked marijuana, and the worker brought suit. "The reporter's own testimony indicated she had relied on second- and thirdhand accounts when writing the story," *Editor & Publisher* reported. A jury awarded the employee $70,000. (See Chapter 25 for further discussion of libel.)

◀ **Warning**

Attributing material to a source does not prove its truth. All a reporter does when attributing information is to place responsibility for it with the source named in the story. Attribution says only this: It is true that the source said this.

◀ **Verification**

The reporter who cares about truth is reluctant to settle for this half step but often is prevented from moving on by deadline pressures and the difficulty of verifying material. If a reporter tried to check every piece of information, most stories would never be written. There are, of course, certain routine verifications a reporter must make:

- Names, addresses and telephone numbers are checked in the newspaper's library, the telephone directory and the city directory.
- Background information is taken from clips in the morgue.
- Dubious information is checked against records, with other sources.

This kind of verification is essential to the reporter's work. Yet error, inaccuracy and fanciful tales creep into the news daily. When Judy Garland died, her death was noted in a syndicated column:

Her end was inevitable, from the day in Chicago's Oriental Theater when George Jessel was to introduce the child singer, Frances Gumm. His tongue resisted the clumsy sound, "Frances Gumm." He suddenly thought of the message he'd just sent to Judith Anderson, who was opening in a Broadway play:

"Dear Judy, may this new play add another garland to your Broadway career."

Jessel therefore blurted the name, "Judy Garland." Then he turned to the child singer waiting in the wings and told her: "Judy Garland . . . That's you, honey."

Even a columnist should tell truths. Had this one sought to check the anecdote he might have learned the truth, that Garland was the maiden name of Judy's mother.

When the Giants and the 49ers met in a National Football League playoff, Mayor Edward Koch of New York wagered a New York deli feast—pastrami, corned beef, dill pickles with cornrye bread—against Mayor Dianne Feinstein's cracked crab and California wine. The Giants and Koch lost. *The New York Times* reported the food was shipped by the Second Avenue Deli. *The Washington Post* said the Carnegie Deli supplied the sandwiches.

Big deal. Who cares what delicatessen shipped the corned beef and pastrami? Whoa, hold the mayo. The delis care. And we care, as journalists. It's trifles such as this that make the reader shake his or her head knowingly—journalists just can't get the simplest things right.

Nonverifiable Information ▶

The reporter can verify this statement: "The mayor submitted a $1.5 million budget to the city council today." All the reporter needs to do is examine the minutes of the meeting or the budget. But he or she cannot verify the truth of this statement: "The budget is too large (or too small)." A city councilman might have indeed stated that he would oppose the budget because it was too large, whereas the head of the Municipal League might have declared her organization's distress at the "paltry budget that endangers health and welfare projects." We can determine that the statements were made, but we cannot determine the truth of opinions and judgments.

The Techniques of Verification ▶

Verification is not the use of another opinion to counter the view of one source with that of another on controversial issues. Journalists should offer several views on controversial matters, and they should seek out the victims of charges. But that is balance, not verification.

When a minister charged that a magazine used as educational material by a public school system in California was Communist inspired, a *Fresno Bee* reporter balanced the charge with a reply from school officials. But he also sought to verify the allegation by checking whether the publication had ever been listed as subversive. The reporter examined several publications that listed so-called subversive organizations and individuals. The magazine was not listed.

Here is how he began his story:

> Rev. August Brustat, a Lutheran minister, has charged the "Scholastic" magazine, which is used in some Fresno schools, with carrying the Communist line to students. But a librarian in Fresno County Free Library and a school official said they can find no evidence the magazine is subversive.

In times of war, the press is partially dependent on official communiqués since so much goes on beyond the reporter's range. When reporters try to verify what they are told by military press officers, independent checking can be made difficult.

Nevertheless, some reporters manage to describe the realities of combat. Often, their versions clash with those of authorities.

When the United States announced its planes had accidentally bombed the Cambodian village of Neak Luong, the U.S. Embassy told correspondents that the damage was minimal. Sydney H. Schanberg, a *New York Times* correspondent, decided to see for himself and sought air transportation to the village. The Embassy intervened to keep him from flying there, but Schanberg managed to find a boat.

◀ In Vietnam

Schanberg stayed in Neak Luong a day and night, interviewing villagers and taking pictures. When local authorities learned he had been gathering material, they put him in confinement overnight. But he managed to send his story to his newspaper. Here is how Schanberg's story begins:

The destruction in this town from the accidental bombing on Monday is extensive.

Big chunks of the center of town have been demolished, including two-story concrete buildings reinforced with steel. Clusters of wood and thatch huts where soldiers lived with their families have been erased, so that the compounds where they once stood look like empty fields strewn with rubble.

Schanberg quotes the air attaché at the Embassy as saying, "I saw one stick of bombs go through the town, but it was no great disaster." Schanberg then goes on to point out that there were almost 400 casualties, and he takes the reader through the village:

The atmosphere in Neak Luong, on the east bank of the Mekong River 38 miles southeast of Phnom Penh, is silent and sad—bewildered at being bombed by an ally. Everyone has lost either relatives or friends; in some cases entire large families were wiped out.

Yesterday afternoon a soldier could be seen sobbing uncontrollably on the riverbank. "All my family is dead! Take my picture, take my picture! Let the Americans see me!"

His name is Keo Chan and his wife and 10 of his children were killed. All he has left is the youngest—an 8-month-old son. The 48-year-old soldier escaped death because he was on sentry duty a few miles away when the bombs fell.

The bombs went down right in the middle of this town from north to south as it lay sleeping shortly after 4:30 a.m. Over 30 craters can be seen on a line nearly a mile long, and people reported others in jungle areas outside the town that this correspondent could not reach.

The story states that a third of the village hospital was demolished and then quotes the Air Force spokesman as saying there was a "little bit of damage to the northeast corner of the hospital" and some "structural cracks" in a wall. In his story, Schanberg is like a bulldog that refuses to let his quarry go.

Although the attaché had described a compound for Cambodian Marines that had been destroyed as consisting of "hootches," the *Times* reporter points out that the Cambodians lived with their families in these shacks.

A woman's scalp sways on a clump of tall grass. A bloody pillow here, a shred of a sarong caught on a barbed wire there. A large bloodstain on the brown earth. A pair of infant's rubber sandals among some unexploded military shells.

The colonel is quoted as saying about the reactions of the townspeople, "They were sad, but they understand that this is war and that in war these things happen."

> "I do not understand why it happens," said Chea Salan, a 21-year-old soldier who lost relatives and army buddies. "Before, every time we saw the planes coming we were happy because we knew the planes came to help us. Now I have lost heart."

Schanberg's story demonstrates how journalistic guidelines can be used with consummate craftsmanship:

- **Verification:** Assertions are checked against the reporter's observations.
- **Dramatization:** Interviews with those involved personalize the event.
- **Truthfulness:** The detailed and specific observations give a reader the sense of the relationship of the report to truth.
- **Balance:** Both views, the military's and that of the victims, are presented.

Schanberg won a Pulitzer Prize and a Sigma Delta Chi Award for his coverage of Cambodia.

In El Salvador ▶

In 1982, journalists for *The Washington Post* and *The New York Times* reported from a mountain village in El Salvador that hundreds of men, women and children had been massacred. Raymond Bonner of the *Times* said he had seen the skulls and bones of the peasants and that villagers near El Mozote said that government forces had wiped out 733 people.

Bonner quoted Rufina Amaya, a survivor. She said she had hidden in trees when the soldiers arrived at El Mozote. They killed her blind husband and her four children, ages 9, 5 and 3 years and 8 months.

The reports in the two newspapers were met with vigorous denials. Salvadoran government officials said the massacre was fabricated, and it accused "leftists" of making up the story. The Reagan administration, which had supported the Salvadoran government in what it said was a civil war ignited by "subversives," also denied the event had occurred.

The Reagan administration went further. According to Anthony Lewis of the *Times,* the "Reagan administration did not rest with disingenuous denials. It did its best to smear the reporters."

The Wall Street Journal editorial page joined in the attack. It condemned the reporters as "overly credulous and said they had been taken in by a rebel 'propaganda exercise.'" In a 36-inch editorial titled "The Media's War," the *Journal* said:

> Much of the American media, it would seem, was dominated by a style of reporting that grew out of Vietnam—in which Communist sources were given greater credence than either the U.S. Government or the government it was supporting.

Ten years later, in 1992, a team of forensic archeologists dug into the ruins of El Mozote. They uncovered dozens of skeletons, most of children. Nearby, the archaeologists said, were shell casings and other indications of a massacre.

As evidence of the truth of the original reporting mounted, Lewis wrote that the incident proved "again how essential it is to be skeptical of convenient government denials."

A young reporter, new to the courthouse beat, learned that one of the criminal court judges had placed a man with a long criminal record on probation. Despite the seriousness of his latest crime, an armed robbery, the defendant was not sentenced to prison. The reporter, conscious of the community's anger at the growing crime rate, dug into the story. He obtained the details of the defendant's criminal record from a source in the police department. He spoke to the district attorney who prosecuted the case. ◀ **Fairness**

The piece he handed in the following week was heavy on factual detail, and the reporter was proud of his work. However, he had one hole—a big one— which the city editor spotted immediately.

"Where's the judge in this?" he asked the reporter. "Didn't you ask him why he did it? Around here we give both sides, always."

The story made the judge appear incompetent or worse, whereas he may have had a valid reason for not sending the criminal to prison. He should have been interviewed. Fairness requires a balanced account.

Here are the guidelines *The Washington Post* "Desk Book on Style" includes on fairness:

• No story is fair if it omits facts of major importance or significance. So fairness includes completeness.

• No story is fair if it includes essentially irrelevant information at the expense of significant facts. So fairness includes relevance.

• No story is fair if it consciously or unconsciously misleads or even deceives the reader. So fairness includes honesty—leveling with the reader.

• No story is fair if reporters hide their biases or emotions behind such subtly pejorative words as "refused," "despite," "admit" and "massive." So fairness requires straightforwardness ahead of flashiness.

• Reporters and editors should routinely ask themselves at the end of every story: "Have I been as fair as I can be?"

But does fair play mean that each side in an argument is given equal attention by the journalist? When *The New York Times* published a profile of a spokeswoman for the Tobacco Institute, the reaction was immediate and angry. ◀ Judgment Necessary

One letter writer condemned the article as an example of the media's desire to present "all points of view," and the result as endowing "all ideas with equal intellectual currency." This, the letter writer wrote, does not help "an addled populace unable to denounce those involved in the tobacco industry as the liars and scoundrels they are."

The article, the letter stated, should have offered a "framework for analysis."

Another letter writer, the chief of gastroenterology at the Veterans Affairs Medical Center in Ann Arbor, was also angered by the spokeswoman's advocacy as publicized by the *Times:*

> I would like to invite her and members of the tobacco industry to make hospital rounds with me or any other physician to meet the beneficiaries of her so-called advocacy. I suspect she might feel differently about her job after meeting patients disfigured by surgery for head and neck cancer, speechless from the loss of their larynxes or dependent on artificial ventilatory support because of chronic obstructive pulmonary disease, clinging to the last vestiges of dignity and life.

Balance ▶

During political campaigns, editors try to balance—in some cases down to the second of air time or the inch of copy—candidate A and candidate B.

Balance is important. But some journalists contend that balance does not mean they must station themselves precisely at the midpoint of an issue. If candidate A makes an important speech today, the speech may be worth page-one play. If, on the same day, opponent B repeats what he said yesterday or utters nonsense, the newspaper or station is under no obligation to balance something with nothing. A journalism of absolute balance can add up to zero. Balance is a moral commitment and cannot be measured by the stopwatch or the ruler.

The same common sense should be applied to matters that require fair play. Should candidate A make a serious accusation against opponent B, the reporter should seek out B for a reply. The targets of charges and accusations should always be given their say, and the reply should be placed as closely to the allegation as possible.

When the *Atlanta Constitution* revealed that a state legislator was helping his son sell computers, the newspaper carried the senator's reply as well as the charge.

When charges are made for which no documentation is offered, the reporter is required to say so, as high in the story as possible. During his first presidential campaign, Ronald Reagan said there had been a federal deficit in every year since World War II. After quoting Reagan, Lou Cannon, White House reporter for *The Washington Post,* added, "According to budget documents Mr. Reagan sent to Congress earlier this year, there have been eight budget surpluses during this period, five of them during Democratic administrations."

A reader complained to the *Post,* "Why is Cannon debating with the president? Why doesn't he just report what the president says?" Sam Zagoria, the newspaper's ombudsman, replied, "No story is fair if it consciously or unconsciously misleads or even deceives the reader. So fairness includes honesty—leveling with the reader." Zagoria said Cannon was right, that "the added facts were necessary for completeness."

SON WORKS FOR FIRM SUBMITTING BID

State Senator Pushes Computers

'I have not been in state government long, but it seems most unusual to me that a state senator accompanies a marketing representative on a sales visit.'

—Bill Oliver

'It is not news to me that my son works for Univac. I made a statement that my son works for Univac before a joint meeting of the House and Senate Appropriations committees, the public, and the press.'

—Sen. J. Ebb Duncan

SALESMAN'S FATHER
Sen. J. Ebb Duncan

Fair Play

The statements in italics preceding this story in the *Atlanta Constitution* carry the charge and the reply.

Here is the AP's policy on balance:

> We make every reasonable effort to get comment from someone who has a stake in a story we're reporting—especially if the person is the target of an attack or allegations. . . . If someone declines comment, we say so. If we can't get comment from someone whose side of a story should be told, we spell out in our copy the steps we took to try to get that comment. . . . Whenever possible we also check our files to see what, if anything, the person has said in the past relating to the allegations. Including past comment may provide needed balance and context.

Lack of balance and the absence of fairness are often inadvertent. Since writing is as much an act of the unconscious as it is the conscious use of controlled and disciplined intelligence, the feelings of reporters can crop up now and then.

In describing an official the reporter dislikes, a reporter might write, "C. Harrison Gold, an ambitious young politician, said today. . . ."

Or, writing about an official the reporter admires, that reporter might write, "Gerald Silver, the dynamic young state controller, said today. . . ."

It is acceptable for a young man or woman to be "ambitious," but when the word is used to describe a politician, it can have a negative connotation. On the other hand, the "dynamic" politician conjures up an image of a young man or woman hard at work serving the public. Maybe the reporter is accurate in these perceptions. Maybe not. The reporter's job is to let the reader draw conclusions by describing what the politician says and does.

Danger exists any time a reporter departs from the recital of observed and documented material. Similes and metaphors can cause trouble because their use sometimes leads the reporter to inject his or her feelings into a piece. One reporter wrote, "Looking as though he would be more comfortable in a scarlet bowling shirt than in the business suit he wore, State Assemblyman Louis Montano faced tenants from the end of a long table." The imagery ran away from the reporter's good sense and decency. The sentence implies that the legislator was more suited to bowling than lawmaking. Montano, like others written about by the press in disparaging ways, had little rejoinder. He could write a letter to the editor. But the damage had been done.

Unfair and unbalanced journalism might be described as a failure in objectivity. When journalists talk about objectivity, they mean that the news story is free of the reporter's opinion or feelings, that it contains facts and that the account is from an impartial and independent observer. Stories are objective when they can be checked against some kind of record—text of a speech, the minutes of a meeting, a police report, a purchase voucher, a payroll, unemployment data, or vital statistics. Stories are objective when material in them is borne out by evidence.

If readers want to weep or laugh, write angry letters to their senators or send money to the Red Cross for tornado victims, that is their business. The reporter is content to lay out the facts. Objective journalism is the reporting of the visible, what people say and do.

◄ Objectivity

Bart Ah You,
The Modesto Bee.

Self-Discipline

Whatever the reporter felt about the homeless—sympathy or annoyance—the account of their situation is written objectively. The reporter lets the homeless men and women speak, and quotes those who serve their physical and emotional needs.

In the 1950s, social and political problems that had been proliferating since the end of World War II began to cause cleavages in society, and reporters found their methodology—objective reporting—inadequate in finding causes and fixing responsibility.

Journalists were concerned about the attention they had given Joseph McCarthy, the Wisconsin senator whose charges of Communist conspiracies had been given front-page play over the country. Their tortured self-analysis led them to assume collective responsibility for the senator's rise to power. They realized it was not enough to report what McCarthy had said—which was objective reporting. McCarthy had indeed made the charges, but many of the charges were later found to be false.

Journalists asked themselves whether they had a responsibility to go beyond mere transcription of what people say and do. They found they were waiting for events to develop, the authority to speak out. They did not venture into areas that are not discernible or not measurable. They did not seek the depths of the iceberg but settled for the observable tip. That kind of journalism, with little predictive capacity, is unable to fulfill journalism's role of supplying people with information on which they can make decisions.

Journalists reported the announcement of policies and programs but infrequently examined the consequences for those affected. The monitoring was left to the bureaucracy, taxpayer organizations, other special interest groups and a few columnists. Journalism failed to alert the public to the problems of poverty, racism, inequality and the domestic consequences of the Cold War. It seemed to be committed to institutions rather than to people and to have a built-in bias for established authority, presumed to be rational, disinterested and responsive.

Elmer Davis, a courageous radio journalist, pointed to the limitations of objective journalism during the McCarthy period. He described the frustrations of reporters who knew officials were lying but were unable to say so in their stories.

Davis said that the principle of objectivity holds that a newspaper or station will run "everything that is said on both sides of a controversial issue and let the reader make up his mind. A noble theory; but suppose that the men who talk on one side (or on both) are known to be lying to serve their own personal interest, or suppose they don't know what they are talking about. To call attention to these facts, except on the editorial page, would not, according to most newspaper practice, be objective."

Davis wondered whether readers have enough background on many subjects and he asked, "Can they distinguish fact from fiction, ignorance from knowledge, interest from impartiality?"

The newspaper is unworthy of the reader's trust, Davis continued in his book *But We Were Born Free,* "if it tells him only what somebody says is the truth, which is known to be false." The reporter has no choice, he wrote, but to put into "the one-dimensional story the other dimensions that will make it approximate the truth." The reporter's obligation is to the person who goes to the news "expecting it to give him so far as humanly possible not only the truth and nothing but the truth, but the whole truth." Then, in a paragraph that influenced many journalists, Davis wrote:

> The good newspaper, the good news broadcaster, must walk a tightrope between two great gulfs—on one side the false objectivity that takes everything at face value and lets the public be imposed on by the charlatan with the most brazen front; on the other, the "interpretive" reporting which fails to draw the line between objective and subjective, between a reasonably well-established fact and what the reporter or editor wishes were the fact. To say that is easy; to do it is hard. No wonder that too many fall back on the incontrovertible objective fact that the Honorable John P. Hoozis said, colon quote—and never mind whether he was lying or not.

Another broadcast journalist, Edward R. Murrow, who had moved from radio to television, pioneered in-depth reporting. He sought to make television journalism more than a bulletin board with news for the middle class. In his work in the 1950s, Murrow demonstrated passion and conviction along with curiosity and journalistic discipline.

◀ Adjustments

Davis, Murrow and a few print journalists gave a broader scope to objective reporting. Journalists—with their unique nonpartisan perspective and their commitment to democratic values, accurate observation and truth—began to see how they could provide insights for the public and for policy makers. To do so more effectively, they knew they had to change some of their traditional practices. Underlying their conviction that change was needed was their assumption that journalists are publicly useful men and women.

The Commission on Freedom of the Press in the late 1940s (see *A Free and Responsible Press. A General Report on Mass Communications: Newspapers, Radio, Motion Pictures, Magazines, and Books,* pp. 21–22) had told journalists that they are most useful when they give "a truthful, comprehensive, and intelligent account of the day's events in a context which gives them meaning. . . . It is no longer enough to report *fact* truthfully. It is now necessary to report the *truth about the fact.*"

Journalists began finding ways to work themselves away from the constrictions that impeded truth telling. One of their responses was to look behind the breaking news story for causes and to find those with the authority to speak about possible consequences.

Viewing the urban crisis as having its roots in the problems of race and class, journalists began digging into the previously invisible worlds of blacks, the Spanish speaking, youth and women. Journalists made analyses of their own, putting their intelligence as well as their craft to work.

Journalists sought to give an added dimension to their stenographic function by examining the background of assertions and the cause of actions and by looking for the "truth of the fact." This kind of journalism, demonstrated in Schanberg's reporting from Vietnam and Bonner's from El Salvador, moves the reader, listener and viewer closer to the truth.

Facts are the stars that provide guidelines as we navigate toward the destination of truth. But they can never fully illuminate our passage. They require context, meaning. The journalist had to take on this task. At the same time, universities began to train large numbers of journalists, responding to society's need for knowledgeable practitioners.

Brevity ▶

In our generalization about the reporter's job at the outset of this chapter, we pointed out that the news story is succinct. The tersely told story is admired by editors and by busy readers and listeners. Here is a two-paragraph story that says a great deal although it contains only four sentences:

JOHANNESBURG, South Africa, Nov. 8—The bodies of 60 victims of an accidental dynamite explosion a mile and a half down a gold mine 100 miles southwest of Johannesburg were brought to the surface today.

Of the dead, 58 were Basuto tribesmen from Lesotho, chosen for the dangerous job of shaft-sinking, or blasting a way down to the gold-bearing reef. The two others were white supervisors. The black Africans will be buried in a communal grave tomorrow.
—*The New York Times*

All creative work is based on the art of omission. In architecture, the 20th century has been marked by structures that follow the dictum: Less is more. Economy of expression is the hallmark of the artist.

When Beethoven was struggling with the music to his opera "Fidelio," he realized that the leisurely pace of the music did not meet the demands of the theater, and for years he pared down his work. David Hamilton, the music critic, describes Beethoven's effort as a "ruthless piece of self criticism . . . Beethoven expunged balancing phrases, trimmed decorative expansions, excised anything that did not move forward, eventually achieving the terse urgency that now marks the opera's crucial scenes."

In eliminating large sections of his music, Beethoven rejected three overtures he had written. One, "Leonore No. 3," became one of the most popular pieces in the orchestral repertory. Despite its obvious beauty and power, Beethoven found it unsuited to his opera.

Joseph G. Herzberg, an editor on several New York City newspapers, said, "Newspapering is knowing what to leave out and condensing the rest."

Too often, beat reporters and specialists write more than is necessary because they forget they are writing for general readers, not for their sources. The reporter covering new transplant technology for a newspaper cannot go into the kind of detail that a reporter for the *Journal of the American Medical Association* must in her story.

But stories can be too brief. A copy editor can always remove excess material but cannot add essential detail and background that an overly brief report ignores.

Selectivity ▶

The way out of the dilemma of being brief but not writing telegrams is through Herzberg's advice, which can be summed up in one word—selectivity. Brevity is a function of selectivity—knowing what to leave out. The ability to select essential facts from the welter of material that the reporter gathers comes with experience.

Selectivity also involves the use of language that makes the point succinctly. Edna Buchanan, the police reporter for *The Miami Herald,* began her account of a record-breaking week of violence in Dade County this way:

> Dade's murder rate hit new heights this week as a wave of violence left 14 people dead and five critically hurt within five days.

A couple of paragraphs compared these figures with murder figures of previous years, and then Buchanan summarized most of the deaths:

> In the latest wave of violence, a teenager's throat was cut and her body dumped into a canal. A former airline stewardess was garroted and left with a pair of scissors stuck between her shoulder blades. Four innocent bystanders were shot in a barroom gun battle. An 80-year-old man surprised a burglar who battered him fatally with a hammer. An angry young woman who "felt used" beat her date to death with the dumbbells he used to keep fit. And an apparent robbery victim was shot dead as he ran away from the robbers.

A natural tension exists between the editor and the reporter over the issue of brevity. The desk, confronted with ever-decreasing space and time, wants shorter stories. The reporter, excited by the event and driven by a compulsion to tell the full story, wants more time and more space.

Some editors contend that, if Genesis can describe the earth's creation in a thousand words, then no reporter needs any more than four pages of copy for any event of human dimension. But some events are so complex that only an extended account will do. Important stories often require scene setting and background that consume time and space. The guide for the length of stories is: Make it brief but complete.

The executives of 40 daily newspapers in Iowa and journalism instructors at the state's three journalism schools were asked to rank characteristics considered most important for beginning reporters. Both groups put the ability to write clearly and interestingly first.

◀ **Clarity**

Clear prose follows comprehension. That is, the reporter must be able to understand the event before he or she can explain it clearly and succinctly. You cannot clarify what you do not understand.

Clarity is enhanced by simplicity of expression, which generally means short sentences, short words, coherence and logical story structure. We shall be looking at these in detail in Chapter 7.

◀ **Human Interest**

To make certain the story is read, the journalist must recount events in ways that substitute for the drama of the personal encounter. One of the ways the journalist does this is to tell the story in human terms. Reporters personalize and dramatize the news by seeking out the people involved in the event. Human interest is an essential ingredient of news.

A change in city zoning regulations is dramatized by pointing out that now low-income families can move into an area that had been effectively sealed off to them by the previous two-acre zoning rule. A factory shutdown is personalized by talking to workers who must line up at the unemployment office instead of at a workbench.

In a story about chemicals polluting the Hudson River and ruining the fishing industry, Barry Newman of *The Wall Street Journal* begins:

GRASSY POINT, N.Y.—In the gray-shingled shack at water's edge, four fishermen sit playing cards around an old kitchen table, ignoring the ebb tide laden with the spring run of shad. The wall is hung with foul-weather gear; rubber boots are piled in the corner. On the refrigerator door somebody has taped up a newspaper clipping about the awful chemical in the fish of the Hudson River.

"I do my fishing from the window here," an old man says, looking off to the quiet hills on the east bank, three miles across the river from this small valley town.

"No nets for me this year," another man says. "No pay," says the third. And the fourth: "A lot of trouble, this."

Responsibility ▶

Ted Williams was one of baseball's greatest players. The Boston Red Sox outfielder won six batting titles over a span of 17 years and was one of the few to win the Triple Crown twice, leading the league in 1942 and in 1947 in batting, runs batted in and home runs. To many baseball fans, he was heroic. To some sports writers, he was, as Roger Kahn put it, "a pill."

It was possible for readers to know the real Williams because, Kahn says, when nine writers covered Red Sox games "it was impossible to conceal" the truth about Williams. "If one writer courted The Thumper by refusing to report a tantrum as news, another inevitably seized the tantrum as news. Regardless of each reporter's skill, an essential, imperfect system of checks and balances worked. If you cared enough about Williams, and I did, you could find a portrait that was honest by consensus."

But many of the Boston newspapers that covered Williams are gone, as are others in many cities. There are fewer than 30 cities with competing daily newspapers. This means that the responsibility for truth telling falls on fewer shoulders. It falls, in most U.S. cities, in fact, on a single reporter, for most local news beats are covered by only one journalist.

Responsibility is not a visible part of a news story. It is an attitude that the reporter carries to the job. It encompasses all the components we have discussed in this chapter.

Responsibility is the reporter's commitment to the story, to journalism and to the public. Responsibility demands of the reporter that the story be accurate, fair and balanced, that it be so clear anyone can understand it.

Nothing in the law requires a reporter to be *responsible*. In fact, journalists sometimes flinch at the word. The reason for their discomfort is that some people and some organizations use the word as a club with which to beat journalists when the newspaper or station presents material they dislike.

Journalists testily reply that they can be as irresponsible as they like. That's understandable, and it is true. But beneath the surface, reporters and editors understand that journalism is a moral enterprise, that theirs is a calling practiced with honesty and diligence within the limits of verifiable truth and scant time.

Finally, a word about the writing. A news story may be accurate, properly attributed, balanced and fair, objective and brief. The reporter may be compassionate and understanding, may have carried out his or her tasks with responsibility. The story may have something interesting and exciting to say. But unless it is written with some skill, the reader or listener will not bother. ◀ **Writing**

Good writing—direct and clear, simple and straightforward—is an important component of the story. Good writing avoids clichés and redundancies. It does not strain for effect. It does not call attention to itself but to the story it tells.

◀ **Further Reading**

Benjamin, Burton. *Fair Play: CBS, General Westmoreland, and How a Television Documentary Went Wrong.* New York: Harper & Row, Publishers, 1988.

Bensman, Joseph, and Robert Lilienfield. *Craft and Consciousness.* New York: John Wiley and Sons, 1973.

Chancellor, John, and Walter R. Mears. *The News Business.* New York: Harper & Row, Publishers, 1983.

Commission on Freedom of the Press. *A Free and Responsible Press.* Chicago: University of Chicago Press, 1947.

Edwards, Julia. *Women of the World: The Great Foreign Correspondents.* Boston: Houghton Mifflin, 1988.

Liebling, A.J. *The Press.* New York: Ballantine Books, 1961.

Mills, Kay. *A Place in the News: From the Women's Pages to the Front Page.* New York: Dodd, Mead & Co., 1988.

Schiller, Dan. *Objectivity and the News: The Public and the Rise of Commercial Journalism.* Philadelphia: University of Pennsylvania Press, 1981.

Siebert, Fred S., et al. *Four Theories of the Press.* Urbana, Ill.: University of Illinois Press, 1956.

PART THREE: Writing the Story

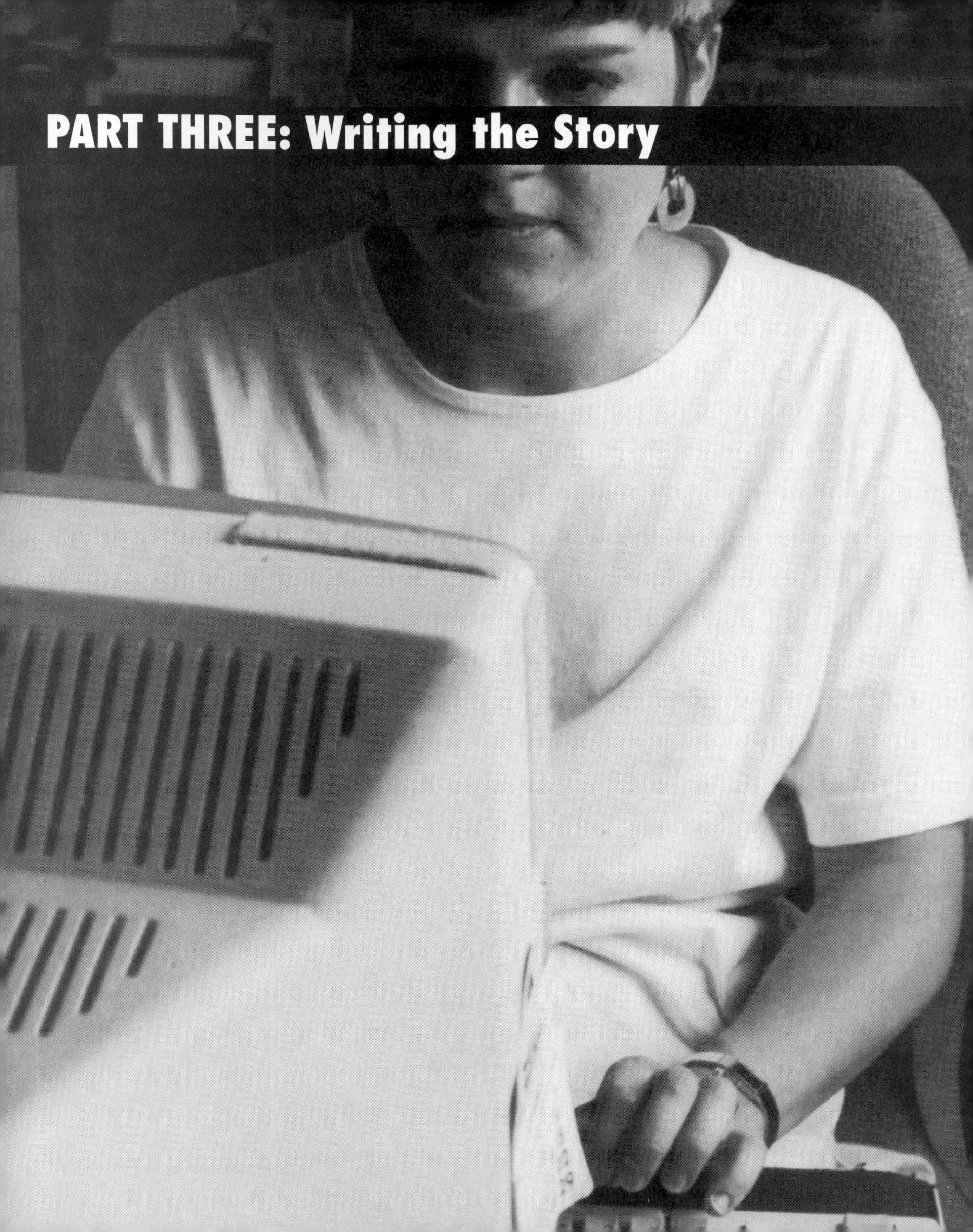

③ What is News?

Naomi Halperin,
The Morning Call, Allentown, Pa.

Impact . . . timeliness . . . proximity.

Preview

Reporters look to a set of news values to help them determine the newsworthiness of events. These values are:

- Timeliness.
- Impact, consequence or importance.
- Prominence of the people involved.
- Proximity to readers and listeners.
- Conflict.
- The unusual nature of the event.
- Currency, the sudden interest people have in an ongoing situation.

At least three-fourths of all stories fall into the categories of impact or importance and the unusual.

We have discussed several essentials of journalism—accuracy, attribution, verification, balance and fairness, objectivity, brevity, clarity, human interest and responsibility. These elements are the reporter's guides to reporting and writing the story. But what leads the reporter to the events worth reporting? Among the cascade of events the reporter encounters in a workday, which should be singled out for attention?

How does the courthouse reporter leafing through a dozen civil complaints decide which is the newsworthy document? How does the police reporter determine which of the score of arrests is noteworthy? After determining that an event or idea is worth reporting, how does the reporter decide whether to write two paragraphs or seven? How does the broadcast journalist know a story is worth 60 seconds at the start of the 6 p.m. newscast or 10 seconds toward the end? If journalism can be described as the art of selection, then what guidelines does the journalist use in practicing selectivity?

◀ **Some Answers, Past and Present**

If we go back to the beginning of formal news communication, we learn that what we read, see and hear today is not much different from the material in the daily bulletins posted in the Roman Forum and what was later printed in gazettes and newsbooks.

Realizing that Roman citizens needed to know about official decisions that affected them, Julius Caesar posted reports of government activities in the *Acta Diurna.* In China, the T'ang dynasty (618–906 a.d.) published a gazette—

handwritten or printed by wood block—to inform court officials of its activities. The more immediate predecessor of the newspaper was the handwritten newsletter, containing political and economic information, that circulated among merchants in early 16th-century Europe.

The first printed newsbook, published in 1513 and titled *The trewe encounter,* was an account of the Battle of Flodden Field. The Anglo-Scottish wars of the 1540s provided printers with material for more newsbooks.

During the 17th century, news sheets spread to the business centers of Europe, reporting news of commerce. In this country, as historian Bernard Weisberger has pointed out, the newspaper "served as a handmaiden of commerce by emphasizing news of trade and business."

To this day, much of our news is about the actions of government and business, and our journalism continues to stress the drama of war and other calamities.

Day and Bennett ▶

The newspaper editors of the 19th century understood the need to appeal to a large audience to stay in business, and their acumen led to definitions of news that hold to this day. The papers in the large cities were printing news for the newly literate working class. One of the first penny papers—inexpensive enough for working people—contained the ingredients of popular journalism. In 1833, the first issue of Benjamin H. Day's *New York Sun* included a summary of police court cases and stories about fires, burglaries and a suicide. Other stories contained humor and human interest.

Several years later, James Gordon Bennett—described by historians as the originator of the art, science and industry of news gathering—used the recently developed telegraph to give the readers of his *Herald* commercial and political news to go along with his reports of the everyday life of New York City, its sins and scandals. His formula of news for "the merchant and man of learning, as well as the mechanic and man of labor" guides many editors today.

Pulitzer ▶

The Library of Congress.

Joseph Pulitzer

Day and Bennett followed the tastes and appetites of their readers, but they also directed and taught their readers by publishing stories they deemed important. This blend of entertainment, information and public service was stressed by Joseph Pulitzer, who owned newspapers in St. Louis and New York. He, too, gave his readers what he thought they wanted—sensational news and features. But Pulitzer was not content with entertainment. He also used his news staff for his campaigns to curb business monopolies and to seek heavy taxes on income and inheritance. In 1883, Pulitzer charged the staff of his New York *World* with this command:

> Always fight for progress and reform, never tolerate injustice or corruption, always fight demagogues of all parties, never belong to any party, always oppose privileged classes and public plunderers, never lack sympathy with the poor, always remain devoted to the public welfare, never be satisfied with merely printing news, always be drastically independent, never be afraid to attack wrong, whether by predatory plutocracy or predatory poverty.

Pulitzer and William Randolph Hearst were locked in a circulation war for New York readers when Cuba rebelled against its Spanish rulers. Spain was severe in repressing the insurrection and the New York newspapers seized on the story of the helpless Cubans trying to free themselves from their oppressive rulers.

◀ Hearst

Hearst's *Journal* was particularly imaginative. After the United States declared war in 1898 and the troops were slow making it to Cuba, Hearst urged them on with an inventive news story that had 5,000 troops on their way.

"Over the next week," writes Arthur Lubow in *The Reporter Who Would Be King,* "the *Journal* reported an exciting sequence of landings, bombardments and fleet battles, all admirably detailed, all entirely fictitious. The *Journal* was selling so well thanks to its apocryphal scoops that its rivals began to play the same game, often rewriting the accounts of the creative *Journal* writers."

Modern editors overseeing newsrooms humming with the latest electronic wonders apply many 19th-century concepts of news. They would define news as a blend of information, entertainment and public service. They would also agree with the definition of news offered by Charles A. Dana, who ran the *New York Sun* from 1869 to 1897. Dana said news is "anything that interests a large part of the community and has never been brought to its attention before."

◀ Today's Editors

One of Dana's editors, John B. Bogart, contributed the classic definition, "When a dog bites a man, that is not news, because it happens so often. But if a man bites a dog, it's news."

Another enduring definition of news was offered by Stanley Walker, a Texan gone East to success as city editor of *The New York Herald Tribune* in the early 1930s. He said news was based on the three W's, "women, wampum, and wrongdoing." By this he meant that news was concerned with sex, money and crime—the topics people secretly desired to hear about. Actually, Walker's formula is as old as the contents of Caesar's *Acta Diurna* 2,000 years ago, which, along with information about public affairs, offered news of sports, crime and sensational events. And in England, while newspapers were carrying material directed at the commercial class, handbills and pamphlets were carrying sensational crime news.

By the mid-1970s, the United States had been through three crises: a war in Vietnam that wound down with guilt and defeat for many Americans; the Watergate scandals; and the failure of some political, social and economic experiments of the 1950s and 1960s that had been hailed as solutions to international conflict, racial tension and poverty.

It was not surprising, then, to see a shift in the criteria used to determine the news. Av Westin, the executive producer of the American Broadcasting Company's "Evening News" program, said Americans wanted their news to answer

Know the Audience. When Barney Kilgore took over *The Wall Street Journal*, it had a circulation of 32,000. The circulation now exceeds 1.8 million. "Don't write banking stories for bankers," he instructed his staff. "Write for the bank's customers. There are a hell of a lot more depositors than bankers."

the following questions: Is the world safe? Are my home and family safe? If they are safe, then what has happened in the last 24 hours to make them better off? Is my pocketbook safe?

People not only wanted more pocketbook stories but escape stories as well. Reflecting the interests of their readers, editors asked for more entertainment in the form of copy about lifestyles, leisure subjects and personalities.

In the 1990s, editors devised the "reader-friendly" story. Readers, they argued, want to learn how to diet, how to raise their children, where to invest their money. The news agenda was being shaped to conform to the interests of middle-class readers and viewers. Also, editors became aware that a major segment of the female population consists of working women. Coverage followed this late awareness.

Reporters follow the guidelines of their editors and publishers. Reporters also agree among themselves on what constitutes news. Thus, at any given time, news in the mass media is similar.

Summing up, two general guidelines emerge:

• News is information about a break from the normal flow of events, an interruption in the expected.

• News is information people need to make sound decisions about their lives.

How does a reporter or editor determine what events are so unusual and what information is so necessary that the public should be informed of them?

News Values ▶

The following seven factors determine the newsworthiness of events, personalities and ideas:

1. **Timeliness.** *Events that are immediate, recent.* The daily newspaper and the hourly newscast seek to keep readers and listeners abreast of events. Thus, broadcast news is written in the present tense, and most leads

on newspaper stories contain the word *today.* No matter how significant the event, how important the people involved, news value diminishes with time. André Gide, the French novelist, defined journalism as "everything that will be less interesting tomorrow than today."

The media are commercial enterprises that sell space and time on the basis of their ability to reach people quickly with a perishable commodity. The marketplace rewards a fast news carrier. Although newspapers place less emphasis on speed than do the electronic media, a newspaper that offers its readers too much rehashed news will not survive. Radio, which was being prepared for its funeral when television captured a large segment of the listening audience, staged a comeback with the all-day, all-news station.

Timeliness is important in a democracy. People need to know about the activities of their officials as soon as possible so they can assess the directions in which their leaders are moving. Told where they are being led, citizens can react before actions become irreversible. In extreme cases, the public can rid itself of an inefficient or corrupt official. Officials also want quick distribution of information so that they can have feedback from the public. This interaction is one of the reasons the Constitution protects the press. Without the give-and-take of ideas, democracy could not work.

Timeliness is also the consequence of advertising necessities. Since most businesses are based on the quick turnover of goods, advertisements must appear soon after goods are shipped to stores. The news that attracts readers to the advertisements must be constantly renewed.

2. **Impact.** *Events that are likely to affect many people.* Here, journalists talk about significance, importance, the kinds of information that interest people or that journalists decide people need to know to be informed. A postal workers' strike will be covered in detail because everyone is affected by the delivery of mail. A campaign for Congress will receive attention in the candidate's district because journalists consider it essential that voters know the candidates' positions before voting.

Some news that has considerable impact in one community may be unimportant in another. To residents in Milwaukee, a November cold snap has little impact because cold weather in that month is hardly an interruption in the expected. But when 40-degree weather was forecast for St. Petersburg, Fla., many of whose residents had fled northern winters, it was front-page news under a large headline.

3. **Prominence.** *Events involving well-known people or institutions.* When the president trips disembarking from an airplane, it is front-page news; when a city councilman missteps, it is not worth a line of print. A local banker's embezzlement is more newsworthy than a clerk's thievery, even when the clerk has stolen more. When Michael Jackson sprains a thumb while working on a Walt Disney movie, it is network news. Names make news, goes the old adage, even when the event is of little consequence.

Prominence applies to organizations as well, and even to some physical objects. The repair of a major bridge in Akron is given coverage in that city, but when the Golden Gate Bridge shuts down that action merits national coverage.

Impact

This extra sold 67,000 copies, and a reprint the next day sold 125,000 copies—despite the constant replay of the explosion on television.

In 1884, the American poet and journalist Eugene Field was moved by the journalism of personalities to write:

Now the Ahkoond of Swat is a vague sort of man
Who lives in a country far over the sea;
Pray tell me, good reader, if tell me you can,
What's the Ahkoond of Swat to you folks or me?

Despite Field's gentle poke, journalists continue to cater to what they perceive as the public's appetite for newsworthy names.

4. **Proximity.** *Events geographically or emotionally close to the reader, viewer or listener.* People are interested in, and affected by, activities close at hand. A city ordinance requiring the licensing of dogs in Memphis, Tenn., would be of interest to that city's residents, of some interest to Nashville, Tenn., residents, and of little interest to dog owners in Butte, Mont.

If 42 people die in an airplane crash in the Andes and one of the passengers is a resident of Little Rock, the news story in Little Rock will emphasize the death of the local resident. This process is known as *localizing* the news.

When two tour buses collided in Wales, injuring 75 people, here is how *USA Today* began its brief:

> Teen-agers from Lancaster, Pa., Houston and St. Louis were among 75 people hurt when two tour buses returning from Ireland collided in Wales.

People also feel close to events and individuals with whom they have emotional ties. Newspapers and stations in communities with large Catholic or Jewish populations will give considerable space and time to news from the Vatican or the Middle East.

After the space shuttle Challenger exploded and sent seven crew members to their deaths, the *Amsterdam News,* a weekly in New York City with a predominantly black readership, headlined on page one the death of the black astronaut who was aboard.

When commemorative ceremonies were planned to mark the sacrifice of four Army chaplains during World War II, *The Jewish Week* began its story this way:

> Rosalie Goode Fried does not remember her father, Rabbi Alexander David Goode—she was only 3 years old when he died in 1943.
> But America has never forgotten him.
> Goode and three Christian chaplains gave up their life jackets—and their lives—when their Army transport was sunk by a German submarine near Greenland 50 years ago.

When a proposal to bar education, health and welfare benefits to undocumented aliens was being discussed in California, reader interest closely

Proximity

followed ethnic lines. The proposal was clearly aimed at the large Mexican population. Given their interest, it was no surprise a poll showed that the issue was closely followed by 43 percent of Hispanics and only 24 percent of whites.

5. **Conflict.** *Events that reflect clashes between people or institutions.* Strife, antagonism and confrontation have provided stories since people drew pictures of the hunt on the walls of their caves. The struggles of people with themselves and their gods are the essentials of drama. The contemporary counterparts are visible to the journalist whose eye is trained to see the dramatic—an official who must decide whether a proposed highway should go through the homes of a dozen families, a parents' movement that seeks changes in the reading list that high school authorities have adopted.

Although critics of the press condemn what they consider to be an overemphasis on conflict, the advance of civilization can be seen as an adventure in conflict and turmoil.

6. **The Unusual.** *Events that deviate sharply from the expected and the experiences of everyday life.* The damage suit filed by an Albuquerque couple because the club they had rented for their wedding reception was occupied when they and their 200 guests arrived stands out from the dozen other suits filed that day.

In 1970, when an all-white jury awarded a black man $70,000 in damages, the racial angle was played up in the wire service story:

Police Victim Gets $70,000

CHICAGO, June 17—An all-white jury awarded $70,000 in damages yesterday to a black man who said that two policemen had violated his civil rights by beating him after they stopped him on a traffic charge. . . .

Nowadays, it is not unusual for a white jury to make awards to black plaintiffs, and such a story would not be put on the transcontinental wires of the press associations.

7. **Currency.** *Events and situations that are being talked about.* Occasionally, a situation of long standing will suddenly re-emerge and become newsworthy. Historians might refer to such a situation as an idea whose time has come.

In the early 1960s, President Kennedy called attention to the plight of the poor. Then President Johnson declared a "war on poverty." Newspapers responded by covering health and welfare agencies and by going into poor areas of their cities in search of news. Television produced documentaries on the blighted lives of the poor. More than thirty years later, the poor, though as numerous, receive less attention.

Newspapers and broadcast stations will sometimes make discoveries of their own and push them so that they become current. When a newspaper decides that some facet of community or national life is worth intensive coverage, it may assign a reporter or a team of reporters to dig into the situation. The result, usually a number of stories, is called a *campaign* or a *crusade*. Much of this news has a steamroller effect, and further news is developed because of the sudden currency of the theme or issue.

These guidelines do not tell us that one of the most enduring stories is the tale of how humanity prevails—how we live now is a story few readers have ever been able to resist. Nor do they give us any hints about the realities of the newsroom, its pressures and its politics.

Changing Times . . . Changing Beats

A century ago, 50 percent of the workforce in the United States made a living from agriculture. Farm news was big news. Today, with 2.5 percent so employed, farm news is important outside agricultural areas only when the cost of food goes up. At the turn of the century, fewer than 115,000 students attended college and journalists paid little attention to them. Today, more than 50 times as many are enrolled and higher education is a major beat.

© Joel Strasser.

The application of news values reflects geography, demography and time. When census figures for income were released, a metropolitan newspaper with a large black readership had this headline:

Blacks make gains
in family income

The *Lakota Times*, which calls itself America's Indian Newspaper, put this headline over its page-one story on the same census data:

Indians fall in poverty stats

In this, the Age of Candor, there is nothing—well, hardly anything—that is considered off-limits for journalism. The exposure of the personal lives of the powerful and the popular in the mainstream media is relatively new.

During the presidency of Franklin D. Roosevelt, not only was his affair with Lucy Mercer considered no business of the public, his obvious physical handicap was never seen: No photos showed the president's cumbersome braces, his inability to walk unaided. If a photographer attempted to shoot a photo of Roosevelt's polio-ridden legs, the president's aides would block the view or push the camera away. Nor was any mention made in print of his handicap.

The audience nowadays seems to want to know everything—particularly the personal—about people in public life. Some say such so-called news is a distortion of what journalism should be about. Others welcome the opening up of the personal to scrutiny. Nothing about the powerful, they say, should be off-limits.

Watch the local evening news on television. Compare the placement and time given news in the broadcast with the play in the newspaper. Some of the news that is emphasized on television is given routine treatment in the newspaper, and some newspaper stories receive slight mention in newscasts. Obviously, some news is better suited to the newspaper than to television, and television is better able to capture some events than is the newspaper.

Television technology and the audience demand pictures, which leads television to lean heavily on action. As Richard Salant, former president of Columbia Broadcasting System News, put it, "You see more fires on local television than you do in the newspapers because fires look better on television."

In a newspaper, the space allotted for news usually depends on the amount of advertising that is sold. Unlike radio and television, which have nonexpandable time slots for newscasts, a newspaper may run 32 pages one day and 48 the next, when department stores place their white-sale advertising. A story that would run half a column on a day when the news hole is tight could be given a full column when ample space is available.

On any given day, the news flow may be slow. That is, important stories simply may not be breaking. On days such as these, routine events are covered that would be ignored on busy news days.

◀ **News Is Relative**

◀ Changed Times

◀ Differing
News Needs

◀ Advertising and
News Flow

After a Connecticut newspaper printed a front-page story about a kidnapping at a shopping center, the merchants at the center told the publisher that the newspaper's survival depended on the economic health of local business and that such stories would drive shoppers elsewhere. The newspaper replied that crime was always covered by the newspaper and that no individual or group could be given special treatment.

At *The Washington Post,* reporter Leonard Downie had been looking into an arrangement between corrupt real estate speculators and local savings-and-loan institutions to gouge inner-city residents. The bankers got wind of Downie's checking and told the managing editor that if the *Post* ran the series, they would pull their advertising.

Downie, who later became the *Post*'s managing editor, recalls Benjamin C. Bradlee, his editor, telling him about the visit and the threat. Bradlee looked at Downie and said simply, "Just get it right."

The reporting continued, the series ran and the banks pulled their advertising, costing the newspaper $750,000 in lost advertising revenue.

The pressure to please advertisers sometimes does lead to stifling the news. Elizabeth Whalen, the executive director of the American Council on Science and Health, was asked by *Harper's Bazaar* to write an article with the title "Protect Your Man from Cancer." Her article began with the link between smoking and cancer. When the editor saw the article, he told a copy editor, "Christ, Jane, I can't

Five Packs a Day

Although *The Charlotte Observer* circulates among farmers who grow two-thirds of the tobacco used to make cigarettes, the newspaper ran this picture of a victim of "smoking-caused emphysema" in a section entitled "Our Tobacco Dilemma."

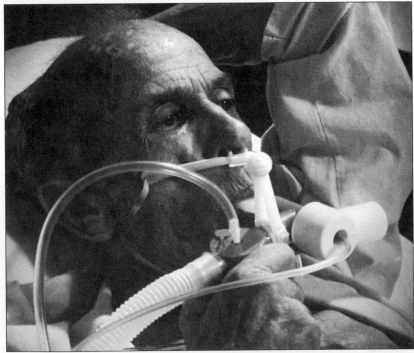

Mark B. Sluder, *The Charlotte Observer.*

Conflicting Goals: Sales vs. Truth

Advertising is the principal source of revenues that supports our media system. That dependence creates an incongruity between the public's preferences and the criteria employed by the people in charge. As consumers of communication, we judge it by its value and meaning for us; advertisers judge it by its efficiency in disseminating what they call "exposure opportunities."

Media content has been driven primarily by the need to maximize audiences for sale rather than by the desire to communicate the truth about our world or express deep thoughts and feelings. To this end, broadcasting and film have vied with each other in pursuit of violence and vulgarity. The largest of our mass media, the daily press, traditionally the forum for contention and irreverence, has undergone a steady attrition of competition and a general retreat to the safety of the middle ground. Left to its own devices, the public persistently drifts toward amusement rather than enlightenment, avoiding confrontation with the pressing, perhaps overwhelming, problems that confront the nation and the world.

—Leo Bogart

open this article with smoking." She moved the material to the end "so it wouldn't jump in the face of every cigarette advertiser."

Whalen was told the cutting was based on her "frequent mention of tobacco and the fact that they (the magazine) ran three full-page cigarette ads each month."

Some publications do not succumb to the pressures of cigarette advertisers. *The Charlotte Observer* carried a 20-page special report titled "Our Tobacco Dilemma." North Carolina's farmers grow two-thirds of the tobacco used for cigarettes and its workers manufacture more than half of the almost 700 billion cigarettes made in the United States each year. Tobacco, the state's leading cash crop, brings in $1 billion a year to growers.

Yet the *Observer* did not shrink from putting under the title of its special section this headline:

N.C.'s top crop; part of our lives but bad for health

On the front page next to a picture of a tobacco warehouse was a photograph of James McManus, 62, a former painter and paperhanger, a five-pack-a-day smoker. He was pictured with the tubes from his oxygen tank attached to his nose and mouth. "McManus speaks only with difficulty and needs an oxygen tank to survive," the paper states. He has "smoking-caused emphysema."

The tobacco industry outspends all other national advertisers in newspapers and is second to the transportation industry in magazine advertising. The tobacco industry spends more than $1 billion on advertising cigarettes, about $25 a smoker per year.

Giving In ▶

When the Chinese government was upset by the British Broadcasting Corporation's news coverage of China, it made its displeasure known to Rupert Murdoch, the owner of a massive global media conglomerate. Murdoch's Hong Kong operation had been broadcasting the BBC newscasts that disturbed Chinese Communist Party leaders.

Murdoch acted quickly. He eliminated BBC news. He said that retaining the BBC news, considered the provider of the finest broadcast journalism in the world, would jeopardize his business in China.

Building Up ▶

Advertisers can elevate the performance of a newspaper. Increasingly, large retailers are more interested in the quality of the readership than in the quantity of readers. They are looking for well-educated, discerning men and women. Let's look more closely at the audience the media want to reach.

The Audience ▶

The nature of the audience is an essential factor in determining what is covered and how events are reported. News directors of noncommercial television and radio stations lean heavily on analysis and venture into advocacy journalism, whereas the commercial stations with their mass audiences stay close to so-called objective, event-oriented reporting. Reporters for special-interest magazines and alternative newspapers are less sensitive to the needs of the mass audience than are the reporters for daily newspapers.

Newspaper readership studies have shown that young people are interested in stories about music and entertainment and that, as they grow older, marry and purchase homes, they become more interested in local news. Stories about taxes, schools and local politics interest older readers, as do stories about food, health and medicine.

The young and women are increasingly important to advertisers. Both are major spender-consumers. Advertisers are especially interested in reaching the young, whose buying habits are still forming.

Advertisers look for the people who buy cars, CDs, stereo units; take weekend jaunts to the Bahamas; buy refrigerators and stoves to set up households. Most of these spenders are young, in their 30s, and their reading and viewing habits are geared to a faster, peppier pace than are those of their elders.

The media have shifted content to attract this younger, on-the-go audience. Profiles of rock groups and movie stars have increased. Stories have been shortened to appeal to an audience said to be too busy to read two columns about the school budget or to devote an hour to a documentary on the rain forest. More illustrations appear in newspapers and magazines, and boxes and other typographic shorthand provide information for readers on the run.

Increasingly, more space is being devoted to sports, style and features, and greater amounts of television time are scheduled for zippy magazine shows. The traditional news staples—local, national and international news—make up a smaller part of the total news budget.

All the new material is not fluff. The well-off, 40-plus audience has children in college, a burdensome expense to many. The result: More news about how to manage finances.

The decade-younger audience has different but equally pressing needs and interests. Usually married late and with a child or two, both parents work, leaving Alice at a day-care center and Zachary with a nanny. The result: More news about parenting.

To the critics of these new news topics, editors cite a historian's assertion that "the most important filter through which news is constructed is the cultural air we breathe, the whole ideological atmosphere of our society."

Sometimes, the audience's vehemence forces an editor to discipline a staff member and cut off his or her work. Following the death of Richard Nixon, Matt Coker wrote a column for the *Daily Pilot* in which he wrote that he drank a toast on hearing about the former president's death. He described Nixon as "a paranoid liar who did irreparable harm to these United States of America . . . this wretched, wretched man. . . ." Coker ended his column with, "Good-bye and good riddance."

The response in conservative Orange County was quick, in some cases nasty. Of the more than one hundred calls and letters, four were death threats. Some demanded Coker's firing. Coker was not fired, but his column was taken away from him.

◀ **Audience Clout**

The pressures we have described work in two directions—what is used and what is tossed out. A publication or station can be assessed as much by its wastebasket as by its columns and newscasts, for the sins of omission are as serious as those of commission. Reporters and editors are moved by common assumptions and the tide of public opinion. As a consequence, the divergent idea or the unusual person may not be assessed with the same criteria applied to the accepted and the expected.

◀ **Newsroom Politics and Ideology**

Some editors favor certain types of news—political stories, features, hard news—and give less attention to other kinds of news. The commitment of a newspaper to a large statehouse staff may mean a lot of news from the state capitol, even at the expense of important international news, because people on the payroll must be put to use.

The politics in the newsroom can affect the news. The power structure, which puts the reporter close to the bottom of the power hierarchy, places decision making in the hands of editors, publishers and news managers who rarely see the events the reporter writes about. Yet they often have firm ideas about what should be covered and how stories should be written, and the reporter is tempted to go along to get along. Some publishers and station owners have pet projects—a favored charity, the downtown business mall—and these will be given special attention. Political and social cronies may be granted time and space disproportionate to their actual news value.

When Fidel Castro had a swimming accident, the *El Paso Times* ran this headline.

Castro Narrowly Escapes Drowning
Too Bad! Too Bad! Too Bad!

Ideology sometimes determines what is printed. Reporters and copy editors are proud of their independence, particularly of the distance they put between the newsroom and the editorial writer's alcove. But the ideological commitments of the newspaper sometimes seep into the newsroom and affect what is covered and its play.

Civil Rights: Not News ▶

During the civil rights movement in the South, when blacks sought an end to discrimination, many newspapers refused to run the growing story.

"Most of the papers in the South blacked out much of what the movement was doing," said John Siegenthaler, who covered the civil rights struggle for *The Tennessean* in Nashville, "even when it was in their own city on their own city square."

Bill Kovach, curator of the Nieman Foundation at Harvard, recalled trying to cover the movement as a young reporter. "The paper I began with in East Tennessee . . . made an arrangement with the Chamber of Commerce not to report on the freedom riders.

"And when I found out, I quit and went to work for the paper John (Siegenthaler) worked for, and we covered the civil rights movement."

Economics and News Policies ▶

As we have seen, the economics of stations and newspapers affect coverage. A small station may not have the resources to cover many events in the community. It may rely on sources other than its staff—publicity handouts and releases, the press associations, volunteers—and rewrite news from the local newspaper, which usually is able to muster more reporters than is the local radio or television station. Shorthanded newspaper staffs rely on the telephone, a poor substitute for on-the-scene coverage.

Even the weekly tabloid newspapers sold at supermarkets have changed their content to attract advertisers as well as readers. Headlines such as SON KILLS FATHER AND EATS HIM offend the typical buyer, a white, middle-aged shopper, and when readers decline, advertisers go elsewhere. After the biggest weekly tabloid, the *National Enquirer,* dropped from 5.0 million to 4.5 million readers, it decided to shift to blander fare, emphasizing diets, family relations and service stories.

> **Supermarket Stuff.** Sal Ivone, managing editor of the *Weekly World News,* describes the news policy of the tabloid this way: "If someone calls me up and says her toaster is talking to her, I don't refer her to professional help. I say, 'Put the toaster on the phone.'"

The Influence of Owners ▶

The strong publisher determined to influence public policy through his or her newspaper has just about disappeared. But ownership still influences how news is covered and what is published. Without the spur of competition, the monopoly newspaper may become lazy, sitting back to await news rather than going out to dig it up. It may ignore what Benjamin C. Bradlee, the former executive editor of *The Washington Post,* describes as the "special responsibilities" of the monopoly newspaper: "to listen to the voiceless; to avoid any and all acts of arrogance; to face the public with politeness and candor."

The chain newspaper might be light on local news, which is expensive to gather, and heavy on wire news and syndicated material, which requires only editing. An anonymous home office concerned with the profits of the chain may

U.S. Cities with Competing Daily Newspapers

Seattle — WA
MT
OR
ID
WY
ND
SD
MN
WI
MI
Madison
Green Bay
Detroit
NY
Wilkes-Barre
VT
NH
ME
MA
RI
■ Boston
■ New York
CT
■ Trenton
■ York
NJ
DE
MD
■ Washington DC
NV
UT
Salt Lake City
San Francisco
CA
Las Vegas
Denver
CO
NE
IA
Lincoln
Chicago
IL
IN
Ft. Wayne
OH
Cincinnati
WV
PA
VA
KS
MO
Columbia
Evansville
KY
Nashville
NC
NM
Albuquerque
AZ
Tucson
OK
AR
Little Rock
TN
MS
AL
Birmingham
GA
SC
Charleston
Kingsport
Chattanooga
TX
El Paso
LA
AK
FL
Honolulu
HI

Legend:
■ Two separate newspapers
● Newspapers under joint operating agreements

● Birmingham (Ala.) News
● Birmingham Post-Herald

● Tucson Arizona Daily Star
● Tucson Citizen
● Tucson Territorial

● San Francisco Chronicle
● San Francisco Examiner

■ Denver Post
■ Denver Rocky Mountain News

■ Washington Post
■ Washington Times

● Honolulu Advertiser
● Honolulu Star-Bulletin

■ Chicago Defender
■ Chicago Daily Herald
■ Chicago Southtown Economist
■ Chicago Sun-Times
■ Chicago Tribune

● Evansville (Ind.) Courier
● Evansville Press

● Fort Wayne (Ind.) News-Sentinel
● Fort Wayne Journal-Gazette

■ Boston Globe
● Boston Herald

● Detroit Free Press
● Detroit News

■ Columbia (Mo.) Missourian
■ Columbia Daily Tribune

■ Lincoln (Neb.) Journal
● Lincoln Star

■ Las Vegas (Nev.) Sun
● Las Vegas Review-Journal

■ Trenton (N.J.) Times
■ Trenton Trentonian

● Albuquerque (N.M.) Journal
● Albuquerque Tribune

■ New York Daily News
■ New York Post
■ New York Times
■ New York Newsday
■ Staten Island (N.Y.) Advance

● Cincinnati Enquirer
● Cincinnati Post

■ Wilkes-Barre (Pa.) Times-Leader
■ Wilkes-Barre Citizens' Voice

● York (Pa.) Dispatch
■ York Daily Record

● Chattanooga (Tenn.) Times
● Chattanooga News-Free Press

■ Kingsport (Tenn.) News
■ Kingsport Times-News

● Nashville (Tenn.) Banner
● Nashville Tennessean

● El Paso (Texas) Herald-Post
● El Paso Times

● Salt Lake City Deseret News
● Salt Lake City Tribune

● Seattle Post-Intelligencer
● Seattle Times

● Charleston (W. Va.) Gazette
● Charleston Daily Mail

● Green Bay (Wis.) Press-Gazette
● Green Bay News-Chronicle

● Madison (Wis.) Capital Times
● Madison Wisconsin State Journal

Dying Competition

The number of cities with competing newspapers has steadily declined, and the number of chain-owned newspapers has spiraled over the past three decades, the result of declining advertising income and a decrease in the circulation of afternoon newspapers. Twenty-seven states have no competing newspapers.

direct the editor of the local newspaper to the bottom line on the ledger rather than to the amount of local news.

The chains are swallowing newspapers at such a rapid rate that three of five newspapers are now within one of the 170 groups. The chains defend group ownership by contending that the financial strength of groups gives local editors greater resources that enable them to take on the local power structure. But Ben Bagdikian of the University of California, a press critic, disagrees with this optimistic view of chain ownership. He sees the ever-present need for profits precluding the development of quality journalism.

Monopolizing the Media. In the first edition of his book *The Media Monopoly,* Ben Bagdikian stated that 50 corporations controlled most of the country's media business. In his second edition, that number had been reduced to 29 and, most recently, it's down to 23.

At the end of World War II, Bagdikian says, 80 percent of the nation's daily newspapers were locally owned. The most recent figures estimate that 75 percent of the dailies are controlled by outside companies, with 15 companies controlling the bulk of the newspapers.

"There's real danger that the number of distinguished papers will decline, because they're part of chains now, too, and the pressure is on them to produce dollars," Bagdikian says.

Leo Bogart, a media research specialist, says that the result of the centralization of newspapers is that "complacent survivors are irresistibly drawn toward the gently flowing mainstream, or even to the shoals of mediocrity, and the public is left without alternative reports and opinions on what's going on."

The monopoly of the three television networks has disappeared under the blizzard of cable channels, but ownership occasionally acts as though it were in a monopoly situation. When General Electric, which owns NBC, heard of the network's plan to make a miniseries of a scathing biography of Nancy Reagan, it stepped in. The chairman of GE ordered the deal with the publisher Simon & Schuster cancelled.

The biography included a section on Ronald Reagan's service as a spokesman for GE in the 1950s and 1960s. While Reagan was touring the country selling GE's image, the company was convicted of price fixing. It was fined almost $1 million and three of its top executives were sent to prison.

Gary Deeb of the Gannett News Service revealed the pressure GE put on NBC and concluded: It is "crystal clear that Corporate America still knows how to smother a brush fire."

Tom Wolfe, the former newspaper reporter who wrote *The Right Stuff* and *The Bonfire of the Vanities,* blames newspaper chains for the decline in reporting, which he describes as "the weak link in American journalism right now. And it is, oddly enough, one of the least discussed. But reporting is the heart of everything.

"The reason that the link has become weak is the fact that there has been such an erosion of competition in the newspaper business. There are many cities where newspapers are, in effect, regional monopolies. This inevitably leads to a reduction in the ranks of reporters."

It also leads, say media observers, to a concentration on profits at the expense of coverage. Whatever the causes, the result worries those who believe that newspapers and broadcast stations are essential to the proper functioning of democracy.

The Enlarged Scope of News ▶

News, we see, is hardly determined in a vacuum. Let's examine a few subjects that have become newsworthy in the last few years. Clearly, the explosion of entertainment news can be traced to the enthusiasms of the generation that tossed jelly beans at the Beatles and grew long sideburns to affect the Elvis Presley look. The coverage of entertainers and sports figures seems a logical development.

But other subject areas have developed in the face of resistance and ignorance. Our first nominee: News of religion.

Religion ▶

Religion, says Terry Mattingly, wasn't news for a long time, despite the clear religious convictions of most people in the United States. He recalls covering the 1984 convention of Southern Baptists, the largest non-Catholic denomination in the United States, when its leadership stated that women should not be ordained because Eve sinned first in Eden. Mattingly, who writes the "On Religion" column for Scripps Howard News Service, learned that moderates in the organization were thinking of forming a breakaway organization and he informed his editor. His story was spiked.

Today, he says, it is "impossible to argue that religion isn't news. Everyone from Billy Graham to Shirley MacLaine has preached sermons to journalists noting that religious groups shape the lives of millions, control budgets containing billions of dollars and play pivotal roles in an unusually high number of gripping local, national and international stories."

Critics of the news media cite the coverage of religion news as Exhibit No. 1 in their indictment of the professional journalist's news judgment. Because religion does not play a major role in the lives of most journalists, they paid it little attention. And when they did cover the subject, their ignorance was profound.

Peter Steinfels, senior religion correspondent for *The New York Times,* remembers being called by a reporter after the American Catholic bishops had issued a pastoral letter on the U.S. economy. As Steinfels was explaining the letter, the reporter interrupted to ask, "What exactly is a bishop?"

A study of reader interests found that of nine topics presented to newspaper readers, religion was right in the middle, behind, in order, news of education, health, business and food and ahead of entertainment, sports, the arts and personal advice. Most readers felt their newspapers did not cover religion adequately.

Religion Now News

Long confined to back pages and covered with routine notices of services and quotes from sermons, religious news has emerged as the stuff of page-one play.

◄ Gays and Lesbians

Another subject long left ignored by the newsroom was news of the gay and lesbian community. This omission, too, is an exhibit in the case some make against the media, suggesting that most of the media follow because they fear to lead.

Journalists considered such coverage taboo. They were concerned about a backlash from their readers and viewers.

No longer a hush-hush subject, such coverage is routine today, even though some segments of the public continue to object—to little avail.

After the *Florida Times-Union* in Jacksonville ran a profile of gay parents, readers protested in letters and with phone calls. A few threatened to cancel subscriptions.

The newspaper did not publish the protesting letters. Most, said reader advocate Mike Clark, contained profanity and were otherwise unprintable.

"If you do a story about gays and imply they deserve coverage, you get the most extreme reaction from readers. The whole issue of homosexuality is a very powerful one in this town. Emotions kind of go off the chart," says Clark.

"News and feature stories have to cover the real world," he continues. "That includes families that differ from the traditional family unit."

◄ Rain, Shine, Snow, Sleet

Unlike their reaction to covering religion and the gay community, the response of journalists to the increased interest in weather news has been welcoming. They have responded with five-color weather maps in newspapers, weather reports every eight minutes on radio and an all-weather television channel.

Actually, all is not bright and sunny on the weather news front. Who's doing the weather news on TV, a trained meteorologist or a personality?, asks Robert T. Ryan, chief meteorologist at WRC-TV in Washington, D.C. There is only one answer, he says, "if the journalistic community is to fulfill its responsibility of keeping the public informed."

Shopping Malls ▶

The Register, a 345,000-circulation newspaper in Orange County, Calif., shocked newspaper editors by assigning a reporter full-time to cover the area's shopping malls. Why not?, asks the *Register*'s editor, Tonnie L. Katz. It's providing useful information, she says.

"Journalists, particularly journalists at major papers, are so out of touch with their customers that unless they change and learn to respect what readers want, it can doom them," Katz says. The paper put on page one a box giving the hours of the local malls during the Christmas shopping season.

The paper also handles traditional stories, such as its investigation of the random murder of a young woman in Orange County. But it is clearly proudest of what it describes as meeting the needs of its customers.

Some critics contend that this shift toward the "customers" reflects the trend in the economics of the mass media toward satisfying the real customer, the advertiser.

Widening Interests ▶

Our last half century has been marked by increased mobility. Two generations ago, families clustered. In today's family, a son attends school in Wyoming. A married daughter runs her own business in Iowa. The parents live in Cleveland. The father's mother is in a retirement home in California, and the mother's parents operate an inn in Massachusetts.

When an earthquake struck the Los Angeles area, the various family members scanned their papers for information about the town in which the retirement home is located. The Wyoming state legislature's consideration of doubling out-of-state tuition concerned the parents, as did the unusually wet spring in Iowa, which caused a delay in planting corn and the possibility of a downturn in their daughter's business.

News reflects the way we live, how we make a living and, as the historian remarked a few pages back, "the cultural air we breathe."

Who Decides? ▶

Traditionally, the subjects for news and editorials were decided by news professionals. In the 1990s, a new decision maker entered the scene—the public.

People in the community now play a key role in setting the news agenda. At the *Argus Leader* in Sioux Falls, S.D., the editors meet with an advisory board to obtain insights into what people think should become news. (The newspaper also has an Editorial Board Advisory Committee.)

The *Argus Leader* is part of the Gannett newspaper group and has been working with the group's News 2000 program in an attempt to become reader driven. David W. Hawpe, editor of Gannett's *Courier-Journal,* says the program is designed to meet readers' needs and desires, designed to "empower" readers and to sharing "the civic dialogue with them rather than dictating to them."

In some cities, the concept of "public journalism" has taken hold. In Norfolk, Va., *The Virginian-Pilot* replaced its beat system with reporting teams

Vox Populi

The voice of the Sioux Falls public is sounded through citizen advisory boards. The people speak; editors listen.

organized to cover issues such as public safety and public life, issues, the editors say, that will be covered the way private citizens see them.

For the most part, though, what becomes news is the result of decisions made by journalists. They contend they know their community's head and its soul and can reflect these in their news decisions. Some journalists go further: They actively set a news agenda for their communities. These journalists can be described as advocates of an activist journalism.

To some journalists, news consists of overt events—an automobile accident, a city council meeting, a court document, the State of the Union Address. Their journalism is denotative, pointing to what has happened.

◀ An Activist Journalism

Necessary as this reporting is, some journalists consider it a passive type of journalism because the journalist essentially is responding to events. They would complement denotative journalism with a more active, seeking-out journalism.

When Heidi Evans of the *Daily News* was told by a caller that every woman who went to a cash-only abortion clinic was informed that she was pregnant, Evans raced over to the clinic the next day with a urine sample of her own.

"The owner, who did the tests himself, told me I was pregnant and tugged at my arm to have the procedure right then," Evans said.

"The following day, I sent another reporter with a sample from one of our male colleagues. His urine also tested positive." After two more weeks of reporting, in which she showed how poor, mostly immigrant women were herded by the clinic owner to a back room where a fly-by-night doctor operated, the state shut down the clinic.

Evans was called by the clinic owner's receptionist with the tip because Evans had a reputation as a reporter who could do something, could correct injustice. She had just completed a series after finding that the city had 3,000 unread Pap tests sitting in a box. Thousands more had just been sent out for analysis after sitting in an office for as long as a year unread.

"The women had been told by clinic doctors to assume their Pap tests were normal if they didn't hear back in six weeks," Evans said. "Ninety three learned later that they had precancerous conditions and 11 had cervical cancer."

The result: The city's testing program was overhauled and women now are given their test results in a week. Four of the officials responsible were fired or demoted. Evans was awarded the prestigious George Polk Award for local reporting for her Pap smear series.

Evans is not reluctant to claim that her journalism is an activist, advocacy journalism. She makes news out of the undercurrents and the hidden activities of those in power.

Troubled Vets ▶

For Christopher Keating of *The Hartford Courant*, the reports from a nearby Veterans Administration hospital were disturbing. There were too many suicides among discharged patients, he thought. He checked into three of them and found the deaths happened after the men left the hospital's psychiatric center.

He checked further and learned that data on suicides among Vietnam veterans was vigorously disputed. No one, for example, could say for certain whether some of the veterans' deaths were accidental drug overdoses, vehicular accidents or suicides. The Centers for Disease Control and Prevention listed the suicide toll at 9,000. Some veterans groups worry that as many as 60,000 have taken their own lives.

Keating could classify some deaths as definite suicides. But, he wrote, "no one will ever know whether a drug overdose or a single-car accident was a suicide. A driver whose car hits a tree in the middle of the night might have fallen asleep or might have driven off the road on purpose."

In his digging, he located the director of a Vietnam veterans group who said that the psychological damage suffered by many of the veterans was responsible for 63,000 suicides.

Keating found that the average age for Vietnam soldiers was 20, 24 for Desert Storm, 26 for World War II. These young men were at a vulnerable age for combat-related illnesses.

Keating continued to dig into the situation because he was convinced more help is needed for these men.

To some, Evans and Keating are making news, not covering it. To others, they are working in the tradition of public service journalism, one of the most important roles the journalist can fulfill.

These journalists seek to place on the public agenda matters that they believe require consideration and action. Social scientists say that conditions usually do not speak for themselves. The sociologist Herbert Blumer states that issues come to public attention, not because of the "intrinsic gravity of the social problem," but because they have been given status by some respected group that has called attention to the problem. These groups can legitimatize an issue as a matter of concern requiring action, Blumer says. ◀ Legitimatizing Issues

Among those that can legitimatize situations Blumer lists educational organizations, religious leaders, legislators, civic groups and the press. Once legitimatized, the issue may be acted on quickly, as occurred when television showed the starvation in Somalia caused by warring clans. The United States sent in troops with food. Or the situation may be unresolved, as has happened despite the efforts of political leaders and the press in the case of poverty, still a problem more than three decades after President Lyndon B. Johnson declared a war on poverty.

Impersonal and objective as journalists would like to make the determinants of news, much of journalism is based on selection, and choice is a highly personal affair. It derives from the journalist's professional background, his or her education and the intangible influences of family, friends and colleagues. ◀ Summing Up

The professional decisions—what people need to know—are framed by other considerations as well: The need to entertain to keep readers and viewers who are constantly being seduced by other entertainment media; the pressures of the business of journalism such as budgeting restrictions, meeting the competition, considering the needs of advertisers.

Even more elusive in our search for absolutes in the area of news determinants are the decisions that have their origin in the arena where ambition and conscience battle.

Vague as these influences may be, the reporter must cope with them. Fortunately, the reporter's handiwork is tangible. Once the heat of reporting and writing has cooled, the reporter can examine the story. Then, alone or with a trusted friend or colleague, the reporter can try to pinpoint the reasons for decisions. This self-questioning—directed by some of the principles we have discussed in this chapter and those we'll tackle in Chapter 27 on the morality of journalism—is part of the journalist's continuing education.

Bagdikian, Ben H. *The Media Monopoly.* Boston: Beacon Press, 1987.
Clurman, Richard. *To the End of Time: The Seduction and Conquest of a Media Empire.* New York: Simon & Schuster, 1992.
Gans, Herbert J. *Deciding What's News.* New York: Pantheon Books, 1974.
Roshco, Bernard. *Newsmaking.* Chicago: University of Chicago Press, 1975.
Schudson, Michael. *Discovering the News.* New York: Basic Books, 1978.
Westin, Av. *Newswatch: How TV Decides the News.* New York: Simon & Schuster, 1983. ◀ Further Reading

The Tools of the Trade

4

Preview

Journalists rely on a variety of tools to do their work. These include the computer, tape recorder, telephone and many information sources such as census data, polls, official documents, clippings and databases.

The journalist:

- Understands how to use basic references.
- Knows public-record laws.
- Understands how the computer can help to gather and to analyze information for stories.
- Is able to conduct and interpret a public opinion poll.

Four reference volumes are compressed on this CD-ROM.

Journalists use several kinds of instruments for their reporting—pencils, pads, tape recorders, video display terminals. They use various reporting devices—the telephone, the computer, reference materials and such analytic tools as mathematics and polling techniques. Then there is the special language the journalist uses to communicate with co-workers.

Learning the language is essential, as the apprentice electrician finds out the first day on the job when he is told to get a bucket of volts, or the chemistry student who is immortalized in the couplet:

Johnny was a chemist; Johnny is no more.
What Johnny thought was H_2O was H_2SO_4.

Newsroom ignorance may not prove fatal, but it can lead to inclusion in journalism's hall of horrors. Take the case of the afternoon newspaper in Walsenburg, Colo., that wanted to carry the name of the winner of the Indianapolis 500 car race in its late edition. The newspaper's AP wire shut off at 3 p.m., too early for the result. So it asked the Indianapolis AP bureau to let it know the winner by telegram.

The Indianapolis bureau acknowledged the newspaper's request with this message: "Will overhead winner of Indianapolis 500." The AP was telling Walsenburg it would telegram the winner's name. In wire service lingo, the word *overhead* is used for *telegram.* But the sports department didn't know that, and a reporter who was handed the message wrote this story:

> Indianapolis, Ind., May 30—(AP)—
> Will Overhead won the Indianapolis Memorial Day race today. At the two hundred fifty mile post Babe Stapp was leading the string of racing cars, but gave way to Overhead on the last half of the 500 mile grind.

A glossary of journalism terms is provided in the back of the book. When in doubt about any term, consult it. You may want to pencil in additions.

Unlike the reporter's vocabulary, the tangible tools are supplied by the employer:

◀ **The Tangible Tools**

The **VDT** (video display terminal) displays what the reporter inputs with the keyboard, which relays electronic impulses to the computer. Printouts can be made of the material.

A **pad** with a hard back like a stenographer's notebook is best for note taking. The stiff backing makes jottings clear, and the spiral binding keeps notes in order.

The **tape recorder** is a necessity for the radio reporter, optional for the print reporter. The tape recorder is useful in covering speeches. It is an aid for stories requiring precise quotes. The broadcast journalist may not tape the voice of the source without asking permission.

A **laptop computer** is useful for out-of-office assignments.

The **telephone** is a basic tool of the trade but it cannot substitute for the face-to-face interview. (See Chapter 25 for legal restrictions.)

The **cellular phone** and the computer, powered by battery, allow reporters to send in their stories from any location. The system can be carried in a briefcase.

The **microcomputer** makes charts, graphs and diagrams. With the microcomputer it is possible for even the smallest newspapers and stations to expand their use of visual material produced in the newsroom.

Newspapers and stations subscribe to a variety of news services. The major supplier is the Associated Press. Syndicates formed by large newspapers such as the Los Angeles Times—Washington Post News Service, the Chicago Tribune Press Service, the New York Times News Service and others are increasingly used.

◀ **Newsroom Resources**

Local reporters use the wire services for special coverage. If a newspaper wants the AP to follow a local team in a national tournament, the service will write a story aimed at that paper's readers. The wire services also will make checks, when reporter time is available. A member newspaper could ask the AP to check a senator's vote on a farm bill, for example.

Basic References ▶

Every reporter has a few references handy—the newspaper or station stylebook, a dictionary and the telephone directory. The stylebook, often the one used by the AP, assures consistency in spelling, capitalization, punctuation and abbreviation. Is it 18 Fifth Ave. or 18 Fifth Avenue? The stylebook tells us. Do newspapers use postal abbreviations for states? The stylebook tells us to use Calif., not CA. A stylebook, included in this textbook for your use, begins on p. 649.

Reporters use the dictionary to verify spellings and to make certain that the words they want have the shades of meaning they intend.

The cross-indexed or reverse directory, a listing of telephone numbers by address, is invaluable on a late-breaking story when the reporter cannot go to the event but needs details from the scene.

Some reporters keep a small library at their desks—a one-volume history, an atlas, a thesaurus and a world almanac. If these are not within arm's reach, the reporter should know where they are in the newsroom.

Every reporter should know how to use these references:

- **A world almanac.**
- *The Reader's Guide to Periodical Literature.*
- *The New York Times Index.*
- *Bartlett's Familiar Quotations.* Who penned, "How do I love thee? Let me count the ways"? Had a Chicago journalist consulted Bartlett's, the newspaper might have been spared embarrassment. The quotation was used under a large page-one picture of a couple sitting on a statue of Shakespeare in a Chicago park—with attribution to William Shakespeare. (If you do not know the author, look it up.)
- *The National Zip Code & Post Office Directory.* Use this for locating cities in states and for finding the ZIP code.
- **City directory.** Several firms produce directories with information about people living in the community. A typical entry will include correct full name; occupation and employer; complete street address including apartment number; spouse's name and initial; whether the person owns or rents, is retired, is employed, is a student. In the street directory, a reporter can find the name of the resident and his or her telephone number from a given address. Some directories are based on telephone numbers; given a number, the reporter can find the name of the telephone subscriber. The directory companies also make up classified business directories that list, at no charge, all businesses.
- *Who's Who in America.* This resource contains biographical information about 72,000 living North Americans and is an essential source for information about leaders in social, economic, cultural and political affairs. Biographical information is supplied by the person listed. Other biographical directories published by the same firm, Marquis Who's Who Inc., include regional directories and directories on biographees professions. For biographies of long-dead people, the *Dictionary of American Biography* is useful. For people who have died within the last several years, consult back volumes of *Who's Who, Who Was Who* or *Current Biography.*

Searching the Past

For her story on changes in fashion, this reporter examined *The Readers' Guide* for articles about men's and women's clothing 20-plus years ago. *The Guide* summarizes magazine articles.

- **Source book and futures book.** Every reporter keeps a current address book of names, titles, addresses and telephone numbers from his or her beat. A date book or date pad listing future assignments and appointments—called a *futures book*—is also necessary.
- **Maps.** Some reporters keep in their desks or have quick access to the city map or street directory and a mass transit map. A Rand McNally road atlas for the U.S., Canada and Mexico can be useful.
- **Grammar text.** Deep in a drawer and consulted on the sly by a few journalists is a grammar text, high school or college variety. Some reporters never do learn how to punctuate the question in a quote within a quote or the possessive of *Jones*.

Phonetic Alphabet for Telephone Use

A—Alpha	N—November
B—Bravo	O—Oscar
C—Charlie	P—Papa
D—Delta	Q—Quebec
E—Echo	R—Romeo
F—Foxtrot	S—Sierra
G—Golf	T—Tango
H—Hotel	U—Uncle
I—India	V—Victor
J—Juliet	W—Whiskey
K—Kilo	X—X-ray
L—Lima [as in Peru, not bean]	Y—Yankee
M—Mike	Z—Zulu

Henry's Elbow

The newspaper wanted to include a review of the local orchestra concert and asked the culture reporter to telephone her review. The review described the "superb playing," and commented, "Particularly beautiful playing came from Henry Schuman's elbow, Benjamin Hudson's violin and Richard Sher's cello."

Schuman's elbow? A new instrument? Most likely the reviewer said *oboe,* and the transcriber heard *elbow.* And this is why reporters using the telephone spell unusual and unfamiliar words. And when they spell they use the phonetic alphabet.

This phonetic alphabet is used by international airports and is the basis of most journalists phonetic alphabets.

ALPHABETICAL DIRECTORY WHITE PAGES

ⓗ HOUSEHOLDER   ⓡ RESIDENT OR ROOMER

correct full name ———————— Landon Edw G & Charlotte D; servmn B F Goodrich
     h1215 Oak Dr

occupation and employer ———————— Landon Fred M & Mary E; supvr Reliance Elec h60
     Norman Av

complete street address
including apartment number ———————— Landon Kenneth A & Carol L; clk First Natl Bk
     h1400 E Main St Apt 14

Landon Kenneth A Jr studt r1400 E Main St Apt 14

Landon Virginia E r1641 W 4th St

student 18 years of age or older ———————— Lane See Also Layne

cross reference of surnames ———————— Lane Allen M & Joan M (Allen's Bakery) h1234
     Grand Blvd

Lane Avenue Restaurant (Ernest G Long) 216
     Lane Av

out-of-town resident employed
in area ———————— Lane James M & Betty B; brkmn Penn Central
     r Rt 1 Jefferson O

Lane Marvin L USA r1234 Grand Blvd

armed force member and
branch of service ———————— Lane Robt B & Margt E; retd h1402 N High St

Lane Walter M r1234 Grand Blvd

Layne See Also Lane

wife's name and initial ———————— Layne Agnes E Mrs v-pres Layne Co h2325
     Eureka Rd

Layne Albert M & Minnie B; slsmn Hoover Co h19
     Bellows Av

corporation showing officers and
nature of business ———————— Layne Co Inc Thos E Layne Pres Mrs Agnes E
     Layne V-Pres Edw T Layne Sec-Treas bldg
     contrs 100 N High St

Layne Edw T & Diane E; sec-treas Layne Co h140
     Oakwood Dr

Layne Ralph P & Gladys M; formn Layne Co h1687
     Maple Dr

Layne Thos E & Agnes E; pres Layne Co h2325
     Eureka Rd

suburban designation ———————— Leach See Also Leech

retiree ———————— Leach Wm E USMC r1209 Ravenscroft Rd (EF)

Lee Alf M & Celia J; retd h2106 Oakwood Dr

business partnership showing
partners in parenthesis ———————— Lee Bros (Louis J And Harry M Lee) plmbs 151
     Abbott St

Lee Harry M & Karen L (Lee Bros) h2023 Stone Rd

husband and wife employed ———————— Lee Louis J & Martha B (Lee Bros) h1616 Fulton

Lee Martha B Mrs ofc sec Lee Bros h1616 Fulton

"r" resident or roomer ———————— Lee Minnie M Mrs h87 Eastview Dr

Lee Muriel E r810 LaForge St

"h" householders ———————— Lee Sterling T & Nadine S; mtcemn Eastview Apts
     h202 Wilson St Apt 1

Lee Thos W & Effie M (Tom's Men's Wear) r Rt 23

owner of business showing name
of business in parenthesis ———————— **LEE'S PHARMACY (Lee A Shaw) Prescriptions
     Carefully Compounded, Complete Line Of
     Toiletries And Cosmetics, Fountain Service,**

bold type denotes paid listing ———————— **Greeting Cards, 1705 N High St (21505) Tel**

Leech See Also Leach

Leech Doris E tchr North High Sch
     h1323 W McLean St

business firm showing name of
owner in parenthesis ———————— Leech Joseph B & Lucy V; slsmn Metropolitan Dept
     Store h824 Wilson St

Leech Joseph B Jr studt r824 Wilson St

unmarried and unemployed
resident ———————— Leech Marcia M clk Community Hosp r1323 W
     McLean St

more than one adult in household ———————— Lewis Anne M Mrs clk County Hwy Dept h914
     Wilson Av

Lewis Ernest W studt r914 Wilson Av

Lewis Harold G & Anne M; mgr Cooper Paint Store
     h914 Wilson Av

Lewis Robt B lab County Hwy Dept r1410 Union
     Hwy Rt 2

church showing name of pastor ———————— Lewistown Methodist Church Rev John R Allen
     Pastor 515 Maple Valley Rd

R.L. Polk and Company.

City Directory

Government agencies require filings that are useful in investigative work. The Sun Newspapers of Omaha investigated Boys Town and found that, despite pleas of poverty, the nonprofit organization had a $209 million investment portfolio. The series was based on information from Form 990 that the institution filed with the Internal Revenue Service. Tax-exempt organizations file details of their finances on the 990. Write the Disclosure Officer at the local IRS office for the 990 of the organization you are checking.

The reporter's basic newsroom reference is, of course, the newspaper or station morgue or library. No story should be written without first checking the morgue. In many newsrooms, library material can be retrieved on the computer.

Most of the standard references have been placed on disks called CD-ROMs for compact disk-read only memory. The Census Bureau makes available CD-ROMs of demographic material on cities, counties and states.

The electronic revolution has put information of vast scope at the journalist's fingertips, providing he or she can use the available tools. The computer puts the journalist in touch with 50,000 bulletin boards, a huge array of databases and more than 20 million users of the Internet.

"Everything has gone digital," says Nicholas Negroponte, director of the Media Laboratory of the Massachusetts Institute of Technology. He says engineers have made it possible to send large amounts of data over fiber-optic networks so that, for example, the entire output of *The Wall Street Journal*—a hundred years' worth—could be delivered in half a second.

The revolution has spawned magazines, journals and newsletters that are available only through a terminal, or what is known as *on-line journalism.* Soon, says a report drawn up for the Association of American Publishers, the "World Wide Web will become the ultimate library of public information." Already, the Internet is being used as a reporting tool.

A *Wall Street Journal* reporter who was preparing a story on Parkinson's disease learned that there is an Internet news group made up of people interested in the disease. He put a message out and was able to obtain useful names and information.

Here are two typical exchanges that moved on the Internet:

Query

Does anybody have story ideas for using death-record data? When you used the data in your state, did you get the names and addresses of the dead people? Here in Oregon, they'll only give you a stripped-down database without the names. Thanks for any ideas.

Reply

You could sort out by cause of death or age of victim. Maybe that would come up with an interesting angle. You might find, for instance, that just as many people in their 70s commit suicide as kids from ages 17 to 24. You might find that people of

Learning the System

Managing Editor Peter Ellis instructs college intern Amy Welch in the computer system at the *Argus Leader.*

◀ **Computer Literacy**

◀ Internet Use

certain ages and ethnicity tend to die of gunshot wounds. You might find that most people who are homicide victims die between 2 a.m. and 6 a.m., while most suicide victims die in the early afternoon. Dunno. I'm just casting about ideas.

After Orange County, Calif., found itself $1.7 billion in the hole and filed for bankruptcy, a reporter for *The Orange County Register* asked, "Does anyone know where I can find a list of the largest bankruptcies in the U.S.?" An answer came quickly: "I'd try Forbes or Barron's."

Five Areas ▶

Phil Ward, who was a member of the Louisiana State University journalism faculty, says the Internet is useful for several journalistic purposes: research in government, educational and private databases; interviewing sources via e-mail; swapping reporting ideas and asking other reporters for information; discussing journalism subjects with other journalists; and finding or posting jobs. Examples:

• A graphics designer for a newspaper was making a map and had to place on it a small town in New Mexico that was included in the copy. A reply came back with the latitude and longitude of the small town.
• A University of Wisconsin student was injured while traveling and a reporter wanted to reach his relatives. The reporter asked over the Internet for information about contacting them. A person with access to the university directory supplied the information.

The Grateful Dead ▶

Louis D. Boccardi, president and chief executive officer of the AP, tells this story about the usefulness of the Internet:

Beth Weise is a reporter in the AP's San Francisco bureau. She writes a column about the Internet and, of course, she logs on frequently.

But her basic assignment, like that of many AP people, is general reporting. Recently she wrote a story about the reopening of the storied old Fillmore Auditorium in San Francisco. Her story said The Grateful Dead had played there on the night the hall opened in the '60s.

Beth sent the story to the General Desk in New York for the national wire. And, wouldn't you know, she got an editor who happened to be a Deadhead.

The editor fired back a message telling Beth that The Grateful Dead didn't even exist at that point and suggested, politely I hope, that she check her facts.

It was eight o'clock on a Sunday night and her source, one of the present managers of the band, wasn't around.

Now—Internet to the rescue.

Beth logged in and posted a query to a Grateful Dead usenet news group. In 20 minutes, she had three responses. One message was from somebody who had been at that original concert and another came from the author of a book on the band. If she had waited a few minutes more, she might have heard from Jerry Garcia himself.

It turned out that the band WAS at the concert, but they had just changed their name from The Warlocks the week before and were not well known at the time as The Grateful Dead.

The Internet is also useful in obtaining information from organizations in the news. After the Oklahoma City terror bombing, the National Rifle Association issued a statement on terrorism that was summarized in news accounts. For those who wanted access to the full statement, Internet provided the means of reaching the NRA.

◀ **The NRA**

"Be aware of where it comes from," warns Boccardi about the Internet. While the new technology can strengthen news reporting, he says, the "seductiveness of its technology" should not cause a change in "the principles of what we do." He set up as guidelines accuracy, objectivity, fairness and accountability.

◀ **Warning**

The lack of certainty about the source of material on the Internet has caused some professionals to desert the Internet, reports *The Wall Street Journal*. Too many users, the article states, are "flooding the bulletin boards with irrelevancies." The article continues:

> Their concern is over the Usenet sector, where "newsgroups" discuss subjects of common interest. Some longtime expert users say untrained newcomers are making discourse impossible by flooding the chat lines with naive questions or silly comments, disbursing inaccurate information or taking a hostile, abusive attitude to anyone they disagree with.

When a Russian jet fighter shot down a Korean airliner, newspapers and stations needed background information—fast. Some were able to have the material on their screens within minutes by using databases. Databases are electronic libraries that are accessible through on-line computers. In this case, the reporters and editors searching for background typed in the search words *Korean Air Lines*. The database computer scanned thousands of stories for the words and, in less than a minute, a list of articles was available.

◀ **Databases**

The advantage of using on-line databases is that they can answer specific questions with great speed. A user can make a more comprehensive search of material than is possible with any other method.

With more than 5,000 machine readable libraries available, the user must know where to look for the needed information. A directory of electronic information providers can be consulted; newspaper and university librarians are usually trained to provide such information.

There are three kinds of databases:

• Some databases provide full texts of news stories, magazine articles and documents.

• Some databases give bibliographic material that refers to magazine and newspaper articles, government reports and scholarly articles. Some bibliographic databases provide only references, and others give summaries of the articles as well as the references.

• Numeric databases contain census data, statistics and a variety of demographic material.

LEXIS®-NEXIS®, an on-line information service, offers more than 2,400 full-text sources, including *The New York Times, Washington Post, Los Angeles Times* and scores of other newspapers as well as magazines, broadcast transcripts, wire services and newsletters. It also contains every patent issued since 1975, every volume of the *Federal Register,* every issue of the *Congressional Quarterly* and every 10-K form filed with the Securities and Exchange Commission. (The 10-K lists a company's finances, ownership, management history and other details.) Medline—available on NEXIS—has more than four million records and is a major source for biomedical material. ERIC is a database that covers education.

The database can be expensive—$35 to $200 an hour—and mostly larger newspapers subscribe. Reporters whose newspapers do not have access to a database usually can find some place in town with access. University and college libraries do database searching; a law firm may be on LEXIS, an on-line information service for lawyers.

Government Databases ▶

The database and the computer are indispensable tools for digging reporters. Seven of the 10 finalists in major news categories for the Pulitzer Prize in a recent year were stories made possible by the computer. Here are some examples of how newspapers have used government database material for stories:

• Reporters at the *Dayton* (Ohio) *Daily News* fed the names of all county workers into their computer, which made a master alphabetized list that showed that several employees held two jobs and were receiving two salaries. The reporters also learned the names of those receiving unusually large amounts of overtime pay.

• The *Los Angeles Times* analyzed criminal court sentences and found that first-offender blacks were much more likely to be jailed than first-offender whites for the same crimes.

Many computer-assisted stories rely on putting two batches of information into the computer and noting the overlaps. Bob Sanders of *The Post-Standard* in Syracuse, N.Y., obtained the Federal Election Commission database on financial contributions to Sen. Alfonse D'Amato's campaign. He then obtained the list of loans for federal rural housing projects made by the Farmers Home Administration to developers. Sanders ran the two together and he found a relationship that enabled him to write:

> Five New York developers who contributed to U.S. Sen. Alfonse D'Amato's campaigns received about 40 percent of the highly competitive loans for a federal rural housing program in the state.

Sanders discovered that the state director of the FHA who approved the loans had borrowed money from some of the developers, and he also learned that those who had loaned the director money were able to receive government money faster than were other developers. As a result of Sanders' disclosures, the director was suspended.

Smarts. "Tools and technology are important only in reference to their application. A baboon with a computer is a baboon."—Ed Miller, former editor and publisher, *The Morning Call,* Allentown, Pa.

For another story, Sanders compared census data with the location of bill- ◀ Using Census Data
boards. He wanted to see whether advertisers were trying to reach minority
neighborhoods with alcohol and cigarette advertisements. The billboard locations
came from the city planning commission, the census data from tract tapes. He
found his suspicion was accurate: A disproportionate number of billboards were
placed in minority neighborhoods, many of them with advertisements for alcohol
and cigarettes.

Sanders kept in mind the adage, "Statistics put people to sleep." "You are
looking for key statistics to illuminate a story," he says. "The data points to or
backs up the story." Here is how his billboard story began:

Jeff Scruggs has a blue ribbon on his front door on Seymour Street proclaiming his opposition to drugs.

But when he opens that door each day he is confronted by a different message: a long smoldering cigarette gracing a 12-by-25-foot billboard, providing a backdrop on a corner neighbors say is a hot spot for drug dealers. . . .

All up and down Salina Street and Erie Boulevard, outside the mom-and-pop stores on South Avenue and on the near west side, more than half the city's 247 street-level billboards give residents two major messages: smoke and drink.

When reports of mass murders with assault rifles became numerous, reporters in the Washington bureau of the Cox Newspapers decided to see whether
these weapons were frequently used in crimes. No one had the information tabu-
lated, so they dug into cardboard files for documents—42,758 in all. With a computer program, they organized the voluminous files and they learned that semi-
automatic guns were 20 times more likely to be used in a crime than were
conventional weapons.

The *Star Tribune* in Minneapolis spent nine months making a computer-
assisted analysis of the activities of 767 sex criminals. The 30,000 word series of
articles by Donna Halvorsen and Allen Short, "Free to Rape," found the state's
courts failed to deal effectively with rapists and child molesters and that those
who were treated in Minnesota's costly psychological treatment program were
more likely to commit new sex crimes than those who were not treated. The reporters also found a far higher rate of repeat crimes than the state's official figures
indicated.

Reporters in the Washington bureau of the Knight-Ridder newspapers analyzed computerized Medicare records of open-heart surgery to pinpoint unusually high death rates in some hospitals. After three children were killed in school-
bus accidents, *The Providence Journal-Bulletin* compared a list of bus-driver
licenses to a tape of traffic violations and discovered that some bus drivers had
been ticketed as many as 20 times. Some drivers were convicted felons. The state
tightened licensing procedures as a result.

The *Atlanta Journal* checked seven computer tapes with 109,000 real estate
loans that had been reported to the federal government and found that whites
were at least five times more likely to receive home loans as were blacks in
the same income bracket. Nine days after the revelation, local banks made

Not Magic. Computers "will not transform bad reporters into good ones," says Andrew Schneider, prizewinning reporter and director of the National Institute of Advanced Reporting. "If you don't have the basic reporting skills and use them well, a hundred computers won't make a difference."

$77 million available for home purchase and improvements in primarily black communities. The newspaper won a Pulitzer Prize for its series.

Basic Functions ▶

These computer-aided projects are based on three basic activities that the computer can perform for the journalist:

- **Alphabetizing:** Similar jobs or similar names can be placed in a series.
- **Rank ordering:** Instructed to put in order any list, the computer will reveal, for example, the highest to lowest infant mortality rates among the cities in a state or among the states in the nation.
- **Correlating:** The computer will match two different databases. A reporter who wants to check whether school hiring procedures are thorough can match a list of the city's schoolteachers against a list of convictions for sex crimes.

Census Data ▶

The census takes the social and economic pulse of 250 million Americans every 10 years. It is used to determine congressional representation and is the basis for the allocation of billions of dollars in federal, state and local funds. The Bureau of the Census breaks down its count into census tracts of around 4,000 people, making vast amounts of information available to the local reporter: How many married women are living with their husbands? How many households are headed by females? What are the median and average family incomes?

The reporter who wants to track social change in his or her community will find census data essential. Working mothers, children in nursery school, shifts in family patterns and demographic changes—data on all this are available. Reporters have used census data to find pockets of the elderly and of ethnic groups. Changes in the racial makeup of neighborhoods can be charted with census data.

For a story about the housing stock in the community, the reporter can find the number of houses that lack toilets, private baths and hot water. The number of people living in housing units (density) also can be determined. By analyzing who lives in a representative's district, it is possible to indicate how he or she is most likely to vote or to determine the pressures exerted on the legislator regarding public housing, Social Security and other social issues. The data also can be used to document depth reporting—the need for additional day-care centers, low cost housing or senior citizen facilities.

Printed census reports are available at public and university libraries and at many local, state and federal agencies. The best place to obtain local census material is the State Data Center, where experts can help with interpretations and make comparisons with previous censuses. Detailed information is available from the centers on computer tapes and floppy discs as well as on CD-ROM (Computer Disc-Read Only Memory).

An investment of about $100 will purchase all the reports for a state. Colleges and universities often have computer tapes. The Bureau of the Census, U.S. Department of Commerce, Washington, D.C. 20233, (301) 763-4040 can help in locating the nearest tape center.

Census News. Some of the trends to check: Aging population—increasing life expectancy means more aged; what's it mean for Social Security, Medicare? New family—increasing numbers of nontraditional households such as unmarried couples, older children at home, elderly sharing homes. Growth of minority population—in a few years, one of three schoolchildren will be from minority groups. How will schools cope? How will the socioeconomic gap between majority and minority be handled?

The Bureau takes more than 250 sample surveys a year to monitor trends in employment, population growth, fertility, living arrangements and marriage. It makes surveys of a number of activities every five years, including housing, agriculture, business, construction, government, manufacturing, mineral industry and transportation.

Some of the best-kept official records are those for disease and death. Doctors, clinics and hospitals are required to keep scrupulous records. These are sent to city and county health offices, which relay them to state and federal agencies.

Since this information has been kept for many years, it can provide the journalist with an insight into community health standards. In fact, infant mortality rates are sometimes described as the measure of the civilization of a society.

◀ **Death and Disease Data**

Table 4.1 Infant Mortality Rates for States			
Average 8.3			
Alabama	9.9	Montana	7.9
Alaska	7.5	Nebraska	8.8
Arizona	7.0	Nevada	6.6
Arkansas	9.5	New Hampshire	4.8
California	6.7	New Jersey	8.0
Colorado	7.5	New Mexico	9.3
Connecticut	7.1	New York	8.3
Delaware	8.3	North Carolina	10.3
Florida	8.7	North Dakota	7.1
Georgia	10.1	Ohio	8.8
Hawaii	6.7	Oklahoma	9.2
Idaho	7.5	Oregon	6.7
Illinois	10.3	Pennsylvania	8.7
Indiana	9.3	Rhode Island	8.5
Iowa	6.9	South Carolina	9.4
Kansas	8.2	South Dakota	10.5
Kentucky	8.8	Tennessee	9.9
Louisiana	9.8	Texas	7.6
Maine	6.6	Utah	6.0
Maryland	9.4	Vermont	4.9
Massachusetts	5.6	Virginia	8.5
Michigan	9.3	Washington	6.9
Minnesota	7.3	West Virginia	9.3
Mississippi	11.9	Wisconsin	8.0
Missouri	8.5	Wyoming	8.1

The rate is calculated per 1,000 live births.
Figures are from the National Center for Health Statistics.

The United States' infant mortality rate is 23d among industrialized nations, and the rates in some of its cities are even higher than those in some developing countries.

The figures are highest in urban areas and poor rural areas, and they are unusually high among minority, teen-age, and unwed mothers. Internal comparisons also can be made since most local health agencies break the city into health districts. Districts with low-income residents can be compared with those with middle-income residents, and comparisons can be made between districts with white and nonwhite populations.

For data on death numbers and rates write:

Scientific and Technical Information Branch
Division of Operations
National Center for Health Statistics
6525 Belcrest Rd. Room 1064
Hyattsville, MD 20782
Phone: (301) 436-8500

Venereal Disease and AIDS ▶

A reporter noticed a wire service story that said syphilis rates in many cities had increased. Gonorrhea cases had declined. The reporter decided to find out how his city ranked in the rates for these diseases. He noticed that the source for the figures was the Centers for Disease Control and Prevention in Atlanta. He wrote, obtained the booklet "Sexually Transmitted Disease Statistics" for the past year and wrote a local story.

The CDC also keeps data on AIDS cases, and reporters can obtain state and city rates from the agency. Table 4.2, on the opposite page, shows the 10 states and cities with the highest AIDS rates.

For morbidity reports on notifiable diseases—sexually transmitted diseases, tuberculosis, childhood diseases—write or call:

Centers for Disease Control and Prevention
Atlanta, GA 30333
Phone (404) 639-3311

Correlations ▶

Interesting stories can be written by making correlations that compare disease and death data with median family income, unemployment rates, crime rates, truancy rates, educational attainment, population density, welfare recipiency and so on.

Correlations can be made that show the roles that gender, race and class play in our society. These findings are useful for a community that wants to make public policy to cope with the needs of its citizens. But some people contend that these stories stigmatize the poor.

Table 4.2 AIDS: Annual Rate of Cases

States		Metropolitan Areas	
New York	82.2	San Francisco	158.0
New Jersey	63.2	New York	153.4
Florida	61.8	Miami	153.3
Maryland	54.4	Jersey City, N.J.	152.1
California	38.6	Ft. Lauderdale, Fla.	106.1
Delaware	38.4	Newark, N.J.	98.0
Georgia	31.8	Baltimore	76.8
South Carolina	31.6	W. Palm Beach, Fla.	75.3
Louisiana	28.7	New Orleans	53.2
Connecticut	27.8	Washington, D.C.	53.1
National Average	30.0	Metropolitan Area Average	41.4

Rate per 100,000 population.
Centers for Disease Control and Prevention.

The response is that articles about the consequences of poverty and ignorance can lead to changes. For example, the community may decide to spend more on prenatal care and maternal and child health clinics. Schools may include in their curricula specifics about the dangers of alcoholism and drug addiction. Stories based on local experiences have greater impact and utility than do the generalized material national organizations provide.

Reporters should know just what records are available to them on their beats. Among the many records usually accessible to the public are:

◀ **Public Records**

- Assessment and tax records, deeds, property transfers.
- Records dealing with licenses—restaurant, dog, liquor, tavern and the many other business and professional licenses.
- City engineer's records—streets, alleys, property lines, highways.
- City building permits, variances, unpaid taxes, liens, violations.
- Automobile ownership.
- Election returns.
- Articles of incorporation. Most states require officers to file their names and holdings in the corporation. Partnerships.
- Bills and vouchers for all governmental purchases. Copies of the checks (warrants) paid out for goods and services.
- Minutes of city council, county commission meetings. All appropriations, budgets.
- Most records in the judicial area—indictments, trials, sentences, court transcripts.
- Wills, receiverships, bankruptcies.

Most police records on a current basis. There are limits to arrest records.

Reporters sometimes discover that they are denied public records. A check of the law helps to open them up. All the states have "sunshine laws" that require records to be available for public examination.

Useful Numbers ▶

For information on legislation in the House or Senate, call (202) 225-1772. For information on when a bill was signed or vetoed, call (202) 456-2226.

For tapes of proceedings on the floors of Congress:

	Senate	House
Democratic	(202) 224-8541	(202) 225-7400
Republican	(202) 224-8601	(202) 225-7430

To obtain documents from the Government Printing Office, write:

Superintendent of Documents
U.S. Government Printing Office
Washington, DC 20402
(202) 783-3238

For information from a specialist in drugs and for crime statistics write or call:

Data Center and Clearinghouse for Drugs & Crime
1600 Research Blvd.
Rockville, MD 20850
1 (800) 666-3332

Freedom of Information Act ▶

No Secrets. The journalist's insistence on freedom to seek out information has a distinguished heritage. In 1644, John Milton's *Areopagitica, "A Speech for the Liberty of Unlicensed Printing,"* contended that truth might be learned if all ideas were let loose for discussion. Joseph Pulitzer put the matter in journalistic terms:

"There is not a crime, there is not a dodge, there is not a trick, there is not a swindle which does not live by secrecy. Get these things out in the open, describe them, attack them, ridicule them in the press, and sooner or later public opinion will sweep them away."

Access to one of the vast areas of information—federal records—was limited until Congress enacted the Freedom of Information Act in 1966. The act, and important amendments in 1975, unlocked millions of pages of federal documents. The FOIA states that the public has the right to inspect any document that the executive branch possesses, with nine exceptions. These exceptions prevent reporters, or anyone else, from examining income tax returns, secret documents vital to national defense or foreign policy, intra-agency letters and other sensitive material.

The 1975 amendments give the federal courts the power to review classified documents to make sure that they are properly classified, and they put a limit on the time an agency can take to reply to a request.

The *Mercury-News* in San Jose, Calif., used a Freedom of Information request to the FBI to obtain material that revealed that President Reagan had been an FBI informer in the late 1940s. The documents obtained by the newspaper identified Reagan as "T-10" and said that he and his first wife had "provided the FBI with names of actors they believed were members of a clique with a pro-Communist line." The *Mercury-News* also learned from FBI files on the author John Steinbeck that the FBI had tracked Steinbeck for years because of his involvement with labor causes. Steinbeck wrote *The Grapes of Wrath,* which won the Pulitzer Prize for literature in 1940.

Continuing Battle

Newspapers "ranging from the smallest community papers to the largest national dailies find themselves almost continually snarled in disputes over one of our basic democratic rights: To find out what the branches of the government and its agencies are doing," says the American Society of Newspaper Editors. At the state and local levels, newspapers use Freedom of Information laws often and have resorted to suits to obtain court orders to unlock information.

The Patriot Ledger in Quincy, Mass., won a state supreme court order requiring a lower court to release the divorce records of a county treasurer under investigation for corruption.

The Free Lance-Star in Fredericksburg, Va., used the state FOI law to check on how active a fair housing commission had been. It learned the commission had made one investigation in 20 years.

The Charlotte (N.C.) *Observer* used more than 40 FOI requests to disclose how the president of the University of South Carolina was spending money: weekends in the Caribbean, $12,000 private-plane flights, travels in Europe with selected students at university expense, $330,000 for the widow of Egyptian president Anwar Sadat for three semesters of teaching at the University.

To use the act, find out which agency has the records sought. A guide is the *U.S. Government Manual,* which may be obtained from the Government Printing Office. Ask for Stock Number D22-003-00424-8. Requests usually are sent to the Freedom of Information Office of the agency. No reason need be given for the request for information. It sometimes makes the request easier to handle if specific information is requested. Charges are usually nominal. The reporter may ask to be notified of charges in advance.

The letter should state that the request is being made "under the provisions of the Freedom of Information Act, 5 U.S.C. 552." See Appendix C for the request procedure and a sample letter.

All states have enacted open records and open meetings laws. Usually, these laws presume that everything public and official is open with stipulated exceptions. Most denials of requests for records fall into these categories:

◀ State Laws: Exceptions

1. **Confidential records.** Records that are exempted by federal or state law such as income tax returns, health and welfare files on individuals.

2. **Privacy.** Records that would allow an unwarranted invasion of an individual's privacy. (Officials have less right of privacy than do private individuals.)

3. **Collective bargaining negotiations.** Disclosure of present or imminent actions in these areas could impair discussions.

4. **Trade secrets.** Information that might injure a person or firm in a competitive situation.

5. **Records compiled for law enforcement agencies.** Records that could impede a fair trial, endanger the life or safety of an agent or an informer.

6. **Inter-agency memoranda and intra-agency reports.** Excludes statistics, policies and instructions to the staff.

7. **Examinations and evaluations.** Materials used in assessing job applicants.

The states' open meetings laws exempt executive sessions that are concerned with collective bargaining; imminent legislation; the medical, financial or credit records of a person or corporation; and any matters made confidential by state and federal law.

Mathematics for the Reporter ▶

The UPI dispatch read:

The average American who lives to the age of 70 consumes in that lifetime the equivalent of 150 cattle, 24,000 chickens, 225 lambs, 26 sheep, 310 hogs, 26 acres of grain and 50 acres of fruits and vegetables.

A Nevada newspaper reader who saw the story was puzzled. That seemed like a lot of meat to consume in a lifetime, he thought. He consulted his butcher who estimated the dressed weights of the various animals listed in the story. They came up with a total of 222,695 pounds of meat. The reader wrote the UPI that he had done some figuring. He multiplied 70 years by 365 days to find the total number of days in the average person's lifetime. The figure was 25,500 days. He divided the total meat consumption of 222,695 pounds by 25,500 days. "That figures out to a whopping 8.7 pounds of meat a day," he wrote.

The UPI retired the reference work from which the item was gleaned.

The reporter who handled the story would have avoided embarrassing UPI had he observed Rule No. 1 for numbers: Always check them.

If the reporter who handled the Postal Service food drive story for his Florida paper had checked the numbers he was given, he would have avoided looking as silly as the UPI reporter. He wrote that letter carriers had collected 11 million tons of food last year in three Florida counties. A reader checked: 11 million tons equals 22 billion pounds. Divide that by the U.S. population of 261 million.

The reader calculated that the letter carriers would have had to have collected 84 pounds of food for each man, woman and child in the United States. Hardly likely.

It turns out that it wasn't tons but pounds—11 million pounds. That's still a lot, but it's 1/2,000th of the newspaper's figure.

Percentages ▶

We live in an age of quantification. Numbers surround us, and they reveal a great deal about how we live. The reporter must be able to make simple calculations like the one an Associated Press reporter made for the 1990 census. The new U.S. population figure was 249,632,692, but the reporter knew this number alone would be meaningless in the lead. Even the total increase of about 23 million would not make a sharp lead.

What was needed was the percentage increase, which he figured this way:

Total 1990	249,632,692
Total 1980	−226,504,825
Increase	23,127,867

$$\frac{\text{Increase}}{\text{Total 1980}} \quad \frac{23,127,867}{226,504,825} = 10.2\%$$

Here was the AP lead:

> The Census Bureau today put the population of the United States at 249,632,692, an increase of more than 23 million people, or 10.2 percent, over the 1980 total.

One of the most common mistakes in calculating a percentage increase or decrease is putting the difference between the old and the new over the new figure. Wrong. The denominator, the bottom figure in the fraction, is the original or old figure. We are figuring the change—the percentage increase or decrease—from the **old** to the present or **new,** so we use the old as the base.

The police reporter is given the annual report of violent crimes in the city for last year: 17,030. Two years ago, the total was 22,560. The reporter knows that she has to give a percentage decline:

Two years ago	22,560	$\frac{5,530}{22,560}$	= 24.5 percentage decline
Last year	−17,030		
Decline	5,530		

The reporter writes:

> Violent crimes in Freeport declined 24.5 percent last year from the previous year.
> The police department's annual survey reveals that 17,030 violent crimes were committed last year, compared with 22,560 the year before, or 5,530 fewer crimes.

Now for a tricky area. Let's say that the interest rate that the city has to pay on bonds it is selling has gone from 6 to 7 percent. That's a 1 percent increase, right? Wrong.

◀ **Percentage Points**

Remember that we take the difference between the new and the old figures and place that over the old in a fraction:

New	7		
Old	−6	$\frac{1}{6}$	or a 16.66% increase
Increase	1		

But it would be confusing to write, "The new rate is 7 percent, which is 16.7 percent greater than the old." So we use a different term, **percentage points.** We write that the increase is 1 percentage point.

"An estimated 50 million Americans smoked 600 billion cigarettes last year," the story about a local anti-smoking proposal said. The city editor calls you, the reporter handling the story, to the desk.

"Let's put this and a lot of the other figures into some understandable terms," he tells you. "In this case, why not follow the sentence with one that says, 'This means the average smoker lit up so many cigarettes a day.'"

Back at your desk, you make a few simple calculations: 600 billion cigarettes smoked a year ÷ 50 million smokers = 12,000 cigarettes per smoker a year.

You want average daily use, so you make the next calculation: 12,000 cigarettes a year ÷ 365 days = 32.87 cigarettes per smoker a day.

You round that off to 33—a pack and a half a day. A reader can see the smoker crumpling up a pack and smoking halfway through a second pack for his or her daily dose. This is more graphic than the millions and billions, which depersonalize the story.

New York City is the murder capital of the country. True or false?

It depends on whether you use **numbers** or **rates.** For journalists, numbers are not as meaningful as rates because rates take into consideration such factors as the size of the population.

True enough, in a recent year New York City had more murders than any other city—almost six a day for a total of about 2,000 a year. Washington, D.C., had 482 murders the same year.

It doesn't require any brilliance to realize that Washington has a much smaller population than New York, which means it would be misleading to describe New York as the country's most murderous city. Let's see what happens when we factor in the population, as is done when crime rates are calculated:

<table>
<tr><td align="center">Washington</td><td align="center">New York</td></tr>
<tr><td align="center">$\dfrac{482 \text{ murders}}{598,000 \text{ people}} = 0.000806$</td><td align="center">$\dfrac{2,000 \text{ murders}}{7,353,000 \text{ people}} = 0.0002719$</td></tr>
<tr><td align="center">$0.000806 \times 100,000 = 80.6$</td><td align="center">$0.0002719 \times 100,000 = 27.19$</td></tr>
</table>

We multiply by 100,000 to eliminate the awkward decimal. When we do this, we get a rate that says there were 80.6 murders in Washington for every 100,000 people, which makes murder more likely in Washington, D.C., than in New York City. In fact, residents of the nation's capital are almost three times as likely to be murdered as are New York City residents. (80.6 divided by 27.19 gives us 2.96.)

How would you describe the average salary at J.C. Walnut and Co., an upholstery shop whose employees are on strike? Walnut says it is $31,140, and he has put a sign in his window saying so and telling his customers that the employees are ungrateful.

Here is how the annual salaries for the company break down:

- $72,500 (1) Mr. Walnut
- 59,600 (1) Son Theodore

- 30,500 (4) Master craftsmen
- 25,200 (6) Upholsterers
- 20,600 (3) Laborers

If we add up the salaries, being careful to multiply by the number of workers in each category, we reach a total payroll of $467,100. To find the average Walnut reached, we divide by 15, the total number of people on the payroll. The average is $31,140. So Walnut is right, right? Wrong.

First let's consider the word *average*. That is a dangerous word because it covers three kinds of figures:

Mean: This is the average Walnut used. To derive it, we add up all the figures in our set and divide by the total number of individual components.
Mode: The component occurring most often in a listing of components.
Median: The midpoint in a grouping.

The mean distorts when there are unusually high or low components, as there are here with Walnut and son Theodore's salaries making the average tilt toward the high end. The mode here is $25,200, which is the most frequently occurring salary.

The median, which is used most often in computing averages, requires you list all the salaries to find the midpoint:

```
                    72,500
                    59,600
                    30,500
                    30,500
                    30,500
                    30,500
                  ┌ 25,200
                  │ 25,200  ◄─── median
           mode   │ 25,200
                  │ 25,200
                  │ 25,200
                  └ 25,200
                    20,600
                    20,600
                    20,600
```

Look at this list of 15 numbers. The midpoint is the eighth on the list because there are seven salaries above it and seven below it. The eighth salary on the list is $25,200, which is the same as the mode.

Our figure of $25,200 is considerably less than Walnut's average of $31,140. And if we use some common sense, we realize that only the employees are on strike, so what is Walnut doing putting his and his son's salary in the computation?

Take out the top two on the list and we get 13 salaries. The mode and the median are still $25,200. The mean is $25,769.

Analyzing Figures ▶

Let's take this a step further before we leave the delightful realm of mathematics. Let's look behind the median. There's more here than meets the eye.

The federal government announces that the median household income last year was $37,383. Not bad. But wait a minute. Common sense, based on our reading and experience, tells us that income is widely disproportionate in this country among whites, blacks and Hispanics and between men and women. We want a breakdown of the median. Look at what we find:

Household Income

White	$39,310
Black	21,550
Hispanic	26,623

These figures tell us something about the nature of our society: The median family income of blacks is 55 percent that of whites, and the median income of Hispanics is 68 percent of whites.

As for households with working women as the providers, here are the median incomes:

Income of Women

White	$22,023
Black	19,816
Hispanic	16,758

The business of dissecting data gives us specifics, and, as we know, journalism is the art of the specific. The same agency that gave us median income figures reports that 37 million people were living in poverty last year, poverty being designated as a household income that is less than $14,763 for a family of four. With each additional family member, the poverty threshold increases by about $2,500.

We ask for particulars. Who are these 37 million people? The largest number, 24.5 million, are white and make up two-thirds of the total poor. But if we make a further check to see what percentage of the total number of whites live in poverty, we derive a much smaller percentage, 12.3 percent. Let's make a similar calculation for all racial groups:

White: 12.3 percent
Black: 35.4 percent
Hispanic: 31.3 percent
Asian: 14.7 percent

Again, the particulars give us a better insight into the nature of the problems the country faces. Let's do some more dissecting:

Percentage of 18–24-year-olds in College

White	Black	Hispanic
34	24	18

How many receive degrees? Check the figures on your campus.

Breakdown. The racial/ethnic composition of the United States is: white, 79.8 percent; black, 11.7 percent; Hispanic, 8.5 percent; Asian-Pacific Islander, 3.7 percent. The total exceeds 100 percent because Hispanics may be of any race.

The National Assessment of Educational Progress was established by Congress to monitor educational effectiveness. It has been testing students since the 1960s in reading, science and mathematics. A recent nationwide test showed that 36 percent of those about to graduate from high school could not do basic arithmetic. That's bad enough—a third of twelfth graders cannot add, subtract, multiply or divide.

◀ **Math Competency**

But when we dissect the figures, a worsening picture emerges: 66 percent of blacks, 55 percent of Hispanic students and 54 percent of Native American students failed to achieve basic competency. In a society that is increasingly technological and is dedicated to giving its minority groups access to jobs and decent living, these figures indicate the difficulty of the task. Behind the facade of the rhetoric and affirmative action legislation are bedrock problems the society has failed to solve.

Consider these national averages for some death rates:

◀ **Death Rates**

Diabetes	19.0
Chronic liver disease and cirrhosis	10.9
Infant mortality	10.0
Maternal death	7.9

Now, let's break them down by race and see what happens:

	White	Black
Diabetes	10.3	23.7
Chronic liver disease and cirrhosis	8.3	13.9
Infant mortality	7.3	17.6
Maternal death	5.6	18.4

We can go even further and break down a death rate and life expectancy into sex as well as race:

	All	White		Black	
		Male	Female	Male	Female
Suicide	12.2	21.4	5.2	12.2	2.4
Life expectancy	74.8	72.6	79.3	66.0	74.5

There are stories here, and some of these stories get to the heart of major problems society faces. If we dig into the difference in life expectancy, for example, we find homicide plays a significant role. Let's look at some homicide figures.

The rate for white murder victims is 5.2; for black murder victims it is 36.9. For murder offenders, the rates are 3.7 for whites, 32.4 for blacks.

◀ **Murder Rates**

We can make a further refinement to see what the rates are for deaths from firearms. Let's break these down by age group as well as by race:

	1–14	15–19	20–24	25–29	30–34
Black	8.2	123.6	164.4	113.4	82.9
White	1.4	11.8	14.9	12.3	10.1

How can we account for these rates, some of which are greater than 10 to one, black deaths to white deaths? A possible answer: Juvenile gang killings have risen steeply from the 1980s to the 1990s. One study by the FBI found that the death rate increased 270 percent from the mid-1980s to the mid-1990s.

These are national figures. All cities keep excellent death records so that it is possible to make analyses of this sort locally. By doing so, reporters are able to pinpoint social, economic and health problems.

Try These ▶

And now examination time. Can you spot the bad math in these three excerpts from publications?

1. Women faculty represented less than 13 percent of the full professors (12.7) while men represented 40 percent.

2. Those who smoke the small, and generally less expensive, brands are facing a tax increase of 3,333 percent; a 20-pack of Dutch Treats, a popular brand of small cigars that sells for about a dollar before state excise and sales taxes, would sell for $2.06.

3. The House of Representatives approved the agreement by an even wider margin, 288 to 146. (The comparison was with the Senate vote of 76 to 24.)

The first example appeared in a publication of the national journalism educators organization. One journalism instructor commented, "It's not the small percentage of women we're worried about but the other 47.3 percent."

No. 2 appeared in *The New York Times*. If the tax goes through, it will raise the price of Dutch Treats $1.06, which is a 106 percent increase, hardly 3,333 percent.

No. 3 is also from the *Times*. It warns us what can happen when a reporter gets frisky with numbers, especially a reporter gifted with innumeracy, the recently coined word that describes mathematical ineptitude. True enough, the House vote in favor of the agreement was 142 votes greater than the negative vote, whereas in the Senate there were 52 more affirmative votes than there were nays. But the reporter is comparing apples and avocados; the House has four times the membership of the Senate.

The better comparison is with the *ratio* of yays to nays:

House: almost 2 to 1.
Senate: more than 3 to 1.

So the Senate vote, we see, was more resoundingly affirmative than the House vote, which is exactly the opposite of what the *Times* reporter tried to get across. The blooper, incidentally, was on page one of the newspaper.

As long as we're looking at the errors of others, look at this headline from a major journalism school's alumni bulletin:

◀ Empty Boast

Two-thirds of 1993 graduates answering alumni survey have communications jobs

Big success story? Hardly. The story reveals that 189 graduates were surveyed and 24 percent replied. That's 45 answers, and two-thirds of those responding have jobs, which comes to 30 with jobs. That's 16 percent of the '93 graduating class. Well, let's be generous and say that not all of the 144 who did not answer the school's survey are jobless. But chances are that most who didn't reply are without journalism jobs. Anyway, the figure of "two-thirds" in the headline is tainted, a bait-and-switch type of come-on. That is, after swallowing the bait in the headline, you discover in the story that the "two-thirds" switches to something far less. None of this prevented the school from crowing in a sidebar:

> A national survey of 2,000 1993 journalism graduates from 86 journalism schools found that only about half the degree recipients found jobs in communications-related fields six to eight months from graduation, compared to 66 percent of the graduates of the school.

Since 1970, when the first electronic editing terminal was placed in the newsroom of *Today* in Cocoa, Fla., newspapers have replaced reporters' typewriters and editors' pencils with video terminals.

◀ The Electronic Newsroom

The terminal is an electric typewriter keyboard with a television screen. As the reporter types a story on the keyboard, the story appears on the screen and is recorded in a central computer, called a *controller*. All the terminals in the newsroom are wired to the controller, and copy stored there can be called back by reporters or editors. (Some newspapers use personal computers, which are self-sustaining, without a controller.) The reporter can move up or down through the copy with a touch of a key (called scrolling) and can use other keys to delete letters and words. Material is inserted or deleted easily, and paragraphs can be moved around with equal ease.

Some newspaper computers allow reporters to use the keyboard for mathematical computations. The computer also can be used to store the telephone numbers of sources as well as their names and addresses.

The computer also is used to store and retrieve information. Newspaper libraries and data banks provide reporters with vast amounts of information at a touch of their fingers.

The computer can be used to provide vast amounts of information:

1. **On-line research:** Vast libraries of databank material are available through on-line reference services such as the LEXIS®-NEXIS® service, Dialog, NewsNet and Datatimes. These services are used for background

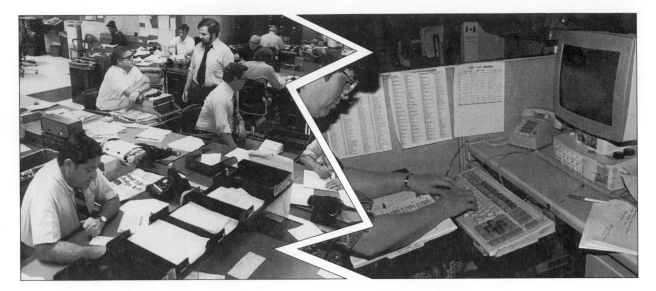

The Old . . . and the New Newsrooms

Before the electronic revolution, newsrooms resembled the *Daily News* city room on the left. Reporters used manual typewriters, and editors marked their copy with pencils. The newsroom clatter was so deafening that shouting was the normal means of communication. Came the revolution: Computers replaced typewriters and pencils, and the keyboard and screen were used to edit copy. Work cubicles took the place of the open newsroom and staffers could communicate on their computers rather than by shouting across the newsroom.

material, most often to find lists or articles that have appeared in newspapers, magazines and specialized sources.

2. **Government databases:** The federal government, states and cities have put their records, from census reports to local court documents and arrest reports, on tapes that are available to journalists.

3. **Staff-developed databases:** Reporters who have gathered material useful for future stories can make their own libraries.

Infant Mortality ▶

Look back to Table 4.1 on page 87, "Infant Mortality Rates for States." The list is alphabetized. We can feed the states and their rates into our computer and rank the rates from highest to lowest. If we do, we find Mississippi has the highest rate with 11.9 and New Hampshire the lowest with 4.8. We also can input the national rate of 8.3 to find out which states are above and which are below the average. And we can see how our state fares in comparison with others.

But these are overall rates, and we are now sufficiently informed to know that we can make a more sophisticated analysis. We can obtain figures for the infant mortality rate by race, for example.

What we find is sobering. The national rate for black infant mortality is 14.8, almost twice the white rate. In fact, a state-by-state comparison by race shows the black rate is two to three times the white rate in almost every state.

We also can obtain infant mortality rates by race for cities. Some rates for cities with populations of more than 500,000 are:

Table 4.3 City Infant Mortality Rates by Race

City	Total	White	Black
Los Angeles	7.84	6.61	18.16
San Diego	6.45	4.48	22.90
Chicago	13.33	7.86	19.60
Detroit	21.28	11.90	23.19
New York City	10.09	8.26	14.75
Philadelphia	14.74	8.94	20.05
Dallas	8.56	6.72	13.00
Houston	9.04	6.96	14.76
Phoenix	9.32	8.60	22.02
San Francisco	7.18	5.27	22.90
Washington	19.62	13.07	22.04
Jacksonville	8.67	6.36	13.44
Indianapolis	12.17	8.98	20.92
Baltimore	14.89	12.78	15.91
Boston	10.44	5.81	16.58
Cleveland	16.68	12.60	20.06
Columbus	10.03	7.74	16.04
Memphis	16.41	9.94	19.19
Milwaukee	10.61	9.08	12.57

Centers for Disease Control and Prevention, National Center for Health Statistics, National Vital Statistics System.

◀ A NEXIS Search

In Chapter 1, we watched a reporter handle a story about an organization that asked the state board of education to prohibit schools from using books that the group contended stereotyped black people. The reporter used a database for much of the background material he put into his story.

Let's take a close look at how Dick, the reporter, used the NEXIS service for his story.

The service consists of a number of libraries, one of which is the news library with the texts of newspapers and magazines and other material. To access the NEXIS service, you need a personal computer with a modem, LEXIS-NEXIS Communication Software and a LEXIS-NEXIS account. One way to look at the NEXIS service is to imagine it as a filing cabinet with drawers, the drawers being the different libraries. Within the drawers are different files, and the files contain individual documents.

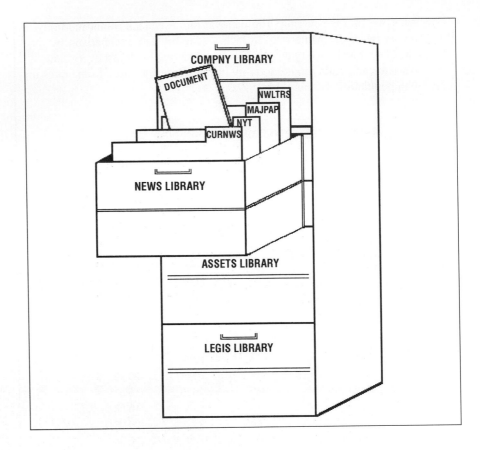

Here is a partial list of the available libraries that showed up on a user's screen:

Please ENTER the NAME (only one) of the library you want to search.
-For more information about a library, ENTER its page (PG) number.
-To see a list of additional libraries, press the NEXT PAGE key.

NAME	PG	NAME	PG	NAME	PG	NAME	PG	NAME	PG	NAME	PG	NAME	PG
- - - - - - - - - - - Types - - - - - - - - - - - -						- - - - - - - - - - - - - Topics- - - - - - - - - - - -						- - - Int'l - - -	
General				Public		BUSFIN	20	Intellect		- -Medical- -		ASIAPC	3
- - -News - - -		- - - Legal - - - -		- - Records - -		CMPCOM	20	-Property-		GENMED	13	CANADA	18
NEWS	1	CODES	5	ALLREC	4	ENERGY	8	COPYRT	7	EMBASE	13	EUROPE	3
TOPNWS	1	LAWREV	10	ASSETS	4	ENTERT	20	PATENT	11	MEDLNE	13	GERMAN	3
		LEGNEW	1	DOCKET	4	ENVIRN	8	TRDMRK	12			MDEAFR	3
		MEGA	5	FINDER	4	INSURE	9			- Political -		NSAMER	3
		MODEL	10	INSOLV	4	MARKET	1	- - Legal - -		APOLIT	2	UK	17
				INCORP	4	PEOPLE	20	BANKNG	6	CMPGN	2	WORLD	3
- -Financial- -				LEXPAT	4	SPORTS	20	FEDSEC	9	EXEC	2	TXTLNE	17
COMPNY	20			LIENS	4	TRANS	12	GENFED	5	LEGIS	2		

INVEST	20		VERDCT	4		HOTTOP	5			- - -Assists- - -	
NAARS	20					LABOR	10	- - -Tax- - -		EASY	13
QUOTE	20		-Reference-			PUBCON	11	FEDTAX	9	GUIDE	13
			BUSREF	20		STATES	5	STTAX	11	PRACT	13
			LEXREF	10						TERMS	13
			MARHUB	10							

Please ENTER, separated by commas, the NAMES of the files you want to search.
You may select as many files as you want, including files that do not appear below, but you
must enter them all at one time. To see a description of a file, ENTER its page (PG) number.

Journalists use the NEWS library, which contains files. Files can be single
publications. *The New York Times,* for example, is a single file within the NEWS
library. Files also can be groups of publications. An example is CURNWS, a file
that contains all the full text sources in the NEWS library for the past two years.

FILES—PAGE 1 of 78 (NEXT PAGE for additional files)

NAME	PG	DESCRIP	NAME	PG	DESCRIP	NAME	PG	DESCRIP
			- - - - -THE NEWS LIBRARY- - - - -					
- - - - - Full-Text Group Files - - - -			- - - - -Full-Text By Type- - - -			- - - - - -Full Text By Region- - - - -		
CURNWS	1	Last 2 years	MAGS	3	Magazines		- - -Papers & Wires- - -	
ARCNWS	1	Beyond 2 years	MAJPAP	3	Major Papers	NON-US	1	English Non-US
ALLNWS	1	All News Files	NWLTRS	3	Newsletters	US	1	US News
			PAPERS	3	Newspapers		- - - -US Sources- - - -	
			SCRIPT	3	Transcripts	MWEST	3	Midwest
- - - - -Group File Exclusions- - - - -			WIRES	3	Wires	NEAST	3	Northeast
ALLABS	4	All Abstracts	- - - - - - -Hot Files- - - - - - -			SEAST	3	Southeast
NONENG	1	Non-English News	HOTTOP	2	Hot Topics*	WEST	3	West
TXTNWS	1	Textline News*				- - - - - - - - - -Assists- - - - - - - - -		
TODAY	1	Today's News*	OJHOT	2	Same Day OJ	GUIDE	2	Descriptions*
					Crt Trscrpts	CONAME	2	Co. Thesaurus*

Files marked * may not be combined.

Dick is looking for recent material on book censorship, so he decides to use
the most recent file. His next step is to start his search after this appears on his
screen:

Please type your search request then press the ENTER key.
What you enter will be Search Level 1.

Type .fr to enter a FREESTYLE(TM) search.

For further explanation, press the H key (for HELP) and then
the ENTER key.

He uses as his search term BOOK CENSORSHIP, so he types:

BOOK CENSORSHIP

Then he presses the ENTER or RETURN KEY. The following turns up on his screen:

BOOK CENSORSHIP

NEXIS interprets the highlighted word as a search term and not as a NEXIS segment name.
Your search request has found 137 STORIES through Level 1.

To DISPLAY these STORIES press either the KWIC, FULL, CITE or SEGMTS key.

To MODIFY your search request, press the M key (for MODIFY) and then the ENTER key.

For further explanation, press the H key (for HELP) and then the ENTER key.

This indicates the user can view the documents in several display formats:

KWIC: Key Words In Context will show the search term with a small block of text on either side—15 to 25 words.

FULL: This format displays the entire document.

SEGMTS: This format allows the user to select portions of the material to view. Some examples of segments are the headline and the byline of the writer.

CITE: This format displays a bibliographic list of the documents the search turns up, the most recent first.

Dick presses the function key (F7) to view the stories in CITE. Here is what his screen shows under this format:

LEVEL 1—137 STORIES

1. AP Worldstream, July 23, 1995; Sunday, International news, 987 words, Court Bans Book, Arguing France's Beloved Tintin Was a Boozer, ELIZABETH GARNSEY, PARIS

2. AP Online, July 23, 1995; Sunday, International news, 974 words, Court Bans Book On Tintin, PARIS

3. The Toronto Star, July 19, 1995, Wednesday, FINAL EDITION, NEWS; Pg. A3, 278 words, Horrors! Trustees ban Stephen King, CP), OTTAWA

4. Calgary Herald, July 16, 1995, Sunday, FINAL EDITION, SUNDAY INSIGHT; Pg. A5, 1023 words, War of words rages in Alberta's libraries, JIM CUNNINGHAM

5. The San Francisco Examiner, July 7, 1995, Friday; Second Edition, NEWS; Pg. A-22, 534 words, The U.N. "airbrushes" history, JAMES A. FINEFROCK

6. The Washington Post, July 05, 1995, Wednesday, Final Edition, STYLE; Pg. C12; JUDY MANN, 783 words, A Question of Responsibility, Judy Mann

Dick continues to look through the citations and his attention is caught by several items. He decides to narrow his search to *Mark Twain*. To do this, he uses the FOCUS (TM) feature, which allows you to do "a search within a search." In other words, you can look for documents within the group of documents found by your original search.

12 of 143 STORIES satisfy your FOCUS search request.

To display these 15 STORIES, press any format key (e.g. FULL).

To display FOCUS terms in the STORY you were viewing, press the ENTER key.

To exit FOCUS and return to the STORY you were viewing, enter EXIT.

For further explanation, press the H key (for HELP) and then the ENTER key.

PAGE 1

FOCUS—11 STORIES

1. Calgary Herald, July 16, 1995, Sunday, FINAL EDITION, SUNDAY INSIGHT; Pg. A5, 1023 words, War of words rages in Alberta's libraries, JIM CUNNINGHAM

2. Calgary Herald, February 11, 1995, Saturday, FINAL EDITION, ENTERTAINMENT; BOOKS; Pg. F6, 743 words, Freedom to read a universal right, KEN MCGOOGAN

3. The Charleston Gazette, January 27, 1995, Friday, Editorial; Pg. P5A, 1081 words, UNEQUIVOCAL RIGHT CURBING FREE SPEECH CAN BE DANGEROUS PATH TO TAKE, Paul Nyden

4. St. Petersburg Times, September 28, 1994, Wednesday, City Edition, TAMPA BAY AND STATE; THE REGION; Pg. 3B, 683 words, 2 teens charged with killing security dogs in burglary

5. Capital Times, September 14, 1994, Wednesday, ALL EDITIONS, Pg. 1D, 1061 words, BOOK CENSORSHIP SCRAPES CHILDREN'S WORLD, By Ann Burt Meyer

6. Pittsburgh Post-Gazette, SEPTEMBER 10, 1994, SATURDAY, SOONER EDITION, Pg. D2, 402 words, LESSONS IN CENSORSHIP BOOK-BANNERS ARE STILL BEDEVILING THE NATION'S SCHOOLS

7. The San Francisco Examiner, September 2, 1994, Friday; Fourth Edition, NEWS; Pg. A-22, 360 words, California is (ugh) No. 1, ROBERT HOLLIS

8. The Houston Post, September 1, 1994, THURSDAY, FINAL EDITION, Pg. A28, 552 words, TEXAS 2ND IN U.S. FOR CENSORING BOOKS; IN PUBLIC SCHOOLS, LIBERAL GROUP REPORTS, JAY ROOT, POST WASHINGTON BUREAU, WASHINGTON

9. The San Francisco Examiner, September 1, 1994, Thursday; Fourth Edition, NEWS; Pg. A-7, 160 words, BOOKS UNDER FIRE

10. Los Angeles Times, October 21, 1993, Thursday, Orange County Edition, View; Part E; Page 4; Column 4; View Desk, 282 words, OC HIGH/STUDENT NEWS & VIEWS; SCHOOLS URGED TO DEVELOP BOOK POLICIES, By Associated Press

11. Idaho Falls Post Register, September 29, 1993, News; Pg. C1, 694 words, IN INCREASING NUMBERS, PARENTS ARE JUMPING ON THE BANNED WAGON, Ron Marr

Dick wants to see in detail the references to Mark Twain in what has turned up as the result of his FOCUS (TM) search. He uses the KWIC (key words in context) display format and he examines the brief entries. His eye catches six useful entries, one of which follows:

FOCUS-8 OF 11 STORIES

Copyright 1994 The Houston Post
The Houston Post

September 1, 1994, THURSDAY, FINAL EDITION

SECTION: NATIONAL, Pg. A28

LENGTH: 552 words

HEADLINE: TEXAS 2ND IN U.S. FOR CENSORING BOOKS; IN PUBLIC SCHOOLS, LIBERAL GROUP REPORTS

BYLINE: JAY ROOT, POST WASHINGTON BUREAU

DATELINE: WASHINGTON

BODY:
. . . control of school boards and then successfully challenge books and curricula, he said.

The PAW report found 22 percent of all the reported incidents were "the handiwork of right-wing political organizations." Six percent, meanwhile, including challenges to The Adventures of Huckleberry Finn by Mark Twain, came from "the political left."

Forty-two percent of the reported incidents of censorship led to books being removed or restricted in some manner, according to the study.

Incidents in Texas ranged from a broad, and partially successful, challenge to health textbooks . . .

To sum up, the basic steps to searching the NEXIS service are:

1. Select a library.
2. Select a file.
3. Enter a search.
4. Decide which articles you want to see and the format you would like to see them in.
5. Evaluate the articles found and determine which ones are worth printing or downloading to a disk. (Downloading refers to transferring material to a disk.)

Dick finds a reference to material about censorship issued by People for the American Way and he calls the Washington headquarters (202-467-4999) to ask about it. He learns that the organization publishes annual findings on censorship in schools along with other attacks on what the group describes as the "freedom to learn" and he requests a copy of the organization's report. The most recent list includes *The Adventures of Huckleberry Finn*. Here are other listings from its report of the "most frequently challenged books and materials":

Reference Material

Annie on My Mind, Nancy Garden
The Chocolate War, Robert Cormier
Developing Understanding of Self and Others [self-esteem program]
Go Ask Alice, Anonymous
I Know Why the Caged Bird Sings, Maya Angelou
Of Mice and Men, John Steinbeck
Pumsy in Pursuit of Excellence [self-esteem program]
Rolling Stone [magazine]
Scary Stories to Tell in the Dark, Alvin Schwartz

The first title rings a bell. Dick feels sure he has seen it somewhere. He puts the title into the NEXIS system and in less than a minute his memory is refreshed: The Olathe, Kan., Board of Education removed *Annie on My Mind* from the school library, but a federal judge ruled that while "local school boards have broad discretion in the management of school affairs, they must act within fundamental constitutional limits." Judge Thomas Van Bebber said that board members "may not ban books based on their personal social, political and moral views." The book is about the love between two teen-age girls.

Dick files this in his folder, and he makes a note to call three ministers of local churches who have been outspoken about what they describe as the need to return to "basic values."

Attacks on 'Freedom Values'

People for the American Way compiles attacks on what it considers "freedom values." In its latest report, it listed 438 such attacks, including more than 50 on sex education in the schools, and opposition to widening voter registration and the inclusion of homosexuals in antidiscrimination ordinances and laws.

COMPILED BY PEOPLE FOR THE AMERICAN WAY

Internet Check ▶

Dick also uses the newspaper's Internet facility to track down censorship of Twain's books. He accesses Banned Books Online through Netscape on the World Wide Web (http://www.cs.cmu.edu/Web/People/spok/banned-books. html).

He finds material going back to 1876 when the Public Library in Brooklyn, N.Y., banned *The Adventures of Tom Sawyer* from the children's room. It was also excluded from the Denver Public Library. In 1885, the public library in Concord, Mass., banned *The Adventures of Huckleberry Finn* as "trash and suitable only for the slums." In 1905, the Brooklyn Public Library also banned *Huckleberry Finn,* and the librarian of Brooklyn College appealed to Twain to defend his book. Twain replied:

> I am greatly troubled by what you say. I wrote Tom Sawyer and Huck Finn for adults exclusively, and it has always distressed me when I find that boys and girls have been allowed access to them. The mind that becomes soiled in youth can never again be washed clean.

Also on the Internet: "The London Athenaeum has called it [*Huckleberry Finn*] one of the six greatest books ever written in America."

Dick knows it's time to stop. He now has enough material for several stories. Time to begin organizing his notes. A great believer in the use of folders for long stories and series, he starts his organizing by writing on one folder, "Black Parents Association." He puts in it the organization's press release about its objections to *Huckleberry Finn* and the two other books. Then he picks up another folder and writes, "Reactions to Release." He decides he needs to deal with the charges of Twain as a racist, and he has plenty of material on that, so another folder is titled, "Twain—Racist."

We take leave of Dick as he scrambles through his notes to find material for his first three folders. Occasionally, he stops as an idea hits him for a theme, and he scribbles hastily on still another folder.

The news was about the budget, taxes and the battle between Congress and the president. The political season was warming up as well. Would the people support or repudiate the president in the congressional elections?

In the past, the answer derived from taking the political pulse was hardly convincing. Reporters would chat with political leaders, those supposedly perceptive insiders with delicate olfactory nerves attuned to the mildest of political breezes. The result might be interesting reading, but it had no predictive value whatsoever.

Now, the science of surveying gives the journalist a surer hand to reach into areas of coverage that before had been handled with impressions and conjecture.

Polls are used for a variety of stories. The well-designed poll can tell with a fair degree of accuracy not only what people think of a president's performance but also whether a proposed school bond issue is popular in a middle-class section of the community or what types of day care are favored by working mothers. Polls have been used to determine whether Catholics approve of abortion, how people feel about the death penalty, what blacks think of affirmative action. *The New York Times* even ran a survey that established that 87 percent of 3- to 10-year-olds believe in Santa Claus.

Recognizing the value of polls and surveys, many newspapers and television stations have hired pollsters and polling organizations. The reporter is still essential, for the poll can only supply the information. The reporter must make the poll into news. To do this, he or she must understand how polls work and their possibilities and limits.

The poll is a systematic way of finding out what people are thinking at a given time by questioning a sample population. It can provide a fairly accurate stop-action photo of a situation. This does not mean that all polling data should be taken at face value. There are some inherent problems in polling, and there are pollsters whose purpose is to promote their clients. Reporters who understand polls know what to accept, what to discard. Reporters who are overwhelmed by data, who believe there is some mystery about figures, will be victimized, just as they will be misled by any public relations gimmick.

Polls are "able to establish with great accuracy the extent to which an opinion is held, and they can successfully predict behavior over the short run," writes Sheldon S. Wolin of the Department of Politics at Princeton University. "Once the period is extended," he cautions, "the reliability of the findings diminishes rapidly."

There are hundreds of polling organizations and firms. The majority are local groups that conduct marketing surveys. The big firms—Gallup, Harris, and Roper—handle commercial clients, too, but are best known for their political polls and surveys. It is this political polling that so often finds its way into newspapers and news broadcasts. During a political campaign, as much as one-third to one-half of the news is about the public's reaction to a candidate or an issue.

◄ **Public Opinion Polling**

◄ **Political Polls**

Unfortunately, the emphasis on predicting winners, on who's ahead, rather than on interpreting the data leads to the waste of huge amounts of fascinating material about how people are voting and why, whether some groups—blacks, Jews, Catholics, farmers—have switched their allegiances.

Although reputable pollsters pretest their questions, ambiguities do creep in. Reporters always should examine the questions behind the polling data to make sure that they are clear and, for polls conducted for private clients, to ascertain whether they are loaded.

Types of Polls ▶

The first check a reporter makes of polling material is a determination of how the poll was conducted. There are a variety of ways to elicit information from the public, some of them unreliable, some less reliable than others.

The coupon poll is just about worthless. People are asked to clip, fill out and mail a coupon that appears in the publication. The results are distorted because the person who goes to all that trouble—including paying for postage—is usually someone with strong feelings about the subject and hardly representative of the general population.

The call-in poll, in which readers or viewers are asked to express their sentiments about an issue by telephoning the newspaper or station, is subject to the same criticism as the coupon poll. When the *San Francisco Chronicle* conducted a call-in poll on the death sentence, it headlined the results on page one. Not surprisingly, three-fourths of those calling favored the death penalty. After *USA Today* reported that its call-in poll showed that Americans loved the financier Donald Trump, it learned that 5,640 of the 7,800 calls came from a single source, another financier. Shamefaced, the newspaper said its polls are "strictly for fun."

The 1-900 call-in poll is useless as a measure of public opinion. "You have to be willing to pay for a phone call in order to participate, and that very seriously limits the representativeness of the people whose responses are being reported," says Harry O'Neill, president of the National Council on Public Polls.

The straw poll is no more reliable than the other types of polls already mentioned, although some newspapers have been using this technique for many years. For a straw poll, a person hands out ballots at one or more locations. People then drop their ballots into a box at the spot. It is difficult to keep the straw poll from being overrepresented by the people in the one or two locations selected—usually supermarkets, factory gates and the like. The *Daily News,* which conducts straw polls for New York and national elections, uses a professional pollster to organize its straw locations.

The man-in-the-street poll is probably the poll most frequently used to gather opinions at the local level. Newspapers and stations without access to their own polling apparatuses will send reporters out to interview people about a candidate or an issue. Those who have had to do this kind of reporting know how nonrepresentative the people interviewed are. Reporters may seek out those who look as if they can supply a quick answer, those who do not need to have the question explained to them. Reporters may ignore those who are poorly dressed and members of minority groups.

Margin of Error. Polls are accurate to a point. The margin of error expresses one of the variables. Depending on the number of persons polled, the margin of error can be as high as 12 percent, as low as 3 percent.

A 3 percent margin of error gives a cushion of 3 percent up or 3 percent down. Thus, in a poll that gives Jones 51 percent and Smith 49 percent of the voters polled, a 3 percent margin of error means the result cannot be forecast with any certainty. Jones' actual result could be 54 percent (up 3) or 48 percent (down 3). Smith could be 52 percent (up 3) or 46 (down 3).

Too close to call.

These polls can be used as long as the story says precisely what they are—the opinions of a scattering of people, no more than that, no more scientific than astrology. The sample of people interviewed in such polling is known as a "non-probability sample," meaning that the conclusions cannot be generalized to the population at large.

◀ Proper Polling

A good poll should be done at night and over weekends, not just during the workday. It is best to poll people in their homes rather than on the street. Polls that are conducted by home interviews are usually more reliable than the catch-as-catch-can polling techniques of the straw poll or man-in-the-street interviews.

Most polls are done by phone to save time and money, although many of the poor and many members of minority groups do not have phones, and 25 percent of those called refuse to cooperate.

To reach its conclusions about how well adults around the country thought the president was handling his problems, *The New York Times*/CBS News Poll spoke to 1,422 people by telephone. At first glance, this effort seems like madness. To pass off the opinions of fewer than 1,500 people as representative of more than 100 million adults seems folly. Yet if the sample is selected carefully, the questions properly put, the results stated fairly and completely, and the interpretations made with discernment, a sample of around 1,500 people can reflect accurately 95 percent of the time the opinions of people across the country with a margin of error of about 3 percentage points. (See Appendix B, "Public Opinion Polling Checklist.")

Polling Problems. When the candidate is black or female, the race or gender of the poll taker can influence results. People will not give "socially undesirable" answers to poll takers, regardless of their true feelings.

◀ The Sample

Obviously, if a small group is to speak for many, that group must be carefully chosen so that it is representative of the larger group. The key word here is *representative*.

If we want to know what people think of an incumbent governor, we can interview voters and nonvoters. But if we want to know whether people will vote to re-elect him or her, it is common sense to interview only eligible voters, those who have registered. But we cannot stop there. If we went out in the daytime to supermarkets, laundromats and parks where mothers gather with their young children, our sample would be skewed heavily toward women. That would be a nonrepresentative sample since men constitute a large percentage of voters. Also, since only a third to a half of eligible voters actually go to the polls in most contests, questions must be asked to determine whether the person being polled will actually vote.

Samples are selected in a number of ways. *The New York Times*/CBS News Poll sample of telephone exchanges was selected by a computer from a complete list of exchanges around the country. The exchanges were chosen in such a way that each region of the United States was represented in proportion to its population.

Once the exchanges were selected, the telephone numbers were formed by random digits. This guaranteed that unlisted as well as listed numbers would be included in the sample.

The making of the *New York Times*/CBS News Poll sample demonstrates how pollsters try to eliminate the human factor from the choice of those who will be interviewed. A good sample should give everyone in the population we are trying to learn something about a chance to be represented in the poll. This is what

Hardly Representative. The stories about French unfriendliness are untrue, said American Express. The proof: A poll of 1,000 Americans who visited France more than once over the last two years (and thus would be inclined to be pro-French). People who lose weight can keep it off, said a diet-products company in a news release. The sample: A group of 20 who went through the company's weight-loss program.

The Exit Poll

Everyone wants to know who won the election and why, as soon as possible. The exit poll provides the information—usually just as the voting ends. For most races, this poll supplies the winners and the reasons voters cast their ballots.

The exit poll is based on interviews with voters as they emerge from polling places. For results of national interest, the AP and the four networks have joined to form the Voter News Service. The VNS uses county-based models to form its polling base. These models allow analysts to call Candidate A a winner even when the vote count shows her trailing Candidate B.

Voters also are asked why they voted for A and not for B. Shortly after the polls closed, VNS called Sen. Edward Kennedy a winner, because, voters said, he supported health care and had Senate experience. Even of the voters who said he had been in office too long, one in four voted for him.

Stealth Candidates. When the former grand wizard of the Ku Klux Klan, David Duke, ran for governor of Louisiana, polls consistently underestimated his actual vote. Why? Voters are unwilling to admit their true feelings when race is an issue, says pollster Paul Maslin. To correct for this, pollsters divide the undecided white vote 4:1 for the white candidate in a race of a white versus a black candidate. Some interviewers will ask general questions to gauge whether interviewees have racist sentiments.

---

is meant by the term *random sample*. To the average person, the word *random* usually means haphazard, without plan. Pollsters use it to mean that the sample guarantees that any of those in the larger population group have as good a chance to be polled as anyone else in that group.

Once the sample has been drawn, it is then weighted to adjust for sample variations. In the *Times*/CBS Poll of the president's popularity, the sample consisted of 445 people who told the pollsters making the calls that they were Democrats, 482 who said they were Republicans and 495 who said they were independents. Using the breakdown in the sample would overrepresent Republicans. To reflect the known proportion of party members in the voting population, the groups of voters were weighted by party identification.

The poll also weighted the results to take account of household size and to adjust for variations in the sample relating to religion, race, age, sex and education. This weighting was done in accordance with what is known of the characteristics of the voting population from the results of the last election, the proportion of men and women in the population, census figures on nationality, religion, income and so on. The raw figures were adjusted to eliminate distortions from the norm.

Despite the inclination to think that the more people interviewed, the more accurate the results, the statistical truth is that it is as much the quality of the sample that determines the accuracy of the poll. After a critical number of interviews have been conducted, little additional accuracy is achieved. Results based on a good sample successfully interviewed are adequate for most purposes.

A Polling Disaster ▶

The classic example of quantity over quality is the *Literary Digest* poll for the 1936 presidential race between Franklin D. Roosevelt and Alf Landon. On the basis of its 2,376,523 replies, the poll predicted a Landon victory. But Landon was soundly defeated and carried only Maine and Vermont. The reason: The sample was made up of names from lists of automobile owners and telephone users, hardly representative of the general populace, most of which was mired in a deep depression.

Expert pollsters say that it is best to have at least 1,000 respondents if the results are to have any significance. But when this number is broken into smaller subgroups—whites, blacks, Catholics, college graduates—then the margin of error can be as high as 12 percent and the results meaningless.

◀ Optimum Numbers

Questions on the poll should be clear and unambiguous. A Roper poll found that one in three Americans believes it is possible that the Holocaust never took place, which seems hard to reconcile with the vast amount of information about the extermination of millions of Jews, gypsies and others the Nazis declared undesirables.

◀ The Questions

The question asked was, "Does it seem possible or does it seem impossible to you that the Nazi extermination of the Jews never happened?"

That's a badly phrased question, especially difficult to understand when it is heard and not read. A critic of the poll pointed out that answering that the Holocaust did occur would require using a double negative: "It is impossible that the Nazi extermination of the Jews never happened."

The critic, Katherine Moschandreas of the Harvard Divinity School, did her own polling. She asked a simple question: "Do you believe that the Holocaust happened?" She found that 89 percent responded yes, 7 percent said they did not know, and 3.5 percent said they did not believe it happened.

A *New York Times*/CBS Poll asked about "government spending on welfare," and 48 percent of those polled said it should be cut. The Poll then asked about "spending programs for poor children," and 47 percent said aid should be increased. (The federal program of Aid for Families with Dependent Children has 14 million welfare recipients, two-thirds of them children.)

Polls do tell us a lot about ourselves. But they have to be approached with caution, both by the people devising and doing the polling and by the users of the poll results. Following are just a few orange lights.

◀ Cautions

People aren't necessarily informed about the subjects they are asked to discuss. But pollsters cannot toss out those who are uninformed, unless the poll is expressly designed to find the sentiments of the well-informed. Few are so designed. Look at these results:

◀ Informed
Respondents

Poll Question: Do you feel the amount the U.S. spends on foreign aid is too much, about right, too little?
The results:

Too much	75%
About right	17%
Too little	4%

Asked how much they thought the United States spent on foreign assistance as a percentage of the federal budget, most respondents said 15 percent.

Next, people were told that the actual foreign spending figure is 1 percent. They were then asked whether they thought this 1 percent is too much, about right, too little.

The results:

Way too much	9%
A bit too much	9%
About right	46%
A bit too little	18%
Way too little	16%

The difference between the result of informed opinion and off-the-top-of-the-head opinion is enormous. Those who felt the government was overspending on foreign aid when informed did a flip-flop, going from 75 percent against to 80 percent saying it was about right or too little. Quite a shift.

Jeans, Shoe Polish and Ice Cream ▶

Journalists have to be especially careful with polls conducted by businesses and industries. A poll released to the press by Levi Strauss & Co. showed that 90 percent of college students said Levi's 501 jeans would be "in" that year. The 501 jeans were the only jeans on the list.

"You can't have an industry study done by that industry and be 100 percent objective," says a pollster. "There are too many judgment calls, too many meetings between the sponsor and the organization doing the study."

Most of these studies are made expressly to produce material that will work its way into newspapers and onto television. Kiwi Brands, a shoe-polish company, claimed that 97 percent of "ambitious" young men believe polished shoes are important in getting ahead. Simplesse, makers of the Simple Pleasures frozen dessert, asserted that 44 percent of those who eat a lot of ice cream are likely to enjoy a tub bath. "We've gotten a number of clips back," said a company spokesman, who added that the study was timed for the media.

Winners and Losers ▶

Journalists must be careful about their tendency to heed the demands of readers and listeners for definitive opinions and for winners and losers. A poll can only state what people say they are thinking or how voters say they will vote at the time they are polled, and sometimes even then the contests are too close to call.

Journalists should remember this: People change their minds; polls cannot guarantee that behavior will be consistent with intentions.

Reputable pollsters know just how far they can take their data. But they are often under pressure to pick winners in election contests. When preelection polls indicate a 60–40 percent breakdown, a pollster feels at ease in choosing the winner. But when an editor, reflecting the desire of readers and listeners, asks for a choice in a 44–42 race with 14 percent undecided, then trouble lies ahead.

Although editors and broadcast producers tend to be most interested in the top of the poll—who's ahead—most of the significant material in the poll usually is found in why the candidate is ahead or behind and how the candidate is faring with certain groups. This can make interesting and significant news. There may be a good story in the candidate who does well with a certain religious group and poorly with another because of his or her stand on abortion or prayer in schools.

Copy Editing Symbols

Spell out	The (PHA) is pushing for the extension, viewing	The Pittsfield Housing Authority is pushing . . .
Transpose	it as the final link in its urban road renewal	. . . urban renewal road
Begin new paragraph	network. ⌐If undertaken, the city is planning	network. ¶ If undertaken, the city . . .
Delete letter	to work in conjunction with a neighbourhood	. . . a neighborhood
Restore marked-out or hard-to-read material	revitalization program for the three-block area that is that is affected.	that is affected.
Change to lower case	The State and Federal Governments would pay	The state and federal governments would pay
Separate words	for the road work.	for the road work.
Abbreviate	The (Pittsfield Housing Authority) says that	The PHA says that
Insert	five houses would be taken by the projet with	. . . by the project with
Spell out	a possibility that as many as (8) more would	. . . eight more would
Delete material; close up	have to eventually come down.	have to come down.
Indent for paragraph	⌐The finite takings involve buildings at 90	The finite takings . . .
Capitalize	summer st., 83 and 90 Union St., and 88 and 95	Summer St., 83 and 90 . . .
Run in, or bring copy together	Bradford St. Of the five, only one is a single-family home.	Bradford St. Of the five, only one is a single-family home.
Punctuation	The others are multiple family dwellings.	. . . multiple-family dwellings.

Summing Up ▶

Journalists have a vast array of reporting and research resources at their fingertips. Used intelligently, these resources can contribute to making stories accurate and thorough. They also can help journalists develop story ideas that were too time-consuming to pursue before the computer.

None of these tools, however, operates by itself. All must be directed by the human pressing the keys. Journalists not only must know how to use these devices wisely and creatively, they must have a wide range of knowledge and experience that will generate the ideas to feed into the machines.

No matter how powerful the machine or tool, it pales in comparison with the human brain. Even the bee's brain operates a thousand times faster than the fastest computer going.

The point is that all these tools can operate at their optimum efficiency when directed by a resourceful, well-trained journalist.

Further Reading ▶

Barzun, Jacques, and Henry F. Graff. *The Modern Researcher.* New York: Harcourt Brace Jovanovich, Inc., 1985.

Croteau, Maureen, and Wayne Worcester. *The Essential Researcher.* New York: HarperCollins Publishers, 1993. (A one-volume sourcebook for journalists written by University of Connecticut journalism faculty members.)

Huff, Darrell, and Irving E. Gers. *How to Lie with Statistics.* New York: Norton, 1954.

McCormick, Mona. *The New York Times Guide to Reference Materials.* New York: Times Books, 1985.

Meyer, Philip. *Precision Journalism,* 2d ed. Bloomington: Indiana University Press, 1979.

Paul, Nora. *Computer Assisted Research: A Guide to Tapping Online Information,* 2d ed. St. Petersburg, Fla.: The Poynter Institute for Media Studies, 1994.

Williams, Frederick. *Reasoning with Statistics.* New York: Holt, Rinehart and Winston, 1968.

5 Story Structure

Phil Sears, *Tallahassee Democrat.*

Bank robbery foiled—a single-element story.

Preview

Planning precedes writing. Reporters see the news story as an organized whole. Each sentence, every paragraph is placed to suit a purpose. Even while reporting, reporters try to visualize the shape and content of their stories, especially the beginning, the lead. The lead gives the story its structure.

News stories have a linear structure:

• The beginning includes a summary of the most important material. It tells the reader what to expect.

• The remainder of the story—the body—amplifies, buttresses, gives examples and explains the beginning. It also contains background and secondary material. The ending can sum up the story.

F irst the idea. Then the words.

As the young reporter struggled with his story, he recalled this advice that his city editor had given him the day before. Having written the obituary of a banker in 45 minutes, he had been proud of his speed. But the editor had said that the story was disorganized. The reporter read his story carefully, keeping in mind his editor's comment. Yes, he was writing without a firm idea of what he wanted to say and how it would fit together.

Suddenly, he was struck by what he had just told himself: "What do I want to say? Where do I put it?" That was the key to putting his notes into some kind of structured shape.

• What do I want to say?
• Where does it go?

This reporter's discovery is made all the time by young journalists. Usually, it is followed by another revelation: The news story form or structure is simple and most stories fit into the following structure:

• The lead.
• The material that explains and amplifies the lead.
• The necessary background.
• The secondary or less important material.

The city editor's advice about thinking before writing has been offered to generations of students. As an essay in the *Fifth Reader,* a grade school textbook of the 1880s, puts it, "In learning to write, our first rule is: *'Know what you want to say.'* " (The italics are those of the author of the essay, Edward Everett Hale, the Boston clergyman who wrote the short novel *The Man Without a Country.*) Hale had a second rule: "*Say it.* That is, do not begin by saying something else which you think will lead up to what you want to say."

Every writer who has written about the writer's craft—whether journalist, poet, novelist or critic—has understood these first principles of writing. George Orwell, the British journalist and novelist, was concerned that the English language was being endangered by unclear thinking. In an essay, "Politics and the English Language," he wrote that the first question scrupulous writers ask themselves before writing is, "What am I trying to say?"

In *The Elements of Style,* the "little book" that generations of college students have used, authors William Strunk Jr. and E.B. White begin their section on writing this way: "Choose a suitable design and hold to it." They continue: "A basic structural design underlies every kind of writing. . . . The first principle of composition, therefore, is to foresee or determine the shape of what is to come, and pursue that shape."

Henry James, the American novelist, said that without form "there is absolutely no substance." Form, he wrote, "*takes,* holds, and preserves, substance—saves it from the welter of helpless verbiage that we swim in as in a sea of tasteless tepid pudding, and that makes one ashamed of an art capable of such degradations."

Sometimes plans change. A writer may develop new ideas in the act of writing and the original plan has to be discarded. But even then a new plan is substituted.

Nevertheless, many reporters start to write without a plan in mind. As a result, their stories exhibit one of the most common faults of journalistic writing—disorganization or lack of focus. Henry Fairlie, a British journalist, calls this deficiency "shapelessness." He attributes it to "an intellectual inability, on the part both of the reporter and copy editor, to master the story." This mastery, Fairlie says, must be put to use "before writing."

As one journalism teacher has been telling his students, "You can't write if you can't think." Ambrose Bierce, a newspaperman and author of *The Devil's Dictionary,* described good writing as "clear thinking made visible."

The Basic Idea ▶

Almost all writing is based on an observation, an emotion or an opinion that the writer wants to communicate. This basic idea may be put at or near the beginning of the piece as it usually is in a news story, or it may be tacked on at the end, as is a request for money for the flight home at Christmas in a student's letter to his or her parents. The basic idea is *always* there.

The news story has a beginning that sets out the basic idea or theme and a body that elaborates and explains the theme. As the newsroom adage puts it, "The story flows from the lead." When reporters attempt to form ideas for stories, they search for the lead of the piece. Fairlie describes the importance of the lead this way: "Every journalist who has ever struggled with [a lead] knows why it can

Wandering in Wonderland

The inability to fix on the point causes writers to go on and on and on. They believe that as long as they keep going, they will hit on something newsworthy. They are like Lewis Carroll's Alice in her conversation with the Cheshire Cat:

"Would you tell me, please, which way I ought to go from here?"
"That depends a good deal on where you want to get to," said the Cat.
"I don't much care where—" said Alice.
"Then it doesn't matter which way you go," said the Cat.
"—so long as I get *somewhere,*" Alice added as an explanation.
"Oh, you're sure to do that," said the Cat, "if you only walk long enough."

No editor will permit a writer to wander aimlessly through a story on the way to *somewhere.*

take so much effort. It is as important to him as to the reader. Writing it concentrates the mind wonderfully, forcing him to decide what in the story is important, what he wants to emphasize, and can eventually give the shape to the rest of the story as he writes it."

Thomas Boswell, columnist for *The Washington Post,* says, "The most important thing in the story is finding the central idea. It's one thing to be given a topic, but you have to find the idea or the concept within that topic. Once you find that idea or thread, all the other anecdotes, illustrations and quotes are pearls that hang on this thread. The thread may seem very humble, the pearls may seem very flashy, but it's still the thread that makes the necklace."

The hunt does not end when the writer corners the lead idea, however. The reporter still has to identify material that explains, supports and amplifies the lead before beginning to write. Since most news events consist of more than the important action or actions singled out in the lead, the reporter also has to identify the secondary material that will have to be included.

A story that consists of one important action or is based on one major fact or idea is a single-element story. Also known as the single-incident story, it is the story handled most often by beginning reporters. The story requires:

- Lead.
- Explanatory and amplifying material.
- Background (if necessary).
- Secondary material (if any).

◀ **The Single-Element Story**

Thieves Get 36 Batteries

Thieves who entered a Charlotte auto parts store stole 36 Delco batteries, police were told yesterday.

Crowell Erskine, 49, manager of the Piedmont Auto Exchange at 410 Atando Ave., told officers the store was broken into between 5 p.m. Tuesday and 8 a.m. Wednesday by thieves knocking a hole in the rear wall of the one-story brick building.

Erskine said the batteries were valued at $539.18.

—*The Charlotte Observer*

1. The lead focuses on the basic idea, the theft of a batch of batteries. The reporter knows the reader opens the newspaper each day with the question, "*What* happened today?"

2. The reporter answers what he or she thinks will be the logical questions a reader might ask, "*Where* did the break-in occur? *When* did it happen? *How* was it done?" The answers to these questions explain and amplify the lead.

3. Background is provided. The reporter knows the reader will want to be told the value of the goods stolen.

Suppose that a break-in occurred in the police department's property room at headquarters. Then the lead would emphasize *where* the theft occurred. If the parts-store theft had taken place in broad daylight while shoppers thronged the streets, this fact—*when* the theft occurred—would go into the lead.

Had the thief scaled a 15-foot wall to gain entry, *how* the theft was managed would be placed in the lead.

If the thief left a note in the store apologizing for his act and saying he needed the money to pay medical bills for his sick wife, *why* the theft occurred— according to the thief—would be put into the lead.

The most important element always forms the basic idea for the lead. To find that basic element, the reporter anticipates the questions the reader will ask and then answers them. These questions have been summarized as *who, what, when, where, why* and *how*—the Five W's and an H.

Burying the Lead ▶

A student was assigned to interview the chairman of the local United Way Campaign, which was in the middle of a fund drive. The reporter thought that the midpoint of the drive might be a good time to check progress. Here is the story he turned in:

> The local United Way Campaign today issued its second weekly report in its current campaign to raise $750,000 for next year's activities.
>
> Tony Davis, the campaign chairman, said that donations in the first two weeks had exceeded last year's fund raising at a similar time.
>
> "We've collected $350,000, and that's about $25,000 ahead of last year," Davis said. "Thanks to the work of our downtown volunteers, the local merchants have been canvassed more thoroughly than ever before, and their gifts have been very generous."
>
> The month-long drive seeks funds for 28 local organizations, including the Big Brothers, Senior Citizens House and a new program to aid crippled children.

The story is clear but it has a glaring fault: What should have been the basic theme was placed in the second paragraph. Occasionally, a reporter will intentionally delay the lead, usually for dramatic effect. This was no such instance. The most significant fact the student reporter gleaned from his reporting was that the campaign was running ahead of last year's receipts. And since this is a straightforward or spot news story, the progress report should have been placed in the lead. Given this advice by his instructor, the student rewrote the story.

```
    The United Way Campaign to raise $750,000 is running
ahead of last year's drive at the midway point.
    Tony Davis, the campaign chairman, said today that in the
first two weeks of the month-long fund drive, $350,000 had
been collected. That is $25,000 ahead of last year's collections
at this time.
    "Thanks to the work of our downtown volunteers, the local
merchants have been  . . ."
```

The same set of facts was given to a reporting and writing class. Here are some of the leads that emerged:

```
    Tony Davis, the chairman of the United Way Campaign,
reported today that the fund drive is running ahead of
schedule.
```

```
    The United Way Campaign has collected $350,000, which is
$25,000 ahead of last year's drive at this time.
```

```
    Local merchants were credited today with helping to push the
United Way Campaign closer and faster toward its goal of
$750,000.
```

In each of these leads, the basic idea is the same: Collections are ahead of those last year. This was the most important element and it must be the basis of the lead.

The single-element spot news story may contain several themes or ideas, but in this type of story the reporter decides that only one is important. A story of this kind may have the following structure:

◀ Single-Element
Story Structure

- Lead: Idea A.
- Explanatory material. Elaboration of Idea A.
- Secondary material. Sub-themes B, C, D, E.
- Background.
- Further elaboration of Idea A.

Short pieces written this way usually can be cut after the lead or two paragraphs, and longer pieces can be cut after a few paragraphs.

The Multiple-Element Story ▶

Multiple-element stories can be edited similarly because we write them the same way as the single-element story. The difference is that we put more than one basic idea high up in the story.

An event that has two or more major ideas or themes calls for a multiple-element story. The structure of the multiple-element story is:

- Lead: Idea A, Idea B.
- Explanatory material. Elaboration of Idea A, Idea B.
- Secondary material. Sub-themes C, D, E, F.
- Background.
- Further elaboration of Idea A, Idea B.

Two-Element Story ▶

Here are 12 paragraphs from an election story that appeared in the *Daily News*. Seemingly complex, the story has a simple structure that is based on the two major story ideas: (A) rejection of the bond issue and (B) Republican control of the legislature.

Gov. Hughes Loses Bonds & Legislature
by Joseph McNamara

(1) The lead contains a colloquial phrase in the first sentence that the reporter felt would attract readers. The second sentence summarizes the two themes, A and B.

(2–8) These seven paragraphs refer to theme A. In 2, the reporter gives a possible consequence of the loss of the bond issue.

In any election, vote tallies are essential, and the reporter supplies them in 5 and 6, which set up a good example in 7 of the extent of the governor's shellacking. In 8, the reporter gives a bit of background to A.

(9) Secondary information about other items on the ballot.

(10–12) Elaboration of theme B. Examples of specific races are given.

(1) New Jersey Gov. Richard J. Hughes took a shellacking all around in yesterday's statewide election. The voters rejected the $750 million bond issue proposal on which he had hung much of his political prestige, and the Republicans gained control of both houses of the Legislature.

(2) Hughes, who had warned during the campaign that if the bond issue were defeated he would ask the Legislature in January for a state income tax and sales tax to meet the state's financial needs, announced early today that he "may have to do some rethinking" about the size of the need. And he made it clear that the "rethinking" would increase his estimate of the amount required.

(3) "I accept the verdict rendered by the people," he said in a written statement.

Behind from the Start

(4) The bond issue proposal, which was broken into two questions—one on institutions and the other on roads—trailed from the time the polls closed at 8 p.m. With the count in from 4,238 of the state's 4,533 districts, the tally early today was:

(5) Institutions: No, 868,586; Yes, 736,967.

(6) Highways: No, 866,204; Yes, 681,059.

(7) As a measure of Hughes' defeat, in the Democrats' Hudson County stronghold—where the Governor had hoped for a plurality of 150,000—he got only a 100,501 to 64,752 vote in favor of the institutional bonds and 93,654 to 66,099 in favor of the highway bonds.

(8) He had promised that if the bond issue were defeated, he would go before the Legislature in January and ask for a state income tax and a state sales tax to meet the state's obligations.

(9) Four other referendums had no great opposition, and passed easily. They were on voter residency requirements, a tax break on farm land and a change in exemptions from the ratables to the finished tax for both veterans and the elderly.

(10) The Republicans have controlled the State Senate for the last half century, and smashing victories yesterday in crucial Essex, Burlington and Camden Counties increased their majority—which had shrunk to a hairsbreadth 11-10—to two-thirds.

(11) Democrats swamped in the avalanche included Gov. Hughes'

brother-in-law Sen. Edward J. Hulse of Burlington County. He was unseated by Republican Edwin B. Forsythe who ran up a convincing 6,000-vote majority.

(12)   In populous Essex County, Republican C. Robert Sarcone defeated Democrat Elmer M. Matthews—who conceded shortly after 11 p.m. without waiting for the final count. And in Camden County, Republican Frederick J. Scholz unseated incumbent Joseph W. Cowgill. . . .

The following is an example of a story that begins with a three-element lead. The reporter would have singled out one element had she felt that one was the most important of the three. She decided the three were of equal importance.

◀ Three-Element Story

Study Links 3 Factors to Heart Ills
By Jane E. Brody

(1)   A new study conducted among 110,000 adult members of the Health Insurance Plan of Greater New York has once again demonstrated that smoking, an overweight condition and physical inactivity are associated with a greatly increased risk of death and disability from heart disease.

(2)   The study, published yesterday in the June issue of The American Journal of Public Health, reported that men and women who smoke cigarettes face twice the risk of suffering a first heart attack as do non-smokers.

(3)   The annual incidence of first heart attacks among pipe and cigar smokers was also found to be higher than among non-smokers, but not as high as among cigarette smokers.

(4)   Men who are "least active," both on and off the job, are twice as likely as "moderately active" men to suffer a first heart attack and four times as likely to suffer a fatal heart attack.

(5)   Men who were classified as "most active" showed no advantage in terms of heart attack rate over men considered "moderately active." The authors reported that other differences between active and inactive men, such as the amount they smoked, could not account for their different heart attack rates.

(6)   The heavier men in the study had a 50 percent greater risk of suffering a first heart attack than the lighter-weight men. An increased risk was also found among women who had gained a lot of weight since age 25.

(7)   None of the differences in risk associated with weight could be explained on the basis of variations in smoking and exercise habits, the authors stated.

(8)   The incidence of heart attacks was also found to be higher among white men than among non-whites and among Jewish men than among white Protestants and Catholics. But the heart attack rate among Jewish women was not markedly different from that among non-Jewish women.

—*The New York Times*

(1) The lead has a three-part theme: A study concludes that smoking, A, overweight, B, and physical inactivity, C, increase risk of heart disease.

(2) Brody tells the reader the source of the material and where it came from and then gives more information about theme A.

(3) More detail on A.

(4) Here she jumps to C, physical inactivity. It might have been better to have followed the A, B, C order.

(5) More on physical inactivity.

(6) Brody moves on to theme B, overweight.

(7) More on B; its relationship to A and C.

(8) Brody considered this secondary information.

A less cluttered lead might have put the attribution in the second paragraph and started, "Smoking, an overweight condition and physical inactivity. . . ."

Some reporters might have found a lead in the information Brody places in the last paragraph. Although most events have obvious leads, a number do not. News judgment is essential on multiple-element stories, and judgments differ. Brody was on target. The last paragraph is secondary.

Brody's story also illustrates another basic guideline for structuring a story: Put related material together.

Story Units ▶

In organizing their stories, news writers move from one theme to another in the order of the importance of the subjects or themes. The lead is elaborated first, and then the next-most-important theme is stated and then elaborated and explained. The rule of thumb is this: Put everything about the same subject in the same place.

When his editor explained the rule—like things together—to Dwight Macdonald, a journalist and critic, his first reaction was, "Obviously." His second, he said, was, "But why didn't it ever occur to me?" His third was, "It was one of those profound banalities 'everybody knows'—after they've been told. It was the climax of my journalistic education."

The Inverted Pyramid ▶

The story structure explained in this chapter—important elements at the beginning, less important at the end—has for decades been taught to students as the "inverted pyramid" form. The term can be misleading. An inverted pyramid is an unbalanced monolith, a huge top teetering on a pinpoint base. It is a monstrous image for journalists, for the top of a story should be deft and pointed. Discard the picture of this precariously balanced chunk and remember that all it means is that the most important material is usually placed at the beginning of the story and the less important material placed at the end.

The news story takes its shape from the requirements and limitations of the craft as measured by the clock—a silent but overwhelming presence—and the available space for copy. Given these realities, most stories must be written in such a way that they can be handled quickly and efficiently. If the 10 inches of available space suddenly shrinks to eight, no problem. The news story structure makes it possible to cut the bottom two paragraphs without losing key information.

If the only justification for the standard news story form were its utility to the people writing and editing the news, it would not have stood up over the years. The form has persisted because it meets the needs of media users. The readers of news usually want to know what happened as soon as the story begins to unfold. If it is interesting, they will pay attention. Otherwise, they turn elsewhere. People are too busy to tarry without reward.

Sometimes the pleasure may come from suspense, a holding of the breath until the climax is revealed deep in the story. When the reporter senses that this kind of structure is appropriate for the event, a delayed lead will be used.

Research tells us that structure can help increase the viewer's and reader's understanding of the story and his or her involvement in it. For those who stay with the story from beginning to end, the start and the conclusion seem to be the best-remembered portions of the piece. Now that page layout can be more accurately designed, the reporter can put a kicker or summary at the end of a story without worrying that it might be squeezed out.

News forms may be said to be utilitarian or pragmatic, in the tradition of the hustle and bustle of American life. But there is also an aesthetic component in the standard news form that its detractors sometimes fail to detect. If the expression "form follows function" implies beauty in the finished work, then the news story is a work of art, minor as it may be. The news story meets the demands of art: It reveals a harmony of design.

◄ **Storytelling Form**

Editors are concerned about the failure of the newspaper to attract new readers. They believe that the standard fare and form are unappetizing, that a generation reared on MTV, 15-second TV commercials, rock music and docudramas seeks more excitement than most newspapers have been offering. As a consequence, there is increasing reliance on what is described as the storytelling form. The reader is invited into the story with an interesting, amusing or exciting incident or example. Stories are written to build to a climax rather than to give the reader the main theme at the outset.

At first glance, this storytelling form seems to release the writer from the task of structuring carefully. Not so. As we will see in the next chapter, the storyteller is just as scrupulous in the choice of material for the beginning of the piece as is the user of the traditional form. Both forms require the writer to identify the major theme and to make clear at the outset that the story will be concerned with that theme. The incident or example selected to begin the storytelling article must fit neatly into the theme of the piece.

That theme may come in the first paragraph, the third paragraph or the last. The ending is as carefully crafted as is the beginning. In all cases, the writer must first identify the theme and then decide where it will be placed in the piece.

Look at a story a reporter wrote about the search for a new city hall. She began with a general observation and then moved into the significant action:

> Modern buildings of glass and steel mark the downtown section.
>
> But the city's business is conducted in an old brick building that many residents liken to a warehouse.
>
> Last night, city officials went shopping for a new city hall. They looked at a modern 10-story office building. . . .

The third paragraph contains the news element, the lead idea. The first two paragraphs take the reader to the theme in an interesting way.

But suppose the reporter is covering a fire in city hall that led to two deaths. This story must begin with the news of the deaths. That news cannot be delayed. The story's structure takes its shape from the nature of the event.

An Old Timer's Advice

Today's news stories follow no rigid form. Content often dictates the shape the story takes. Not so decades ago. Here's the advice of a veteran United Press reporter, Reynolds Packard, in his novel, *The Kansas City Milkman:*

> The lead of a story should be a one-sentence paragraph. The second and third paragraphs should be two sentences each and the fourth paragraph should be one or three sentences to make variety. Then back to the paragraphs of two sentences.

No one follows Packard's recommended structure today. But the rest of his advice to news writers remains valid today:

> The verb of the lead must be transitive and in the active voice.
> The lead must never start with a participial phrase which slows up the tempo.
> And remember, you are writing international politics so it can be understood by the Kansas City Milkman. If the Kansas City Milkman can't understand it, the dispatch is badly written.

Story Necessities ▶

Take any event and play the reporter's game. What are the necessary facts for an automobile accident story, a fire story, an obituary? Let us say an automobile hits a child. What must the story include? It will have to contain the child's name, age and address; the driver's name, age, address and occupation; the circumstances and location of the accident; the extent of the child's injuries; the action, if any, taken against the motorist. Any other necessities?

Given an assignment, the reporter has in mind a list of necessities for the story. The necessities guide the reporter's observations and direct the questions he or she will ask of sources. But there can be a problem.

Unless the reporter can spot the significant differences between stories of a similar type, one accident story will be like another, one obituary like a dozen others. The reporter on the "automobile hits child" story tries to discover the unusual aspects of the event that should be given priority: Was the youngster playing? If so, was he or she running after a ball, playing hide-and-seek or jumping rope? Was the child looking for a dog, cat, younger brother? Was the child crossing the street to go to school? How seriously was the child injured? Will the youngster be able to walk normally?

Once the reporter has (a) thought about the necessities of stories he or she is assigned and (b) sought out the facts that differentiate this story from others like it, the story is on its way to being organized. The final step is to construct a lead around the important or unique element. There is no simple formula for determining what should go into the lead. The criteria for news we developed in Chapter 2 are helpful. Basically, news judgment is an exercise in logical thinking.

When a fire destroys a hotel worth $30 million and takes 14 lives, the reporter focuses the lead on the lives lost, not the destruction of the hotel, no matter how costly. The reporter reasons that a life cannot be equated with money. If no one was killed or hurt in the fire, then the significance may well be that it was a costly structure, not a three-story hotel for transients that had seen better times. If there were no injuries and the hotel had some historical interest, the lead might be that a landmark in town was destroyed by fire. Finally, if no one was hurt and the hotel was a small, old building like many others in town, the fire would rate only two or three paragraphs.

The thinking process that underlies writing news stories is precisely the same as the thinking process that guides reporting. Reporting and writing are inextricably bound together, and when done properly they provide the ingredients for the well-organized story.

Let us imagine a reporter assigned to the education beat. Told to check a report that public school teachers might not report for work next fall, she thinks of several essential questions:

◀ Covering a Strike Threat

- Is the report true?
- How many teachers are involved?
- What are the reasons for the strike?
- When will the decision be made about whether to strike?
- What are the responses of authorities to the threat?
- What plans are being made for the students should there be a strike?

The answers to these questions and other observations made during her reporting are the building blocks for the story. The reporter knows what her lead will be from the minute she receives the assignment—the possibility of a teacher strike and schools not opening. She has a simple formula for finding the lead: What do I know today that I did not know yesterday and that everyone would like to know?

These are the first few paragraphs of the story she writes:

Teachers in all 15 public schools in the city today threatened to strike next September unless they are given an 8 percent wage increase in next year's contract.

Spokesmen for the local unit of the American Federation of Teachers, which represents 780 Freeport school teachers, said the strike threat will be presented to the City Board of Education at Thursday's negotiating session.

"Without a contract that contains pay levels reflecting the increased cost of living, we will not report for work in September," said Herbert Wechsler, the president of the local unit. "No contract, no work."

If the Thursday session leads to no resolution of the issue, the reporter's story about this development will begin this way:

The possibility of a strike of public school teachers next September loomed larger today when six hours of contract talks failed to settle the wage issue.

The teachers' union seeks an 8 percent pay increase over the current pay levels for next year's contract. The school board has offered 4 percent.

The nonstop discussion between the union and the city school board failed to produce a settlement, said Herbert Wechsler, the president of the local unit of the American Federation of Teachers. The union, which represents the city's 780 public school teachers, issued its strike threat Tuesday and presented it formally at today's session.

Joseph Foremen, the state superintendent of education, who is attending the contract talks at the invitation of both sides, said:

"The two groups are widely separated. We need a cooling-off period. Unless one side or the other makes some kind of concession, we may have no teachers in the schools Sept. 9. And a concession is the last thing on their minds now."

The General, Then the Specific ▶

The best advice she received from an editor, a reporter remarked was, "Follow every generality with a specific."

Every story has a logical structure, the editor told her, of general to specific. For example, when a council member says that next year's budget will set a record high, the reporter asks how high that will be, what the amount will be:

Riggio said next year's budget will set "a record high." He estimated it would amount to $725 million.

Here's another example:

Miles said, "Vince Lombardi was wrong when he said that winning is everything." It's more important, the coach said, to develop an athlete's sense of fair play and his or her love of sport.

DAD ▶

To the news writer, form and content are one. Each reinforces the other. We've already noted that no matter how well reported a story is, if it zigs here and zags there, the reader or viewer will not bother to try to make sense out of the chaos. But let's pause a moment to look at the perfectly organized story: If it lacks dialogue, action or description, the bored reader will also move on.

Dialogue, action, description: DAD. Let's look at a story that contains these essential elements, a religion story. Back in Chapter 3, we said that journalists came late to the topic of religion despite the great interest many people have in it. This story by Jena Heath that appeared in *The Charlotte Observer* stirred a tempest.

Letters showered down on the newspaper for a month, and Heath received calls of support and outrage from Virginia and the District of Columbia as well as from North Carolina after the piece was put on the Knight-Ridder wire and run on the front page of the religion section of *The Washington Post*.

Heath, who now works for *The News & Observer* in Raleigh, N.C., initiated the story. She felt it was time to write something about the role of Catholic women in their church. Her editor suggested she talk to women who want to be priests. Newsroom colleagues came up with names of sources.

Heath worked on the story for two weeks. The story ran at the top of page one of the Sunday newspaper. Look at how Heath blends description, action and dialogue in these opening paragraphs:

It was seven winters ago, but Sister Carol Symons hasn't forgotten.

She was ministering to the sick in Boone. The day the call came, the town's only priest was away. Sister Carol raced the seven minutes from her home to the hospital, where she found anguish. A Mexican migrant worker had given birth to a stillborn girl.

As she entered the dimly lit recovery room, the nun murmured to the woman's husband, tears glistening on his face. She walked across the room and took the woman's hand. Looking up from her stretcher, the woman choked out the words in Spanish.

Quiero confesar mis pecados, she pleaded. I want to confess my sins.

Sister Carol couldn't help. In the Roman Catholic Church, only priests can offer the peace of absolution.

"For me, the heart of the story is that there I was, a person in ministry and I couldn't help her," Sister Carol said. "I would be ordained if I could."

Change is coming for Catholic women, not fast enough for some, too fast for others. One door, though, remains firmly shut: the door to the priesthood.

The image of a female priest at the altar is an emotional one for Catholics. Traditionalists say Jesus chose 12 men as his disciples, that Jesus himself was a man and that the church's long history of an all-male clergy means the priesthood was never intended for women.

Many Catholic women, meanwhile, have seen female priests in the Episcopalian Church since 1976, when it began ordaining women. They've seen female rabbis since 1972 and a host of female ministers, including Southern Baptists, since 1964.

Yet Catholic women who feel called to the priesthood say they must live with the pain of knowing they cannot serve God as their hearts dictate.

Robert Lahser,
The Charlotte Observer.

Sister Carol Symons

A lot of work goes into writing a news story. As a reporter with more than 30 years experience on California newspapers put it to a beginner, "Those of us who survive work on our stories from the minute we get the assignment." The work the reporter was talking about takes the form of projecting at each level of reporting and writing the story as it will appear in its final form.

Reporters try to visualize and structure their stories at these stages:

- Immediately on receiving the assignment.
- While gathering material at the event.
- Before writing.
- During writing.

It is time to examine the most important step in the writing process—creating the lead.

Scanlan, Christopher, ed. *How I Wrote the Story.* Providence, R.I.: Providence Journal Co., 1983.

Snyder, Louis L., and Richard B. Morris. *A Treasury of Great Reporting.* New York: Simon & Schuster, 1949.

Wilson, Ellen. *The Purple Decades: A Reader.* New York: Farrar, Straus and Giroux, 1982.

OVER TIMES SQUARE

HOLDING ON
FOR DEAR LIFE

Michael Norcia, *New York Post.*

Breaking news event—direct lead.

6 The Lead

Preview

The lead gives the reader the sense of the story to follow. There are two basic types of leads:

• **Direct:** This lead tells the reader or listener the most important aspect of the story at once. It is usually used on breaking news events.

• **Delayed:** This lead entices the reader or listener into the story by hinting at its contents. It usually is used with feature stories.

The lead sentence should contain one idea and follow the subject-verb-object sentence structure for clarity. It should not exceed 35 words.

T he effective story lead meets two requirements. It captures the essence of the event, and it cajoles the reader or listener into staying awhile.

> We slept last night in the enemy's camp.
> —By a correspondent for the *Memphis Daily Appeal,* after the first day of the Civil War Battle of Shiloh.

> Millionaire Harold F. McCormick today bought a poor man's youth.
> —Carl Victor Little, UP, following McCormick's male gland transplant operation in the early 1920s. UP's New York Office quickly killed the lead and sent out a sub (substitute lead).

> The million-to-one shot came in. Hell froze over. A month of Sundays hit the calendar. Don Larsen today pitched a no-hit, no-run, no-man-reach-first game in a World Series.
> —Shirley Povich, *The Washington Post & Times Herald,* on the perfect game the Yankee pitcher hurled against the Brooklyn Dodgers in 1956.

"I feel as if I had been pawed by dirty hands," said Martha Graham.
—Walter Terry, dance critic of *The New York Herald Tribune,* after two members of Congress denounced Graham's dancing as "erotic."

What price Glory? Two eyes, two legs, an arm—$12 a month.
—St. Clair McKelway, *Washington Herald,* in a story about a disabled World War I veteran living in poverty.

Snow, followed by small boys on sleds.
—H. Allen Smith, *New York World-Telegram,* in the weather forecast.

These leads defy almost every canon decreed by those who prescribe standards of journalistic writing. The first lead violates the rule demanding the reporter's anonymity. The UP lead is in questionable taste. Povich's lead has four sentences and three clichés. Terry's lead is a quote lead, McKelway's asks a question—both violations of the standards. Smith's weather forecast is a little joke.

Yet, the leads are memorable.

They work because they meet the requirements of lead writing: They symbolize in graphic fashion the heart of the event, and they entice the reader to read on. Here are two leads from New York City newspapers that appeared the morning after the mayor announced his new budget. Which is better?

Mayor Lindsay listed facilities for public safety yesterday as his top spending priority for next year, shifting from his pledge of a year ago to make clean streets his first objective in capital expenditures.
—*The New York Times*

Mayor Lindsay dropped his broom and picked up the nightstick yesterday, setting law enforcement facilities as the top priority in the city's construction plans for the coming fiscal year.
—*Daily News*

◀ **Memorable Beginnings**

The business of luring the reader into a story is hardly confined to journalistic writing. Andrew E. Svenson, the prolific author of many of the Nancy Drew, Bobbsey Twins and Hardy Boys juvenile books, said that the trick in writing is to set up danger, mystery and excitement on page one to convince the child to turn the page. He said he had rewritten page one as many as 20 times.

Plato knew the importance of the first words of a written work. "The beginning is the most important part of the work," he wrote in *The Republic.*

The Old Testament begins with simple words in a short sentence: "In the beginning God created the heavens and the earth."

Everyone remembers great beginnings:

It was the best of times, it was the worst of times, it was the age of wisdom, it was the age of foolishness, it was the epoch of belief, it was the epoch of incredulity, it was the season of Light, it was the season of Darkness, it was the spring of hope, it was the winter of despair.

As most high school students know, that is how Charles Dickens began *A Tale of Two Cities*. Another book, written 92 years later, is also familiar to high school readers, possibly because of the beginning that trapped them into reading further:

> If you really want to hear about it, the first thing you'll probably want to know is where I was born, and what my lousy childhood was like, and how my parents were occupied, and all that David Copperfield kind of crap, but I don't feel like going into it, if you want to know the truth.

The writer—J.D. Salinger. The book—*Catcher in the Rye.*
Another great beginning:

> It is a truth universally acknowledged, that a single man in possession of a good fortune must be in want of a wife.

That's the way Jane Austen began *Pride and Prejudice.*

Finding the Lead ▶

New Yorker writer John McPhee says, "The first part—the lead, the beginning—is the hardest part of all to write. I've often heard writers say that if you have written your lead you have 90 percent of the story." But that's not easy, he says.

"You have tens of thousands of words to choose from, after all—and only one can start the story, then one after that, and so forth. . . . What will you choose?" McPhee asks.

But before the words can be selected, the facts must be sorted out. How does the reporter select the one or two facts for a lead from the abundance of material he or she has gathered? What's the focus of the story?

Actually, the fact sifting begins well before the reporter sits down to write. Experienced reporters agree with journalists John W. Chancellor and Walter R. Mears who say:

> We have found that a way to write good leads is to think of them in advance—to frame the lead while the story is unfolding.

The Five Lead Questions ▶

We can begin our examination of the lead-writing process by looking into the thinking of news writers. Their first step consists of answering two questions:

1. *What* was unique or the most important or unusual thing that happened?
2. *Who* was involved—who did it or who said it?

After answering these questions, the reporter seeks words and a form that will give shape to the responses. This leads to three more questions:

3. Is a direct or a delayed lead best? (Does the theme of the story go in the first sentence or somewhere within the first six paragraphs?)
4. Is there a colorful word or dramatic phrase I can work into the lead?
5. What is the subject, and what verb will best move the reader into the story?

Let's accompany Sarah as she works on a story about a talk she has just covered. A Harvard sociologist gave the talk about teen-age pregnancy to a campus audience. He said that the bill for social services, special schools, lost work hours and hospital care for the infants, who are often born prematurely, adds up to several billion dollars a year.

"Last year," he said, "about 500,000 teen-agers gave birth, and almost as many teen-agers had abortions. About two-thirds of these teen-agers were unmarried. The dollar costs have been enormous, to say nothing of the social costs."

Sarah is writing for the campus newspaper. She has a couple of hours before deadline. If she were working for a radio or TV station, she would not have the luxury of time to think about her lead and story. As Chancellor and Mears state in their book *The News Business:*

> When you've got to run to a telephone to start dictating, or when you've got to go on camera and start talking, the one thing you really need is to have a lead in your head. It doesn't have to be fancy, but if you frame it properly, the rest of the story will flow from it in a natural and graceful way.

Sarah knows that if she can identify the heart of the talk, her story will just about organize itself since the next several paragraphs after the lead will have to consist of quotes that buttress and amplify the lead material she has selected. Easier said than done, she muses.

Well, what's her lead? She had better start writing, and she does:

A Harvard sociologist studying teen-age pregnancy gave a speech last night to more than 200 students and faculty members in Hall Auditorium.

Trouble. That's called backing into the lead. All this kind of lead tells the reader, she realizes, is that the speaker spoke to an audience, which is hardly unique and certainly not interesting or important enough to merit anyone's attention. He did say something interesting—in fact, he made several interesting points. Sarah had been surprised by the large number of teen-agers who gave birth and the number of abortions among these young women. Lead material?

Not really, she reasons, because the speaker devoted most of his talk to the cost of teen-age pregnancy. This information was clearly the most important. She could work the figures into the second and third paragraphs to explain the reasons for the high cost. Sarah writes:

A Harvard sociologist said last night that teen-age pregnancy is costing the country billions of dollars a year.
Gerald Cantor told 200 students and faculty members in Hall Auditorium that the costs associated with the pregnancies of 500,000 young women under the age of 20 "are vastly greater than we had thought."
He attributed the costs to social services. . . .

Sarah pauses to read what she has written. She is satisfied that she has found the most important part of the talk for her lead, that she has identified the speaker properly and placed the talk. . . . Wait. She isn't happy with the word *said* in her lead. Not very exciting. Should she make it *warned?* Or is that too strong?

Sarah has answered the first three of our five questions for lead writing:

1. **What:** The high cost.
2. **Who:** Harvard sociologist.
3. **Direct or delayed:** Direct.

We take leave of Sarah as she ponders the fourth and fifth questions. If you wish, lend her a hand.

A Race for Congress ▶

Here is a lead a reporter wrote about a congressional race. He thought he had answered the first two questions writers ask themselves when writing a lead:

> Replies of Rep. Ronald A. Sarasin and William R. Ratchford, candidates in the Fifth Congressional race, to a Connecticut League of Women Voters questionnaire were released today.

He did include *what* had happened and *who* was involved. But he did not make his answer to the first question sufficiently specific. What did they say in their replies? The reporter might have reached this answer in the story, had his editor let him continue. But the editor pointed out that voters want to know the opinions and positions of their candidates quickly in stories about politics. Such events do not lend themselves to delayed leads.

A better lead for the political story might have been:

> Ronald A. Sarasin and William R. Ratchford, candidates for Congress in the Fifth District, agree that the deficit is the major domestic issue facing the nation.

The next paragraph might have included the background information that the reporter had mistakenly put into his lead:

> Their positions on the budget and on other issues were released today by the Connecticut League of Women Voters. The League had sent its questionnaires to all major candidates for office.

The subsequent paragraphs would expand the deficit theme and introduce additional material from the replies of the congressional candidates.

Kickers ▶

All these leads are direct leads for breaking or hard news stories. But there are times when writers back into the lead on a breaking news story—intentionally. Edna Buchanan began a story for *The Miami Herald* this way:

> Bad things happen to the husbands of the Widow Elkin.
>
> Someone murdered husband No. 4, Cecil Elkin, apparently smashing his head with a frying pan as he watched "Family Feud" on TV.

> Husband No. 3, Samuel Smilich,
> drowned in a weedy South Dade canal.
> Husband No. 2, Lawrence Myers, can-
> not be found. . . .

Anyone out there who isn't hanging on every word? Notice the detail Buchanan supplies: It was not just any pan but a frying pan with which No. 4 was dispatched. And he wasn't just watching television but "Family Feud." The canal where No. 3 was found was "weedy."

Buchanan goes on to write about Widow Elkin and then concludes the piece:

> It is the murder of her fourth husband
> that got Margaret Elkin in trouble. She is
> accused of trying to hire a beekeeper to kill
> him. The trial is set for Sept. 9.

The prosaic way to have started this story would have put the date set for the trial in the lead. But Buchanan's reporting turned up a remarkable series of events, and she gave us a modern morality tale with a climax.

Journalists call these lead-type endings *kickers,* probably in recognition of the jolt the climax gives the reader.

◀ **Types of Leads**

Beginning journalists often are offered lists of leads. They are told about the who, what, where, when, why and how leads; the anecdotal, clause, gag, shotgun and quote leads; and a score of others.

This categorizing may be useful for a research project, but the lists are of little use to the working reporter. No reporter looks at his or her notes and thinks, "Well, this looks like a *who* lead here. Or maybe it's a *what* lead."

What ran through the mind of the reporter who wrote this lead?

> NORFOLK—Charley Greene has hit
> the roof in an effort to prove that he isn't
> six feet under.
> —*The Virginian-Pilot* (Norfolk, Va.)

Is that a *who* or a *what* lead? What is the difference and who cares? The reporter learned that a retired Navy warrant officer had not been receiving his retirement pay because the government thought him dead. The situation seemed humorous enough for feature handling. Then the reporter played with some words that would express the plight of a man caught in coils of red tape. The reporter decided on a delayed lead.

There are only two basic leads, direct and delayed. All the others fall under these two types.

◀ Direct Lead

The direct lead is the workhorse of journalism, the lead that is used on most stories. As we have seen, the direct lead focuses on the theme of the event in the first paragraph. The surest way to test a reporter's competence, editors say, is to see whether his or her leads on spot news events move directly to the point and are succinct and readable.

Oklahoma City
Direct Leads

Five minutes after the AP moved a news alert at 9:12 a.m. that an explosion had damaged the federal courthouse in downtown Oklahoma City, a series of bulletins and urgents were sent, some moving within minutes of the preceding one. Here is the first bulletin and the sixth lead in this rapid series of direct news leads:

BULLETIN

OKLAHOMA CITY (AP)— An explosion rocked the federal courthouse in downtown Oklahoma City, blowing a large portion of the front of the building away.

There were reports of numerous injuries.

URGENT
6th Lead—Writethru

OKLAHOMA CITY (AP)— An explosion ripped through a federal office building and turned downtown Oklahoma City into chaos this morning.

The nine-story Alfred Murrah Federal Building looked like it had been rocked by a bomb. From top to bottom, floors caved in. Burning debris and burning cars lined streets.

Associated Press.

Minutes after the bombing.

Here are some direct leads:

> A local couple was awarded $150,000 in damages yesterday in Butte County Court for injuries they suffered in a traffic accident last March.

> Guy Barton Rhodes, an organist with the First Methodist Church for 45 years, died at his home at 33 Raritan Ave. today. He was 91 years old.

> Another in a series of snowstorms is expected to hit the Sierra today.

The direct lead answers the reporter's first two questions—what happened and who was involved?—in the first sentence of the story.

Direct leads need not be dry and dull. Here's a direct lead by Aljean Harmetz of *The New York Times* for a business story, which we usually think of as a dry subject with prose to match:

> Two veteran motion picture industry executives were chosen today by the board of Walt Disney Productions to head the troubled company a mouse built.

Attracting
The Reader ▶

Jack Miller of *The Toronto Star* visualized the subject of his story:

> If researchers can perfect a new laser detection technique, doctors may start spotting cancerous breast tumors not much bigger than the period at the end of this sentence.
>
> Early detection of tumors—finding them when they're just starting out and are still small—always has been a key to improving the odds for beating cancer. . . .

When a fire struck a high-rise apartment building in Queens, New York, the AP put this lead on its story:

> A late-morning fire in the upper floors of an 18-story apartment building in the Lefrak city project in Elmhurst, Queens, killed three people Thursday, the Fire Department said.

Now look at how the *Daily News* began its story about the same fire:

> Strong winds combined lethally with a fire in a Queens high-rise building yesterday, creating a "blowtorch" that roared through an apartment building and into a hallway, killing three people and injuring 22.

The image of a blowtorch searing its way through the building is powerful. A battalion fire chief used that word in an interview and the reporter had the good sense to put it in the lead. Good reporting makes for good writing.

Wendy Lin's careful examination of a police report and her sharp eye made for this arresting lead on a court story for *Newsday:*

> She was arrested in garters and black lingerie, but yesterday a 66-year-old grandmother was arraigned on prostitution charges in Queens Criminal Court wearing blue jeans and a pair of sensible, gumsoled shoes.

The delayed lead is often used on features and news features, the kinds of stories that are not about developing or fast-breaking events. The delayed lead usually sets a scene or evokes a mood with an incident, anecdote or example.

Here is a delayed lead on a feature about a man who runs a demolition company. It was written by AP Newsfeatures writer Sid Moody:

> Jack Loizeaux is a dentist of urban decay, a Mozart of dynamite, a guru of gravity. Like Joshua, he blows and the walls come tumbling down.

Notice that the reader does not know from this lead just what Jack Loizeaux does—the delayed lead does not reveal essential information to the reader. That is one of its attractions.

◄ Delayed Lead

Retribution. When *The Washington Times* began publication, many of its staffers were members of the Rev. Sun Myung Moon's Unification Church. One of them turned in this lead for a fire story:

A 39-year-old Fairfax man was punished by God Thursday night for smoking in bed by burning to death.

Jobless in the Valley of the Poor

Debbie Noda, *The Modesto Bee*.

For its series on poverty in the San Joaquin Valley, reporters for *The Modesto Bee* interviewed dozens of people. Here is how Karyn Houston began her story:

> The father and his 19-month-old daughter are on the sidewalk at the entrance to the supermarket parking lot. As people drive by, the man pleads with a hand-lettered, cardboard sign:
> "Need food. Will work. Please help."
> The little girl is bundled in a light blue parka and mittens. Bottles of juice and milk are nearby. Her warm breath puffs tiny white clouds into the cold December air. . . .

The UPI put this delayed lead on a news story that could have taken a direct lead—the passage by the House to extend daylight savings time two months:

> WASHINGTON—The House wants to add a little daylight to the dark and dreary days of March and April.

Here is how an investigative reporter for the *Chicago Tribune* began a series of articles exposing corruption in Chicago's ambulance services:

> They are the misery merchants and they prowl the streets of our city 24 hours a day as profiteers of human suffering. . . .

Just any incident or anecdote will not do for the delayed lead. The lead must be consistent with the news point, the theme of the story. It must *lead* the reader straight to the heart of the event. Notice how John Rebchook of the *El Paso Herald-Post* takes this delayed lead to the news point in the fifth paragraph, the current status of the drive to collect unpaid traffic fines. Rebchook illustrates his point about unpaid traffic warrants by using in his lead a specific driver who has avoided paying:

> In less than three miles, Joseph L. Jody III ran six stop signs, changed lanes improperly four times, ran one red light, and drove 60 mph in a 30 mph zone—all

Example

without a driver's license. Two days later, he again drove without a driver's license. This time he ran a stop sign and drove 80 mph in a 45 mph zone. For his 16 moving violations—the first 13 committed on Sept. 20, 1982—Jody was fined $1,795.

He never paid. Police say that Jody has moved to Houston. Of the estimated 30,000 to 40,000 outstanding traffic warrants in police files, Jody owes the largest single amount.

Still, Jody's fines account for a small part of at least $500,000 owed to the city in unpaid traffic warrants.

In February, Mayor Jonathan Rogers began a crackdown on scofflaws in order to retrieve some $828,000 in unpaid warrants. As of mid-March, some $368,465 had been paid.

News point (Theme)

As broadcast news reached more and more homes with the latest information, newspapers resorted to writing techniques to grab readers who already had an outline of the event. One of the techniques is the news feature. The writer "featurizes" the straight news event by putting a delayed lead on the story.

By the time *The New York Times* was on newsstands and doorsteps, everyone knew the end to a legal battle over custody of 2½-year-old Jessica. The Supreme Court had dashed the hopes of Jessica's adoptive parents to keep her. This meant the child would have to be turned over to her biological mother, who had given her up for adoption shortly after Jessica was born.

◀ **Leads on News Features**

Don't Delay Too Long

Unless the writer intends to build to a last-paragraph climax, the sooner the news point is reached after a delayed lead the better. Here's a good example by George James of *The New York Times* in which the lead is in the second paragraph:

Sheila Maria Boyd and Jerry Conner, both of Brooklyn, were married yesterday in Queens Borough Hall. Afterward, they celebrated at Cobblestone's Restaurant, a few blocks away at 117–18 Queens Boulevard in Forest Hills.

Among the uninvited guests were nine police officers from the 112th Precinct, who gave them handcuffs and arrested them on 18 counts of robbery.

"I think they were having our famous baby back ribs," said Pete Massaro, the owner of the Cobblestone's, "and the white house wine."

Ms. Boyd, 23 years old, of 327 Lincoln Avenue, and Mr. Conner, 27, of 1765 Prospect Place, were wanted for the robbery of 13 patients and 5 employees in the office of Dr. Arnold. . . .

Don Terry put this lead on his news feature:

> BLAIRSTOWN, Iowa, Aug. 2—When she is grown up, maybe Jessica DeBoer will understand why the adults in her young but complicated life have caused so much hurt in the name of love.
>
> But starting today, the 2½-year-old has more immediate lessons to learn, namely how to live without the only people she has ever known as Mommy and Daddy, Roberta and Jan DeBoer of Ann Arbor, Mich.

In Rwanda ▶

Early in his coverage of the slaughter in Rwanda, the AP's Mark Fritz understood that the battle between the Hutus and Tutsis had to be put in human terms. He had to put faces on the carnage, and for the most part his news features showed the various guises of death.

Health centers were set up in Rwanda in an attempt to lure refugees back to their country from neighboring Zaire, to which they had fled. Fritz began his story about the centers this way:

> GOMA, Zaire (AP)—Bernard Sebazzogue watched as cholera killed his daughter on Monday, his wife on Tuesday and his grandmother Thursday. By week's end, he gathered up his three remaining children and fled for help. To Rwanda.
>
> What lay before him, rising from the dirt over the first 50 miles into his country, were five hospitals that began springing up just a few days before Sebazzogue's family began dying.
>
> These outposts at Goma's doorstep are part of a quick and somewhat haphazard effort to create a corridor of health care in Rwanda from which more than 1 million people fled over several panicked days in early July.

Note that a direct lead could have been fashioned out of the material in the third paragraph. Fritz chose to featurize the story, and the impact is obvious. His coverage included feature stories and straight news accounts as well as news features. His work was recognized with the Pulitzer Prize for International Reporting for 1995.

A Story of Drugs ▶

At first glance, the death records that police reporter Robert Popp of the *San Francisco Chronicle* saw in the police file seemed routine. But rewriteman George Williamson, copy editor Jim Toland and Popp turned it into a sad tale. Here is their story:

Small Boy's Big Loss to Drugs

Johnny B., 6, awoke at a pre-dawn hour yesterday and saw his fully clothed mother lying on the floor next to the bed they shared in the Roy-Ann Hotel at 405 Valencia Street.

Her nose was bleeding badly. Johnny got up, found some tissues, and wiped her face clean. Then he went back to sleep.

When he awoke again at 8:30 a.m., Anne B., 25, was still on the floor. Her face was covered by new blood.

Postscript: Jim Toland had given students in his news writing class at San Francisco State University the facts taken from the police report. One student, curious to see if there is such a place as the Roy-Ann Hotel, drove by. She found the *Chronicle* had misspelled the name of the hotel. It was the Royan.

Johnny dressed himself neatly—as usual—and groomed his Dutch boy haircut before going downstairs to tell the hotel clerk about his "sick" mother.

The coroner's office later determined that she had died from an overdose of an undetermined drug.

Johnny recounted that the night before, two men had visited the studio apartment in the Inner Mission District. He said he asked one man why he was using a rubber cord to make his arm veins bulge, and the man responded that he was taking a blood test.

The men left some time after Johnny went to bed.

In her story for *USA Today,* Barbara S. Rothschild describes a sex therapist's boo-boo with this delayed lead:

There may finally be a question that embarrasses Dr. Ruth Westheimer. It's about the accuracy of her book.

Teens who read the new sex book co-authored by the USA's best-known sex therapist could get more than they asked for.

A baby, perhaps.

First Love: A Young People's Guide to Sexual Information, by Dr. Ruth and education professor Nathan Kravetz, has a major error on page 195.

In a chapter on contraception, the $3.50 book says it's "safe" to have sex the week before and the week of ovulation.

It should read "unsafe"—since those are the times a woman is *most* likely to become pregnant. . . .

◀ Dr. Ruth's Blooper

As should be clear by now, there are no absolute rules about when the direct or the delayed lead should be used. True enough, on large-scale events the direct lead is usually called for, and on features the delayed lead works best. But the lines tend to blur beyond these extremes.

Usually, newspapers establish a style their reporters follow. When a study of bank lending practices found that whites are more likely than blacks to receive mortgage money, Michael Quint of *The New York Times* began his story with a direct lead:

◀ Direct or Delayed?

> WASHINGTON, Oct. 21—The most comprehensive report on mortgage lending nationwide ever issued by the Government shows that even within the same income group whites are nearly twice as likely as blacks to get loans.

For its page-one story the same day, *The Wall Street Journal* writer John R. Wilke preferred a delayed lead that focused on the effect of the discriminatory practices on an individual. Here is how his story began:

> BOSTON—When Sterling Saunders needed a home-repair loan, he turned to two of New England's largest banks, Shawmut Bank and Bank of Boston. He had a steady job, equity in the house and little debt, but they turned him down.
>
> In desperation, he arranged a $35,000, two-year loan from a small Massachusetts mortgage lender, Resource Equity Inc., at a stratospheric 34.09% interest rate. When Resource wouldn't refinance Mr. Saunder's

Delayed lead

Kerwin Plevka, *Houston Chronicle.*

Errant Toss

The catcher throwing wildly to second and the runner scoring the winning run on the error were the most important events in the game and became the theme for the lead.

loan he fell even deeper into debt through refinancings with other high-rate lenders. Now the 42-year-old city employee, his wife and three daughters face eviction from their home of 16 years by a third lender.

"This might never have happened if we'd been able to find a bank loan in the first place," Mr. Saunders says. The banks decline to address specifics of his case, but judging by recent studies of lending patterns, one reason he couldn't get bank loans may have had to do with his address: He lives in a low-income, mostly black Boston neighborhood with few bank branches. A big survey by the Federal Reserve and analyses by others show these areas get a disproportionately small share of mortgage money from banks. . . .

Theme

The *Journal* did run a direct-lead story reviewing the study inside the newspaper.

The Dangers ▶

The Wall Street Journal's narrative style has influenced papers across the country, but its news style sometimes has spread by contagion rather than by healthy example. The delayed lead requires a talented hand. Moreover, it cannot be used at the reporter's whim.

In an attempt to sell their editors on their stories, ambitious reporters use delayed leads on routine news stories, and some reporters play with delayed leads when they are unable to write direct news leads. By taking the narrative or chronological approach or by focusing on an individual, they hope that the reader will somehow figure out just what the news point is.

Editors are aware of these tactics and the abusers of the delayed lead find themselves confined to taking scores from the local bridge and bowling leagues and explaining to the wrestling promoters why the sports editor doesn't consider wrestling results worthy of space.

The Combo Lead ▶

Some reporters have mastered a technique that combines the direct and delayed leads. The story begins with a few general sentences. Then the reporter hits the reader with a karate chop at the end of the first paragraph. Edna Buchanan, the Pulitzer Prize-winning police reporter for *The Miami Herald,* is master of this kind of lead. Here are two typical Buchanan leads:

The man she loved slapped her face. Furious, she says she told him never, ever to do that again. "What are you going to do, kill me?" he asked, and handed her a gun. "Here, kill me," he challenged. She did.

On New Year's Eve, Charles Curzio stayed later than planned at his small TV repair shop to make sure customers would have their sets in time to watch the King Orange Jamboree Parade. His kindness cost his life.

Buchanan covered a story about an ex-convict, Gary Robinson, who pushed his way past a line at a fried-chicken outlet. He was persuaded to take his place in line, but when he reached the counter there was no fried chicken, only nuggets, whereupon he slugged the woman at the counter. In the ensuing fracas, a security guard shot Robinson. Buchanan's lead was:

Gary Robinson died hungry.

Buchanan says her idea of a successful lead is one that could cause a reader who is breakfasting with his wife to "spit out his coffee, clutch his chest, and say, 'My god, Martha. Did you read this?' "

For her lead on a story about a drug smuggler who died when some of the cocaine-filled condoms that he had swallowed began to leak in his stomach, Buchanan wrote:

His last meal was worth $30,000 and it killed him.

Let us listen to a reporter as she mulls over the notes she has taken at a city council meeting:

> There were 13 items on the agenda. Well, which were the important ones? I'll circle them in my notes—
>
> - General traffic program to route heavy trucks to Stanley Street and keep Main for lighter traffic.
> - 56 stop signs to be bought.
> - Paving program for Kentucky Street that will later fit into the bypass.
> - OK'd contract to White Painting Co. to paint City Hall. $28,000.
> - Hired consulting firm for traffic study.
>
> Clearly, I need a direct lead here. Four of them seem to deal with traffic. Should I summarize them or should I pick out the truck route or the traffic study? They seem equally important, so maybe I'll play with a summary lead. I'll drop the stop signs way down and then go into the painting contract.

She writes:

> The City Council today took three significant actions to cope with the city's downtown traffic congestion.
> The Council:
> 1. Approved the employment of Rande Associates, a consulting firm from Burbank, Calif., to make a study of traffic patterns.
> 2. Called for bids on paving 12 blocks of Kentucky Street, which is planned as part of a downtown bypass.
> 3. Endorsed the city traffic department's proposal to route heavy vehicles to Stanley Street before they enter Main Street.

◀ A Difficult Choice

Roundup Leads A *roundup* is a story that joins two or more events with a common theme. Roundups usually take multiple-element direct leads. They are often used for stories on traffic accidents, weather, crime. When the events are in different cities and are wrapped up in one story, the story is known as an "undated roundup."

Torrential rains in Missouri and Kansas left five persons dead, hundreds homeless and crop losses of more than $1 million.

The day after the Supreme Court narrowed a woman's right to an abortion, *The New York Times* put this lead on its roundup of anti-abortion activities in its folo story:

WASHINGTON, July 4—Opponents of abortion, moving to take advantage of the Supreme Court ruling Monday, are preparing measures for state legislatures around the nation that would increase restrictions on abortion.

At this point, some doubts assail the city hall reporter. She remembers that the truck traffic issue has been argued for several months. Downtown merchants complained to the mayor about the truck traffic, and Stanley Street home owners petitioned the Council to keep the trucks away. The local newspaper and radio station have editorialized about it. In her haste to structure a complicated story, her news judgment went awry, she thinks. She writes:

> The City Council today decided to route truck traffic to Stanley Street and away from downtown Freeport.

The reporter is pleased with the lead she has written. But then more doubts. Maybe the overall pattern is more important than the single item about Stanley Street. After all, she thinks, the Council's three major actions will affect more people than those involved in the Stanley Street situation. She decides that she needs some advice and she shows the city editor both leads.

"That's a tough one," he tells her. "Sometimes you flip a coin. Why don't you use your first lead and move up the third item, the one on Stanley Street, and put it first in the list?"

If we look closely at the two leads the city hall reporter prepared, we notice that the single-element lead about the routing of truck traffic to Stanley Street denotes a specific action the council took. The summary lead about the council taking three "significant" actions to "cope with" traffic congestion is the reporter's conclusion or interpretation. The *Daily News's* summary lead on the New Jersey election in Chapter 5 also contains an interpretation that the governor "took a shellacking all around in yesterday's statewide election." Editors allow experienced reporters to interpret the news.

Good Reporting Equals Good Leads ▶

Many weak leads are the result of inadequate reporting. Consider this lead:

> Barbara Elizabeth Foster, 19, St. Mary's University sophomore, will be queen of the city's Rose Festival.

Immediately, the city editor knows he is in for a tedious trek through the copy. The reporter failed to single out an interesting characteristic of the new queen to add to her age and year in school. Glancing through the copy, the editor notices that her mother was named Maid of Cotton 25 years ago. At the end of the story, there is a fleeting mention that her father enjoys gardening.

The editor runs his fingers through thinning hair. Masking his exasperation, he circles two sections and suggests to the reporter that there just might be a lead in the mother-daughter relationship and that a logical question to have asked the new queen was whether her father grew roses. Without good reporting no story can shine, much less be complete.

Color and S-V-O ▶

Next, to the fourth and fifth of our five guides to writing leads. The fourth question the reporter has to answer is, "Is there a colorful word or dramatic phrase that I want to work into the lead?"

When Florida conducted the first execution in the United States in a dozen years in which a person was put to death against his or her will, many reporters were assigned to the event. The nation had engaged in a debate about the morality of the death penalty. How best to put the Florida execution into words? Here is the lead Wayne King wrote for *The New York Times:*

> STARKE, Fla., May 25—The state of Florida trussed Arthur Spenkelink immobile in the electric chair this morning, dropped a black leather mask over his face and electrocuted him.

The choice of the verb "trussed" is inspired. Not only does it mean to secure tightly, its second definition is "to arrange for cooking by binding close the wings or legs of a fowl."

The fifth guide takes us directly into the construction of the lead—the selection of the subject and verb for the lead.

The basic construction of the lead should be subject-verb-object, S-V-O. That is, the lead should begin with the subject, should be closely followed by an active verb and should conclude with the object of the verb.

The S-V-O structure has an internal imperative: It directs the reporter toward writing simple sentences, which are sentences with one main clause. This kind of construction keeps leads short, another major requirement for a readable beginning.

Here are two direct leads:

> In the past decade, David Blake has overpaid the city $7,635 in property fees on his small pharmacy in East Harlem.
> —*Newsday*

S = David Blake; V = has overpaid; O = the city.

> SAN FRANCISCO—A federal judge has ordered the City of San Francisco to hire 60 women police patrol officers within the next 32 weeks.
> —*UPI*

S = judge; V = ordered; O = San Francisco.

The S-V-O construction is the staple of journalistic writing. Three-fourths or more of the sentences a reporter writes follow this pattern. Most direct news leads—whether for print or broadcast—have this construction. It parallels the usual pattern of discourse and conforms to the command, "Write as you talk." Also, the S-V-O construction is functional. It is consistent with the thinking pattern of the reporter as he or she structures the lead. It is the most direct way of answering the first two questions the reporter asks when trying to find the lead: What happened? Who was involved?

A Poet's Perception. "Reduced to its essence, a good English sentence is a statement that an agent (the subject of the sentence) performed an action (the verb) upon something (the object)."—John Ciardi

Actors and Writers. Actors are told, "Act the verb." The same advice helps writers: "Write the verb." The verb gives life and energy to the sentence.

Although the S-V-O guideline may seem rigid, it does permit a variety of styles. Let us look at several leads written the night of a famous heavyweight championship fight:

BULLETIN
CHICAGO, Sept. 25 (UPI) SONNY LISTON KNOCKED OUT FLOYD PATTERSON IN THE FIRST ROUND TONIGHT TO WIN THE HEAVYWEIGHT CHAMPIONSHIP OF THE WORLD.
M950ct

CHICAGO, Sept. 25—Nobody got his money's worth at Comiskey Park tonight except Sonny Liston. He knocked out Floyd Patterson in two minutes, six seconds of the first round of their heavyweight title fight and took the first big step toward becoming a millionaire.
—Robert L. Teague, *The New York Times*

CHICAGO, Sept. 25—Sonny Liston needed all of two years to lure Floyd Patterson into the ring and only two minutes, six seconds to get him out of it in a sudden one-knockdown, one-round-knockout at Comiskey Park last night.
—Jesse Abramson, *The Herald Tribune*

CHICAGO, Sept. 25—Floyd Patterson opened and closed in one tonight. It took Sonny Liston only 2:06 to smash the imported china in the champ's jaw and, thereby, record the third swiftest kayo in a heavyweight title match—a sudden ending that had the stunned Comiskey Park fans wondering wha' hoppened. The knockout punch was there for everyone to see. It was a ponderous hook on Patterson's jaw. But the real mystery was what hurt the champ just before that; how come he suddenly looked in trouble when Liston stepped away from a clinch near the ropes?
—Leonard Lewin, *The Daily Mirror*

CHICAGO, Sept. 25—It was short, sweet and all Sonny Liston here tonight. The hulking slugger with the vicious punch to match his personality teed off on Floyd Patterson, knocked the champion down and out at 2:06 of the first round and won the world heavyweight championship without raising a bead of sweat on his malevolent countenance.
—Gene Ward, *Daily News*

All the reporters agreed on the news angle or theme—Liston's quick knockout of Patterson. The thinking of these reporters was along the S-V-O line: S = Liston; V = knocked out; O = Patterson.

The first lead, written for the UPI, whose reporters are told to remember that there is a deadline every minute, has little more than the S-V-O structure in the lead. Written within seconds of the 10-count, the story was designed to meet the needs of newspapers and broadcast stations on deadline.

The other reporters, who worked for New York City newspapers when the city had four morning dailies, were under less pressure and were able to fashion more distinctive leads. Some put personal observations and their interpretations into the leads—a practice permitted byline reporters.

When Thurgood Marshall died, the leads were also basically the same:

Retired Supreme Court Justice Thurgood Marshall, the first black to serve on the nation's highest court and a key figure in the civil rights movement, died yesterday of heart failure at 84.
—Phil Mintz, *Newsday*

WASHINGTON—Thurgood Marshall, who championed the causes of the downtrodden, the imprisoned and the defenseless in almost a quarter-century on the Supreme Court, died yesterday at the Bethesda Naval Medical Center near here. He was 84.
—*The Boston Globe*

WASHINGTON—Thurgood Marshall, one of the most influential Americans of the 20th century and the first black to be elevated to the U.S. Supreme Court, died Sunday at the Bethesda Naval Medical Center in suburban Washington. He was 84.
—Glen Elsasser and Nicholas M. Horrock, *Chicago Tribune*

WASHINGTON—Retired Justice Thurgood Marshall, the first black to sit on the U.S. Supreme Court and a towering figure in the civil rights movement, died Sunday of heart failure. He was 84.
—The Associated Press

But look at the diversity in the beginnings of these sidebar stories in which reporters assessed Marshall's career:

By his long and wide-ranging career, which took him from the Deep South half a century ago as a civil rights attorney to the US Supreme Court in 1967 as the first black justice, Thurgood Marshall became a doubly powerful symbol, both for black achievement and as a protector of individual rights, many of his clerks said yesterday upon learning of his death.

"He's Mr. Civil Rights, a tremendous hero to lots of people, but especially to black Americans," said Randall L. Kennedy, a Harvard law professor and law clerk for Marshall during the Supreme Court's 1983 term. "I would bet that in some way, any and every black attorney has been influenced by him."
—Dick Lehr, *The Boston Globe*

WASHINGTON—Thurgood Marshall's greatest contributions to the Supreme Court and American justice were not the scores of majority opinions he wrote.

None of those opinions, despite his 24 years as a justice, was among the most important Supreme Court decisions of his time. Marshall cared little for legal niceties. He was no judicial craftsman.

But he may have had as much impact on the court, at a time when that bench was a pre-eminent force in shaping society, as any other justice in history.
—Timothy M. Phelps, *Newsday*

Looking back at the direct news leads in this section, we can generalize about their essentials.

First, we notice that each lead has something *specific* to tell the reader. The reporter moved directly to the heart of the event.

Next, the *time* element is almost always in the lead. Then, there is usually a *source* of the information or action, and the source is often identified. And finally, the *place* of the action is often included.

◀ Four Essentials

specifics
time
source
place

When a reporter writes a lead, he or she navigates between divergent currents. One pull is toward writing a longer-than-average sentence, as the lead must offer significant information. The other is toward a short sentence, since short sentences are more readable than long ones. The long sentence may be difficult to grasp; the short sentence may be uninformative or misleading.

Lead sentences should adhere to a 35-word limit whenever possible, for visibility as well as readability. Long leads occupy so much of the narrow

◀ Lead Length

35 word limit

newspaper column that they appear forbidding. For broadcasting, all sentences tend to be short for quick comprehension.

The AP tells its reporters, "When a lead moves beyond 20–25 words it's time to start trimming." Some of the extra baggage that can be jettisoned:

- Unnecessary attribution.
- Compound sentences joined by *but* and *and*.
- Exact dates and times unless essential.

This means that the AP and other news organizations never run long leads, right? Wrong. When the occasion demands full information in the lead and the news writer is adept at constructing a sentence that has rhythm and balance, long leads are given a green light. Look at this lead by Peter Coy of the AP:

NEW YORK (AP)—The stock market plunged out of control Monday in a selling panic that rivaled the Great Crash of 1929, pushing the Dow Jones average down more than 500 points, draining more than $500 billion from the value of stocks and sending shock waves around the world.

That's 46 words, a blockbuster, but so was the event. Despite its length, the lead is not hard to read. One of the reasons is the writer's use of action verbs that propel the reader through to the end.

When an event is compellingly important, all rules and guidelines are tossed aside and the writer is allowed to jam the facts into the first sentence. Look at this lead from *The Washington Post* that runs 39 words long:

Five men, one of whom said he is a former employee of the Central Intelligence Agency, were arrested at 2:30 a.m. yesterday in what authorities described as an elaborate plot to bug the office of the Democratic National Committee.

Not much artistry here, just the facts. But what facts. This was the opening salvo in the *Post*'s exposure of the Watergate scandal that led to the resignation of Richard Nixon from the presidency.

Leads for Folos ▶

When the Supreme Court ruled that principals can censor high school newspapers, *The Christian Science Monitor,* the *Kennebec* (Maine) *Journal, The Augusta* (Ga.) *Chronicle* and scores of other newspapers around the country assigned staff reporters to find out what effect the ruling would have on local high schools.

These local stories are known as *folos.* The *folo* can run alongside the major story, or it can be published a day or so after the major piece has run.

The lead to a *folo* includes some information from the major piece:

Local high school principals say they will continue to allow student journalists a free hand, despite a Supreme Court decision that gives them the power to censor school publications.

Updated or freshened stories fall into the category of the *folo* story. Usually, it is possible to find someone to comment on a new development or to track down people affected by a new program or policy.

Causes and consequences are useful for leads to these stories:

> Service and maintenance workers were returning to their jobs today following a vote to end a 10-day strike against three Baltimore-area hospitals.
> —*The Baltimore Sun*

Disasters are updated without difficulty. If the cause of the airplane crash is unknown, investigators can be asked about the progress of the inquiry. If there were serious injuries, the condition of the victims can be checked, and if there are additional fatalities, a new death toll can be used as the basis of the lead.

A reporter handed in this lead:

> The city planning office today recommended adding a section to the zoning code regulations on classification for residential use of property.

The editor puzzled over it and then instructed the reporter to say specifically what the proposed section would do. The reporter tried again.

> The city planning office today recommended that property zoned for two-acre, one-family dwellings be rezoned to allow the construction of cooperative apartment houses for middle- and low-income families.

The city editor looked this over and seemed pleased. "Let's take it a step further," he said. "What's the point of the recommendation?" He answered his own question. "To change the code so ordinary people, not only the rich, can move into that wooded area north of town near the Greenwich Estates section. Let's try to get people into the lead." The reporter returned in 10 minutes with these two paragraphs:

> Low- and middle-income families may be able to buy apartments in suburban areas north of the city.
> This is the intention of a proposal made today by the city planning office. The recommendation to the city council would rezone property in the area from the present restrictions that permit only single-family dwellings on two-acre lots.

In this process of writing and rewriting, the reporter went from a jargon-loaded, impenetrable lead to one that stated succinctly and clearly what the proposed regulation was intended to bring about. Accuracy was not sacrificed for simplicity and readability.

◄ **Readability**

Readability stems from the ideas that make up the sentence, the order in which they are written and the words and phrases chosen to give the ideas expression:

Ideas: When possible, the lead should contain one idea. "The sentence is a single cry," says Sir Herbert Read, the British critic and author, in his *English Prose Style*. Too many ideas in a sentence make for heavy going. Also, the idea selected should be easy to grasp; complexities should be simplified.

Sentence Order: The subject-verb-object construction is the most easily understood.

Word Choice: Since the lead moves on its subject and verb, the choice of nouns and verbs is essential for readability. Whenever possible, the subject should be a concrete noun that the reader can hear, see, taste, feel or smell. It should stand for a name or a thing. The verb should be a colorful action verb that accelerates the reader to the object or makes the reader pause and think. It is not so much the presence or absence of the verb that matters, but the choice between a transitive and an intransitive verb.

Don't Write Writing ▶

Immersed in words, the reporter is tempted to write writing, to make meaning secondary to language. This is fine when a Dylan Thomas plays with words, but it is dangerous for a journalist, whose first allegiance is to straightforward meaning. Word play can lead to tasteless flippancies such as this lead.

> JACKSONVILLE, Fla.—Like justice, the new judge of the Duval County Court is blind.

Some reporters seem to think that using a direct quotation in the lead or injecting *you* into the lead makes for classy writing. They're wrong. Editors consider this weak writing. When you are tempted, consider this lead and imagine the editor's explosion when it popped out on the screen:

> You don't have to go to a doctor to find out whether you are pregnant. Test kits can be bought over the counter.

Good journalism is the accurate communication of an event to a reader, viewer or listener. As Wendell Johnson, a professor of psychology and speech pathology at the University of Iowa, put it, "Communication is writing about something for someone . . . making highly reliable maps of the terrain of experience." Johnson would caution his students, "You cannot write writing."

The reporter who puts writing before fact gathering will achieve notoriety of a sort, if he or she is clever enough. Such fame is fleeting, though. Editors and the public eventually flush out the reporter whose competence is all scintillation.

This is not a red light to good writing. In fact, the fashioning of well-written stories is our next objective.

Summing Up ▶

Good leads are based on the writer's clear understanding of the theme of the story. All else follows. This is why finding the theme is No. 1 in our list of guidelines for writing readable leads:

1. Find the essential element(s) of the story.
2. Decide whether a direct or a delayed lead better suits the event.

3. If one element is outstanding, use a single-element lead. If more than one is, use a multiple-element lead.

4. Use the S-V-O construction.

5. Use concrete nouns and colorful action verbs.

6. Keep the lead short, under 30 or 35 words.

7. Make the lead readable, but do not sacrifice truthful and accurate reporting for readability.

Howarth, W.L. *The John McPhee Reader.* New York: Vintage Books, 1977.

Murray, Donald. *Writing for Your Readers.* Chester, Conn.: The Globe Pequot Press, 1983.

Roberts, Gene, and David R. Jones. *Assignment America.* New York: Quadrangle/Times Books, 1974. (An anthology of good writing by correspondents for *The New York Times*.)

◄ **Further Reading**

Writing to deadline.

Preview

Well-written stories have these qualities:

• They show the reader the event or individual through anecdotes, quotations and incidents.
• Quotations and human interest are placed high in the story.
• The language is precise, clear and convincing.
• Sentences are short. Transitions take the reader smoothly from one theme to another.
• The writing style is appropriate to the event.

Good writing depends on reporting that turns up relevant information. The story flow is aided by the use of the narrative structure. Language is simple and direct.

W hether three-paragraph item or Sunday feature article, the story is carefully put together. The rudiments of the well-crafted story are:

• **The structure:** The lead states the essential elements of the event. The body amplifies and expands the lead.
• **The content:** Facts, derived from direct observation or reliable sources, are accurately presented and used to show and tell the reader or listener what happened, who was involved, when and where it happened, and the causes and possible consequences of the event—its how and why.

But more is expected of the journalist. The story should be well-written. Readers and viewers are not passive recipients of news. They demand that it be presented in an interesting way, or they will move on to another story or station.

The well-written story is clear, easy to follow, easy to understand. Good writing helps the reader see the event the reporter is trying to describe. George Orwell said, "Good prose is like a window pane."

The window pane, unlike the stained glass window, does not call attention to itself. Good writing calls attention to the people in the story, the event, the information.

The men and women who write for a living—whether journalists, poets, novelists or essayists—work at learning and mastering their trade. They have an "idea of craft," as the writer-teacher Frank Kermode puts it, a drive toward "doing things right, making them accurate and shapely, like a pot or a chair."

Stephen King, the prolific writer of best-selling horror stories, says, "Writing is a matter of exercise . . . if you write for an hour and a half a day for ten years you're gonna turn into a good writer."

Every writer is familiar with the agony of chasing elusive words. The writer knows that words can be brought to life only by strenuous and continued effort. The aim is perfection of expression, the absolute fit of words to the event. Walt Whitman described the writer's goal this way:

> A perfect writer would make words sing, dance, kiss, do the male and female act, bear children, weep, bleed, rage, stab, steal, fire cannon, steer ships, sack cities. . . .

Creative workers and craftsmen and craftswomen know that the path to individuality begins with emulation. In teaching students at the Royal Academy, Joshua Reynolds, an 18th-century English painter, advised, "The more extensive your acquaintance is with the works of those who have excelled, the more extensive will be your power of invention, and the more original will be your conceptions." Journalists read widely to master style and technique, to learn the tricks of the writer's trade.

Poet or police reporter, the writer is engaged in a struggle to find words and phrases to match his or her observations. When Hemingway covered the police court for the *Kansas City Star,* he would take his notes home and work over them hour after hour to simplify the testimony of witnesses until he had captured in a few words the essence of the evidence. He would use the language he had heard in court. This practice, as much as the influence of Ezra Pound and Gertrude Stein, may have been responsible for Hemingway's objective prose, what the critic Maxwell Geismar called "his famous flat style: the literal, factual description of the 'way things are.' "

This style, more brother than cousin to journalism, is evident in the ending to *A Farewell to Arms*. Frederic has just pushed the nurses out of the room where Catherine has died so that he can be alone with her:

> But after I had got them out and shut the door and turned off the light it wasn't any good. It was like saying good-bye to a statue. After a while I went out and left the hospital and walked back to the hotel in the rain.

Novelist or journalist, said Hal Boyle, for years one of the AP's top reporters, the writer has the same task: "The recognition of truth and the clear statement of it are the first duties of an able and honest writer." But unlike the novelist, the journalist cannot spend hours in the search for the right word, a couple of days to devise a beguiling beginning.

◀ **Writers Write**

Reach the Reader. "The key questions are: Is this stuff interesting? Does it move, touch, anger, tickle, surprise, sadden or inform? If it does you are in for a treat, a good read."—Thomasine Berg, *The Providence Journal*

◀ **Doing It Right— in a Hurry**

The journalist is asked to write—and to write well—now, quickly, before the clock's hands sweep to the inexorable deadline. No other writer is asked to perform with such speed. Yet journalists manage to do the job, creating stories that are, in Kermode's words, "accurate and shapely."

Before we find out how this is done, let's consider a few housekeeping details first.

Preliminaries ▶

It is impossible to write for the public unless you understand what you are writing about. Comprehension precedes clarity. You cannot "be wholly clear about something you don't understand," says John Kenneth Galbraith, the Harvard economist whose books and articles about what is called "the dismal science" of economics are models of clarity.

Next, you have to be in command of writing mechanics, which cover a wide field from being at ease with language to the ability to organize material into a story to spelling. A study of working journalists showed that those considered superior by their editors were the reporters whose writing mechanics were in high gear.

A reminder: Don't write writing. Don't make the purpose of your writing clever prose. Your job is to communicate information. "I never heard a reader praise the quality of writing," says Henry McNulty, for many years the ombudsman for *The Hartford Courant*. "They are only interested in the facts in a story and their accuracy." Write well, the best you can to attract and retain readers, listeners and viewers. But never at the expense of a truthful telling of the story.

And some solace: Don't worry if glittering copy doesn't spin from your keyboard. "I don't know anybody who writes well who writes easily," says Joan Beck, a columnist for the *Chicago Tribune*. After journalism school, she went to work at the *Tribune* and was, she says, "surprised to see people whose bylines I had admired for a long time sitting there, head in hand, trying to write. It was a great revelation to me that writing did not come easily to anybody I know."

And lastly: Writers who try to write well are always asking themselves whether the words they are using make their stories clear, succinct, direct. When they are dissatisfied with their answer, they revise and rewrite. As Ernest Hemingway told an interviewer who asked him what the problem was that caused him to rewrite the last paragraph of *A Farewell to Arms* 39 times: "Getting the words right."

Lasting. "Technique holds a reader from sentence to sentence, but only content will stay in his mind."—Joyce Carol Oates

Show, Don't Tell ▶

In our effort to find some guides to help us write well, we might start with Leo Tolstoy who, in describing the strength of his master work *War and Peace,* said, "I don't tell; I don't explain. I show; I let my characters talk for me."

Consider the science reporter who wanted to describe the size of a small worm. She wrote, "Although they strongly caution against inferring too much about human life spans from worms no bigger than a comma at the end of this clause, they say that evolution. . . ." That' showing.

If one of the writer's most impelling directives is to make the reader see, then the science writer did just that. Show, don't tell. Telling not only makes for dull reading, it makes readers passive. Showing engages readers by making them visualize, draw conclusions, experience insights.

© Greg Lovett.

Taking the Gospel to College Students

The careful reporter listens closely to the message of this young evangelist as she proclaims the gospel at the University of Arkansas. The writer quotes her, describes her intensity, watches students' reactions. The reporter also interviews her and the students to whom she is preaching about her successes and failures.

"Isn't anybody in this town can beat me. I'm invincible." This is Bella Stumbo of *The Los Angeles Times* quoting a politician. She doesn't have to tell us the man has a gigantic ego.

Good writers let the words and the actions of their subjects do the work. John Ciardi says, "Make it happen; don't talk about its happening."

When the reporter makes it happen, the reader moves into the story. The writer disappears as middleman between the event and the reader.

Covering the funeral of a child killed by a sniper, a reporter wrote, "The grief-stricken parents wept during the service." Another reporter wrote, "The parents

◀ Let Them Talk, Act

wept quietly. Mrs. Franklin leaned against her husband for support." The first reporter **tells** us the parents are "grief-stricken." The other reporter **shows** us the woman's grief.

In a movie review, Stanley Kauffman of *The New Republic* writes, "We are told later that he (George C. Scott) is a cool man—which, presumably, is why his wife left him—but we are only *told* it; it's characterization by dossier, not by drama."

To show the effects of the disappearance of dairy farms in the northeast, the reporter wrote of the farmers who stick around after selling their farms and can be seen "in the general store buying their morning beer."

Details show us more than generalities do. A story about a former Minnesota beauty queen pleading guilty to shoplifting described her loot as "several items." When the story reached an AP editor, she found out what had been stolen and put the items in the story—a swimsuit, silk scarves and hairpieces.

In a three-sentence paragraph, Sam Blackwell of the Eureka, Calif., *Times-Standard* shows us a lot about teen-age romance:

> They had met cruising the loop between Fourth and Fifth Streets in Eureka. She fell in love with Wes' pickup truck, then fell in love with Wes. Wes gave her an engagement ring the day she graduated from high school.

Louis Lyons, a Boston newspaperman and later curator of the Nieman Foundation for journalists at Harvard, never forgot the lesson his night editor taught him. "When I was a cub reporter I had a story to do on the quarterly report of the old Boston Elevated system, whose history then as now was a nearly unbroken record of deficits," Lyons recalled. "This time they were in the black. I knew just enough to know how extraordinary that was.

"I wrote: 'The Boston Elevated had a remarkable record for January—it showed a profit. . . .'

"The old night editor brought my copy back to my typewriter. He knew I was green. In a kindly way, quite uncharacteristic of him, he spelled out the trouble.

"He pointed out that the word remarkable 'is not a reporting word. That is an editorial word.' " Then he advised Lyons to write the story so that the reader would say, 'That's remarkable.' "

One way journalists show their readers is through reporting the effects on people of the situation about which they are writing. The Department of Health and Human Services reported that 1.1 million minors run away or are thrown out of their homes every year. Most runaways are physically or sexually abused by a parent. About a third have an alcoholic parent, and many are from foster homes.

To give the report life and meaning, Sonia L. Nazario of *The Wall Street Journal* found some troubled teen-agers in California. Her account begins:

HOLLYWOOD—Five teen-agers crouch over a candle in a dark, fetid cavern under a busy roadway. Around them, the dirt floor seems to move as rats look for food. As the teen-agers pass around a half-gallon bottle of Riesling, they talk about their latest sexual scores. This is the place the teens call, simply, the Hole. "This is my home," reads a graffito scrawled on a concrete wall.

Here at the Hole, an ever-changing group of about 30 teen-agers, who have run away from home or been thrown out, have banded together to form a grotesquely modern kind of family. Predominantly white, middle-class and from troubled backgrounds, the "Trolls," as they call themselves, come to the Hole to find empathy and love. They have adopted a street father, a charismatic ex-con named John Soaring Eagle, or "Pops" to his flock. In return for his affection and discipline, the Trolls support Pops—and themselves—by panhandling, prostitution and mugging.

◀ Good Quotes up High

The reporter is alert to the salient remark, the incisive comment, the words of a source that sum up the event or that will help the reader visualize the person who is speaking. Also, a person's words help to achieve conviction, the feeling of truth. After all, if these are the words of a participant, the reader reasons, the story must be true. The higher in the story the quote appears, the better, although good quote leads are rare.

Notice the use of the poignant remark of the child in the second paragraph of this story:

> Mary Johnson, 9, lay alongside the bodies of her slain family for nearly two days. She believed she, too, would die of the bullet wounds inflicted by her mother.
>
> But Mary lived, and told ambulance attendants on her way to the hospital yesterday: "Don't blame mother for the shootings."

In an interview with an opponent of the U.S. government's policies in El Salvador, a reporter used this quote high in her story:

> "Why are we on the side of those who are killing the nuns?" he asked.

Reporters have an ear for the telling quote. In a story about the record number of murders in Miami-Dade, Edna Buchanan of *The Miami Herald* quoted a homicide detective as saying, "In Dade County, there are no surprises left."

Let Them Talk. "Realistic dialogue involves the reader more completely than any other single device. It also defines character more quickly and effectively than any other single device. (Dickens has a way of fixing character in your mind so that you have the feeling he has described every inch of his appearance—only you go back and discover that he actually took care of his physical description in two or three sentences; the rest he has accomplished with dialogue.)"—Tom Wolfe

The actress Farrah Fawcett was quoted in a story, "The reason that the all-American boy prefers beauty to brains is that he can see better than he can think."

Human Interest up High ▶

A working rule for reporters: Try to place as close to the lead as possible the high-quality example, incident or anecdote that spotlights the theme of the story. Usually, this will be something about the people involved in the event. When delayed leads are used, the human interest incident begins the story. With direct leads—which often stress the formal aspect of the event—the human-impact illustration or example should be close to the lead.

We are all a little like Alice (of *Alice's Adventures in Wonderland*). " 'What is the use of a book,' thought Alice, 'without pictures or conversations?' " The reporter lets the anecdotes serve as pictures, and the quotations as conversations.

Hemingway's Apprenticeship ▶

Ernest Hemingway's boss at *The Kansas City Star* was C.G. (Pete) Wellington, of whom Hemingway later said, "Wellington was a stern disciplinarian, very just, very harsh, and I can never say how grateful I am to have worked under him."

Wellington forced the young Hemingway to adhere to the *Star's* 110 rules for vigorous writing—among them short sentences, plainness of expression, few adjectives, no slang or stale phrases.

"These were the best rules I ever learned for the business of writing," Hemingway said. "I've never forgotten them. No man with any talent, who feels and writes truly about the thing he is trying to say, can fail to write well if he abides by them."

Mark Twain's Principles ▶

Let us listen to what another former reporter said about writing.

Mark Twain had volunteered to read the essays submitted for a writing contest by the young women at the Buffalo Female Academy. He was delighted by what he read, and in his report to the Academy he pointed out the virtues of the two prize essays. He described them as "the least artificial, least labored, clearest, shapeliest and best carried out."

The first-prize essay "relates a very simple little incident in unpretentious language," he said. It has "the very rare merit of *stopping when it is finished*." (Twain's emphasis.) "It shows a freedom from adjective and superlatives, which is attractive, not to say seductive—and let us remark, in passing, that one can seldom run his pen through an adjective without improving his manuscript.

"We can say further that there is a singular aptness of language noticeable in it—denoting a shrewd facility of selecting just the right word for the service needed, as a general thing. It is a high gift. It is the talent which gives accuracy, grace and vividness in descriptive writing."

Good writing has four characteristics. It is:

• **Accurate:** The language fits the situation. This is Twain's "accuracy of wording," "using just the right word."

• **Clear:** Through proper use of form and content, the story is free of vagueness and ambiguity.

• **Convincing:** The story is believable. It sounds true.

- **Appropriate:** The style is natural and unstrained. In Twain's words, "unpretentiousness, simplicity of language . . . naturalness . . . selecting just the right word for the service needed."

The categories are not islands unto themselves. Causeways connect them. If we write that a congressman "refuted" charges that his proposal will cause unemployment, when he actually "denied" the charges, the language we use is inaccurate and the story is not clear. When we quote people as they use the language—not in the homogenized dialogue that passes for the spoken word in too many news stories—the language is appropriate and our stories are more likely to convince readers they are true.

Before we go on, a reminder and a qualifier.

The reminder: A great deal of work is done before the reporter writes. Good journalistic writing is the result of good reporting and clear thinking. Clever writing cannot conceal a paucity of facts, stale observations or insensitive reactions to people. But bad writing can nullify superior reporting.

The qualifier: In the rest of this chapter—and in other chapters, too—rules, formulas and injunctions are presented. They are offered as guidelines, as ways to get going. They should not be considered inviolate laws. But it is best for the beginner to accept them for the time being, until his or her competence is proved. After this apprenticeship has been served, the experienced journalist can heed Anton Chekhov's comments about writing in his play "The Seagull." "I'm coming more and more to believe that it isn't old or new forms that matter. What matters is that one should write without thinking about forms at all. Whatever one has to say should come straight from the heart."

◀ **Accuracy**

The city editor of a medium-size Iowa daily stared at the lead in disbelief. A reporter who had covered a city commission meeting the night before had written that the commission adopted a controversial resolution "with one descending vote." The proper word is *dissenting,* the city editor informed his errant reporter.

Without accuracy of language, the journalist cannot make the story match the event. The obvious way to check words for accuracy is to use the dictionary. But reporters who misuse language often do so without knowing their words are misfits. They could be saved from embarrassment by widening their reading.

Writers struggle to find the words with just the right shades of meaning for the situations they are describing. The handwritten manuscript of *The Great Gatsby* reveals that F. Scott Fitzgerald ruthlessly eliminated long sections of beautiful writing because they interfered with the story's flow. He worked unceasingly to find the accurate word, replacing *looked* with *glanced* in one place, changing *interrupted* to *suggested* in another. Fitzgerald knew Tolstoy's rule: Show, don't tell. He eliminated sections in which he told the reader about his characters and instead let the action and dialogue do the work.

Hemingway's writing was simple, but it was not simplistic. He shaved language to the bone, but at no sacrifice to meaning. This required hard work. Reaching for a baseball metaphor, Hemingway said of a writer that "he has to go the full nine even if it kills him."

Talk of the Town

A young reporter assigned to the police beat used his enterprise to develop a story about youth gangs for the *Omaha World-Herald*. The editor told Charles Robbins that his story had more impact on the community than any other in months. The editor outlined the reasons:

1. It began with a "vivid, graphic description of specific, real-life events, things that happened to real people." He said too many enterprise stories use pseudonyms, "losing at least 50 percent of their effectiveness when they do."

2. "The story had a hard-news peg. A man had just been mugged.

3. "It had confirmation from named sources.

4. "You used direct quotations, but you were selective in what you used. You weren't just a stenographer tapping out everything your sources said in long, repetitive quotations.

5. "You used specific, colorful description. You noted the color of their (the gang members') 'uniforms,' including the color-coded shoelaces, the $300 jogging suits and the cellular telephones.

6. "The story was told economically in 24 inches. There were other angles you probably could have gone after, but doing so might have delayed publication and made the story more difficult to digest."

Ever since the day the story was printed, the editor said, it has been Topic No. 1 "in every age and demographic group in Omaha."

Use Words with Referents ▶

Avoid. *Jargon:* The specialized language of a profession or trade few outside it understand. *Gobbledygook:* Words for the sake of words piled up to obscure the fact the writer doesn't have a clue as to what he or she is saying. *Purple prose:* Inflated language used to impress, as *hydraulic specialist* for *plumber.*

An accurate vocabulary comes from a feel for words, for the way people use language, which sometimes differs from dictionary usage. "The true meaning of a term is to be found by observing what a man does with it, not by what he says about it," says P.W. Bridgeman, a physicist.

Journalists use words that correspond to specific objects and identifiable feelings and ideas. When the journalist writes about the state treasurer's annual report, she is describing a specific person who has issued a document that can be examined. But when the reporter takes it upon herself to describe the report as *sketchy* or *optimistic,* she is moving into an area in which there are no physical referents. She may use such words in an interpretative story, but only if she anchors them to specific facts and figures.

Words such as *progress, freedom, patriotism, big business, militant, radical* cause trouble because they float off in space without being anchored to anything specific, concrete or identifiable. Reporters will quote sources who use these words and phrases, but they ask sources to explain just how they are using these vague terms.

Unwary reporters can become accomplices in brainwashing by using vague language. When an oil company distributed a press release announcing the construction of an "oil farm" outside a Massachusetts town and the reporter dutifully wrote in her lead that the "oil farm will occupy a tract southeast of the city," the reporter was not only using language inaccurately, she was helping the oil firm obscure the truth. The so-called "farm" was to be used for oil storage tanks, which have a grimy image. A farm, with visions of white barns and green pastures, is what the oil company wanted readers to imagine so that potential opposition would be diverted. *Farm* as used by the oil company and the reporter is a euphemism.

Let us leave the topic of word usage with two comments about words from Mark Twain:

> A powerful agent is the right word. Whenever we come upon one of those intensely right words . . . the resulting effect is physical as well as spiritual, and electrically prompt.
> The difference between the right word and the almost right word is really a large matter—the difference between lightning and the lightning bug.

When Congress was discussing *taxes,* it sought to soften the impact of that dread word by substituting the words *revenue enhancement.* In Northern California, where marijuana is a major agricultural product, the polite term for its cultivation is *cash-intensive horticulture.* A company does not demote an employee; it hands him or her a *negative advancement.* When the Challenger shuttle exploded, the bodies were placed not in coffins but in *crew transfer containers.* When a pleasant word or phrase is used in place of one that may be grim, the substitute is called a *euphemism.*

◀ **Euphemisms**

Some journalists may consider themselves compassionate for letting euphemisms slip by. After all, what is the harm in permitting people who work with convicts to describe prisoners as the *consumers of criminal justice services?* What, for that matter, is wrong with *senior citizens* for older people or *sight deprived* for the blind? Surely, these euphemisms hurt no one.

Actually, they do damage us because they turn us away from reality. If the journalist's task can be reduced to a single idea, it is to point to reality. Words should describe the real, not blunt, blur or distort it.

Veiling Reality. The State Department stated that it would no longer use the word *killing* in its reports on human rights. In its place, the department said, will be "unlawful or arbitrary deprivation of life."

For its program to train dolphins to kill enemy swimmers, the Navy said the purpose was "swimmer nullification."

Some years ago, a Chicago police reporter who was covering a rape was reminded by his desk of the newspaper's prohibition of what the publisher considered earthy language. *Rape,* he was told, was taboo. In his second paragraph, he wrote, "The woman ran down the street screaming, 'Help, I've been criminally assaulted! Help, I've been criminally assaulted!' "

These misuses of language are dangerous shoals on which many reporters have run aground. If we could mark the reefs that threaten writers, the most dangerous would be where reporters have gone under while fishing for synonyms for the verb *to say.* Let it be said at once, loud and clear, the word *said* cannot be overused for attribution. If tempted to replace it with *affirmed, alleged, asserted,*

◀ **Said**

contended, declared, pointed out, shouted, stated or *whispered,* see the dictionary first. Better still, recall Ring Lardner's line: "Shut up he explained."

Facts First, Words Second ▶

One of the impediments to accuracy stems from the reporter's unceasing desire for language that will perk up the reader. The desire is healthy, but it can lead to the selection of words—as well as facts—that are more colorful and exciting than the event merits. Reporters sometimes are so stimulated by the urge to be creative that their language and their stories diverge from the reality that inspired them. As writers, they feel that an occasional liberty with facts and language should be granted them. In his novel *The Deer Park,* Norman Mailer describes the lure of a well-crafted story for a movie director, Charles Eitel. Mailer indicates the corruption of such temptation: "The professional in Eitel lusted for the new story . . . it was so beautifully false. Professional blood thrived on what was excellently dishonest."

To some writers, words are ends in themselves. But the objective is to communicate information accurately, not to display technical brilliance with the zoom lens or tape splicer, not to play with words. Technique has its place; its proper role is to aid in accurate communication. As Pauline Kael, the movie critic, put it, "Technique is hardly worth talking about unless it's used for something worth doing."

Good writing follows good reporting. William Burroughs, the novelist, said of the writer, "Generally speaking, if he can't see it, hear it, feel it and smell it, he can't write it."

Spelling ▶

A few words about the bane of the copy editor, the misspelled word. A word incorrectly spelled is a gross inaccuracy. It is like a flaw in a crystal bowl. No matter how handsome the bowl, the eye and mind drift from the sweeping curves to the mistake. A spelling error screams for attention, almost as loudly as an obscenity in print.

Maybe not. These days we see *alright* for all right, *its* for it's, *cemetary* for cemetery. Even *The New York Times,* surely one of the most scrupulously edited newspapers, has its share of misspellings. A story about nuns who support the ordination of women stated, "They want nuns to have a visible role at the *alter.*"

Some reporters put their trust in computer programs that check spelling. But such programs will not flag correctly spelled words that are misused, such as *alter* for altar. Nor will they catch misspelled plurals such as the one used by a reporter whose newspaper we shall not name: "He said the *testes* were hard, but he managed to pass them."

Intelligent reporters—good spellers or bad spellers—use the dictionary. Many editors associate intelligence with spelling ability because they consider the persistent poor speller to be stupid for not consulting the dictionary—whatever his or her native intelligence.

So There. When Harvard awarded Andrew Jackson and honorary degree, John Quincy Adams boycotted the ceremonies, describing Jackson, known as the people's president, as "a barbarian who could not write a sentence of grammar." Jackson replied, "It is a damn poor mind indeed which can't think of at least two ways to spell any word."

The saying has it that doctors bury their mistakes and architects cover them with ivy. Journalists have no such luck. Their blunders are forever committed to public view:

**Question is,
how to tell
roommates
your gay**
—**Forum** (Fargo, N.D.)

**Blind girl
servives first
round of bee**
—**Gazette** (Indiana, Pa.)

Recession undercuts diversity

Concensus at National Association of Black Journalists meeting: Faltering economy blamed for perceived retreat from newsroom diversity

—Editor & Publisher

◀ **Clarity**

The words and phrases the journalist selects must be put into a setting, into sentences and paragraphs that make sense to readers. "If you're going to be a newspaper writer you've got to put the hay down where the mules can reach it," said Ralph McGill of the Atlanta *Constitution*. Although his reporting ranged over subjects as complex as race relations and foreign affairs, McGill wrote for ordinary people. His journalism was never vague. A reader of the King James version of the Bible, he learned early the strength, vigor and clarity of the precise word in the simple declarative sentence.

"A word fitly spoken is like apples of gold in pictures of silver," McGill said of the journalist's craft, quoting from Proverbs in the Old Testament. We know several ways to make these pictures—these sentences and paragraphs—clear to our readers.

◀ Grammar

First, there are the essentials of grammar and punctuation. In our grandparents' day, students stood at the blackboard and diagrammed sentences. They broke sentences down into nouns, verbs, pronouns, adjectives, adverbs, prepositions, conjunctions and interjections. From there, they went into phrases—verbal, prepositional, participial, gerund and infinitive. Then they examined clauses—main and subordinate. This is how they learned sentence construction. In most schools today, the only grammar students learn is taught in foreign language classes. For a journalist, this is inadequate training.

One way the beginning journalist can cope with this inadequacy is to invest in a handbook of grammar. It will not only solve grammatical problems quickly, but help to expand the student's writing range.

Punctuation ▶

Punctuation is the writer's substitute for the storyteller's pauses, stops and changes in voice level. The proper use of punctuation is essential to clarity. Misuse can change emphasis or meaning:

> She could not convince him of her innocence, however she tried.
> She could not convince him of her innocence; however, she tried.

We know that readers pause at the ends of sentences and paragraphs. These short intervals in the flow of the story help readers absorb what they have read. Broadcast copy needs even shorter sentences, because the listener cannot reread unclear material. Even Gertrude Stein, the author of nonstop prose ("Rose is a rose is a rose is a rose"), came to recognize the value of the period. In *Lectures in America* (Boston: Beacon Press, 1957), p. 217, Stein wrote:

> When I first began writing, I felt that writing should go on, I still do feel that it should go on but when I first began writing I was completely possessed by the necessity that writing should go on and if writing should go on what had colons and semi-colons to do with it, what had commas to do with it, what had periods to do with it. . . .
>
> What had periods to do with it. Inevitably no matter how completely I had to have writing go on physically one had to again and again stop some time then periods had to exist. Besides I had always liked the look of periods and I liked what they did. Stopping sometimes did not really keep one from going on, it was nothing that interfered, it was only something that happened, and as it happened as a perfectly natural happening, I did believe in periods and I used them. I never really stopped using them.

Punctuation Pains. It is said of the novelist Gustave Flaubert that he spent an entire morning laboring over where to place a comma, then took the afternoon to fret about whether to remove it.

James Thurber, the great *New Yorker* writer, said of his editor Harold Ross, "He used to fuss for an hour over a comma. He'd call me in for lengthy discussions about the Thurber colon."

Spurred by an anxiety to cram facts into sentences, some inexperienced reporters write blockbusters that send the reader down line after line in increasing confusion. When you have a sentence running three lines or more, think of the self-editing of Isaac Babel, a Russian writer whose short stories are highly polished gems:

> I go over each sentence, time and again. I start by cutting all the words it can do without. You have to keep your eye on the job because words are very sly. The rubbishy ones go into hiding and you have to dig them out—repetitions, synonyms, things that simply don't mean anything.
> Before I take out the rubbish, I break up the text into shorter sentences. The more full stops the better. I'd like to have that passed as a law. Not more than one idea and one image to a sentence.
> A paragraph is a wonderful thing. It lets you quietly change the rhythm, and it can be like a flash of lightning that shows the landscape from a different perspective. There are writers, even good ones, who scatter paragraphs and punctuation marks all over the place.

The maxim that each sentence should, if possible, carry only one idea has been assumed to be an injunction limited to journalism. Not so, as we see from Babel's comment. Good journalistic writing is based upon the principles of good writing. Journalism is a part of the world of letters.

The press associations have concluded after a number of studies that one of the keys to readable stories is the short sentence. Here is a readability table:

Average Sentence Length	Readability
8 words or less	Very easy to read
11 words	Easy to read
14 words	Fairly easy to read
17 words	Standard
21 words	Fairly difficult to read
25 words	Difficult to read
29 words or more	Very difficult to read

This table refers to average sentence length. One sentence after another under 17 words would make readers and listeners feel as though they were being peppered with bird shot. The key to good writing is variety, rhythm, balance. Short and long sentences are balanced. A long sentence that is well-written can be as understandable as an eight-word sentence, if it is broken, usually by punctuation, into short clauses and phrases.

Some reporters have trouble writing short sentences because they cannot handle transitions, the links between sentences and paragraphs. Because these reporters have no mastery of the device that enables a writer to move smoothly from sentence to sentence, their tendency is to think in large clots of words. The journalist with control of transitions thinks in smaller sentence clusters.

A Pulitzer Prize Story: Workings of the Brain

Here is the beginning of the first story in a series by Jon Franklin that won a Pulitzer Prize for explanatory journalism for *The Evening Sun*. The word count in these 12 sentences runs 16, 24, 34, 9, 13, 18, 14, 21, 19, 5, 13, 21. The average sentence length is 17 words, standard reading fare. Notice the way Franklin varies the length of his sentences to set up a rhythm—long, short. The longest sentence in the sample—the third, 34 words—is followed by a short sentence—nine words.

Since the days of Sigmund Freud the practice of psychiatry has been more art than science. Surrounded by an aura of witchcraft, proceeding on impression and hunch, often ineffective, it was the bumbling and sometimes humorous stepchild of modern science.

But for a decade and more, research psychiatrists have been working quietly in laboratories, dissecting the brains of mice and men and teasing out the chemical formulas that unlock the secrets of the mind.

Now, in the 1980s, their work is paying off.

They are rapidly identifying the interlocking molecules that produce human thought and emotion. They have devised new scanners that trace the flickering web of personality as it dances through the brain. Armed with those scanners, they are mapping out the terrain of the human psyche.

As a result, psychiatry today stands on the threshold of becoming an exact science, as precise and quantifiable as molecular genetics. Ahead lies an era of psychic engineering, and the development of specialized drugs and therapies to heal sick minds.

But that's only the beginning: The potential of brain chemistry extends far beyond the confines of classic psychiatry.

Many molecular psychiatrists, for instance, believe they may soon have the ability to untangle the ancient enigma of violence and criminality.

There are four major types of transitions:

1. **Pronouns:** Use pronouns to refer to nouns in previous sentences and paragraphs:

> *Dr. Braun* began teaching history in 1927. *He* took *his* Ph.D. that year. *His* dissertation subject was the French Impressionists.

2. **Key words and ideas:** Repeat words and ideas in preceding sentences and paragraphs:

> He has been accused of being an *academic purist. Those words* make him shudder.
> "*Academic purist* is made to sound like an epithet," he said.

3. **Transitional expressions:** Use connecting words that link sentences. A large array of expressions function as connectors. Here are most of the major categories of conjunctions and some of the words in each category that can be used as transitions:

Additives: Again, also, and, finally, furthermore, in addition, next, thus, so, moveover, as well.

Contrasts: But, however, nevertheless, instead, on the other hand, otherwise, yet, nonetheless, father.

Comparisons: Likewise, similarly.

Place: Adjacent to, beyond, here, near, opposite.

Time: Afterward, in the meantime, later, meanwhile, soon.

> He tried twice to obtain permission to see the paintings in the private museum. *Finally,* he gave up.

> Dr. Braun's *next* project centered on the music of Berlioz. *But* his luck remained bad. An attempt to locate a missing manuscript proved a *similar* failure.

> *In the meantime,* he continued his study of Spanish so that he would be able to do research in Spain.

4. **Parallel structure.** Sentences and paragraphs are linked by repeating the sentence pattern:

> *No one* dared speak in his classes. *No one* ventured to address him in any but the most formal manner. *No one,* for that matter, had the courage to ask questions in class. His lectures were nonstop monologues.

Transitions are used after the reporter has planned his or her piece by blocking out the major sections. Transitions link these blocks as well as the smaller units, the sentences. Transitions are the mortar that holds the story together so that the story is a single unit.

A news story should move smoothly from fact to fact. When natural sequence is disrupted, the story loses clarity. Here are two paragraphs from a story in an Oklahoma daily newspaper:

◄ Logical Order

> "There is nothing new in the allegations," Bartlett said. "We've heard them all before."

> "When we first heard them we thought there was nothing to it, but then we had a second look," Tillman said.

Although the first paragraph is closed by quotation marks, which means that the speaker (Bartlett) is finished, most readers jump ahead to the next quote and presume that Bartlett is still talking. They are jolted when they find that Tillman is speaking. The solution is simple: When you introduce a new speaker, begin the sentence or paragraph with his or her name. Also, jumps in time and place must be handled carefully to avoid confusion:

NEW YORK (April 13)—A criminal court judge who last month ruled that a waiter had seduced but not raped a college student sent the man to jail for a year **yesterday** on a charge of escaping from the police after his arrest.

On March 19, Justice Albert S. Hess acquitted Phillip Blau of raping a 20-year-old Pembroke College student. The judge said a man could use guile, scheme, and be deceitful, but so long as he did not use violence, rape did not occur.

At that time, women's groups protested the decision.

"Despite the protests of outraged feminists who demand your head, or other and possibly more appropriate parts of your anatomy," the judge told Blau **yesterday,** "I shall punish you only for crimes of which you have been found guilty."

The changes in time are clearly indicated at the start of the second and third paragraphs. From "yesterday" in the lead, the reader is taken to "March 19" in the second paragraph and is kept there in the third paragraph by the transition "At that time" beginning the paragraph. When the quote begins the fourth paragraph, the reader is still back in March with the women. Midway through the paragraph the reader suddenly realizes the judge is speaking and that he spoke yesterday. The jolts in time and place could have been avoided with a transition at the beginning of the fourth paragraph:

> In sentencing Blau **yesterday,** Justice Hess commented on the protests. He said: . . .

This may seem to be nitpicking. It is not. The journalist knows that every sentence, every word, even every punctuation mark must be carefully selected. Readers read from word to word, and are maneuvered, teased, pushed, sped and slowed through the story by the way it is written. Major disturbances of logic and order in the story confuse readers, just as a quick jump cut on television can destroy the continuity of the event for the viewer.

Logical order is based upon the organizing concept that the reporter selects. The most frequently used organizing principle is chronology, a narrative device that is particularly useful on longer pieces.

The chronological approach has two forms. The writer can use the story-telling approach by beginning sometime before the climax:

> Two college sophomores began the day yesterday in a hurry.
>
> Judy Abrams had studied late the night before and had slept late. She gulped her breakfast of coffee and jumped into her car, five minutes before her 9 a.m. class.
>
> Franklin Starrett did not have time for breakfast before he, too, sped off in his car for the campus. He had an appointment with his English instructor at 9 a.m.
>
> Within minutes of their departures, the cars they were driving collided on Stanford Avenue south of the campus. . . .

Or the writer can put a direct news lead on the story and then, a few paragraphs down in the story, begin the chronological account:

> Two Mallory College students were critically injured when the cars they were driving collided head-on yesterday morning on Stanford Avenue south of the campus.
>
> Community Hospital officials said the students suffered multiple fractures and internal injuries. They called on students to volunteer blood for transfusions.
>
> The students began the day in a hurry. . . .

Movement ▶

Stories must move, and the nature of the event determines the pace at which the story about it moves. A story about a tornado or hurricane striking a community will move at the speed of the wind, but the piece about the burial service for the victims will follow the deliberate cadence of the prayers of the preacher as he speaks of those called too soon to their maker.

Fast or slow, the story has to move along. It cannot stop to explore secondary roads. Stan Grossfeld, associate editor of *The Boston Globe,* profiled the filmmaker Spike Lee as he taught a class at Harvard. In one of the class sessions, Lee describes how he edited the opening scene of *Jungle Fever.*

In the opening scene, which was shot but later cut, he descends in front of the Brooklyn Bridge on a crane and announces, "All you people who think I'm anti-Semitic can kiss my black ass two times."

Lee said the scene was extraneous: "When you write a script, you think everything's gonna be great, but once the film is shot and put together, sometimes a lot of the stuff is redundant. We had a whole subplot between me and my wife, eight scenes that had to go, 'cause it wasn't moving the plot forward. It didn't matter that I was in the scene, the [expletive] had to go."

Some people find the news they read, hear and see as unconvincing as some of the advertising that accompanies it.

◀ **Conviction**

"What's the real story?" reporters are asked, as though they were prevented from revealing the truth by powerful advertisers or friends of the publisher or station manager. These pressures rarely influence reporters. More often, the pressures of time and the inaccessibility of documents and sources impede truth telling, and just as often, reporting and writing failures get in the way of the real story. Here are the components of a story that is accurate, complete and credible:

Reporting:

1. Relevant factual material from personal observation and physical sources.

2. Authoritative and knowledgeable human sources for additional information.

3. Significant and complete background information.

Writing:

1. Simple language.
2. Illustrations, examples and quotes that document the lead.
3. Human interest.
4. Appropriate style.

Let's examine these story necessities.

> **Details, Details.**
> When reporting a murder, Edna Buchanan says she wants to know "what movie they saw before they got gunned down.
> "What were they wearing? What did they have in their pockets? What was cooking on the stove? What song was playing on the jukebox?
> "I always ask what the dog's name is, what the cat's name is."

The journalist uses details just as any writer does—to build a picture that shows us what is going on and that convinces us of the truth of the account. The journalist's eye catches the tears of the child whose puppy takes third place instead of first at the dog show. Such specific observations convince the reader that the reporter's account can be trusted.

◀ **Relevant Material**

The journalist is conscious of the backdrop, the scene. It may be that the news conference took place in the mayor's office, the rescue made in a calm sea at dusk. Then the particulars: The mayor spoke from his desk, with seven microphones from radio and television stations in front of him and a dozen journalists in attendance; the Coast Guard boat was manned by six seamen and an officer.

A journalism teacher, a veteran of many years on newspapers, still shudders at his recollection of the night he was sent out to the suburbs by a San Francisco

A People's Suffering

For six years, the Guatemalan army waged a brutal war against Indian villagers it said were helping leftist guerrillas. The villagers said the thousands of killings were indiscriminate, and years after the deaths forensic specialists exhumed many bodies. Writer-photographer Vince Heptig accompanied forensic anthropologist Luis Minguel Alonso as he dug up remains. In *The APF Reporter,* Heptig tells the story simply and directly. Here are some excerpts:

Layer by layer, Luis brushed away the rich soil to reveal what the onlooking people already knew—the boy had been shot in the head. As he continued, Luis revealed the rope that tied the young boy's hands behind his back had also reached around his neck.

Luis deducted that the boy had been killed by "tiro do gracia," or a shot to the head at close range. The other twelve bodies the anthropologists unearthed suffered similar fates.

This mass grave contained 13 skeletons, bringing the total number of bodies exhumed in this tiny village to 26.

A Boy's Death: Hands Tied, Shot in Head

newspaper. Fumes from an unvented heater had poured through a house, killing the entire family. Only the dog survived. The reporter gathered the relevant information—names and ages of the victims, occupation of the father, approximate time of death, schools the children attended, how long they had lived in the house, whether the vent was legal and even the name of the dog (taken from its collar). Racing to a pay phone to make the final edition, he was dictating the story when he was stunned by the rewriteman's question: "What kind of house was it? Wood? Stucco? Brick?" The reporter had no idea, and there was no time to dash back to the house to find out.

Here are the first four paragraphs of a speech story:

◄ Authoritative Sources

This country must return to law and order if America's free institutions are to survive, Lexington businessmen were told Monday night.

And, it is the responsibility of businessmen on the local level to educate Americans, particularly the youth, in the importance of these free institutions and what they mean.

Speaking at a general membership meeting of the Greater Lexington Area Chamber of Commerce, Dr. Kenneth McFarland, author, educator and businessman, said that the current situation must be turned around.

"We can no more co-exist with this than we can co-exist with a cancer," he said. "We've got to take the handcuffs off the police and put them back on the criminal where they belong."

These are serious statements, and we wonder who is making them. We are given the source's background in the third paragraph. But the identifying material raises more questions than it answers: Author of what? Educator where? What kind of business? Does he own or manage the business?

Since the story is so vague about the qualifications of the source, readers will be reluctant to accept his analysis. He may have been qualified, but the story does not give his qualifications.

Readers and listeners find some news unconvincing because the sources that journalists use are officials or so-called experts who have not experienced the situations they are describing. A local story about unemployment that quotes only officials and data is inadequate. Unemployment is more than figures released by an official sitting at a desk. It is men and women standing in idle helplessness on street corners or waiting anxiously in front offices day after day for job interviews.

It is, of course, easier for a reporter to call an official for material than it is to seek out people affected by events. The result is education stories written without interviewing students, public health stories that lack comments from those who use clinics and emergency rooms.

◄ Complete Background

In an AP story about the Army's pleasure over an unusually heavy crop of volunteers, the "story cited every factor except the main one: The economy was down, unemployment up, and enlistments always rise under those circumstances," said Jack Cappon, AP's general news editor.

An event that is not placed in context lacks meaning. Context can provide the how and why of the event. As Cappon put it, "In news writing, nothing is more basic than making sure that any event, speech, situation or statistic is reported in sufficient context to fix the meaning accurately."

Simple Language ▶

One of the biggest best sellers in this country's history was a political treatise, *Common Sense,* by Thomas Paine. Within three months of its publication in 1776, 120,000 copies were sold in the Colonies, whose population was about 2.5 million. Today, a book selling as well would reach 10 million readers in this country. Paine used the language of the people. He began his pamphlet, "In the following pages I offer nothing more than the simple facts, plain arguments, and common sense."

The good reporter is firmly rooted in the language of ordinary people, which, because it is comprehensible, has the ring of conviction.

Look at the power of this section of a speech given by Sojourner Truth, an abolitionist and an advocate of equality for women. This is from her talk on women's rights, given in 1867:

> I am above 80 years old; it is about time for me to be going. I have been 40 years a slave and 40 years free, and would be here 40 years more to have equal rights for all. I suppose I am kept here because something remains for me to do; I suppose I am yet to help to break the chain. I have done a great deal of work; as much as a man, but did not get so much pay. I used to work in the field and bind grain, keeping up with the cradler; but men doing no more, got twice as much pay. . . . We do as much, we eat as much, we want as much. I suppose I am about the only colored woman that goes about to speak for the rights of the colored women. I want to keep the thing stirring, now that the ice is cracked. . . . I am glad to see that men are getting their rights, but I want women to get theirs, and while the water is stirring I will step into the pool.

Quotations ▶

Wallace Stevens, the insurance company executive who wrote poetry that influenced a generation of poets, commented with some incredulity on events that were swirling around him: "In the presence of extraordinary actuality, consciousness takes the place of imagination." Fact has supplanted fiction.

Why, then, is so much journalism dull and unconvincing? Possibly because writers do not use in their stories what they see and hear. They paraphrase good quotes. They explain instead of letting the example show the reader.

Here are two paragraphs from a book by Studs Terkel, *Working: People Talk About What They Do All Day and What They Think of While They Do It.* Terkel, a radio reporter based in Chicago, interviewed a 14-year-old newsboy, Terry Pickens:

> I don't see where being a newsboy and learning that people are pretty mean or that people don't have enough money to buy things with is gonna make you a better person or anything. If anything, it's gonna make a worse person out of you, 'cause you're not gonna like people that don't pay you. And you're not gonna like people who act like they're doing you a big favor paying you. Yeah, it sort of molds

your character, but I don't think for the better. If anybody told me being a newsboy builds character, I'd know he was a liar.

I don't see where people get all this bull about the kid who's gonna be president and being a newsboy made a president out of him. It taught him how to handle his money and this bull. You know what it did? It taught him how to hate the people on his route. And the printers. And dogs. . . .

No paraphrase or summary would have the impact of Terry Pickens' own words. For that matter, few psychologists with their understanding of the problems of adolescence can express so succinctly and convincingly—and with such emotion—the realities of growing up. Journalists can.

When the Virginia State Bar Association voted to admit its first black member despite a determined effort by some senior members to block the move, a news story quoted a Richmond lawyer as praising the applicant as a "commendable person with a high standing as a lawyer." Then the story quoted him as adding, "But he is a Negro and therefore I am opposed to accepting him as a member of this association. . . . I have a good many Negro friends, but I don't invite any of them to my home or club to socialize with me."

In three sentences, the reporter crystallized an aspect of racism by letting one of the participants speak.

Sara Grimes covered juvenile court in Philadelphia. The judges were generations away from the reality of street life. Here are sections of a story Grimes wrote to show the distance between the court and the young offenders. A judge is speaking to two boys in court:

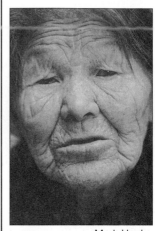

Mark Henle,
The Phoenix Gazette

Meaningful Quote

"With envy, I listen to my grandchildren and great-grandchildren speak the beautiful language. Speaking English is like a magical door to anywhere for them."—Irene Begody, 77, Navajo Reservation.

"You should stand still and be respectful when approached by a police officer. Then the officers will respect you. . . .

"I imagine they roughed you up a little bit, huh? I'd have given you a couple of good ones, too, before I took you in.

"In the old days, we used to have Irish policemen and we'd get it over the legs and then we'd get it again at home when the police took us to our fathers.

"We didn't call it police brutality then, and I'm concerned about the disrespect shown here for the policemen. . . .

"The next time you see a policeman, think positively. You can even say, 'Officer, what can I do for you?' The police are paid to protect us. When I see them I feel safe.

"You work, you pay taxes, the police are there to protect you."

Let sources talk and you often will find a vivid image, a colorful phrase, a passionate vehemence, a deep sadness. After a riot at the New Mexico State Penitentiary during which 33 prisoners were beaten, burned and hacked to death by fellow inmates, a reporter asked what it had been like inside as prisoners wielded blowtorches, hammers and hacksaws. An inmate replied:

Man, what can I tell you? It was like the devil had his own butcher shop and you could get any cut you wanted.

In her story in *The Washington Post* about depression among youngsters, Laura Sessions Stepp balances the statements of authorities with the comments of adolescents like Darrell.

"Right over there," she quotes Darrell as he points across the street, "some boy got shot. I was at the skate rink across the street when it happened. You never know when it's going to be pointing your way. You shouldn't have to worry about getting shot when you're a kid."

Caution: Important as quotations are, it is improper to put into direct quotation what has been heard second- or thirdhand. This device, used by "imaginative" reporters influenced by the New Journalism, is unethical. Reconstructed quotes are best left to the novelists.

Human Interest ▶

Dull

Interesting

When a television reporter returned with a feature about a local store that was selling books, posters, pictures and other material based on television's "Star Trek," his editor praised his enterprise. But the tape concentrated on the material sold. There was little about the customers, the "Star Trek" fans.

"We missed," the editor said. "We should have followed a customer around and used him as the center of the story."

Frederick C. Othman, a veteran reporter for UPI, advised reporters to put as many personal references as possible into each sentence, "he, she, King George, uncle, boy, girl or any such word describing a human being. The more such words, the more interesting the story."

Here is some more advice from Othman: "If a gent wears a dark-brown coat, say it's chocolate-colored. Not only is that descriptive, but it gets food into the story. Any word connoting food adds interest value.

"Tell about the taste of things and, especially, smells. Both good and bad. Take the man smoking a Turkish cigarette; it smells like burnt chicken feathers. Say so."

Sometimes reporters fail to personalize events that easily lend themselves to human interest. When a puppy fell into the shaft of an abandoned well in Carlsbad, N.M., the rescue operation became a front-page story in many newspapers. One press service story that used the name of the puppy, Wimpy, was widely preferred to the competition's story that lacked the pup's name.

Compare these versions of the same story:

I	II
All doctors hope their patients never have occasion to use the Poison Control Center recently established in the emergency room of the Community General Hospital. However, it should be reassuring to citizens, particularly parents, to know the center exists for use in an emergency.	A frantic mother called her physician and cried that her two-year-old had been at the oven cleaner. The child's lips were smudged with the liquid.
	The label said poison. What should she do?
Springfield is one of only eight cities in the state which have official "recognized" centers to handle poisoning cases. The other seven cities are . . .	Her call set in motion a series of checks and other calls. In a short time her physician knew precisely what chemicals were in the cleaner, which were poisonous, and what should be done.
	The child was treated and beyond a few small burns on the lips and tongue the baby is doing well.
	This happened the other day, and it was the first case for the Freeport Poison Information Center in the Community General Hospital.

The journalist who wrote the second piece did a better job of writing because his reporting was superior. Also, he contributed a greater public service because the picture he painted of a mother and child is etched in the minds of parents. The second story is also more appropriate to the event—it shows what the Center does.

The style of the second piece is consistent with the event. The average sentence length of the first five sentences, which describe the poisoning incident, is around 11 words. The next three average 21 words because the reporter was seeking to give an air of calm after the frenzy of the incident. This brings us to the fourth and last of our guidelines for good journalistic writing.

◀ **Appropriate Style**

Every event has its own tone, texture and pace that good reporters try to reflect in the way they write their stories. The way a story is written is known as its *style*. An understanding of style might start with Cicero, the Roman statesman and orator: "Whatever his theme he will speak it as becomes it; neither meagerly where it is copious, nor meanly where it is ample, not in this way where it demands that; but keeping his speech level with the actual subject and adequate to it."

This congruity between theme and speech is what the writer means by fitting the story to the event. Cardinal John Henry Newman in his book *The Idea of a University* wrote, "Matter and expression are parts of one; style is thinking out into language."

Every creative person tries to match expression with content. Spike Lee says he filmed "Malcolm X" in three different styles. Each represented a distinct period in Malcolm's life.

In the following story of a murder, the short sentences reflect the starkness of the event:

Fight for Hat Cited as Motive in Boy's Slaying

Sixteen-year-old Kenneth Richardson was killed Thursday over a floppy brown hat, police said.

"It was just a plain old hat," Metro Homicide Detective Hugo Gomez said.

Richardson was wearing it. Someone tried to take it. Richardson refused.

Others entered the fray. The youth ran. They chased him.

"It was a running and shooting type thing. They were shooting directly at him," Gomez said.

Richardson still had the hat when taken to International Hospital, where he died in surgery, Dade's 554th homicide this year.

He was shot in the parking lot of the Miami Gardens Shopping Plaza at 12:15 a.m., soon after the nearby Gardens Shopping Skating Center closed for the night, police said.

No arrests have been made.

"They were all Carol City kids," Gomez said. "There was talk of several guns."

About 25 youths were in the area at the time, police say. "But there was nothing but the dust settling when we got there," Gomez said.

—*The Miami Herald*

Since journalists are obliged to tell their stories briefly, they must choose words that count, words that quickly and efficiently paint pictures. The story is most effective when the journalist selects words in which the denotative and connotative meanings, the explicit and implicit meanings, mesh.

Plain Talk. "If any man were to ask me what I would suppose to be a perfect style of language, I would answer, that in which a man speaking to five hundred people, of all common and various capacities, idiots or lunatics excepted, should be understood by them all, and in the same sense which the speaker intended to be understood."—Daniel Defoe

"If language is not correct, then what is said is not what is meant; if what is said is not what is meant, then what ought to be done remains undone."—Confucius

When New York City was close to bankruptcy, the city appealed for federal aid. President Ford brusquely said no, that the city's profligacy and incompetence had caused its fiscal misery and that it had to put its house in order itself. Pondering the story on the president's refusal, William Brink, the managing editor of the *Daily News,* cast about for the five or six words he could fit into the *News'* page-one headline for the story. He tried:

FORD REFUSES
AID TO CITY

The headline was dull, and the top line was half a unit too long. He tried again:

FORD SAYS NO
TO CITY AID

This fit, but it was as dull as the first. Brink recalls that in the back of his mind was the idea that "Ford hadn't just declined to help us. He had, in effect, consigned us to the scrap heap." He then wrote two words on a piece of copy paper. After a few moments, he put three other words above them.

The headline in the margin here was instantly famous. Television news stations displayed it that night, and *Time* and *Newsweek* ran it in their summaries of the city's plight. It not only presented the information succinctly (denotative), it also suggested the president's disdain for New York (connotative) in language New Yorkers understand. The headline was appropriate to the subject.

The key to stylistic excellence is a wide vocabulary and a sensitivity to language that guides word choice. For instance, when the treasurer of a large utility is convicted of stealing $25,000 in company funds, a reporter can write:

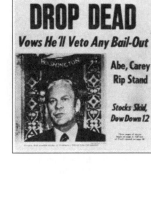

- The *employee* was xxx.
- The *official* was xxx.
- The *executive* was xxx.

Each noun has a different connotation. *Employee* would be appropriate for a lower-ranking worker. Although he is an *official* of the company, the word usually is used in connection with public officials. *Executive* seems most appropriate.

Let us look at some verbs:

- He *pilfered* $25,000 xxx.
- He *took* $25,000 xxx.
- He *appropriated* $25,000 for his own use.
- He *embezzled* $25,000 xxx.
- He *stole* $25,000 xxx.

Pilfered seems to trivialize the event. *Took* is prosaic: We *take* a rest, *take* cream in our coffee. *Appropriated* suggests an official action: Congress *appropriates* funds. *Embezzled* and *stole* are strong words and probably the best to use.

Good writing is anchored in control, but sometimes the words take off on their own:

Thoughts flew like spaghetti in his brain.
"Marvin," she hissed.
The muscles on his arms rose slowly, like a loaf of bread
taking shape.

The stylist is prized in every newsroom, just as an individual style is valued in every field. Yet reporters often are unimaginative in their selection of facts, and their writing is uninspired. A vapid writing style begets stereotyped observations and vice versa. Compare these two stories about Memorial Day. Which one is more appropriate to the event?

◀ The Stylist

Topeka Reminded of Debts to Dead

An Army general officer and a Navy lieutenant commander reminded Topekans of their debt and responsibility to America's war dead in two Memorial Day services Tuesday morning.

Brig. Gen. John A. Berry, commanding general of Fort Riley, spoke to representatives of 18 veterans organizations at ceremonies at Mount Hope Cemetery.

Earlier, Lt. Cmdr. John G. Tilghman, U.S. Navy Reserve, talked briefly at services on the Topeka Avenue Bridge.

"It is good for us to gather this morning to think of—and thank—those men and women who gave their lives in wars past that you and I may have the full benefits and privileges and responsibilities of our American heritage," said Cmdr. Tilghman.

"Many men in World War II and the Korean War did not always understand all the causes behind the war in which they fought, but they were sure they wanted those of us at home to continue to enjoy the birthright and heritage which is ours, and gave their lives that we might do so.

"You and I must realize our responsibilities in making sure our children and those to come in future generations will be sure of the same promise.

"Today, thousands are fleeing from those who would take away their birthright and their heritage. You and I may someday join their flight unless we get off the fence and take a stand for that which is right—morally right and right patriotically."

Tilghman told his audience protection of its heritage may not always be in combat dress and on a battlefield.

—*The State Journal*

Fresno Rites Honor Fallen War Heroes

Walk with me early this Memorial Day through the Liberty Cemetery before the ceremonies begin and a thousand feet scatter the dust over these quiet gravestones.

Here are the dead of many of our nation's wars.

A Flag flutters beside each grave and flowers grace them all. No one is forgotten.

Some died in uniform. Others, like Sergeant William J. Dallas of the 2nd Tennessee Infantry in the Spanish-American War, went to war and returned to live a long life—80 years long.

Many stones stand upright, their marble veined with the passage of time. What stories lie behind some of these stones? The passerby cannot tell. The inscriptions simply say:

Michael O'Connor, US Navy, Spanish-American War. Or, in the Civil War section: Isaac N. Ulsh, Company B, 13th Kansas infantry.

Other markers do tell their stories:

Jack T. Martin, Jr., 1922–1942, USS Langley, Lost At Sea.

James S. Waggoner, CEM, USN, USS Kete, 1917–1945, Lost At Sea.

Sergeant Keith A. Matthew, 877th Bomber Squadron, USAAF, 1918–1945, Lost At Sea.

Two Petersons

Side by side are these two:

T. Sergeant Maurice Peterson, 9th Air Corps, 330th Bomber Group, 1917–1944, Ploesti, Roumania.

Objectivity = Credibility. Primo Levi, an Italian chemist, was sent to a concentration camp by the Nazis. On his return to Italy, he decided to write of his experiences. Asked why his books seem so dispassionate, lacking any anger or desire for revenge, he replied:

"I have deliberately assumed the calm and sober language of the witness, not the lamenting tones of the victim or the irate voice of someone who seeks revenge. I thought that my account would be more credible and useful the more it appeared objective, the less it sounded overly emotional; only in this way does a witness in matters of justice perform his task, that of preparing the ground for the judge. The judges are my readers."

Sergeant Sterling Peterson, Airborne Infantry, Company B, 1919–1944, Normandy, France. . . .

The sun rises higher and friends and relatives of the dead come bearing flowers.

Families come and decorate graves with snapdragons, roses, stocks, hydrangea, marigolds and others. While the adults place the flowers, the children roll in the grass and shout to one another.

Then the ceremonies begin.

Veterans organizations march to the cemetery, and the Colors are massed at the War Veterans Memorial Shaft.

"Let us pray that we may always honor those who have given the last full measure of devotion to their country," Dean Emeritus James M. Malloch says.

"Let us pray that the United States may ever be the land of the free and the home of the brave and the advocate of peace in the councils of nations."

Pay Tribute

At the Belmont Memorial Park, military units stand at attention while tributes are paid to the dead.

Mayor C. Cal Evans reminds the quiet crowd Memorial Day has a new significance, paying "homage to the heroes of peace as well as to the heroes of war."

The main speaker, Legislative Commissioner Ted C. Wills, says:

"Although the bodies of our loved ones are consigned to the earth, their souls have winged their way to the Father in Whose house there are many mansions, where, for all eternity, theirs will be the fullness of joy."

The oratory is carried to the treetops and fades away and the soldiers march off.

—*The Fresno Bee*

The first story is like dozens of Memorial Day stories. The oratory, while perhaps passionately uttered, has little emotional impact because it ignores those the event commemorates—the victims of war. The second story teeters on the edge of sentimentality in the lead, but soon settles into understated narrative that seeks to match the solemn nature of the event.

New Journalism ▶

The antecedents of the journalist's relaxed, nonstilted writing style are the nonfiction novel of the 1950s and the New Journalism of Tom Wolfe and others in the 1960s. In a *Wall Street Journal* review of an anthology of Wolfe's works, *The Purple Decades: A Reader,* Ellen Wilson describes Wolfe's inspiration for this new way of writing:

In the early Sixties, Tom Wolfe went to the New York Coliseum to cover a Hot Rod and Custom Car show, and came back with the New Journalism. As he tells it in the introduction to "The Kandy-Kolored Tangerine-Flake Streamline Baby," he felt frustrated by his inability to recreate the atmosphere of the show, with its "nutty-looking, crazy baroque custom cars, sitting in little nests of pink angora angels hair," in standard journalese. He needed a style flexible and uninhibited enough to capture everything a straight news story would miss: the carnival atmosphere and the thoughts and emotions of the participants.

He came up with a style incorporating slang and contemporary speech patterns, stream of consciousness and abrupt switches in perspective. The first step was painstaking research and close attention to detail. After that, he was free to select from the novelist's whole bag of tricks.

Journalism historians say the roots of New Journalism actually go back a century. One of the founders of the school was Richard Harding Davis, a war correspondent of the late 19th century. His biographer, Arthur Lubow, points out in *The Reporter Who Would Be King* (New York: Scribner's, 1992) that Davis followed a maxim included in a popular journalism correspondence course of the day: "Truth in essentials, imagination in non-essentials is considered a legitimate rule of action in every office."

When Davis was reporting for the *Evening Sun,* he covered the story of a physician accused of killing a young woman in a botched abortion and of secretly burying the body. We pick up Davis' account as a gravedigger discovers the woman's body:

> He had struck a nickel-plated screw of the coffin, and at that moment the bell over the superintendent's house began to toll. They were very near your secret then, Dr. McGonegal—very near. And the bell that tolled for the funeral passing through the gate of the cemetery was just a coincidence, but it sounded like a knell, Dr. McGonegal—very like a knell.

The doctor was found guilty and at 70 began a sentence of 14 years at hard labor.

Journalists read the work of journalists. Ernie Pyle, a correspondent for the Scripps Howard newspapers in World War II, was loved by the soldiers he accompanied to battle. Pyle wrote of the death of Captain Waskow during the Italian campaign of 1944 in a story that has become a journalistic classic. Here is part of Pyle's story:

> Then a soldier came and stood beside the officer, and bent over, and he too spoke to his dead captain, not in a whisper but awfully tenderly, and he said:
> "I sure am sorry, sir."
> Then the first man squatted down, and he reached down, took the dead hand, and sat there for a full five minutes, holding the dead hand in his own and looking intently into the dead face, and he never uttered a sound all the time he sat there.
> And finally he put the hand down, and then reached up and gently straightened the points of the captain's shirt collar, and then he sort of rearranged the tattered edges of his uniform around the wound. And then he got up and walked away down the road in the moonlight, all alone.

The death of good men haunted Pyle, and when he was shot by a sniper on Ie Shima in 1945, the soldiers who had risked their lives to bring back his body found in his pocket a column he had written for the end of the fighting in Europe. Here is some of it:

> Those who are gone would not wish themselves to be a millstone of gloom around our necks.
> But there are many of the living who have had burned into their brains forever the unnatural sight of cold dead men scattered over the hillsides and in the ditches along the high rows of hedge throughout the world.
> Dead men by mass production—in one country after another—month after month and year after year. Dead men in winter and dead men in summer.
> Dead men in such familiar promiscuity that they become monotonous.
> Dead men in such monstrous infinity that you come almost to hate them.

Read the Ads

Writers study advertisements for their tight, colorful writing. Advertising copywriters are trained to put maximum meaning in minimum space. This ad appeared around prom time, says Patrick Fagan, creative director of Keller Crescent Co., who wrote the copy. "Since the peer pressure to drink and drive would be strong during prom parties and the like, we created this ad."

The writer John Hersey said of Pyle that he was "the great artist" of the "human aspects of warfare—of bravery, loss, wounds, humor, self-sacrifice, pain and yes, death—and, by the way, he always added the name and home address of the person he was talking about."

A study of writing can begin with this advice in Sir Herbert Read's *English Prose Style:*

> The great strength of the English language lies in its splendid array of transitive verbs drawn both from the Anglo Saxon and Latin. Their power lies in their recognition of nature as a vast storehouse of forces. . . . Shakespeare's English is immeasurably superior to all others. . . . It is his persistent, natural and magnificent use of hundreds of transitive verbs. Rarely will you find an *is* in his sentence. A study of Shakespeare's verbs should underline all exercises in style.

The Bard and the Bible ▶

Abraham Lincoln, who had little formal education but wrote forceful and compelling prose, read Shakespeare and the Bible. John McPhee, the *New Yorker* writer many journalists read with admiration, says he returns regularly to Shakespeare for replenishment and instruction. Writers admire Shakespeare's use of action verbs:

- Every cloud engenders not a storm.
- We are advertis'd by our loving friends.
- An honest tale speeds best being plainly told.
- The grass stoops not, she treads on it so light.
- The labour we delight in physics pain.
- Policy sits above conscience.

Few journalists realize how much they owe the King James Bible. Almost every virtue of the prose style the journalist uses can be traced to its influence: direct simplicity, exactness and economy of language, rapid pace, even the S-V-O construction. The writings of John Bunyan, Emily Brontë and scores of others were influenced by the Bible. The novelist Willa Cather said she read passages from the Bible to be in touch with good prose before she wrote. Peter Abràhàms, a black South African author, said he had a teacher who "whenever I used big words or made clumsy and almost meaningless sentences, sent me to the Bible. I read the Bible and I saw."

This is no place to make a plea for taking up the Bible. But look at these sentences and consider the possibility of some extracurricular reading:

- For many are called, but few are chosen.
- Who is this that darkeneth counsel by words without knowledge?
- We all do fade as a leaf.
- Man shall not live by bread alone.
- A word spoken in good season, how good it is.
- The rich rules over the poor, and the borrower is the slave of the lender.
- How forcible are right words.
- Let thy words be few.

Gilbert Millstein, a network television newswriter, recommends reading Hawthorne, Melville and the more recent Nathanael West. Of West's novels he says:

> For example, any television newswriter who reads *Miss Lonely-hearts* or *The Day of the Locust* by Nathanael West would find in them an economy and vividness of language achieved without adjectives that would surprise the life out of him. I would offer those two books as models for any person who wants to write factual news. The economy of *Miss Lonelyhearts* is unbelievable. There isn't a single word that could be dropped. The same is true for *The Day of the Locust*. But young people appear not to read these kinds of books anymore.

Look at an author's manuscript; you'll be surprised by the extent of the revisions. In a review of an exhibit of the works of major American and British authors, the reviewer wrote that "the single unifying link is revision. From Nathaniel Hawthorne and Charles Dickens to Virginia Woolf and Saul Bellow, the lesson goes: writing is rewriting, leaving out more than putting in, always trying to simplify and clarify."

Much of what we've said presumes a rational, disciplined approach to news writing. Sometimes, diligent thinking and careful planning are of no avail. The right lead will not come; the exact words lurk just beyond our reach; sentences stumble over each other; and the whole business looks a mess.

◀ **Write, Write and Rewrite**

Then—only minutes before the edition closes or the newscast is to go on—the story comes together. The theme of the piece is clear. There it was, hiding in the fourth graf. And there, that quote in the fifth graf, the perfect second graf. We toss out 50 lines. Adrenalin flows and the words fly. Everything fits. On deadline, too.

Every writer has gone through this scene. Sean O'Faolain, the Irish writer, points out that ideas sometimes become clear "by, and only by, the very act of writing."

Some writers can function only under this kind of pressure. Given a day to do a story, they dillydally until the deadline is an hour off. Then they can write. True enough, they rarely miss their deadlines. But the wear and tear they undergo and the anxiety they inflict on their editors is frightening to behold. Better to develop good writing habits now, gradually and without too much pressure, so that on-the-job writing most often is a calm, deliberate process. That means writing, seeing your mistakes and rewriting.

Someone said nothing good was ever written as a first draft. Journalists often do not have the leisure of a second look at their copy. Too often, the job requires writing on the run, doing a story with facts gathered close to the deadline. Nothing can be done about that. But when there is time, the rewrite is almost always a good idea and usually necessary.

With practice, writing comes easier and is accomplished with less anguish and more speed. But even the veterans rewrite when they have the time.

Mentors ▶

Behind most writers is a figure pushing and propelling them, someone from the past who made a lasting impression, whose standards the writer spends a lifetime trying to meet.

"When I got there I felt like crying," Robert Caro recalls about one of the first stories he covered for the newspaper *Newsday.* "I mean, this was the first time I had ever been at a human tragedy." A deaf man with a troubled marriage had parked his pickup on a railroad track and just missed being killed.

"I came back and wrote the story, and I didn't know how to write," Caro says. The news editor, who had looked over the story, walked over to Caro's desk. "He said something like, 'This is a terrific piece of writing, but you don't have a lead on it.' He said that in the lead you do so-and-so." Caro wrote the lead and was told, "Now you need a second paragraph." And so it went until the story was finished.

Caro, who has written sharply etched biographies of Robert Moses and Lyndon B. Johnson, says he learned techniques from his editors at *Newsday* that he uses in his books.

Gay Talese, a former *New York Times* reporter who has written an acclaimed history of that newspaper and many other books, recalls the *Esquire* editor Harold Hayes: "He had a way of bringing out the best in me. He was demanding and I had a strong desire to please him.

"He was a Marine, a Southern minister's son, and he had very severe standards. . . .

"Harold had a way of making me feel at once he was supportive, but there was a little fear in the relationship, and threat—he had to be satisfied, standards had to be met."

Let's look to some writers for what they can tell us about writing.

◀ **Summing Up**

We'll begin with words. John Ciardi, poet, essayist and writer on writing:

> Count the adjectives and verbs; good writing (active writing) will almost invariably have more verbs. . . . A diction in which every noun is propped up by an adjective may be almost flatly said to be a bad one.

Mark Twain advised, "Whenever you see an adjective, kill it." And that vast source of material, Anonymous, is quoted on writing as saying, "The adjective is the enemy of the noun."

As for verbs, the action verb is our object. Mervin Block, the television writing coach, received a script with this lead: "The Dow was down more than 62 points." Block commented: "The verb *was* is a linking verb and doesn't convey any action. The writer needs a vigorous verb like *fell*. Or *sank*. Or *slid*. Or *skidded*. Or *dropped*. Or *plunged*. Or *tumbled*. But *was* doesn't move."

Block's point is that there are plenty of action verbs available to the writer.

Words make up sentences, and Red Smith's teacher at Notre Dame, John Michael Cooney, wanted sentences from his students that were "so definite they would cast a shadow." He was an enemy of vague writing and began class by intoning, "Let us pray for sense."

Sense for whom? Harold Ross, the founder and longtime editor of *The New Yorker* wanted his magazine never to contain "a sentence that would puzzle an intelligent 14-year-old."

The sentences should be put to good use, and that means using them for quotations, anecdotes and illustrations. Donald Murray, the writer and writing coach, comments on the use of examples, illustrations and anecdotes:

> You tell them the anecdote and they say, "Boy, this is a bad situation." That's the art in it—not to tell the reader how to think, how to feel, but to give the reader the old Mark Twain thing, "Don't say the old lady screamed. Drag her on stage and make her scream."

◀ Telling Trifles

Then there is the insight provided the reader or viewer by the writer's observation of the seemingly insignificant, what the British novelist John Galsworthy described as "the significant trifle." It could be a slip of the tongue, the use of an unusual word, a mismatched pair of socks, the curt dismissal of a student or hired hand.

Style

And, of course, there is style. Molly Ivins, the colorful Texas columnist, said of a local politician that "if his IQ slips any lower, we'll have to water him twice a day." But when she wrote of "a fella . . . havin' a beergut that belongs in the Smithsonian," her editors made it, "a man with a protuberant abdomen."

Copy Editors

Perhaps the last word should be given to the copy editor. Here's Joel Rawson's lament about the copy he sometimes reads at the *Providence Journal Bulletin:*

> The thing that I resent most is sloppiness. I resent getting a story with misspellings in leads and errors of fact, and I resent getting a story that I know somebody didn't sit down and reread. Even on deadline I expect somebody to go back and reread that story and fix up what is obviously wrong with it. You're taking up a lot of people's time and you're also ruining your credibility and mine if work like that goes through the copy desk or other editors on this newspaper. And if somebody else doesn't catch (the mistakes) and they go into print, it hurts us all.

Final Words

Well, Rawson has the next to final word. The last word is *Caution.* A few cautionary remarks about writing writing.

Red Smith: "The essential thing is to report the facts; if there is time for good writing as well, that's frosting on the cake."

Leo Tolstoy: "As soon as man loses his moral sense, he becomes particularly responsive to the aesthetic." The critic Irving Howe said of Tolstoy that in old age Tolstoy was "free of literary posture and the sin of eloquence."

Writing is a means to convey information, not an end in itself. James David Barber, former director of Duke University's Center for the Study of Communication Policy, worries about a development he sees in journalism:

> In the 30's and 40's reporters were after scoops. After World War II they went to college and became analysts. Now they are moving beyond that to a literary, poetic mode—in which cleverness and turn of phrase is celebrated—rather than dealing with the warp and woof of reality.

Every reader, every listener and every editor wants good writing, writing that soothes, angers, sings, sobs and sighs. But above all, they want writing that informs.

Further Reading

Breslin, Jimmy. *The World According to Breslin.* New York: Ticknor & Fields, 1985.

Clark, Roy Peter. *The American Conversation and the Language of Journalism.* St. Petersburg: The Poynter Institute for Media Studies, 1994.

Clark, Roy Peter, ed. *Improving Newswriting.* St. Petersburg, Fla.: Poynter Institute for Media Studies, 1982.

Ivins, Molly. *Molly Ivins Can't Say That, Can She?* New York: Random House, 1991.

Kluger, Richard. *The Paper: The Life and Death of The New York Herald Tribune*. New York: Random House, 1987.

Ross, Lillian. *Reporting*. New York: Dodd Mead & Co., 1981.

Scanlan, Christopher, ed. *(Year) Best Newspaper Writing*. Chicago: Bonus Books; St. Petersburg: Poynter Institute for Media Studies.

Terkel, Studs. *The Good War: An Oral History of World War Two*. New York: Pantheon, 1984.

Terkel, Studs. *Working: People Talk About What They Do All Day and What They Think While They Do It*. New York: Pantheon, 1972.

8 Features, Long Stories and Series

Bob Thayer, *The Journal-Bulletin*, Providence, R.I.

Feature writers spot the absurd.

Preview

Features are written to entertain. The writer lets the actions and comments of the personalities carry the story. Features usually begin with a delayed lead—an incident or anecdote that illuminates the point of the feature. The body contains additional incidents, many quotes and the news peg. The ending may summarize the piece or provide a climax.

Long stories are written to provide readers with information about a complicated idea or situation. The reporter outlines the theme before reporting so that material relevant to it can be gathered. In writing, a tone or style appropriate to the main idea is adopted, and ample quotes and incidents are used to keep the story moving.

Series are written when the subject is too complex for the long story format. Each article has a major theme; sidebars may be used to develop subthemes.

S ome editors say there are three types of news stories. Although there are no precise lines that can be drawn to separate the three, they can be distinguished as follows:

Spot news story: Contains material of such significance that it must be reported immediately to the public.

News feature: Uses information that supplements the spot news, usually by providing the human element behind the breaking news event or by giving background through interpretation and explanation.

Feature: Aims to entertain through the use of material that is interesting but not necessarily important.

The Feature ▶

The feature has had a reputation much like Canadian mining stock, slightly suspect. Although it has worthy antecedents in the satire and parody of poets and essayists who used the pen to attack individuals in public and private life, the feature was approached gingerly by many editors. Many editors subscribed to the philosophy of Richard Draper, who wrote in his Boston *News-Letter* in the 18th century that he would use features only when "there happens to be a scarcity of news."

Conservative editors of the 19th century reacted with distaste to the features published by the penny press from the 1830s to the Civil War. Directed to the working class, which had been enlarged by the country's industrial revolution, these inexpensive newspapers ran stories about domestic tragedy and illicit sex, stories that editors such as Horace Greeley found unworthy of journalism. When he established the *Tribune* in New York in 1841, Greeley announced that his newspaper would avoid the "immoral and degrading Police Reports, Advertisements and other matters which have been allowed to disgrace the columns of our leading Penny Papers." But Greeley was soon running some of the material he had condemned.

◀ At First Distasteful

The feature story was a weapon in the great circulation wars between Pulitzer and Hearst in New York at the turn of the century. Crime stories, sports, society news, science news—all of it embroidered with sensational details often as much invented as factual—were used to attract readers. This type of feature became synonymous with Yellow Journalism.

The Hearst newspapers were perhaps the most successful of the sensational and flamboyant papers of their day. W.A. Swanberg, in his biography *Citizen Hearst,* describes them:

> They were printed entertainment and excitement—the equivalent in newsprint of bombs exploding, bands blaring, firecrackers popping, victims screaming, flags waving, cannons roaring, houris dancing and smoke rising from the singed flesh of executed criminals.

A reporter for a Hearst newspaper described a typical Hearst paper as "a screaming woman running down the street with her throat cut." The Chief, as Hearst was known to his employees, had the man fired.

In the days of Front Page journalism, the feature writer's job was to wring tears from the bartender, smiles from the policeman and gasps of wonderment from the tenement dwellers. The tales of the city, as spun out by the feature writers of the day, were long on drama, short on fact.

As the United States grew into a world power and its citizens had to confront the consequences of World War I and then a pervasive depression, some of the press graduated to more serious pursuits. The feature came to be seen as too frivolous for the responsible newspaper. Newspapers that held on to the old formulas declined in popularity. The Hearst chain dwindled from 22 newspapers to eight.

In 1947, when Joseph G. Herzberg, city editor of *The New York Herald Tribune,* put together a series of essays by *Tribune* staffers for the book *Late City Edition,* not one of the 29 chapters was devoted to the feature story.

Nevertheless, the feature thrives today. First, editors discovered that serious journalism does not have to be abstract. They rediscovered the fact known to Greek playwrights 2,300 years ago—events have a human dimension. Indeed, it is the human aspect of the event that makes it worth communicating. In his play *The Frogs,* Aristophanes has the playwright Euripedes say, "I made the drama democratic. I staged the life of every day, the way we live." This is an excellent description of contemporary journalism.

◀ Now Thriving

"Give Delight". In his obituary of an English writer, David Cecil, Isaiah Berlin gives us one aspect of the feature. Berlin says that Cecil believed the "central purpose of art was to give delight, not to instruct, not to disturb, nor to explain, nor to praise or condemn a movement, an idea, a regime, nor to help build a better world in the service of a church, a party, a nation, a class, but to irradiate the soul with the light which God had granted the artist the power to shed, and the reader or listener to absorb, understand, delight in, and thereby be drawn nearer its divine Creator."

Anita Henderson,
Beloit (Wis.) *Daily News.*

Easy, Dad

Features tease tears and
grimaces as well as smiles
and laughter.

Guidelines ▶

Frontier Nurse ▶

Editors found that an unvarying diet of seriousness was rejected by the mass audience. To reach that audience, the newspaper or broadcast station must present a variety of news, the same variety that marks our lives. We need to read about the cost of living going up, and we make time to enjoy a piece about the price of an ice-cream cone.

Recognizing the maturity of the feature, the advisory board to the Pulitzer Prizes in the 1970s created a prize for the best feature. The guideline is: "For a distinguished example of feature writing giving prime consideration to high literary quality and originality."

Nowadays, many editors see only a fine line between news and features. Lew Powell, of *The Charlotte Observer,* says, "The distinctions between news and features are increasingly blurred these days.

"Features are busting out of the back-of-the-book ghetto and changing the way stories are written throughout the paper. The old 'Mayor Harris said today . . .' kind of straight news story is just as likely to begin with an account of a testy exchange between the mayor and a councilman or with an analysis of how the mayor's statements fit in with his re-election campaign or with his previous statements."

Some young reporters say they prefer to write features rather than hard news because the feature is easier to handle. This is the blather of the uninformed. The momentum of the news event carries most spot news stories. True, it is not easy to learn to organize a tight news story, and the skill to devise succinct leads that quickly take the reader to the news point is not easily mastered. But the feature writer must carry these burdens and more.

The feature is an exception to some of the writing rules, and this imposes on the writer the task of pioneering in each piece, beginning anew to find a form, a story tone, the appropriate words and the telling scenes for this particular story. Readers demand more of feature writers than of straight news writers and so do editors.

The few guidelines for feature writing cut to the heart of writing itself:

- Show people doing things.
- Let them talk.
- Underwrite. Let the action and the dialogue carry the piece.
- Keep the piece moving.

Few writers have gone wrong by making the individuals in their stories carry the action. This requires a discerning eye to see the telling action and a discriminating ear to catch the illuminating quote.

Showing people doing things and letting them speak requires that the reporter be on the scene. Jim Warren of the *Lexington Herald-Leader* accompanied Glenna Allen of the Frontier Nursing Service as she made her rounds in the eastern Kentucky mountains. His story begins this way:

HYDEN—The road that snakes up from Coon Creek is hard-packed dirt in some places and bottomless mud in others, all of it pitted with cavernous potholes.

Slide one way and you hit a mountain wall; slide the other and you go off a cliff into space.

Driving is tricky, especially when a mountainous coal truck—in this case a Tennessee Orange Mack with a full load of bituminous coal—looms around a blind curve.

Glenna Allen handled the situation with skill that comes from long practice, steering her battered tan Toyota almost to the drop-off at the right edge of the road. . . .

Tom Woods II,
The Lexington Herald-Leader.

Backwoods Care

◀ **Conforming
Kindergarteners**

Warren lets Allen talk:

> "My mother hates it that I'm doing this," Miss Allen said with a laugh. She left Dayton, Ohio, to work in the mountains. "She thinks I'm going to get myself killed by a rattlesnake or run over some cliff, and she keeps asking when I'm coming home. . . ."

Lena H. Sun, *The Washington Post* Beijing bureau chief, took her readers into a kindergarten to show how Chinese children are made into conforming, obedient citizens.

> BEIJING—It is a playtime at the Tongren Kindergarten. As 3-year-olds run relay races in the schoolyard, the teacher suddenly calls out to one girl.
> "You didn't run on the dotted line," the teacher says disapprovingly. The girl, pigtails bobbing, immediately retraces her steps on faded red spots painted on the concrete. The teacher smiles and nods. No one else makes the same mistake.

"Show people doing things," our first guideline, is the thrust of Sun's lead.

◀ **Gambling Woman**

When reporters were assigned to cover the opening of an off-track betting parlor in a suburb of New York City, most were content to report such obvious facts as the size of the crowd and the name and address of the first bettor on line. Leonard Levitt of *Newsday* resisted the routine and did some checking about the 62-year-old grandmother who was first in line. He refused to settle for the obvious. As good feature writers know, snappy writing cannot sustain the underreported feature.

Through interviews with the woman, her husband and children, Levitt learned that she was a chronic gambler who bet $50 and $100 a day. Her husband told Levitt, "It was hard when the kids were growing up. I used to hold three jobs." The woman told Levitt, "My husband doesn't approve of my betting. Neither do my kids. None of them bets. But they love me." In these few quotes, a family's tragedy is unfolded.

◀ **Sleepers**

The feature writer also sees the absurd and hears the preposterous. In his piece about the Southern Furniture Market in High Point, N.C., where the new styles in furniture are previewed each year, Lew Powell tells us about Dr. Samuel Dunkell, "psychotherapist and author of the best-selling 'Sleep Positions.' " Just to make sure we know this event is hardly the stuff of which significant news is made, Powell sets the mood in the first paragraph:

> Today in Washington reporters are awaiting Koreagate revelations. In Memphis, the latest on Elvis. In Minneapolis, the Billy Graham audit. In High Point we're crowded into a mattress showroom waiting for the inside poop on sleep positions.

From the serious to the silly. Powell does this in a few sentences. The words "inside poop" tell the reader that what follows is going to be fun:

Enrico Caruso slept with 18 pillows. Neil Sedaka rubs his feet over each other. The late Hannah Arendt, author of "The Origins of Totalitarianism" and not someone you'd expect to be spilling this kind of stuff, favored the "water wings" position.

And have we got a photo opportunity for you! As Dunkell discusses the "royal" position, the "flamingo," the "mummy," the "sphinx" and the "swastika," model Norma demonstrates. Her yellow sleepshirt keeps riding up, ensuring undivided attention. When she's joined by a male model for the "hug" and "spoon" position, a sock-footed TV cameraman clambers onto an adjacent Maxipedic for a better angle.

"Republicans sleep face down, Democrats on their backs," Dunkell says. Scribble, scribble. "Surprisingly few people fall out of bed—perhaps 20 percent in their lifetime." Scribble, scribble . . .

The feature writer sees universals as well as aberrations. What is there about that pianist, this drummer with dreams that strike chords common to all of us? The feature writer knows that great writers inspire us to see ourselves in Tolstoy's Natasha, Fitzgerald's Nick Carraway and Melville's Captain Vere. The feature writer must be open to human experience. It was said of Rembrandt that he rejected nothing human. Neither does the feature writer.

Frank Barrows of *The Charlotte Observer* says careful planning of the feature is essential. "Simply because a feature is not written to be cut from the bottom—as a news story might be—does not mean that the material can be randomly set down on paper.

"For a feature to be something other than puffery, you must do the type of serious preparation and thinking that lead to organization. For instance, you might not want to put all the straight biographic data in one place."

Barrows knows that such material is usually tedious. Beginners tend to bunch up background. More experienced hands break up background such as biographical material and place bits and pieces into the moving narrative. For example, he says, when a reporter comes to a place in the story where she is showing how the subject's hometown influenced his life, that is the place to put something about his birthplace and a few other routine details. In other words, the necessary background is spotted or blended into the ongoing story.

Another fault of beginners is the leisurely pace they set at the outset of the piece, as though they are feeling their way toward the theme of the story.

"Too often in features the writer does not tell his reader soon enough what he is writing about," Barrows says.

Betty Tichich,
Houston Chronicle.

Sweet 15

Anabell Garza has turned 15 and is ready for an important step in her life, the *quinceañera,* when Hispanic young women become adults. The story is told by Karen Hastings in *Texas,* the *Houston Chronicle Magazine.*

Planning ▶

Look at how Eric Lawlor of the *Houston Chronicle* slides the reader right into his piece about a truck stop outside town. He sets a scene in the first paragraph, pulls us into the restaurant in the second paragraph and in the third paragraph we meet a waitress who introduces us to a dialogue that gives us a good idea of what's going on:

◀ Truck Stop

The truck stop on the North Freeway is ringed with rigs. Trucks glide past one another with the grandeur of sailing ships; 16-wheel galleons bearing—not spices from the Indies or gold from the New World—but auto parts and refrigerators.

Truckers weave as they enter the restaurant; like sailors on shore leave, they are still finding their legs.

Tina Hernandez, an 18-year-old waitress here, serves an order of ham and eggs.

"Where are my grits?" asks the recipient.

"You don't get grits unless you ask for them," she tells him. "If you want grits, you gotta say, 'I want grits.' "

If this sounds unnecessarily acerbic, it's not, in fact: Tina and her customers are actually fond of one another. An affection that masquerades as good-natured abuse.

"Give me a bowl of split-pea soup," says a man whose face looks curiously flat.

Perhaps someone sat on it. "Is there any meat in there?"

"There's meat in there all right," says Tina. "The problem is finding it."

"How are you and Billy (not his real name) doin'?" he wants to know.

"We don't talk anymore," says the waitress. "He got scared. Just checked out."

"Oh, I don't believe that. I'll bet you are goin' out and just don't want anyone to know about it."

"I'm tellin' ya: that man is scared of women."

"Maybe, he just doesn't like YOU," offers Myrtle, another waitress.

At a nearby table, a driver is telling a colleague about a recent fling.

"I had to leave her finally because she was so cold-blooded. You could get pneumonia sitting next to a woman like that."

In his feature about a school for bartenders, Lawlor gets down to business at once, taking the reader into the classroom in the lead:

◀ Using All
the Techniques

K.C. Stevens is explaining the difference between a godfather and a godmother.

"To make a godfather," she tells her class at the Professional Bartenders School, "use amaretto and scotch. A godmother, on the other hand, combines amaretto and vodka."

Then Lawlor steps back for a few paragraphs to let the reader survey the scene, telling us something about the teacher and her students:

K.C., a onetime barmaid, has been teaching people to mix drinks for four years now.

"I didn't want to find myself at the age of 40 wearing orthopedic shoes behind some crummy bar," she says. "Being a bartender is a young person's game."

Her class nods agreement. If that isn't to exaggerate this barely perceptible movement

of heads. This is a pretty lethargic group. They slump at the school's mock bar as if drink had ravaged them. They wouldn't look out of place in Pompeii.

It's hard to imagine these people doing anything as animated as tending bar. Indeed it's hard to imagine them doing anything as animated as standing up.

Steve Campbell,
Houston Chronicle.

Budding bartenders learn how to concoct a variety of refreshments at this school for bartenders. Instructor K. C. Stevens displays the proper mix of energy and cordiality.

Learning The Trade

K.C., a good soul, is inclined to agree. "A lot of them are spaced off somewhere," she says. "I was telling a couple of them just this morning, 'Look, you're gonna have to put more time into studying.' But once they get the picture, things usually work out. Many people come in here expecting to party. They don't realize there's a lot of work involved."

From the first sentence, the reader is hooked on this story. This is the objective of the writer who seeks to entertain readers—grab them and keep them reading.

This story takes a full column of type. Every line was read. Why? If we can answer the question, perhaps we will make a start toward understanding what makes a good feature.

First, the subject is interesting. Even if you can't tell a Hot Toddy from a hot buttered bun—and care less—you wonder about these people who are able to throw together scores of different concoctions from their amazing array of bottles.

Second, Lawlor knows what he is doing. The most interesting subject in clumsy hands will be dulled. Let's analyze Lawlor's craft:

- The story moves quickly.
- The quotations are vivid.
- The characters interact. They talk, do things.

In any discussion with feature writers, the words *tone* and *style* always come up. A feature writer uses one tone—one kind of voice—for a piece about a classical guitarist, another for a guitarist with a rock group. Tone is established by selection of facts, quotes, illustrations, by word choice, length of sentences, even by the length of paragraphs. The rock musician may be quoted in short, one- or two-sentence paragraphs to match the rock beat, whereas the classical musician's quotes may run on longer to give the reader the sense of the sonority of classical music.

The profile of a man who crashes big parties will have a humorous cast to it, whereas the profile of a survivor of the Holocaust who recalls the concentration camps will be written in somber grays. The verbs will be different. The piece about the party crasher will have crisp action verbs. The rule about avoiding the intransitive verb *to be* may be broken in the Holocaust piece in a deliberate effort to underplay the reporter's writing and to allow the source's recollections to carry the piece.

The new field of neuroscience interested Jon Franklin, chief science writer for *The Evening Sun* in Baltimore. Franklin had been talking to Dr. Thomas Ducker, chief of neurosurgery at the University of Maryland Hospital, about brain surgery, and Ducker had agreed to call him the next time he planned an especially difficult surgical procedure. When Ducker called, Franklin set out to follow the story of Edna Kelly, who was afflicted with what she called her "monster," a tangled knot of abnormal blood vessels in the back of her brain. She was born with the malformation, but in recent years the vessels had ballooned inside her skull and were crowding out the healthy brain tissue.

Kelly agreed to be interviewed, and she allowed Franklin to use her name. She also permitted Franklin to watch the surgery. Ducker agreed to cooperate.

Here is how the first story in Franklin's two-part series begins:

In the cold hours of a winter morning, Dr. Thomas Barbee Ducker, University Hospital's senior brain surgeon, rises before dawn. His wife serves him waffles but no coffee. Coffee makes his hands shake.

Downtown, on the 12th floor of the hospital, Edna Kelly's husband tells her goodbye.

For 57 years Mrs. Kelly shared her skull with the monster. No more. Today she is frightened but determined.

It is 6:30 a.m.

"I'm not afraid to die," she said as this day approached. "I've lost part of my eyesight. I've gone through all the hemorrhages. A couple of years ago I lost my sense of smell, my taste, I started having seizures. I smell a strange odor and then I start strangling. It started affecting my legs, and I'm partially paralyzed.

"Three years ago a doctor told me all I had to look forward to was blindness, paralysis and a remote chance of death. Now I have aneurisms; this monster is causing that. I'm scared to death . . . but there isn't a day that goes by that I'm not in pain and I'm tired of it. I can't bear the pain. I wouldn't want to live like this much longer." As Dr. Ducker leaves for work, Mrs. Ducker hands him a paper bag containing a peanut butter sandwich, a banana and two fig newtons. Downtown, in Mrs. Kelly's brain, a sedative takes effect.

Franklin's intentions are made clear at the outset. This is to be a detailed account of the confrontation between a skilled surgeon and disease. Franklin takes the reader into the operating room:

Now, at 7:15 a.m. in Operating Room 11, a technician checks the brain surgery microscope and the circulating nurse lays out bandages and instruments. Mrs. Kelly lies still on a stainless steel table.

A small sensor has been threaded through her veins and now hangs in the antechamber of her heart. Dr. Jane Matjasko, the anesthesiologist, connects the sensor to a 7-foot-high bank of electronic instruments. Wave forms begin to move rhythmically across a cathode ray tube.

With each heartbeat a loudspeaker produces an audible popping sound. The steady pop, pop, pop, pop isn't loud, but it dominates the operating room.

Dr. Ducker enters the operating room and pauses before the X-ray films that hang on a lighted panel. He carried those brain images to Europe, Canada and Florida in search of advice, and he knows them by heart. Still he studies them again, eyes focused on the two fragile aneurisms that swell above major arteries. Either may burst on contact.

The one directly behind Mrs. Kelly's eyes is the most dangerous, but also the easiest to reach. That's first.

The first story ends at 11:05 a.m. Ducker has managed to find and clip off one of the two deadly aneurisms. The next article begins with Ducker peering into the neurosurgery microscope in search of the second. The going is slow, dangerous.

At 1:06 p.m. there is trouble and Ducker worries that his patient's heart has been slowed too many times. He decides not to continue. If she recovers, he says, he will try again.

If she survives. If. If.

"I'm not afraid to die," Mrs. Kelly had said. "I'm scared to death . . . but . . . I can't bear the pain. I wouldn't want to live like this much longer."

Her brain was too scarred. The operation, tolerable in a younger person, was too much. Already, where the monster's tentacles hang before the brainstem, the tissue swells, pinching off the source of oxygen.

Mrs. Kelly is dying.

The clock in the lounge, near where Dr. Ducker sits, says 1:40.

"It's hard even to tell what to do. We've been thinking about it for six weeks. But, you know, there are certain things . . . that's just as far as you can go. I just don't know. . . ."

He lays the sandwich, the banana and the fig newtons on the table before him neatly, the way the scrub nurse laid out instruments.

"It was triple jeopardy," he says, finally, staring at his peanut butter sandwich the same way he stared at the X-rays. "It was triple jeopardy."

It is 1:43, and it's over.

Dr. Ducker bites, grimly, into the sandwich.

The monster won.

Franklin holds the reader in suspense until the jolting final sentences. The three sentences are short, quick—consistent with the abrupt end of Mrs. Kelly's life. Franklin was awarded a Pulitzer Prize for the feature story, the first time a Prize was given in this category. You might want to go back to our four rules for writing the feature and note in the margins of the sections from Franklin's pieces where he follows these guidelines.

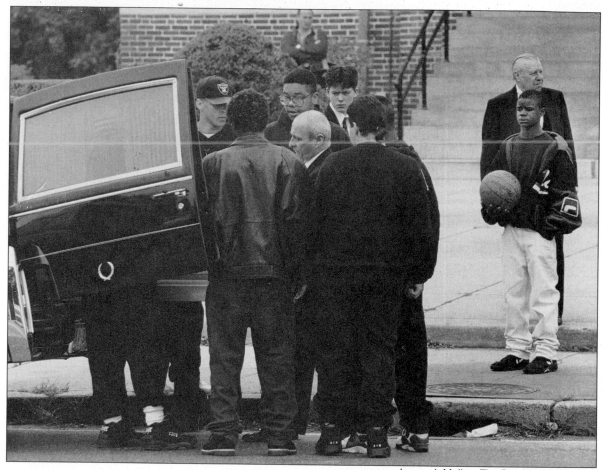

James J. Malloy, *The Providence Journal.*

Saying Goodbye to a Good Buddy

The story of the teen-ager's funeral begins with a lead-in paragraph: "Tommy DeGrafft, 15, is remembered as a good boy and an outstanding athlete who died because he was in the wrong place at the wrong time. A priest calls for an end to the anger and hatred that has given way to shootings in the past year." (The youth was killed in a drive-by shooting.) Then, reporter W. Zachary Malinowski begins his story from the funeral site, Pawtucket: Tears streamed down Wayne Tucker's face as he lead the funeral procession down the center aisle at St. Teresa's Church yesterday. Behind Tucker stood eight teen-age pallbearers in black sweatshirts and loose-fitting jeans, bearing the silver casket holding their friend, Tommy DeGrafft, who died in a barrage of gunfire last weekend. In Tucker's hands was a basketball covered with the scrawled signatures of DeGrafft's former teammates. One said simply, "To Tommy from All of Us."

The news feature usually has its origins in some news event. When Carl Hiassen of *The Miami Herald* dug into the court case involving a doctor and his millionaire wife, he came up with a tale of greed preying on loneliness. His story begins:

◀ **The News Feature**

To Dr. Edward Gordon, love meant never having to say he was out of money.

Six years ago, the solicitous Miami Beach physician married a patient who was worth more than $8 million. Her name was

Elizabeth Buffum, and she was a lonely alcoholic.

With Gordon, she stayed lonely and she often stayed drunk. She just barely stayed wealthy.

Today, as lawyers doggedly try to retrieve her scattered fortune from all over the globe, the former Mrs. Gordon lies in a Fort Lauderdale nursing home, permanently brain-damaged. Relatives say her life was destroyed by four ruinous years as the doctor's wife. They say it wasn't a marriage, it was a matrimonial Brink's job.

"Unbelievable," says one son, Peter Beaumont. "It's sort of a classic: elderly lady with lots of bucks heads down to Retirement City and gets fleeced by local doctor."

It began as a September love affair. He was 62, silver-haired and single, with a new medical practice in Florida. She was 60, a bit overweight and twice divorced, given to irascibility and depression. . . .

The lead is inviting. Nobody, every writer knows, ever tires of reading about love, money and violence.

The second and third paragraphs are like the coming attractions at a movie, or the come-on advertising of television.

The fourth paragraph drives home the theme: A woman ruined by her marriage. And in the fifth paragraph, a quote is used to sum up the theme. The sixth paragraph introduces us to the chronological narrative the writer will spin.

Feature Ideas ▶

The feature writer makes journalism out of daily experience. Shopping in a supermarket, the reporter notices the stacks of candy and gum and other small items near the checkout counter. One story idea pops up, then others. Listen to the reporter think:

> How important is impulse buying? How do merchants determine what goes on the bottom shelves, on the top shelves? How much do people spend on junk food? What is junk food anyway? Do students really spend a lot of money on chips, soda and beer?

Humor: Approach with Caution

Asked for advice about writing humor, most writers reply, "Don't try."

That's a two-pronged answer. Humor may be the most difficult kind of writing there is. There are probably 50 excellent Washington correspondents, a score of top-notch foreign correspondents. Every newspaper has a master reporter. But there are fewer than half a dozen good humorists writing for newspapers.

The other prong of the response is that if you have the urge to write a funny piece, or you are ordered to do so, don't try too hard. The strain will show.

Mark Twain, the country's greatest humorist, said, "There are several kinds of stories, but only one difficult kind—the humorous."

In his essay, "How to Tell a Story," he wrote, "The humorous story depends for its effect upon the manner of the telling. . . . The humorous story is told gravely; the teller does his best to conceal the fact that he even dimly suspects that there is anything funny about it."

And there the reporter's train of thought stops and abruptly shifts:

> Does anyone go to the kitchen faucet and drink water anymore? Or is everyone going to the fridge for a bottle or can?

In the files, the reporter finds that consumption of soft drinks overtook coffee in 1975, milk in 1976 and water in 1984.

He finds individual consumption of soft drinks last year was 680 cans or bottles a year. Dividing by 365 the reporter gets one and four-fifths cans or bottles a day for every man, woman and baby in the land. Next, he will talk to local bottlers to localize his piece.

Ideas are everywhere. A letter writer to Ann Landers says that college students consume an average of 34 gallons of alcoholic beverages a year and quotes the chancellor of the University of Wisconsin as saying that the biggest problem on campus today is alcoholism. A reporter wonders: What's happening on the local campus?

A business publication carries a study on the number of women who are directors and officers in major companies—429 out of 12,315, or 3.5 percent. This gives the reporter an idea for a local folo: What's the percentage in town?

Just look around. Notice that group sitting in the cafeteria, those high school students? They are griping. About what? Listen in: His mother doesn't like his girlfriend: ◀ **Be Alert, Aware**

> "She thinks I'm too young to be going steady. She thinks I should spend my time on school work. But me and my girl were meant for each other."

A young woman says to no one in particular, "I don't fit in, not even here. I don't think I look good enough. I don't like the way my body is. Everyone else is popular. Not me."

Another teen-ager says he just had some good news that has relieved him after a couple of weeks of stress: "I thought that my girlfriend was pregnant. Lost a lot of sleep, and weight. I just found out she isn't."

Jimmy Breslin, a Pulitzer Prize-winning columnist, is an advocate of looking around. "Notice the women eating alone at night, the people without friends. Loneliness, he says, is a major problem, especially among women.

As you can see, features can be made from the somber as well as the zany side of the human experience.

The writer seeking feature ideas reads beyond his or her field. Look at the classified ads, this one for example: ◀ **Read Everything**

> FOR SALE—wedding dress, size 7,
> never worn. Phone 382-4911.

There's a story behind this forlorn ad, just as there was one behind the offer of a Celebese ape for sale. Tara Bradley-Steck of the AP's Pittsburgh bureau called the number in the ad and was told she needed no special permit to own the ape. Intrigued, she investigated the business of selling and owning wild and exotic animals. She wrote that despite the protests of humane societies, thousands of people own, breed, exhibit or sell these animals.

Read letters to the editor: After the Supreme Court held that Boy Scouts could require their members to say the Scout Pledge in full, including the words "to do my duty to God and my country," a woman wrote that the Girl Scouts did things differently. Each member, the letter writer wrote, can "choose whether she would use the word 'God' or not." After a survey the Girl Scouts made, they decided "in the name of inclusiveness, among other things, to provide a choice." She added, "It points out just how differently women approach problem solving and decision making in comparison to 'male' methods."

A great feature idea here: Do men and women solve problems differently? There are plenty who can comment on this.

Death in a
Dumpster ▶

Read the newspaper closely, even the smallest items. It was a short, horrific story that caught Jules Loh's attention: A homeless drifter had sought a night's peace in a Dumpster. As the man slept, a garbage truck making its rounds picked up the Dumpster. . . . In a pocket of the soon mangled body was an army discharge paper with the name Gregory DeGregorio.

That was all Loh, an AP special correspondent, had to go on when he decided to investigate DeGregorio's short life. The story, when Loh finally finished his extensive reporting involving interviews around the country and a long session at the keyboard, ran more than 150 paragraphs. Yet many papers ran it, the story of a Vietnam veteran, a drunk, a petty criminal and a schizophrenic. It moved on AP's wires on Veterans Day with an editor's note that pointed out that "among the heroes are the homeless. . . . How could a society so proud of its safety nets so completely overlook one of its most helpless?"

The story, crammed with details, begins:

Verlin Bell's routine began, as usual, in pitch darkness. His last stop, still an hour before sunup, was in the parking lot behind the Southern Paint Co. store on Seagrave Street.

He nudged his big green garbage truck with practiced accuracy up to the Dumpster and slid its two steel lifters into sleeves on either side. He levered the Dumpster noisily up and over the cab, tilted its contents into the brightly lit truck bed, then lowered it back in place.

As he backed away, he shoved the compactor blade in gear and glanced at the mirror.

"I always check the mirror. I look through the window in back of the cab to make sure the hydraulic hoses are clear. This time . . . well, this time I saw the top half of a man. He was caught between the blade and the roof, hanging over the blade, facing me."

Why so many details? Loh says, "The reader gains confidence because the writer knows so many specifics, knows I was there. I required myself to be as specific as I could, and that required extra reporting. I wanted the reader to know an awful lot about this guy. All this detail gives the reader the sense of being able to believe everything."

Loh takes the reader back to the dead man's birth:

> He was born in Philadelphia and baptized 10 weeks later at Annunciation Church on South 10th Street, the spiritual anchor of a neighborhood where they still hear confessions in Italian. His parents, Frank and Mary DeGregorio, named the boy Gregory John. He was their only child.
>
> His father was a large, friendly, 35-year-old veteran of World War II, a tile setter by trade. Around the union hall they called him Big Frank. Mary was five years younger and according to friends as gregarious and optimistic as her husband. Both doted on their son.

To Vietnam:

> After six months in the field, on July 17, DeGregorio arrived on a stretcher at the 3rd Field Hospital near Saigon, bleeding from his stomach. A shrapnel wound. They patched it, leaving a jagged scar.
>
> But they did not send him back to his own infantry outfit. Instead they assigned him to a security unit in Saigon. There, by the only observation available, "DeGregorio sort of went berserk." Four days later, at a hospital in Japan, the diagnosis came down: chronic schizophrenia.

To a homeless shelter in St. Petersburg where Loh interviewed the man who ran it with his wife:

> "Greg would come in the morning for coffee and doughnuts, maybe take a shower," Jerry Styles recalled. "He was never dirty. His clothes were not the best, secondhand but clean. He never looked run down or scuzzy or shaggy.
>
> "But I knew he had mental problems. We feed about 80 men in the morning. They sit at the picnic tables out back or stand in groups, but Greg stayed apart. He sat by himself on a bench against the house as far as he could get from the others. He was totally quiet, just sat and stared. He was never loud or violent. In fact he was quite docile. He was not unfriendly, just indifferent. He didn't choose to mix."
>
> Indifferent?
>
> "That's what he was," said Styles, "indifferent."

Loh comments on this interview:

> The reason the high school transcript gave for Gregory's dropping out was "indifference." It was a real stroke of luck—for me, anyhow—when Jerry Styles used the same word. So that the reader wouldn't miss that, I made Jerry repeat it by repeating it myself. Finding Jerry Styles and his wife, Camille, who ran the homeless shelter in

St. Petersburg, turned out to be a godsend not just in reporting the story but writing it as well."

Loh wanted to end with the "two elements of Gregory's story. The first is the irony of one last mix-up by the record keepers":

> Anyone who would care to visit the grave should be forewarned: In the cemetery's alphabetical visitors' directory Gregory's name is not there. Like his missing Army record, it has been misfiled. Someone divided his last name, DeGregorio, into two words and you will find him listed under the G's. His grave is number 573 in section 104.

Then to the second element, the grave itself in a National Cemetery near Tampa:

> He rests in a sweet and silent bivouac of the dead 10 ranks back from the smooth curve of a blacktop road and 15 files east of two live oak trees that shade his tombstone in the late afternoon.
> His epitaph reads vertically in eight lines:
>
> GREGORY
> DeGREGORIO
> PVT
> US ARMY
> VIETNAM
> JULY 15 1947
> NOV 12 1992
> PURPLE HEART
>
> AP-NY-1215EST

The last paragraph, Loh says, evokes "the one contribution he made in his life—his military service—by using soldierly words: 'bivouac,' 'ranks,' 'files.' And I allow myself a soothing alliteration—'sweet,' 'silent,' 'smooth'—in contrast with the turmoil of his life and the violence of his death."

Avoiding the Pitfalls ▶

The feature writer who botches a story suffers the agonies of those who make public spectacles of themselves. Because the feature is widely read, when it fails it collapses in full view. In the newsroom, colleagues excuse the spot news writer's failures more readily. After all, breaking news is written under pressure of deadline before all the facts are in. The feature writer has plenty of time to report and write and usually is given enough space.

The following suggestions are from a dozen feature writers around the country:

- "Good stories come from good material. Good material comes from good reporting—and that is just as true if not more so with feature writing as with news writing," says Sheryl James of the *St. Petersburg Times*. As Tom Wolfe puts it, "Style can't carry a story if you haven't done the reporting."

• Single-source stories are not as good as multisource stories. No one cares to read about the author who talks about his life unless his personal account is supplemented by interviews with fellow writers, critics, his family, friends, even some readers.

• Do not have such a love affair with quotes that you fail to paraphrase routine material. Worse: Do not use quotes chronologically from the interview as a prop for failing to organize the piece. Good features can be written that are almost all quotes, but the quotes in these stories are usually rearranged.

• Know what you are going to say and the tone in which it is to be said before starting. Otherwise, the story will never get off the ground.

• Develop an enthusiasm for the piece. Features can be marred by an objectivity that keeps the reader at a distance. "The idea of a feature is to involve the reader," a reporter said. "This is often taken to mean good craftsmanship through colorful writing. That's not enough. The writer needs to take a point of view, not simply to say, 'Look at this guy who was put into an institution for the retarded at the age of six, and when he was 18 some worker in the place saw that the kid wasn't retarded at all but had a learning disability.'

"The writer of this kind of piece has to be indignant at the tragedy. How can you be objective about this kind of inhumanity? A reader should be moved to indignation—not by the reporter's sounding off. We don't want that. But this kind of piece has to have the kind of facts and a story tone that gives a strong sense of human waste and bureaucratic inefficiency."

• Make sure the story has a good plot and is unusual enough to hold our interest. This means the central idea should have possibilities for drama, conflict, excitement, emotion.

• Don't tell us when you can show us people doing things.

Steve Ueckert,
Houston Chronicle.

Duck Talk

"You've got to tell those ducks what they want to hear," says Jimmy Goddard, a master duck caller Eric Lawlor interviewed for his piece about that fine art.

Lawlor let Goddard speak:

"Talk to them the way you'd talk to your lady. Say 'I love you honey, please come on back. . . .' You have to mean everything you say.

"Nothing alive spots a fraud faster than a duck. . . . You must be able to tell a duck's mood. I watch the bird. If he's happy, I'm happy. I tell him, 'If you'll just come on down here, the two of us can have a fine old time.' That's if he's happy. If he's lonesome, then you have to be lonesome. Ask him if he'd like to cry on your shoulder."

- Avoid first-person stories. They are usually less interesting than you think. There are exceptions, of course:

I don't drive a Mercedes. I don't smoke Cuban cigars, or drink Dom Perignon (unless you're buying). I'm more likely to dine at Burger King than a four-, three-, or two-star restaurant. But I do have one thing higher rollers would envy. I own a racehorse.

No, I don't own the horse by myself. I have a few partners; there are an even dozen of us, actually. We're not the types you'd expect to be in this game. We're a locksmith, an investment banker, a journalist, the director of a rape crisis center, a retired businessman, two therapists, a prosecutor, three lawyers in private practice, and a law student. Four of us are women.

David Hechler's experience as a horse owner lasted a year or so. Gypsy Flame proved to be nice to look at but slow afoot.

Brights ▶

The *bright* is to the feature what the short story is to the novel—a distillation, a tightly written gem that brightens the reader's day. The bright can be one paragraph or several. The following article is about as long as a bright should run:

POOLE, England—(AP)—"It was God who took out my tonsils," the little boy told his mother after his operation at Poole General Hospital.

"When I was taken into the big white room, there were two lady angels dressed in white. Then two men angels came in. Then God came in."

"How did you know it was God?" the mother asked.

"Well, one of the men angels looked down my throat and said, 'God, look at that child's tonsils.'

"Then God took a look and said, 'I'll take them out at once."

The conversation was reported by the hospital's staff newsletter.

The last paragraph is an anti-climax. It belongs in the running story, probably at the end of the second paragraph. Then the reader would be left with that wonderfully innocent quotation from the child.

The Long Story ▶

Newspapers have responded to the clear advantage of broadcast journalism in covering the spot story by emphasizing reporting in depth. This has meant that newspaper reporters need to be able to handle series of stories and depth pieces that run a column or more. Broadcast journalists who do documentaries also must master the techniques essential to handling the long piece. The long story is, of course, the staple of the magazine.

A simple recital of events is not enough for the long story. Readers, viewers and listeners will not waste time on a lengthy story or documentary unless the reporting has developed insights for them and the writing is a cut above the pedestrian prose often accepted in the short news story. The story also must be well-organized. It must carry the reader through a long journey.

When John McPhee, whom many consider one of the best reporters in the country, was at *Time,* he wrote many of the magazine's longer pieces. "Each had to have a beginning, a middle and an end, some kind of structure so that it would go somewhere and sit down when it got there," he said.

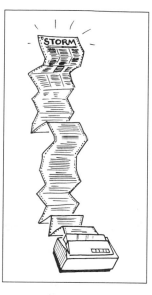

Sidebars Keep Down Length

A story can be too long, contain too many subthemes. When that happens, the main piece can be accompanied by sidebars, stories that accompany the main piece. When a convicted murderer and a burglar cut their way out of a maximum security prison in Connecticut, Tom Puleo wrote two sidebars to the escape story: (1) "By closing seven guard towers to save $900,000, the state may have laid the groundwork" for the escape. (2) "Beth W. Banta and a small group of residents worked nearly two years perfecting a telephone system that would alert them to prison disturbances and escapes. Tuesday, one of their worst fears came to pass. A violent felon escaped the maximum-security Somers state prison, and the telephone system didn't work."

"The first point about reporting a depth story," says Jeffrey Tannenbaum of *The Wall Street Journal,* "is that it usually requires a lot of work. For a profile of Rockefeller University, I conducted at least 20 interviews in person, and the typical interview lasted 90 minutes. I also did several more interviews by phone and read a great deal of background material."

The long story, he says, "is an interplay between the specific and the general." By "general" he means the key points or themes that the reporter has selected as the basis of the piece. A story about a breaking news event may have one or two points. The long story may have half a dozen. "Specific" refers to the details that illustrate and amplify the general points.

"For every generalization in the story," Tannenbaum continues, "there should be specific illustrations to buttress it. This means the reporter has to identify the themes and then must dig out the proof for them. The more specific and colorful the details that are used as proof or buttressing material, the more effectively the generalization or theme will be brought home to the reader."

Like all experienced journalists, Tannenbaum tries to sketch out his major ideas or key points as early as possible. This may come before any reporting is done, or soon after the reporting begins. A theme can come from a tip, an editor's assignment, the reporter's hunch. Or it may simply be the logical step following a series of developments on a beat.

"For each key point, I want two things: Good quotes stating the point and colorful illustrations, anecdotes, examples," he says. "I know exactly what I am looking for from each interview subject."

In the reporting, additional points often will develop, and these, too, must be buttressed with specific quotes, illustrations, data and anecdotes.

Organizing the Story ▶

The major difficulty writers have with the long story is controlling its several major points, the half-dozen building blocks that must be arranged in logical and interesting order. It is not easy. McPhee says he goes "nuts trying to put it all in focus."

McPhee's first step is to structure the piece by typing up his notes and organizing them by subject or theme. He types the themes on index cards and tacks them to a bulletin board. Some reporters spread their cards on a flat surface. The story is plotted by arranging the cards in the order that seems best for the story.

By attaching the notes to the appropriate cards with the thematic material, the reporter has the story laid out in a form easy to scrutinize and to rearrange if necessary. This physical arrangement tends to give the reporter a sense of control over the story, and control of themes and reporting detail is the key to mastering the long piece. The long article must move logically and coherently from beginning to end, from idea to idea.

"Strange as it may seem to the beginner anxious to set words to paper, structuring the story challenges a reporter's creative talents as much as the writing. What's most absorbing is putting these stories together," says McPhee. "I want to know where I'm going from the start of the piece. It's my nature to want to know."

A Short Feature: A Man Beset

A feature story need not be long. By making every word count, a reporter for *The Fresno Bee* captured the mood of a man with a problem:

Ben Karp is a patient man. Like most of us he can shrug off life's little onslaughts in hopes of a better day.

But Karp has been shrugging and dodging and hoping for six months now, and his patience finally snapped. He called the *Bee* and asked for a reporter to see him at his general merchandise business at 1837 Mariposa Street.

"Very important," he said. On the scene, Karp whipped off his hat, pointed a slightly trembling finger at a brownish spot the size of a half dollar on it and then wordlessly pointed skyward.

There, cooing happily and roosting comfortably in corners and on window sills, were pigeons. Dozens of pigeons.

"I've called the mayor, the public works commissioner, the health department," Karp said. "They promised me to do something. Nothing is done. It's ruining my business. People don't like to walk in here past that line there.

"I'd like to get a shotgun and scare them off. But you can't shoot a gun in the city. The health department says it can't do anything because it can't prove pigeons carry disease. The humane society says I can't trap or poison them. The mayor's office says he was going to have a meeting on it. Nothing happened.

"This is bad for the city, I tell you. Thousands of people go in and out of the bus depot and they see this and I hear them say to each other, 'Fresno can't be such a clean city. Look at this.'

"I don't blame people for not wanting to come into the store. What can I do about it?"

And Karp looked up at his feathered friends and shrugged.

The following system is useful to organize the long article:

1. Identify all themes. Summarize in a sentence or two.
2. Place each summarized theme on a separate index card. Put the cards in the order that the themes will follow in the story.
3. Cut up notes by theme and place them next to theme cards. Reread and again arrange cards and notes in the order in which they will be written.
4. Look through the cards for the major theme that will serve as the lead or the integrating idea for the article. Write it on another card.

As the notes are lined up (Step 3), a reporter may discover a lack of adequate documentation or illustrative material to buttress some of the themes. More reporting will be necessary.

◀ **Writing Preparations**

Reporters check their notes at this stage for the high-quality quotes and illustrations that can be placed high up in the various sections of the story. One might be used to begin the article if the piece lends itself to a delayed lead. Some reporters use a colored pencil or pen to mark these high-quality quotes, anecdotes and incidents to call them out for use.

Caution: Resist the temptation to use a dramatic quote or telling incident simply because it is attention getting. The material must illustrate the theme it accompanies. If the fit is loose, put the example with a more appropriate theme or toss it out—however much work went into digging it up, however exciting the material.

Remember: Keep clearly in mind or in view the major theme for the piece (Step 4). Toss out any material that is irrelevant to this integrating idea.

Once the story is organized, do not assume that the structure cannot be changed. If the piece does not seem to be flowing properly, shift some of the elements around.

◀ **Changing Directions**

Some of the other problems that come up are:

• A theme has too much material to organize: Divide it into subthemes that can be handled more easily. Consider dropping, or at least drastically subordinating, some themes.

• A theme is too minor to be worth the space being given it: Blend it into another theme or discard it.

• The transition from one theme to another is awkward: To go from one theme to another smoothly, reorder the themes so that the linkage is more natural.

• A long block of background material does not move; it impedes the flow of the article: Break up this background, history, explanatory material and blend sections into the narrative.

A Television Documentary ▶

Everyone who sets words on paper for a living goes through the anxieties of cutting back, of discarding quotes, of tossing out details that get in the way of the theme and that impede the flow of the story. But this cannot be done until the theme is clearly identified. Let us watch the producer of a television documentary as he tries to focus on a theme for his subject—the decline of many of the country's older cities—and then makes changes in his script.

The deterioration of the inner city has had the attention of planners, politicians and journalists since the 1950s. If the city is the heart and brain of civilization, then the troubles afflicting the city cores of Denver, Detroit, Cleveland, Philadelphia, Boston, Baltimore, St. Louis, Los Angeles, New York and dozens of others threaten a way of life—cultural, commercial, educational, religious. For in the cities are the opera houses and philharmonic halls, the factories and the offices, the schools, and the temples and the cathedrals. The city gives a center to modern life.

To make journalism out of the tribulations of the large city is no easy task. The decline is the result of complex social, political and economic forces. Reporters with a national audience cannot write about all the cities in trouble. They must make one or two illustrate the plight of the many. They must draw common elements from the tangled problems of many cities and then find a city that symbolizes most of these elements.

Howard Weinberg, a producer of "Bill Moyers' Journal," decided to look at the problems of the inner cities, and he cast about for some central themes and a city to symbolize them. Weinberg first defined the scope and limits of his piece. He then settled on a point of view. His idea was to show the forces, especially racism, at work in causing neighborhood deterioration.

"I went to Chicago," Weinberg says. "My associate and I spent a week there, interviewing realtors, mortgage bankers, open housing leaders, community leaders, journalists, government officials and others on the south, west, north sides of Chicago."

When he returned to New York he felt frustrated. He had no idea how he would tell such a complicated story in half an hour. Tentatively, he decided to use the neighborhood of Austin on the West Side where black and white community groups had organized to preserve and improve their neighborhood. Also, one organizer, Gale Cincotta, lived in Austin, and Weinberg wanted to have a person as a focus for the program.

"In discussions with Bill Moyers, I was forced to rethink and refine my outline," he says. In looking back at his original outline, Weinberg found he had written, "It is beginning to be understood in communities of the inner cities that deterioration is not an accident, it is the inevitable result of a lack of faith. Expect deterioration—and you'll get it."

This idea of a self-fulfilling prophecy kept coming back to Weinberg, and he continued to do more reporting. Gradually, a theme and a strong point of view emerged. "It became clearer that 'redlining' was the story I wanted to tell, not the FHA abuses, not the efforts to relocate blacks in the suburbs or to 'stabilize' a threatened neighborhood."

◀ Redlining

Redlining takes its name from the red circles that banks and other lending agencies reportedly draw on maps around certain neighborhoods. The banks decide that people in these neighborhoods will not be given mortgage money because the banks consider the neighborhoods to be deteriorating. The practice makes it difficult for residents to improve their homes or for buyers to move into the neighborhood. Further deterioration results.

Weinberg was struck by the material he turned up in his reporting. "A savings and loan association was licensed to serve a neighborhood—and clearly, it was not doing that when it openly admitted that it received 80 percent of its deposits from its neighborhood and reinvested 20 percent in its neighborhood," Weinberg says.

Weinberg visualized the booming suburbs—which the savings of inner city residents were helping to build—and the deteriorating inner city. This would make for dramatic pictures.

He decided to shift the main focus from Austin to Rogers Park, which was beginning to go the way of Austin. Here is how the script of "This Neighborhood Is Obsolete" begins:

BILL MOYERS: The skyline of Chicago thrusts a handsome profile above the shores of Lake Michigan, suggesting the serene self-assurance of a city and its architecture, its wealth and its power and its tolerance for new ideas in urban living. But opulent skylines point up and away from the reality in their shadows. And in Chicago, as in every large American city, the grand vista is misleading.

Out beyond the soaring, secular temples of commerce, before you reach the shopping centers of suburbia, the future of Chicago is being decided every day in less spectacular surroundings: in neighborhoods where drugstores and delicatessens, taverns, laundromats, barbershops, and small churches on treelined corners express a lifestyle in danger of extinction.

For the way the economic game is played these days, these neighborhoods hardly have a chance. There's a profit in moving people out and hang the human cost.

In the next half hour, we'll look at two Chicago neighborhoods where the neighbors are fighting back.

I'm Bill Moyers.

This neighborhood is obsolete.

The people who live here don't think so, but some of the banks and savings and loan associations do. They stopped lending money because they believe the community's deteriorating and the risk is too great. But without money to improve people's homes or to give them a chance to buy another, the decay speeds up and the fear becomes a self-fulfilling prophecy.

In this and similar neighborhoods in Chicago, people accuse the savings and loan associations and the banks of redlining. Redlining means an entire geographic area can be declared unsuitable for conventional loans and mortgages. A redline is, in effect, drawn like a noose around a neighborhood until for want of good housing the working and middle classes are driven to the suburbs and the neighborhood is left to the very poor.

A side effect of redlining is something called disinvestment. You probably haven't heard of that term before. I hadn't until I came here. Disinvestment is a process of collecting deposits in one neighborhood and investing them somewhere else. The lending agents say it's necessary to spread the risk, but it leaves a neighborhood like this short of capital and hope. Gasping for its very life.

> The people who could afford to, move on. And that's what the savings and loan associations would like to do. After they've helped to build up the suburbs and make them affluent and attractive, they want to move there, too, or at least to open a suburban branch. Only then does an old neighborhood like this discover where its money has gone, but by then it's too late.

Like much good journalism, the documentary and the campaigns of local stations and newspapers had results. The month after the Moyers documentary, the Illinois Savings and Loan Commissioner issued a regulation against redlining that prohibits savings and loan associations from refusing to lend money in a neighborhood because of its age or changing character. The following year, Congress passed two pieces of legislation to end redlining by banks.

Notice that Weinberg had to reduce his ideas to the dimension of his program. Like the writer of a 300-word story or a 30-second news item, he had to focus on a single theme and toss out all extraneous material. The journalist never escapes the chore of boiling down material, of eliminating anything not related to the theme.

That basic theme can always be expressed in a simple sentence or two. David Belasco, the American theatrical producer, once remarked, "If you can't write your idea on the back of my calling card, you don't have a clear idea."

Some subjects are too broad, too deep, too complex for even the long story. Faced with such a problem, the reporter finds that the series of articles is the way out. When Sam Roe of *The Blade* decided to examine the decline in Great Lakes shipping, he knew that he could not handle the topic in a single article. Only a series would do the job.

◀ **The Series**

Roe's task was to show how the collapse of the steel industry struck lake shipping with devastating effect. Most of the ships served U.S. steel firms, carrying iron ore to the giant plants. Toledo's port on Lake Erie handled 43.8 million tons of cargo in 1966. Two decades later, it handled 17.9 tons.

"To capture and hold a reader's attention throughout a series is no easy task," Roe says. "That's why it is important to have stories with action, particularly in the first installment." Roe's first part in his four-part series begins with a delayed lead:

ABOARD THE AMERICAN REPUBLIC—"Damn! She's swinging too wide."

Capt. Robert Tretter cuts the throttle, curses the current, and prays that the *American Republic,* a freighter longer than two football fields, can negotiate one final hairpin bend on the Cuyahoga River. A strong current is denying her a lefthand turn and is pushing her toward a concrete embankment.

"You got 12 feet over here," says wheelsman John Norton. "She'd better not get closer."

The men on the bridge are as tense as sailors aboard a battleship in combat. For the past two hours, the *Republic,* carrying 21,000 tons of iron ore from Lorain, has inched her way down the narrow river toward Cleveland's inner docks.

Tom O'Reilly, *The Blade.*

A Port's Relentless Decline

As the steel industry collapsed, Great Lakes shipping went into decline. For the main story in his series on the slump in shipping, Sam Roe of *The Blade* went aboard a freighter and accompanied the crew on its voyage.

Just what does this have to do with his theme, the decline of Great Lakes shipping? In a deft maneuver, the journalistic equivalent of Capt. Tretter's handling of his freighter, Roe sets his story in the right direction:

Now, just when it appears the *Republic*'s port side will ram the embankment, the current lets her go. . . .

This time, the *American Republic* prevailed.

But ahead of her lies a far more formidable obstacle, one that her crew and all others in the shipping industry fear they can't beat: the relentless decline of Great Lakes shipping.

Numbers tell the story. This year there were only . . .

"This lead is more captivating, I thought, than diving into the statistics," Roe says.

Roe says he finds it useful to "walk the reader through" main stories. "For example, the main Great Lakes story was reported and written from the vantage point of a single ship on a single voyage.

"A cook in the mess talking about tough times allowed me to cite unemployment figures. Two decks below, in the cargo holds, an engineer pointing out new equipment allowed me to discuss technological changes in the industry. And so on. The story never really had to move off the ship."

◀ Outlining

Roe says an outline ensures a successful series. As soon as he has in mind a clear picture of what he wants to say, the outline is written. Too soon and the reporter cannot single out what is significant. Too late and the reporter will waste time gathering information irrelevant to the theme.

The outline helps the reporter to see holes in the reporting before writing begins. It also has a practical use. "A solid, detailed outline helps a reporter sell a series to editors," Roe says. Editors are reluctant to give the OK to a reporter who has in hand only an idea and some scattered notes. Series require a large amount of space, and editors won't provide it unless they have some assurance of the probability of a successful series.

Roe suggests writing nut grafs, the paragraphs that contain the basic idea, for each story. "Keep in mind when writing them: Why is this story significant? What am I trying to say?"

◀ Organizing and Writing

Outline in hand, the reporter then divides his or her notes in the appropriate sections, according to the outline.

"I read through all the notes on a particular story," Roe says. "I think along the way: Does this information belong in this story? Is more reporting needed?"

To organize each piece, Roe uses color markers, red for all the material that pertains to the lead, green for statistical information and so on. This makes it possible to link similar material quickly. Items that do not fit his pattern are moved to another story or scrapped.

"This process requires a lot of room," he says. He spreads his notes out. "Take time to see everything you've collected," he advises.

Roe's series, "Struggling to Stay Afloat," won first place in an AP contest for enterprise reporting among newspapers with circulation greater than 75,000.

◀ Tecumseh Street

For his two-part series on children living amid poverty, violence and parental neglect—an increasingly grim prospect for youngsters growing up in large cities—Roe focused on a single street in Toledo. "At first glance," he says, "it seemed to be a lifestyle piece. But more than anything it was a records-search project. I spent several weeks gathering material from documents—juvenile court and police records and census tract records."

Many of the records were not computerized and he had to go through thousands of individual cards to carry out his idea that developed from a figure he had seen: Each year, 400 local youngsters are sent off to state prisons, more than one a day.

Perhaps, he reasoned, he could find a street from which an unusual number of youngsters graduates to state prison. He found one, Tecumseh Street, which in 18 months sent off eight youngsters. Roe looked at the general picture, and then he zeroed in on particulars.

The general:

- Four of five children are born out of wedlock.
- Median income is $10,856, and in one section of the 1½ mile street, the income is $4,448.
- The street is one of the most crime ridden in Toledo.

For the particulars, he looked at the eight youngsters who went off to prison: Five grew up without fathers and four of them "saw one of their parents sent to prison," Roe said. He tracked down families to show that the problems ran through five generations—poverty, school dropouts, teen-age pregnancies.

Here is how his first piece began:

There, in that house, lives a family so poor that the 11-year-old daughter once was arrested for shoplifting socks and underwear. A few years later she was arrested again, this time for selling her body.

Down the street lives a boy who at age 14 was recruited by drug dealers to traffic cocaine. Now he's 17 and doing time at a state youth prison.

Further down lives a boy who says the only time he sees his mother is when she comes into the neighborhood to buy drugs. He's been arrested for receiving stolen property, robbery, and the rape of a 13-year-old girl.

Welcome to Tecumseh Street, perhaps the most difficult place to grow up in Toledo.

"It's rough," says 17-year-old Tecumseh resident Mandrell Walker. "And it's at its roughest point."

Mandrell is awaiting trial on charges that he shot a man in the back of the head.

It's just one street. But this one street in the Central City owns burdensome numbers:

▶ Court records show that in the last 18 months, officials have sent eight children living on Tecumseh to state juvenile prisons—the most from any street in Toledo.

▶ Another seven kids are suspected of being members of gangs such as the Bloods, the Buck Street Gangsters, and the Avondale Posse.

▶ And over the last five years, the street has seen a dozen child-abuse and child-endangering cases.

On top of that, the street lies in one of the poorest, most crime-ridden neighborhoods in town.

"It almost seems that some kids are doomed before they even start," says Keith Zeisloft, assistant administrator of the Lucas County Juvenile Court.

For his second piece, Roe focused on a young man awaiting trial for aggravated robbery, a youth who "has been arrested 15 times, suspended from school 14 times, detained at the juvenile jail six times and sent to state youth prisons twice." Roe continues:

Sounds like a rotten kid.

But what is remarkable is that he is not worse.

Court records show he has only seen his father three times in his life, and his mother is an admitted crack addict who abandoned him when he was 7.

Before she did, the boy says, she and her boyfriends—men he never really knew—put welts on his legs by whipping him with an extension cord.

Alan Detrich, *The Blade.*

Problem Parents Problem Kids

"When your parents don't care about you, you don't care about yourself," says this young man, a product of Tecumseh Street, awaiting trial on a robbery charge. He has been arrested 15 times.

Alan Detrich, *The Blade.*

Real-Life Games

Tecumseh Street children share their street with drug dealers and the customers of the dealers. The youngsters often witness drug busts. Here, 7-year-old Tracy ties up his 5-year-old sister Rebecca in a game of drug dealer. He is playing the arresting officer, his sister the arrested dealer. Luckey, 9, is a witness for the arresting officer. Tracy says that across the street from their play area is a real drug house.

And the mother—now serving 3 to 15 years in a Cleveland prison for burglary—tells Lucas County Juvenile Judge James Ray in a recent letter that two men once physically abused her son in her apartment building.

"I was there," she writes, "but I was so drunk I didn't hear my son's screams."

There may be problem kids on Tecumseh Street, but often the problem is the parents.

"It's terrible," Judge Ray says. "Actually, I'm amazed at the number of kids who survive those situations."

The Aftermath ▶

Predictably, there was an angry reaction. "Many Tecumseh Street residents were furious, believing their street had been unfairly singled out," Roe said. A petition with 180 signatures was sent to *The Blade* demanding that the story be redone and that Roe be banned from any future stories about the area. The editors refused, and residents responded by planning a march on the newspaper.

"They enlisted a civil rights leader to help. But he was acquainted with my previous work. In fact, his group had given me an award several months earlier for a series on police corruption. He urged the residents to attack the problem, not the messenger." They did.

They met with the mayor, city manager, police chief. And soon after, the police stepped up patrols, the city cleaned alleys and fixed street lamps. City officials vowed to fight drug dealers and gang members, and residents extended their Block Watch program.

Unmarried—with Children ▶

In 1960, one of 20 children born in Toledo was illegitimate, born out of wedlock. Today, that figure is almost one of two, nearly twice the national rate. The figures suggested a story to Roe, who had learned of the one-of-two figure while doing research for his series on Tecumseh Street. He already knew the high price in poverty that children and women pay in single-parent families. But when he began his research for his new series he was surprised to find an assumption challenged. "I discovered that the fastest growth of out-of-wedlock births in the United States in the last 10 years was women aged 25 to 34. Teenage mothers have been blamed for the rise.

"I decided at this point to break my series into two parts. The first would be an overall discussion of the issue with the focus on the 25–34 age group. The second part would ask: How are the children affected?"

Roe carefully planned his interviewing. To find the mothers, he wanted a representative group that included whites and members of minority groups since his data showed that the rise in out-of-wedlock births had been across the board—whites and minorities. (After the series ran, Roe was the target of complaints that the stories portrayed blacks negatively.) He looked for professional, financially secure women and those whose children are more likely to drop out of school, live in poverty and become involved in crime.

"It's [out-of-wedlock births] among the two or three most important social changes in this country since World War II," he quoted Lisbeth Schorr, a lecturer at Harvard University and an expert on poverty.

He looked for patterns in the growing rate of out-of-wedlock births among women 25 to 34 years old and listed them as:

◀ Causes

- More women are entering the work force and delaying marriage.
- More couples are living together outside marriage.
- Divorce rates have surged.

"More and more women are spending time outside of marriage," Roe quotes a fertility expert at the University of North Carolina. "Therefore, more women are at risk of getting pregnant while single."

In addition, Roe found that there is "less stigma attached to unwed mothers than in previous years, when shotgun weddings were common, pregnant girls slipped out of town to give birth, and children of unwed mothers were 'bastards' or 'illegitimate.'

"'Every time I look into my living room and see all the toy trains on the floor I know he's legitimate,' unwed mother Mary Schoenhofer says of her 3-year-old son."

Roe also quotes Karen Wilcox, who has three children: "There are people who are married and have children but don't love them. As long as I love them, teach them the proper morals, teach them right from wrong, then I don't see why I should be ashamed of anything."

The mother, Roe reports, had her first child in 1981 when she was living with the father; the parents were not married. They married and in 1990 she had another child. "Records show the baby's father was not Ms. Wilcox's husband. The couple divorced in 1990.

"Since then, Ms. Wilcox—who says she does not believe in abortion and occasionally uses birth control—had had another child out of wedlock."

Roe describes the situation of a 33-year-old working woman who became pregnant and decided not to marry the father.

"The only reasons not to have the baby were all selfish reasons," he quotes her as saying.

But her work schedule is arduous and she sees her son so little, she says, that "When I have to work five days in a row, then see him, it's like: Who is this kid?

"He has a hard time understanding I have to go to work. Usually it ends up with him crying when I leave. . . . I get tired of not seeing him, too, but it is something I have to do."

David Zapotosky, *The Blade.*

Single Mom

"The only reasons not to have the baby were all selfish reasons," she told Sam Roe. "So I decided to keep the baby. And I'm not sorry I did."

At first, says Roe, "Mary was hesitant to be interviewed for my series. But I told her that her comments would shed light on the problems single parents face, and she agreed."

Many women, Roe found, have to quit low-paying jobs without health benefits and go on welfare because they cannot afford to pay for medical insurance that would ease the costs of their pregnancies.

"That's how we have lost a lot of girls at McDonald's," Roe quotes one mother as saying. "They quit because they have to make a choice: either welfare and medical insurance or a job and no medical insurance."

◀ The Burger King Ladies

Roe follows with a quote from Ann Desmond, a local hospital nurse, in which she calls these women "the Burger King ladies."

The cost across the United States is $11 billion a year in aid for dependent children. Locally, 16,030 mothers receive assistance, a 41 percent increase over five years.

Roe quotes one young mother as saying women "come out of school having babies and do not stop. They set out to get on welfare and have a bunch of babies and stay home." Then he quotes the county director of human services, who says, "A single woman receives $274 a month for one child, $334 for two, $413 for three, $483 for four. We're talking in the neighborhood of $70 more for each kid. It strikes me as not worth it."

Missing Fathers ▶

The fathers? Roe quotes an unmarried mother as saying, "These guys today don't care if they get a woman pregnant. They think welfare can take care of it." As for collecting child support, some $18 billion in uncollected payments are reported nationally.

Roe tried to track down a man the court found through a blood test to be the father of a 5-year-old girl. He was ordered to pay $60 a week in child support and owes the mother $9,000. Roe went along as police checked his last address. No luck. Roe managed to locate him in Florida and spoke to him on the phone. The father told Roe, "I'm not running or anything. I just haven't been able to pay. I got to be able to live myself. I don't even have a car." He now makes $6 an hour. "How am I supposed to make it on that? They might as well throw me in jail. Or maybe I could go on welfare. Maybe then they would leave me alone."

While some of the women manage work and child rearing, most are dropouts with no special skills who live in poverty. For many, there is no way out—not for them, rarely for their children.

Roe's second piece in the series begins:

In his 15 years, Michael Belcher has seen his father once.

It was six years ago, when Michael was 9. He was with his mother at Chris's Grocery on Cherry Street when she pointed to a man in a checkout line.

"That's your daddy," she said.

"Who?"

"Your daddy."

No way, he thought. His daddy was big and strong and rich. He drove fast cars. Shopped in fancy places. At least that's what he imagined. At least that's what he told his friends.

But this guy? He looked too average. Too human.

Michael left without saying a word. "But I thought about it all day. I wondered why he never came around. Why he didn't want to be with me."

Today, Michael wouldn't know his dad if he walked by. "Damn," he says, "I don't even know his name."

Yet Michael's story is not so unusual. With nearly 1 out of 2 kids in Toledo born out of wedlock, an increasing number of children are growing up knowing little about one of their parents, usually their father.

"There's no point in meeting my dad now," says one 17-year-old girl, a Central Catholic High School honor student. "I've come this far without him."

In this story, Roe asks, "Will today's children be OK?" His answer: "Experts aren't sure.

"Being born out of wedlock is clearly detrimental to children," he quotes one expert. "The question is how detrimental is it?"

Some research, Roe says, finds that children born out of wedlock "are more likely to live in poverty, drop out of school and commit more crimes than kids born to married couples."

They are more likely to die in infancy, have low birth weights, have poor diets, bounce from school to school, suffer abuse. Roe uses Patrice Wilcox and Michael Belcher to personalize the problems of youngsters growing up without a father at home.

Patrice is 10, a polite, thoughtful girl who says she wants to be a doctor. "My mom said I need a male figure in my life, but I don't," Patrice says. "I have her and she'll always love me."

Roe interviewed Michael at the county juvenile hall where he was awaiting a hearing on a charge of carrying a concealed weapon. At 10, he was arrested for aggravated burglary; at 12 he was arrested for the same crime.

Roe ends the series this way:

"I still think about him sometimes," Michael says one night in jail, his head down, his voice soft. "I picture him coming to see me or buying me this or that. I picture him as a good man. I don't picture him bad."

And how does he picture his future?

"I'm going to have two kids. I'm going to be there for my kids. I'm going to give them everything they need.

"They are going to know who their father is, what he is all about. I'm not going to be like my dad."

Investigative reporters frequently use the series for their revelations. Most of their subjects are complicated, and the series allows the reporter to present the material in digestible pieces. Also, after the first article runs, readers or listeners have a chance to call or write with additional information. Many investigations have started small and ended with large-scale exposés because of tips from readers and listeners.

Some series are so complex that their writers have trouble putting the material in focus, an essential step before a lead can be written.

When Donald Barlett and James Steele investigated a new federal tax law that exempted many rich individuals and a number of large corporations, they found they had a huge amount of material. They were able to find seven themes, one for each piece in the series. They then started to write. But as they moved along they had trouble distilling some of the pieces into leads.

Rather than stop their writing, they continued with the series. They would write the leads later.

Their editor, Steve Lovelady, was looking over the third of the articles, soon to appear in *The Philadelphia Inquirer.*

"What does this mean to the average reader?" he asked himself. And he answered—"That you'll never get a break"—unlike the well-connected taxpayers the reporters had uncovered.

Lovelady showed Barlett what he had scribbled on an envelope, and Barlett said, "Forget part three, this is now part one."

Barlett and Steele worked it over, polished it. Here is the lead for the series they came up with:

Imagine, if you will, that you are a tall, bald father of three living in a Northeast Philadelphia row house and selling aluminum siding door-to-door for a living. Imagine that you go to your congressman and ask him to insert a provision in the federal tax code that exempts tall, bald fathers of three from paying taxes on income from door-to-door sales. Imagine further that your congressman cooperates, writes that exemption and inserts it into pending legislation. And that Congress then actually passes it into law. Lots of luck.

Long. Very long. The reader is directly addressed twice in the first few words. But it works. The series had an enormous readership, and the newspaper was swamped with requests for copies. The *Inquirer* distributed 50,000 copies.

Quality Counts, Not Length ▶

The long story and the series have been on the defensive in recent years. As advertising revenue declined and newspaper readership stagnated despite population growth, publishers cast about to exorcise the devils besetting the business. One of the causes of their problems, they concluded, is long stories, and they ordered shorter, brighter writing and few or no continuations (jumps) from page one to inside pages. Instead of so much print, the readership doctors prescribed more pictures, maps, graphs—in color whenever possible.

The publishers and their hired hands were chasing the wrong culprit. Long stories that are interesting, clear, well-organized and written with vigor are read. The *Inquirer*'s lengthy income tax series was read. Avidly. The *Oregonian* in Portland picked it up from the Knight-Ridder News Service. John Harvey, that paper's news editor, said:

Your series touched off the greatest response of any series I have ever run in the *Oregonian*. Our readers were outraged. Were a certain senator on the ballot this year I doubt he could be reelected. Congratulations on a first-class job of reporting.

The book from the series became a big seller.

Further Reading ▶

Buchwald, Art. *You Can Fool All of the People All the Time*. New York: G.P. Putnam's Sons, 1985.

Halberstam, David. *The Powers That Be*. New York: Alfred A. Knopf, 1979.

Mitchell, Joseph. *McSorley's Wonderful Saloon*. New York: Grosset & Dunlap, 1943.

Moffitt, Donald, ed. *The American Character: Views of America from The Wall Street Journal*. New York: George Brogiller, 1983.

Reaching into the Past for a Feature

Features based on historical material in libraries and letters make for good reading, especially if there are interesting photographs to accompany the article. This photograph of a homestead in Wyoming reveals a lot about the roles of men and women on the frontier. The head of the household is seated comfortably at the center, and around him the women are shown with the tools of their work. One poses with her spinning wheel, and grandma is shown knitting. To the man's left a young woman poses with the butter churn, and to her left a mother fans a child in her lap.

Swanberg, W.A. *Citizen Hearst.* New York: Charles Scribner's Sons, 1961.

Swanberg, W.A. *Pulitzer.* New York: Charles Scribner's Sons, 1967.

Note: Ben Hecht's book of the rough-and-tumble Chicago journalism period, *Gaily, Gaily,* is no longer in print, but copies can be found in libraries. It was published by Doubleday in 1963. Also hard to locate is *The Front Page,* a play about the same period written by Hecht and Charles MacArthur.

9 Broadcast Writing

National Broadcasting Company, Inc.

"Today" anchor and guest.

Preview

Broadcast stories are written to be easily understood. Radio and television writers should:

- Use everyday language.
- Write short sentences.
- Limit every sentence to one idea.
- Use the present tense whenever appropriate.
- Usually confine their stories to one major theme.

In addition to writing local stories, broadcast writers rewrite into broadcast form the stories they obtain from news wires. The material is compressed, sentences are shortened and tenses are changed.

Television journalists must cope with a technology that emphasizes the image. Writing and news judgment often are based on the available pictures.

Broadcast news is written to be read aloud by newscasters and to be heard or seen by listeners or viewers. Stories are written according to rules different from those for print journalism.

Watch the evening news, stopwatch in hand. Most of the *tell* stories on television—brief stories read by an anchor or reporter without tape—run two to five sentences for 10 to 30 seconds. Few broadcast stories run more than two minutes. If all the news on a half-hour newscast were to be printed, it would not fill even two-thirds of a page of a standard-size newspaper.

Broadcast news serves a purpose different from that of the newspaper. Its intent is to provide the public with basic information quickly and succinctly. The broadcast writer's job is to get the story idea across without detail. To communicate events in such short bursts to an audience that cannot read or hear the material again, the broadcast journalist follows a special set of guidelines.

Like the jockey or the weight watcher who thinks twice about every slice of bread, the broadcast journalist examines every word and idea. Too many words and the story may squeeze out another item. Too many ideas and the listener or viewer may be confused. Broadcast newswriters set their writing rhythm to a series of rules: Keep it tight. Write simple sentences. One important idea to a sentence. When attribution is necessary, begin the sentence with it. Every expressed idea must flow logically into the next.

Most of radio's national and international news is rewritten from the news wires. The wire stories are condensed and simplified. On television, most of the brief items—the *tell* stories—are also taken from the wires and rewritten. Let's see how this is done.

◀ **Rewriting the Wires**

News Wire

SAN FRANCISCO (AP)—Leaders of the University of California on Thursday voted to drop race-based admissions following a tumultuous meeting in which Jesse Jackson and other demonstrators drove the panel from its meeting room.

The 14–10 decision by the UC Board of Regents was a major victory for those working to roll back affirmative action programs around the nation, including Republican Gov. Pete Wilson, who has made that fight the key plank of his presidential campaign.

"It means the beginning of the end of racial preferences," said Wilson, who grabbed the national spotlight from his vantage point as president of the regents. "We believe that students at the University of California should achieve distinction without the use of the kind of preferences that have been in place."

Jackson said after the vote, "California casts either a long shadow or a long sunbeam. This is a long shadow. July 20 will live a long time in California history."

Radio Wire

(San Francisco)—The University of California Board of Regents voted tonight to end race-based preferences in school admissions.

The vote came soon after demonstrators interrupted the regents' meeting, singing "We Shall Overcome." The regents were forced to another room to vote on the admissions policy.

Earlier tonight, the regents voted to eliminate the school's affirmative action-based policies concerning the hiring of faculty and contractors.

Mervin Block, a veteran broadcast news writer, rewrote the following wire story for broadcast:

News Wire

DETROIT—City officials imposed a curfew and mobilized more than 35,000 volunteers and nearly 3,500 block clubs in hopes of stifling Detroit's traditional Devil's Night arson spree Tuesday night.

In the past decade, the night before Halloween has become an excuse for firebugs to go on a rampage, torching abandoned houses, parked cars and trash bins. Many fires have spread to occupied homes.

The Idea. "One way to get a grip on a story is to assume it's the biggest story of the day: try to visualize the banner across the front page of the local paper. Which few words would the banner use to summarize the story?"—Mervin Block

This year, Mayor Coleman A. Young and city workers have launched their most aggressive anti-arson campaign. . . .

A 6 p.m.-to-6 a.m. curfew began Monday for unescorted youths under 18. . . .

Here's how Block rewrote it:

Broadcast Version

The eve of Halloween: For many years, Detroit ha; been bedeviled at this time by firebugs. They've set fire to cars, even abandoned houses. Many fires spread to occupied homes. This year, Detroit says it's taking its toughest steps. A curfew has been imposed on unescorted children. And City Hall says it has 35-thousand volunteers to help stop arson.

Block did not move directly into the news. First, he wrote a brief introductory phrase. Then he backed into the lead. In fact, he dug into the fourth paragraph for information before he used the 35,000 volunteers from the wire service lead.

Now, let's watch Block rewrite an AP news wire story into a 20-second tell story for network television news. Here is the wire copy Block had before him:

News Wire

Yorba Linda, Calif (AP)—Construction of the long-delayed Richard M. Nixon presidential library and museum will require the demolition of the home of a 93-year-old widow who doesn't want to move, officials say.

"I love my house. I don't want them to take it from me," said Edith Eichler, who knew Nixon as a boy here and supported him for president.

"Why should I have to move into a more crowded, dinky retirement place away from my family and friends? Do you think Richard Nixon would want his mother to move?"

Yorba Linda, Nixon's birthplace 30 miles southeast of Los Angeles, was chosen for the $25 million library last month after a nine-year search. Years of delays by San Clemente city officials forced Nixon to give up building the library in that coastal community, where he kept the western White House during his presidency.

At a news conference Monday night, city officials said they would appraise Eichler's one-story, wood-frame cottage within a month and make her an offer.

Eichler, a former schoolteacher who has lived in the house for 65 years, will be the only person displaced by the museum.

Eichler said she knew the Nixon family well.

"Richard was a nice enough little boy, always running around like any other kid. Who would believe he would become a president?

"And who would ever imagine they'd want to build this big library for him right in my own back yard?" she asked.

Here is Block's story:

Broadcast Version

They're putting up a library for former President Nixon near Los Angeles, but they say they first have to tear down the home of a 93-year-old widow. She says she loves her home and does not want to move. Officials of the city of Yorba Linda say they'll appraise her wood-frame cottage and make her an offer. The woman says she knew Nixon as a boy and supported him for president.

Here is how Block thought the story through:

> I tell newswriters, "Avoid premature pronouns." Yet I started my script with "they." Why? Although I refrain from starting a story with a pronoun, I know that in conversation we often start tidbits with "they." F'rinstance: "They say onions and garlic are good for you—but not for your companions."
>
> I certainly don't want to start with a yawner: "Officials in Yorba Linda, California . . ." In the first sentence, I want to mention *Nixon, library* and *L.A.,* but I don't see how I can sensibly start with any of them. So I turn to our old friend "they." I make it clear that it's "they" who say the home must be torn down.
>
> I don't use the widow's name because it doesn't mean anything outside Yorba Linda. I defer mentioning the name of the town, because it's not widely known. I save words wherever I can: I don't call it a *presidential* library; what other kind would they put up for a former president? And I'm just as stingy with facts: I don't mention San Clemente, the western White House, the widow's background and other details in the wire copy.

◀ "Newsbreak"

"Newsbreak" runs on the CBS television network several times a day. In less than a minute, several major stories are read. One day, Block compressed seven wire stories into 50 seconds. Here are some items from the script and his explanation of how he wrote them:

Script	Explanation
A former employee of the Westchester Stauffer's Inn, near New York City, was arrested today and charged with setting the fire that killed 26 corporate executives last December.	Rather than start a story with a place name, "In White Plains, New York," I always try to fix the place up high but unobtrusively. In the fourth line, I wrote "outside," then realized that "near" is closer and shorter. I didn't use his name because he was an unknown and his name wouldn't mean anything to anyone outside White Plains, which is largely unknown itself except as the site of a Revolutionary battle.
The government's index of leading economic indicators last month rose slightly, one-point-four percent. The increase reversed three straight months of declines.	To save words, I didn't say the U.S. Department of Commerce issued the statistics. It's sufficient to say "the government." I originally wrote, "rose slightly last month." Then I caught myself, remembering Strunk's rule to "place the emphatic words of a sentence at the end."
A British truck driver admitted today he was the "Yorkshire Ripper," pleading guilty to manslaughter in the deaths of 13 women. By not pleading guilty to **murder,** Peter Sutcliffe could be sent to a hospital for the criminally insane—and not prison.	This is a simple, straight-forward, no-frills account of a dramatic development in a sensational story. But there's no need here for any supercharged language to "sell" the story. (As the architect Ludwig Mies van der Rohe used to say, "Less is more.") My second sentence gives the "why" for his plea. I underlined "murder" because I thought it was a word the anchor should stress. (Some anchors welcome this. In any case, in the pressure-cooker atmosphere of a network newsroom, the stress is usually on the writer.)

Voice-Over
Videotape ▶ Television writing is complicated by the need to write to visuals. Block was told to write a lead-in and 20 seconds of voice-over videotape for the "CBS Evening News" from this wire service story:

CRESTVIEW, Fla. (AP)—Tank cars carrying acetone exploded and burned when a train loaded with hazardous chemicals derailed here today. Thousands were evacuated as the wind spread thick yellow sulfur fumes over rural northwest Florida.

Only one injury was reported. A fisherman trekking through the woods near the wreck inhaled some of the fumes and was hospitalized for observation.

Oskaloosa County Civil Defense director Tom Nichols estimated that 5,000 people had fled homes or campsites in the 30-square-mile evacuation area, which included several villages and about half of Blackwater River State Forest.

"It's a rural area and houses are scattered all through it," said Ray Belcher, a supervisor for the Florida Highway Patrol. "It's about half woods, half farms."

Civil Defense officials put the approximately 9,000 residents of nearby Crestview on alert for possible evacuation as approaching thunderstorms threatened a wind-shift that would push the fumes in that direction. . . .

Block was writing "blind" in the tape. That is, he did not have access to the videotape his copy would refer to. Here is Block's thinking:

First, I see the dateline, Crestview, Fla., and I know that in writing for broadcast I have to put the dateline up near the top in as unintrusive a way as possible. It has to be done deftly.

When I started writing for broadcast, I was told by an editor that it's inadvisable to begin a story by saying, "In Crestview, Florida . . ." The editor told me that was a lazy man's way of starting a story. In London today . . . in Paris today . . . He didn't say never. But in 90 or 95 percent of the cases, it's best not to begin that way.

We see in the first line of the AP story that one of the trains is carrying acetone. My reaction is that most people don't know what acetone is. That probably is a reflection of my ignorance. If we were to use it on the air, it could sound like acid-own. In any case, there's no need to identify the chemical, or any of the chemicals, perhaps. The most important element is the explosion and the evacuation.

In the second paragraph of the story, it says that only one injury was reported. I didn't mention the injury. It seems slight. The third paragraph gives the name of the county. In writing news for broadcast you have to eliminate details and focus on the big picture.

In my script, beginning with the second paragraph, I had to write 20 seconds of voice-over. As so often happens, I had no chance to see the videotape in advance, so I had to write in a general way without getting specific. I made an assumption at this point, and although it's dangerous to assume, I have seen so many derailments on TV films or tape that I figured the opening shot would be of derailed cars. So I presumed my paragraph covering the tape of the accident would be appropriate.

I was looking for facts in the AP story that would be essential in my script. As you can see, my script consists of about a five second lead-in and 20 seconds of voice-over for the tape. Within the tight space, I can use only the most important facts because a script cannot consist of a string of dense facts.

Here is the script as Block wrote it:

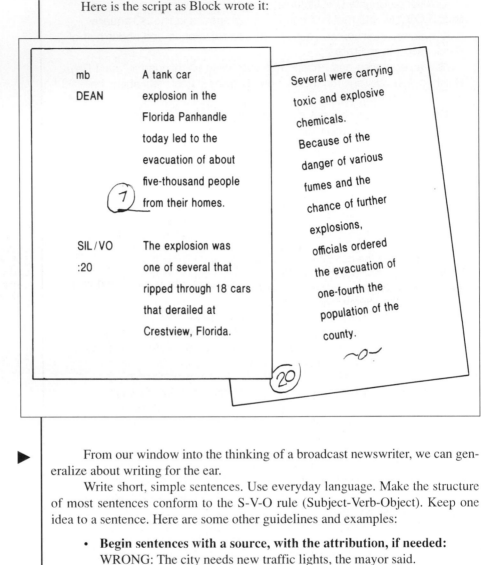

```
mb              A tank car              Several were carrying
DEAN            explosion in the        toxic and explosive
                Florida Panhandle       chemicals.
                today led to the        Because of the
                evacuation of about     danger of various
                five-thousand people    fumes and the
         7      from their homes.       chance of further
                                        explosions,
                                        officials ordered
SIL/VO          The explosion was       the evacuation of
:20             one of several that     one-fourth the
                ripped through 18 cars  population of the
                that derailed at        county.
                Crestview, Florida.
                                                      20
```

Sentence Structure and Language

▶ From our window into the thinking of a broadcast newswriter, we can generalize about writing for the ear.

Write short, simple sentences. Use everyday language. Make the structure of most sentences conform to the S-V-O rule (Subject-Verb-Object). Keep one idea to a sentence. Here are some other guidelines and examples:

- **Begin sentences with a source, with the attribution, if needed:**
  WRONG: The city needs new traffic lights, the mayor said.
  RIGHT: The mayor says the city needs new traffic lights.
- **Avoid starting a story with a participial phrase or a dependent clause:**
  WRONG: Hoping to keep the lid on spiraling prices, the president called today for wage-price guidelines for labor and industry. (Participial phrase.)
  RIGHT: The president is calling for wage-price guidelines to keep prices down.
  WRONG: When the bill was passed, he was absent. (Dependent clause.)
  RIGHT: He was absent when the bill was passed.

- **Use ordinary, one-syllable words whenever possible:**
  WRONG: The unprecedented increase in profits led the Congress to urge the plan's discontinuance.
  RIGHT: The record profits led Congress to urge an end to the plan.
- **Use vigorous verbs.** Avoid adjectives and adverbs:
  WEAK: He made the task easy for his listeners.
  BETTER: He simplified the task for his listeners.
  WEAK: She walked slowly through the mud.
  BETTER: She trudged through the mud.
- **Use the active, not the passive, voice:**
  WEAK: He was shown the document by the lawyer.
  BETTER: The lawyer showed him the document.
- **Use familiar words in familiar combinations.**
- **Write simply, directly.** Omit useless words.
- **Write in language that can be read easily.** The writer should test his or her writing by reading it aloud. Not only will the reading catch sounds that do not work, it will reveal whether a newscaster can read one idea in a single pulse. The newscaster must be able to breathe, and each breath closes out an idea.

Simple, direct writing can be elegant. This is the language of Mark Twain, Charles Dickens, and Edward R. Murrow. Here is a lead by Charles Kuralt, a correspondent for CBS television who was doing a piece about exploitation of the environment:

Men look at hillsides and see board feet of lumber. Men look at valleys and see homesites.

- **Use a phrase to indicate someone is being quoted:** as he said, as he put it, and these are his words. For routine quotes, paraphrase.
  WEAK: He said, "I am not a crook."
  BETTER: He said, and these are his words, "I am not a crook."
- **Place titles before names.** Spell out most numbers. Do not use initials for agencies and organizations unless they are widely known, such as FBI and CIA. Use contractions for informality. Paraphrase quotations unless they are essential or unusual. Keep sentences to fewer than 20 words.

◀ **Tenses**

The anchoring tense for broadcast copy is usually the present or the present perfect tense:

The state highway department **says** it will spend six million dollars this year improving farm-to-market roads.

The state highway department **has announced** it will spend six million dollars this year improving farm-to-market roads.

When the present tense is used in the lead, the story often continues in that tense. When the present perfect tense is used in the lead, the story shifts to the past tense to indicate when the event occurred:

A federal judge **has issued** a temporary order stopping efforts to put a reservist on active army duty because he refused to shave off his beard.

Yesterday, the judge **gave** the army ten days to answer a suit filed by the American Civil Liberties Union for the reservist.

Following the past tense, the story can shift back to the present perfect or even to the present tense if the writer believes the situation is still true or in effect. The AP radio story continues:

The ACLU **filed** the suit on behalf of a high school teacher, John Jones of Bristol, Rhode Island.

The suit **asks** the court to declare unconstitutional a regulation forbidding beards and **claims** the teacher was marked absent from several drills that the suit **says** he attended.

But shifts from the present directly to the past sound silly, as in this piece from the radio wire of one of the press associations:

The New Jersey Taxpayers Association **says** a recent government report shows the state's per capita property taxes are the highest in the nation.

The association **reported yesterday** that only Massachusetts had a higher property tax average than New Jersey.

The writer is better off using present perfect in the lead and then shifting to the past:

The New Jersey Taxpayers Association **has reported** that a recent government . . .

The association **said** yesterday that only Massachusetts . . .

Attribution ▶

Generally, broadcast copy places attribution at the beginning of sentences. This makes for clarity.

News Wire

ALBUQUERQUE (AP)—The death of a man whose body was found set in 500 pounds of concrete in a 55-gallon drum may be connected to a counterfeiting case, a federal agent says.

"I believe there is a connection. We won't be 100 percent certain until we know if the guy is who we think he is," said David Saleeba, special agent in charge of the U.S. Secret Service office in Albuquerque. . . .

Broadcast Wire

(Albuquerque)—A federal agent says the death of a man whose body was found set in 500 pounds of concrete in a 55-gallon drum may be connected to a counterfeiting case. Albuquerque police and federal agents say they believe the body recovered is that of 21-year-old Derek Suchy.

Block conducts broadcast workshops around the country, scrutinizes news scripts and, in his monthly column "WordWatching" in the *RTNDA Communicator,* he examines bloopers, blunders and questionable writing. "Too many of us think we're not only the messengers but also part of the message," he writes. For example:

Carrollton police tell us one person was injured during a car chase overnight.

Sometimes, the broadcast writer will introduce the station into copy, or the media, as this Nebraska news writer did:

It was a full-fledged media event that brought every TV station in the state to northwest Nebraska today.

"The media are not the story," says Block. "The *story* is the story."

In one of his columns, Block culled these sentences from clips. Look at the words in italics:

• The attorney for defendant Henry Watson *dropped a bombshell* in his closing argument.
• City officials and union leaders have been *burning the midnight oil.*
• The workers were *visibly shaken* but not hurt.
• Lopez was sitting with friends on a courtyard bench at the Marlboro Houses in Coney Island when *shots rang out* Sunday.

Yes, you are right. They are clichés, the "language of newspeople churning out copy in a race against the clock," Block says. And he goes on to quote George Orwell's warning to writers: "Never use a metaphor, simile or other figure of speech you are used to seeing in print."

Some events are too complex to plunge into immediately. Or there may be a confusing array of personalities or numbers. The listener then has to be set up for the theme of the piece.

◀ **The Lead**

Newspaper Lead
As Gov. Alfred Caster neared the end of his seven-day working vacation aboard a riverboat today, his aides said that he was unconcerned about some editorial criticism that he had become an absentee governor whose administration was adrift.

Broadcast Lead

Some newspaper editorials have criticized Governor Caster as an absentee governor. But officials aboard a riverboat with the governor say that the criticisms don't bother Governor Caster. He is nearing the end of his seven-day working vacation on the boat.

National Broadcasting Company.

He's Your Choice?

NBC Correspondent Andrea Mitchell interviews delegates to a national party convention.

Broadcast Reporting ▶

Advice from the AP

Sentence Length: Always keep in mind that someone has to read the words you write for broadcast—and has to read them aloud. Very long sentences, especially those with lots of clauses, cause broadcasters to stumble.

If a sentence goes over two lines on your terminal screen, it may be too long. Take another look at it. Read it aloud, slowly. Can you get through it without gasping for air or stumbling?

If you can, then ask yourself if the listener will be able to comprehend all the facts you've presented in that one sentence. Would you convey the information more clearly in two sentences? If so, rewrite.

The Lead: The shorter the better. Don't summarize the day's major development in a long, complex sentence. Instead, provide a short and compelling reason for the listener to keep listening.

Helping the Broadcaster: Read copy one more time to root out typos and awkward phrasings and to provide pronunciation guides, called *pronouncers,* wherever the anchor is going to encounter a strange or difficult name or word.

Let's look at how broadcast reporters work. First, we go to an all-news radio station.

Each evening, the news director makes up an assignment sheet for reporters for the next day. The editor goes through the futures file, notes continuing stories and consults the wire services' schedules of stories. About 6 a.m. reporters begin to check with the editor for their assignments.

In the field, the reporters, who carry tape recorders, may each cover three or four stories—a feature, a running story from city hall, a talk by a congressman and a traffic accident that tied up a major artery. For each, the reporter phones the editor, who decides whether the reporter should go on live or be recorded.

If the reporter is to go on live, the editor places the reporter on a newscast. If recorded, the reporter talks to an aide, who makes sure the material is being recorded properly by an engineer. The recording, called a *cart* (for *cartridge*), is labelled by slug and time and given to the editor.

Radio reporters cannot rely on pictures so they supply much of the descriptive material for their stories. Sound bites from their interviews are essential to give the listener a sense of immediacy and participation. The radio reporter develops a keen ear for the high-quality quote, the quotation that sums up the situation. The rest is ruthlessly discarded.

One of the most important tasks of the broadcast journalist is to ask relevant questions. Good interviews are made by the right questions.

As tape can be edited, the reporter can ask a question again if the answer is too long or complicated.

The television reporter works with a more complex technology than does the radio journalist. The TV reporter is always aware of the need for the picture.

Cover shots (see **Glossary**) may be needed to cover the sound track. If the story is about nutritious breakfasts, a cover shot of people shopping for cereal might be appropriate. Words augment the picture.

Here is how the script of ABC's "World News Tonight" began when a hostage was released in Beirut. See whether you can decipher the left-hand column:

0	LS, David Jacobsen and Terry Waite	Peter Jennings V/O:	This is the picture that David Jacobsen's family has been waiting to see. The former hostage alive and well and on his way home.
8	LS, ABC studio	Announcer:	From ABC, this is World News Tonight with Peter Jennings.
14	CU,	Jennings O/C:	Good Evening. The former hostage, David Jacobsen, once told his family that his job as administrator at the American University Hospital in Beirut was the most satisfying one he'd ever had. He had gone to the Middle East in 1984 for a change of pace, some change. As of yesterday, he'd been a hostage for 17 months. Tonight he's in West Germany and the doctors there say he is in remarkably good condition. Here's ABC's Pierre Salinger:
41	LS, helicopter	V/O:	The first leg of freedom. The
47	LS, helicopter		helicopter from Beirut set
50	CU, Jacobsen		down in Cyprus bringing back David Jacobsen. But it was obvious that release was a bittersweet experience for him.
52	CU Jacobsen	SOT:	"My joy is somewhat diminished by the fact that other captives are still being held in Lebanon."

1'05 CU of Jacobsen on videotape	V/O: It was only a month ago that Jacobsen appeared on this videotape released by his cap- tors criticizing the Reagan Ad- ministration.
1'12	SOT: "Mr President, are you going to make another mistake at the cost of our lives? It seems that you are continuing to make mistakes in our situation."

In case you couldn't figure out the abbreviations: LS, long shot; CU, close-up. Often used, though not here, is ECU, extreme close-up.

Reporting and ▶
Writing to Tape

The feature or timeless piece may include an interview, voice-over silent tape, or tape with sound of an event and the reporter's summarizing the event. The story may take days of planning and hours of shooting, editing and writing, and then when it is finally broadcast it may run for only a minute and a half.

For a story on a new reading program in the city schools, an interview with the superintendent of schools may set out the intent of the curriculum change. Additional interviews will allow viewers to hear the specific plans of teachers. School children will be interviewed. Locations might include classrooms, teachers discussing the program, the superintendent in his office.

The producer will want a variety of shots—medium, close-up and cutaway—to build a picture story to accompany the reporter's narration and interviews.

Stories for newspapers usually follow a straight-line form—most important material at the beginning, least important at the end. But for longer broadcast pieces, the form is a circle because the ending usually has a reminder of the theme.

The reporter's task is to marry natural sound, visuals and interviews. Sometimes the reporter muffs the opportunity. In a piece about a cloistered order of nuns who vow perpetual silence, the reporter wrote a narration with no pauses. He wrote about silence but never stopped talking. In effect, the viewer could not hear the silence. The event would have been captured had he stopped talking in some places, a few seconds at a time, to allow viewers to hear the clatter of knives and forks at a silent dinner, the footsteps of nuns in darkened hallways. The tone of the story should match the event.

Packaging Short ▶
News Features

Let's accompany a television news student, Cathy, as she puts together a news feature. The story is about a program designed to prevent children from committing crimes when they grow up. Cathy has an interview with the psychologist who developed the program. She also has videotaped the children in the program as they talk to the psychologist and play. Cathy has interviewed the children for their reactions to the program.

After her reporting, Cathy has 40 minutes of tape. On her way back to the station Cathy starts blocking out her story:

> I'll tell the editor to start with pictures of the children in a circle for 20 seconds while in my script I'll give some facts about the project.
>
> Then a 20- to 30-second sound bite from the psychologist explaining the "substitute family" technique. As he talks about the substitute parents, the editor will show pictures of the children and parents greeting one another affectionately.
>
> Then I'll write a short transition into the interviews. I think that to get into this section I'll pose the question, "But does the program work?" and have three or four short interviews with the answers.

She'll close with a quote from the psychologist and then her own wrap-up from the scene to answer questions she feels have been left unanswered. She estimates the feature will run from 2:30 to 2:45, just what the producer wants.

Much of what Cathy did was the result of planning. For her interviews, she devised questions that sought to get to the heart of the story quickly. Interviews have to be kept short, to the point. This requires gentle but firm direction by the reporter. Here are some interviewing guidelines:

◀ **Interviewing**

1. Don't ask questions that can be answered yes or no.
2. Don't ask long, involved questions.
3. Don't suggest answers to interviewees.
4. Build on the subject's answers—don't ask questions just because you prepared them. Listen to his or her answers and ask questions about what he or she says.
5. Ask only one question at a time. Don't ask multiple questions.
6. Develop a sense of timing. Cut in if the subject starts to be repetitive or long-winded. Don't cut the subject off just when he or she is about to say something important.
7. Make the subject comfortable before shooting the interview.

   a. Describe the general area your questions will cover, but don't tell the subject exactly what the questions will be. The first, spontaneous response to a question is often the truest.

   b. Explain the setting—which mike the subject should speak into and so on. Tell him or her to look at *you* or other questioners—not the camera—unless he or she is going to show the audience how to do something that requires direct communication between speaker and audience.

   c. Before the interview chat easily to dispel any nervousness. Show an interest in the subject's area so he or she will gain confidence.

   d. Don't act like you know it all. *Prepare,* so you *do* know enough so that your subject feels you understand what he or she says.

   e. Know what you are looking for. Most short news items must be carefully focused because of time limits.
8. Try to stick to one topic.
9. Adjust the tone of the questions to the interviewee's experience. A politician may need to be pushed and asked direct questions.

Field Reporting

Emerald Yeh, who combines reporting with her work as an anchor at KRON-TV in San Francisco, interviews a child-care worker for a story on low salaries paid by child-care centers to their employees in the San Francisco Bay area.

Long Pieces ▶

Most broadcast stories, as we have seen, are short. The better stations give their staff the time to do longer pieces and series. Public broadcasting stations have a commitment to long-form television, as do several commercial stations such as WCCO-TV (Minneapolis), WBRZ-TV (Baton Rouge) and WSMV-TV (Nashville).

WSMV-TV has won many awards for its in-depth pieces. One of its prizewinning series was "A Matter of Taste." It was a penetrating examination of whether Tennessee was losing its natural beauty to development.

"When we started brainstorming about the series, the first location that came to mind was Pigeon Forge," says Don Heider, the writer for the WSMV-TV series. "This community had seen a remarkable amount of development in a short time, primarily due to its strategic location as an entry way to the Smokey Mountains. It was obvious this was a place where there had been unchecked development."

◀ "Visual Chaos"

Heider needed someone to express those concerns, and he thought an artist would see the situation from a visual perspective. He also needed someone who would speak in support of the path the town took to its newfound prosperity. The Pigeon Forge Chamber of Commerce supplied some names. He also found an architect who was with a group pushing for stronger sign laws in the state.

"Key to the success of the piece," says Heider, "was a lot of set-up time on the front end, interviewing a number of people over the phone until I knew I had the right people to tell the story, and also ensuring that we had strong visuals.

"Also essential was good communication between myself and the photojournalist." They discussed ideas before Heider made his first calls, and the discussion continued throughout the planning and shooting. "We were still talking about what the story should say and look like when we edited it."

Here is the beginning of Heider's script:

SLUG ANCHOR	WRITER	WSMV-TV NEWS	STATUS TIME
TACKY #1	HEIDER	MON JUL 25 09:02	READY 4:54

NAT SOUND

SOUNDBITE 4/10:43 LEE ROBERSON/ARTIST [I SUPPOSE MOST PEOPLE WHO LIVE HERE KIND OF TAKE IT FOR GRANTED BUT I NEVER REALLY HAVE. I'M HERE BY CHOICE. I LIVE ADJACENT TO THE SMOKY MOUNTAINS NATIONAL PARK AND THAT'S BECAUSE I WANTED TO, IT'S **JUST NOT** SOMETHING THAT HAPPENED.]

NESTLED AWAY IN A SMALL COVE NEXT TO THE SMOKIES LIVES LEE ROBERSON.

SOUNDBITE 4/11:53 LEE [THESE MOUNTAINS ARE LIVEABLE AND THEY'RE HOSPITABLE AND THEY'RE COMFORTABLE, THEY KIND OF WELCOME YOU.]

LEE IS AN ARTIST. HE DRAWS HIS INSPIRATION FROM THIS LAND WHERE HE WAS RAISED.

SOUNDBITE 4/12:24 LEE [MY GRANDPARENTS LIVED IN CADE'S COVE.]

WHERE LEE LIVES, IT'S PEACEFUL . . . QUIET . . . RESTFUL.

BUT JUST A FEW MILES AWAY, THINGS ARE DIFFERENT.

NAT SOUND—PIGEON FORGE

SOUNDBITE 2/13:34 LEON DOWNEY/PIGEON FORGE [IT IS A BOOM TOWN, SURE, AND IT HAS BEEN A BOOM TOWN FOR THE PAST SEVERAL YEARS.]

IT'S TENNESSEE'S NEWEST MECCA FOR TOURISM. PIGEON FORGE.

NAT SOUND

PIGEON FORGE IS A PUTT-PUTT PARADISE. A GO-CART KINGDOM. A UTOPIA FOR ANYONE UNDER THE AGE OF 15.

SOUNDBITE 2/17:27 DOWNEY [WHEN A FAMILY COMES IN HERE WITH A CARLOAD OF CHILDREN, WITH ONE OR TWO CHILDREN OR WHATEVER, THEIR HEADS ARE ON A SWIVEL AS SOON AS THEY GET HERE. THEY JUST CAN'T BELIEVE ALL THE FUN THINGS THERE ARE TO DO IN PIGEON FORGE. IT'S SORTA LIKE MYRTLE BEACH IN THE MOUNTAINS.]

THIS IS A COMMUNITY DESIGNED AROUND THE NEEDS AND WANTS OF CHILDREN. CHILDREN WHO CAN TALK THEIR PARENTS INTO SPENDING MONEY.

PIGEON FORGE WAS A GROWING TOURIST TOWN UNTIL 1986. THAT WAS THE YEAR DOLLY PARTON CAME BACK TO EAST TENNESSEE. SHE CONVERTED AN OLD AMUSEMENT PARK INTO DOLLYWOOD. THE PARK AND THE TOWN TOOK OFF.

NAT SOUND

IN JUST A YEAR DOLLYWOOD DOUBLED ITS ATTENDANCE. IN 1987, THE YEAR AFTER DOLLYWOOD OPENED, COMMERCIAL CONSTRUCTION IN PIGEON FORGE QUADRUPLED.

PIGEON FORGE ISN'T JUST A TOURIST TOWN NOW. IT'S A PHENOMENON. DEVELOPMENT HAS BEEN GOOD FOR BUSINESS. BUT DEVELOPMENT ALSO THREATENS SOMETHING HERE.

SOUNDBITE 4/17:04 ROBERSON [WHILE THERE'S NOTHING WRONG WITH PROVIDING ACCOMMODATIONS AND ENTERTAINMENT AND THE VARIOUS THINGS PEOPLE ARE LOOKING FOR I GUESS WHAT WE'RE A LITTLE CONCERNED ABOUT IS THAT WE MIGHT LOSE SIGHT OF WHY THEY COME HERE. NOW IF WE ALLOW WHY THEY CAME HERE AND COME HERE TO BE DESTROYED, WE ALL LOSE.]

PIGEON FORGE GOT ITS START AS THE GATEWAY TO THE SMOKIES. A STOPOVER POINT AS YOU ENTERED ONE OF THE SOUTH'S MOST SPECTACULAR NATURAL WONDERS.

BUT NOW AS YOU DRIVE THROUGH PIGEON FORGE YOU CAN BARELY SEE THE SMOKIES. THE VIEW IS BLOCKED BY SIGN AFTER SIGN.

SOUNDBITE BURR/5:14 EUGENE BURR/ARCHITECT-PLANNER [IT'S ESSENTIALLY A VISUAL CHAOS.]

EUGENE BURR IS A KNOXVILLE ARCHITECT AND PLANNER WHO HAS ALSO NOTICED SOME OF PIGEON FORGE'S GROWTH PROBLEMS.

SOUNDBITE BURR/2:56 BURR [YOU DON'T HAVE A SENSE OF CITY WHEN YOU ENTER PIGEON FORGE, THERE'S THIS WALL OF GARISH ADVERTISING WHERE EACH BUSINESS IS TRYING TO COMPETE WITH THE NEXT.]

BURR BELIEVES IF THE CITY DOESN'T TAKE STEPS TO IMPROVE ITSELF, ITS GROWTH MAY NOT LAST LONG.

More and more stations and the networks are blending the day's headlines with features and theme stories. Some of this shift has been toward more coverage of entertainers, but a significant amount has been toward substantive topics such as poverty, the homeless and problems of race and class.

◀ **Shifting Emphasis**

"The CBS Evening News" began one of its depth pieces this way:

RATHER: In the streets of America, those domestic priorities include what to do about the plague of violent crime by the young against the young. Dallas today became the latest city to turn to one increasingly popular and controversial solution. Scott Pelley has a report.

SCOTT PELLEY: Each night the body count grows—American teenagers victims of gangs, drugs and violence. It is a deadly trend that is prompting a growing number of cities to impose curfews on youth.

AL LIPSCOMB (Dallas city councilman): The figures are astoundin' on young people—the killin', the maimin'.

PELLEY: Dallas City Councilman Al Lipscomb is sponsoring a curfew measure.

LIPSCOMB: Since we cannot have any type of a curfew on parents, who cannot control their youth, we have to do the next best thing.

PELLEY: The proposal says kids under 17 must be home by 11, unless they work. Parents could be fined. Businesses who let kids in after the curfew face fines up to $2,000.

SARAH SLOBEN (dance-club manager): It's—it's solving a problem with a chain saw that needs to be dealt with with a scalpel.

PELLEY: Sarah Sloben manages a dance club for teenagers.

SLOBEN: It's an infringement of the rights of teenagers. It's an unnecessary burden on business owners, and it's gonna tie up the police. The police are not baby-sitters. They're policemen.

Copy Preparation ▶

Copy is written to give the newscaster as much help as possible. The rules for copy preparation differ from station to station. Some require the slug in the upper left-hand corner and the time the story takes to run above it.

Copy for television is written on the right half of the page. The left half is kept open for technical instructions. Some stations also ask that radio copy be written this way, but most radio copy is written across the page.

A line of 45 to 50 characters will take four seconds to read. By keeping lines to the same length, it is easy to estimate the time it will take to read the story without the use of a stopwatch.

End each page with a full sentence. Better still: End on a paragraph. Do not leave the newscaster hanging in the middle of a sentence or an idea as he or she turns the page. Keep paragraphs short.

Each page should be slugged. For pieces running more than one page, each page should be numbered, and the writer's name or initials should appear on all pages.

Place the word *more,* circled, at the bottom of stories of more than one page, and use a clear, large end mark—30, #, END—when finished.

Some stations require copy to be written in capital letters for easier reading, although studies have shown that all-capital text is more difficult to read than is cap and lower case text. For television, visual directions should be written in all caps.

**Telling the
Whole Story** ▶

Little of what goes through the broadcast station's editing rooms reaches the public. Interviews are ruthlessly cut as editors search for the telling 20-second sound bite. Background material, if any, is compressed. Sometimes, the meaningful shades of gray that make the story truthful don't make the broadcast, especially when they complicate the theme or story line.

A.M. Rosenthal, former executive editor of *The New York Times* and now a columnist for the newspaper, describes his reaction to a segment on the show "60 Minutes" in which the Cuban ballerina Alicia Alonso explains how she protested the brutality of the dictator Batista by refusing to dance for several years. When Fidel Castro came to power, she was placed in charge of the national ballet company.

"Not one word," comments Rosenthal, about how she feels about Castro's "imprisonment of poets, painters and writers. An unquestioning plug for Mr. Castro and a rewriting of history by omission."

Rosenthal asked Morley Safer, who did the segment, about this omission. "He told me that he did indeed ask the ballerina about Castro tyrannies," Rosenthal writes. "But she was wordy and polemical so he thought he would cut that part. It made for a better show, he said. A judgment call, he said."

People in public life have long considered broadcast news a more direct route to the citizen and a more congenial medium than print. Franklin D. Roosevelt was famous for his radio fireside chats in which he soothed a country mired in a deep depression. Dwight D. Eisenhower initiated the televised presidential news conference to reach the public directly, without the interpretations and possible criticism of the print press. Eisenhower used television, historian Stephen Ambrose wrote, to "set the national agenda" and also to "obfuscate an issue when he was not sure how he would deal with it."

A Dozen Deadly Sins

Thou shalt not:

1. Scare listeners.
2. Give orders.
3. Start a story with:
   - "as expected."
   - "in a surprise move."
   - "a new development today."
   - "our top story tonight is."
   - *there is* or *it is*.
   - a participial phrase.
   - a personal pronoun.
   - a question.
   - a quotation.
   - an unknown or unfamiliar name.
   - someone's "making news" or "making history,"
   - *another, more* or *once again*.
4. Characterize news as "good" or "bad."
5. Use any form of *to be* as the main verb in your lead.
6. Bury the verb in a noun.
7. Use *yesterday* or *continues* in your first sentence.
8. Use *no, not* and negatives in your first sentence.
9. Use newspaper style, language or rituals.
10. Cram too much information into a story.
11. Lose or mislead a listener.
12. Make a factual error.

Adapted from Block, Mervin. *Writing Broadcast News—Shorter, Sharper, Stronger* (Chicago: Bonus Books, 1987).

A Conveyor Belt for Politicians ▶

Mario Cuomo of New York, when governor, told newspaper reporters, "Don't flatter yourselves into thinking you're the best way to reach the public.

"When I go to you, I don't reach the public directly; you do. When I go electronically, I reach the public. If I want to reach the public, I shouldn't be talking to you. I should be talking to a radio microphone."

Critics have accused broadcast journalists of allowing office holders and candidates to pass on to the public what one disparagingly described as "sound bites that were simply advertising."

Broadcast journalists are aware of their being used as the conveyors of messages, and some are as careful of their being exploited as are print journalists.

But many stations allow themselves to become conveyor belts for politicians. A study by the *Washington Journalism Review* of 26 stations found that 22 of them used video press releases sent by their representatives in Congress without stating that the materials were press handouts, not news handled by the station's news people.

Ethical Imperatives ▶

The Power of TV. In 1958, Edward Murrow said, "This instrument can teach, it can illuminate, yes, and it can even inspire. But, it can only do so to the extent that humans are determined to use it to those ends. Otherwise it is merely wires and lights in a box. There is a great and perhaps decisive battle to be fought against ignorance, intolerance and indifference. This weapon of television can be useful."

Today, the U.S. is the only Western nation without a network newscast in the prime-time evening hours.

Although in Somalia famine, disease and warring factions were taking a huge toll, especially of children, television was slow to cover the story of still another African nation in trouble.

The consequence, said several aid group officials, was that the international community was slow to act. A volunteer in Somalia told Dr. Bob Arnot, the CBS News medical reporter, that half of the doomed children might have been saved had aid arrived a year earlier.

The cameras finally did arrive. But it was too late for as many as a third of the nation's 4.5 to 6 million people.

"It is unfortunate," said Sen. Nancy Landon Kassebaum of Kansas, "it takes these pictures to really bring it home."

What delayed the coverage? Television writer Walter Goodman of *The New York Times* says, "It is difficult to imagine a million or more white children dying in some part of the world without attracting troops of American reporters and more television pictures, no matter how difficult or dangerous the job. . . .

"Two dead children in Bosnia made a bigger story on one television evening than scores of thousands of dead and dying in the eastern Horn of Africa did for weeks; in Bosnia, a camera was on the scene."

Comments: Pluses And a Few Minuses ▶

Dan Rather, anchor, "CBS Evening News": The feel-good alleged news correspondents, the good-news pretenders are a dime a dozen and on every station. They're everywhere now. . . . One of the reasons, Dear Listener, is that not enough of you care, nor of us, those of us still in the craft, in the profession of what is supposed to be the public service of broadcast news.

Joan Barrett, KVUE-TV, Austin, Tex.: One of the first questions we ask at our morning meeting is, "What are people talking about today?" And then it's, "What do people need to know? What should they know. What do they want to know?" You know, producers play a key role in our shop. Yet we don't get many students who say "I want to be a producer." But they're the ones shaping the decisions in the newscasts for the most part.

Tom Bettag, executive producer, "Nightline": I like to think of Nightline as a broadcast that attempts to illuminate the major issues of our time. At 11:35 at night, people want to go to sleep. They turn on Nightline to find out if there's something they need to know, if there's something people are going to be talking about in the morning. They aren't interested in being entertained. Nightline has its largest audiences when there is real news.

Kirk Winkler, KTVK-TV, Phoenix, Ariz.: The most important problem (among journalism students) is a simple lack of curiosity. One in ten students now graduating has enough of it to make it as a successful reporter. Also: They do not know how to report on deadline and some don't know what a city directory is and don't read a daily newspaper.

Walter Cronkite, "CBS Evening News" anchor and managing editor for 19 years: Some anchorpersons are inadequately educated and poorly trained. Their only qualifications seem to be pretty clothes and stylish hairdos—and this applies to both sexes. Too many are interested in becoming stars rather than journalists. They aren't interested in news except as it resembles show business. However, a talented generation of young people is coming out of journalism schools with the hearts and guts—and educational background—to be called journalists.

© Capital Cities/ABC, Inc.

Tom Bettag

Preparation: Examine notes and all material for the broadcast to determine the key material. Highlight it. Know the time allotted for the segment you are writing. Decide on the lead.

Writing: Begin with the best. Make it short, to the point, interesting. Use S-V-O construction, present tense, familiar words and phrases.

Last-minute check: Read what you have written. If you sound too formal, stumble on a word or run out of breath, then rewrite.

◀ **Summing Up**

◀ **Further Reading**

Arlen, Michael J. *The Camera Age: Essays on Television.* New York: Farrar, Straus & Giroux, 1981.

Block, Mervin. *Writing Broadcast News—Shorter, Sharper, Stronger.* Chicago: Bonus Books, 1987.

Block, Mervin. *Rewriting Network News: WorldWatching Tips from 345 TV and Radio Scripts.* Chicago: Bonus Books, 1990.

Block, Mervin. *Broadcast Newswriting: The RTNDA Reference Guide.* Chicago: Bonus Books, 1994.

Ellerbee, Linda. *And So It Goes: Adventures in Television.* New York: G.P. Putnam's Sons, 1986.

Hewitt, Don. *Minute by Minute.* New York: Random House, 1985. (Hewitt is the executive producer of "60 Minutes.")

Kimball, Penn. *Downsizing the News: Network Cutbacks in the Nation's Capital.* Washington: Woodrow Wilson Center Press; Baltimore: Johns Hopkins University Press, 1994.

Persico, Joseph E. *Edward R. Murrow: An American Original.* New York: McGraw-Hill, 1988.

Smith, Sally Bedell. *In All His Glory: The Life of William S. Paley, the*

Legendary Tycoon and His Brilliant Circle. New York: Simon & Schuster, 1990.

Sperber, Ann M. *Murrow: His Life and Times*. New York: Freundlich Books, 1986.

Note: For an insight into the decline of network news see:

Boyer, Peter J. *Who Killed CBS?* New York: Random House, 1988.

Frank, Reuven. *Out of Thin Air: The Brief, Wonderful Life of Network News*. New York: Simon & Schuster, 1991.

Joyce, Ed. *Prime Times, Bad Times*. New York: Doubleday, 1988.

PART FOUR: Reporting Principles

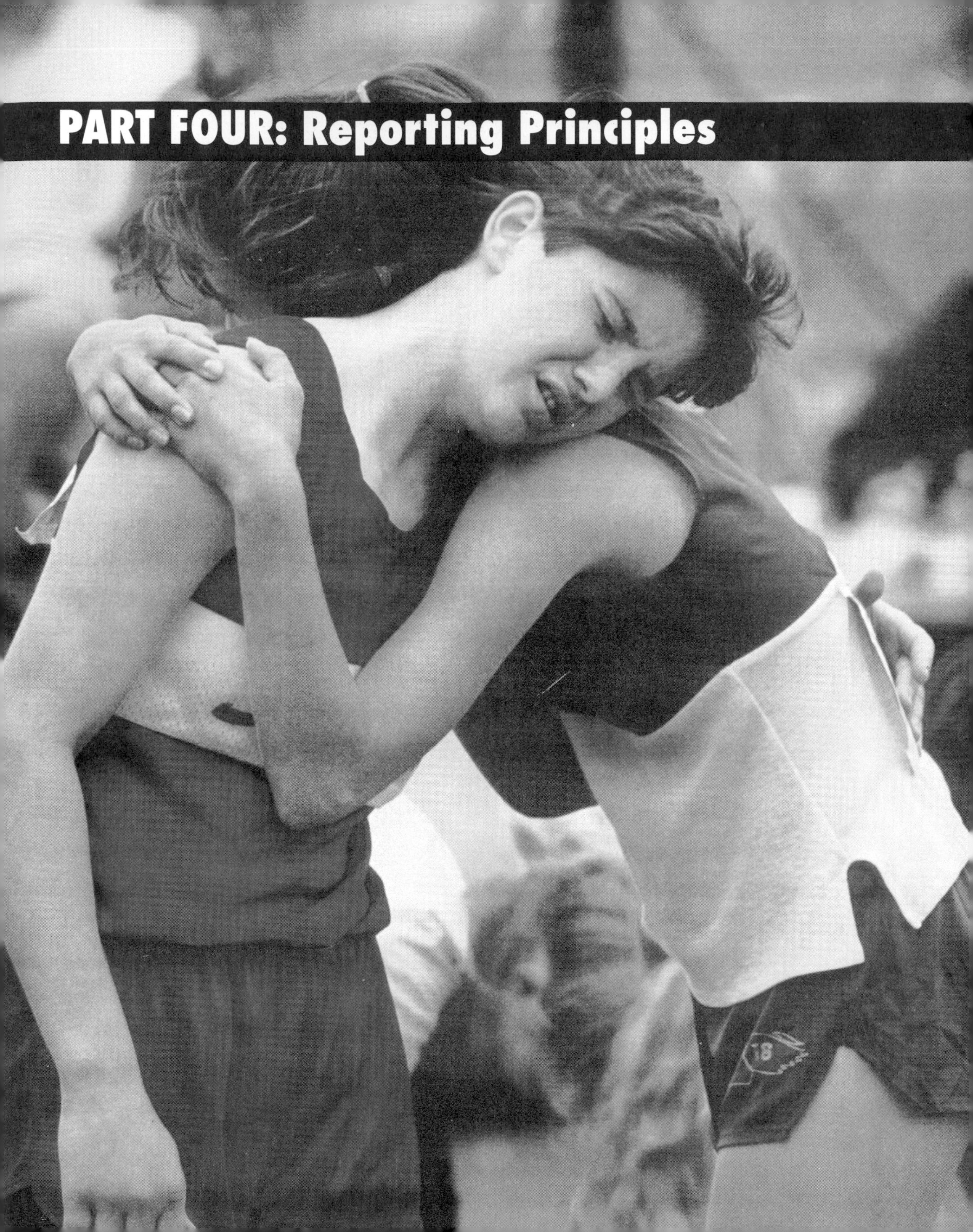

10 Digging for Information

Preview

The reporter's job is to gather information that helps people understand events that affect them. This digging takes the reporter through the three layers of reporting:

1. **Surface facts:** press releases, handouts, speeches.
2. **Reportorial enterprise:** verification, investigative reporting, coverage of spontaneous events, background.
3. **Interpretation and analysis:** significance, causes, consequences.

The reporter always tries to observe events directly rather than rely on sources, who sometimes seek to manipulate the press. One common tactic of sources is the media event, an action staged to attract media attention.

Verification, background checking, direct observation and enterprise reporting amplify and sometimes correct source-originated material.

Reporters are allowed to interpret events when appropriate.

Jeff McAdory,
The Commercial Appeal

Good journalism cuts across all the lines.

The reporter is like the prospector digging and drilling the way to pay dirt. Neither is happy with the surface material, though sometimes impenetrable barriers or lack of time interfere with the search, and it is necessary to stop digging and to make do with what has been turned up. When possible, the reporter keeps digging until he or she gets to the bottom of things, until the journalistic equivalent of the mother lode—the truth of the event—is unearthed.

The reporter, like the prospector, has a feel for the terrain. This sensitivity—the reporter's street smarts or nose for news—helps unearth information for stories. Equally helpful is the reporter's general knowledge.

Let's watch a reporter for a Florida newspaper do some digging.

The word from Tallahassee was that the single winning ticket in the $5 million Florida lottery had been sold in Port St. Lucie. Sarah Jay, a reporter for *The Port St. Lucie News*, had heard rumors about the winner—that someone in a meat market knew the winner's name; that the winner could be found by talking to someone in the Roma Bakery. Jay tried the market. No luck. She fared better at the bakery, where a woman told Jay that her niece was the winner.

◀ **Finding the Winner**

Jim Urick, *The Port St. Lucie News.*

Going to the Source for a Player's Perspective

Sarah Jay of *The Port St. Lucie News* asks a lottery player how she selects winning numbers. Jay was able to track down a local winner of $5 million despite a number of obstacles—an unlisted telephone number and tips that led to dead ends. By using tax records, Jay found the winner's home in a housing development.

She gave Jay the woman's name—Pat Lino—but no phone number or address. Jay checked the telephone company—the number was unlisted. But she did find some Linos in the directory and called, thinking she might reach a relative.

"One guy was totally unrelated," Jay says. "Another was the winner's brother-in-law, and although he wouldn't give me her phone number he did mention that she lives in St. Lucie West, a new housing development."

Knowing that property tax records that list addresses are available, Jay checked the files for Pat Lino. She found the address and drove to the location, only to find no one there.

"It was all locked up. It looked as though I'd hit a dead end, but just to be sure I talked to a neighbor. He didn't know them, he said. Nor did another. But then I tried one more neighbor, and she knew Pat Lino. She had Pat Lino's daughter's phone number."

The neighbor called and Pat Lino was there. But she said she didn't want to be interviewed. "I told the neighbor that I only wanted to speak with her for a minute, that I'd been looking for her all day," Jay said. Lino gave in.

"In this small bedroom community, the naming of a $5 million lottery winner was the talk of the town. And we had it first."

As reporters go about their work of digging up information, they are guided by an understanding of the nature of reporting: Reporting is the process of gathering facts—through observation, reasoning and verification—that when assembled in a story give the reader, viewer or listener a good idea of what happened.

The reporter's job is to look beneath the surface for the underlying reality. Lincoln Steffens, the great journalist of the muckraking period, said the reporter's task is "the letting in of light and air." Reporters base their work on the same conviction that guided Steffens. Their job is to seek out relevant truths for people who cannot witness or comprehend the events that affect them.

Layer I reporting is the careful and accurate transcription of source-originated material—the record, the speech, the news conference. Its strengths and its limitations are those of objective journalism.

◀ **Layer I Reporting**

Layer I is the source for the facts used in most news stories. Information is mined from material that originates with and is controlled by the source. Fact gathering at this level of journalism may involve going to the mayor's office to pick up a transcript of the speech he is to deliver this evening or it may involve calling the mortuary holding the body of the child who drowned last night. The stories based on these facts rely almost wholly on information the source has supplied.

Fact gathering at Layer I is the journalistic equivalent of open pit mining. The reporter sinks no shafts into the event but is content to use the surface material, some of which is presented by public relations and information specialists. Much of the reporter's task is confined to sorting out and rearranging the delivered facts, verifying addresses and dates and checking the spelling of names. Most stories appearing in newspapers and on radio and television are based on source-originated material.

Despite criticism of it, Layer I reporting serves an essential function. At its most basic level, it gives the community information about the happenings in town. The local newspaper will publish photos of dogs awaiting adoption at the County Animal Shelter and tell parents that the school lunch on Monday will be hot dogs, junior salad bar, veggie dippers and fruit salad. Tuesday, meatball sandwich, salad, buttery corn and raisins. . . .

The newspaper also will provide an hour-by-hour police incident report:

> 1:03 a.m.: A loud party was reported on Lincoln Street. On request, the responsibles agreed to quiet down.
> 2:24 a.m.: William Young of 42 Broadway was arrested for driving under the influence of alcohol. He was booked in the county jail. . . .

The News Story and Its Layers of Truth

Layer I—Handouts, press conferences, speeches, statements.

Layer II—Reportorial enterprise, verifying material, background, reporter's observations, spontaneous events.

Layer III—Significance, impact, causes, consequences, analysis, interpretation.

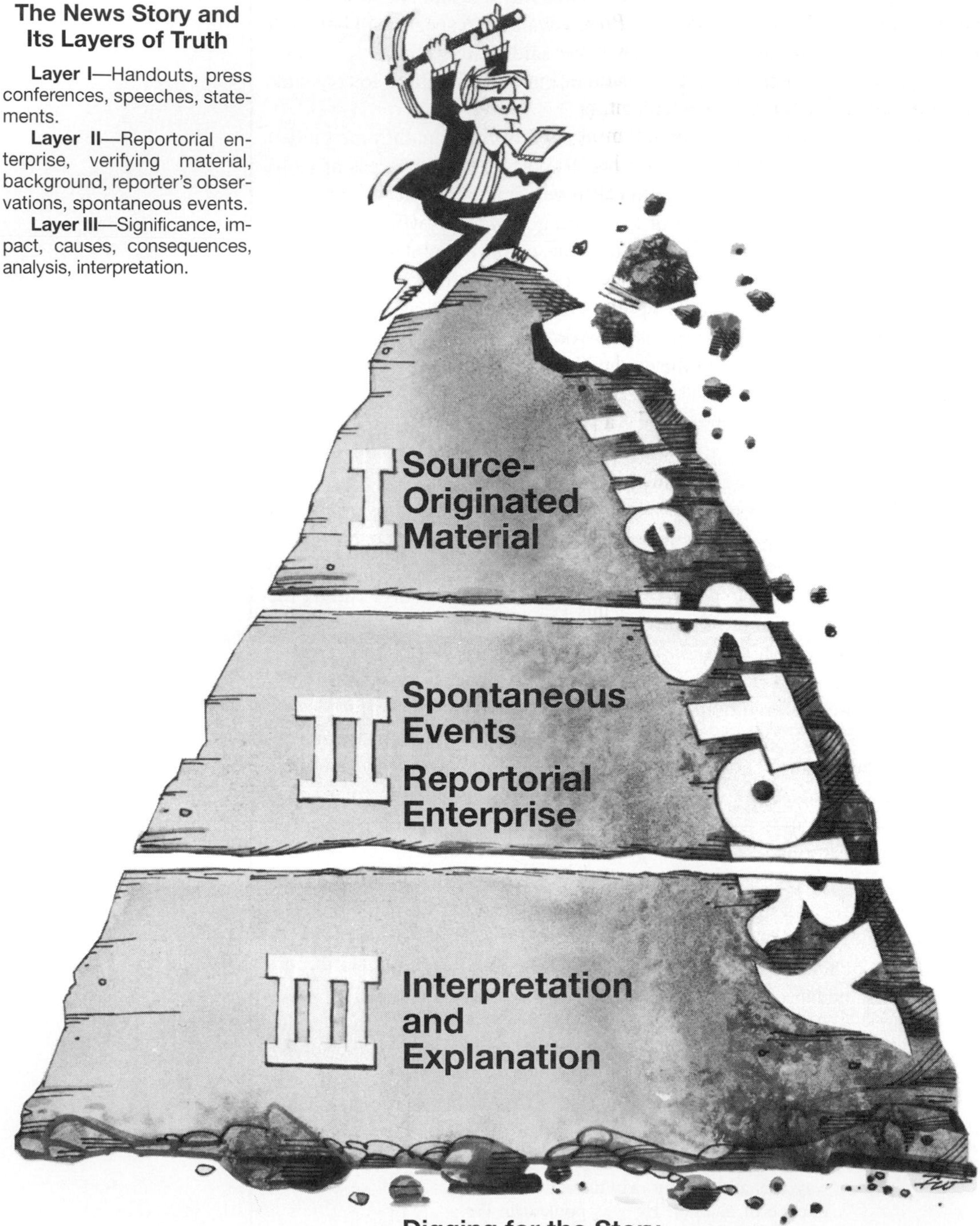

I Source-Originated Material

II Spontaneous Events

Reportorial Enterprise

III Interpretation and Explanation

The Story

Digging for the Story

Good reporters can show initiative in Layer I reporting, as did Jere Downs who covers Montgomery County for *The Philadelphia Inquirer.* She had heard that the Sacred Heart Hospital in Norristown was about to close its doors. But when? Downs says she "crept into the hospital and went to the boardroom." She had been told that the closing was imminent, perhaps that day. Yes, she learned, the board members were being told of the immediate closure.

This was big news. The hospital was the borough's fourth-largest employer with 870 full- and part-time employees, and almost 100 patients would have to be transferred.

Downs had a few hours to make the morning newspaper with her story.

First, she talked to board members. Then she interviewed employees "who had just learned that this shift would be their last. I knew many people who worked at the hospital and called them from a nearby pay phone for quotes.

"My best break came through a retired policeman who was working as a security guard at the hospital. He told me that 85-year-old Jimmy Caiola, who helped found the hospital in the 1930s, was a patient on the fifth floor.

"I knew Jimmy and called up to his room about 9:30, just in time to put the finishing touch on the story that I then dictated over the phone."

Downs' story made page one. An *Inquirer* editor called her work the "finest deadline reporting" in years. The story begins:

The financially troubled Sacred Heart Hospital in Norristown abruptly announced last night that it will shut down today, transferring 97 patients and laying off 870 full- and part-time employees.

Hospital president J. Russell Walsh made the announcement shortly after 9 p.m., following a vote to close by the board of directors.

"Despite aggressive cost-saving measures and months of extensive review of operating alternatives," Walsh said, "resources will not be available to sustain the services necessary to guarantee quality care for our patients, and we must take the necessary steps to not place them in jeopardy." He said the hospital had an operating deficit of $2.2 million for the first quarter of this year. In recent years, he said, the hospital had instituted layoffs and significant cost-cutting measures.

The 270-bed nonprofit hospital and rehabilitation center, at DeKalb and Fornance Streets, was founded in 1936 by the Missionary Sisters of the Most Sacred Heart, a Catholic order based in Reading, Pa.

Hospital officials said the transfers and discharges of patients would begin this morning and were expected to be completed by the end of the day. They said nurses were visiting patients last night, informing them of what was in store this morning.

Stories like those of reporters Jay and Downs inform their communities, tell people what's happening to whom. Such coverage is essential, especially in the area of public affairs. The public must have access to the statements and activities of its officials, and these officials must have access to the people so they know what's on the mind of the public. This give and take makes responsive, consensual government possible.

◀ A Hospital Closes

But this arrangement breaks down when Layer I material is passed off as truth, when reporters do not make clear that much of it is material that sources have been disposed to disclose.

Manipulation and Acceptance ▶

News organizations, as well as sources, have thrived under the arrangement implicit in Layer I journalism. Material for news can be obtained quickly and inexpensively by relying on source-originated information. This relaying of unverified material was particularly significant in the coverage of closed societies such as the Soviet Union and China.

© Mark Avery.

Avoiding Propaganda

To find out about the suppressed democratic movement in China, Jan Wong of *The Globe and Mail* of Toronto interviewed dissenters in public where they could not be bugged and approaching secret police could be spotted in time for the source to slip away. Wong's reporting led the police to put her under surveillance.

In totalitarian countries, reporters are not allowed to travel or to interview people without permission. The pictures journalists drew of these countries were often exactly the opposite of the grim reality. John K. Fairbank, an esteemed scholar of Chinese history who at one time wrote that the Chinese peasants had found Mao's revolution "a magnificent achievement," admitted later in a University of Arizona meeting of journalists who had covered China in the 1930s and 1940s, "Our reporting was very superficial. As has been pointed out it was mainly through the English language, it was seldom from a village, and I don't recall ever talking to a peasant in the three or four years I was in wartime China."

Steven Mosher, a historian, says in his book *China Misperceived: American Illusions and Chinese Reality* that while journalists were sending back glowing reports of the progress in reducing crime and massive improvement in health, millions were dying of starvation.

Despite considerable coverage of the Soviet Union, its swift collapse came as a shock to newspaper readers and television viewers. They were surprised by the revelations of the ruinous state of the economy and the pervasive hatred of the Communist Party among the people. There was no indication of this in many reporters' accounts of Soviet life. The manipulators of the media had been able to hide the true state of affairs in these repressive societies.

But there is no excuse for accepting Layer I material when verification is possible.

◀ **Pseudo-Events**

As the mass media, particularly television, became the dominant dispensers of experience in American life, sources sought to manipulate reality to accommodate the medium. The information sources realized that press releases and announcements unaccompanied by visual material of events would not merit more than 20 seconds on most newscasts, if that. As a result, sources learned to stage events for the press that resembled spontaneous events (Layer II) but were, in fact, as much under the control of the source as the press release and the prepared speech. These staged events are known as *media events* or *pseudo-events*.

The press could use the stories and pictures of the first female window washer in San Francisco, even if the event had been dreamed up to publicize the availability of rental space in a new office building. By providing the media with an endless stream of events, the managers of staged events enable the 11 p.m. news to be different from the 7 p.m. news and the afternoon newspaper to take the morning news a step further. The flow of contrived events feeds the insatiable news maw, for the public has been conditioned to demand vivid, dramatic news with every newscast and edition. Television stations—creating and responding to the demand—devised news programs with titles such as "Eyewitness News" and "Action News."

Following a presidential State of the Union speech, Russell Baker of *The New York Times* asked one of the president's advisers if the speech "was not mostly a media event, a nonhappening staged because reporters would pretend it was a happening."

PR and the News. In their book *PR: How the Public Relations Industry Writes the News* (New York: William Morrow and Company, 1985), Jeff and Marie Blyskal estimate that 40 to 50 percent of all news stories originate in public relations firms. They conclude that "whole sections of the news are virtually owned by PR."

"It's *all* media event," the adviser replied. "If the media weren't so ready to be used, it would be a very small splash."

Daniel J. Boorstin, the social historian, originated the term *pseudo-event* to describe these synthetic occurrences. He says that a "larger and larger proportion of our experience, of what we read and see and hear, has come to consist of pseudo-events." In the process, he says, "Vivid image came to overshadow pale reality." His book about image making opens with this short dialogue:

> ADMIRING FRIEND: "My, that's a beautiful baby you have there!"
> MOTHER: "Oh, that's nothing—you should see his photograph."

Boorstin says the pseudo-event has these characteristics: "It is not spontaneous, but comes about because someone has planned, planted or incited it. . . . It is planted primarily (but not always exclusively) for the immediate purpose of being reported or reproduced. Therefore, its occurrence is arranged for the convenience of the reporting or reproducing media. . . . Its relation to the underlying relativity of the situation is ambiguous. . . ."

Media Manipulation ▶

The orchestration of events for public consumption is a frequent occurrence in government and politics. Needing public attention and approval, politicians often resort to media manipulation, and they often get away with their contrivances.

Perhaps one of the most dramatic pictures of the civil rights movement in the South in the early 1960s showed a determined Gov. George C. Wallace blocking the entrance to a University of Alabama building, refusing to allow two black students to enroll. For Wallace, a symbol to southerners of resistance to federally imposed desegregation, this was a powerful image. He refused to give way when confronted by federalized National Guard troops with a court order.

Grudgingly, however, in the face of firepower, he stood aside.

The reality was far different: In secret meetings, the Justice Department and Wallace had worked out a scenario that would make President John Kennedy and Wallace look good. Wallace would be allowed to take a stand against desegregating the university but would permit the black students to enroll under The Guard's protection.

Wallace thus was able to make political capital in the South, and Kennedy appeared decisive to people who wanted the country to move faster toward desegregating its educational system.

Another well-plotted scenario developed during the 1972 Republican presidential convention. But this pseudo-event was exposed by enterprising reporters.

Presidential Plotting ▶

Because President Nixon was certain to be renominated, Republicans faced a publicity problem: How could reality—the routine renomination of the president—be made exciting? If there were no drama, how then would the White House press managers keep the public tied to the television screen and how would they be able to provide the raw material from which reporters could fashion their stories?

The GOP's solution was to override reality with a staged event of enormous dimension. The White House wrote a 50-page scenario for the convention, a full script that called for "impromptu remarks" from delegates, "spontaneous" shouts of "Four more years," and allotted—to the minute—screams of enthusiasm. At the moment the president would be renominated, the chairman was instructed to attempt "unsuccessfully" to quell the "spontaneous" cheering.

The script fell into the hands of the press. *The Wall Street Journal,* among others, ran news stories on how the White House had organized the convention for television viewers. As the *Journal's* reporter, Norman C. Miller, put it in his story, the "convention was perhaps the most superorganized ever . . . the delegates' only function during the formal proceedings was to serve as a necessary backdrop for the TV show."

Miller went offstage and tried to dig up the real story—Layer II. He interviewed delegates, watched a pep rally for Republican women and found no one had showed up at the "Poor People's Caucus."

The manipulation of political conventions is matched by the strategies of campaign consultants and media handlers to keep the press from direct access to the candidates. Press handouts and daily telegenic events are common fare for campaigns. In the 1988 and 1992 presidential campaigns, political pros often called the shots in campaign coverage. Some examples:

In 1988, George Bush went to Disneyland where he met U.S. Olympic athletes and some Walt Disney characters. That night, television had colorful pictures. NBC showed Bush talking to the athletes: "You're representing the country of the little guy. No matter what the circumstances of your birth and background, you can go anywhere and do anything."

In another visual, Bush was shown unloading fish at a San Diego cannery. And so it went. Dukakis' media chiefs tried to match these visuals when they realized they were being overwhelmed on the evening television news. The Democrats put Dukakis in an Army tank, but the visual was a flop: It showed the head of a diminutive Dukakis peeping out of the turret.

In the 1992 presidential campaign, the Democrats faced a serious problem: A poll showed that 40 percent of the voters considered Bill Clinton a "wishy-washy" politician who would not "talk straight." They disliked Hillary Clinton even more, describing her as "being in the race for herself, going for power," a wife intent on "running the show."

Clinton had already been battered by talk of an extramarital affair. Something, his advisers agreed during the summer of 1992, would have to be done to keep the campaign from disintegrating.

The result was a 14-page outline of behavior modification and media manipulation. Clinton was to be made into an ordinary guy. Hillary Clinton was to be less aggressive, the couple "warm and cuddly."

The image construction was necessary, Democratic strategists reasoned, because the Republicans were sure to emphasize Bush "family values" and imply the Clintons lacked these values.

But by the time the Republicans "made their move, the program of image-modification drafted by Mr. Clinton's consultants had so changed the Clintons'

In Charge. "We were manipulated. They called all the shots on what we could do or cover. The result was the president had no accountability to the public."—Helen Thomas, UPI White House correspondent on covering the Reagan presidency

public persona that the feared attack failed to wound him at all," *The New York Times* reported. Clinton had become just plain Bill, even "Bubba," as a friendly talk show host described him.

Clinton made the news by playing the saxophone on one of the late-night shows. He turned a sanctimonious assertion that he had tried marijuana as a student but had not inhaled into a joke, making fun of himself. His handlers had found through focus groups that people viewed Clinton sympathetically when he talked about his mother and the alcoholic stepfather who abused his brother and his mother.

On talk shows and in interviews, Clinton presented what his strategists had worked out as "the human side, the real Bill Clinton." As for Hillary Clinton, they made her speak out on family issues.

The results included a *People* cover story, "At Home with the Clinton Family," and a *U.S. News and World Report* story, "The Bill Clinton Nobody Knows."

During Clinton's administration, Hillary Clinton emerged as a powerful spokeswoman for health care reform. Again, pollsters found that some people wanted her less visible, and the White House took notice. But in the 1996 presidential campaign, Hillary Clinton re-emerged, speaking often, traveling widely.

History may have taught the Clintons something. During Franklin Roosevelt's presidency, his wife Eleanor was an outspoken advocate of causes—racial justice, strong unions, international cooperation. The criticism was loud, continuous and sometimes vicious, all to no avail. Mrs. Roosevelt continued to travel widely and to speak out. President Roosevelt supported her. Mrs. Roosevelt remained the most popular woman in the country, and her husband was elected to four terms in the White House.

Trial Balloons ▶

One of the ways government officials manage the media is through the floating of trial balloons. The technique involves letting reporters in on inside information, usually about an appointee or a new program. The material is to be used without attribution. The information is published or used on television, and public reaction is gauged. If the public rejects the idea floated, no one can be blamed as there is no source named. If there is acceptance, the nominee may be named, the program adopted.

Early in his administration, President Clinton floated several nominees before the public. One, a candidate for attorney general, pulled out when negative response developed. The administration also leaked the possibility of freezing cost-of-living increases for Social Security recipients. When the reaction was negative, the administration sent up another balloon—increasing the taxes on Social Security benefits. That met with less opposition.

Dangers of Layer I ▶

When reporting is confined to Layer I, the distinction between journalism and public relations is hard to discern. The consequences for society can be serious, as Joseph Bensman and Robert Lilienfield, sociologists, explain:

> When "public relations" is conducted simultaneously for a vast number of institutions and organizations, the public life of a society becomes so congested with manufactured appearances that it is difficult to recognize any underlying realities.

News Management Tactics

Officials influence the news several ways:

Explanatory briefings: Complex events often require explanations by officials who use the opportunity to present the official point of view. These briefings may be off-the-record, which allows the sources to escape responsibility for the information should it prove one-sided or wrong.

Controlled timing. By holding news conferences close to deadline, sources make it difficult for reporters to verify material.

Feeding favorites: Information is offered on an exclusive basis to certain reporters, usually those at influential newspapers such as *The Washington Post, The New York Times* and *The Wall Street Journal.* The tendency for the newspaper with an exclusive is to play it up.

Security blanket: Embarrassing information can be covered up by labeling it top security even if the material will not imperil security.

Heading off stories: Material with self-serving information is leaked when officials are worried about an unfavorable impending development or story.

As a result, individuals begin to distrust all public facades and retreat into apathy, cynicism, disaffiliation, distrust of media and public institutions. . . . the journalist unwittingly often exposes the workings of the public relations man or information specialist, if he operates within a genuine journalistic attitude.

Tom Wicker of *The New York Times* said that the press—because of its concentration on Layer I—has been weak at picking up new developments before they have become institutionalized, and their sponsors have learned to stage media events to attract attention.

The journalistic corrective requires that reporters make their own observations whenever possible and verify all information when observation is not possible. Properly reported, the story would reveal behind-the-scenes stagecraft. Far from being an unwitting exposé of the public relations person's work as the sociologists put it, the story would be like Miller's, an intentional description of the orchestration.

◀ **Correctives**

Some staged events do produce news—the civil rights demonstrations across the South in the 1960s, picketing by the local teachers' union. And certainly the dozens of news stories that are based on source-originated material—such as the text of the mayor's speech and the details the mortuary supplies about the child's death—are legitimate news. But the reporter must always ask whether Layer I information reflects the truth of the event and whether reportorial enterprise is needed to supply the missing facts and relevant background.

Layer II Reporting ▶

When the event moves beyond the control of its managers, the reporter is taken into Layer II. The transition from Layer I to Layer II can be seen at a news conference. The reading of a statement provides the source-originated material (I). The give-and-take of the question and answer period is spontaneous (II). When the source declines to answer questions, the reporter should understand that he or she is back in Layer I, dealing with material controlled by the source.

The reporter who seeks verification from a second source that the governor will appear at the Lions Club ceremony is moving into Layer II. So is the reporter who, after she is told by the police that the hotel was burglarized at 5:46 a.m., looks up the time of sunrise that day. Her enterprise enables her to write, "The holdup man left the hotel in early morning darkness."

The reporter who writes that the state purchasing agent has awarded to a local dealer a contract for a fleet of automobiles is engaged in Layer I journalism. The investigative reporter who digs into the records to learn that the contract was awarded without bids is working at the second level.

When an official of a city undergoing a recession recommends a city-financed plan that he says will increase employment, the reporter will ask him for precise details, questions that belong mostly in Layer I reporting. Then the reporter will check the data the official has supplied. He will look into the program the official said has been working in another city in the South. This checking moves the reporter into Layer II.

Finally, the reporter will seek comments from other city officials about the feasibility of the proposal and its prospects for adoption. Untold numbers of stories have been written about proposals that went nowhere because they were badly drafted or were introduced or recommended by people with no influence. Local newspapers usually play up a legislator's proposals or intentions, but give no attention to the fact that he is a freshman with no influence, a member of the minority party, or that the committee chairwoman has vowed never to let such legislation move through her committee.

If we look back at the reporters at work in Chapter 1, we can see how often journalists move from Layer I to II:

- The reporter who went on the campus to see the demonstrations for himself rather than accept handouts.
- Much of the work Dick did on his story about the Black Parents Association after receiving the handout from the group was on his initiative.
- The investigative stories by Cammy Wilson, Heidi Evans and Carolyn Tuft were carried out entirely in Layer II.

These reporters moved beyond merely relaying information originated and controlled by a source. Each checked the information, supplied missing facts, explained complicated details. None of these efforts is the activity of a reporter content to gather facts at Layer I.

Jere Downs, whose hospital-closing story we read about in a description of Layer I reporting, also operates in Layer II. As we saw then, her cultivation of sources paid off for her when people helped her with material for her deadline story. This time, a woman called to complain that a constable had been threatening to arrest her for an unpaid $10 parking ticket.

Downs told the woman to call her again if the officer made good on his threat. The constable did, the woman called, and Downs had this story:

◀ The Zealous Constable

◀ The Arrest

He came with a gun and an arrest warrant, and led Cynthia Keichline away in handcuffs while her daughters watched, crying, from the front porch.

Keichline's crime?

A $10 parking ticket in Upper Moreland Township, plus late penalties and court fees.

Keichline, 36, was awakened at 7:30 a.m. Tuesday and answered the door to her Northeast Philadelphia home to find Montgomery County Constable Michael Solow there, accompanied by a Philadelphia police officer.

"I just couldn't believe this was happening," she said in a telephone interview. "Then he ordered me to get dressed. I asked him not to put the cuffs on me."

"I thought my mom did something bad," said Lisa Keichline, 12. "I was afraid she would get hurt."

Solow refused to wait until Keichline's ex-husband could drive from his home about 15 minutes away to care for her daughters, Lisa and Katie, 10.

"We waited almost a half-hour," Solow said yesterday. "How long do we have to wait?"

Keichline had already paid $42 for the ticket and late fees. Solow could have erased the warrant by waiving his $44 fee. But he said arresting Keichline was a matter of principle.

"I'm not looking at it as a parking ticket; I'm looking at it as a warrant," said Solow, 54, of Ambler, who was elected constable two years ago. . . .

This is Layer I reporting, and it is done well. But Downs knew that the situation called for further reporting, some digging into the activities of the constable. She worked on the follow-up for six weeks. People who read about Cynthia Keichline's arrest called Downs with tales of their own experiences.

◀ The Folo

"I followed telephone leads, checked his resumé and education, talked to his ex-wife and former business associates," Downs said. She also looked into the laws affecting the duties of constables.

The result was a long story that began with another incident in the constable's law-enforcement career:

Erica Volz says she remembers seeing a flashing red light behind her and pulling her Ford Escort to the side of Flourtown Road. An unmarked Buick swung in behind her.

A man in a pressed shirt and sharply creased gray trousers strode briskly to her window and told her she was speeding. He asked for her driver's license, registration and phone number.

Volz, who was 18 at the time, assumed the man was a Whitemarsh Township police officer.

"He didn't explain anything," Volz said in an interview, recalling that night in October 1992. "He told me I was too young to be out on a school night, and that I would lose my license for 30 days and receive a $500 fine."

Obtaining Background

For an article on drug addiction, Jere Downs talks to a counselor at the North Philadelphia Drug and Alcohol Rehabilitation Center. Downs originates many of her stories.

Downs found that the constable had been the target of complaints about his activities but that authorities were powerless to act. She wrote that "there is no effective way to discipline constables—elected officials who offer their services to the courts." Her story continued with this background material:

Constables serve, in effect, as independent, unsupervised bounty hunters for local district courts—the lowest level of the judicial system outside the big cities. Those courts, presided over by elected district justices, resolve misdemeanors and small-scale civil disputes and conduct hearings for felonies.

"They [constables] are the last arm of the court that does not have an adequate training program in place, nor a disciplinary process for someone they would have to answer to," said Emil J. Minnar, president of the state constables association.

Women for Sale ▶

Lena H. Sun,
The Washington Post

Sold—$363

This young woman was luckier than most. Some of those who trade in women shackle them and even cut their leg tendons to keep them from escaping.

Rape Data ▶

When Lena H. Sun, *The Washington Post*'s correspondent in China, heard of the practice of selling women to men seeking wives, she looked for a victim so she wouldn't have to rely on secondhand accounts. On the outskirts of Beijing, she found Ma Linmei who was, Sun wrote, "a virtual prisoner. The main road is more than an hour away by foot, down a steep, rocky path. She has no money, and she can barely speak the local dialect. No one will help her escape."

Her husband had been unable to find a bride locally and traveled thousands of miles to Yunan Province in southwestern China to buy a wife.

Sun interviewed Ma, who told her, "I miss my home. I miss my mother. I'm always sick. If I had money I would run away."

But in a way, Ma was luckier than many women, Sun found. Thousands of others "are abducted by traders in human flesh, who trick them with promises of good jobs and a better life far from home. The traffickers often rape and beat the women before selling them into virtual bondage, often with the full knowledge and cooperation of local Communist Party officials. . . ."

Some of the victims, she reported, are as young as 14. Some are locked up, others shackled to keep them from running away. "Some have had their leg tendons cut to prevent them from escaping," Sun reported.

On campus, in national conferences and at conventions . . . wherever the subject came up, the data was alarming: One in four or five or six women will be raped. To Sam Roe and Nara Schoenberg the figures seemed unconvincing, and they decided to look into the subject. Moving from Layer I (accepting the presumed legitimacy of the high-rape risk) to Layer II (verifying the figures) proved difficult.

In their three-part series, which took them six months to report and to write, they found that there is no support for the frightening figures, that the actual danger is perhaps one-tenth as great.

Roe and Schoenberg move beyond debunking a presumption. They point out that public funds have been misdirected in the battle against rape. They found women in poor neighborhoods were 30 times more likely to be raped than women in well-to-do neighborhoods and that campus rape rates were a 30th of the rape rates for the general population among 18- to 24-year-olds.

Instead of going to help those most affected (poor, mostly minority women), money was going to help those least at risk, a disproportionate amount going to rape counseling on campus, for example. Roe and Schoenberg quote Pat Morey, who has run campus and community rape programs in Urbana, Ill.: "A college student has privilege—social privilege—and this translates into getting a bigger slice of the pie. That's not the way it should be."

They continue, "At a time when many colleges are hiring rape educators, community rape programs in cities like Madison, Wis., Austin, Texas, and Newport, Ky., are painfully short of staff. Victims wait up to several months for counseling and support groups."

The reporters interviewed officials at more than 50 universities. They obtained figures about what colleges spend to combat rape and found they have been steadily climbing—$245,200 at Temple, $200,000 at the University of Michigan, $145,000 at the University of Minnesota, $77,000 at Indiana University, $70,000 at the University of Illinois. "These figures are very conservative estimates," the reporters write, "as they do not include items like counseling."

◀ Checking Charities

Good stories are everywhere. In the day's mail at home are a couple of appeals from charities. The alert reporter decides to check one that sounds fishy, from a group supposedly raising funds for "police officers." The reporter knows that some so-called charitable organizations have unconscionably high administrative costs.

The reporter also knows that all nonprofit groups must file an IRS form called the *990*. It's "a guide to spending patterns and potential abuses of public money and trust," says Felix Winternitz, the editor of *Cincinnati Magazine*. The form indicates how travel money is spent, what officers' salaries are—where the money is going. *The Washington Post* found that the Marines' Toys for Tots drive never delivered toys to tots. *The Los Angeles Times* discovered the Points of Light Foundation spent $22 million on salaries, travel, promotions and staff perks and only $4 million on the needy.

No organization is exempt from scrutiny. The New York attorney general checked the Freedom Forum, formerly the Gannett Foundation, and found strange goings-on: "self-dealing," "unnecessarily expensive custom furniture for its executive offices," as well as Foundation-paid "personal items" and travel for family members of the trustees.

While making no admission of wrongdoing, the Foundation officers returned almost $175,000 to the charity.

The attorney general reported that it initiated its inquiry "after press reports criticizing the construction and decoration of the Foundation's $15 million Virginia headquarters and the use of Foundation funds and personnel to purchase Chairman Allen Neuharth's book, *Confessions of an S.O.B.*, in an apparent attempt to improve its bestseller standing."

Neuharth made restitution to the Foundation of $30,000 for the book purchases and "3,957.50 for costs incurred by the Foundation for the purchase of a massage table and universal treadmill for the Chairman's office," the settlement stated.

Checking ▶

Those in power are pleased when journalists work within the confines of Layer I, which limits the reporter to little more than stenographic reporting. A city university announces it will accept all high school graduates in an attempt to diversify the student body. The politicians who devised the program and their educator-administrator colleagues bask in the community's approval.

But what is the effect? How is the open-admissions policy working? The reporter moves into Layer II for an assessment and finds: Half the students drop out before their junior year, and only 22 percent obtain their degrees within five years. Half the students are in remedial courses for the entire freshman year.

He finds that many of these students arrive in college lacking language and mathematical skills. Taxpayers are paying for a high school education twice.

The reporter's investigation leads the university to tighten its admissions standards, and high schools in turn to demand more of their students before issuing diplomas. Without the digging journalism of the reporter, many college students would continue to drop out, frustrated by their inability to do college-level work, the standard of work in the college would have remained significantly low so that its reputation would continue to decline and graduates would find it harder to obtain jobs and to enter graduate school.

The Layer II reporting was in the tradition of public service journalism.

Investigative Reporting ▶

The reporter who digs soon finds his or her appetite whetted for the kind of information that such digging produces. Clark Hallas and Robert B. Lowe of *The Arizona Daily Star* heard about strange doings in the University of Arizona athletic department. In time, they unearthed a major scandal. Such checking and digging led to a Pulitzer Prize in local reporting.

When Judy Johnson of *The Anniston Star* heard some people in an Alabama community were having trouble getting credit from banks and finance companies, she decided to investigate. She spent months examining records of mortgages and land transfers. "I compiled them into lists year by year, looking for patterns, building a history," she said.

She talked to people turned down by banks. Through the years of borrowing from a local businessman, one woman had accumulated $50,000 in loans. Among her loans was one for a four-year-old car she and her husband had bought from the businessman's used car lot. The model she bought cost her slightly less than a new car would have cost her.

Johnson showed how the poor, who cannot obtain credit from large lending institutions, are victimized by private lenders. Her series won national recognition.

Investigative reporters rely for much of their work on physical evidence—files, documents, pay vouchers, minutes of meetings. A reporter heard that some of those on the New York City payroll were political appointees who never showed up for work. An idea: Examine parking tickets in resort areas issued to vehicles with New York license plates. He compared the names on the tickets with names on the city payroll—possible with the computer and city payroll tapes. Lo and behold, he found tickets for city employees on days they were supposed to be working.

Frank Woodruff, *Sun-Bulletin.*

Street Kids

Reporter Gail Roberts of *The Sun-Bulletin* in Binghamton, N.Y., had been hearing stories about youngsters making their homes on streets, in basements and in parks. Rather than rely on officials to describe the situation, she tracked down the street people herself. They told her they had left abusive homes to fend for themselves. They said they survived by selling sex, fencing stolen items and begging.

**Abortions and
Dust Cloths** ▶

"Are you going to perform an abortion?" Ellen Whitford asked the doctor who had just given her a pelvic examination. Whitford, a reporter for *The Virginian-Pilot* in Norfolk, had gone to the clinic to investigate statements women had given her of unusual activities there. Whitford was not pregnant, but the doctor said he would do an abortion.

Whitford had the proof she needed—that the clinic was performing unnecessary abortions. Her series of stories about the clinic led to the George Polk award for local reporting.

A television team from KPRC-TV in Houston exposed home improvement contractors who were performing slipshod work and charging inflated prices. When the homeowners, many of them poor people, could not meet the payments, their homes were seized. The work of Rick Nelson and Joe Collum led to an official investigation of the con artists and a halt to the foreclosures. This reporting, too, won a Polk award.

James Dwyer of *The Dispatch* in Hudson County, N.J., found something strange when checking the bids of suppliers to a vocational school. Some seemed to be typed on the same typewriter. He also noticed that the prices for ladders, dust cloths, shovels and other items were high. Even when the supplies were purchased in quantity, prices were higher than they would have been for goods sold as individual items in hardware stores. For example, the school paid $564 for ladders that local stores sold for $189. He visited the school and found enough dust cloths to keep the school's furniture glowing for a couple of centuries.

Dwyer tried to locate the firms that made the unsuccessful bids. He could not find them. He theorized that the agent through whom the goods were sold had invented bidders, and using these fake firms to enter high bids on faked stationery, the agent made his firm the low bidder. Dwyer's investigation confirmed his theory, and a grand jury took over.

Dangerous Projects ▶

Occasionally, an investigative assignment is perilous. To document for the *Reader's Digest* his account of southern Asia's child-prostitution trade, Paul Ehrlich drove to an area where pedophiles were suspected of meeting children.

He stopped at one house, and when he learned the owner was away, he posed as the owner's friend. From questioning the servants, he learned that some Europeans stayed at the house for a month or more. When Ehrlich returned to the car, the man he was with told him, "Don't ask too many questions. It can be dangerous."

Ehrlich found many people were anxious to put an end to the illicit exploitation of boys and girls. But they were also fearful. "Some required several referrals before trusting me," Ehrlich said. "Many would meet with me in secluded places late at night or early in the morning."

Here is how the article, "Asia's Shameful Trade," begins:

In a Burmese village near the Thai border in 1992, a truck halted in front of a 14-year-old girl as she walked toward the rice paddies where her parents worked. Grabbing the child, the driver forced her into the truck. Hours later, she found herself locked up in a brothel in Bangkok, Thailand. Soon she was being raped up to ten times a day. When she cried out, a man came in and slapped her. "Shut up!" he said. "And don't try to escape or I'll beat you."

The article led some countries to investigate the possibility of prosecuting their citizens who go abroad for sexual liaisons with children.

For Bob Greene, whose long career at *Newsday* took him into the living rooms of crooked politicians and to the waterfront where mobsters ruled, danger was simply part of his job. He recalls being told that he would be "rubbed out" if he showed up at a waterfront warehouse.

He took up the challenge. He went to the dock, pulled a pistol out of his pocket and asked, "Where's the son of a bitch who says he's going to kill me?"

◀ **The Moral Component**

If the activities of journalists can be broken down into three functions—to describe, to explain and to persuade—then we could say that the investigative reporter works all three. Much of the digging journalist's time is spent ferreting out factual material to describe. Some of this material requires explanation: placing in context and showing relationships, causes, consequences.

The third area, persuasion, is less obvious. We must ask the journalist's motive for digging in a particular area. When we do, we find that invariably the investigative journalist says the situation was bad, wrong, needed changing. The revelation the journalist seeks to make is motivated by the desire to correct an injustice, to right a wrong. And to do that he or she must persuade the public to alter the situation.

◀ **A Tax Giveaway**

As soon as the massive Tax Reform Act was passed by Congress and signed by the president, Donald L. Barlett and James B. Steele of *The Philadelphia Inquirer* began to examine it. They discovered hundreds of tax breaks for corporations and specific individuals. But the language was so intricate that identities were hidden.

Here is a typical provision:

> The amendments made by Section 201 shall not apply to a 562-foot passenger cruise ship, which was purchased in 1900 for the purpose of returning the vessel to United States service, the approximate cost of refurbishment of which is approximately $47,000,000.

The two investigative reporters set out to find who was profiting, why they were being helped and what the cost would be to taxpayers. They searched through financial disclosure statements by members of Congress, looked at documents of the Securities and Exchange Commission, used databases to examine thousands of newspapers, magazines, newsletters and government reports.

The digging took 15 months, and Barlett and Steele found that Congress had made the largest giveaway in the history of the federal income tax. (The beneficiaries of the provision involving the 562-foot passenger cruise ship, incidentally, were a group of wealthy investors in the *S.S. Monterey* who were given an $8 million tax break.)

They named the people and the companies that had been allowed to escape taxes by a law that stenographic journalists working in Layer I had hailed as a "tax reform." The rich were being helped by the new law at the expense of the average taxpayer.

In the face of massive public reaction—the lengthy series was reprinted around the country—Congress shelved its so-called reform legislation and passed a new tax bill without a single tax break for an individual or company. Barlett and Steele won the Pulitzer Prize for national reporting for their seven-part series.

Handling the Handout ▶

"Don't be a handout reporter," Harry Romanoff, a night city editor on the *Chicago American,* would tell young reporters. One of Romanoff's charges was Mervin Block, who recalls an encounter with Romanoff:

> I remember his giving me a fistful of press releases trumpeting movie monarch Louis B. Mayer's expected arrival at the Dearborn Street Railroad Station. An hour later, Romy asked me what time Mayer's train would be pulling in. I told him, and when he challenged my answer, I cited the handouts: one from the Santa Fe, one from Mayer's studio (MGM), and one from his destination, the Ambassador East Hotel. All agreed on the time. But that wasn't good enough for Romy.
> "Call the stationmaster and *find out.*"

When handouts from food chains in Chicago announced price cuts on thousands of items, the Chicago newspapers bannered the stories on their front pages. One such headline:

Inflation Breakthrough—Food Prices to Drop Here
—Chicago Sun-Times

Despite the rash of stories about how the shopper "may save 15% in price battle," as one paper said in a headline over one of its stories, consumers were actually paying more on a unit, or per-ounce, basis.

The Chicago commissioner of consumer affairs demonstrated that the city's consumers were being misled by the store announcements and consequently by the newspaper stories that took the handouts at face value. Many of the items that were reduced in price were also reduced in weight. Peanut clusters went from 72 cents a packet to 69 cents, an apparent saving of 3 cents. But the packet went from 6 ounces to 5¼ ounces. With a little arithmetic, a reporter could have figured out that this was actually an increase of 6 cents a packet. Some items were publicized because they stayed at the same price "despite inflation," according to the handouts and the stories. True enough. A 70-cent can of beef stew was still 70 cents. But the new can contained half an ounce less than the old can.

Seeing and Sourcing ▶

Information seekers know that the quality—the truthfulness—of their report depends upon the accuracy of their observations and the worthiness of their sources. The value of Layer II reporting can be no greater than the value of the observation and the source. This is why reporters train themselves to observe carefully and to use the best sources.

A class of journalism students was shown a photograph that had appeared in a metropolitan daily newspaper. It was of high school youngsters clustered around a table at which college recruiters were seated. The cutline described the event as a College Fair for public high school seniors.

"What did you notice about the photograph that was worth a story?" the journalism instructor asked.

The students were silent, unwilling to state the obvious, that this was a recruiting scene. Then one student's hand shot up: "All the students are female."

And that was the story, which the newspaper had missed. Almost all the students attending the College Fair were young women.

Jeffrey A. Tannenbaum of *The Wall Street Journal* puts the names of the most helpful sources in his files. "Someday, they may come in handy," he says. But what about finding sources for a subject entirely new to the reporter?

"First, look for institutional sources," Tannenbaum says. "If you're writing about pizzas, there's a national association of pizza chefs." For his story about the growing power of the states' attorney generals, he asked the New York attorney general if there was an association of all 50 officers. He was given a telephone number.

In gathering information from new sources, he says, "One source leads to another. Perhaps only the seventh one in the chain has what you need."

When do you know you have gathered all you need? "Only after the information the sources have provided is getting redundant, and the sources are failing to supply new sources."

For his piece on the attorney generals, a source told him about the Pennsylvania AG's refusal to support the application of a Moose Lodge for renewal of its liquor license. The Lodge, Tannenbaum was told, had been rejecting black applicants for membership and had refused to serve drinks to blacks even when they were brought as guests. That situation became the basis of the lead to his story.

For Tannenbaum's story, the telephone was an essential reporting tool. But for too many reporters, it substitutes for direct observation, for "walking up tenement steps and ringing doorbells," as Jimmy Breslin puts it.

◀ **Using Shoe Leather**

"There's no substitute for face-to-face reporting," says a midwestern reporter. "Sources usually like to know with whom they are dealing, and as a reporter, I want to be able to sense how best to approach the person and the subject I'm interested in. You can only get that sense, that feeling, by dealing directly with people."

Most sources are cooperative. But some make life difficult for the digging journalist. The source unaccustomed to being interviewed who shies away from questions requires time to soothe and reassure. Some sources simply refuse to talk to reporters. The public official or boardroom general who refuses to cooperate must be pressed for answers to legitimate questions affecting the public.

◀ **Getting Answers**

Reporters have a few techniques to make reluctant sources open up to their questions. When a public official will not respond to legitimate questions about public events and issues, the reporter can tell the source that the public has a right to expect openness from those its taxes support.

For those in private life who exercise power—media company heads, utility directors and the like—the refusal to reply can be met with the reporter's, "Fine. I'll just say that you 'refused to answer' this question." Faced with a non-responsive response, the reporter counters, "OK. I'll just say that you 'did not explain your answers.' "

When nothing works, reporters usually turn to other sources to try to obtain the needed information. And when there is demonstrable falsification by a source, the reporter is free to say so in the story.

Correcting Sources ▶

The reporter moves from Layer I to Layer II reporting when he or she refuses to allow incorrect information to reach the public. In an interview with *The New York Times,* a financier said he wanted upbeat news in the newspaper he was trying to save from failing, the *New York Post.* He said the *Post's* founder, Alexander Hamilton, "wasn't into printing negative things." The story continued:

> "He was up about the country; he wasn't looking for the bad," Mr. Hoffenberg said. (In fact, Hamilton's newspaper was known for publishing scathing editorial commentary as well as juicy tidbits about the sex life of Hamilton's rival, Thomas Jefferson.)

The reporter didn't wait for or seek out another source to deny the source's assertion about Hamilton. She corrected it on her own in the same story in which the misstatement was made.

Caution: Journalists cannot expect public support in their persistence in digging for information. "The press in America is operating in an environment of public opinion that is increasingly indifferent—and to some extent hostile—to the cause of a free press in America," George Gallup, the pollster, concluded after measuring public attitudes toward the press. He found that 37 percent of his respondents said curbs on the press were "not strict enough," whereas 32 percent said they were "about right" and only 17 percent said they were "too strict." The others had no opinion.

A reason for this anti-press sentiment from the public may be found in another set of questions Gallup asked. The poll found that only 24 percent of those asked knew "what the First Amendment to the U.S. Constitution is or what it deals with." Less than half, 42 percent, of the college educated answered correctly.

Layer III Reporting ▶

People are not content with knowing only what happened. They also want to know how and why it happened, what it means and what may occur as a result—causes and consequences. When the story is important, reporters should mine Layer III, the area of interpretation and analysis.

Layer III reporting tells people how things work and why they work that way, or why they don't work. When President Bush announced two legislative actions with political overtones during the 1992 campaign, he did so, *New York Times* reporter Andrew Rosenthal wrote, "after the network news programs had already been prepared. The hour of disclosure assured that they would receive minimum press exposure. . . ."

Layer III reporting moves into the area of judgment and inference. Obviously, this kind of journalism requires reporters who have command of their subjects as well as a mastery of the craft.

The need for interpretative and explanatory journalism in a complex society emerged at the same time the preparation of journalists was becoming more formal and less insular. Before World War II, most journalists came up through an apprenticeship system. Hired as copyboys—almost all were male—they learned the processes and procedures of the newsroom, which were the sum and substance of the education of most reporters and editors.

When the GI Bill of Rights produced a sea of education-hungry young men and women after World War II, journalism schools expanded. They offered more than trade-school training. The result was a new generation of journalists who had studied sociology, geography, foreign languages. Editors, in time, respected this background and gradually began to allow their reporters greater leeway in reporting. Reporters are now allowed to point, explain, lead.

The AP story from Chicago began:

◀ Easy Credit

> William Rodriguez trudged home through rain and snow and wee-hour darkness.
> He was only 23, in good health and known as a happy-go-lucky fellow.
> Yet he would be dead before sunrise.

Rodriguez had purchased rat poison on his way home from work, and as he walked he ate the poison. Why? the AP asked and assigned two reporters to find out. Their digging turned up the answer—easy credit. Rodriguez owed about $700 to merchants for furniture, clothing, a television set. He couldn't meet the payments, and the creditors were threatening to tell his employer.

The story galvanized the city's enforcement agencies. Rodriguez had been sold low-grade merchandise and had been given credit at usurious rates. The legislature reacted by lowering interest rates. The resulting law is known as the "Rodriguez Law."

When the New Jersey state legislature passed a bill banning state Medicaid payments for abortions, it ignored nine federal district court decisions in eight states that ruled similar bills were unconstitutional. The reason for the legislators' action was described in this Layer III sentence from *The New York Times:* "Approval of the measure reflects the influence of the Catholic Church, which opposes abortion, in New Jersey: About 55 percent of the state's registered voters are Catholic."

The battle over the need for interpretative reporting has long been over, although some newspaper and broadcast station editors are adamant about its dangers and rarely permit it. Dangers there are, but the risks are only slightly greater than those inherent in other areas of journalism. The benefits to the reader outweigh these risks.

Necessary Risks ▶ In Warrentown, W. Va., 63 indigent mothers were sterilized with their permission. Reporters were sent to the city to do follow-up stories. Here are the headlines over two of these folos in New York City newspapers:

Town in Uproar over Sterilization

Virginians Calm on Sterilization

Troublesome as interpretative reporting can be, reporters have little choice but to try to explain the events they cover. Walter Lippmann, one of the few original thinkers about American journalism, observed that during the 1930s with the advent of the New Deal, "events started happening which were almost meaningless in themselves. It was the beginning of the era when Why became as important as What, when a Washington correspondent left his job half done if he only told what happened and failed to give the reasons and hint at the significance." Journalism has no rule that what Washington reporters can do is prohibited to local reporters.

One device reporters use to add interpretation to their news pieces is simple enough. They ask a source to size up the situation. Sometimes the how and why of the event may be so elusive that no single explanation is sufficient. Then the reporter must talk to several sources to find a range of explanations and analyses. This kind of reporting will give the reader or listener alternatives on which to base his or her conclusions.

Putting I, II and III to Work ▶ Let us watch a reporter mine these three layers for his story.

City Planner Arthur calls the local stations and newspaper to read to reporters a statement about a new zoning proposal. The release contains facts 1, 2 and 3. At the newspaper, reporter Bernard looks over the handout, tells his city editor that 1 and 2 are of no news value but that 3—elimination of two-acre zoning north of town—is important and worth exploring in an interview with Arthur. The editor agrees and assigns Bernard to the story.

Before leaving for the interview, Bernard checks the newspaper library for a story about a court decision he recalls that may be related to the proposed regulation. He telephones another city official and a real estate developer to obtain additional information. With this background and Arthur's statement, Bernard begins to develop ideas for questions. He jots down a few, 4, 5 and 6.

During the interview, City Planner Arthur repeats 1, 2 and 3. Reporter Bernard asks for more information about 3, the elimination of the minimum two-acre requirement for home building. Bernard also brings up his own subjects by asking questions 4, 5 and 6. New themes develop during the interview: 7, 8 and 9.

Back in the newsroom, Bernard looks over his notes. He sees that his hunch about 3 was correct. It was important. Arthur's answer to question 5 is newsworthy, he decides, and fact 7—the possibility of low- and medium-cost housing in the area—which developed during the interview, may be the lead, especially since the broadcast stations probably will not have it. Bernard needs comments on the impact of 7 from developers. A couple of calls and the possible consequences, 10, emerge. The developers confirm their interest in building inexpensive housing. Looking over his notes, he spots background from the library, 11, that is now relevant and also will go into the story.

The story will contain facts 3, 5, 7, 10 and 11. Bernard decides he will fashion 7 and 10 into a lead, and he worries about how to blend 11 into the story at a fairly early stage without impeding the flow of Arthur's explanation. Background is important, but sometimes it is difficult to work smoothly into the story. He writes this lead:

> A proposed change to eliminate the two-acre zoning requirement for home building north of town could open the area to people who can afford only low- and medium-cost housing.

Bernard's story will consist of the following:

Facts	Layer
3	I
5, 7, 11	II
10	III

Bernard has used almost all the techniques reporters have at their command to gather facts for stories. He was given information by a source. Then he used the newspaper library—a physical source—for background. He then interviewed his original source—a human source—and made independent checks by calling up additional sources.

Now that we have sketched out the layers of reporting, it is time to turn to the process itself, which we can summarize here before we go on:

- Know what to look for.
- Gather the information.
- Record it accurately.
- Weigh the information.

All this precedes writing.

Summing Up ▶

Here is some down-to-earth advice about reporting gathered from suggestions by working reporters:

• Stay ready for any breaking news story by keeping up to date on developments in the community.

• There is a story behind almost any event. Remember, it was a third-rate break-in in a Washington building that began the Watergate revelations and ended in the resignation of a president.

• Always check all names in the telephone book, the city directory and the library to make absolutely sure they are spelled correctly.

• Follow the buck. Find out where money comes from, where it is going, how it gets there and who's handling it. Whether it is taxes, campaign contributions, or donations, keep your eye on the dollar.

• Be counterphobic. Do what you don't want to do or are afraid to do. Otherwise you'll never be able to dig into a story.

• Question all assumptions. The people who believed the emperor was clothed are legion and forgotten. We remember the child who pointed out his nudity.

• Question authority. Titles and degrees do not bestow infallibility.

Further Reading ▶

Behrens, John C. *The Typewriter Guerrillas.* Chicago: Nelson-Hall, 1977.

Boorstin, Daniel J. *The Image: A Guide to Pseudo-Events in America.* New York: Atheneum, 1961.

Crouse, Timothy. *The Boys on the Bus.* New York: Random House, 1973.

Hersey, John. *The Algiers Motel Incident.* New York: Knopf, 1968.

Hess, Stephen. *The Washington Reporter.* Washington, D.C.: Brookings Institution, 1981.

McGinniss, Joe. *The Selling of the President 1968.* New York: Pocket Books, 1973.

Weir, David, and Dan Noyes. *Raising Hell: How the Center for Investigative Reporting Gets the Story.* Reading, Mass.: Addison-Wesley, 1983.

11 Making Sound Observations

Rick Muasacchio,
The Tennessean.

The dramatic enthralls readers, viewers.

Preview

To gather the reliable and relevant information essential to a story, the reporter must:

• Know what readers and listeners are interested in, what affects them and what they need to know.
• Find a theme for the story early in the reporting.
• Look for the dramatic, the unusual, the unique aspect of the event that sets it apart from other events like it.

Reporters face restraints on their fact gathering. Time is always limited; it is not always easy to find vantage points from which to see the event; sources will not cooperate.

For some stories, journalists use unobtrusive observation (the identity of the reporter is unknown to those being observed) and participant observation (the reporter becomes part of the event being reported).

The Congo was torn by civil war. Because the war had serious international implications, the United Nations dispatched a peacekeeping force and sent Secretary-General Dag Hammarskjold to the African republic to try to arrange a cease-fire.

At dusk, reporters at the Ndola airport in Northern Rhodesia awaiting Hammarskjold's arrival saw a plane land and a fair-haired man emerge. The reporters, who had been held behind police lines a hundred yards away, ran to file bulletins on the secretary-general's arrival. Anticipating Hammarskjold's next move, the press associations soon had stories describing Hammarskjold's conferring with President Moise Tshombe about a cease-fire. Many of these stories ran in early editions of the next day's newspapers.

But the man the reporters saw disembark was not Hammarskjold. He was a British foreign affairs official on a fact-gathering tour. At the time the reporters were filing their stories, Hammarskjold was aboard another plane that later crashed in a forest 10 miles north of Ndola, killing the secretary-general and the others on board.

How did it happen? The UPI reporter told his boss later, "I saw a man I thought looked like Hammarskjold. Other reporters claimed they were sure it was. After comparing notes, we all agreed to file stories."

The incident reveals some of the problems reporters face in covering spot news stories. To make sound observations, the reporter has to see and hear the event clearly, but this is not always possible. In this case, rather than wait to be

271

certain of their man's identity, the reporters did what reporters do when their observations are uncertain and they are under pressure—they made an inference.

Because the man had light hair and his build approximated that of the secretary-general, the reporters jumped to the conclusion that he was Hammarskjold. This violated the reporter's maxim, "Beware of inferences. Do not jump from the known to the unknown."

To guard against individual error, they checked with each other and formed a consensus. The difficulty in covering events often causes journalists to consult each other for reassurance, which leads to what is known as *herd* or *pack journalism*. Reporters tend to chat about the lead, the credibility of the source, the reliability of the documentation they have been offered. They seek agreement in resolving the uncertainties.

Learning how to make sound observations—more difficult than it seems—begins with an understanding of how the reporter works, the methods he or she uses in searching for relevant information for the task of truth telling, which often involves the risk of independently made observations.

Seeing the Whole Scene ▶

In his short story "The Murders in the Rue Morgue," Edgar Allan Poe has his character C. Auguste Dupin expound on the art of observation as Dupin goes about solving the grisly murders of Madame L'Espanaye and her daughter, which have stumped the Parisian police. He dismisses the way the police work:

> "There is no method in their proceedings, beyond the method of the moment. . . . The results obtained by them are not unfrequently surprising, but, for the most part are brought about by simple diligence and activity. When these qualities are unavailing, their schemes fail."

Although hard work is essential to good reporting, activity is not enough. A method is essential. Dupin says that the detective makes "a host of observations and inferences. So, perhaps, do his companions; and the difference in the extent of the information obtained lies not so much in the validity of the inference as in the quality of the observation. The necessary knowledge is of *what* to observe."

In other words, the vacuum-cleaner collector of information wastes time. Dupin says the proper method is to follow "deviations from the plane of the ordinary." This is how "reason feels its way, if at all, in its search for the true. In investigations such as we are now pursuing, it should not be so much asked 'what has occurred,' as 'what has occurred that has never occurred before.' "

Dupin talks of seeing the "matter as a whole." This, too, is excellent advice for the journalist. For the reporter, like the detective, every assignment is a mystery to be unraveled. To observe, to analyze, to synthesize, to pattern the observations the journalist must have a method. The method begins with seeing the matter as a whole as quickly as possible. This gives the reporter an idea of what to look for, what to observe.

For the journalist, the "educated thought" that Dupin takes to his work is the understanding that no event exists in isolation, that all events are part of the continuum: cause—event—consequence.

When reporters see clearly and see as a whole, they are on their way to communicating not only truthfully, but graphically. Gene Roberts, managing editor of *The New York Times*, learned this on his first job as the farm columnist for the 9,000-circulation *Goldsboro News-Argus* in Wayne County, N.C. Roberts' editor was Henry Belk, who was blind.

Often, Roberts recalls, when he showed up for work in the morning, Belk would call him over and inform the young reporter that his writing was insufficiently descriptive.

"Make me see," he would order.

Roberts says, "It took me years to appreciate it, but there is no better admonition to the writer than 'Make me see.' There is no truer blueprint for successful writing than making your readers see. It is the essence of great writing."

◀ 'Make Me See'

The reporter on assignment is confronted by a flood of facts. A meeting can last two hours, cover seven different topics and include four decisions. A speaker may deliver an address containing 4,500 words. To handle these stories, the reporter may have at most a column for each story, about 750 words, or 90 seconds on a newscast.

There are three guides to the selection of relevant facts:

1. *Know the community:* Develop a feeling and understanding of what readers need and want to know.

2. *Find the theme:* Carefully identify the theme of the story as soon in the reporting as possible. This way facts that support, buttress and amplify the theme can be gathered, the rest ignored as irrelevant.

3. *Look for the drama:* Develop a sensitivity to the unique, the unusual, the break from the normal and routine.

◀ Relevant Observations

Mourner

For the reporter who seeks out the unusual, the sting of defeat may make as good a theme as the joy of victory.

The unusual is not always at center court. It may be on the sidelines where the losers bury their heads in grief. It could be found in the half-hidden gesture of capitulation when the candidate betrays a bold front. It could be buried in the small print in a document, the last sentence in a press release that begins with optimism and self-congratulation but ends with the admission of an unprofitable business year.

Looking deeply, listening intently, the reporter discovers truths that fascinate readers and viewers.

© Greg Lovett.

Making Sound Observations   273

Know the Community ▶

We saw in Chapter 2 that facts that are relevant to readers in one section of the country may be unimportant to readers in another area and that the story that fascinates some readers may bore others. The reporter must know what interests readers or viewers and what they need to know. This news sense is part intuition, part common sense and part knowledge acquired from living and working in the community.

Reporters who move from one area to another often have trouble adjusting to their new readers and listeners. The story is told about the veteran reporter for a Chicago newspaper who decided to forsake the big city for a more relaxed life in Texas. He accepted a job as the city editor of a west Texas daily newspaper. One day a fire broke out in town and the reporter's blood stirred in the city editor. He decided to go out on the story himself.

On his return, he batted out a story, Chicago style—dramatic and well-written. The managing editor was pleased with his city editor's handiwork except for one hole in the story.

"How much water did they use to put out the fire?" he asked. In parched west Texas, that fact was as important to readers as the number of fire units answering the call would have been to Chicago readers.

Find the Theme ▶

Our second guideline is based upon the form of the news story, which places certain demands on the reporter that he or she must satisfy in fact gathering. We know that the story consists of the statement of a central theme or idea (the lead) and the elaboration of that theme or idea (the body). The reporter must find the theme quickly so he or she can ask the relevant questions and make the appropriate observations to flesh out the story.

The sociologist Irving Kristol observed, "A person doesn't know what he has seen unless the person knows what he is looking for." In his book, *The Art of Scientific Investigation,* the British scientist W.I.B. Beveridge writes that developing ideas or hypotheses helps a person "see the significance of an object or event that otherwise would mean nothing."

When the Salvation Army dispatched 4,000 of its soldiers to New York City to do battle against "sin and evil," a reporter for *The New York Times* accompanied some of the troops through the streets. Impressed by the work of the Army men and women, the reporter decided early in her reporting to emphasize their dedication and singled out this detail in her account to illustrate her theme:

"The Army believes in total abstinence," a young soldier was saying to a disheveled-looking man, whose breath reeked of alcohol. "You are the temple of the Lord and if you destroy yourself, you're destroying Him."

"Am I?" the older man asked, as they stood in front of the entranceway of the Commodore. "No, I'm not."

"Sure you are," the soldier replied, resting his hand on the man's shoulder. The man reached out his hand, too, and began to cry. So did the Salvation Army soldier.

This approach—confining observations to the theme—is not unique to journalism. All writing intended to communicate information is written with the theme clearly in mind. Irrelevant details are gravestones marking dead writing.

But if the reporter discovers facts that contradict the basic idea, then the idea is discarded and a new theme is adopted. In this way, the reporter is like the scientist whose conclusion can be no stronger than his or her evidence.

Of course, some events will have secondary themes. The same rule about gathering only material that buttresses the theme applies to the secondary ideas.

Experienced reporters almost always have a theme or tentative idea as soon as they receive an assignment or at the outset of a story they originate. If a reporter is sent to cover a fire in a college dormitory, the reporter immediately thinks of deaths and injuries and the cause as the theme or possible lead. If the assignment is about the rescue of a drowning man, the lead could be the courage or ingenuity of the rescuer. Six youths die in an automobile accident; the reporter cannot help but immediately think of alcohol and drugs or speeding.

◀ **Devising Themes**

As soon as the Bethesda Naval Center announced that Supreme Court Justice Thurgood Marshall had died, reporters knew the theme of their story and the direction it would take. The fact that a Supreme Court Justice had died was not the theme but that the first black to join the Court and a leading figure in the civil rights movement had died. And that is just how the AP story began:

> WASHINGTON—Retired Justice Thurgood Marshall, the first black to sit on the U.S. Supreme Court and a towering figure in the civil rights movement, died Sunday of heart failure. He was 84.

Reporters knew what to write because of their knowledge of Marshall and his career.

These themes or ideas tell the reporter "what to observe," to use Poe's language. They guide the reporter in asking questions, in doing background checks. In short, they allow the reporter to structure the reporting.

The theme or idea is fairly broad. Usually, it comes to the reporter's mind almost as soon as he or she is given an assignment or senses a story. The idea originates in the reporter's experience, knowledge of the subject, understanding of the essentials or necessities for this kind of story and in a vague area we can only describe as the reporter's feel for the subject.

Some reporters call these ideas or insights hunches. (We will discuss hunches and reportorial intuition in Chapter 17.) Ideas also can originate in a reporter's prejudices or biases.

"Look, I have advance prejudices," says Seymour Hersh. "Any reporter who says he doesn't is kidding. But that doesn't mean I would deliberately report something wrong or not tell the truth about something. I would not change a story to make it fit what I think.

"I spent an incredible amount of work—dozens of interviews—digging into a number of allegations by a number of people that the American military was involved in the overthrow of Allende (president of Chile). I did a lot of work and I couldn't find it. It's not there. I'm not going to write that story. It's gone, kaput," said Hersh.

"As long as I can make these kinds of judgments I'm okay."

Science in the Newsroom. O.K. Bovard, the great editor of Pulitzer's *St. Louis Post-Dispatch,* was said to take a scientific approach to news. He would advance a theory or hypothesis on the basis of a bit of information and then prove or disprove it through reporting. He said he and his staff used the approach "all day long in this room. The imaginative reporter does it when he refuses to accept the perfunctory police view of the mystery and sets himself to reason out all the possible explanations of the case and then adopts a theory for investigating the most likely one."

The reporter's theme or idea throws a broad shaft of light on the subject, allowing the reporter to see his or her way through the dense undergrowth of material. Reporters know that they also need to make a pencil-light penetration of the material to come up with the specific news pegs or news angles for their stories. To do this they fall back on their knowledge and experience to help them distinguish the new from the old, the unusual from the usual, the unexpected from the routine.

These "deviations from the plane of the ordinary," as Poe put it, provide the newsworthy element for the story, the lead.

The reporter can spot these deviations, these interruptions in the expected, by knowing a lot about the situation that is being reported. The extraordinary shouts out for attention to the reporter who is open to the significant, the novel.

Look for the Drama ▶

Bob Thayer,
The Providence Journal.

Turning Point?

Did the steal open up a big inning? Or did the second baseman's grab of a poor throw keep the runner at second and prevent a rally? This play could be the lead for the game story.

Individuality ▶

Linking Observations. "Effective observation involves noticing something and giving it significance by relating it to something else noticed or already known."—W.I.B. Beveridge

Learning to distinguish the break from everyday routine is difficult for the reporter covering his 10th fire, his 33d ball game and his third board of education meeting this month. Events seem to settle into a familiar pattern. Spotting the differences between this fire, this game, this meeting and the others is difficult. After all, most people cannot differentiate the Delicious from the Jonathan, the Jersey from the Guernsey. To them, all apples are alike and all cows are just cows.

The reporter has to learn to look at the world through the eyes of the innocent child while applying the discerning eye of the wise elder who can differentiate the significant from the meaningless, the dramatic from the routine.

Red Smith, a sportswriter who covered so many baseball games he lost count, explained the basis of the journalist's artistry: "Every ball game is different from every other ball game—if the reporter has the knowledge and wit to discern the difference."

When Gustave Flaubert, the French novelist, was teaching Guy de Maupassant to write, he told the young man to pick out one of the cab drivers in front of a railway station in Paris and to describe him in a way that would differentiate him from all the other drivers. To do so, Maupassant had to find the significant details that would single out that one man.

Experienced reporters usually agree on the themes of the stories they cover. Beyond that, each reporter puts his or her individual stamp on the story. Some of that individuality comes from writing style. Much is based on the particular observations the reporter makes. What is relevant to one reporter may be irrelevant to another.

When Homer Bigart, the winner of two Pulitzer Prizes and one of the country's great reporters, was sent to cover the military trial of Lt. Willam Calley, who had been accused of murdering civilians in the My Lai massacre during the Vietnam War, Bigart observed how Calley was brought into court. He linked this observation to his observations at another army officer's trial he had covered, and he wrote:

> Although he had just been found guilty of twenty-two murders, Calley was treated far more gently than was Army doctor Captain Howard B. Levy four years ago after receiving a

sentence for refusing to give medical training to Green Berets on the grounds that the training would be used unlawfully in Vietnam.

Unlike Levy, Calley was not handcuffed and left the court unfettered. An officer explained: "His conduct has been exemplary throughout and he'll continue to be treated as an officer."

Bigart's editors at *The New York Times* apparently considered his references to the Levy trial to be irrelevant, for the section read simply:

> Lieutenant Calley was not handcuffed when driven to the stockade.

Whose judgment was better, Bigart's or his editors'? Bigart's reference to the Levy trial provides the reader with some idea of the intense feeling of the military against the peace movement—of which Levy was a symbol—and its consideration for the accused murderer of civilians, a career army man.

Following its defeat in the 1992 presidential election, the Republican Party sought to find the causes of its rout. The religious right was blamed by some party members because of its domination of the nominating convention. The conservative wing had pushed through a tough anti-abortion platform plank and seemed to position the party as intolerant of diverse lifestyles and nonconformist beliefs.

In the reassessment by Republican governors, the moderate wing sought to define the GOP as "the big tent," a party that could embrace diverse beliefs and elements. But at a news conference, Gov. Kirk Fordice of Mississippi told reporters, "The United States of America is a Christian nation. . . . The less we emphasize the Christian religion the further we fall into the abyss of poor character and chaos in the United States of America."

Gov. Carroll A. Campbell Jr. of South Carolina differed, he wanted reporters to know. "The value base of this country comes from the Judeo-Christian heritage that we have and that is something we need to realize." Richard L. Berke, who covered the conference for *The New York Times*, watched Campbell as he returned to his seat on the dais next to Fordice.

"I just wanted to add the 'Judeo' part," Campbell told Fordice. Berke then writes, "Mr. Fordice responded tartly, 'If I wanted to do that I would have done it.' "

The exchange, brief as it was, provided a shaft of light for the reader, an insight into the positions and the feelings of the two wings of the party.

Berke had positioned himself so that he could overhear the conversation of the governors. Sometimes finding a vantage point from which to see and to hear is difficult and the reporter has to shoulder his or her way to the front of the crowd.

A reporter for a college newspaper was unable to find a seat near the front of the lecture she was assigned to cover and took a place in the back of the room. The subject was political satire, and the speaker seemed to be outspoken in his summary. The reporter wrote this lead:

> "Political satire of today stinks," Dennis Quinn, assistant professor of English, said at yesterday's Poetry Hour.

◀ **Looking, Listening**

Unrepentant. Three years later, Gov. Fordice was assaulting the separation of church and state. He said that the wall of separation is more like a revolving door. "It swings one way," he told reporters. "The church can clearly go through that door into government any way it wants to, but that door slams absolutely shut when the government tries to enter that church." He said the country is "in grave peril" because "we continue to deny a supreme presence. . . ."

Gov. Campbell's successor in South Carolina, David M. Beasley, went further along the religious conservative path, issuing a proclamation declaring May 27 "March for Jesus Day throughout the state." It called on "all people of faith to join in this celebration."

A few days later, the newspaper received a letter from Professor Quinn. With some restraint, he wrote that he had actually said, "Political satire is practically extinct." The *University Daily Kansan* printed his letter, and despite the reporter's embarrassment she stayed in journalism and went on to do distinguished work as an AP correspondent.

The *Asbury Park Press* reported that sewage effluent was being tested by placing "mice and shrimp" in the liquid for four days. If half survived, the effluent would be considered harmless.

No, no, moaned the source for the story when he saw the article in the New Jersey newspaper. "I said, mysid shrimp," he told the managing editor.

Listening In

Rodger Mallison of the *Fort Worth Star-Telegram* took photos and conducted interviews for a series on local crime. Here's what he wrote about the arrest of the young driver he photographed taking a sobriety test:

"In two hours I'll be out," the man says.

"I don't think so, dude. I'm not taking you to the drunk tank. I'm taking you to jail for DWI," Johnson says.

"You can't do that. I'm a very intelligent man."

"I can see that. It takes a lot of intelligence to get behind the wheel drunk. You could've killed somebody."

"That's right, and I'll kill you," the man says. "Stupid ——. You'll get killed; we've already got your name. Come to Stop Six. You'll be six feet under. Your —— is going. I hate a black man that takes another black man down. . . . I'll kill you. I will slit your whole throat."

It is a long nine-minute ride to the jail.

"I had to bite my tongue a few times," Johnson says at the jail. "You definitely have to have a thick skin. You can't take it personally."

Wrong Turn

A reporter decided to visit the site of the World War II reception center where he had been inducted 40 years before, which was now being used by a national research laboratory. In his story in *The New York Times,* the reporter described the "barracks-like buildings with no windows" and "locked gates" that reminded him of the isolation he felt as a young soldier.

A laboratory employee, puzzled by the description that bore no relationship to the place in which he worked, followed the reporter's route as outlined in the story. The reporter, it turned out, had made a wrong turn off the parkway and had driven to the back entrance to a racetrack. The "barracks-like buildings with no windows" were stables.

So, not only get up close, but when what you think you've heard sounds strange, check it out. No source should be allowed to back away from a statement, but sometimes what we think we've heard needs verifying.

Verify that seemingly wild statement, rumor or situation. Don't write it off. The reward could be a footnote in journalism history, or a Pulitzer Prize.

Editors attending a luncheon at a convention of the American Society of Newspaper Editors were astonished when they saw Fidel Castro, the guest of honor, reach across the table and swap plates with the president of the Society.

Had an editor acted on that astonishment at the 1961 banquet and done what reporters are supposed to do—ask why—that editor might have been informed that Castro feared assassination. And that editor might have had a major story. For in 1975, the Central Intelligence Agency admitted that during the administrations of presidents Eisenhower, Kennedy and Johnson the United States government had indeed tried to murder Castro.

No one could believe the rumors: The Internal Revenue Service was botching a huge number of returns. Some weren't being examined, some were tossed away. Arthur Howe of *The Philadelphia Inquirer* decided to check the rumors and he learned that the IRS had mishandled one of three returns for the previous year. In Atlanta, a worker flushed returns down a toilet. In Memphis, complicated returns were destroyed.

The IRS denied it all. But Howe persisted, and he corroborated everything. He was awarded the Pulitzer Prize for National Reporting.

Deborah E. Lipstadt maintains in her book *The American Press and the Covering of the Holocaust* that many newspapers refused to publish reports of the Nazi Final Solution because the reports of death squads and gas chambers were "beyond belief." If the newspapers and radio stations had been less skeptical of the reports of refugees, she writes, they might have had an accurate description of Hitler's rise to power and his policies. Even when faced with government reports

◀ Checking It Out

"**Skepticism** is the chastity of the intellect, and it is shameful to surrender it too soon or to the first corner."— George Santyana

of Nazi atrocities, the press maintained a "persistent incredulity," says the author. The accounts of eyewitnesses seemed too horrifying to be believed.

Lipstadt holds the press "ultimately as culpable as the Government" for failing to report on the Holocaust. She does recognize a few journalists, among them Edward R. Murrow, who did spot the dangers of the Nazis early and were inclined to believe what happened later.

The Holocaust, the Castro incident and the Watergate burglary point to an unseen dimension of reporting. Although the reporter is guided by logic, he or she must be open to the most implausible facts and observations. Time after time reporters find aberrant facts and extraordinary observations and put them aside as too unusual for further examination. No report should be dismissed—no matter how outlandish it seems—without at least a quick check.

Limitations of the Story ▶

Although we may agree that the reporter's task is to continue the search for relevant facts until the theme is adequately supported, we also must admit that the search can never be completed, that there are facts beyond the reporter's reach. Just as a map can never be the complete guide to a territory, so a news story is rarely the definitive statement of reality.

Here are some of the obstacles reporters face:

- The source the reporter cannot locate.
- The missing record, document or newspaper clipping.
- The incident the reporter cannot see or hear properly.
- The facts the source will not divulge.
- The material the copy editor cuts out of the story.
- The reporter's own limitations.
- The book or magazine the reporter fails to read. Yesterday's newspaper left unread beyond page one.
- The phone call not returned.
- The question not asked.
- The appointment missed.

For those who like ideas expressed in formulas, we can represent the concept of the limitations of the story with the Reporter's Equation:

Truth = Story + X

Actually, the capital letter X represents a series of small x's—those that we have listed as the obstacles reporters face.

From our quick trip into the realm of math, let's take a turn down the hall to talk to a semanticist about truth and certainty.

Certainty's Boundaries ▶

As the semanticist Wendell Johnson put it, "There is always at least a small gap between the greatest probability and absolute certainty." But we can be certain, Johnson does say, about some statements.

"It is certain that 2 = 2," Johnson says, "because we say so. We agree to treat it as certain." But there is no certainty that two lawyers equal two lawyers. "No two things are the same, and no one thing stays the same," he says.

This concept is helpful to the journalist, for it guarantees—if it is followed—the reporter will take a fresh eye to people and events, that the first impression is helpful but not decisive.

"In the realm of direct experience," Johnson says, "whether we look backward in memory or forward in anticipation, nothing is absolutely certain. Each new situation, problem, or person is to be approached, therefore, not with rigidly fixed habits and preconceived ideas, but with a sense of apparent probabilities."

We will be discussing how journalists formulate "apparent probabilities" in Chapter 17 when we examine hunches, feelings and thinking patterns. But it should be said here that reporters covering their fifth football game, 10th basketball game, 15th city council meeting or 20th speech need to keep Johnson's advice in mind: (1) no two things are the same and (2) approach a reporting situation with an open mind but with some idea of the story.

Red Smith, whom many consider the best of all the sportswriters, went to every game. "He was horrified that someone might actually cover a game by watching TV or listening to radio," Gene Roberts said. Smith "needed the material, the sense of being there," Roberts said. It was his "being there" that gave Smith material that made his story of **this** game different from the story about yesterday's game.

Smith also approached each game with some idea of "probabilities," which he derived from the names of the starting pitchers, the possible continuation of streaks, animosities left over from the last time the teams played and a dozen other factors.

The clock is the journalist's major obstacle. Unlike the historian or the sociologist, who face few daily or weekly deadlines in their work, the journalist submits to the requirements of publication and airtime while still seeking to present a complete and accurate account.

◀ **The Tyranny of Time**

Complex events require the time to find relationships that link seemingly disparate events. The reporter may find that the newspaper or station will not provide time. Discouraged, the reporter sometimes settles for a rudimentary form of truth, the recital of what sources declare (Layer I journalism), which is truth of a sort.

The journalistic style also may obstruct truth. The journalist is instructed to tell a story in simple, dramatic, personalized prose. Some important events are complicated. The reporter who seeks to make these events—usually ideas, trends, concepts—come alive may distort them by using exciting details that are colorful but misleading. For years, the newsmagazines emphasized this kind of detail. Their correspondents named the wines the diplomat drank, counted the cigarettes he smoked during a tense hearing. The significance of the event often was lost in the human-interest trivia.

◀ **Style as a Barrier**

The act of reporting can itself be an impediment to accurate observations. Walter Lippmann characterized the journalist as a "fly on the wall," a detached observer whose presence does not affect the event being observed. But if reporting requires close-at-hand observation, scrupulous note taking, photographs, or tape, how unobtrusive can the reporter be? The fly descends and buzzes around the event.

◀ **The Reporter as Intruder**

We know what happens when a television crew arrives at an event. Drones become animated. Reserved people begin to gesticulate. Reality is altered.

At a political rally in Central America, a reporter noted the calm, almost serene atmosphere. Even when a speaker released a dove from the center of the plaza, the crowd was hushed. Then the television and still photographers arrived, and the event suddenly took another shape. Fists were shaken. A Cuban flag was unfurled for the photographers, and revolutionary slogans were shouted into the recording equipment. When the photographers departed, the rally returned to its placid state. In the next day's newspaper, accompanying the reporter's story of a quiet protest against United States policy, was a shot of what seemed to be a fist-shaking mob.

Even the reporter's pencil and paper can distort the event. Every reporter experiences the trying moment when, after chatting with a source to put him or her at ease, it is time to reach for a pencil and notepad. In an instant, the mood changes. The simple tools of the reporter's trade have spooked the source.

Unobtrusive Observation ▶

This type of reaction can be avoided by nonreactive or unobtrusive observation, methods that have the merit of allowing the reporter to be a fly on the wall. Let us follow a reporter as he uses this reporting technique.

Among the dozens of reporters gathered in central California to attend a Republican state conference was a reporter who wanted to prove to his editor that he could handle politics. The newspaper's political reporter was assigned to the main political story. The reporter we are following was to do sidebars.

Unlike the other reporters at the convention, our man was unknown to the delegates. He was able to mix freely, smiling and shaking hands with delegates. He knew he was being mistaken for a young delegate, and when one of the central committee secretaries told him there was an important meeting, he went along with her. They walked into the meeting together, and he sat near her, apparently doodling absent-mindedly on a pad in front of him.

All day long he moved in and out of caucuses, meetings and powwows. He heard Orange County delegates denounce the president, a Republican, as a liberal, a spendthrift, an enemy of the party's conservative principles. He listened as deals were made to try to attract labor and minority votes.

His story, played prominently on page one, was exclusive and other newspapers were forced to quote from it. Republican leaders were chagrined. Our young reporter was jubilant.

The week before when another political group—a national organization of right-wing partisans—held a convention, the reporter had plumped down in a soft chair in the lobby of the hotel and listened. He had heard delegates talk about bringing back the gold standard, the threat of communism from minorities, the radicalism of the labor movement and the dangers of sex education in the public schools.

What may be the classic example of participant observation is Howard Griffin's book *Black Like Me,* written some 40 years ago. To explore the world of Southern blacks, Griffin had his skin dyed. He then traveled through the South, living with black people. He found a society marked by poverty and oppression, and he wrote that "whites as a group . . . contrive to arrange life so that it destroys the Negro's sense of personal value, degrades his human dignity, deadens the fibers of his being."

Some journalists condemn this kind of reporting. Their criticism stems from their concern about widespread intrusions into privacy by insurance firms, credit investigators and the federal government, which has poked into people's lives through wiretaps and mail openings. What right, then, do journalists have to do what they condemn others for doing?

◀ Ethics Debated

The journalist defends prying on the ground that the search for truth justifies the means if the story reveals wrongdoing or aids the public in decision making. As for a check on the prying journalist, the reporter would have none but his or her conscience. "Let me use my judgment," the journalist says. "I will not use material irresponsibly."

Opponents of the ends-justify-the-means argument contend that reporters cannot adopt methods they condemn, that they cannot set themselves apart from the rules that apply to others.

We do know that the Census Bureau, health and welfare departments and other agencies collect material for the common good but intrude on privacy. Can journalism use this defense of its methods?

Is there a link between the journalist's unobtrusive observation and governmental inquiry, or are some areas clearly off-limits for the journalist? A guideline: For private activities, think twice; for official activities held in private, act in the public interest.

Journalistic ethics are discussed further in Chapter 27.

Another research method—participant observation—links social science and journalism strategies. An Oregon reporter who managed to fold his six-foot frame into a third grader's seat at school was a participant observer. The reporter who worked as a telephone operator and then wrote a series of articles based on her observations was basing her stories on personal experience. At the simplest level, a reporter can spend a day with a meter reader, a public health nurse. Mary Voboril of *The Miami Herald* took an exercise class with Jane Fonda.

◀ **Participant Observation**

In participant observation—the opposite of unobtrusive observation—the reporter discards his or her role as the uninvolved, detached observer and joins the activity of the person or group he or she is covering. The newspaperman who became a third grader for a story participated in the children's school work, ate lunch with them and played ball at recess. The school children took him for a friend, a bit older and awkward about some things, but a companion nevertheless. They talked to him as an equal. His relationship with the students enabled him to gather material that the usual interview and observation techniques would not have revealed.

William Foote Whyte, in his classic study of an Italian-American slum, *Street Corner Society* (Chicago: The University of Chicago Press, 1943), talks about the difference between the traditional perception of what is news and the

Charles Buchanan, *Winston-Salem Journal.*

Getting the Garbage

For her story about sanitation men, Phoebe Zerwick of the *Winston-Salem Journal* rides along on the orange garbage truck as the men make their morning rounds. She absorbs the sights and the sounds—and the smells, too. "A mist lingers on an unusually cool August morning. A few dogs bark, lunging at fences. Once in a while someone starts a car engine and backs out of a driveway. . . . The smell, sometimes sweet, sometimes sour, is still faint at 8 a.m. before the heat of the day cooks up stronger odors." She observes the workers: "The men keep up a furious pace, with Casey, 28, taking long strides in knee-high rubber boots and McLaurin, 34, running."

reality of the way people live, which participant observation allows the reporter to view:

> If the politician is indicted for accepting graft, that is news. If he goes about doing the usual personal favors for his constituents, that is not news. The newspaper concentrates on the crisis—the spectacular event. In a crisis the "big shot" becomes public property. He is removed from the society in which he functions and he is judged by standards different from his own group. This may be the most effective way to prosecute the lawbreaker. It is not a good way to understand him. For that purpose, the individual must be put back into his social setting and observed in his daily activities. In order to understand the spectacular event, it is necessary to see it in relation to the everyday pattern of life. . . .

Whyte learned how to be accepted by the street corner people. "If you ask direct questions, people will just clam up on you," he writes. "If people accept you, you can just hang around, and you'll learn the answers in the long run without even having to ask the questions."

When Whyte used some obscenities to try to gain acceptance, one of his new friends advised him, "Bill, you're not supposed to talk like that. That doesn't sound like you." Whyte had to be careful about influencing the group he was observing. "I tried to be helpful in the way a friend is expected to be helpful." The results of his observations allowed the reader to have a moving picture of the street corner society, not the still photograph that the brief glimpse allows.

Concerned by the direction of journalism toward focusing on centers of authority, reporters realized that they were concentrating on the formalities of life—its ceremonies, meetings, announcements. They realized they were not describing the reality of human experience and they became anxious to develop techniques that enabled them to expand their reporting. Sara Grimes, a reporter in Philadelphia, said after she had been covering the juvenile court for a year, "I wonder why so many reporters insist on quoting people in positions of power rather than observing people who are affected by power."

◀ New Directions

She listened closely to the young defendants in court, and she sought to understand the effect of the system on youngsters by talking to them. One day she learned that an 11-year-old boy—who was brought into court in handcuffs—had been held in a detention center for nine months although he had not committed a crime. He was a runaway. Grimes asked to talk to the youngster, who had been sent to foster homes after his parents were judged neglectful. He had not liked the foster homes and had run away. Here is part of the story she wrote:

◀ Listening to Young Offenders

"Jones, Jones," the guard's voice could be heard as he walked up and down the cell-block. Amid a few undistinguishable low grumblings behind the rows of bars came a small, high voice. "Yes, that's me."

Johnny was brought out to an anteroom. No longer crying, he sat with downcast eyes in dungarees and a gray sweat-shirt. Quietly and slowly he answered questions.

He wished he had somebody to bring him soap because the institutional soap gives him a rash. He would like to leave YSC (Youth Study Center) and would go "any place they send me."

How does it feel to be handcuffed? In a barely audible voice, he answered: "It makes me feel like a criminal."

It is a natural step from this kind of reporting to participant observation, for the only way the reporter can understand some situations is to experience them. Without this personal experience, some reporters contend, the people they write about become cardboard figures.

These reporters who contend that journalism has not dug deeply enough into the lives of people would agree with Chekhov's observation in his short story "Gooseberries":

> We see the people who go to market, eat by day, sleep by night, who babble nonsense, marry, grow old, good-naturedly drag their dead to the cemetery, but we do not see or hear those who suffer, and what is terrible in life goes on somewhere behind the scenes. Everything is peaceful and quiet and only mute statistics protest: so many people gone out of their minds, so many gallons of vodka drunk, so many children dead from malnutrition. And such a state of things is evidently necessary; obviously the happy man is at ease only because the unhappy ones bear their burdens in silence, and if there were not this silence, happiness would be impossible. It is a general hypnosis. Behind the door of every contented, happy man there ought to be someone standing with a little hammer and continually reminding him with a knock that there are unhappy people, that however happy he may be, life will sooner or later show him its claws, and trouble will come to him—illness, poverty, losses, and then no one will see or hear him, just as now he neither sees nor hears others. But there is no man with a hammer. The happy man lives at his ease, faintly fluttered by small daily cares, like an aspen in the wind—and all is well.

Some reporters see themselves as the man with the hammer.

Among the Navajos ▶ Reporters for *The Albuquerque* (N.M.) *Tribune* spent eight months with Navajo Indians in and around Gallup, N.M., which has the highest rate of alcohol-related deaths in the United States. The series by David Gomez and Patricia Guthrie showed death, disease and despair.

The six-part series also revealed the failure of officials to deal with the problem. The series won a George Polk award for local reporting.

With an Addict ▶ Loretta Tofani of *The Philadelphia Inquirer* watched as the young woman dropped her maternity pants past her swollen stomach. The woman, eight months pregnant, picked up a syringe and injected heroin into her right calf.

"He won't stop moving, this baby," the woman told Tofani. "When he moves a lot it means he's sick. He needs a fix."

Tofani stayed with the 30-year-old addict for months, watched her wheedle money from relatives for her drugs, stayed in her kitchen when she entertained a visitor for the $20 she needed for a fix.

And she stayed through the birth of the baby and watched the woman fight to retain custody of her daughter, who was born addicted to heroin, methadone and a pill the woman was popping before the birth.

The Live In ▶ Journalism students at Columbia University engage in participant observation in an assignment known as the Live In, which sends students into homes and workplaces. To move closer to their sources, students have tutored addicts in drug rehabilitation centers and children in schools. They have slept on the floors of mission houses in the Bowery, in sleeping bags at a residence of the Catholic Workers and on cots in shelters for the homeless.

Students have walked the beat with police officers, gone on home visits with social workers and accompanied ambulance drivers on their calls. These experiences were not one-shot affairs. Students met the policeman's family, talked to the welfare mother's children and went into wards to talk to patients.

Charles Young, a white, middle-class student from Wisconsin, did his Live In in a junior high school in West Harlem in New York City. Let's join Young while he waits for the assistant principal in his office. The room is filled with students. Young describes the scene at the beginning of his Live In:

> Gus Marinos, known simply as "Marinos" to everybody, a Greek immigrant in his twenties with dazed but kindly eyes beneath his Coke-bottle glasses, returns to his office on the fourth floor. The room erupts with a deafening chorus of his name.
>
> "MAH-*REE*-NOS! HER FINGERNAILS BE POISON!" a girl screams, holding up her scratched right hand.
>
> "So die," says Marinos, examining some smudged papers on his desk.
> "WHY 'ON'T CHEW DIE!"
> "You wanna go home?"
> "YEAH, BUT CHEW CAN'T TELL ME HER NAILS AIN'T POISON!"
> "So go home."
> "HER NAILS GOT DIRT AN' SHIT IN 'M!" The girl leaves with a pass home.
>
> "MAH-*REE*-NOS!" another girl demands, "GIMME A PENCIL!" He hands her a pencil from his desk. "I 'ON'T WANT NO PENCIL LIKE THAT! I WANNA BLACK PENCIL!"
> "This *is* a black pencil."
> "I MEAN A YELLOW PENCIL THAT WRITES BLACK!"
> "We don't sell those here."
> "I 'ON'T WANT TO BUY NO PENCIL! I WANT CHEW TO GIMME IT!" She grabs the pencil from his hand and in the process drops a text book. "NOW SEE YOU MADE ME DONE DIRTY MY BOOK!"
> "I made you done what?"
> "DIRTY MY BOOK!" She leaves for class.
>
> These girls read an average of two years below the national norm for their grade level (slightly ahead of the boys), but the ghetto has already taught them how to get what they want from life: yell until somebody gives it to you. The lesson is apt, because when they are graduated in three years or so, they won't be equipped to do anything anyway.
>
> That these girls (all sent to the office for disciplinary reasons) want something is obvious. What they want is less obvious and increasingly important as the market for unskilled labor dries up.
>
> The first step in finding out what they want is learning a new vocabulary, some of which would be useful to define here. To "come out your mouth" is to communicate. "On time" is an adjective or adverb of approbation meaning you have done something according to socially accepted procedure. "On cap" is synonymous with "in your head," referring to intelligence. . . .

Young interviewed the assistant principal in charge of discipline, who, he writes, "carries a cane in one hand and a leather whip in the other when she wades into a group of warring Dominican and Puerto Rican youths."

Life as a Cop. Steven Cole Smith spent 19 weeks in the Dallas Police Academy, training alongside 43 other recruits. He wanted to know more about the police he covered for the *Dallas Times Herald*. Repeatedly, he said he had been told on his beat, "You can't understand what it's like unless you do it." He discovered he couldn't pass the academic tests without studying hard, and the physical training was taxing. "Rain or shine, we exercised and ran incessantly." He said he could understand the police-reporter tension: "Police see the subsequent media story as second-guessing a decision that had to be made in a heartbeat, always under stressful conditions." During his training and in later weeks on a police beat, he wrote for his newspaper about his life as a police officer.

His description continues:

> She resembles an army tank—solid, low-to-the-ground, unstoppable, paradoxically maternal.
>
> She is in fact known as the mother of the school. Teachers speak with awe of the dedication that brings her to the otherwise deserted building on weekends and vacations. Students speak with equal awe of her omniscience. Because they trust her, she knows exactly who is pushing what drugs and who is fighting with whom.
>
> Standing at the main entrance to the building at 3 o'clock one Friday afternoon in anticipation of a gang fight, Williams catalogues a gathering of a dozen or so Puerto Rican school alumni.
>
> "That one is on parole now. . . . That one is pushing. Look at his station wagon. . . . That one has a sawed-off .38 in his pocket. We'd tell the police about it, but it will pass fifty hands by the time they can react. . . ."
>
> On Thursday, one of their little brothers dropped a piece of chalk from the fourth floor that hit a Dominican on the head. In the ensuing melee, another Puerto Rican was badly cut on the arm with a broken bottle. The Puerto Ricans seek vengeance.
>
> Having no stake in the matter, the blacks are blasé and leave the area immediately. They've seen it all before and even the prospect of serious violence is a bore. The Hispanics gather in groups along the sidewalk and buzz with rumors, with more energy than they have shown all day in class.
>
> Williams crosses the street and puts her arm around one of her former students who has an Afro bigger than the rest of his body. She makes small talk for a couple of minutes, then kisses him on his pock-marked cheek as the gang scatters off down the street. A group of Dominicans, observing the enemy from a block away, disappears to its lair on 133rd Street.
>
> The aborted fight is typical of junior highs anywhere in that the participants seem willing to do battle over nothing. What is frightening is that the involved alumni range in age from 16 to the mid-twenties. They never grew up, just became better armed. They are the fruit of the American system of education.
>
> "Even five years ago they at least expressed an interest in college," says Williams back in the dormitory-room-sized office which she shares with three other school officials and usually seven or eight students who have been thrown out of class. . . .

Young befriended a bright young black student in the school. After Young graduated and went to work for *Rolling Stone,* he decided to look up the youngster for a story for the magazine about his dream of becoming a basketball star. He found the youth in high school, playing basketball, struggling with his classes and still filled with hope. Young's piece, "Above 125th Street: Curtis Haynes' New York," begins:

"I'm growin' plants all the time," says Curtis Haynes, pouring half a glass of water over a geranium. The floor and window ledge of his bedroom are covered with leafy pots. "Plants are everything. They give us oxygen and food. They also a home for insects." He brushes an aphid off a leaf. "Insects gonna inherit the earth."

He continues the tour of his room—recently painted electric blue by his mother—by pulling a picture off a shelf full of basketball trophies. Judging by his fleeting eyes and reticent tone of voice, he doesn't know what to make of me—a pale, white, 26-year-old, bearded magazine editor with thick glasses from a myopic childhood of too much TV watching and book reading in Madison, Wisconsin. Nor do I know what to make of him—a handsome, ebony-skinned, 16-year-old, short-haired high-school student with sharp vision from a childhood spent on the basketball courts of Harlem. "This my brother, Footie," he says, holding a blurred photograph of a teenager bearing a strong resemblance to Curtis. "Remember, remember, remember . . ." is inscribed around the margins. "We named him that because he had such big feet," he says. Curtis' Pro Ked basketball shoes equal my own 11½ Adidas—and I am 6' 2" while he is just 5' 10". "He died in a fight two years ago. Puerto Rican friend got in an argument at a party and the other dude pulled a gun. My brother jumped between them. I never go to parties no more."

The concept of the Live In is based on the work of anthropologists such as Margaret Mead and Oscar Lewis and the author Robert Coles. They spent considerable time with the people they were observing. In describing the field work that went into her book *Coming of Age in Samoa,* Mead wrote:

> I concentrated on the girls of the community. I spent the greater part of my time with them. I studied most closely the households in which adolescent girls lived. I spent more time in the games of children than in the councils of their elders. Speaking their language, eating their food, sitting barefoot and cross-legged upon the pebbly floor, I did my best to minimize the differences between us and to learn to know and understand all the girls of three little villages on the coast of the little island of Tau, in the Manua Archipelago.

◀ **Problems of Involvement**

But participant observation can cause problems. In addition to the possibility that the reporter's presence may affect the event, the participant observer can become too deeply involved with his or her sources, risking the possibility that feelings may precede responsibility to the facts.

Participant observation also has been criticized as exploitation of the source. After all, the journalist is using the lives of people as the basis of a story, which could lead to the reporter's acclaim, help him or her win a pay raise and possibly a promotion. But the alcoholic, the addict, the welfare mother and the police officer are not reimbursed for their contributions. Nor is much done about the problems that overwhelm some of these people.

The journalist James Agee agonized over prying into the lives of Southern sharecroppers. He and the photographer Walker Evans were assigned to do an article on cotton tenantry, the system by which farmers worked the fields of landowners in return for a share of the crop less what was advanced to them for seed, living quarters and tools. The sharecroppers were poorer than dirt poor, for not even the earth they tilled was theirs. The magazine article was not published, but in 1940 the work became a book, *Let Us Now Praise Famous Men.* Agee knew the justifications for his intimate observations, but they did not console him. Early in the book, he describes his reservations:

> It seems to me curious, not to say obscene and thoroughly terrifying, that it could occur to an association of human beings drawn together through need and chance and for profit into a company, an organ of journalism, to pry intimately into the lives of an undefended and appallingly damaged group of human beings, an ignorant and helpless rural family, for the purpose of parading the nakedness, disadvantage and humiliation of these lives before another group of human beings, in the name of science, of "honest journalism" (whatever that paradox may mean), of humanity, of social fearlessness, for money, and for a reputation for crusading and for unbias which, when skillfully enough qualified, is exchangeable at any bank for money (and in politics, for votes, for job patronage, abelincolnism, etc.). . . .

In rebuttal to these criticisms, reporters who use the technique say that public awareness is increased by stories about the lives of people. They say this awareness can lead to reform by involving the public emotionally in the situations described by the reporter.

Also, participant observation can help correct a detachment that can lead to callousness. A student who said he considered drug addicts weak and worthless conducted a Live In with a young female addict. The woman's daughter was being put up for adoption because her mother had been judged unfit to raise her. The woman's agony at the prospect of losing her daughter—which the student felt intensely—led him to do a series of revealing articles about the city's adoption laws.

The experience of participant observation allows the reporter to step outside routines and familiar environments to achieve new insights and to avoid another trap—the tendency to stereotype. Working under pressure, reporters fall back on stereotyping people, which permits them to simplify complicated events and to communicate complexities in easily understood terms. Forgetting that life is endless variety and change, some reporters look at the world through a kaleidoscope that is never turned. As a consequence, their observations reflect only a narrow, static vision. In Chapter 17, we will examine these stereotypes and the ways of thinking that determine how reporters look at events.

Postscript: Some 50 years after Agee and Evans interviewed and photographed the poor in the rural South, a Harvard student read their book and decided to make it the focus of his senior thesis. The student, Bill Berkeley, went to Alabama to interview some of those Agee had talked to.

He found a few who remembered the Agee-Evans team. One woman, who had been photographed as a child for the book cover, asked Berkeley, "What right did that man have to put my picture on the cover of his book?" She was pictured wearing a potato sack.

Berkeley decided on journalism as a career, and, after working on an Alabama daily, became a free-lance foreign correspondent. His reporting in Liberia on human rights abuses led to a warning that he would be killed if he returned to Liberia, and in Zaire he and his wife were arrested, questioned for 48 hours and ordered to leave the country immediately because of "unauthorized reporting."

Whether the reporter is involved in participant reporting or covering a city council hearing, the principles and the methods of reporting are the same.

◀ **Everyday Reporting**

The reporter has a sense of what is newsworthy from his or her familiarity with the community and the beat. On assignment, the reporter tries to come up with a story idea quickly. Then the reporter documents the idea.

But the reporter is not so transfixed by the broad theme that he or she ignores details. When Christopher Ringwald of the *Watertown Daily Times* covered the disappearance of a young mother, he noted in his story, "The only item missing with Miss McDonald was a quart bottle of Bacardi rum." She had taken nothing else with her when she left.

Six weeks later, a partially decomposed body was found in a remote area. The identity was uncertain, and the police were not talking. But Ringwald did learn one fact that made his story have some certainty about the identification of the woman:

> To the side of the corpse, which was found in a reclining position as if the woman had fallen asleep there, according to Chief King, was a quart bottle of Bacardi rum.

Ringwald said that when he interviewed the family he asked what the woman took with her. On learning it was rum, "it seemed unnecessarily nosey to ask what brand. But I did."

Not only do reporters ask questions that they think will elicit useful replies, they note relevant and specific physical characteristics: Are there fewer spectators than anticipated? Were the bookcases empty? Is the block on which the murder took place a quiet residential street? Was the highway slick with rain when the accident occurred? Was it dark or dusk when the game ended?

They note whether the bird in the cage of the apartment in which the crime took place was a parakeet, canary or parrot. And they listen if it was a parrot. A reporter for a California newspaper put up high in his story the cries of the parrot at the scene of a suicide-murder: "Where's mommy? Where's daddy?"

◀ **Summing Up**

The key to first-rate observation is the quality of the theme the reporter has in mind. The reporter's theory or idea—call it the possible lead to the story—"suggests and coordinates observations," says the scientist and teacher-writer Stephen Jay Gould of Harvard. "Theory can prod, suggest, integrate and direct in fruitful ways."

But it "can also stifle, mislead and restrict," Gould adds. He calls the business of devising themes as a prelude to making observations the "double-edged sword . . . as both liberator and incarcerator. . . ." It is liberating when the theme is borne out by information gathered on the basis of detached observation. It is incarcerating when the reporter's observations are made with eyes and ears determined to see and hear on the basis of hope and belief that the theme or lead is on target.

In the next chapter, we will look at how reporters build the background on which they structure sound observations and their stories.

Charlie Starr, *The San Diego Union-Tribune.*

Looking for—and Finding—the Different Angle

Journalists seek out the new and different. If it's routine, it isn't newsworthy. On assignment from his newspaper to find a feature photo, Charlie Starr thought a shot of baseball's All Star game from a hillside in the twilight would be interesting. When he made it up the hill, he found a group set up to enjoy the game with their own tailgate party. Starr waited for the light from the TV screen to be about the same level as the light from the stadium. This is the result.

Further Reading ▶

Agee, James. *Let Us Now Praise Famous Men.* Boston: Houghton-Mifflin, 1960.

Beveridge, W.I.B. *The Art of Scientific Investigation.* New York: Vintage Books, 1962.

Lipstadt, Deborah E. *The American Press and the Covering of the Holocaust, 1933–1945.* New York: The Free Press, 1985.

Sanders, Marlene, and Marcia Rock. *Waiting for Prime Time: The Women of Television News.* Urbana, Ill.: University of Illinois Press, 1988.

12 Building and Using Background

Preview

Reporters are always at work building two kinds of background knowledge:

- **General:** The overall knowledge that the reporter takes to the job. It is based on wide reading and general experience.
- **Specific:** The specialized information that helps the reporter handle his or her beat. It includes, for example, knowing about one judge's preference for jail sentences and another's for probation, or the mayor's determination to re-assess property to increase revenues.

A command of background allows the reporter to see connections among facts and incidents; this grouping of material may lead to stories that are more revealing than is the bare recital of the news event.

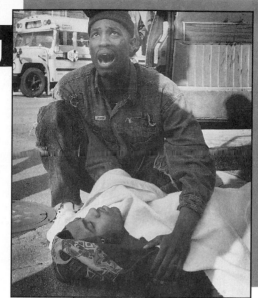

Todd Panagopoulos, *The Star,*
Chicago Heights, Ill.

The shooting is set against mounting school violence.

The reporter is expected to know it all. An error, a missing fact or a misinterpretation cannot be explained away.

Demanding as this may seem, it is the lot of the professional to be unfailingly certain in performance. The doctor is expected to identify the ailment that plagues the patient. The attorney is an authority on the law. The teacher is a wise, unfaltering guide who takes students through the complexities of phonics, irregular French verbs and William Blake.

But we know all professionals are fallible. Doctors misdiagnose, and sometimes their operations fail. Lawyers lose cases they should win. Teachers are human, too, like the grade school teacher who assigned her class the task of writing sentences containing words from a list she supplied. One youngster, whose father had taken him to a baseball game the day before, chose the word *cap,* and he wrote, "Catfish Hunter wears a cap." The teacher returned the boy's paper with the sentence corrected: "A catfish hunter wears a cap."

Should the teacher have known Catfish Hunter was a baseball player? Well, perhaps we do make excuses for teachers, as well as for doctors and lawyers. But we do not excuse the journalist who errs through ignorance.

Should the journalist really be expected to know everything? "Yes," replies the reporter Murray Kempton. "When you're covering anything, and you're writing about it at length, you use everything you know. And in order to use everything you have to be interested in an extraordinary range of things."

Twain's and Mencken's Complaints ▶

In Mark Twain's *Sketches,* he describes his experiences as a newspaperman in "How I Edited an Agricultural Paper." Twain is telling a friend that little intelligence is needed to be a newspaperman:

> I tell you I have been in the editorial business going on fourteen years, and it is the first time I ever heard of a man's having to know anything in order to edit a newspaper. You turnip! Who write the dramatic critiques for the second-rate papers? Why, a parcel of promoted shoemakers and apprentice apothecaries, who know just as much about good acting as I do about good farming and no more. Who review the books? People who never wrote one. Who do up the heavy leaders on finance? Parties who have had the largest opportunities for knowing nothing about it. Who criticise the Indian campaigns? Gentlemen who do not know a war whoop from a wigwam, and who never have had to run a foot race with a tomahawk, or pluck arrows out of the several members of their families to build the evening camp-fire with. Who write the temperance appeals, and clamor about the flowing bowl? Folks who will never draw another sober breath till they do it in the grave.

H.L. Mencken, a journalist whose prose skewered presidents, poets and bartenders with equal vigor, used some of his most choice execrations to denounce his fellow journalists. In an editorial in the *American Mercury,* October 1924, he wrote of journalists:

> The majority of them, in almost every American city, are ignoramuses, and not a few of them are also bounders. All the knowledge that they pack into their brains is, in every reasonable cultural sense, useless; it is the sort of knowledge that belongs, not to a professional man, but to a police captain, a railway mail-clerk or a board boy in a brokerage house. It is a mass of trivialities and puerilities; to recite it would be to make even a barber or a bartender beg for mercy. What is missing from it is everything worth knowing—everything that enters into the common knowledge of educated men. There are managing editors in the United States, and scores of them, who have never heard of Kant or Johannes Müller and never read the Constitution of the United States; there are city editors who do not know what a symphony is, or a streptococcus, or the Statute of Frauds; there are reporters by the thousand who could not pass the entrance examination for Harvard or Tuskegee, or even Yale. It is this vast ignorance that makes American journalism so pathetically feeble and vulgar, and so generally disreputable no less. A man with so little intellectual enterprise that, dealing with news daily, he goes through life without taking in any news that is worth knowing—such a man, you may be sure, is as lacking in true self-respect as he is in curiosity. Honor does not go with stupidity. If it belongs to professional men, it belongs to them because they constitute a true aristocracy—because they have definitely separated themselves from the great masses of men. The journalists, in seeking to acquire it, put the cart before the horse.

The practice of journalism arouses considerable passion among outsiders, sometimes leading them to excesses of inconsistency. George Bernard Shaw, the eminent playwright and critic, was of two minds regarding journalism. In a note to a journalist, he wrote:

> Dear Sir,
> Your profession has, as usual, destroyed your brain.

But he also wrote:

> Journalism can claim to be the highest form of literature. For all the highest literature is journalism, including Plato and Aristophanes trying to knock some sense into the Athens of their days and Shakespeare peopling that same Athens with Elizabethans. Nothing that is not journalism will live as long as literature or be of any use while it does live. So let others cultivate what they may call literature. Journalism for me.

◀ **GBS: Two Views**

These comments were made years ago. Journalists are now college trained, often in schools of journalism (a hopeful sign, Mencken said in the same editorial we have quoted from). And yet: What are we to make of the current generation, one of whose representatives wrote in a college newspaper about a presentation of "The Merchant of Venus," instead of "The Merchant of Venice"?

And what can we say to the journalism student who wrote of the sculptor Michel Angelo?

Should the journalist be expected to know the plays of Shakespeare, the world of art and the names of baseball players? And how to derive a percentage, calculate a ratio and find the median in a group of figures? Would it terrify would-be journalists to suggest that the answer has to be yes?

This storehouse of knowledge is the reporter's background. As Kempton, Twain and Mencken suggest, it should be kept full and constantly replenished—if such a feat is possible. Reporters need to have at their fingertips a wide assortment of information and more: They should know dates, names, policies made, policies defeated, what leads the best-seller list and what agency compiles the list of the 10 most-wanted criminals. All of this has to be put into some kind of schematic, some kind of pattern, or reporters will eventually see themselves in the sad comment of T.S. Eliot, "We had the experience but missed the meaning."

◀ **Improvements?**

The term *background* has three definitions:

• A reporter's store of information. This knowledge may be amassed over a long period or picked up quickly in order to handle a specific assignment. Without background knowledge, a reporter's fact gathering can be nondirected.

• Material placed in the story that explains the event, traces its development and adds facts that sources have not provided. Without background, a story may be one-dimensional.

• Material a source does not want attributed to him or her. It may or may not be used, depending on the source's instructions.

◀ **Background Defined**

More Than Writing. "The vocabulary of a writer is his currency but it is a paper currency and its value depends on the reserves of mind and heart which back it."—Cyril Connolly

Reporters have a deep and wide-ranging fund of knowledge. Much of this stored information concerns processes and procedures: the workings of the political system; the structure of local government; arrest procedures; government finance. The good reporter is aware of the past and its relation to the present. The *Dred Scott* and the *Brown* v *Board of Education* Supreme Court decisions are kept in mental drawers, ready for use. When a candidate refers to the New Deal, the reporter knows what is meant.

The knowledge of how things work can turn a routine assignment into a significant story. When a reporter for a Long Island newspaper was sent to cover a fire in a plastic factory, she noticed that the plant was located in a residential zone. On her return to the office, she told her editor, "I've got the information on the fire, but I want to check out why that factory was built there in a residential

What They Don't Know

The National Assessment of Educational Progress tested 8,000 17-year-olds of different races, both sexes and all regions of the U.S.

Some of the findings:

- 20 percent or fewer could identify Joyce, Dostoyevsky, Ellison, Conrad or Ibsen.
- 36 percent knew Chaucer is the author of *The Canterbury Tales*.
- 37 percent could equate Job with patience during suffering.
- Fewer than 25 percent knew that Lincoln was president between 1860 and 1880.
- 32 percent could place the Civil War between 1850 and 1900.
- 57 percent could place World War II between 1900 and 1950.
- 30 percent could identify the Magna Charta.

Their elders didn't do much better: 63 percent of those 18 to 24 could not find France on an unmarked map, more than half couldn't locate New York City and one in seven couldn't point to the United States on a world map.

And What They Do Know

John Treacy, professor of economics at Wright State University in Dayton, Ohio, asked 109 students to identify Adam Smith, the father of economic study, who was discussed in their reading, and Spuds McKenzie, a dog used in a television commercial for beer. The results:

- 29 percent identified Adam Smith correctly.
- 95 percent identified Spuds McKenzie correctly.

zone. Was it zoned industrial when the factory was built, or did the company get a variance?" The reporter knew that variances—exceptions to general zoning patterns—are sometimes awarded to friends or political donors. Though the reporter was not a city hall reporter or a specialist in real estate, she knew about zoning through her overall understanding of city government. Her curiosity and knowledge led to a significant story.

When Joe Munson, a photographer for *The Kentucky Post* in Covington, Ky., was covering the Indianapolis 500, the daring tactics of a driver caught his eye. Munson knew that there is an imaginary line that race car drivers must follow around bends in order to keep their cars under control.

 ◄ Covering the 500

"I noticed driver Danny Ongais straying six inches from that imaginary line and I suspected he was destined for a crash," Munson recalled.

"So I kept my camera focused on him."

Munson was ready when Ongais lost control and his car cracked into the wall. Munson was able to run off 20 shots of the fiery crash that seriously injured

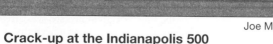

Joe Munson, *The Kentucky Post.*

Crack-up at the Indianapolis 500

Joe Munson, a photographer for *The Kentucky Post,* sensed that Danny Ongais was asking for trouble. With his knowledge of race car driving, Munson was able to tell that Ongais was cutting turns too closely. Munson trained his camera on Ongais, and when the car spun out of control on a turn, Munson was able to photograph the fiery crash.

Ongais. One of them took first place in the sports category of a National Press Photographers Association regional competition.

A frequent criticism of U.S. journalists is that although their mastery of the journalistic craft is unexcelled, their general knowledge is limited. American journalism lacks a tradition of scholarship, critics contend.

Such knowledge is important because it is the bedrock on which news stories are built. The American philosopher John Dewey said, "We cannot lay hold of the new, we cannot even keep it before our minds, much less understand it, save by the use of ideas and knowledge we already possess." Irving Kristol, a writer on social and political affairs, says, "When one is dealing with complicated and continuous events, it is impossible to report 'what happened' unless one is previously equipped with a context of meaning and significance."

Sinking Baskets ▶

Here's an example of what Dewey and Kristol are talking about. It's from John McPhee's series of articles, "A Sense of Where You Are" for *The New Yorker,* which later became a book. McPhee engaged in an extended Live In with Bill Bradley, the Princeton basketball player. One day McPhee accompanied Bradley to a school gym where he watched Bradley shoot 14-foot jump shots.

Bradley kept missing. "Six in a row hit the back rim of the basket and bounced out," McPhee wrote.

Bradley paused and "seemed to be making an adjustment in his mind. Then he went up for another jump shot from the same spot and hit it cleanly." Bradley continued to shoot and hit, then paused. He turned to McPhee and said, "You want to know something? That basket is about an inch and a half low."

A few weeks later, McPhee wrote, he returned to the gym with a steel tape, borrowed a ladder and measured the height of the basket. "It was nine feet ten and seven-eighths inches above the floor, or one and one-eighth inches too low."

Bradley's intimate knowledge of the court, his feel for the exact height of the basket (his basketball storehouse) enabled him to adjust to what he realized was a new situation. Bradley, by the way, went on to a distinguished professional career with the New York Knicks and then took his studious approach to the U.S. Senate where he represented New Jersey.

Knowing the Records ▶

Marcia Chambers, who covered the Criminal Courts Building for *The New York Times,* scored many exclusives because she had mastered the procedures of the criminal justice system. Chambers used files, records and background that led to an exclusive she wrote on the arrest of a mass-murder suspect. Without her background knowledge, her arrest story would have had some interest but little significance. Here is her description of how she went about digging up the information for her story:

> On the day Calvin Jackson was arrested, I covered the arraignment where the prosecutor announced that Jackson had been charged with the murder of one woman and had "implicated himself" in several others. At the time, we wanted to find out more about Jackson's prior criminal record, but given the hour—5:30 p.m.—we couldn't get the information. In a sidebar story that appeared the next day, Joe

Treaster, the police reporter, said Jackson's previous arrest had occurred 10 months before. But the disposition of the case, the story said, was unknown.

From my experience, I knew that nearly all cases are disposed of through plea bargaining, the process whereby a defendant agrees to plead guilty in exchange for a lesser charge. Several weeks before I had obtained from the Office of Court Administration data that showed that last year only 545 out of 31,098 felony arrests went to trial, including drug cases.

On Monday, at 10 a.m., I went to the court clerk's office. My premise was that Jackson's last arrest, like the thousands of others that pass through the criminal court system, had probably involved plea bargaining, a reduction of charges and a minimal sentence.

From the docket book, I obtained the docket number of the mass-murder case, and since case records are public information, I asked the clerk for the case. I took it to the side of the room, and quickly copied the file that contained information about his previous arrests. (In addition to carrying change and a phone credit card for phone calls, reporters should carry at least two dollars in change at all times for the copying machine as well as a backup pen or pencil.)

On Tuesday, having obtained the dates of Jackson's previous arrests from the rap sheets, I checked the docket book again, obtained the cases and copied them.

At about 2 p.m., I called my desk to say I thought I had a good story. I had a general outline, but said I was uncertain whether it would be ready to go that night. I left the courthouse and went to the *Times*.

First I went to the law library at the *Times* to check the Penal Code and Criminal Procedure Law. I knew from the complaint that Jackson had been charged with two felonies in his prior arrests, which had been delineated on the court papers by statute number. From the law books I learned the maximum sentence for each crime. In this case, the original charges were "C" felonies, punishable by up to 15 years in prison.

By 3:30 p.m., I was still missing information. I wanted to talk to the victim who had pressed the charges against Jackson and his two accomplices on his last arrest, but a check at the Park Plaza Hotel where he lived, and where a half dozen of the murders had occurred, turned up the fact that the complainant had moved out four months before and left no forwarding address or telephone number.

I wanted to talk to the judges involved. Two were unreachable; one was on the bench.

At 4:30 or 5 p.m., I told my editors the status of the story. We decided that while it was important to speak to the participants, the records clearly spoke for themselves. The decision was made to write the story at about 5:15 p.m., for a 7 p.m. deadline.

After I finished writing, a young intern came over to my desk and said to me, "Boy, that was a good leak."

I was startled by his comment and told him how the story came about. His statement indicated to me one of the major failures of journalism today—an over-reliance on leaks and insufficient attention paid to enterprise.

Suspect in Slayings Once Got 30 Days Instead of 15 Years

By Marcia Chambers

Calvin Jackson, who is said by the police to have "implicated himself" in the murder of at least nine women, was arrested in Manhattan 10 months ago on felonious robbery and burglary charges that could have sent him to prison for 15 years, an examination of court records disclosed yesterday.

Instead, the 26-year-old former convict was sent to jail for 30 days after the felony charges against him and two others were reduced to misdemeanors.

He had pleaded guilty in plea bargaining in Criminal Court to the lesser charges, which arose from the robbery last November of a young man, a resident of the Park Plaza Hotel, where Mr. Jackson lived and where six of his alleged victims were killed.

Mr. Jackson's experience is no different from that of thousands of others who yearly pass through the city's court system.

. . . the year of Mr. Jackson's last arrest, there were 31,098 felony arrests in Manhattan, according to the crime analysis unit of the Police Department. Of these, only 545 cases went to trial on the original felony charges, including possession or sale of narcotics.

Four out of every five of the 31,098 felony arrests were subject to plea-bargaining and were disposed of at the very outset of the court process—at arraignment before a Criminal Court judge or at a subsequent hearing. That is what happened in the Jackson robbery case. . . .

—*The New York Times*

Blundering in Print ▶

Reporters with ample background knowledge do not embarrass themselves or their editors by blundering in print or on the air. Witness these bloopers, the result of a lack of specific knowledge:

- In one of her columns, Harriet Van Horne referred to Canada as having a "tough and happily homogeneous population. . . ." (The columnist ignored the large Indian and Inuit populations and the almost six million French-speaking Canadians, who have their own schools in an officially bilingual country. Not only is the country not homogeneous, the French- and English-speaking Canadians are hardly happily ensconced together. Many of the French-speaking people contend they are second-class citizens, which led to the separatist movement in the province of Quebec.)
- When the basketball coach at Boston College accepted the head coaching job at Stanford, a CBS sports announcer said that the coach had "followed Horace Mann's advice to go west." (The advice is attributed to Horace Greeley, founder and editor of *The Tribune:* "Go west young man." Horace Mann was an educator.)
- In a feature on food served during the Jewish holidays, a reporter for the *Press-Enterprise* in Riverside, Calif., described Yom Kippur as

"marked by rich, indeed lavish meals." (Yom Kippur, known as the Day of Atonement, is the most solemn of all Jewish holy days and is observed by fasting.)

• During a televised National Basketball Association game, a player let the man he was covering drive past him for a basket. The player looked disgusted with himself, and from the broadcast booth the sportscasters could see his lips moving. "What do you think he's saying, Bill?" one asked his colleague, Bill Russell, one of the great defensive stars in basketball and the first black coach in the NBA.

Russell replied, "I know how Walt feels. I can hear him muttering a four-syllable word." Russell's colleague laughingly corrected him, "You mean four-letter word, Bill." Slowly, deliberately, Russell said, "No, I mean four-syllable word."

There was a long pause, a smothered gasp and then a commercial. (Russell's long playing career had given him a vast store of knowledge about the game, from strategy to the obscenities players use.)

◀ **Missing an Opportunity**

A magazine article about the death of the rap singer Eazy-E from AIDS carried the singer's warning that he hoped would "reach out to all my homeboys and their kin because I want to save them before it's too late," that "this thing is real and doesn't discriminate. It affects everyone."

Eazy-E (real name Eric Wright) was extremely popular among teen-agers. During his stay at a Los Angeles hospital, he received more cards and flowers than did Lucille Ball when she was hospitalized there before her death in 1989.

"Before Tomika, I had other women," the article quotes Eazy-E. "I have seven children by six different mothers. Maybe success was too good to me."

Here was an opportunity for the magazine to point out that AIDS is increasing among women through heterosexual contact and that a growing number of AIDS-infected babies are being born. The opportunity was missed.

◀ **Amassing Background**

Specific and general knowledge are gained in many ways. Education is a major contributor. Well-rounded high school and college curricula usually provide the knowledge and tools with which journalists must be equipped, from history and geography to foreign languages and mathematics.

A study of editors of newspapers with circulations between 25,000 and 90,000 by Mike Shelly, Traci Carson and Liz Russell of the Department of Communication at Illinois State University showed that the editors recommended for future journalists the following minors with a journalism major (in percent of editors polled):

Political science	23 percent
History	18 percent
Economics	17 percent
English	14 percent
Business	12 percent

The Past Illuminates The Present

To those who despair over today's racism and environmental damage, a knowledge of the past provides perspective. For years after gold was discovered in California, mining companies used hydraulic water cannons to wash down mountains for the gold ore they contained. Silt clogged once pristine rivers, causing floods downstream and irreparable damage was done to the terrian. After considerable public pressure, the practice was outlawed.

Now only a fringe movement of the far right, the Ku Klux Klan once elected governors and paraded its cause down the main avenues of state capitals. Here Klanswomen march along Pennsylvania Avenue in 1928 in Washington, D.C.

Top photo: Plumas County Museum. Bottom photo: National Archives in Washington, D.C.

Education does not stop with a degree. Journalists read widely and continue their studies in various ways. But not all knowledge comes from books.

The young men and women who are determined to be journalists are alert to the world around them. They make friends with all sorts of people, and they welcome new ideas, new ways of seeing events. They are interested in history, current affairs and what makes people and organizations tick. They speculate about what motivates people, they wonder about the role of money in society, and they are interested in how geography, history and the weather affect what people think and do. Although they are present oriented, they know something of the past. They learn by going to roller rinks and museums, from talking to third graders and pensioners, by watching fishermen and street vendors.

They also learn by attending seminars and conferences for journalists, by obtaining material on a wide variety of subjects from groups that dispense background matter. One such organization, the Foundation for American Communications, sponsors conferences and issues background material. Funded by the Ford Foundation, FACS' address is 3800 Barham Blvd., Suite 409, Los Angeles, Calif., 90068, (213) 851-7372.

◀ Continuing Education

Good reporters collect stray pieces of background that often have no particular use at the moment. Sooner or later, another bit of information will come along that when paired with the first will make a good story.

For example, a reporter who made it his business to look in on the state penitentiary every few weeks was talking to a guard one day when an old man walked by. He was an inmate with a long record, the guard said. Swindler, thief and bad-check artist, he was always in trouble, and now he was in the pen for life. A few weeks later, the reporter was chatting with the warden about another prisoner. Despite a long record of violent crime, he was in for an eight-year term, which meant he would be out in a little more than half that time.

The disparities in sentences interested the reporter, but he did little with the information. Such disparities were not new to him. Well-to-do defendants were never convicted for drunken driving but instead were allowed to plead to reckless driving charges; the poor were usually convicted of drunken driving. He had done a story on that. The short prison terms usually imposed on white collar criminals was also an old story.

Every so often, the reporter would go through the penitentiary's records of the arrests, convictions and sentences of the inmates for possible features. One day, while leafing through the record book, he noticed that the elderly swindler had been sentenced under something called the "habitual criminal law," which required stringent and specific sentences for frequent offenders. The reporter checked all the habitual criminal convictions and found that there was no consistency in sentences. The reporter's interest was piqued.

The convict with a long record of violent crimes was not sentenced under the habitual criminal law at all, despite the mandatory law. Putting these facts together, he wrote a series of articles pointing out that judges and district attorneys throughout the state were ignoring and misapplying the habitual criminal law. As

◀ **Pairing Facts**

a result, of the 72 frequent offenders in the state penitentiary who should have been sentenced under the law, only 14 were doing time under its provisions.

Many Prosecutors and Judges Ignore New Mexico Habitual Criminal Laws

(New Mexico has a stringent law concerning habitual criminals. But a Journal survey has shown that it is being consistently ignored by law enforcement officers. This is the first in a series of articles on this important law.)

SANTA FE, Jan. 4—New Mexico's habitual criminal laws, which were designed to increase punishment for the frequent offender, are ignored, inconsistently used, and misunderstood by many of the state's law enforcement officers and judges, a study of official records disclosed today.

Although the laws are clearly mandatory and require district attorneys to bring charges under the act when they can be applied, few district attorneys follow the statutes.

The habitual criminal laws apply to persons who have been found guilty of more than one felony.

Yet of the 72 men now behind bars at the state penitentiary who have committed three or more felonies, only 14 were sentenced under the habitual criminal act. The number of second offenders who could have been sentenced under the law but were not were too numerous to check.

In a few cases where men have been convicted under the law, district judges have handed down illegal sentences and have not applied the law consistently.

For some time the legal profession has been aware of these facts, but little has been done either to repeal the laws or to make them work fairly.

The habitual criminal act was passed in 1929 and establishes a table of increased prison sentences for law violators who have committed more than one felony. . . .

—*The Albuquerque Journal*

Always Use Background ▶

Few stories are complete without some background information. Reporters who disregard this advice do so at the peril of inadequately informing their readers and listeners. Events have causes and consequences.

When Sen. Robert Dole was seeking the 1996 presidential nomination, the Kansas Republican announced that he would try to block President Clinton's choice for Surgeon General. The nominee, the head of a medical school, had performed abortions during his career as a physician. The Associated Press report of Dole's opposition included this background sentence about the nominee:

His nomination is vehemently opposed by Christian right organizations, groups Mr. Dole has been courting in his presidential bid.

Anticipatory Journalism ▶

A solid grasp of the past and the present is essential to a growing area of reporting—*anticipatory journalism*. It consists of spotting trends, identifying movements in their earliest stages, locating individuals with an important message.

Journalism has not been good at this kind of reporting. It ignored the feminist movement, was late to sense the civil rights surge, was hesitant about the lifestyle changes of teen-agers.

But anticipatory journalism need not confine itself to trends and movements to be useful. It can be as simple as making journalism out of the realization that the city's revenues are inadequate to meet expenses and that payrolls and services will have to be cut or taxes increased. With this knowledge, the reporter can interview the mayor, city council members and community leaders about what solutions they recommend.

This is public service journalism, for its practice gives the public ample time to discuss and decide issues rather than having to react to decisions already made.

An essential to the practice of anticipatory journalism along with a grasp of background is a good string of sources, a subject we shall next look into after a final doleful note.

The best journalists know a lot. They know the past as well as the present. They are exceptions to the charge levelled by *The New York Times* columnist Bob Herbert who describes the United States as "a nation of nitwits." As evidence, he cites a Gallup Poll that found:

◀ **Summing Up**

- Sixty percent of Americans are unable to name the president who ordered the atomic bomb dropped on Japan. (Truman.)
- One of four didn't know Japan was the target of the bomb.
- A fifth didn't know that such an attack had occurred.

"We are surrounded by a deep and abiding stupidity," he writes.

For journalists to ply their trade well they know that they must be informed. Otherwise, they know, they are a menace to their readers, listeners and viewers.

Lewis, Anthony. *Gideon's Trumpet.* New York: Random House, 1964.
Steel, Ronald. *Walter Lippmann and the American Century.* Boston: Atlantic Monthly Press, 1980.
Ullmann, John H. *Reporter's Handbook: An Investigator's Guide to Documents and Techniques.* New York: St. Martin's Press, 1983.

◀ **Further Reading**

13 Finding, Cultivating and Using Sources

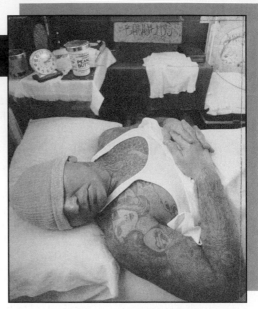

John Davenport, *The Houston Cronicle.*

Good sources are found everywhere.

Preview

The reporter relies on two types of sources:

• **Physical sources,** which consist of records, documents, reference works, newspaper clippings.

• **Human sources,** which consist of authorities and people involved in events. They are often less reliable than physical sources because they may have interests to protect and they are untrained observers and sometimes tell reporters what they think the reporter wants to hear. When using human sources, reporters find the person most qualified to speak—an authority on the subject, an eyewitness, an official, a participant.

J ournalists have a saying that a reporter can be no better than his or her sources. These sources include officials, spokesmen and -women, participants in events, documents, records, tape recordings, magazines, films and books. The quality of the reporter's story depends on the quality of the sources.

Reporters spend a lot of time looking for and cultivating people who can become sources and contacts. A county courthouse reporter in California spends a couple of hours a day passing time with his sources. He also chats with guards, secretaries, elevator operators, all of whom he describes as contacts, people who can provide tips for stories. An elevator operator tipped him off about a well-known businessman who had been summoned by a grand jury and was taken to the jury room by a back elevator.

Jeff Klinkenberg of *The St. Petersburg Times* shows us Milt Sosin, the Associated Press courthouse reporter in Miami, at work:

He pokes his head into offices and makes small talk with secretaries. He chats with a lawyer in an elevator. He shares respectful words with a newspaper reporter outside a courtroom. With a charming smile, he even opens a hallway door for a sweaty man in a three-piece suit.

For Sosin, who is probably the best reporter you *never* heard of, charm is part of his giant bag of journalist's tricks. His job is getting information. Being chummy, though it may come unnaturally, could pay off one day: He may need these courthouse people to provide news that might lead to an Associated Press exclusive.

"It's no big deal," Sosin says later, sounding almost embarrassed. "They're just sources. You treat them right. You stop by and ask them if anything is going on, that's all. If they give you something you can use, you protect them. You never betray their confidences."

Sosin's way with sources pays off. One of his biggest scoops was the indictment of Gen. Manuel Noriega of Panama for drug crimes. All the major newspapers were working on the story.

Klinkenberg writes:

> "I was sure he had been indicted," Sosin says now. "But the U.S. attorney was keeping it secret. He wanted to announce it at a press conference. I made a few phone calls. All my sources said Noriega's name was on the indictment. I told AP to go with the story."

During his first weeks covering Congress for *The Wall Street Journal,* Fred L. Zimmerman learned that finding and cultivating sources and contacts is essential. "If you can establish a friendly relationship with a committee chairman's secretary, she will tell you where he can be found in a hurry," Zimmerman says. "Or she will put you through on the phone sometimes when she wouldn't do it for a reporter she doesn't know."

There are two kinds of sources, human and physical. The distinction between the two, and their relative reliability, was nicely put by Sir Kenneth Clark, the British writer and critic: "If I had to say who was telling the truth about society, a speech by the Minister of Housing or the actual buildings put up in his time, I would believe the buildings."

The difference is often on the reporter's mind, for even though much of his or her work depends upon interviews, the reporter seeks physical evidence whenever possible. This kind of material includes newspaper clippings, books, records and documents as well as the reporter's direct observation.

Let us examine these two types of sources in detail.

A person with information the reporter needs for a story or for background is called a *source.* Sources include the woman who saw an airplane fall short of the landing strip and Deep Throat, the informant who cooperated with *Washington Post* reporters Woodward and Bernstein on their Watergate investigation. The stockbroker friend of a reporter who explains complicated financial matters is a source, although his name may never appear in a story.

Arthur L. Gavshon, the diplomatic reporter for the AP, defines a source in an article on sources in the *AP World Magazine:*

> To me anyone on the inside of any given news situation is a potential source. But they only turn into real sources when they come up with a bit, or a lot, of relevant information.

Gavshon says he finds sources anywhere and everywhere. He develops his sources "just as you would get to know a friend and nurture a relationship in

Ken Elkins,
The Anniston Star.

Conflicting Concepts

How do we help the millions of children living in poverty? One group says welfare benefits have created a culture of poverty into which generations of children have been born. They would cut benefits, force parents to work. Another group says cutting benefits would put more children at risk. Reporters are expected to cover such controversies with fairness and insight.

◀ Human Sources

Dual Purpose

Human sources can provide background information that helps a reporter understand a situation, and they can supply specific material for a story.

everyday life (always assuming you can live a normal life as a journalist)—through the exercise of patience, understanding and a reasonable capacity to converse about shared interests."

Sources need not be mayors or directors of companies. The city hall reporter knows that the town clerk who has served a succession of mayors has a comprehensive knowledge of the community and the inner workings of town government. The courthouse reporter befriends law clerks, court stenographers and security guards. Business reporters cultivate switchboard operators, secretaries, mailroom help.

Reporters have gone out of their way to do favors for their sources. At one newspaper in California, the reporters who handle obituaries send birthday candy and flowers to the mortuary employees who call to report the deaths of important people. A death called in near deadline means the newspaper or station telephoned first will have that much more time to write the obituary. A difference of two minutes can be the difference between making or missing the last edition or the 6 p.m. newscast.

Some reporters cultivate sources by reversing the news-gathering process. One Midwestern newsman says that instead of always asking sources for news, he puts his sources on the receiving end. "I see to it personally that they hear any gossip or important news. When I want news, I get it," he says.

The source needed for information on a single story need not be cultivated with the care reporters lavish on sources essential to a beat. But courtesy and consideration are always important. In speaking to a source for the first—and perhaps the only—time, the reporter identifies himself or herself immediately and moves to the questions quickly. A different pace is necessary for the source essential to a beat. Gavshon cautions:

> Don't ever rush things. Don't make the ghastly mistake of thinking only in terms of tomorrow's headline. . . . One-night stands rarely satisfy anybody.

Be Careful ▶

Under pressure, reporters often must rely on human sources who seem trustworthy. Sometimes they are not what they seem. When a federal agency called for a moratorium on silicon-gel breast implants, a woman made herself available to reporters, saying she was a breast cancer patient and had implants. She said she was satisfied with them. Three local television stations and *The Boston Globe* used her comments.

Terry Schraeder of WCVB-TV in Boston checked out the woman and found she was a paid spokeswoman for Dow Corning, manufacturer of the implant material, which had provided her with training in handling the media and a list of reporters to contact.

Pseudo-Sources ▶

Then there are the sources who are hardly qualified to speak on a subject but appear authoritative. When some members of Congress wanted to find out the plight of farmers hard hit by rising costs and falling income, they called Sissy Spacek and Jane Fonda to testify. The women had played farmers in films.

"It was not the pink leather sofa ($3,070), the trip with seven aides to ◀ Tips Puerto Rico ($16,000) or the chartered helicopter to Atlantic City ($1,500) that precipitated Laura D. Blackburne's fall from the chairmanship of New York City's Housing Authority last week. It was her abrupt, often harsh treatment of subordinates—who then opened the door for reporters who had been tipped to what they would find."

This is the beginning of Calvin Sims' account in *The New York Times* of the toppling of a major city official.

Disgruntled employees in Blackburne's office supplied reporters with lists of trips, lavish spending and dates. The reporters then filed Freedom of Information Act requests and obtained the records.

"We vowed to get her back, and we did," said one source.

Tips come from whistle-blowers—people who are angry at what they consider incompetence and violations of the law—as well as from disgruntled workers. We saw in Chapter 1 how a city employee tipped Heidi Evans to the failure of the city health department to renew Pap smear testing, and how that tip opened up a scandal. Her source was a whistle-blower.

Tips come in all shapes and sizes, not only as revelations of wrongdoing. A member of the local university's social science department tells a reporter on the university beat that he read a study that found that the favorite newspaper reading of those 21 to 25 years of age are the comics, television and movie listings and the classified ads. Maybe there's a story there, he suggests to the reporter.

The source is the reporter's life blood. Without access to information ◀ Keeping the Source through the source, the reporter cannot function. The reporter is just as necessary to most sources, for without the journalist the source has no access to the public. Sources in public life need reaction to their ideas and policies.

Out of this mutual need a source-reporter relationship develops: The source will provide the reporter with information and will brief him or her on developments. In return, the reporter will write a fair account of the material.

As events become more complex, the reporter's dependence on sources increases. When a reporter learns of a probable future event, such as the presentation of the municipal budget to the city council, he or she may ask a source for background so that the difficult story can be written authoritatively. The courthouse reporter who learns through the grapevine that the grand jury is about to return an indictment against the city clerk will ask the district attorney for a briefing, promising not to break the story before the indictment is returned. Sources usually are happy to comply because they prefer an accurate story to a rush job.

Bob Greene of *Newsday* says that it's necessary to build a "personal bond" with sources to keep them. "Show an interest in them, their work, their activities, their family. Get the names of children, husbands, wives, and use them. Every now and then, say, 'Let's have dinner, breakfast.' "

When something happens on a beat that could cost a reporter his or her source, another reporter usually is assigned to the story. "In sports, we'd rather have an investigative reporter come in and do our tough reporting," says Mary

Kress of *The Florida Times-Union* in Jacksonville, "so that the sports beat reporter doesn't get into trouble with the coach or the players."

Protecting Sources ▶

Sometimes a reporter is asked to protect a source's identity. An investigative reporter learns from a police officer that a convict serving a life term for murder was convicted on perjured police testimony. In return for the tip about the frame-up, the reporter must promise not to name the source.

The reporter can make this promise because shield laws in most states protect confidential sources. All states have some kind of protection, but in some states, a reporter who tries to protect a confidential source may face contempt charges and jail. State press associations usually distribute pamphlets about reporters' rights.

Sometimes a reporter is reluctant to embarrass a friendly source with a tough story. Walter Lippmann said there must be a "certain distance between the reporter and the source, not a wall or a fence, but an air space." Once a friend becomes an official, he said, "you can't call him by his first name anymore."

Some reporters protect their sources. Jack Anderson, a Washington columnist who specializes in inside information, states his philosophy as follows: "We will give immunity to a very good source as long as the information he offers us is better than that which we've got on him."

The inexperienced reporter has still another problem that sometimes leads to the overprotection of sources. Mixing with the kinds of people the reporter had once only read about or seen on television—governors, movie stars, generals—can be a heady affair. As a consequence, the reporter may lose objectivity. Veteran reporters may suffer from another form of this ailment. They become source oriented. Forgetting that they are responsible to the general reader, they write copy for their source's approval.

Reliability ▶

Human sources are not the most reliable of sources. Beat reporters find that their sources often have interests they wish to protect, programs and ideas they want to push, enemies they want to hurt.

The reporter who has to rely on transient sources for quick information on a breaking story knows that most people are notoriously inaccurate observers. A woman who says she saw an airplane crash "in a ball of fire" may not be relaying what she saw but what she has seen in movies of air crashes.

An eyewitness can seduce a reporter by the sheer drama of his or her story. Instead of being enthralled, reporters should be cautious, for their knowledge of human nature should tell them that most people tend to overdramatize events.

Erving Goffman, the sociologist, says everyone is a performer trying to put his or her stamp of individual identity on things. Individuals find it hard not to exaggerate their observations or feelings when they know that the more dramatic their account the more likely they will appear on TV. People also remember selectively, recalling mostly that which fits their preconceived notions or that which they find pleasant.

How can the reporter test the source's reliability? Sources essential to a reporter's beat should be chosen because of their knowledge of the subject, their contacts, and their reputations for intelligence and honesty. Here are some measures of reliability for transient sources:

◀ **Tests**

- Was the person an observer of the incident, or did he or she hear about it from someone else?
- Is the person a competent observer? An airline employee would be a better source for information about an airplane crash than would a student or a salesperson.
- Can the source supply precise details that have the ring of truth and seem consistent with the facts?
- Are several sources offering the same information? Generally, when several people provide the same version of an event, chances are good that the accounts are reliable.

Sometimes, sources lie. Some lie because they want the publicity a story-starved reporter will give them. Pete Hamill recalls one incident early in his journalism career: "Years ago I published a column based on a horrific story related to me by a man in East Harlem; three weeks later someone sent me a copy of a 30-year-old short story on which the lie was based."

◀ **The Liars**

He recalls another columnist's piece about a man who described his heroism in a fire. The next day, says Hamill, "this splendid gentleman was arrested for setting the building on fire."

These are the kooks and sad sacks. There are others—professionals, office holders, politicians—who lie as part of their jobs. A prominent criminal lawyer told journalists at a national convention, "If I give you deliberate misinformation on behalf of a client and you print it, that's your problem."

He said that he routinely and successfully manipulates reporters so that they write stories favorable to his clients. Some cases, he says, create a "feeding frenzy" among the press. "It's frightening . . . the hunger that's out there, whether it's the print media or television," he says. "I have found, to some extent, that media people can be used."

Then there are the hoaxsters, some of them engaging in sick humor, such as those who call newspapers to report the deaths of people very much alive. Obituary writers are vulnerable to the caller who says he or she is telephoning from a distant city about the sudden death of a local person. Editors caution those new to this beat to verify all deaths with a relative, a local mortuary, some official source.

◀ **The Hoaxsters**

Some hoaxsters are harmless, even hilarious. No journalism survey is complete without a salute to the inimitable Joe Skaggs, a teacher of media communication and a genius at staging events for a gullible press.

At one news conference, crowded with reporters and television crews, Dr. Josef Gregor announced that he had distilled cockroach hormones into a pill so potent it would make people immune to ailments as diverse as acne and menstrual cramps. His study group, the "Metamorphosis," distributed the scientific literature to reporters.

At another packed news conference some time later, Joe Bones announced he had formed the Fat Squad for people who needed help dieting. For a fee of $300, the Squad—a group of burly enforcers—was prepared to use physical force if necessary to keep clients on their diets. The story was carried on network television and in major newspapers around the country.

Outside the Democratic convention in New York City, the Rev. Joseph sat quietly on his bicycle. Behind him, attached to the bike, was a handsome oak portable confession booth, the Portofess, the Rev. Joseph told the curious.

Some delegates, too hurried to walk to a church a few blocks away, took advantage of the service.

The Portofess attracted the press, and stories were sent on the AP wires and Reuters. CNN and CBS and scores of other stations and newspapers featured the Portofess with its gold lettering that advertised Father Joseph's good office.

Gregor-Bones-Joseph was, of course, Joe Skaggs, who says he stages these elaborate scenes to show how careless the media are in checking sources. "Aren't they also susceptible to more dangerous manipulation?" he asks.

The Use of Experts ▶

Sometimes reporters use sources because of who or what they are, not because of what they know. Most people tend to believe those in authority. The more impressive the title, the higher the social position, the more prestigious the alma mater, the more faith people have in the expert or authority. This trust in authority is known as the "hierarchy of credibility"—the higher on the scale the authority is, the more believable the source is thought to be. When the journalist surrenders to this tendency, he or she allows those in power to define events and situations.

Reporters must be careful to use sources only within their areas of expert knowledge. Asked questions within the narrow range of their expertise, sources are useful. A banker can talk about banking, a general about the strategy and tactics of war. But it is dangerous to rely on a banker for comments on the nation's economy or on a general as an authority on international affairs. They may be less useful than the lesser-known labor department area representative or the assistant professor of international affairs at a local college.

A reporter's best sources are those who have demonstrated their knowledge and competence as accurate observers, interpreters and forecasters of events. Reporters should drop sources who are proved wrong in their observations and assessments, whether they served in the president's cabinet, ran a multimillion-dollar import business or graduated *summa cum laude* from Harvard.

Bob Greene suggests six measures of a source's credibility:

Track record: Has this source proved accurate in the past?
Confirmability: Can the source provide the names of other witnesses or documents that confirm the information?
Proximity: Was the source in a position to know the facts he or she is relaying?
Motive: Is the source's motive in supplying the material rational?
Contextuality: Does the information fit the facts?
Believability: Does the source seem to be stable, in control?

Gavshon uses a fairly simple device to test reliability. "My own rough-and-ready rule is to test out the new-found source with questions to which I already know the answers."

Despite all these tests, the reporter must keep in mind that he or she is relying on someone else, and that fact alone makes the story vulnerable. No reporter can ever feel certain that another person's observations are as objective and as accurate as his or her own.

Situations come up in which there is no right or wrong, truth or fabrication. In controversies over issues, sources may not lie, but they can differ significantly. Dr. Judith Lewis Herman, associate clinical professor of psychiatry in the Harvard Medical School and an authority on sexual and domestic violence, says that balance is essential in such stories. She warns against relying too heavily on anecdote, speculation and the opinions of "a small group of professional experts."

She recommends:

> In matters of significant controversy, an honest and vigorous effort must be made to include reasonable opposing views.
> The motives of those who press their views upon journalists must be routinely examined and, where appropriate, revealed to the reader.

◀ Balance Needed on Controversies

The leak is one of the instruments of government. Officials and agencies, departments and cabinet members, mayors and council members—everyone leaks information to reporters, and no one wants his or her name, agency or department attached to the information as a source. The other common characteristic of the leak is that it serves the leaker's purpose.

A list of the evils of the leak would be longer than the companion list of the good the leak serves. Officials can hide, float trial balloons, and plead innocence if the material backfires. But the leak also can be the avenue of communication for the whistle-blower. It can be a route along which classified or secret material reaches the public. The reporter has to walk a thin line between serving the source's purposes and serving the public's needs. But walk it the reporter must, because the leak is more than here to stay; the leak thrives and will continue to do so.

Presidents take office vowing to stem the tide of leaks. Ronald Reagan urged lie detector tests for those suspected of leaking, and before he took office, George Bush threatened reprisals against those leaking material to the press. He said that leaks reflected a lack of discipline among officials that could lead to problems such as the disclosure of security information.

Bush was particularly angry during his campaign when it was revealed, through a leak, that he was considering Sen. Dan Quayle of Indiana as his running mate, a report that turned out to be accurate.

Leaks can be wildly inaccurate and sometimes damaging to the subjects of the leaked material. Elie Abel of Stanford University has some guidelines for the use of such material:

• Be skeptical about the motives of the person leaking the information. "The leaker's interest should be identified, even when he cannot be named," Abel says.

◀ Leaks

- Editors should ask reporters questions about the material, and reporters "who expect to be trusted by their editors ought to show comparable trust in the discretion of their editors."
- Editors should require that at least two independent sources confirm leaked material.

Physical Sources ▶

The range of physical information is enormous. The availability of physical sources is limited only by the reporter's knowledge of their existence.

Many reference resources are free to the journalist: the law library of the district attorney or the nearby law school, the public and private libraries in town whose librarians delight in visits or calls from journalists, the files of local and state agencies in town and the considerable resources of the nearby college or university. Many of the larger state educational institutions have on their campuses various state-supported and private programs for governmental studies that are well-stocked with materials for stories as well as for background. Master's and doctoral theses make good sources for copy.

Databases provide quick access to dozens of excellent sources, from census material to local arrest records. Donald Barlett and James Steele turned to *The Philadelphia Inquirer* databases for material for their prize-winning series about the federal Tax Reform Act. "Once you would come up with a name of somebody, you could go right to one of these databases and see what was known about him very quickly," Steele said. The database made it possible to pack large amounts of convincing detail into their stories, such as the description of the widow who inherited $4 million more from her late husband's estate under the giveaway terms of the act.

Not All Sources Are Equal ▶

Not all physical sources are of equal reliability. Tables of vital statistics are more reliable than the city official's summary introducing the tables. The world almanac is more reliable than a newspaper clipping of the same event, for the almanac is usually the work of professional researchers, and the news story may have been written in a hurry before all the facts were in.

Veneration for Print ▶

Journalists have a tendency to venerate the printed word, no matter what its source, perhaps because the journalist spends his or her life so close to words on paper. Whatever the reason, the journalist's esteem for the somber black characters of print can be misplaced. In fact, print sometimes solidifies an original error. Once a story is written and filed in the newspaper library, it is difficult to correct.

Here is an apology for an error by Tom Wicker of *The New York Times,* who assumed that the published word was true:

A Memorial Day column detailing the problems of Vietnam war veterans stated that 500,000 of them had attempted suicide. This statistic was derived from an article in *Penthouse* magazine. The author of that article obtained it from a pamphlet of Twice Born Men, a veterans' group in San Francisco, now defunct. That organization's former director, Jack McCloskey, says he got the figure from the National Council of the Churches of the U.S.A. The council disavowed any knowledge of the statistic, which must therefore be considered unsupported. Its publication in this space is regretted.

The figure 500,000 should have seemed preposterous on its face. But reporters sometimes are influenced by their attitudes. Wicker may have been predisposed to believe the figure because of his opposition to the Vietnam War.

Art Jester of the *Lexington Herald-Leader* used physical and human sources to puncture the dramatic story of a public speaker, Col. John Cottell, who passed himself off as having served as a spy for the British and told tales of being parachuted behind Nazi lines, being imprisoned in Moscow's dreaded prison, Lubyanka, and being the model for John Le Carré's novels, *The Spy Who Came in From the Cold* and *Tinker, Tailor, Soldier, Spy.* He gave 70 to 75 talks a year at $2,500 each.

The tales were just too dramatic, Jester felt, and he started to dig. His conclusion in a copyrighted story: "Much, if not all, of his story is fiction."

◄ The Spy
Who Wasn't

• Le Carré denied any knowledge of Cottell. "I'm getting fairly irritated by the man. I've never heard of him, and there's no question of him being the basis of characters in my work. He is either mad or a fraud."
• Cottell said he was in a spy exchange at the Berlin Wall in 1957. The Wall was built in 1961.
• He claimed he was an ordained Anglican priest, and in his talks he often wore clerical garb. An Anglican bishop Jester contacted said, "Cottell has no connection with this diocese and we believe him to be a fraud." In answer to Jester's questions, Cottell acknowledged that he only holds a mail-order ordination certificate from the Universal Life Church Inc., which sends out certificates to anyone who mails a fee.
• His birth certificate listed him as two years younger than he claimed, which would have made him 16 years old when, he asserted, Winston Churchill sent him to parachute behind German lines in World War II.

Much can be learned by tracking a person through the many documents he or she leaves behind. Such searches are described as "following the paper trail." The trail is strewn with material: a birth certificate, hospital records, school records, real estate transfers, marriage and death certificates.

◄ Paper Trail

The material can be found in newspaper clippings, court records, reference works and government agency files. Two examples of what can be learned:

Home: What it cost; what was paid and what was borrowed for the down payment; who holds the mortgage and how much it amounts to; liens on the property; the amount of property taxes paid and any delinquencies.

Automobile: Registration number; title information; name and model of vehicle; year of manufacture; license plate number. Automobile records also include data on the owner—name, age, height, weight, offenses.

Special-interest organizations turn up material the journalist can use. For example: *ASH, Smoking and Health Review* looked into cigarette smoking by children. It reported that "more than one million children each year" take up smoking, "and approximately one fourth will die—often a painful and lingering death—as a result of this addiction."

◄ **All Sorts
of Sources**

ASH stands for Action on Smoking and Health, a national nonprofit organization concerned with the problems of smoking. The publication quoted U.S. Secretary of Health Louis W. Sullivan about the ease with which children can obtain cigarettes: "It is a moral and medical outrage that our society permits such ready access by our children."

Sullivan went on to endorse a model state law as "the single most important reform to improve the health of its citizens that any state could undertake in the decade of the 1990s."

In most states, Sullivan says, the sale of cigarettes to minors is prohibited. But the statutes are rarely enforced by busy police; and when merchants are cited, the cost to them—a small fine—is considered worth the risk.

The model law proposes licensing stores to sell cigarettes to adults, and when a sale is made to a minor, making the penalty be loss of the license. The law is similar to the statute regulating the sale of alcoholic beverages.

All of this interests a reporter. She decides to check on whether youngsters are smoking, so she goes to schools and student hangouts and watches. She then tries to learn where students buy their cigarettes. And finally she checks on the state law and whether the model law ASH wrote about has been introduced. If so, what happened to it? If not, why not?

Become Your Own Expert ▶

Reporters have a knee-jerk tendency to call on experts and authorities in their reporting. These sources can be useful, of course. But given time, a reporter can become his or her own expert source.

Nicholas Lemann, a national correspondent for *The Atlantic* magazine and the author of *The Promised Land: The Great Black Migration and How It Changed America,* says depth reporting takes reporters into areas in which they traditionally call on experts for background. Lemann suggests that reporters themselves become the experts, "rather than relying on someone else. . . ." He says:

> Whatever you're writing about, as soon as you start to follow that string, you're apt to find that you've wandered into the realm of history and sociology. Let's say your subject is high-rise public housing in Chicago. How did it get there in the first place? Finding the answer to that question can't help but take you into subjects like the great black migration from the South to Chicago, the rise and fall of the Kelly-Nash political machine, the legislative initiatives of the Truman Administration, and, even more arcane, the architectural theories of Le Corbusier and his followers.
>
> Although some of this can be run down through the traditional journalistic means of interviewing and examining records at City Hall, you also have to do a good deal of the reporting at research libraries and archives. I have to confess that when I first realized this, I had to fight off the feeling that libraries are for wimps and nerds, as opposed to real reporters, but after a while I got to like it. Ideas have consequences and bad ideas have bad consequences.

Lemann says that journalists "tend to be intellectually insecure, but this can be overcome through plain old-fashioned legwork—doing enough legwork,

A Basic Resource— The Library

albeit in the library, to become really conversant with the ideas that animate your story."

He believes that journalists may now be doing the work of novelists as the leading chroniclers of our society. He suggests that journalists may next dream of "taking over from social scientists . . . as the leading explainers of American society; and they might dream of accomplishing all three goals—of being portraitist, investigator, and explainer—at the same time, in the same work. Nobody is doing this perfectly now, and maybe nobody ever will, but I think if we try to, if we hold it in mind as a goal, we'll be pushing the notion of investigative reporting to its fullest possible meaning."

Let us accompany four reporters as they work with various kinds of sources for their stories. The first story is the type that puts reporters on their mettle, the late-breaking event that must be handled quickly and accurately.

◀ **How Reporters Use Sources**

The story takes us to a New Jersey newsroom where a reporter is making late police checks, which consist of calling area police departments not personally covered by the police reporter. Here, the reporter must rely on human sources. There is little opportunity to examine police records.

◀ A Fatal

The reporter is told that a car plowed into a motorcycle at a stoplight and the two young people on the motorcycle were killed. The driver was arrested three miles down the highway and charged with drunken driving. The reporter knows this is a good story, but little time remains before the last edition closes. The rule in the newsroom, she remembers her editor telling her, is simple: "In baseball, if you get your glove on the ball and don't handle it cleanly, it's an error, no matter how hard it's hit to you. If you get a story before deadline and don't have it written for the next edition, you're not a reporter."

She has seen baseball games in which fielders managed to touch a ball but were not given errors when they failed to throw the batter out. But she had not called that to her editor's attention. She knows better.

She quickly learns the names of the victims and the driver as well as the location and circumstances of the accident. Knowing that the investigating officers are still writing their report, she asks if they are available at the station. They will have details she needs, especially about the chase for the driver. She then calls the mortuary to obtain background about the victims. Mortuaries usually have the exact spelling of a victim's name, and his or her age, address and occupation.

She glances at the clock to see whether she has time to call the parents of the victims for more precise information. Also, relatives often are around after an emergency to help out, and they might be able to tell her something about the deceased. But she decides that first she will try the clippings to see if the victims' names are in the newspaper library.

During her interviews with the investigating officers, one of them mentions that this was the third motorcycle accident in the last month. She notes that on her pad for a quick check in the library, too.

The check of the library discloses this was actually the fourth motorcycle accident in the county, one of the others having been fatal to a young man. The clippings also turn up a story about the young woman who was killed. She was the daughter of a prominent local family, and the story indicates she used a middle name, which was not in the reporter's notes.

The reporter then decides to locate the parents of the man who died in the accident. She realizes that she had decided not to make those calls because of her distaste for intruding on the family's tragedy. At some newspapers, reporters do not have to make such calls, she recalls a colleague telling her, but that is not the case at this one. The younger sister of the man answers the telephone and is able to supply some details about him.

The reporter used physical and human sources. One key to the story is her knowledge that the investigating police officers might be at the police station writing up the report of the accident. She knows that the best sources are those close to the scene. Although they had not seen the accident, they had arrived quickly and had conducted the investigation. The names of the officers will add authenticity to the story.

With her notes and the library clippings in view she begins to type, some 20 minutes before the last edition closes. She knows she has time because she had been organizing her notes as she was reporting.

A Shooting ▶

Although reporters sometimes use the telephone when they should be on the street talking to people or at meetings observing the give-and-take of open debate, there are times when direct observation is impossible. We have just seen a reporter handle a fatal accident by telephone. When the deadline is imminent and the source or the event is more than a short walk or trip away, the only recourse is the telephone.

Using the telephone can be an art. Properly used, it is a boon to reporting. Let us watch a television news reporter cover a shooting 50 miles north of her station, WKTV in Utica, N.Y.

Early one fall evening, Donna Hanover is told by a cameraman that he has picked up an interesting police report: Two people had been shot in separate incidents as they drove past an Indian encampment near the town of Big Moose. Hanover knows immediately this is a big story. Some Mohawk Indians had moved onto state-owned land in the Adirondack Mountains six months before and had refused to leave.

Hanover's major problem is her impending deadline and the distance to Big Moose. Her newscast is at 11 p.m., which gives her no time for the trip up, reporting and the return trip. She has to use the telephone.

By 10:15 p.m., her calls to the state police have turned up little information—a few details on the shooting and the names and ages of the injured. Apparently both were wounded by shots fired at the cars in which they were riding. Hanover then calls a medical center near Big Moose to check the condition of the victims, a 22-year-old man and a 9-year-old girl. She also hopes to learn something more about the incident. She is told that the young man was taken to a hospital in Utica and that the girl is on her way.

She asks for the names of the relatives of those who were injured, and a hospital attendant gives her the name of the injured man's father. She then calls "information for the home telephone number, hoping that some member of the family would have stayed at home in Big Moose," Hanover says.

She is lucky. The father is not there, but the victim's brother answers her call, and he had been riding in the car with his older brother at the time of the shooting.

This piece of good fortune enables Hanover to use an eyewitness, a better source than someone with a secondhand account. He tells Hanover that they had been fired at twice by the Indians. The first time the shots missed. But on the return trip, the car had come under heavy fire and his brother was hit in the shoulder.

The girl was in a car that passed by the Indian encampment a few hours after the boys were fired at. One bullet entered the trunk, went through the rear seat and struck the girl in the back.

As a result of her calls, Hanover is able to make the 11 o'clock news with a report of the incident. She does not have all the information she needs, but she does have the interview, information from the state police, the condition of the 22-year-old and the name of the 9-year-old girl who was also injured.

The next day, with plenty of time, Hanover and two photographers drive to Big Moose to do an on-the-scene report. She interviews the injured man's brother again, this time in front of a camera, photographs the damaged automobile and interviews local residents and the state police.

"The interview with the brother was important," Hanover says later, "because he was a primary source. The police report wasn't, and our job is to give our viewers the best and most accurate information about what has happened." The interview also added an essential ingredient for television news—visual identification.

"I always try to make the viewers feel close to the scene, to make them feel they were there as it happened," says Hanover.

One patrolman was photographed indicating bullet holes in the car. The Indians were not available for interviews. Later, they told her they had been shot at and were returning the fire.

Her script begins:

> New York state police are manning roadblocks near Eagle Bay and are escorting cars on Big Moose Road where two people in passing cars were shot Monday. Nine-year-old April Madigan of Geneva, New York, is in critical condition at St. Luke's Memorial Hospital Center. . . .

We turn from these spot news stories to a story that begins with a chat between friends.

◀ An Enterpriser

Jeffrey A. Tannenbaum, a reporter with *The Wall Street Journal,* is in the newsroom when a call comes in from a former college classmate, Ralph Sanders.

Sanders, who is blind, tells Tannenbaum he is active in an organization called the National Federation of the Blind and that the group is planning a demonstration. Sanders says that the blind are tired of being denied rights granted to sighted people.

An Enterpriser

Tannenbaum's story about the increasing militancy of the blind began with a call from a former classmate about a demonstration that was being planned. While it was clear to Tannenbaum that the demonstration was a media event designed to attract the press, he decided to dig into the situation.

The story that developed from Tannenbaum's reporting is called an *enterpriser*—the theme originated with the reporter. Tannenbaum found people whose experiences supported the theme of the story. He also located authoritative sources who could comment on the overall situation.

THE WALL STR

VOL. CLXXXVI NO. 7 ★★ EASTERN EDITION THURSDAY, JU

New Crusaders
Angry Blind Militants, Seeking 'Equal Rights,' Try Tougher Tactics

Sightless Stage Walkouts, Sue Landlords, Bosses, Reject 'Excessive' Pity

The Fight With Sky Glider

By JEFFREY A. TANNENBAUM
Staff Reporter of THE WALL STREET JOURNAL

Keith and Elizabeth Howard were all set to board an Allegheny Airlines flight from Washington, D.C., to Philadelphia. The airplane wasn't fully booked. Yet an airline official suddenly insisted they must take separate flights.

The reason: The Howards are both blind.

The couple say they were told the pilot didn't want more than one blind passenger on the flight because he assumed that blind people might cause a safety problem or require extra service. While his wife went on ahead, the 43-year-old Mr. Howard waited for the next flight.

Far from being helpless nuisances, the Howards both successfully manage their own lunch counters in Washington. They angrily protested to Allegheny, which confirms their story. Allegheny apologized, and says that Ransome Airlines, which operated the flight under contract, has changed its policies to prevent a repeat of the incident. But the Howards figure their problems are far from over. They say the airline incident was typical of the "common discrimination—a normal thing" that society practices almost routinely against the blind.

But nowadays, blind people like the Howards are moving with increasing fervor to protest such discrimination. They are voicing complaints, turning to the courts and even staging strikes and demonstrations. As a result, employers, landlords and businesses generally are finding they must either change their policies or face protests and lawsuits.

"A Dash of Leprosy"

"Society will give charity to the blind, but it won't allow us to be first-class citizens," charges Ralph W. Sanders, president of the Arkansas unit of the National Federation of the Blind. "Like the blacks, we've come to the point where we're not going to stand for it anymore," he adds.

Ironically, this militancy occurs at a time when conditions for the blind are improving significantly, particularly in the realm of jobs. Several states in recent have gr— improve— broad—

What's News—

* * *

Business and Finance

OIL'S EXPORT PRICE was cut by Ecuador in what may be the first major crack in the oil cartel's pricing structure. Ecuador's cut was through a reduction in the income-tax rate charged oil companies.
(Story on Page 3)
* * *

A tax on most crude oil and refined petroleum products of up to three cents a barrel was proposed, as expected, by President Ford to help pay for damages caused by oil spills.
(Story on Page 3)
* * *

A Honduran commission urged steps to nationalize the concessions and property of units of United Brands and Castle & Cooke to increase that country's participation in the banana-export business.
(Story on Page 2)
* * *

Developing nations' efforts to negotiate new international agreements fixing commodities prices will be resisted by the U.S., a top Treasury official said.
(Story on Page 2)
* * *

General Motors is being countersued by a former dealer for $33 million in connection with a tangled series of criminal and civil cases involving alleged warranty fraud. Separately, GM said its supplemental benefit fund for laid-off employes could soon resume payouts for a brief period.
(Stories on Page 4)
* * *

Ford Motor confirmed that it quietly paid for repairing about 69,000 rust-damaged 1969-73 models even though normal warranties had expired.
(Story on Page 4)
* * *

Great Atlantic & Pacific Tea reported a $6.5 million loss, less than predicted, for its May 24 first quarter; a year earlier it earned $10.3 million.
(Story on Page 4)
* * *

International Paper's second quarter earnings slid 37% to $47.2

World-Wide

A MIDEAST AGREEMENT isn't "anywhere near," Kissinger said.

The Secretary of State, beginning a European trip during which he will meet with Israeli Prime Minister Rabin, said reports that an Egyptian-Israeli accord had been all but wrapped up are "totally wrong." Hearst Newspapers quoted Egyptian President Sadat as indicating that basic terms of a new interim Sinai agreement had been worked out. But Prime Minister Rabin said some key issues remain to be settled.

Sources suggested that an agreement would involve an electronic surveillance system, operated by the U.S., to warn of any attack through the Gidi and Mitla mountain passes in the Sinai.

Rabin conferred with West German Chancellor Schmidt in Bonn, who urged the Israeli premier to take advantage of the current chance for a settlement with Egypt. Kissinger arrived in Paris and will meet with Soviet Foreign Minister Gromyko in Geneva before seeing Rabin Saturday in Bonn.

The Palestine Liberation Organization said in Beirut that it had failed to win the release of an American Army colonel kidnapped last week. It said the colonel was being held by two radical Palestinian groups that don't belong to the PLO. The deadline the abductors set for the U.S. to meet their ransom demands passed.
* * *

A TURKISH-ARMS COMPROMISE was offered to the House by Ford.

After meeting with 140 House members, the President proposed legislation partially lifting the ban on military aid that was imposed after Turkey used U.S. weapons in invading Cyprus. Under the plan, undelivered arms already paid for by Turkey would be shipped and more weapons could be bought for cash, but Turkey wouldn't be eligible for grants. Ford would report to Congress every two months on arms sales and on the chances for a Cyprus settlement.

The three leading House opponents of arms for Turkey weren't invited to the meeting with Ford. One of them, Rep. John Brademas (D., Ind.), denounced the proposal as a fraud.

Speaker Carl Albert predicted the House would approve Ford's plan. The Senate last month voted 41-40 to end the arms embargo. Turkey has demanded that negotiations on the status of U.S. bases begin next Thursday if the embargo hasn't been lifted by then. It wasn't known whether Turkey would accept Ford's compromise.
* * *

PORTUGAL'S ARMED FORCES will form local units bypass—ng political —ties.

Sanders suggests the demonstration will make a good story. Sensing a broader story than the coverage of an event that it being staged for the media, Tannenbaum arranges to have lunch with Sanders.

"I was fascinated with the possibility of writing a story about the blind comparable to early stories on the civil rights movement," Tannenbaum says later. "In the course of a long interview, Sanders provided the theme for the story. I used it in the sixth paragraph of the finished story.

"What I needed to do after the interview was to document the central thesis. I needed to find examples of ways in which blind people are discriminated against. And I needed to find cases of discrimination in which blind people were militant."

At lunch, Sanders provides some sources and examples of militancy. Tannenbaum finds other examples by calling organizations of the blind. He learns about discrimination by checking with social agencies and human rights commissions. He is able to find more than a dozen examples of discrimination.

"As a rule of thumb," Tannenbaum says, "I like to have half-a-dozen highly readable, colorful, to-the-point examples in a story. Each one should illustrate a different aspect of the general problem, buttressing the main theme but not duplicating one another."

He checks with people who might have another point of view on what the blind charge is discrimination. Tannenbaum says, "More than fairness is involved here; a good reporter knows that the best stories are multidimensional. Conflict and controversy do make a better story, but they also accurately reflect reality."

Tannenbaum now has sources with specific complaints and incidents. He has a feeling an incident at a Washington, D.C., airport described by Keith and Elizabeth Howard should be well up in his story, perhaps the lead.

He interviews the head of Sanders' organization and a blind professor of American history at Seton Hall College in New Jersey, who provides an excellent quote that gives an overview. He consults some references for data about the blind. He has now interviewed 40 people and is ready to write.

Tannenbaum finds the writing goes quickly. "A well-reported story—one reported logically with a central theme in mind—tends to write itself," he recalls an editor telling him. He begins with the Howards in a delayed lead and presents the theme in his words in the fifth paragraph and then in Sanders' words in the sixth paragraph. The next two paragraphs are background.

Tannenbaum's first version had the blind professor's quote lower in the story, but he remembered the guideline that good quotes should be put up high in a story and so he raised the quote as high as he could.

The reporter, Mullins, is told by his city editor to find out whether people are reading as much as they used to—a vague assignment, but Mullins thinks he knows what his editor has in mind. The editor has talked so often about "cretinization by television" that Mullins gathers he wants to know whether youngsters can read as well as they used to. The reading scores in local schools have been steadily declining in recent years, and the editor has played up those stories. So he will emphasize young readers in his reporting.

◀ Does Johnny Read?

"If you find out anyone is still reading, tell us what's being read," is the editor's parting comment as Mullins leaves. He visits bookstores and talks to clerks, and he chats with librarians.

In one library, he notices some youngsters chatting at a table near the window. Unobtrusively, he moves over to listen.

"What did you find out about the clipper ships?" one of the boys asks another. A few minutes later, a girl asks the boy next to her if he knows when the first transcontinental railroad was completed. Apparently they are doing research for an assignment on transportation. Mullins asks one of the boys, and he is told the work is for an honors history class in one of the local high schools. That is worth noting, Mullins decides.

As he passes three older students, he glances at the books they are reading—Jack Kerouac's *On the Road*, Hermann Hesse's *Demian*, and a book that appears to be about race car driving, judging by its title. That, too, goes into Mullins' notes. Suddenly, it strikes him that this is just what he needs to be doing, to rely more on his observations and to support them with interviews of library users.

Mullins strolls around the library. As he passes one shelf, he observes that most of the books, which bear numbers ranging from 200 to 300 on their spines, are hardly used but that a few are well-worn. The well-read books are on eastern religions. He jots down their titles, and he makes a note to look into that by talking to the librarian. She might have some of the titles of the books that have been borrowed frequently.

The physical evidence seems to show that youngsters on school assignments are major library users, as are older people with time on their hands. The older readers congregate around the newspaper rack, and much of their borrowing and reading is of the historical romances, adventure novels and mysteries. Considerable activity by all age groups focuses on the how-to books that offer instruction on investments, gardening, home repair and sex. He learns videotapes are a big item with library users.

Mullins' story is a blend of human and physical sources, the one kind supplementing the other. His observation of the library users injects human interest into the story. He *shows* his readers students and adults using books, newspapers and magazines, and he names these publications, remembering the guideline that journalism is the art of the specific.

Summing Up ▶

Good reporters rely on human and physical sources. A study by Kathleen A. Hanson of the University of Minnesota journalism faculty found that Pulitzer Prize winners used a greater variety of physical sources in their stories than did nonwinners. The winners used more documents, reports, books and other printed matter and fewer interviews than did the nonwinners.

Yet many reporters rely on the interview for almost all their reporting. Stephen Hess found in his study of Washington reporters that journalists used no documents in almost three-fourths of their stories. When reporters are given more time to do stories, he says, "they simply do more interviews."

The reporters we have been studying know the value of physical sources. We also can make these generalizations about their work:

- They make direct observations whenever possible.
- When it is necessary to use secondhand accounts, they find the best human sources available, backed by physical evidence.
- They understand that the official version is not necessarily the true account, so they seek verification.
- They know the limitations of human and physical sources.

Interviews are, of course, essential to reporting. We will next examine how to conduct them and we will consider their place in the reporter's arsenal of methods for digging out useful and relevant material.

Abel, Elie. *Leaking: Who Does It? Who Benefits? At What Cost?* Winchester, Mass.: Unwin Hyman Inc., 1987. This is a 20th Century Fund study that examines leaks and their consequences to government and to journalism.

Downie, Leonard J.V. *The New Muckrakers.* Washington, D.C.: New Republic Book Co., 1976.

Sigal, Leon V. *Reporters and Officials.* Lexington, Mass.: D.C. Heath, 1973.

◀ **Further Reading**

14 Interviewing Principles

National Broadcasting Company, Inc.

Getting close to the source.

Preview

Reporters conduct two kinds of interviews:

• **News interview:** The purpose is to gather information to explain an idea, event or situation in the news.

• **Profile:** The focus is on an individual. A news peg often is used to justify the profile.

For effective interviews, reporters prepare carefully, and they ask questions that induce the source to talk freely. Questions are directed at obtaining information on a theme that the reporter has in mind before beginning the interview. If a more important theme emerges, the reporter develops it.

The reporter notes what is said, how it is said and what is not said. Sources are encouraged by the reporter's gestures and facial expressions to keep talking.

In the stadium locker room, the half-dressed hurdler was stuffing his warm-up suit and track shoes into a battered black bag. Seated on a bench nearby, a young man removed a pencil and a notepad from a jacket pocket.

"I'm from the paper in town," the young man said. "You looked sharp out there. Mind if I ask you some questions?"

The athlete nodded and continued his packing.

"First time you've been to this part of the West or this city?" the reporter asked. Another nod. This was not going to be easy, the reporter worried. The editor had told him to make sure he brought back a good story for tomorrow's paper, the day the National Association of Intercollegiate Athletics would begin its outdoor track meet at the local college. The tall, lithe young man standing in front of the bench was a world record holder in the hurdles, the editor had said, and worth a story for the sports section.

The reporter tried again. "What do you think of our town?" The athlete seemed to see the reporter for the first time.

"I don't know anything about this town," he replied. "I'm here to run. I go to the East coast, the West coast, here. They give me a ticket at school and I get on a bus or a plane and go. My business is to run." He fell silent.

Rebuffed, the reporter struggled to start the athlete talking again. In the 20-minute interview, the hurdler never really opened up.

324

Back in the newsroom, the reporter told the editor about his difficulties. They seemed to begin with his first question about whether the athlete had been to the town before, he said. His boss was not sympathetic.

"First, you should have checked the clips and called the college for information about your man," the editor said. "That way you could have learned something about him, his record or his school. You might have used it to break the ice. Or you could have asked him about the condition of the track, something he knows about."

Then the editor softened. He knew that interviewing is not easy for young reporters, that it can be perfected only through practice.

"I think you have a good quote there about the business of running," he told the reporter. "Did you get anything else about the places he's been? That could make an interesting focus for the piece."

Yes, the reporter said, he had managed to draw the hurdler out about where he had been in the last few months. With the editor's guidance, the reporter managed to turn out an acceptable story.

This incident illustrates the four principles of interviewing:

1. Prepare carefully, familiarizing yourself with as much background as possible.
2. Establish a relationship with the source conducive to obtaining information.
3. Ask questions that are relevant to the source and that induce the source to talk.
4. Listen and watch attentively.

Since much of the daily work of the journalist requires asking people for information, mastery of interviewing techniques is essential. The four principles underlie the various techniques the reporter uses. Clearly, the sportswriter's troubles began when he failed to prepare by obtaining background about the athlete he was to interview. Lacking background, the reporter was unable to ask questions that would draw out his source. Furthermore, he had failed to establish a rapport with the hurdler, so that the session was more like dentistry than journalism, with the reporter painfully extracting bits and pieces of information from an unwilling subject. Fortunately, the reporter had listened carefully so that he managed to salvage something from the interview.

If we analyze news stories, we will see they are based on information from three kinds of sources: physical sources, such as records, files and references; the direct observations of the reporter; interviews with human sources. Most stories are combinations of two or three of these sources.

Glance at today's newspaper. Listen carefully to tonight's evening newscast. You will be hard-pressed to find a story that lacks information from an interview. A front-page story about a court decision, for example, has a quotation from the governor about the consequences of the decision. That story about the city's plan to put desk officers on the street quotes the police chief. An obituary contains an employee's comments about the generosity of the deceased.

Homework Pays. Bryant Gumbel, a former sportscaster, is co-host of the NBC "Today" show, where he has shown himself to be a skilled interviewer, a talent he developed covering sports. He compares news and sports interviewing:

"There are more similarities than differences between news and sports coverage. In both cases the people who you're talking to want to give you the predictable locker room statements and talk about the 'team effort.' If you do your homework, and ask what you think are intelligent questions, then you get something more out of them."

Types of Interviews ▶

Straight news stories seem to rely on physical sources and observations. Yet if you examine them closely, you will more often than not find information a source has supplied through an interview, brief as that interview may have been.

The major story on page one of a September issue of *The Hawk Eye* in Burlington, Iowa, was about a three-alarm fire that destroyed a two-story building that housed an automobile sales agency and a body repair shop. The reporter interviewed several people for information to supplement his observations. Here are the people he interviewed and a summary of their comments:

- **The owner:** 15 cars destroyed; exact loss as yet unknown.
- **A fire department lieutenant:** The building could not have been saved when firefighters arrived. They concentrated on saving the adjoining buildings.
- **An eyewitness:** "I didn't know what it was. It just went all at once. I seen it a-burning and I was scared to death."
- **The fire chief:** The state fire marshal will investigate the cause of the fire.

Although the reporter was not present when firefighters battled the fire during the early morning hours, the interviews with the lieutenant and the eyewitness give his story an on-the-scene flavor. Since these interviews help to explain the news event, we describe them as *news interviews*.

Another local front-page story also relies on a news interview. A head-on automobile crash on Iowa Route 2 near Farmington took the life of a Van Buren County woman and caused injuries to four others. The story is based on an interview with the Iowa Highway Patrol.

The other type of interview story is the *profile* or *personality interview* in which the focus is a person rather than an event or situation.

Phoebe Zerwick of the *Winston-Salem Journal* frequently writes profiles for a feature called "Tarheel Sketch." In one, she profiled a federal district judge with a reputation as a hero to the disadvantaged.

"Over the past 20 years," Zerwick writes, "advocates for black children sent to inferior schools, poor people awaiting public assistance, disabled people who have been kicked off the Social Security rolls, and mentally disturbed children locked away in state hospitals have climbed the stairs to that courtroom. And over the years, McMillan has provided them with relief."

Rarely does a reporter cover an assignment without asking someone for information. Sometimes, the interview is for background material: A city clerk may be asked to verify a figure for a story about the next mayoral election, or a lawyer may be asked for details about a suit he has filed in the county courthouse.

In the course of the day, a reporter may interview a dozen or more people for the stories on which he or she is working. Usually, these are quick question-and-answer sessions conducted over the telephone.

When a reporter talks about doing an interview, usually he or she is referring to a more extended session with one or more sources that will form the basis of a story. These long sessions can be news or personality interviews, depending upon the purpose of the piece.

JAMES McMILLAN

Big Mac's understanding of the Constitution
made him into a champion of the oppressed

By Phoebe Zerwick
JOURNAL REPORTER

CHARLOTTE — Something about the way the attorney was arguing his case didn't sit too well with Judge James B. McMillan.

The case before McMillan, a federal judge in the Western District, concerned a judge who had been opening court with prayer.

The judge, H. William Constangy, said that prayer helped him set a dignified tone for the day's proceedings and also expressed his reverence for the Lord.

But five public defenders in Charlotte were offended by the prayer. They thought that it came too close to government endorsement of religion and violated the First Amendment to the Constitution. Several weeks ago they brought their complaint to McMillan.

As McMillan said afterward, the case was riveting. The evidence was succinct, and the attorneys were well organized. But still, as Constangy's attorney delivered his closing argument, McMillan kept interrupting, fixing on a seemingly minor detail, the possessive pronoun his.

"I'm interested in the theory that it's his courtroom," McMillan asked, at least four or five times, each time raising more extreme examples. Does the judge have a right to pray even though he offends some and bores others? What if he wanted to turn toward Mecca and kneel upon a prayer rug? Does he have the right to do that?

Looking up from the bench, McMillan said, "It's not my courtroom. It's a place where I work."

McMillan's place of work is the federal courthouse in Charlotte, which faces Trade Street, a broad, tree-lined avenue that runs into the city's downtown. He works in a courtroom on the second floor.

Over the past 20 years, advocates for black children sent to inferior schools, poor people awaiting public assistance, disabled people who have been kicked off the Social Security

RESUMÉ

FULL NAME:
James B. McMillan.

AGE: 73.

PUBLIC POSITION:
U.S. District Court judge in the Western District.

BIRTHPLACE:
McDonald, Robeson County

EDUCATION:
B.A., University of North Carolina at Chapel Hill; Law degree, Harvard University.

FAMILY:
Married to Holly Neaves McMillan; one son, one daughter.

rolls, and mentally disturbed children locked away in state hospitals have climbed the stairs to that courtroom. And over the years, McMillan has provided them with relief.

In 1970, he ordered the Charlotte-Mecklenburg Board of Education to bus black children into schools in white neighborhoods and white children into schools in black neighborhoods. The case was the first busing case to be upheld by the U.S. Supreme Court and led to the desegregation of schools across the state and nation.

That was the first major case McMillan heard, and no case since then has triggered the kind of controversy that raged around him during those years. But since then, he has become a kind of hero among advocates for the poor by ruling in favor of the disadvantaged in numerous lesser-known cases.

Theodore O. Fillette, the deputy director of Legal Services of Southern Piedmont, said, "I can say without a doubt he has had the greatest impact on improving the rights of low-income people than anyone else in the state. I would include people without power, racial minorities, prisoners, and physically and mentally handicapped people."

In 1975, McMillan ordered the N.C. Department of Human Resources to process applications for welfare and Medicaid, the federal insurance program for the poor, within the required 45 days.

Some applicants were waiting as long as six months. During that time, some were evicted because they couldn't pay their rent. Others went hungry or cold.

The state is still under court order,

See McMILLAN, Page A20

Before we examine the two types of interviews in detail, let's look over some of the rules under which interviews are conducted.

The Interviewer's ▶ Ground Rules

Both parties in an interview have certain assumptions and expectations. Generally, the reporter expects the interviewee to tell the truth and to stand behind what he or she has told the interviewer. The interviewee presumes the reporter will write the story fairly and accurately. Both agree, without saying so, that the questions and answers mean what they appear to mean—that is, that there are no hidden meanings.

Having said this, we must admit to the exceptions. Sources may conceal, evade, distort and lie when they believe it is to their advantage. The reporter must be alert to the signs of a departure from truth.

The rules that govern the reporter's behavior in the interview can be detailed with some certainty. Reporters, too, conceal, mislead and, at times, lie. Few reporters justify these practices; most agree the reporter should:

1. Identify himself or herself at the outset of the interview.
2. State the purpose of the interview.
3. Make clear to those unaccustomed to being interviewed that the material will be used.
4. Tell the source how much time the interview will take.
5. Keep the interview as short as possible.
6. Ask specific questions that the source is competent to answer.
7. Give the source ample time to reply.
8. Ask the source to clarify complex or vague answers.
9. Read back answers if requested or when in doubt about the phrasing of crucial material.
10. Insist on answers if the public has a right to know them.
11. Avoid lecturing the source, arguing or debating.
12. Abide by requests for nonattribution, background only or off-the-record should the source make this a condition of the interview or of a statement.

Respect the Subject. "There are certain universal principles that should be followed in reporting on ordinary people. Treat your subjects with respect. Listen carefully and at great length. Don't pretend to be chummy and familiar—as a journalist, you automatically belong to a different breed from your subjects. Don't impose an agenda—find out what they think is important."—Nicholas Lemann, National Correspondent, *The Atlantic*

Reporters who habitually violate these rules risk losing their sources. Few sources will talk to an incompetent or an exploitative reporter. When the source realizes that he or she is being used to enhance the reporter's career or to further the reporter's personal ideas or philosophy, the source will close up.

Sources also risk trouble when they exploit the press. Reporters understand that their sources will float occasional trial balloons and give incomplete, even misleading, information. But constant and flagrant misuse of the press leads to retaliation by journalists.

Earning Trust ▶

When Sheryl James of the *St. Petersburg Times* was interviewing sources for her prizewinning series on abandoned infants, she realized that many of those she was interviewing were unaccustomed to talking to a reporter. "I was dealing with good but somewhat unsophisticated people," she says, "who would have been easy to manipulate. It was a challenge to be sure they understood what I was doing and to keep promises made during the reporting process that I could have broken with impunity."

James focused on a woman who was charged with leaving her baby in a box near a dumpster. She had to develop a relationship with the woman. "I simply tried to be straightforward about what I was doing," James said, "and get her to trust me, to know that I would keep my word to her.

"Aside from that, when I finally did interview her, I felt as I do with many people I interview—I try to establish a relaxed rapport, to be human myself so that they know I'm not a media monster."

The extended news interview can provide readers and listeners with interpretation, background and explanation. When Douglas Watson, a *Washington Post* reporter, was covering the extortion and tax evasion trial of a Baltimore County official, he heard the testimony of a stock manipulator who was a confessed white-collar criminal and political fixer. Watson was told that the witness was being held by the United States Marshal's Service in a special facility while testifying for the government. Watson learned there were several of these facilities—known as "safe houses"—and he decided to do a story about them. After the trial, he spent several hours talking to officials.

"In the interviews, I learned about other interesting and unreported aspects of the organization besides 'safe houses,' " Watson said. "One of the Service's activities is giving new identities to people who had been government witnesses. This enables them to start new lives in another part of the country."

Here is how Watson's story begins:

"Restricted Area—U.S. Govt. Training Center," says the sign on the barbed wire-topped fence surrounding a barracks at Ft. Holabird on the edge of Baltimore.

The sign doesn't say it, but the barracks is one of several "safe houses" that the U.S. Marshal's Service operates for the special care and feeding of very important prisoner-witnesses such as Watergate conspirator E. Howard Hunt, political saboteur Donald Segretti and stock manipulator Joel Kline.

Three to five "safe houses" have been in existence around the country for about a year, usually holding about 50, mostly white collar, "principals," as they like to call themselves. They are federal prisoners who usually were involved in organized crime and who are considered too valuable as government witnesses or too endangered by threats to be incarcerated in the usual prison. . . .

The news interview can emphasize an aspect of a continuing story that the reporter considers to have been overlooked or neglected. When the debate over nuclear weapons heated up, Jimmy Breslin of the *Daily News* interviewed I.I. Rabi, one of the nuclear physicists who built the first atomic bomb.

Breslin wondered if Americans weren't too casual about nuclear weapons. A master journalist, Breslin let Rabi speak:

"You're a Queens Catholic. Get on your knees and pray," Breslin quoted Rabi as telling him.

"Nuclear weapons are entirely beyond the people in our government today. It doesn't take much to know that."

◀ **The News Interview**

On the Scene

A radio reporter interviews a speaker following his address at a campus rally to protest alleged unfair hiring practices.

Rabi recalled that during the 1980 Reagan-Carter debate, Carter had talked about his daughter Amy's concern over nuclear weapons. "The newspapers said it was stupid," Rabi said. "I never did. It was the little girl who was going to be killed. . . ."

Rabi is quoted extensively because he has something to say, has the authority to say it and says it well. Young reporters are often surprised at how eloquent the subjects of interviews can be if they are encouraged to speak.

The Profile ▶

The profile should be seen as a minidrama, blending description, action and dialogue. Through the words and actions of the subject of the profile, with some help from the reporter's insertion of background and explanatory matter, the character is illuminated. Profiles should include plenty of quotations.

For a retrospective piece on the 1980 championship University of Georgia football team, *U.S. News & World Report* interviewed the starting offense and the punter in the team's Sugar Bowl victory over Notre Dame. Nine of the 12 did not graduate; none of the six black starters received degrees.

In a series of miniprofiles, the magazine reported on the players' careers in school and later. Herschel Walker, the star of the team, left the team after three years. "I had to worry about what was best for Herschel—and leaving school was best for Herschel," he is quoted as saying. He was signed for a reported $5.5 million by a professional team.

Not so fortunate was Walker's gridiron blocker, Jimmy Womack. Like Walker, he did not graduate. But he had no professional career and regrets his role in Walker's shadow. "If I had gone to Florida State, I could have been in the NFL somewhere," he said. There were, the magazine reports, "compensations . . . in the form of wadded-up $100 bills, passed along in 'padded handshakes' from alumni and boosters." Off the field, he remembered, there were "these girls that liked football players, not one at a time either."

Nat Hudson, who went on to play in the NFL for five years, says that when he goes to a Georgia game or to the athletic area, he feels "like a social outcast." The attitude, he says, is that "we've exploited your talent and we're through with you, so you go back to your business." Racism, he says, is the source of his cool reception.

Ingredients ▶

The profile consists of:

- The person's background (birth, upbringing, education, occupation).
- Anecdotes and incidents involving the subject.
- Quotes by the individual relevant to his or her newsworthiness.
- The reporter's observations.
- Comments of those who know the interviewee.
- A news peg, whenever possible.

Interviewing only the source will lead to a thin, possibly misleading story. When a young *New York Times* reporter turned in a piece about an alcoholic nun who counsels other similarly afflicted nuns, the story did not move past Charlotte Evans, an editor.

"As it stands," Evans told the reporter, "all you have is a moderately interesting interview with Sister Doody. You sat in a chair, and she sat in a chair and you had a chat. That's not very good, considering the story material.

"Did you talk to any nuns in treatment or just out of it?

"Where is the anguish, the embarrassment, the guilt?

"It doesn't sound as if you had done any real reporting, digging, pushing. Where are the people, the quotes, the color?"

For her profile of Les Brown, a black preacher and radio personality, Itabari Njeri of *The Miami Herald* talked to other ministers, a community activist and the directors of the local chapters of the Urban League and the National Association for the Advancement of Colored People, as well as to Brown. Assessments of Brown diverged widely: "I will not allow anyone to manipulate or prostitute the black community, and that is what Les Brown is doing to the nth degree," an Urban League official said. The activist had a different view: "He is different . . . he's got guts. He is a challenge to the traditional black leaders here."

Bella Stumbo of *The Los Angeles Times* would try to spend several days with her subjects. Not only did her extended presence allow Stumbo to see her man or woman in whole, the subject would soon tire of keeping his or her guard up.

◀ Reporting and Writing the Profile

For her profile of an adviser to a governor of California, Stumbo stayed with Justin Dart even when he took a plane to New York. On the flight, Dart ran into former president Gerald Ford. On returning to his seat, he talked to Stumbo about the unexpected encounter, and this is how his remarks came out in the profile:

> "Jerry's a nice man, but he's not very smart," he remarked.
>
> Never one to understate his case, refine his language or temper his judgments, Dart amended himself.
>
> "Actually, our seatmate is a dumb bastard," he added.

Let's accompany her as she does a profile of Washington, D.C., mayor Marion Barry at the time he is accused of using cocaine, Stumbo accompanies him to one of his favorite late-night bars. She listens and she watches as he drums fingers on the tabletop and is "dancing in his chair, sipping his wine, restless, his eyes roaming the room, raw energy barely bridled." Note the blend of description, action, quotation:

"I'd run now even if I didn't want to," he says, smiling sulkily through the gloom. "And I'll get 65 percent of the vote—at least. Isn't anybody in this town can beat me. I'm invincible."

That includes Jackson. "Hah, Jesse don't wanna be no mayor," he snaps. "Jesse don't wanna run nothing but his mouth. Besides, he'd be the laughingstock of America! He'd be run outta town if he ran against me. . . .

. . . Even Barry's speech changes in private, now a soft mumbled patter of dropped words and careless grammar, calling for an acquired ear. And in no way is he understated. He is Pride itself, holding hard to tattered garb.

"Co-caaaane? How folks use that stuff anyhow?" he asks mockingly, coy, flaunting it all.

"You put it up your nooose? Nooo! Ooooooeeeee!"

And with a mock shudder he dances off to the men's room returning ten minutes later to wonder, laughingly, sardonically, how much a Marion Barry urine specimen might be worth to the media or the feds—interchangeable elements, in his mind, in the racist conspiracy against him. . . .

Stumbo encourages her subjects to talk, and the quotes strip her subjects bare. She listens as "the mayor's mind is suddenly prowling the rich realms of sex.

> . . . He wonders if his second wife still loves him, then concludes that the poor woman must—she never had it so good in bed. 'I was good then. I'm even better now,' he proclaims."

Of course, many of her subjects—some of whom consider themselves victims—complain. They say they have been misquoted, as did Barry. But her editors had confidence in Stumbo's accuracy.

Some interviewees blame themselves. A councilman says, "She doesn't lead you into saying anything. There were things I didn't want to see in the paper, but in the course of four days a familiarity develops. It becomes an honest reflection of who you are rather than the canned responses public officials usually give you."

Stumbo quoted the chief of staff to former Governor Jerry Brown as saying, "The first thing I'm gonna do is get that guy to wash his hair. It's disgusting, all that . . . grease. Not even dandruff could get through."

When the profile appeared, the subject offered Brown his resignation. "She totally destroyed me," he said. "But it was nobody's fault but my own."

Former Los Angeles Police Chief Daryl Gates says of Stumbo and her reporting technique: "One of the things Bella does, she's very, very good at it, and that's to kind of get inside you. She asked to go with me and be with me, and I gave her the opportunity."

Gates then found "you open yourself up to whatever takes place. She has the ability to make you feel good and very comfortable with her. She's very charming, relaxes you right away and somehow makes you feel that this piece is going to come out beautiful, you are going to look wonderful."

The Brown chief of staff agreed. "She told me I was the most popular man in the California government . . . and then she made me look like some demented Vietnam War veteran."

Reporting is the Key ▶

Reporting makes the profile. Joseph Mitchell, whose profiles for *The New Yorker* are considered the standard for the form, is described by Brendan Gill in *Here at The New Yorker,* a history of the magazine, as having the ability to ask "just the right questions." The questions would open up his sources, and Mitchell would closely attend their recollections and reflections. He encouraged sources to a loquacity no one suspected they possessed. Mitchell knew that everyone has a good story and that good reporting will flush it out.

In the dedication of one of his books, Calvin Trillin, a *New Yorker* writer, wrote, "To the *New Yorker* reporter who set the standard, Joseph Mitchell." Note Trillin's description of Mitchell as a "reporter." Trillin, like all good writers, knows that reporting is at the heart of the journalist's work.

When Mark Patinkin and Christopher Scanlan were assigned to profile the black community in Rhode Island for *The Providence Journal-Bulletin,* they focused on individuals—the people who symbolize the facts and figures they were gathering.

For a story about the high rate of unemployment among blacks, they talked to a black man who was looking for work:

Voices: Stephen Gordon on Unemployment

"I felt like everything I was trying to build was worthless," said Stephen Gordon. "I was back at the bottom. Quite a few times, I'd just break down and cry. I couldn't even get a job on a garbage truck. I felt less than a man."

Stephen Gordon sits in the darkness of his kitchen in a Newport housing project, speaking of being black and jobless.

Back from Vietnam in 1971, he had gone through three years of the hardest of times. He had no high school diploma. He had no job. He had two children. His family survived on welfare.

Then came a federal job program that reached out and gave him hope, gave him training as a welder. He was a tradesman. For nine months, he strove to build the good life.

He was fired. He appealed the firing to the State Human Rights Commission, which found the company guilty of racial discrimination. That was two years ago, but the case remains on appeal. Meanwhile, Gordon went on unemployment, then welfare. He remembers the feeling.

"My inspiration was destroyed again," he said. "It was the same old rut."

Recently, he climbed out of the rut by finding a job as a cook in a Newport inn. For other black adults in the state, joblessness remains chronic.

Unemployment among Rhode Island blacks is higher than for any other group. There were 8,880 blacks in the labor force. . . .

Match the Event. Note how the writers of these miniprofiles let their subjects speak. They adhere to this rule: The story should match the nature of the event.

In this case, the event is people talking about their lives. What is more natural, then, for the story to include many quotations.

There is hope in the black community, however, and with the careful use of quotes and the selection of incidents, Patinkin and Scanlan showed black success:

Voices: Ed Blue on Moving Up

"I wanted the good life," said Ed Blue. "I wasn't going to settle. I figured, I'm a citizen, I'm a taxpayer. I have as much a right as anybody else. Just give me a chance."

Twenty-eight years ago, Ed Blue came to Rhode Island with a suitcase and $300, another poor black immigrant from a small town in the South. Today he is the state's chief bank examiner and lives with his family in the state's wealthiest suburb, Barrington. Barbara, his wife, is running for Town Council.

For most blacks, Rhode Island has not been a place of opportunity. It wasn't for Ed Blue either. It was a place of slammed doors.

They slammed as soon as he got out of college. One large retailer put an "X" on his application for a clerk's job. He demanded to know why. The interviewer admitted it was to mark black applicants. Next he went to a bank. The bank told him he'd never be anything more than a guard.

Ed Blue saw other blacks told the same thing and saw them accept it. Don't bother, they told him, you won't make it, they won't let you make it. Blue would not accept that. "I was new here," he recalled, "I figured hell, I'll give it a shot. I'm going to break that down."

He put his shoulder against the door and he pushed hard. And when it finally gave, and a higher door slammed, he broke that one, too. He did it, he said, by proving he was so qualified they had no choice but to hire him. Ed Blue made it because he believed in Ed Blue.

"This is one of the things I've instilled in my children," he said. "Don't say you can't. I don't want to hear 'You can't.' "

For their report on crime in the Providence ghetto, the reporters interviewed a prostitute:

Voices: Debbie Spell on Hustling

"Being a hooker is all I know," said Debbie Spell. "It's how my mother supported me. That's all I seen when I was a kid, broads jumping into cars. Put me in a factory and I just couldn't hack it."

In poor neighborhoods, where unemployment and welfare rates are high, many blacks turn to hustling to survive. Debbie Spell turned to prostitution. Although she is 20, she looks 15. She is already the mother of three children. She normally works on Pine Street in Providence, where most of her customers are white.

"If it wasn't for them, then I wouldn't have food for my kids," she said, "or Pampers for my baby." Nor would she have her color television and living-room furniture.

"I'm not proud of it," she added, "but it's the way I make a living. Why should I work in a factory for $100 a week when I can make that much on a Thursday night?"

Although blacks make up only 3.4 percent of the population in Rhode Island, they make up 24 percent of the population at the Adult Correctional Institutions and 7.5 percent of admissions to state drug abuse programs.

In Providence, blacks account for about 10 percent of the population, but a much higher percentage ends up in the city's arrest books. Last year, of the 243 juveniles Providence police arrested for major crimes, 37 percent, or 90, were black. As blacks get older, their arrest percentage grows. . . .

The story about Debbie Spell has a tragic epilogue. A year after she was interviewed, she was arrested on charges of assault and loitering for prostitution. Two days after her arrest, she hanged herself in the shower room of the jail.

Scanlan returned to the streets that Debbie had walked to find out more about this woman who became a hooker at 12, was a drug addict, had three illegitimate boys, and was dead at 22.

"What I found were two grief-stricken women who told me an illuminating story about life on the streets," he said. His interview with Debbie's prostitute friends begins:

PROVIDENCE—It's a little after 5 on a Friday afternoon. Pine Street, between Pearl and Portland Streets, is a desolate stretch littered with broken glass, where young women wait on the sidewalks for men who drive slowly by to stop and pick them up for a few minutes of sex.

This part of South Providence was where Debbie Spell used to wait, too—

until last Wednesday when the police arrested her. On Friday, she hanged herself at the Women's Prison in Cranston.

Maurine sits in the doorway of a vacant building, a tired-looking woman in her early twenties, wearing shorts and a halter top.

"Sometimes it's not even worth the money to me," she said. "I got stabbed

Andy Dickerman, *The Providence Journal-Bulletin.*

Follow-Up to a Tragedy

Christopher Scanlan of *The Providence Journal-Bulletin* had written a profile of a young prostitute who spoke matter-of-factly about her work. A year later, Scanlan learned that the woman had hanged herself in jail two days after her arrest.

To find out something about Debbie and the life she led on the city's streets, Scanlan interviewed prostitutes who were friends of the young woman.

three times. I got busted in the face with a bottle. Just crazy guys. I told the police, but they didn't do nothing. I even got his plate. They still didn't do nothing. They said, 'If that's the type of life you want to lead, you got to take the bitter with the sweet.' "

Last summer, Debbie Spell told a reporter that she was a prostitute because the money was good. But times have changed, Maurine said.

"Hmph," she snorted when a reporter told her what Debbie had said. "Ain't no money here. Too many girls now. Some girls bring their little sisters down here, underage girls, 11 or 12 years old, some of them."

A young man approached and slowed his car.

"Wanna go?" Maurine asked halfheartedly. He looked at her, shook his head and drove on.

Another young woman came up. A few minutes before, Tammy had been dropped off by a trick, and now she was back on the corner. She said she was Debbie's best friend. On her way to Pine Street, she learned that Debbie was dead. She spoke bitterly, her voice husky with grief, sharp with anger. Tears shone in her eyes. Like Maurine, she did not want her real name used.

"This was Debbie's life, right here on Pine Street," Tammy said. "This is all of our lives, right here."

She too was bothered by all the younger girls on the streets, but for a different reason.

"They don't know what they're getting into," she said. "This is no game. It's just step up and make money. But they don't know that yet." A man stopped his car at the corner. She talked to him for a while, leaning on his car door, but he, too, drove away. . . .

Preparations ▶

Fred Zimmerman, a long-time reporter for *The Wall Street Journal,* has these suggestions about how to prepare for an interview:

1. Do research on the interview topic and the person to be interviewed, not only so you can ask the right questions and understand the answers, but also so you can demonstrate, clearly but unobtrusively, to the interviewee that you cannot easily be fooled.

2. Devise a tentative theme for your story. A major purpose of the interview will be to obtain quotes, anecdotes and other evidence to support that theme.

3. List question topics in advance—as many as you can think of, even though you may not ask all of them and almost certainly will ask others that you do not list.

4. In preparing for interviews on sensitive subjects, theorize about what the person's attitude is *likely* to be toward you and the subject you are asking about. What is his or her role in the event? Whose side is he or she on? What kinds of answers can you logically expect to your key questions? Based on this theorizing, develop a plan of attack that you think might mesh with the person's *probable* attitude and get through his or her *probable* defenses.

Research ▶

A.J. Liebling, a master reporter who moved from the newspaper newsroom to *The New Yorker* magazine, is quoted in *The Most of A.J. Liebling,* edited by William Cole: "The preparation is the same whether you are going to interview a diplomat, a jockey, or an ichthyologist. From the man's past you learn what questions are likely to stimulate a response."

Research begins with the library's clippings about the subject. If the topic has more than local importance or if the interviewee is well-known, *The New York Times Index, Facts on File* or a database may have a reference that can be useful. *The Readers' Guide to Periodical Literature* may list a magazine article about the topic or the person. *Who's Who in America* and other biographical dictionaries can be consulted. People who know the interviewee can be asked for information.

These resources provide material for three purposes: (1) They give the reporter leads to tentative themes and to specific questions. (2) They provide the reporter with a feel for the subject. (3) They provide useful background.

Asking Questions ▶

In the best of all possible worlds for the reporter, all sources love to talk, and they speak openly and to the point. Sometimes, reporters realize these dreams. Television cameras seem to make people talkative, as does the prospect of seeing one's name in print. Sometimes the urge to talk wells up from a need that lies deeper than the desire to be seen on television. People occasionally have a compelling need to share an experience or to call attention to a topic that requires exposure.

In a personality interview, the reporter will ask early in the interview for vital data—age, address, education, jobs held, family information and so on. Some of these data may not seem necessary since the clippings and references

© Joel Strasser.

may contain such material. But clippings can be dated or wrong. Also, questions of this sort are nonthreatening and relax the interviewee.

Harold Ross, the brilliant and eccentric former newspaperman who founded and edited *The New Yorker,* slashed exasperatedly at the pages of profiles and interviews that lacked vital data. "Who he?" Ross would scrawl across such manuscripts.

The reporter also must provide the reader or viewer with reason to give credence to the source's comments—background is essential.

As obvious as these questions about identification may be, the beginning reporter may want to jot them down before setting out on an interview. Otherwise, the reporter may be embarrassed by having to call the source later for basic information.

Sometimes a reporter will ask questions that are of little news value in order to break the ice with an interviewee. These lead-in questions must be carefully chosen. The politician, athlete or diplomat usually expects to be queried about relevant matters and has little time for chitchat.

Once the reporter moves into the serious business, he or she must ask questions that are aimed at revelation, disclosure and insight for the reader or listener.

Sandpaper Sam. Some viewers find the questions of Sam Donaldson of ABC abrasive. He defends his tough, boring-in style:

"There's a perception that I'm always asking some rude or confrontational question. That's absolutely wrong. I'm not trying to make the president say something foolish or trip him up. But I think it's proper to ask him a question that confronts him with the critics of his policy."

Direct Questions ▶

Most questions flow from what the reporter perceives to be the theme of the assignment. A fatal accident: Automatically, the reporter knows that he or she must find out who died and how and where the death occurred. The same process is used in the more complicated interview.

A reporter is told to interview an actor who had been out of work for two years and is now in a hit musical. The reporter decides that the theme of the story will be the changes the actor has made in his life. He asks the actor if he has moved from his tenement walk-up, has made any large personal purchases and how his family feels about his being away most nights. These three questions induce the actor to talk at length.

Another reporter is to interview a well-known entertainer. The reporter decides to ask about the singer's experiences that led him to write songs that call attention to war, poverty, sexism and racism. "Bread," says the singer in answer to the first question the reporter asks. "Money," he explains. There is a good market in such songs. The reporter then quickly shifts themes and asks questions about the economics of popular music and the singer's personal beliefs.

Open-Ended and Closed-Ended Questions ▶

When the sportswriter asked the hurdler, "What do you think of our town?" he was using what is known as an *open-ended question,* which could have been answered in general terms. The sports editor's suggestion that the reporter ask the athlete about the condition of the track would have elicited a specific response— fast, slow, or slick—as it was a *closed-ended question.*

The open-ended question does not require a specific answer. The closed-ended question calls for a brief, pointed reply. Applied properly, both have their merits. Two months before the budget is submitted, a city hall reporter may ask the city manager what she thinks of the city's general financial situation—an open-ended question. The reply may cover the failure of anticipated revenues to meet expectations, unusually high increases in construction costs, higher interest rates and other factors that have caused trouble for the city. Then the reporter may ask a closed-ended question, "Will we need a tax increase?"

As we have seen, reporters often begin their interviews with open-ended questions, which allow the source to relax. Then the closed-ended questions are asked, which may seem threatening if asked at the outset of the interview.

Television and radio interviews usually end with a closed-ended question because the interviewer wants to sum up the situation with a brief reply.

The reporter who asks only open-ended questions should be aware of their possible implications. To some sources, the open-ended question is the mark of an inadequately prepared reporter who is fishing for a story.

Some television reporters tend to ask open-ended questions, even when a specific one is more appropriate. A Chicago TV reporter in an interview with orphans asked a youngster, "Do you wish you had a mother and father?" The most familiar of all these open-ended questions asked by poorly prepared TV reporters is, "How do you feel about . . . ?"

Good questions are the result of solid preparation, and this requires more than reading the local newspaper and chatting with authorities. Reporters who hold to these narrow confines usually operate only in a linear fashion. That is, today's coverage is built on yesterday's newspaper stories and the council meeting of the day before. Good stories—informative journalism—are spurred by the questions that break the chain of events. Remember Copernicus. All he asked was what would happen if the sun and not the earth were the center of the universe, and centuries of linear thinking shot off onto a new plane.

Sometimes a young reporter finds that posing the right question is difficult because the question might embarrass or offend the interviewee. There is no recourse but to ask.

◄ Tough Questions

Oriana Fallaci, an Italian journalist famous for her interviews, says that her success may be the result of asking the world leaders she interviews questions that other reporters do not ask.

"Some reporters are courageous only when they write, when they are alone with their typewriters, not when they face the person in power. They never put a question like this, 'Sir, since you are a dictator, we all know you are corrupt. In what measure are you corrupt?' "

Remarkably, heads of state, kings and guerrilla leaders open up to Fallaci. One reason for this is her presumption that the public is entitled to answers and her unwillingness to be treated with indifference. When the heavyweight champion boxer Muhammad Ali belched in answer to one of her questions, she threw the microphone of her tape recorder in his face.

Handling Denials. Make sure what is denied is what was asked. The reply, "That's absurd" is not a denial. Nor is, "I refuse to answer speculative questions."

Another reason for her effectiveness is "her talent for intimacy," as one journalist put it. "She easily establishes an atmosphere of confidence and closeness and creates the impression that she would tell you anything. Consequently, you feel safe, or almost safe, to do the same with her," writes Diana Loercher in *The Christian Science Monitor.*

In her interview with Henry Kissinger, the U.S. secretary of state at the time, Fallaci had him admit that his position of power made him feel like the "lone cowboy who leads the wagon train alone on his horse." His image of himself as the Lone Ranger caused an embarrassed Kissinger to say later that granting Fallaci the interview was the "stupidest" act in his life.

A political reporter who accompanied Sen. Don Nickles on a tour of Oklahoma towns noticed an apparent inconsistency in Nickles' public statements. Nickles often described himself as a conservative who was tough on federal spending. Yet in Eufaula, Nickles announced "good news" from Washington, a commitment of federal funds for a new housing project.

The reporter then asked if the Republican senator's approach was consistent—condemning government spending in one place and welcoming it in another. Nickles' answer: He would vote against federal housing funds but as long as they were available, "I will try to see that Oklahoma gets its fair share."

The quote ends the story, and the reader is left to decide whether the senator is an opportunist.

Some reporters gain a reputation for asking tough questions and not wasting time on preliminaries. When Jack Anderson, the Washington columnist whose specialty is exposés, calls a congressman, the politician knows that he is unlikely to be asked for the text of a speech he is to give in Dubuque. Anderson is after meatier game.

Still, there are questions that few reporters like to ask. Most of these concern the private lives of sources—a Utah congresswoman's divorce, the mental retardation of a couple's son, the fatal illness of a baseball player. Some questions are necessary, some not. The guidelines for relevance and good taste are constantly shifting, and reporters may find they are increasingly being told to ask questions that they consider intrusive. This is the age of intimacy.

Reporters who dislike asking these questions, preferring to spare sources anguish, are sometimes surprised by the frank replies. A reporter for *Newsday* was assigned to follow up an automobile accident in which a drunken youth without a driver's license ran a borrowed car into a tree. One of the passengers, a 15-year-old girl, was killed. In doing his follow-up story, the reporter discovered that most of the parents were willing to talk because, as one parent said, the lessons learned from the accident might save lives.

Making Sources Open Up ▶

The early stage of the interview is a feeling-out period. The interviewee balances his or her gains and losses from divulging information the reporter seeks, and the reporter tries to show the source the rewards the source will receive through disclosure of the information—publicity, respect and the feeling that goes with doing a good turn.

When the source concludes that the risks outweigh the possible gains and decides to provide little or no information or is misleading, the reporter has several alternatives. At one extreme, the reporter can try to cajole the source into a complete account through flattery—or by appearing surprised. At the other extreme, the reporter can demand information. If the source is a public official, such demands are legitimate because officials are responsible to the public. The reporter can tell the source that the story—and there will be some kind of story—will point out that the official refused to answer questions. Usually, the source will fall into line.

A public official cannot evade a question with a plea of ignorance. A city controller, whose job it is to audit the financial records of city agencies and departments, told a reporter he had no idea whether a bureau had put excess funds in non-interest-bearing bank accounts. Told by the reporter it was his business to know that and that the story would state so, the controller supplied the information.

Sometimes a source will seem to talk freely but will cover the important material with a layer of unimportant information. When this happens, it is worthwhile to encourage the source to talk on. The reporter listens. Emboldened by the rapt attention of the reporter, who is studiously taking notes, the source may begin to exaggerate or fabricate.

These assertions duly noted, the reporter may suddenly appear puzzled by statements that, he or she informs the source, contradict what the source had said earlier or what is known as fact. Given the opportunity to pull back gracefully, the source may do so by giving the reporter the desired information. If the source does not, the reporter says that he or she has no alternative but to print the source's exaggerations and accompany them with the evidence that contradicts or corrects the statements. Confronted by the implicit threat to be made to look silly, evasive or duplicitous, the source often agrees to supply the necessary material.

These techniques may appear unethical to the uninitiated. Properly applied to public officials, they are justified by the obligation of journalists to hold officials accountable to the public.

Wendell Rawls Jr., a veteran newsman, says of interviewing:

> Don't tell people what you know. Ask questions. Then back off. Use diversion. I love to do that—talk with people about things you're not there to talk to them about. You ask a question that may be very meaningful. Then you move away from it. I do it sometimes even if the person doesn't get particularly fidgety, because I don't want him to think that I think what he has told me is necessarily important to me. I'll move to another question and say, "What is that on the wall? That's an interesting sort of . . ." Whatever. Anything that will divert him, and he will start talking about that. And then maybe ask two or three questions about junk, and then come back and ask another very pointed question.

The assignment was a delicate one—to interview Archbishop Valerian D. Trifa, the head of the Rumanian Orthodox Church in America. Trifa was trying to find a country to accept him after he agreed to be deported during his trial on charges that he lied about his part in crimes against Jews in Rumania during World War II. Howard Blum of *The New York Times* let Trifa turn the interview into a two-hour rambling monologue.

◀ Letting the Source Talk

Trifa denied taking part in any pogroms against Jews, said he had not been helped by the Vatican to enter the United States, and seemed assured that although he had spent two years trying to find a country that would accept him, his search would end successfully.

Blum posed a question: "Why do you think you were deported?" Trifa pushed back in his chair, seemingly angry, and began to talk heatedly. He brought up the Holocaust, that his deportation was the result of people reviving the period during the Nazi era when six million Jews were killed. He said that "all this talk by the Jews about the Holocaust is going to backfire. . . . Be it legislative or whatever, against the Jews." Blum asked him what he meant by "whatever."

Trifa raised his voice. "I don't want you to say Bishop Trifa is saying people will kill Jews because of what was done to him. No sir. I am just saying 'whatever.' That something will be done."

As for the deaths of Jews in the Holocaust, Trifa is quoted as saying he had no idea whether they were killed. He needed no prodding now. "I do know that not a single Jew was killed in Rumania. At least not because he was Jewish. Statistics prove that." Blum pointed out in the next paragraph that 300,000 Jews were killed in Rumania. Blum asked about articles in a newspaper Trifa edited, whether they were anti-Semitic.

"They were not anti-Semitic. They were anti-Jewish. And they were true," the Archbishop said.

Blum allowed Trifa to indict himself. "You throw a few questions out, making them more specific each time," Blum said. "When the net got quite tight, the subject started beating against it. When he started flaying away, he trapped himself. Or at least some of the people who read the interview thought so."

Handling "No Comment" ▶

Rare is the reporter whose persuasiveness is so overwhelming or whose charm is so overpowering that he or she is never told, "No comment." When a source refuses to answer, reporters must resort to techniques and devices that will nudge information from unwilling sources. One *Wall Street Journal* reporter says if he fails to convince the source that revelation will benefit him, he remarks that he already knows the other side of the issue and that "no comment" will mean that only the other side will be reported.

The reporter also can open up silent sources by telling them that they will be quoted as saying "no comment," which might lead people to believe they are hiding something. Some reporters tell "no comment" sources that they will keep trying to dig up the information, and when they do they will make it a point to include the silent source's "no comment." Few sources want to be embarrassed this way.

Reporters know there is more than one source for a story. A reporter assigned to find out about local automobile sales made no headway with the local dealers. Obviously hit hard by flagging sales, they did not want to admit that all was not well. The reporter told his editor the story could not be broken. The editor suggested he check the motor vehicles department and the tax office. In many cities, new car sales are recorded for tax purposes. Once the reporter had the basic data, the local automobile dealers opened up.

Another technique is to tell the source that although the available information is incomplete, the station or newspaper will have to run it anyway. The source is told that with his or her help the story will be more accurate.

"One of my sources will never tell me anything if we start from scratch on a story," a business reporter said. "But he will talk if I have something. Sometimes I bluff that I know more than I really do," he said.

Investigative reporters are masters of the bluff. Jack Anderson heard that private attorneys who had lost cases before various commissions suspected political fixes. (A reporter's maxim: When investigating suspicious deals, talk to the losers.)

Anderson learned that Commissioner Richard Mack of the FCC had promised his decisive vote to an applicant before the commission proceedings began. The applicant, considered the least qualified of the four applicants by the FCC examiner, had hired an attorney to lobby his case. The attorney, Thurman Whiteside, was a friend of Mack and a notorious fixer.

Anderson found out that Whiteside controlled a trust fund. "I was half satisfied he was using this as a funnel for payments to Mack, but I had no proof," Anderson recalls in his book *Confessions of a Muckraker* (New York: Random House, 1979). He called Mack

. . . and tried to con the truth out of him before he could get his defenses straight.

After giving him the nerve-jangling news that I was Jack Anderson of Drew Pearson's office, I bluffed, 'I have an accountant who is prepared to testify that Whiteside has paid you money from the Grant Foster trust. I'd like to hear your side of it.'

There was a moment of dead air as Mack fell for the bait and groped for a way to reconcile the irreconcilable. 'Those were only loans,' he ventured, not seeming to realize that even in sweetening up the transactions he was admitting to the impermissible offense—taking money under any guise from an attorney in the Miami television case.

Mack dug himself into a deeper and deeper pit as he tried to parry Anderson's educated guesses. By the time the interview was over, Anderson had confirmed his suspicions: Mack was on the take.

Sources seek to set the agenda. They want to control the reporting situation so their words pass untouched to the public. Sources prefer Layer I reporting. The good reporter will not allow the subject to call the shots.

Interviewing Vice President Dan Quayle during the 1992 presidential campaign, the television interviewer Charlie Rose wondered about just who made up the "cultural elite" that Quayle was condemning as being against American values:

◀ Seeking Specifics

> Quayle: They know who they are; we know who they are. . . . The cultural elite looks down on America.
> Rose: Who?
> Quayle: Look, Charlie, you know exactly who I'm talking about.
> Rose: No, Mr. Vice President, I don't know who you're talking about.
> Quayle: Oh, sure you do.
> Rose: I don't know who looks down on America.
> Quayle: If you don't think some of the cultural elite, whether it's here in the studios of New York City or the studios of Hollywood that don't sneer and look down on America and say, "I am smarter than the American people, I know more than the American people, I'm better than the American people," that's what I resent. Maybe it's a little bit of my midwestern heritage, my midwestern background.
> Rose: Well, I would resent it too, some of my southern heritage. But I don't know that that's the reality that the people who run the networks feel a kind of condescension towards the American people. How do the people who run <u>The New York Times,</u> for example, differ from the people who run your own family newspaper?

Quayle did not respond with a direct answer to this last question, but went on to talk about voting.

Specifics, Rose wanted names, specific names. He did not want Quayle to get away with glittering generalities. Journalism, as good reporters know, is the practice of the art of the specific.

A question for young reporters to answer as they set out on their careers:

> What is the reporter's job on an assignment? Is it to be the conveyer of source-supplied information and nothing more? Or should the reporter take to the event some concept of what the public is entitled to know and then ask about these matters?

The answer that this textbook gives is clear: The reporter must convey fully and accurately the views and opinions of those in authority. In addition, the reporter must move beyond being a passive recipient. He or she must play an active role by determining what people need to know or should know and preparing questions that address these needs.

Quotes, Quotes ▶

Look back and you'll notice that your interest perked up when you saw quotation marks. As the novelist Elmore Leonard says, "When people talk, readers listen." In interviews, the writer listens for the telling remark that illuminates the person or the situation. Leonard says he lets his characters do the work of advancing his story by talking. He gets out of the way.

"Readers want to hear them, not me."

Listen to the singer Lorrie Morgan talk about her problems: After her husband, the singer Keith Whitley, died of alcohol poisoning, Morgan was only offered slow, mournful ballads by her songwriters, she said in an interview with *The Tennessean* of Nashville.

"I mean, it was all kinds of dying songs," she said. But then she fell in love with Clint Black's bus driver, and she decided to change her tunes.

"I said, 'I'm not going to do that. I'm not basing my career on a tragedy.' I live the tragedy every day without it being in my music." Her life, she said, has turned around, thanks to her new love. "He's a wonderful, wonderful guy. This guy is very special, and I'm into him real bad." However, Lorrie's love life took a detour—her affections switched to a Senator.

Summing Up ▶

Good interviews make for good stories. They provide insights into people and events. Here is some advice from practitioners of the trade.

Helen Benedict, author of a book on writing profiles, says: "People who are interviewed a lot get tired of the same old questions. You want to stand out as an interviewer and get a good story, and that depends on preparation and intelligence."

Benedict writes out her questions and takes her list with her to the interview. During the interview, she gently guides her subject after establishing his or her trust. "Don't interrupt too much, and don't challenge too early so the person is put on the defensive. Don't talk too much."

She likes to interview in her subjects' homes so she can observe their clothes, objects on walls and desks—their taste. She watches their mannerisms, how they move, sit, drink their coffee, answer the phone, speak to others.

Illuminating Ringo. *Interviewer:* One of your hits is "Roll over, Beethoven." What do you think of Beethoven? *Ringo Starr:* He's great. Especially his poems.

To get at the person behind the personality, good interviewers talk to the friends, associates, relatives of the subject. Samuel Johnson, the brilliant 18th-century English writer, advised writers that "more knowledge may be gained of a man's real character by a short conversation with one of his servants than from a formal and studied narrative, begun with his pedigree and ended with his funeral."

Fred L. Zimmerman, a *Wall Street Journal* reporter and editor, suggests the following:

1. Almost never plunge in with tough questions at the beginning. Instead, break the ice, explain who you are, what you are doing, why you went to him or her. A touch of flattery usually helps.

2. Often the opening question should be an open-ended inquiry that sets the source off on his or her favorite subject. Get the person talking, set up a conversational atmosphere. This will provide you with important clues about his or her attitude toward you, the subject and the idea of being interviewed.

3. Watch and listen closely. How is he or she reacting? Does he seem open or secretive? Maybe interrupt him in the middle of an anecdote to ask a minor question about something he is leaving out, just to test his reflexes. Use the information you are obtaining in this early stage to ascertain whether your pre-interview hunches about him were right. Use it also to determine what style you should adopt to match his mood. If he insists upon being formal, you may have to become more businesslike yourself. If he is relaxed and expansive, you should be too, but beware of the possibility the interview can then degenerate into a formless conversation over which you have no control.

4. Start through your questions to lead him along a trail you have picked. One question should logically follow another. Lead up to a tough question with two or three preliminaries. Sometimes it helps to create the impression that the tough question has just occurred to you because of something he is saying.

5. Listen for hints that suggest questions you had not thought of. Stay alert for the possibility that the theme you picked in advance is the wrong one, or is only a subsidiary one. Remain flexible. Through an accidental remark of his you may uncover a story that is better than the one you came for. If so, go after it right there.

6. Keep reminding yourself that when you leave, you are going to do a story. As he talks, ask yourself: What is my lead going to be? Do I understand enough to state a theme clearly and buttress it with quotes and documentation? Do I have enough information to write a coherent account of the anecdote he just told me?

7. Do not forget to ask the key question—the one your editors sent you to ask, or the one that will elicit supporting material for your theme.

8. Do not be reluctant to ask an embarrassing question. After going through all the preliminaries you can think of the time finally arrives to ask the tough question. Just ask it.

© Joel Strasser

Profiling Diversity

"What there can be no debate about is whether journalism should cover the increasing ethnic diversity of American society as a major story. We in journalism have only barely scratched the surface of it. As we explore this story, the key questions are what they always are in journalism: What's going on? How important is it? How different is it from what went on before? Where can I go to learn about it? How much time can I get my editors to let me spend? . . .—Nicholas Lemann, National Correspondent, *The Atlantic.*

9. Do not be afraid to ask naive questions. The subject understands that you do not know everything. Even if you have done your homework there are bound to be items you are unfamiliar with. The source usually will be glad to fill in the gaps.

10. Get in the habit of asking treading-water questions, such as "What do you mean?" or "Why's that?" This is an easy way to keep the person talking.

11. Sometimes it helps to change the conversational pace, by backing off a sensitive line of inquiry, putting your notebook away, and suddenly displaying a deep interest in an irrelevancy. But be sure to return to those sensitive questions later. A sudden pause is sometimes useful. When the subject finishes a statement just stare at him maybe with a slightly ambiguous smile, for a few seconds. He often will become uneasy and blurt out something crucial.

12. Do not give up on a question because the subject says "no comment." That is only the beginning of the fight. Act as if you misunderstood him and restate the question a little differently. If he still clams up, act as if he misunderstood you and rephrase the question again. On the third try, feign disbelief at his refusal to talk. Suggest an embarrassing conclusion from his refusal and ask if it is valid. Later, ask for "guidance" in tracking down the story elsewhere, or suggest non-attribution, or get tough—whatever you think might work.

13. Occasionally your best quote or fact comes after the subject thinks the interview is over. As you are putting away your notebook and are saying goodbye he often relaxes and makes a crucial but offhand remark. So stay alert until you are out the door. (Sid Moody of the AP says that interviewing gems can come after the notebook is snapped shut. "I've found almost as a rule of thumb that you get more than you've gotten in the interview.")

These are starting points only, not absolute rules. They, and the material in the next chapter, will get you going. After a while, you will develop your own interviewing style. Zimmerman says, "Pick the techniques you think you can use and then practice them. Eventually, they'll become so natural you won't have to think about them."

Further Reading ▶

Benedict, Helen. *Portraits in Print: The Art of Writing Profiles*. New York: Columbia University Press, 1990.

Capote, Truman. *In Cold Blood*. New York: New American Library, 1971.

Fallaci, Oriana. *Interview with History*. Boston: Houghton Mifflin Company, 1976.

Garrett, Annette. *Interviewing: Its Principles and Methods*. New York: Family Association of America, 1982.

Kadushin, Alfred. *The Social Work Interview*. New York: Columbia University Press, 1983.

Mitchell, Joseph. *Up in the Old Hotel*. New York: Vintage Books, 1993.

Note: The books by Garrett and Kadushin, which are used in schools of social work, are excellent guides for journalists.

Noting the high-quality quotes.

Preview

Sources respond to interviewers they consider trustworthy and competent. They pick up cues about the reporter from the reporter's appearance, behavior and questions.

A successful interview depends on:

• Questions that put the source at ease, show the source the reporter knows the topic and elicit information that supports the story's themes.

• Role-playing by the reporter. The reporter may adopt a personality with which the source feels at ease.

• Patience and accurate observations. The reporter lets the source talk while he or she observes the physical surroundings and any revealing interactions between the subject and third parties.

When A.J. Liebling interviewed the jockey Eddie Arcaro, the first question he asked was, "How many holes longer do you keep your left stirrup than your right?"

"That started him talking easily, and after an hour, during which I had put in about twelve words, he said, 'I can see you've been around riders a lot.'

"I had," Liebling said later, "but only during the week before I was to meet him." In his preparations, Liebling had learned that most jockeys on counterclockwise U.S. tracks help balance their weight and hug the rail by riding with the left stirrup longer than the right. A rail-hugging journey is the shortest distance from start to finish.

◀ Starting off Right

Careful preparations such as Liebling's enable reporters to establish an open, friendly relationship with sources, who are pleased that reporters took time to learn something about them.

Usually, it is not necessary to spend much time on the preliminaries with sources the reporter knows. But people who are infrequently interviewed—the atomic physicist in town for a lecture at the university, the engineer sent out by the company to survey the area north of town for industrial development—must be put at ease.

Reporters use all sorts of techniques to start interviews. One reporter usually glances around the source's home or room upon arriving. He tries to find something about which he can compliment the source. Before one interview, he noticed an ivy growing up one wall of the source's office.

"How do you keep the leaves against the wall?" he asked. "Magnets and small clasps," she replied, and she talked about her plants for several minutes.

Who's in Control? ▶

Some sources take over the interview situation, and if they supply the needed information, the reporter should be willing to assume the passive role. Most sources, unaccustomed to being interviewed, need guidance with explanations, helpful questions, encouraging gestures and facial movements.

The source who dominates the interview and intentionally or inadvertently avoids the issue in which the reporter is interested is a challenge. The reporter must wrest control, subtly if possible. Control need not be overt. Indeed, a reporter bent on demonstrating that he or she is in charge will fail to achieve the balance of listening, watching and guidance that is necessary for the successful interview.

A subject may allow the reporter to direct the interview on the strength of the reporter's reputation or on the basis of his or her experience with the reporter. Some first-time sources consider reporters to be authority figures and become submissive. Generally, a source's cooperation and willingness to be guided depend on the immediate reaction a source has to the reporter's demeanor and first questions. Some of the questions that the interviewee may ask himself or herself are:

- Why is the reporter talking to me?
- What is her purpose? Is she here to hurt, embarrass or help me?
- What sort of story does she intend to write?
- Is she competent, or will she misunderstand and misquote me?
- Is she mature, trustworthy?
- Is she bright enough to grasp some of the complexities, or should I simplify everything?
- Will I have to begin at the beginning, or does she seem to have done her homework?

Intrusion. "Reporting never becomes any easier simply because you have done it many times. The initial problem is always to approach total strangers, move in on their lives in some fashion, ask questions you have no natural right to expect answers to, ask to see things you weren't meant to see, and so on. Many journalists find it so ungentlemanly, so embarrassing, so terrifying even, that they are never able to master this essential first move. . . . —Tom Wolfe

Appearance and ▶ Behavior

One afternoon a journalism student cornered his instructor.

"Professor X (and here he named the journalism school's senior professor) told me I had better get my hair cut," the student said. "He said I would offend people I'm sent to interview."

The student's hair was long. "Have it cut and stop worrying," the instructor replied. "Most of the people you will be interviewing will be very proper people."

The student plunged deeper into gloom. "But it will ruin my love life," he said.

The instructor and the student thought over the problem, the student in deep despair.

"Why not have it trimmed, and see what happens?" the instructor suggested.

The student took an inch or so off his locks and had no further trouble with Professor X. Nor, presumably, did his love life suffer, for there were no further anguished visits from the young man, who, after graduation, became a long-haired and successful rock music critic for *The Village Voice.*

A few years later, when the hirsute look had become common on assembly lines and in offices and faculty clubs, the issue became women in pants. And so it goes: Youth expresses its independence through dress and grooming. And traditionalists—who usually are the majority and always in authority—take offense and condemn the new ways, until sometimes they join in and the fad becomes a trend and later a tradition. Until then, reporters in the vanguard risk offending sources, most of whom are traditionalists in politics, social activities, business and education.

A carefree, casual attitude and dress can tell a subject that you, the reporter, do not take him or her seriously. Hair and dress, tone of voice, posture, gestures and facial expressions convey messages to a source. Anthropologists say that what people do is more important than what they say, and the first impressions the reporter conveys with his or her dress, appearance, posture and hand and facial movements may be more important than anything the reporter says.

A reporter can choose his or her garb, practice speaking in a steady, modulated voice and learn to control gestures. But age, race, sex and physical characteristics are beyond the reporter's control, and some sources are affected by these.

Where there is identification with the reporter, the source is much more likely to speak freely than he or she is with an interviewer of another sex, race, religion or age. People feel comfortable with those who are like them.

Most small- and moderate-size newspapers and stations are staffed by young reporters, and it may well be that the prejudice among sources against youth is the most pervasive. Youth must prove itself. And until a source is sure that a young reporter can be trusted, the source may be uncooperative.

Reporters have prejudices and biases that can impede their work. One of the most common antagonisms among the young is hostility to authority. There is value in the maxim that it is always wise to question authority, but sometimes youth moves beyond skepticism to cynicism.

Sent to interview a pioneer developer of the polygraph, a reporter sensed that the man was easygoing and relaxed. In an attempt to be humorous, the reporter's opening remark was, "You're described as the country's leading polygraph expert. That's a lie detector, right?"

◀ **Role-Playing**

The interviewee suddenly stiffened. "If that's all you know, I'm going to call your city editor and have him send someone else over," he said. The reporter apologized, adopted a matter-of-fact approach, and the interview was conducted satisfactorily for both of them.

The reporter was intelligent and had carefully prepared for the interview, but had decided to appear naive to open up the source. He was role-playing, and although this interview just narrowly averted disaster, role-playing is generally successful if the reporter acts out a role appropriate to the subject and situation. Experienced sources expect a neutral, businesslike attitude from their interviewers. Sources who are unaccustomed to being interviewed respond best to the stereotypical journalist they see on television or in the movies, the knowledgeable expert. Some talk more freely to the opposite type, the reporter who confesses he or she needs help from the source.

Obviously, the best role for the journalist is the one he or she finds most comfortable, which for most journalists is the impersonal, unemotional and uninvolved

Peter Francis of *The Stockton* (Calif.) *Record* questions two leaders of the Ku Klux Klan about their plans to organize additional California chapters. The KKK national leader (with cigar) and the head of the California Klan said their program, which included racial segregation, was attracting new members "every day." Although the men were wary of the reporter's intentions, Francis was able to draw them out about their plans for enlarging their base in California.

Rich Turner, *The Stockton Record.*

professional. Sometimes, the reporter finds he or she must become involved or the story will slip away. When one reporter was assigned to cover the rush week activities at a local college, she was struck by the depression of the young women who were rejected by sororities. She felt she was unable to break through the reserve of the young women until she remarked to one of them, "I know how you feel. I went through the same thing in school."

From Friend to Authority Figure ▶

Reporters can adopt the role of friend, confidant and companion when sources appear to need boosting before they will talk. When a source indicates he will cooperate only if he is sure that he will benefit from the story, the reporter is reassuring, promising that her story will be fair and balanced and that this kind of story can only be helpful.

Some stories require pressing sources to the point of discomfort or implying a threat should they fail to respond. Journalism often becomes the business of making people say what they would prefer to keep to themselves. Much of this is properly the public's business, and the reporter who shifts roles from friend to authority figure or threatening power figure may justify his or her role as being in the public interest.

Compassionate Listener ▶

The compassion and understanding that Diana Sugg of *The Sacramento Bee* takes to the police beat has resulted, she says, in "incredible stories about ordinary people."

She wrote about Connie Cornelius, a 44-year-old mother of four who was a girl scout troop leader, PTA member and volunteer school worker. One night, returning from a high school alcohol-free party for seniors, Cornelius drove her car into an intersection at the same instant a speeding car driven by a drunken driver careened through. Cornelius died instantly. Sugg interviewed family members and friends for her story of a tragic loss.

The suicide of a homeless man, Joseph King Jr., recorded in a brief note in the police reports, interested Sugg. "The detective who had worked the case knew me, and he told me how sad it was because before the suicide King and his friend had been talking about trying to get jobs." Sugg tracked down King's friend. "He told me how shy and skinny King was, and that he always needed protection. 'I wasn't finished teaching him yet about how to live on the streets, about how to deal with the cold,' his friend said."

Sugg began her story of the death of an anonymous street man this way:

Joseph King Jr. was a tall guy, but he wasn't a fighter, and on the streets where he lived, his best friend had to watch out for him.

Even in the Sacramento parks where they sometimes slept, King was in the middle, with a friend on either side of him as protection through the night.

But the 49-year-old man was weary, friends said. Tired of moving from homeless shelter to homeless shelter. Tired of missing his former wife.

About 7 p.m. Thursday, after discussing with his best friend ways to get a job, the homeless man dove 20 feet over a ledge behind the Sacramento Memorial Auditorium.

With his buddy crying at his side in the dark loading area, King died.

"He was my best friend. That was the only friend I ever had that was something to me," said Michael Lockhart, 31, who had been living on the streets with King for the past four years.

Sugg says good police reporting should focus on the victims, make them "the human beings that they are." To accomplish this she devotes time to extensive interviews with friends, relatives, investigating officers. "If we can give readers some sense of the loss, if we can give them some insight and context into what is going on out there they might not become so callous. They might better understand why there are so many shootings and stabbings. And they won't be able to dismiss these victims as anonymous faces."

Sugg spent two hours interviewing the family of a youngster who had died. When Randy Ray Harlan was four weeks old, his father—strung out on drugs and alcohol—had beaten Randy mercilessly. Since that beating, the child had been blind and brain damaged. Randy's grandmother provided constant, loving care. Now, Randy could fight no longer. Five years after he was beaten so badly, he died.

As Sugg drove back to the newsroom, she passed the funeral home. She knew she had little time to write. But she was unsure of just how to handle the story. Maybe stopping here would help. She eased her car to the curb.

She recalled her interview with Randy's grandmother:

"He was beautiful before all this happened," the grandmother told Sugg, "perfect in every way." When Randy's sister asked, "Where's Randy? Where's Randy?" Sugg noted the grandmother's reply: "I told you, he's in heaven." Then the grandmother turned to Sugg and said, "He was very special to Carrie. She would hold onto him and hug him and kiss him, but she knew he couldn't do it back. All we could do was tell her he was sick."

Balancing Act. "An interview is frequently the course you chart between what you came in knowing and what you're finding out as it's happening."—Terry Gross, National Public Radio's "Fresh Air"

Again, the grandmother recalled Randy:

"That little boy was a real fighter. I can imagine what he would have been like if this had never happened. He would have gone places.

"But it happened."

Sugg got out of her car and walked over to the funeral home. She went in:

> Pushing the doorbell and peering through the lace curtains, I realized that the viewing hours had started only minutes before. A man in a suit silently motioned me past the blank guest book. I turned the corner and found myself alone, staring at the baby blue coffin. It was small. I could have reached out and carried it away.
>
> But I stood back, several feet from the open casket, noticing the music that hummed lightly in the background. The song sounded like it was coming from a music box in a nursery two or three rooms away. Pushing my fingers deep into my palms to avoid getting upset, I didn't want to get any closer.
>
> Already I could see Randy's skin was tinged the grayish color I had faced too often. I was angry at myself for intruding into this peaceful place, for thinking that Randy was somehow going to tell me what I should feel, what I should write. Several minutes went by before I walked up slowly to his coffin.
>
> Dressed in dark blue pants and a matching blue tie, his arms were wrapped around his teddy bear. Long, brown lashes hung heavy over his eyes. Looking down at him, I felt I owed him an explanation. Randy Harlan deserved to know why his father got strung out one afternoon on Jack Daniels and methamphetamine and began throwing him—a four-week-old infant—against the nursery walls. But I was lost. I didn't know what to say.
>
> For a second, I thought I could almost see his chest move. I wanted to believe that maybe Randy was only sleeping in that white satin, and I stayed by his side for several minutes, watching him. I fought back an urge to reach out and pick him up, to hold him and rock him, make him forget about the pain he had endured in only five years of life.
>
> This little boy is finally resting, I thought.

Here is how her story began:

A little boy rests at last.

Randy died shortly after dawn Sunday, at age 5. His foster mother was rocking him when the blind boy opened his eyes wide.

"He looked straight up at her, as if to say, 'I gotta go. I can't hang on any longer,'" said his grandmother, Velda Wills.

Randy let out a sigh, his thick, long lashes closing over his blue eyes. His short life was over—a life of pain and seizures, of barely hearing and never seeing. He couldn't hold his head up; he couldn't move his arms or legs.

Wednesday, Randy lay in a small, blue coffin, looking as though he had just fallen asleep in his church clothes. His arms were wrapped around his small teddy bear.

"Most of these people don't understand, but they don't have a 5-year-old baby to bury because of drugs," Wills said.

And here is the ending:

"That little boy was a real fighter," his grandmother said. "I can imagine what he would have been like if this had never happened. He would have gone places.

"But it happened."

Wednesday night, in his coffin, Randy was dressed in blue pants and a matching bow tie.

Long, brown lashes hung over his eyes, and just for a second his chest seemed to move—as if he were only sleeping.

Randy's funeral will be held at 11 a.m. Friday at the New Testament Baptist Church in North Highlands. The family has asked that any donations be made to child-abuse and drug-abuse prevention programs.

The line limiting how far a reporter can go before role-playing becomes unethical is difficult to draw. There is a line between a reporter posing as a coroner to speak with the widow of a murder victim and a reporter feigning ignorance in an interview, a common tactic. Yet, in both cases the reporter is lying. What is the difference?

◀ Limits to Role-Playing

One well-known Washington reporter said she did not mind letting a senator pat her on the fanny if it meant he would be more inclined to give her a story—an attitude many of her female colleagues find abhorrent. But is that much different from some role-playing that is considered acceptable?

There are other questions. How well, after all, can a reporter assess a source so that role-playing is useful? We saw how one reporter failed. Even psychiatrists admit to no special ability to make lightning diagnoses.

The answers to these questions reside in the personal ethic of the reporter, which we will deal with in Chapter 27. Here, we can say that lying and deception are unacceptable but that the reporter is no different from the physician or the lawyer who is not obligated to tell patient or client all he or she knows in the professional relationship.

For his series "Unmarried . . . With Children," Sam Roe had to touch on touchy subjects. He wanted to know about the birth control practices of the single mothers, "not the most comfortable topic to be discussing with a male reporter," he says.

◀ Sensitive Questions

"Instead of blurting out, 'So, were you using birth control? What kind? What happened?,' I said: 'Some women say they were using birth control and got pregnant anyway; others thought they were safe; still others say they just didn't think about it. What was the situation in your case?' "

Roe has found that "being polite, friendly, compassionate, honest helps. There is no substitute for being likeable."

The goal of the interview, Roe says, "is to get your subjects talking and to build up their confidence in you." He says that in his work with youngsters for his stories about Tecumseh Street, his first questions were "easy ones." He would phrase his first question as though he were seeking the advice of the youngster: "Before we start, I was hoping you could clear something up for me. I have been talking to a lot of guys in your neighborhood about the gang situation and some say that gangs are a thing of the past, while others say they are just less visible. What do you think?"

Roe said he used this tactic on a 17-year-old awaiting trial for shooting a man in the back of the head. "By the end of the interview he was acknowledging that he only had himself to blame for his problems—a rare admission for a kid.

Roe subscribes to the "share-the-pain" interviewing strategy. When the reporter talks about a similar painful event in his or her life, the reporter is seen to be human and compassionate. "The interview can then work toward being a conversation between two people."

Besides, he says, "If you ask people to spill their guts, you can spill some of your own."

He always leaves his name and phone number, so that "if they want to talk further they can call at any time. This lets them know they are important to you."

Despite the sensitivity of some questions, Roe asks them all. "It never ceases to amaze me what strangers will tell you if you just ask."

Sexuality ▶

Alfred Kinsey, the author of studies of human sexuality, needed to determine the percentage of gays and lesbians in the population. He began his interviews by asking subjects when they had had their first homosexual experience. This created the understanding that such experience was common, and the subject would nod and recall the year of his or her age at the time of the experience. Or else the subject would strenuously object. (Kinsey's 8,000 interviews set the percentage at about 10. A more recent study in 12 of the largest cities in the United States set the figure of gays and lesbians and bisexuals at 9 percent.)

Tough Questions ▶

Reporters who work on investigative stories use a reporting technique that requires a straight face and a knowing tone of voice. Bruce Selcraig, a special contributor to *Sports Illustrated,* calls this the "assumed-truth question."

"You're trying to confirm whether the FBI has begun an investigation at Steroid University," he says. "You may get nowhere if you simply ask an agent, 'Can you confirm this or that?' Instead, try: 'What's the bureau's jurisdiction in this case?' 'Which agent will be supervising the investigation of the university?' "

Selcraig suggests reporters watch how their subjects handle questions:

> Notice stress indicators like frequent crossing and uncrossing of legs, constant handling of desk items (paper clips, pencils), picking at one's clothing, and obvious signs like sweating or stuttering. He may not be lying yet, but you may be getting uncomfortably close to the right question. Try asking: "Have I made you nervous?" or "You seem bothered by something today."

With difficult stories and closed-mouthed sources, Bob Greene of *Newsday* takes an approach he calls "building a circle." He will conduct many interviews for his investigative stories. The first one, he says, is general, "far off the goal. Then you move closer and closer until the person you are checking becomes tense. He or she is then primed for the final interview." Along the way, Greene says, a subject hears that you have been calling on people to check him. "He suggests that you might want to come over and talk to him."

"Interviewing is intimidation. Do they or you have the edge? But be cooperative. Say things like, 'We want to be right. Maybe we're wrong, but we've drawn this conclusion. You can see how a reasonable person can come to this conclusion, can't you?'

"Then they will admit about 80 percent of what you're alleging. They'll gradually back down. You can say, 'Please, give us something that proves we are wrong.'"

Greene follows these rules:

- Never debate or argue.
- Never make statements.
- Ask brief questions that are based on evidence.
- Be cooperative.

You are entering the office of the chairman of the English department. You had telephoned to ask if you could interview him about the department's plans to cope with the increasing numbers of high school graduates who arrive on campus poorly trained in reading and writing. He had told you to drop in about 3 p.m.

As you enter, you notice two paintings of sea scenes on a wall and two novels, a dictionary and a world almanac on his desk. Books in a floor-to-ceiling bookcase line one wall. These impressions do not particularly concern you because this will be a news interview focused on the situation, not the individual. Nevertheless, the setting could provide an occasional break in the quest for facts.

The chairman is worried, he says, about the growing numbers of students unable to understand college-level material. The chairman pauses often in his answers and occasionally goes to a shelf to take down a book that he reads to amplify a point.

"A friend of mine calls this the cretinization of American youth, and I used to laugh at him," he says. He reads from a copy of *McGuffey's Readers*. "This grade-school material is now at the high school level," he says. "I wonder if anyone cares." He then reads from a Wordsworth poem that he says used to be memorized in grade school. No more, he says.

As the interview proceeds, you notice that the chairman is toying with what appears to be a battered cigarette lighter. You wonder whether to ask about it.

Suddenly, you decide that the interview should include more than the plans of the department to offer more courses in remedial writing and grammar. The story will include the chairman's personality as well as his plans and ideas. That will help to personalize it, to make it more readable.

Quickly, you reexamine the office to make note of the artists of the paintings, the titles of the books on the desk, and you ask about the cigarette lighter. (You learn the chairman uses it to relieve tension; he is trying to stop smoking.)

As the chairman talks, you note his mannerisms, his slow speech, his frequent stares out the window. A student enters the office and asks for permission to drop a course, and you watch him persuade the freshman to give the course another week.

Noticing the family pictures on the chairman's desk, you ask for their identities. Smiling, the chairman complies and then says, "You must be a believer in Whitehead's remark that genius consists of the minute inspection of subjects that are taken for granted just because they are under our noses."

You make a note of that, too, more for yourself than for the story.

◀ **The Careful Observer**

Back in the newsroom, the editor agrees that the story is worth two columns, and he sends a photographer to take a picture of the chairman.

Details, Details ▶

The reporter was acting in the best reportorial manner by noting specific details of the setting and the interviewee's mannerisms as well as watching for any interaction with third parties. In looking for details, the reporter was seeking the material that gives verisimilitude to an interview.

It was not enough to say that the chairman toyed with a cigarette lighter. The reporter wrote of the "lighter that he fingered to remind him of his no-smoking pledge." The reporter did not write that the chairman had read from an elementary school reader used in U.S. schools generations ago. He gave the book's title. The reporter did not merely quote the chairman when he spoke about the low scores of entering freshmen on the English placement test. The reporter noted the dejected slope of the chairman's shoulders, and he checked with the college admissions office to obtain the scores.

Too much for you, these warnings to be alert to every little detail? Then ponder the bewilderment of the *Baltimore Sun* reporter who turned in a story about a murder and was asked, "Which hand held the gun?"

The question is asked in newsrooms when a reporter writes a story that lacks convincing detail.

Listening and Hearing ▶

There is an adage that says most people hear but few listen. Words assail us on all sides: Newspapers on the porch every day, magazines in the mail, books to be read, the omnipresent radio and television sets, and the questions, advice and endless chatter of friends, neighbors, relatives and teachers. It is a wonder that anyone hears anyone amidst the clatter. But reporters must hear, must listen carefully. Their livelihood depends on it.

So many people are talking and so few listening with attention and courtesy that the reporter who trains himself or herself to hear will find people eager to talk to someone who cares about what they are saying.

To become a good listener:

- Cut down your ego. You are in an interview to hear what others say, not to spout your opinions.
- Open your mind to new or different ideas, even those you dislike.
- Grant the interviewee time to develop his or her thoughts.
- Rarely interrupt.
- Concentrate on what the person is saying and make secondary the person's personality, demeanor or appearance.
- Limit questions to the theme or to relevant ideas that turn up in the interview.
- Don't ask long questions.

Good listeners will have in their notes the quotations that give the reader or listener an immediate sense of the person being interviewed—what are known as high-quality quotes. Oscar Lewis, the anthropologist who wrote about Spanish-speaking peoples, began his article, "In New York You Get Swallowed by a

A Beatle Talks. *Interviewer:* What do you call your haircut? *George Harrison:* Arthur.

Horse" (*Anthropological Essays,* New York: Random House, 1964, and *Commentary,* November 1964), about Hector, a Puerto Rican, this way:

We had been talking of this and that when I asked him, "Have you ever been in New York, Hector?"

"Yes, yes, I've been to New York."

"And what did you think of life there?"

"New York! I want no part of it! Man, do you know what it's like? You get up in a rush, have breakfast in a rush, go to work in a rush, go home in a rush, even shit in a rush. That's life in New York! Not for me! Never again! Not unless I was crazy.

"Look I'll explain. The way things are in New York, you'll get nothing there. But nothing! It's different in Puerto Rico. Here, if you're hungry, you come to me and say, 'Man I'm broke, I've had nothing to eat,' and I'd say, 'Ay, Benedito! Poor thing!' And I'd give you some food. No matter what, you wouldn't have to go to bed hungry. Here in Puerto Rico you can make out. But in New York, if you don't have a nickel, or twenty cents, you're worthless, and that's for sure. You don't count. You get swallowed by a horse!"

◀ Alert Listening

The reporter may seem slightly passive in the interview, but in fact he or she is working hard, checking the incoming information against his or her preconceptions of the story. Is the source confirming or contradicting the reporter's ideas? Or is he avoiding them for some reason? Or is the source providing better thematic material than the reporter's? Just what does the source mean? What is he trying to say? Does he have any self-interest that affects his statements?

Some people will skirt a topic, and the reporter has to hear what is meant as well as what is said. The concealed meanings can be found by noting gestures, facial expressions, slips of the tongue, half-uttered remarks and the peculiar uses of words. Good listeners pick up the source's inconsistencies. And they are alert to the undercurrents that may be more important than the torrent of information the source seems only too willing to provide.

◀ Taking Notes

Most interviews provide much more material than can be used. Experienced reporters note only the salient facts and the high-quality anecdotes, quotes or incidents that will illustrate them. No reporter can keep up with the source's flow of information and still retain some control of the interview unless the reporter constantly filters the information.

A source, seeing the reporter stop his or her note taking, may be discouraged from continuing. To avoid this, the reporter may want to seem to keep up note taking while the source is supplying nonessential material. Actually, the reporter will be writing about the setting or the ideas he or she has from statements made earlier in the interview. With sources who inadvertently say more than they want to reveal, the reporter slows down note taking or seems disinterested so that the source is not alerted to the significance of his or her remarks.

Before leaving, or during the interview, the reporter may ask the source to repeat something to make certain the quotation is precise or the meaning is clear. When a source contends that he or she meant something else, the reporter must take time to determine whether the source is backtracking.

The adage that first impressions are the best usually works for the reporter. Lillian Ross, the brilliant *New Yorker* writer whose profiles are studied for their understated yet incisive perceptions, says that "first impressions and first

Note-Taking Guide. Studies of memory and the use of handwritten notes show that those who rely on their memories may omit some material, but copious note takers sometimes irritate sources or influence their responses.

The author Truman Capote said that note taking makes people say "what they think you expect them to say." Annette Garrett, author of a book on interviewing, said that note taking can interfere with the interviewer's participation in the interview. Experienced reporters rely on notes to jog their memories, but few take verbatim notes.

instincts about a person are usually the sound reliable ones that guide you to the rest of what the person has to offer." These early impressions can give the reporter a sense of the entire scene, the whole person, whereas the later impressions tend to be narrower, to focus on details and particulars.

The fresh observation is unimpeded by preconceptions. The reporter new on the scene will sometimes out-report the old-timer who has formed notions and drawn conclusions after repeatedly seeing the same events and persons.

To Tape or Not to Tape?

The tape recorder can provide large chunks of quotes, and the quotes will have the flavor of the person's speech. The tape recorder also protects against charges of misquotation. However, some sources freeze in front of a recorder or become so careful the interview is stilted.

One technique, suggested by a magazine interviewer for subjects who do not mind being taped, is to put the machine out of sight so that the subject is not conscious of the merciless machine with its ability to record every word.

"I tape, therefore I am," says Studs Terkel, whose radio programs and books utilize the tape recorder. For his books, Terkel, an excellent interviewer, transcribes his taped material, then edits it carefully. "It's like prospecting," he says. "The transcripts are the ore. I've got to get to the gold dust. It's got to be the person's truth, highlighted. It's not just putting down what people say."

Lillian Ross has no use for the tape recorder and says flatly, "Do not use a tape recorder. The machine, surprisingly, distorts the truth. The tape recorder is a fast and easy and lazy way of getting a lot of talk down. . . . A lot of talk does not in itself make an interview. . . . A writer must use his own ears to listen, must use his own eyes to look."

Retroactive Requests

Sometimes a person being interviewed will suddenly stop and realize he has said something he does not want to see in print or hear on television or the radio.

"Please don't use that," he will say. "It's off-the-record."

Should the reporter honor that request? It depends: If the source is a good contact and the material is not crucial to the story, the reporter probably will go along, particularly if the source is not a public figure or official. However, if the source has said something important, or the information is of concern to the public, then the reporter will usually reply that since the source knew he was talking to a reporter, he cannot suddenly go off-the-record retroactively.

When Jessica Mitford was interviewing Bennett Cerf, one of the owners of the Famous Writers School, he chatted freely with the amiable but sharp-penned writer. In the middle of his discourse, Cerf realized he sounded contemptuous of the people who took the school's correspondence course.

Here is how Mitford describes what happened, in her *Atlantic Monthly* article "Let Us Now Appraise Famous Writers":

While Mr. Cerf is by no means uncritical of some aspects of mail-order selling, he philosophically accepts them as inevitable in the cold-blooded world of big business—so different, one gathers, from his own cultured world of letters. "I think mail-order selling has several built-in deficiencies," he said. "The crux of it is a very hard sales pitch, an appeal to the gullible. Of course, once somebody has signed a contract with the Famous Writers School he can't get out of it, but that's true with every business in the country." Noticing that I was writing this down, he said in alarm, "For God's sake, don't quote me on that 'gullible' business—you'll have all the mail-order houses in the country down on my neck!" "Then would you like to paraphrase it?" I asked, suddenly getting very firm. "Well—you could say in general I don't like the hard sell, yet it's the basis of all American business." "Sorry, I don't call that a paraphrase, I shall have to use both of them," I said in a positively governessy tone of voice. "Anyway, why do you lend your name to this hard-sell proposition?" Bennett Cerf (with his melting grin): "Frankly, if you must know, I'm an awful ham—I love to see my name in the papers!"

When the source states beforehand that something is off-the-record and the reporter agrees to hear it on that condition, the material may not be used. Never? Well, hardly ever. Witness how Clifford D. May handles his source in this article, "Whatever Happened to Sam Spade?" in the *Atlantic Monthly.* A private detective, Jeremiah P. McAward, has been describing his difficulties in shadowing people:

"It's harder than you'd think," McAward continues. "Don't print this, but I once lost a pregnant Indian who was wearing a red blanket and had a feather in her hair, in Macy's." I reply that he cannot tell me something like that and expect that I won't use it. "Really?" he asks. I nod. "All right, then." There is a pause and then he adds. "But she just evaporated. A two-hundred-pound Indian."

Reporters develop a sense of when to quote someone and when to consider the material off-the-record. The objective of the reporter is to gather important information for the public, not to embarrass or intimidate individuals. A reporter suggests this guideline:

◀ Confidences

> A public official who talks to a reporter about public matters is presumed to be on-the-record. A person who has little contact with the press—even though he or she may be a public employee—should be presumed to be speaking off-the-record during a chat. Where there is uncertainty by the source or by the reporter, set the situation straight.

Reporters always keep in mind the fact that they rely on their sources, and a minor story that is based on quotes that the source presumes are off-the-record may shut off that source for good. However, no reporter will allow an official or a public figure to presume what he or she says is off-the-record unless that is clear at the outset of the interview.

Many reporters cleanse the language of free-speaking sources before putting their quotes into stories. They also correct grammatical errors and ignore absurd and meaningless statements that are not central to the story.

◀ Using and Abusing Quotes

The authors of a book about Clifford Irving, who hoaxed a major publisher into believing he had written an authorized biography of multimillionaire Howard Hughes, reported overhearing this conversation between a *New York Times* reporter and a lawyer for Hughes, named Davis.

"Mr. Davis, I wanted to ask you if you have any comment on the things Mr. Maheu has been saying about you and your behavior in Las Vegas."

"It's just bullshit."

"But Mr. Davis, we can't put 'bullshit' in *The New York Times*."

"Why not? You do it every day."

"No, I don't mean it in that sense. I mean it's a term we can't print."

"Oh, would you like it better if I said his remarks were utter nonsense?"

The next day, the authors say, the *Times'* story on the interview quoted Davis as saying Maheu's remarks were "utter nonsense."

Contrast this Mr. Clean approach to quotations with that of the weekly supermarket tabloids. Listen to Jack Alexander of the *Weekly News* describe his interviewing technique:

> I always tell them I'm doing a series of articles, that I'm a religious editor or a travel editor. That puts them at ease. I say I'm with *The News* in Palm Beach and I try not to say more than that. I want to put questions in (the source's) mouth, so he just says "yes" or "no." Then we will quote him as saying that. (I ask the source,) "Could this happen?" He says, "Oh yeah." Then as far as we're concerned, it did happen.

Wendy Henry, editor of the *Globe*, explains the philosophy of these newspapers: "The great thing about working here is the simplemindedness that sales are everything, and a great honesty about what sort of paper we are and who we are aiming at."

Holy Writ or Amendable?

"We regard quotations as absolutely sacrosanct. If there is any reason at all to be tempted to change them, then you take the quotation marks off and paraphrase it."

—*The New York Times*

"Quotations should be exact. The words should not be rearranged for more felicitous phrasing."   —*The Washington Post*

"We can trim quotes to fit stories. The biggest problem . . . is how you use quotes and how you edit quotes in the story. . . ."   —*Newsweek*

The magazine engages in "what is commonly known as cleaning up the quotes."   —*The New Republic*

"(W)riters and reporters by necessity alter what people say, at the very least to eliminate grammatical and syntactical infelicities. If every alteration constituted the falsity required to prove actual malice, the practice of journalism, which the First Amendment standard is designed to protect, would require a radical change, one inconsistent with our precedents and First Amendment principles."

—Justice Anthony Kennedy, U.S. Supreme Court

To some sources, reporters apply the whip of exact quotations. They know the validity of the statement by Arnold Gingrich, former editor in chief of *Esquire* magazine, "The cruelest thing you can do to anybody is to quote him literally."

One of the delights for the reporters covering Chicago Mayor Richard Daley was quoting him exactly as he spoke. Angry at being attacked, Daley was quoted as saying, "They have vilified me; they have crucified me—yes, they have even criticized me." And, on another occasion when he sought to inspire the citizens of his city, he said, "We will reach greater and greater platitudes of achievement."

Daley had an uneasy relationship with reporters, who frequently pointed to corruption in his administration. Once, while lecturing reporters, he said that "the policeman isn't there to create disorder; the policeman is there to preserve disorder." Reporters delighted in quoting Daley's introduction of the poet Carl Sandburg as Chicago's "poet lariat."

Chicago journalists are equal-opportunity quoters—everyone is fair game. When a candidate for mayor attacked aides of an opponent for visiting a "house of prosecution," he was quoted as he spoke. And when another candidate remarked that he would be a "drum major for education" and would "get out in front and beat the banner," he, too, was quoted as he misspoke.

Here is a section from a piece in *The New Yorker*'s "Talk of the Town." It is about a press conference attended by entrants in the Miss Universe beauty contest. Miss U.S.A. has just been introduced to reporters and is telling them that the Miss Universe contest has helped her express her feelings and widen her knowledge:

"For instance, Miss India has a red spot on her forehead. And do you know what? She says it's an Indian custom. . . .

"One of the experiences I've had was just this morning," Miss U.S.A. says. "I'm rooming with Miss South Africa, and I just saw their money. You see people, but you never realize their money was different."

The reporters try to think of another question. Finally, one of them says, "What do you think of the feminist movement?"

"Oh, I think femininity is the best thing on this earth," she says.

"What about masculinity?"

"That's just as wonderful."

Lest you conclude from all this that reporters are always intent on humiliating their sources and that you are much too compassionate to join this cutthroat company, here's evidence to the contrary:

When a politician took the microphone at a meeting to defend a fellow political candidate and said, "He is not the orgy some people think he is," reporters did substitute *ogre* for *orgy*. When Sen. Dennis DeConcini, the Arizona Democrat, endorsed a balanced budget amendment to the Constitution at a news conference by announcing, "It's going to be a great day because we're going to finally wrestle to the ground this gigantic orgasm that is just out of control, that absolutely can't put itself together."—well, what would you have done?

Anonymous and Confidential ▶

Sources do not always want to be identified, for a variety of reasons. The low-level official whose boss demands all material from the office go out under his name requests anonymity for the information she provides. The whistle-blower does not want to endanger his job by being identified.

As the press digs deeper to get to the truths of events, anonymous and confidential sources increase. People with information demand they not be named. The most notable example of an unknown source is Deep Throat, the source for a considerable amount of information about Richard Nixon during his presidency. The reporters who handled the Watergate revelations, Carl Bernstein and Bob Woodward, never disclosed the identity of this key source—if indeed it was one person. Some reporters believe that Deep Throat actually was a convenient way to handle a number of sources who demanded anonymity as the price for information.

The use of anonymous sources is much debated.

"No newspaper worth its name could fulfill its mission without using confidential sources," says Harry M. Rosenfeld, editor of the *Times-Union* in Albany, N.Y. "Without them, much of the very best in journalism would not be possible. At the same time, nothing so much brings our blood to boil. We decry their use and we despair of their ubiquity."

Joel Kramer, executive editor of the Minneapolis *Star Tribune,* says, "Anonymous sources are like fireworks. Used properly, they can produce a spectacular display. But they can also explode in one's pocket."

On the other hand, *USA Today* will not use such sources: "Unidentified sources are not acceptable at *USA Today,*" a policy memo states.

Michael Gartner, editor of the *Ames Daily Tribune* in Iowa and former president of NBC News in New York, likes the *USA Today* policy. He worries that "the anonymous source is taking over journalism, that it is appearing even in innocuous stories about obscure newspapermen. It's a lousy trend that is eroding the credibility of newspapers and adding to the unresponsibility of newspapers."

In a study made of such sources for the ethics committee of the American Society of Newspaper Editors, the journalists who participated were unsure of the terms themselves. *The Wall Street Journal* defines an anonymous source as someone whose name will not be used in the story by agreement "but whose identity we may later need to disclose—in the event of a libel suit, for example—in order to show that we had good reason for using the information.

"A confidential source is one whose name isn't published and whose identity we are pledged to keep secret, even if that means losing a lawsuit or going to jail."

Some Guides ▶

Some suggestions:

• Sources should be told exactly what is being promised them in terms of anonymity or confidentiality.
• Use of anonymous and confidential sources should be avoided if at all possible.

- Anonymous sources must not be used to criticize a person's character or credibility. The exception is rare, and then only with the permission of the editor.
- A source should be told that although his or her name will not appear, the reporter is obligated to give the source's name to the editor.

Let us watch a television reporter as he puts into practice some of the principles and techniques we have been discussing in this and the preceding chapter on interviewing.

◀ A Television Interview

It is 6:30 a.m. and we are in an automobile with J.J. Gonzalez, a reporter for WCBS-TV, in New York City. Gonzalez and the crew are driving to J.F. Kennedy International Airport. Louis Treitler, the electrician, is at the wheel. Gonzalez is next to him. William Sinnott, the soundman, and Joe Landi, the cameraman, are in the back seat.

Gonzalez unfolds the typewritten note from the assignment editor and reads it again: "Go to Overseas National Headquarters at 175th St. off Farmers Blvd. (Right near the airport.) We will be able to get interviews with the passengers. Afterwards, we were told, we would be able to get on the runway to film the boarding which has been delayed until 8:30 or 9. Crew should arrive 7:30 a.m."

The passengers the assignment refers to are airline personnel who had been on a DC-10 the previous week en route to the Middle East. Their plane had run into a flock of seagulls on the runway, an engine ingested several of the birds, and before the plane could take off, one engine stopped turning over and dropped to

United Press International.

Burning Jetliner

Clouds of black smoke rise from the burning fuselage of a jetliner when its takeoff was aborted. Ten crew members and 139 passengers scrambled to safety before the airplane erupted in flames. A television reporter used tape of the burning wreckage in his follow-up piece the next day when the passengers were asked how they felt about resuming their trip to Saudi Arabia.

the ground. The pilot managed to stop the plane and quickly ordered everyone out. Within seconds, the 10 crew members and 139 passengers were spilling out of the exits and down the escape chutes. The plane caught fire and in five minutes was a charred hulk. No one was injured. But if those aboard had been the usual run of passengers, Gonzalez says, there might have been a catastrophe. The metropolitan editor had instructed Gonzalez to find out how the airline personnel felt about taking off a second time.

The Planning ▶

It is a 45-minute drive to the airport, and Gonzalez and the crew have plenty of time to chat about the assignment. They will be going to three locations—first, to the airlines building where the passengers will be assembling, then to the airplane the passengers will board and finally to a runway to watch the plane take off. Film of the plane heading off into the rising sun will make a good closing shot, they agree. But they are not sure that they will be allowed on a runway, and they discuss going to the airport control tower. Sinnott doubts that the tower will be available either, and they talk about using the public observation platform.

Gonzalez knows there is tape at the station that was shot of the burning plane the previous week. He will want to insert some of that dramatic tape into what he anticipates will be unexciting tape from today's assignment.

"This is really a bunch of talking heads," Gonzalez says. He means that the tape shot today will show individuals talking for the camera.

Gonzalez will need a number of transitions, or bridges, to move the viewer from one place to the next smoothly. Gonzalez begins to think of possible bridges—long shots of the airport, the passengers milling about.

Gonzalez makes mental notes of the questions he will ask. If he is lucky, he will be able to interview the pilot of the plane that burned. He knows the pilot will not be on this morning's flight, but if he should happen to be around the airline office, an interview with him could liven up the story. It also would be useful as a transition to the tape of the burning plane and might even carry through as a voice-over (VO) of the firefighters battling the flames.

On the Scene ▶

Fortunately for Gonzalez, the pilot is there, and after chatting with him to obtain some background about the first flight, Gonzalez asks him, "What went through your mind at this time?"

The pilot answers, "Basically, I thought we should be doing it some other way."

His reply makes everyone in the office laugh and it seems to break the tension.

"It's the understatement of the week," mutters a young woman who was aboard the first flight. But when Gonzalez and the crew look toward her she has put on a sparkling smile. In answer to Gonzalez's question about the mood of her fellow passengers, she says that as professional airline people they are not too nervous.

Gonzalez is excited about his interview with the pilot. "This is the only real news here," he says. "No one else has had an interview with the pilot."

In his interviews, Gonzalez did not ask many questions. He knew that viewers are more interested in the interviewee than the interviewer. To keep from intruding when a source began to slow down in the interview, he would encourage the source with a smile or a head shake.

"I also use facial questions a lot," he remarked later. "When someone tells me something that is unclear or hard to believe, I will look incredulous or give the person a blank stare. This encourages them to go on and talk.

"Sometimes, the best question you can ask is one word, a simple 'Why?' "

On the drive to the airport, Gonzalez had estimated the story to be worth "a pound and a quarter," a minute and 15 seconds. But it is Saturday, usually a dull news day, and there may not be many other local stories to compete with this story, so Gonzalez interviews several of the waiting passengers.

"How do you feel about taking the flight now? Uneasy?" he asks a young woman.

"No, I feel good," she answers as the cameraman shoots her reply. "I just want to get going."

Back in the newsroom, Gonzalez engages in another set of preparations. Before he writes his script, he jots down what he has on tape and the voices that will accompany it. In one column, he lists the order in which he thinks the tape will be put together and in another column, he indicates the lead-in for the anchorman, his own voice and those of the interviewees.

Later, Gonzalez learns his hunch about the length of the story was correct. There are few breaking news stories, and CRASH, as he slugged it, is given more than two pounds on the 7 o'clock news.

◄ **Summing Up**

A pleasant appearance, a neutral first question, a willingness to listen usually put an interviewee at ease. Jules Loh of the AP says the first question he asks is, " 'When were you born?' He replies, '1945.' I say, 'What date?' He says, 'October 1.' Now you pull the notebook out.

"You're getting a matter of fact. Then a couple more questions like that. This impresses the subject that you are interested in accuracy. The first thing they've heard about reporters is that they get everything wrong."

Sometimes you deliberately avoid taking notes, says Dan Wakefield, journalist, novelist and screenwriter. "If people were saying something I thought really embarrassing I would try not to be writing because I didn't want them to see my hand moving and clam up," he says. "I would wait until they said something kind of innocuous and that's when I would write down the awful thing they said."

Studs Terkel, the master radio interviewer and author of books of interviews, puts people at ease by saying, " 'Oh yeah, that happened to me.' If I bring some of my own stuff in, maybe that person will feel more akin."

Sometimes, the results can be a disaster for the source . . . and troubling for the reporter. Here's the experience of Emily Yoffe, senior editor of the *Texas Monthly:*

> Once I did a story about congressional press secretaries. And one
> of the press secretaries I interviewed lost his job over the story. I felt
> absolutely awful; it was never my intention to have anyone lose his

job and, in fact, he lost his job because he was being too honest about what it was he did and because it made his boss look like the publicity hound he was.

It was a case where I was sitting there interviewing him, thinking, "I can't believe you are telling me this stuff." And he was very young and I was very young. If I were doing such a piece now and it was someone very young, I don't know if I'd warn him—through the tone of my questions—about what he was saying.

But then again, what he did was describe his job and I just wrote down what he told me. It was his boss who fired him—simply for telling the truth—not me.

Further Reading ▶

Cole, William, ed. *The Most of A.J. Liebling.* New York: Simon & Schuster, 1963.

Mitford, Jessica. *Poison Penmanship.* New York: Vintage Books, 1980.

Webb, Eugene J., et. al. *Unobtrusive Measures: Nonreactive Research in the Social Sciences.* Chicago: Rand McNally, 1966.

16 Speeches, Meetings and News Conferences

Preview

- **Speech** stories include the name and identification of the speaker, the theme of the talk, the setting and ample quotations. When a prepared text is used for the story, it is checked against the actual delivery.
- **Meeting** stories usually begin with the major action taken. They include the purpose of the meeting, background to the major action and quotations from those who spoke, including comments by the public.
- **News conference** stories begin with the major point made unless a better lead turns up in the question-and-answer period. Stories include background and topics from the question-and-answer period.

Bob Thayer,
The Providence Journal.

Catch the gestures along with the words.

◀ **Speeches**

"**O**urs is not to wonder why but to cover the speech or die," the reporter muttered as he put on his overcoat and stepped into the cold for a three-block walk to a downtown hotel where a testimonial dinner for the mayor was to be held. "I'll bet it's creamed chicken again," he said to himself.

The reporter's exasperation was caused as much by the fare he felt the speaker would offer as by the menu.

Speeches, hardly the most exciting stories a reporter covers, are a major part of the journalist's day-to-day work. Realizing that not every speech can be covered, speakers and organizations often deliver a prepared text to the newspaper and broadcast station ahead of time so that the story can be written in the office. (The reporter inserts the phrase, "In a speech prepared for delivery tonight . . ." or something similar.)

Speeches by prominent people are usually covered, whatever the subject. Nothing could have been more mundane than the testimonial dinner set for Betty Ford, wife of President Ford, at the New York Hilton one warm June evening. She was to be honored at the dinner launching a $6 million fund drive for an American Bicentennial Park in Israel. Her remarks were expected to be routine. Indeed, as the evening wore on, reporters became restless. A few of them left, asking those who remained to cover for them should anything unusual turn up.

Naturally, the unusual did occur, and it was front-page news in newspapers around the country and a major item on evening newscasts.

As Mrs. Ford was being introduced, the president of the Jewish National Fund of America, who had just finished speaking, slumped down in his chair at the head table.

In the confusion, Mrs. Ford went to the microphone and spoke to the stunned guests: "Can we bow our heads for a moment and say a prayer for Rabbi Sage," she said. The New York *Daily News* began its story this way:

> First lady Betty Ford led a stunned benefit dinner audience in prayer at the New York Hilton last night for a Zionist leader who collapsed at the affair honoring Mrs. Ford, and died of an apparent heart attack at a hospital a short time later.

Basics for the Speech Story ▶

Every speech story must include:

* What was said: speaker's main point.
* Who spoke: name and identification.
* The setting or circumstances of the speech.
* Any unusual occurrence.

Any of these can provide the lead and theme of the story, although most speech stories emphasize what was said. Itabari Njeri of *The Greenville* (S.C.) *News* began her story with a delayed lead and moved to the speaker's main point in the second paragraph:

> The three greatest lies, according to Dr. Eula Bingham, assistant secretary of labor: "The check is in the mail; Darling, I haven't looked at another woman in 27 years; and, I'm from the government and I'm here to help you."
>
> The punchline got the desired laugh. But Dr. Bingham, who also directs the Labor Department's Occupational Safety and Health Administration, said she really is trying to help business and labor by eliminating or streamlining unnecessary government health and safety regulations.
>
> Addressing the annual spring meeting of the South Carolina Occupational Safety Council, the former college professor and zoologist said: "We are attempting to revamp regulations that are burdensome and not meaningful. Our mandate is to protect the health, life and limb of working men and women. We are not interested in harassing or catching anybody."

The most important task the reporter faces is finding the theme. A tip-off to the theme may be the title of the speech. Often, speakers will use forensic devices to drive home their major points—pounding the podium, raising the voice, suddenly slowing down the delivery, the summary at the end.

When the reporter is unsure of the theme, it makes sense to interview the speaker after the talk. When combining material from a speech and an interview, the journalist should tell the reader or listener where the information came from. Otherwise, those who attended the speech or heard it on radio or television will find the report puzzling.

Occasionally, a reporter will find a lead in what the speaker considers a secondary theme. Then, the reporter should lead with what he or she considers the more important element but summarize high in the story what the speaker considers the major theme.

Robert E. Kollar, Tennesee Valley Authority.

The Point Is . . .

Reporters watch for indications in gestures, voice level and body language for an idea of what the speaker considers the major point.

For example, the president of a large investment firm is speaking to a local civic club about "The Role of the Small Investor." The morning papers have a story from New York about a sudden selling wave on the stock exchange late yesterday that sent prices tumbling. The speaker sticks to his subject that noon but in a digression predicts that the bottom of the market has not been reached. Obviously, the lead is his prediction of a continued decline. The reporter will probably want to ask the speaker after his talk for his comments on the market decline to give still more information to readers about his newsworthy prediction.

A speech consists of spoken words. So must the story. Unless there is an incident during the talk that would make the circumstances and the setting the most newsworthy item, the story should emphasize what was said with ample quotations at the top of the story. But resist the quote lead unless there is a highly unusual statement.

Now and then a reporter sits through an incoherent speech in which illogic and vagueness prevail. What should he or she do—confuse the reader with an accurate account? The reader will only blame the reporter. ◀ Tough to Handle

The reporter should seek out the speaker and attempt to clarify the confused points and ask others who know about the situation the speaker sought to discuss. If these tactics fail, the only recourse is to write a brief story.

John R. Hunt, who turned from prospecting in the wilds of northwestern Quebec to newspapering, has been covering the North country of Ontario for the *North Bay Nugget* for 40 years, "As a small-town newspaperman, I have covered hundreds of speeches," Hunt says.

"It is an interesting fact that a dull and boring speech can often become an interesting story. But I don't know of anything more difficult to write about than a funny speech." The best tactic is to use plenty of quotations and hope the humor carries through.

Reporters have the right to be present at an official, public meeting and can use anything they see and hear there. But they have no legal right to attend a meeting or talk by a private group, and they have to leave if asked. But the reporter can report what he or she learns from those who were there. A talk heard by dozens of people cannot be kept confidential, and the reporter usually points this out to those making the request. He or she also points out that since those attending the session will talk to the reporter about the speech, the speaker may find the material somewhat garbled in the telling and should welcome an accurate report. This argument usually wins the reporter's battle. ◀ Off-the-Record

Washington Post Policy. In a gathering of a private organization, where the reporter is present as a reporter and guest, he or she must protest any attempt by the speaker to go off-the-record. The reporter should point out that the meeting was open to the press and should declare he or she will not be bound by the limitation.

Remember, the reporter is not bound by requests for off-the-record status of any item if the request is made after the information has been disclosed.

Meetings provide newspapers and broadcast stations with enormous amounts of news. Public bodies—school boards, city councils, legislatures, planning and zoning commissions—conduct much of their business at open meetings. Then there are the meetings of private groups—baseball club owners, the directors of corporations, protesting citizens. ◀ Meetings

The essentials of meeting stories are:

- Major business transacted: votes, decisions, adoption of policies.
- Purpose, time and location of meeting.
- Items on agenda.
- Discussion and debate. Length of session.
- Quotes from witnesses and experts.
- Comments and statements from onlookers, authorities and those affected by decision, vote or policy.
- Background.
- Unusual departures from agenda.
- Agenda for next session.

Not all meeting stories will contain every one of these items. Notice the items stressed in the first five paragraphs of this meeting story from *The Brattleboro Reformer* of Brattleboro, Vt. The reporter used a delayed lead to emphasize the unusually large number of people who turned out. The first paragraph sets the scene for the major business transacted by the town school board, which is described in the second paragraph:

Public Protests Budget Cuts In Elementary Programs

By Gretchen Becker

Nearly 300 people came to an emotional Brattleboro Town School Board meeting at Green Street School Tuesday night to protest proposed cuts in the elementary school art, music, and physical education programs.

Purpose
Time
Location

Caught between the strong public opinion at the meeting not to make these cuts and a strong Town Meeting mandate to cut 5 percent from their budget, the school directors reluctantly approved almost $35,000 in budget reductions.

Major business transacted

Approved were elimination of the elementary art instructor's position, the second physical education position, a part-time vocal instructor's position, the fifth and sixth grade basketball program, and rental of space at Centre Church.

The board took no action on the administration's proposals to eliminate the instrumental music position and the part-time principal's position at Canal Street School. Approval of these cuts would have brought the total cuts to $46,000.

Salary Controversy

At Town Meeting March 22, the representatives voted to cut 5 percent, or $74,200, from the elementary budget. Those urging the cuts requested that teachers' salaries be frozen. However, WSESU Superintendent James Cusick has noted several times that the proposed budget included only $25,000 for increases in salaries. . . .

Background

Most often, the lead will focus on the major action taken at the meeting, as in this lead:

City Councilwoman Elizabeth T. Boskin persuaded council members to approve additional funds for the city police department last night.

Major action taken

The council had been cutting requested funds for the 1997–98 budget because of anticipated declines in tax revenues.

Purpose of meeting

But Boskin said violent crimes had increased 18 percent last year.

"The only way to handle this is with more police officers," she said.

Amplification of major theme that includes direct quote on theme

The department had asked for a 15 percent increase in funds over the current year's allocation for hiring an additional dozen officers.

Background

The council has been making cuts in the requests of city departments and agencies ranging from 10 to 20 percent.

Boskin's plea was persuasive, and the council voted unanimously to approve the request for an additional $287,000, an increase of 14 percent.

Amplification of theme

Then the council returned to wielding the hatchet. . . .

Transition to other actions

Sometimes a meeting continues past the reporter's deadline, and the reporter has to make do with what he or she has. It is possible, however, to catch the sense or drift of a meeting, as Robert T. Garrett did in this story in *The* (Louisville) *Courier-Journal:*

LEXINGTON, Ky.—The Fayette county school board appeared likely last night to reject the teaching of "scientific creationism" alongside the theory of evolution in local science classes.

Probable major action

The five-member board, which had been deadlocked 2-2 on the issue, heard opposing views from residents for several

Setting

Seating Plan. Wayne Worcester of the University of Connecticut recommends making a seating plan for covering meetings when you are unfamiliar with the participants. "Key the people to numbers, and as you take quotes and notes assign your numbers to them. When you write, refer to your seating plan."

hours last night before a packed house at school headquarters.

The board had taken no vote as of 11:15 p.m.

But the fifth and previously undecided member of the school board, Harold Steele, hinted that he would vote against the proposed "two-model" science curriculum.

Steele said he had concern that "very definite parameters will endure" that ensure the separation of church and state.

As the school board prepares to face the question of tuition tax credits in coming weeks, it must remember that public education "is not permitted to teach sectarian courses," Steele said.

Before last night's debate, school board Chairman Barth Pemberton and board member Carol Jarboe were on record opposing introduction of creationism in the schools.

Board members Mary Ann Burdette and David Chittenden had said they support the teaching of creationist views. Mrs. Burdette moved that the creationist proposal be adopted, and Chittenden seconded it.

Scientific creationism is a theory closely aligned to the biblical account of creation.

It holds that man and the Earth were created by an outside force, such as God, in a short span of time less than 10,000 years ago and have changed little since. . . .

Buttressing of lead with quotes and paraphrases

Probable position of others on major action

Background

The school board did vote 3-2 to reject creationism in classrooms.

News Conferences ▶

The UPI Day Book, a listing of daily events used by New York City newspapers and broadcast stations as an aid in making local assignments, carried this item one Wednesday evening:

> Manhattan District Attorney Robert Morgenthau holds news conference to produce evidence that confirms existence of ancient civilization in Israel between 2000–1500 B.C., 155 Leonard Street 10:30 a.m.

To local editors, it sounded like a good yarn. Moreover, many New Yorkers feel a kinship with Israel. So, when the district attorney began his conference, half a dozen reporters and two television crews were on hand.

The reporters were told that a Manhattan school teacher visiting Israel had taken a clay tablet out of the country. The tablet was later found to be an antiquity. Under Israeli law, no historical objects may leave the country, and the teacher was therefore in possession of stolen property, a criminal offense.

```
            DISTRICT ATTORNEY—NEW YORK COUNTY

For Release: November 20

Contact: Gerda Handler
         732-7300
         Ext. 603/4

    Robert M. Morgenthau, District Attorney, New York
County, announced today the recovery of a priceless
antiquity from ancient biblical times. The object is a
sherd—a fragment of a clay tablet—bearing a cuneiform
inscription of unique archaeological significance.
    Mr. Morgenthau today returned this antiquity, dating
from between 1500 and 2000 B.C., to Amos Ganor, Acting
Consul General of the State of Israel.
    The sherd was originally found at the site of the
archaeological excavation of the ancient city of
Hazor, located about ten miles north of the Sea of
Galilee in Israel.
    It was removed from Israel in violation of that
country's Antiquities Ordinance, which requires the
finder of any antiquity to notify the Government of
the discovery and afford it an opportunity to acquire
the object. A complaint was filed with the District
Attorney by the Government of Israel through Dr.
Avraham Biran, former Director of the Department of
Antiquities in Israel. An investigation was undertaken
by the District Attorney which resulted in the
recovery of the sherd.
    The sherd records a case of litigation, conducted in
the presence of the king, concerning real estate in
Hazor. It is of great historical value because it
confirms that the excavation, begun in 1955 near the
Sea of Galilee, is the ancient city of Hazor.
According to Professor Yigal Yadin, who headed a four
year archaeological expedition at Hazor, the sherd is
a major link in the identification of the excavation
as the ancient city of Hazor, that was mentioned in
the Egyptian Execration Texts of the 19th Century
B.C., the Annals of the Pharaohs Thut-mose III, Amen
hotep II and Seti I and in several chapters of the
Bible.
```

Figure 16.1

Press Release

District Attorney Robert Morgenthau's press release on the recovery of an antiquity by his office. Compare this with the story a reporter wrote that was based on the release and additional information provided at the news conference.

But the district attorney had decided not to prosecute. He had worked out an arrangement between the teacher and the Israeli government. Although all of this could have been announced in a press release, a news conference was called so that the district attorney could play midwife in the delivery of an important historical tablet to an Israeli representative. The district attorney, an elected official, would appear to the public as a man of compassion and wisdom. The reporters would profit, too, for the story and photograph would get good play.

The incident illustrates the mutuality of interests that the news conference serves. It permits an individual, group or organization to reach many reporters at one time with an announcement that will receive more attention than a press release because of the photo possibilities and the staging, and it is an efficient and economical way for the press to obtain newsworthy material.

Usually, the news conference has a prescribed form. A prepared statement is read or distributed to the reporters beforehand. (See Figure 16.1 on previous page.) Then reporters ask questions.

At the district attorney's news conference, reporters wanted to know the size of the tablet, when it was discovered, how it was recovered and other facts. The news stories that appeared differed substantially from the press release.

Here is how Marcia Chambers began her account that appeared in *The New York Times*. Note that some material in the lead is not contained in the handout and was obtained through questioning. Also, the story stresses the action and places the district attorney in the third paragraph, whereas the press release begins with the district attorney's name:

A fragment of a clay tablet 3,500 to 4,000 years old that confirms the existence of the biblical city of Hazor in Israel was returned yesterday to the Israeli Government after a teacher who smuggled it out of Israel agreed to surrender it to avoid prosecution.

The odyssey of the 2-by-2-inch fragment, with a cuneiform inscription, began in 1963 when the young teacher was on his honeymoon. The teacher, an amateur archaeologist, found the tablet at the site of an archaeological excavation some 10 miles north of the Sea of Galilee.

It ended yesterday, at a news conference, when Robert M. Morgenthau, the Manhattan District Attorney, turned over the priceless piece to Amos Ganor, Israel's acting consul general here. . . .

The essentials of news conference stories are:

—Major point of speaker.
—Name and identification of speaker.
—Purpose, time, location and length of conference.
—Background of major point.
—Major point in statement; major points in question-and-answer period.
—Consequences of announcement.

© Joan Vitale Strong.

The formalities of the news conference are not necessarily the real story. Sometimes the scene is the story, as Richard L. Berke discovered in Denver when the Republican presidential candidates gathered for a news conference. Most of his colleagues remained in Washington, figuring the Denver gathering was just another routine campaign appearance. "Many simply watched it on C-Span to make sure they did not miss any big news," Berke says.

What they did miss, says Berke, was "the best scene thus far in the warm up to the 1996 race." Here is how he reported that scene for *The New York Times:*

◀ The Sideshow's the Story

DENVER, May 14—Like the cows that are usually on display here at the National Western Stock Show Events Center, six Republican Presidential candidates allowed themselves to be herded into position on the dirt and sawdust floor, standing shoulder to shoulder for a photograph.

But the best known of them all—Senator Bob Dole of Kansas—was nowhere to be found. And his opponents were growing impatient. . . .

The waiting candidates engaged in a discussion, all of which Berke heard and reported. Senator Phil Gramm of Texas wanted to go ahead. No, said Senator Arlen Specter of Pennsylvania. "If Dole's not in the picture, it won't get published."

What this scene amounted to, wrote Berke, was "a telling illustration of the early state of the Republican competition.

"To many rank-and-file Republicans, the field consists of Mr. Dole, the Senate majority leader. Then there are the other guys in red ties and dark suits."

Berke says, "The lesson here is that reporters covering events, and particularly politics, should always look beyond the obvious and search for the all important behind-the-scenes details."

Panel Discussions ▶

In symposia and panel discussions, the presence of several speakers can pose a problem. But experienced reporters usually make their way through the tide of talk by emphasizing a thematic approach. They will find a basic theme—often an area of agreement—and write a summary based on that theme:

> Four members of the local bar agreed last night that probation is no longer a useful means of coping with criminal offenders.
> Although the speakers disagreed on most matters at the symposium on "How to Handle Increasing Crime," they did agree. . . .

Even when there is disagreement, a summary lead is possible, for disagreement is a theme, too. Here is such a lead:

> There was no accord at the College Auditorium last night as four faculty members discussed "Discord in the Middle East."
> The political scientists and historians disagreed on the causes of unrest in that troubled area, and they disagreed on solutions.
> All they agreed upon was that the situation is thorny.
> "We really don't know whether peace will break out tomorrow, or continued conflict is in the offing," said Professor Walter. . . .

After the theme is developed for a few paragraphs, each speaker is given his or her say. Obviously, the more newsworthy statements come first.

When one speaker says something clearly more interesting than what the others are discussing, the newsworthy statement is the lead rather than a general theme. Here is how such a story runs:

> A California research team may have found a potent opponent of the virus that causes the common cold sore.
> The information was disclosed today at a discussion of bioscientists and physicians at the School of Public Health on the campus.
> Dr. Douglas Deag, a naval biochemist, said that the enemy of the herpes simplex virus (types 1 and 2) may well be the popular seafood delicacy, seaweed. The red variety—known as Rhodophyta—contains a species that has an active agent that prevents the herpes virus from multiplying.
> Herpes is responsible for keratitis—a severe eye infection—and a genital disease as well as the cold sore. But the research is in the early stages, Dr. Deag said.
> He was one of five speakers who discussed "Frontiers of Medicine," which was concerned primarily with careers in the medical sciences. . . .

Stories involving several speakers will sometimes require multiple-element leads. However, it is generally best to avoid them since the number of speakers and multiplicity of themes can be confusing. Obviously, when necessary to the accurate retelling of the event, a multiple lead will be used.

Space exploration can be man's salvation, a physicist said today, but an astronomer worried that man might overreach himself and pollute the universe as well as his own planet.

The disagreement was voiced at a symposium last night, on "Space Travel," sponsored by the Science Club and held in the Civic Auditorium. More than 250 people turned out, obviously drawn by the promise of hearing one of the speakers discuss Unidentified Flying Objects.

But if they came expecting to hear a defense of UFO's they were disappointed, for Dr. Marcel Pannel said flatly, "They do not exist."

◀ **Summing Up**

Here's a guide to establishing a procedure for covering speeches, news conferences and panel discussions:

1. What's the **subject?** The title is an indicator.
2. What's the **purpose?** Generally, the speaker will be trying to report, explain or persuade, perhaps all three.
3. What's the **main idea?** Here we get to the specific point that will constitute your lead.
4. What's the **evidence** used to prove the point? This provides the body of the story.

Remember: These stories are based on spoken words. Your story must include plenty of quotations. The story always matches the nature of the event.

17 Hunches, Feelings and Stereotypes

John Walker, *The Fresno Bee.*

Compassion can make for good stories.

Preview

Reporters rely on hunches, and feelings as well as rational, disciplined thinking:

• Hunches and intuition spring from the interaction of new information with the reporter's accumulated knowledge. Hunches lead reporters to seek relationships among apparently unrelated facts, events and ideas. The patterns the reporter discovers help readers move closer to the truth of events.

• Feelings and emotions can motivate the reporter to seek out systemic abuses and illegalities.

But hunches and feelings can distort reporting, as can a reporter's stereotypes.

R eporters go about their work in a rational, almost scientific manner. They cover events with detachment, break down their observations and weigh them against their general knowledge and the background of the event and then draw conclusions on the basis of their observations, not in accordance with their hopes and beliefs. Then they reconstruct these observations in coherent, logical stories.

Analysis and synthesis, the application of reason to experience—these are the processes that underlie the journalist's work.

Yet, this summary is misleading. It ignores hunches and intuition and emotional reactions that include feelings such as prejudice, hatred, friendship and love.

Hunches and Intuition ▶

Every reporter has had the experience on assignment of intuitively sensing the meaning of an event, of suddenly seeing through the thicket of details to the underlying concept that shapes the event. Some reporters seem to possess an extrasensory perception that enables them to detect the real story, the actuality that lies beneath surface details. "I can smell something a mile away. It's just a fact of life," says Seymour Hersh, whose stories of the My Lai massacre by U.S. troops in Vietnam was the first of his many investigative stories.

Hunches, guesswork and intuition come into play as soon as the reporter is given an assignment. Before leaving the newsroom, before gathering information, the reporter has feelings and insights about the story, and these shape the reporter's coverage of the event.

There is nothing wrong with this. These intuitive concepts are sound starting points for reporting. "Feelings are not only reasonable but are also as discriminating and as consistent as thinking," said the psychiatrist Carl Jung. Even scientists admit the nonrational to their universe. Albert Einstein wrote approvingly of "intuition, supported by being sympathetically in touch with experience."

A long-time reporter on a southwestern newspaper was trying to explain the difference between useful and useless feelings and hunches. His listener, a summer intern from the state university, clearly wasn't getting it. The reporter searched his memory for an example and finally found one that went back 40 years to an incident that involved Sen. Joseph McCarthy, the Wisconsin Republican whose name became an epithet to describe baseless charges of treason.

Having had a stretch as an instructor at the university, the reporter knew that so-called "war stories," personal experiences, were taboo in the classroom. Accordingly, he told his story in the third person. It went as follows:

◀ **Hunches Can Lead to Stories**

> On a slow news day, a statehouse reporter decided to look into a proposal for a regional education plan for several southwestern states. He called the governor's office for comments. The secretary said the governor was on a brief vacation. Instantly, the reporter had a hunch something was going on. The vacation was too sudden, the secretary's voice too distant and cold. He called a state official he knew to be close to the governor. When he was told the official was "out of town" he was not surprised. Then the reporter called the Republican state party chairman. His whereabouts were unknown to his secretary.
>
> The reporter knew that the state party was to be host to a large gathering of western Republicans to discuss the party's presidential candidates. The officials could be gathering to talk about the party conference. But why all the secrecy? Add another fact: The reporter knew that one of the issues the party faced, one that would probably surface at the regional meeting, was the role Sen. Joseph McCarthy would play in the campaign.
>
> McCarthy had been making charges of subversion and treason in government that had split the country, and the party. Some Republicans felt that McCarthy could help the party because his charges focused on the Democratic administration and its appointees. But the reporter also knew that the governor and the state party chairman were disturbed by McCarthy's allegations of disloyalty by Democrats.
>
> An idea emerged that linked or patterned his background knowledge with the inexplicable disappearance of the officials: The officials were meeting to talk about McCarthy, possibly to take a position on his role in the coming campaign.
>
> After many calls and some sleuthing, he managed to track down some party officials. Instead of asking what they were discussing, he used a tactic reporters resort to when they believe their hunch is on target. He asked, "Have you decided on a strategy to keep McCarthy out of the campaign?"
>
> He was not surprised when an official confirmed his hunch by responding, "Yes, we have."

◀ **Sen. McCarthy's Campaign Role**

Go with the Juices. A journalism instructor advises his students, "Get the facts, but get a feeling for the subject. Follow your hormones as well as your head."

When President Kennedy was assassinated in Dallas, Tom Wicker of *The New York Times* and other reporters heard reports they had no time to check. They had to make quick decisions. Wicker said rumors flew through the city and that he had to go on what he knew of the people he talked to, what he knew about human behavior, what two isolated facts added up to—above all on what he felt in his "bones."

In looking back years later, Wicker said, "I see that it was a hard story to put together, but at the time it was all so compelling that you really didn't have much time to think about what you were doing. You just had to do what you could do.

"In a crisis, if a reporter can't trust his instinct for truth, he can't trust anything."

Jerry Landauer, a superb investigative reporter for *The Wall Street Journal,* had a gut feeling when he first saw Spiro Agnew, then being nominated for vice president:

> There was something too tanned, too manicured, too tailored for the guy to have been living on a governor's salary, with no other known source of income. So I started going down to Towson, seat of Baltimore County, the bedroom community where Agnew got his political start; talked to lawyers who frequently appeared to be on the losing side of zoning cases, to engineers who didn't seem to be getting a fair share of state business. After a couple of visits some started talking.

Landauer was told Agnew was receiving payoffs.

We have seen a reporter who smells out stories (Hersh), one who trusts his "bones," his "instinct for truth" (Wicker), one whose sense of proportion told him something was off-balance (Landauer). We watched a statehouse reporter dig out the truth behind a series of dead ends.

What do they have in common? The answer is experience, knowledge—background that enabled them to put the unusual new material in perspective.

Actually, what seem to be intuition, hunches and luck is the crystallization of experience. A hunch is the sudden leap from the reporter's storehouse of knowledge to a higher plane of insight. A new situation, fact, observation or statement suddenly fuses with material from the storehouse.

In a review of R.A. Ochse's *Before the Gates of Excellence: The Determinants of Creative Genius,* Mary L. Tenopyr, testing director of AT&T, wrote of intuitive breakthroughs: "Nothing that was not already in the creator's mind comes forth, but what is produced is old information put to a new use or configured differently than it was before."

Reporters store thousands of facts about people, events, policies and the many incidents of their daily experience. This vast storehouse is organized subconsciously. When a new piece of information strikes the reporter as important, it triggers the subconscious into releasing related material.

Hunches and instinct usually work for the good reporters, rarely for the lazy or the talentless.

Ability plus practice and experience equals excellence in all fields. During the 1982 hockey season, a talented young center for the Edmonton Oilers set records no one thought possible. Wayne Gretzky had fans comparing his feats with those in other sports. His goals, 82, and his assists, 120, for the season were the equivalent of a .425 batting average in baseball, 55 points a game over a basketball season, 3,000 yards gained in a season of professional football.

Pure instinct, say those who watch him. Not so, says Gretzky.

"Nine out of ten people think my talent is instinct," he said. "It isn't. It's all practice. I got it all from my dad."

When Gretzky was a 3-year-old in Brantford, Ontario, his father iced down the backyard and had the youngster practicing. At the age of 10 he was skating five hours a day.

Good reporters make use of this same combination of talent, hard work and experience. The reporter who discovered the purpose of the meeting of the state's party leaders had more than intuition going for him. He knew from the voice of the governor's secretary that something was unusual about the governor's "brief vacation." Dozens of conversations with the secretary had given him a sense of her voice when routine matters such as a vacation were the subject. Her tone was different this time, and that triggered his hunch that something was happening.

Reporters who rarely develop good stories attribute the success of their colleagues to luck. It doesn't work that way. "Luck is what happens when preparation meets opportunity," says Raymond Berry, a former coach of the New England Patriots.

Still Better. Four years later, Gretzky did even better, breaking his 202-point total with 215 on 52 goals and 163 assists. Still later, he became the first National Hockey League player to record 2,500 points.

◀ One Ejects, One Dies

When David H. Morrissey was working for the *Albuquerque Journal,* a brief news item caught his eye. An Air Force captain had died when his training aircraft crashed. The second crew member ejected safely. "That sounded strange to me," Morrissey recalled. "So I filed an FOIA" (Freedom of Information Act request). Four months later, the *Journal* ran Morrissey's account of what had happened: The captain's parachute had failed to open when he was ejected from his crippled jet.

The story continues:

The documents also say the crash of the AT-38B piloted by Capt. Curtis Iott of Trumbull, Conn., apparently was caused by failure of a mechanical part in the jet's rudder, which made the jet veer into the ground.

The rudder may have failed because a poor-quality cotter pin broke, according to the documents released to the Albuquerque Journal under the federal Freedom of Information Act.

The reporter's mind is like a computer in its capacity to store information. The mind, moreover, can make links, find patterns and relationships. When Morrissey saw the news item, he reacted immediately. Why did one crew member eject safely and the other not? He knew the Air Force investigates crashes and that there would be a document. He also knew the FOIA would pry that document loose.

The fusion of stored and new material is the reporter's highest achievement. Breakthroughs are accomplished through the application of logical thinking, inspiration and intuition to observations and background information.

Awed by a technological society in which computers and data processing machinery seem to minimize human ability reporters should retain their faith in the mind. "The largest computer now in existence lacks the richness and flexibility in the brain of a single honeybee," writes Peter Sterling, a brain researcher at the University of Pennsylvania Medical School.

Einstein's Model ▶ for Thinking

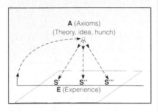

A (Axioms)
(Theory, idea, hunch)

E (Experience)

Everyday Thinking

Scientist or shopkeeper, mechanic or journalist . . . we all think this way, making the leap to some conclusion from our experiences. Einstein said the leap follows no logic, "only intuition." The more diverse the experience, the more insightful the theory or hunch for a story.

This diagram is a way of looking at the kind of thinking we have been describing.

Albert Einstein drew this diagram for a friend who asked the famous physicist to explain the roles of sense experience, intuition and logic in making discoveries or in formulating a theory. Einstein did not limit his ideas about thinking to science. The "whole of science is nothing more than a refinement of everyday thinking," he said.

Einstein's diagram shows a cyclical process. The process begins and ends at **E,** of which Einstein says, "The **E** (experiences) are given to us." **E** represents the range of sense experiences and observations that Einstein referred to as a "labyrinth of sense impressions," a "chaotic diversity."

Out of this plane of experiences a curved line rises toward **A** at the top of the model. This leap is the intuitive reach of the thinker, the reporter's hunch, the scientist's sudden breakthrough.

"**A** are the axioms from which we draw consequences," Einstein said. "Psychologically, the **A** are based upon the **E.** There is, however, no logical path from the **E** to the **A,** but only an intuitive (psychological) connection, which is always subject to revocation."

Notice in Einstein's model that the formulation of ideas is not based on induction, the concept of reaching generalizations from a set of observations. That method, said Einstein, is only "appropriate to the youth of science."

In his first paper on relativity, Einstein referred sketchily to some experiments and then wrote that they "lead to the conjecture," which he called the Theory of Relativity. "There is no logical path to these elementary laws; only intuition, supported by being sympathetically in touch with experience."

In the diagram, lines lead downward from **A** to **S′, S″, S‴**. These are deductions from the central idea, and they can be tested in the plane of experience.

This model and Einstein's concepts are useful to the journalist, for they illustrate in simple fashion the reportorial process. Reporters develop ideas, **A,** based on their experiences, observations and readings symbolized by **E**. From **A,** reporters draw consequences, **S′, S″, S‴**—which we can call leads or story ideas. These leads or themes are the basis of reporting, which is the validating or disproving of the leads in the plane of experience, **E**.

The statehouse reporter's **A** was his sudden insight that the governor was not on a "vacation" but at a meeting with other party leaders. Taken to the plane of his experiences in politics, he drew the conclusion or story lead, **S′,** that the meeting involved Sen. Joseph McCarthy. Further examination of his background knowledge led him to theorize that the meeting led to a strategy to contain McCarthy, **S″.**

For a detailed explanation of Einstein's theory, see "Constructing a Theory" by Gerald Holton in the Summer 1979 issue of *The American Scholar.*

The reporter usually welcomes his or her hunches and intuitive guesses but is less cordial toward feeling—that uncontrollable emotion that can hold us captive without warning, lift us to ecstasy at a glance or a touch and plunge us to bleakest despair with a word or a gesture.

This wilderness of feeling frightens most people, and it terrifies those who depend on their rationality, as reporters do. But reporters are human and must function within the limitations of the rationality of human behavior.

Feelings, in fact, can be an asset. "How can you write if you can't cry?" asked Ring Lardner. The poet Robert Frost commented, "No tears in the writer, no tears in the reader." Feelings help us to develop value systems and to keep them nourished. Moral indignation can direct a reporter to crowning achievements. The muckrakers, whose journalism may well have been the supreme journalistic achievement in this century, were propelled by a monumental moral indignation. Anyone who reads their work can sense the intensity of feeling behind it.

One muckraker wrote of a girl of 17 who had been working in department stores for three and a half years. Uneducated, from a poor family, the girl worked at a New York City department store "at a wage of $2.62½ a week; that is to say, she was paid $5.25 twice a month. Her working day was nine and a half hours long through most of the year. But during two weeks before Christmas it was lengthened to from twelve to thirteen and a half hours, without any extra payment in any form. . . ."

Rheta Childe Doar described maids' quarters that consisted of a den partitioned off from the coal bin; a maid's bed that consisted of an ironing board placed over a bathtub. Maids were rarely let out of the houses in which they worked.

Mary Alden Hopkins described unsafe factories in which women worked . . . and died. In Newark, N.J., 25 young women died when a fire broke out in a factory. Some leaped out of their top floor workplace. Some stayed and died. "They lost their lives because they worked in a building that was not decently safe for human beings to work in," wrote Hopkins. She said there were at least 100 more unsafe factories in Newark, some without fire escapes.

The exploitation of child labor was another theme of the muckrakers. Edwin Markham wrote in *Cosmopolitan* of Helen Sisscak, who worked in the silk mills in Pennsylvania, "a girl of eleven who had for a year worked nights in the mill, beginning at half-past six in the evening and staying till half-past six in the morning. Haggard, hungry, and faint after the night's work shifting and cleaning the bobbins, this child had an hour's walk in the chill of the morning over the lonesome fields to her home." Her pay: three cents an hour.

Then there was Annie Dinke, a silk-twister, 13, who worked on her feet 13 hours, and Theresa McDermott, 11, whose wage was $2 a week.

John Spargo wrote in *Bitter Cry of the Children* of the 12- and 13-year-olds who worked for 50 and 60 cents a day in West Virginia coal mines:

> Crouched over the chutes, the boys sit hour after hour, picking out the pieces of slate and other refuse from the coal as it rushes past the washers. From the cramped position they have to assume most of them become more or less deformed and bent-backed like old men. . . . The coal is hard and

◀ **Feelings**

The Library of Congress.

Ida Tarbell

One of the band of muckrakers who exposed the monopolistic practices of big business, Tarbell revealed the ruthless drive to power of John D. Rockefeller and his Standard Oil Company. She and Lincoln Steffens ran *American* magazine from 1906 to 1915 and attacked municipal and federal corruption and the robber barons of industry.

accidents to the hands, such as cut, broken, or crushed fingers, are common among the boys. Sometimes there is a worse accident; a terrified shriek is heard, and a boy is mangled and torn in the machinery or disappears in the chute to be picked out later, smothered and dead.

This strong emotional reaction to the abuses of power of public officials and the titans of commerce and industry propels investigative reporters to their discoveries. The Teapot Dome scandal was exposed by a reporter for the *St. Louis Post-Dispatch* who spent years gathering evidence to prove that powerful oil interests had bribed the Secretary of the Interior in the Harding administration. The reporter, Paul Y. Anderson, was driven throughout his journalistic career by the need to expose wrongdoers.

Today's Crusaders ▶

John Walker,
The Fresno Bee.

Home Alone

Six-year-old Aida must take care of her 10-month-old brother while her parents work in the fields of California.

Auditing Feelings ▶

These feelings—compassion, indignation at injustice, the need to right wrongs—constitute a powerful, continuing force in journalism. Look at the photograph that opens this chapter and the one in the margin here. The photos are from a series in *The Fresno Bee* titled "Children: The Forgotten Farmworkers." The chapter opening photo shows 4-year-old Melissa Hernandez gathering onions for her parents who cut off the tops. In the marginal photo, Aida Cruz Santiago sits in the family camper alone while her parents pick olives. The 6-year-old baby-sits her 10-month-old brother while the family works.

Alex Pulaski, who wrote the articles, describes the children he has watched working in the fields as "part of a work force intentionally ignored by federal lawmakers, who have carved out exemptions for agriculture. They allow children to labor in the fields at a younger age, in more hazardous jobs and for longer hours than their counterparts at fast-food outlets, retail stores and nearly every other business."

The newspaper estimates that 100,000 children "labor illegally in U.S. fields, forgotten because their sweat keeps down the price of the raisins, chilies and pickles we buy at the grocery store." These children work "in the cucumber fields of Ohio, the chili fields of New Mexico and the onion fields of Oregon and Idaho." Melissa was photographed in an onion field near Ontario, Ore.

Despite the usefulness of strong feelings, the reporter is wise to check his or her emotions every so often, for they can distort observations and impede the processes of analysis and synthesis that are the foundation of reporting and writing.

A city hall reporter who finds the personal lifestyle and ideas of a councilwoman abhorrent may discover he is looking only for negative facts about her. A political reporter whose personal allegiance is to the Democratic Party may find she is overly critical of the Republican Party and its leaders. The idea of welfare payments to the able-bodied poor—or subsidies to farmers—might so violate a reporter's beliefs that his coverage is distorted.

Here are some questions a reporter might ask himself or herself every so often:

- Have I so committed myself to a person, an organization or an idea or belief that I ignore negative information about the person or group?

- Does my need for ego gratification—which runs high among journalists—lead me to see an event a certain way? (The blandishments of governors and presidents can lead to a journalism of cronyism and self-censorship. Clever sources know how to play to a reporter's need for praise.)

- Does my need for immediate and frequent reward—a byline, a front page story, the lead on the evening news—make me write a story before all necessary facts are gathered? (The journalist often must write before every fact is in. Journalism is legitimately described as history in a hurry or, more poetically, "Journalism is history shot on the wing," says E.B. White. But sometimes reporters make stories from skimpy material, particularly when they have not had a good story in a week or two.)

- Is my competitive drive so great that I will ignore, underplay, or try to knock down another reporter's legitimate story on my beat?

Reporters cannot be neutral about life. Nor should they be. Enthusiasms, feelings, generalizations can be useful, as we have seen. But all reactions that swing to an extreme should be examined carefully for their causes. Reporters must watch for uncritical enthusiasm and unreasonable hostility.

Some reactions may be based on what the semanticists call "short-circuited responses," ideas that burst forth without thought. A reporter may be positive about doctors or judges and negative about salespeople or stockbrokers without distinguishing among the individuals in these groups. This kind of thinking is known as *stereotyping,* a dangerous way to think, particularly for a reporter.

When Louis Farrakhan, the leader of the Nation of Islam, spoke in Washington, *The Washington Post* carried two widely differing accounts. The first, by a reporter assigned to the event, described the speech as promoting an economic program for blacks. Two days later, a columnist reported that the most newsworthy part of the talk was the enthusiastic approval of the 10,000 people present to Farrakhan's mockery of the Holocaust and his attacks on "the wickedness" of the Jews.

A similar tale of varied coverage emerged in New York when Farrakhan spoke there. The story in the *Amsterdam News,* which has a black readership, carried this lead:

> Minister Louis Farrakhan packed them in at a controversial rally held last Monday evening at Madison Square Garden despite a vicious campaign by city hall to discourage the general public from attending.

A *New York Post* reporter turned in this lead:

> Black Muslim leader Louis Farrakhan turned Madison Square Garden into a mini-Nuremberg as he brought his message of hate to the city he called "the capital of the Jews."

The *Post* toned down the lead. The reporter, Peter Fearon, remarked in an interview with John Cassidy that "the outrageous aspects of the night were

◄ Race and Religion

Give the Relevance. *The New York Times* style-book on mention of race, religion or ethnicity states:

Race should be specified only if it is truly pertinent. The same stricture applies to ethnic and religious identifications.

Since that guideline was established, the newspaper has added another rule: The relevance of race, religion or ethnicity must be made explicit in the article itself.

Bob Christy,
Daily Kent Stater.

College Speaker

To some in his audiences, Nation of Islam speaker Khalid Abdul Muhammad provided truths about white racism. To others, his rhetoric was openly anti-white and anti-Semitic and historically absurd. At first, journalists paid little attention to Muhammad's campus talks. But when the content was revealed in an advertisement, reporters began to cover his appearances.

Stereotypes ▶

Victim of Images ▶

underplayed by most papers. All of the news media should have gone out of their way to say what a lot of outrageous nonsense this man is preaching. He represents a philosophy we have heard before. It is very close to being Hitlerite."

Newspapers and stations sometimes cater to what they construe to be the sensitivities of their audiences. The result is that readers and viewers are denied essential information.

For some time, the press ignored facts about the appalling living conditions of the poor in minority communities, apparently in the belief that such reporting would be seen as demeaning these people. Consequently, policy makers had no public pressure to increase police protection for blacks and Hispanics, the major victims of crime. Little attention was paid to health conditions in these distressed areas, and the result was infant mortality and maternal death rates two and three times greater than in middle-class white areas.

In Texas, the press was so restrained that it was possible for a small-town couple to dictate the kinds of textbooks children throughout the state could read. The couple claimed to speak for fundamentalists who wanted certain social, political and religious views presented in the public schools. Darwin thus became a nonperson in science textbooks. The theory of evolution was treated gingerly, and "creation science," which holds that the earth and its inhabitants were created at once several thousand years ago, was included in science textbooks as a theory as valid as evolution. Texas could not adopt dictionaries because the couple found they contained obscene words.

Few newspapers wanted to take on the fundamentalists or seem anti-Christian until, in 1985, the Texas attorney general ruled that "creation science" was not science but religion and its inclusion in textbooks violated the constitutional separation of church and state.

Attitudes, fears, assumptions, biases and stereotypes are part of the baggage we carry with us from an early age. We see the world the way our parents, friends, schools and religious communities have defined it for us. We are also creatures of the culture that surrounds us—our jobs, the reading we do, the television programs we watch and our government and economic system.

All these influence the way we think and how we see and hear. And the way we think, see and hear affects the accuracy of our journalism. In a famous experiment, journalism students were shown to have made more errors when they wrote stories about a report that was contrary to their biases and predispositions than they did when the report supported their feelings.

The journalist sees much of the world through lenses tinted by others. The maker of images and stereotypes, the journalist is also their victim.

Since Plato's time, philosophers have speculated about how and what people see. In the "Simile of the Cave" in *The Republic,* Plato describes a cave in which people are shackled so that they can only look straight ahead at one of the walls in the cave. They cannot see themselves or each other. Outside, a fire burns, and between the fire and the cave dwellers there runs a road in front of which a curtain has been placed. Along the road are men carrying figures of men and animals made of wood, stone and other materials. The shadows that these figures cast upon the wall are all the cave dwellers can see.

"And so in every way they would believe that the shadows of the objects we mentioned were the whole truth," Socrates says of what the prisoners can see.

The parable is striking, almost eerie in its perception of image making. It takes little imagination to replace the cave with the movie theater or to visualize the shadows on the wall as the images on a television screen.

Plato goes still further with his insight into how images pass for reality. He examines what happens when the prisoners are "released from their bonds and cured of their delusions." Told that what they have seen was nonsense, they would not believe those who free them. They would regard "nothing else as true but the shadows," Socrates tells us. The realities would be too dazzling, too confusing.

Shadow Reality. A woman customer of a dating service that uses videotapes tells this story: She was reading the biographies of men in the service's reading room when she saw a young man who obviously was the man she was reading about. He seemed eminently suited for a young woman also in the room, and the woman whispered to the young man that he ought to introduce himself to the young woman. He did, and he spoke to the young woman for some time. When he suggested a date, she replied, "Oh no. Not until I see your videotape."

The Seduction of Stereotypes ▶

Now let us jump ahead some 2,250 years to the speculations of Walter Lippmann, whose classic description of how people see is contained in his book *Public Opinion*. Here is that description:

> For the most part we do not first see, and then define, we define first and then see. In the great blooming, buzzing confusion of the outer world we pick out what our culture has already defined for us, and we tend to perceive that which we have picked out in the form stereotyped for us by our culture.

Lippmann says that the "attempt to see all things freshly and in detail rather than as types and generalities is exhausting. . . ." Stereotypes allow us to fit individuals into categories defined for us, categories that are comfortable because they save time in a busy life and defend our position in society, Lippmann says. They also "preserve us from all the bewildering effects of trying to see the world steadily and see it whole," he writes.

But the reporter must try to see it whole. When a student movie reviewer at Barnard College saw a film made by Luis Buñuel, she wrote, in amazement, "How Buñuel at age 70 can still direct such marvelous, memorable, intelligent and worthwhile films is beyond me." Her comment illustrates one of the stereotypes common to youth, the belief that with age comes decrepitude.

Stereotypes are held by every age group, by religious groups, nationalities and the sexes.

Sexism ▶

Sexual stereotypes are extraordinarily powerful. The stereotypes begin in infancy, carry through school and are retained in the workplace and home. For example, women are seen as emotional and dependent, men as stoic and self-sufficient.

Sexist writing identifies women through their relationships with men. Language itself often reflects male-centered thinking. The column on the left contains what is considered to be sexist language. The column on the right contains nonsexist forms:

Sexist	Preferred
policeman	police officer
fireman	firefighter
postman	letter carrier
newsman	reporter

There are also inconsistencies in referring to men and women:

Sexist	Nonsexist
man and wife	husband and wife
men and ladies	men and women
Jack Parsons and Ms. (Miss, Mrs.) Burgess	Jack Parsons and Joan Burgess
Parsons and Joan	Jack and Joan (or) Parsons and Burgess

Historical Note. In 1873, the Supreme Court ruled that a woman was not constitutionally entitled to practice law. The opinion of Justice Joseph B. Bradley stated, "The natural and proper timidity and delicacy which belongs to the female sex evidently unfits it for many of the occupations of civil life. The paramount destiny and mission of women are to fulfill the noble and benign office of wife and mother. This is the law of the Creator."

How to Tell a Businessman from a Businesswoman

An acute observer of the office scene compiled this telling commentary:

A businessman is aggressive; a businesswoman is pushy.

He is careful about details; she's picky.

He loses his temper because he's so involved in his job; she's bitchy.

He's depressed (or hungover), so everyone tiptoes past his office; she's moody, so it must be her time of the month.

He follows through; she doesn't know when to quit.

He's firm; she's stubborn.

He makes wise judgments; she reveals her prejudices.

He is a man of the world; she's been around.

He isn't afraid to say what he thinks; she's opinionated.

He exercises authority; she's bossy.

He's discreet; she's secretive.

He's a stern taskmaster; she's difficult to work for.

Some of the most pervasive stereotypes have been of homosexuals. But in recent years those in the gay and lesbian community say that progress has been made so that they are not as often the victims of heavy-handed discrimination and derision. Legislation has been enacted in a few cities and states to prohibit discrimination because of sexual preference, but a deep-seated antagonism remains.

The debate over such laws stirred a public response that shocked those who had thought gay-bashing was a thing of the past. In the heated atmosphere, the press often performed well, avoiding stereotyping.

A news story grows out of the interaction between reporters and events. If reporters see the event in pre-fixed forms, they will prejudge the event, making it conform to the stereotyped pictures they carry. Robert L. Heilbroner describes an experiment performed with college students that shows how powerful these pictures can be. The students were shown "30 photographs of pretty but unidentified girls, and asked to rate each in terms of 'general liking, intelligence, beauty' and so on," Heilbroner says.

◄ **Substitutes for Observation**

"Two months later," he continues, "the same group were shown the same photographs, this time with fictitious Irish, Italian, Jewish and 'American' names attached to the pictures. Right away the ratings changed. Faces which were now seen as representing a national group went down in looks and still farther down in likability, while the 'American' girls suddenly looked decidedly prettier and nicer."

Stereotypes are, as the semanticist S.I. Hayakawa points out, "substitutes for observation," and reporters tend to fall back on them unless they are careful.

Journalists who settle for stereotyped responses to events might heed the warning of F. Scott Fitzgerald: "Begin with an individual and before you know it you have created a type; begin with a type and you have created—nothing."

Out of the Closet—
But Still Attacked

The drive by gays and lesbians for acceptance and political power has stirred resistance. Anti-gay legislation has been introduced in several states; opposition to gays and lesbians in the military found supporters in Congress; religious groups attacked courses that included discussions of homosexuality.

"When you present information about the contributions of famous gay, lesbian and bisexual people, you are promoting," said a minister opposing a proposal for Des Moines schools. In reply, 30 local ministers said, "To the extent that homosexuality is a factor in people's lives, in history, in the arts, in politics, and in relationships, it should be presented realistically and honestly as part of the way the world is."

© Mark Geller.

Racial, Religious ▶ Stereotyping

The most persistent stereotyping in the United States is directed at Jews, African Americans, Native Americans and Spanish-speaking people. Newspapers and broadcast stations have lent themselves to this stereotyping.

In the 1900s when mass migration brought many Jews to the United States, anti-Semitism spread rapidly, and newspapers were no deterrent. It was not unusual to see a criminal suspect described as a Jew or Jewish. "Jew banker" and "Jew peddler" were common descriptions, as was "Jew store." Bargaining was known as "Jewing down."

Such language about Jews has disappeared from newspapers. But stereotyping of African Americans, Native Americans and Hispanics remains, especially in descriptions of those involved with crime.

Jesse Jackson accused the press of projecting minorities in "five deadly ways every day. It projects us as less intelligent than we are, as less hard-working than we are, as less patriotic than we are, as less universal than we are, as more violent than we are. . . ."

"If Indians want to get the media's attention, they should focus on issues much more important than whether a team has an Indian for a mascot or over a beer named Crazy Horse." The advice stunned the audience of Native Americans. It was offered by a major television network news show host at a conference on the American Indian and the media.

The advice, well-meaning though it may have been, revealed the insensitivity of whites to the feelings and frustrations of minority groups, in this case Native Americans.

"It has to do with self-esteem," said Tim Giago, publisher of *Indian Country Today,* a national weekly published in Rapid City, S.D. "It has to do with children growing up believing they are better than mascots." Crazy Horse, Giago said, is a spiritual leader of the Lakota.

"What would happen if this company named a beer Martin Luther King Jr. malt liquor?" Giago asked. He went on, "Sure, there are more important issues facing us, but if we can't be treated as human beings in the small things, we will never be heard when it comes to the big things." Giago concluded his newspaper column with this warning:

"Like the blacks who were forced to sit in the back of the bus, we will no longer serve as mascots for the sports fanatics of this nation. We refuse to move to the back of the bus anymore."

Curtis Zunigha, an Indian activist, said, "I'm sure the mascot issue is perceived as sensational. But to many Indian people, it represents the core of institutional racism. As long as we tolerate these types of images, attitudes towards jobs, social welfare, progress, and important issues will continue to be dealt with at a surface level."

Some protests have paid off: Nike agreed to discontinue an advertisement that described the Mayans as "crazed, savage warriors" and "delirious, bloodthirsty spectators." In Minneapolis, the *Star Tribune* does not use nicknames for American Indians in its sports reporting. Braves, Chiefs, Tribe, Redmen, Skins are out. Tribal names, such as Seminoles, continue to be used. The newspaper asked teams to provide it with suitable replacements.

The hiring of minority journalists—who now make up about 11 percent of the total employed—has provided a more balanced approach to news coverage, although more than half the country's newspapers employ no minority journalists. Large newspapers and major broadcast outlets are the major employers of minority journalists.

The situation at the upper levels of management is not as positive. Only 5 percent of managerial jobs are filled by members of minority groups.

While stereotyping by the media and racial and religious insensitivity have diminished significantly, some press critics contend that excessive sensitivity has become so common in newsrooms that "even a little bit of candor can be dangerous," as Howard Kurtz, media reporter for *The Washington Post,* puts it. "The result is a new skittishness in the press, a powerful urge to skirt sensitive subjects and airbrush the ugliest realities," Kurtz says.

◀ Native Americans

Mascots No More

Native Americans vow that they will continue to fight against the use of Indian nicknames and symbols for teams—Redskins, Braves, the tomahawk chop, Indians. Some colleges have changed their names, but resistance is strong in professional sports.

◀ Minority Hiring

◀ Overly Sensitive?

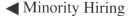

Richard Cohen, a *Post* columnist, contends that there are "issues that the media just can't discuss." Among the nonsubjects, says *New York* magazine columnist Joe Klein, have been the "disintegration of the black family and the growth of a violent, anarchic, alienated, welfare-dependent underclass over the past quarter-century."

Kurtz writes that newspapers "tend to shy away from such gut-wrenching stuff because they are worried—too worried, perhaps—about offending readers. Increasingly, local papers are filled with such yuppie subjects as day care, traffic, the Mommy track, home-equity loans and personal computers. The mere mention of race raises a red flag that sets editors on edge."

Minority Journalists ▶

Minority journalists are under pressure to represent the minority community, some of them say. This is a role, they say, that makes it doubly difficult to tell truths about the minority community. Juan Williams, a *Post* reporter, has come under fire for criticizing Spike Lee movies and for disagreeing with Jesse Jackson.

"Nothing wears more on my soul than people who criticize me as a writer not so much for the content of what I wrote, but for the fact that I'm willing to challenge and debate some decree from a black leader," Williams says.

"There's a whole notion that to really be a black person, you have to have certain political views; otherwise you're 'not really black.' There's a tremendous instinct toward censorship. That's what it boils down to. It's very dangerous. It's limiting, both intellectually and politically. It invites demagoguery."

Kurtz describes in his book *Media Circus: The Trouble with America's Newspapers* (Times Books, a division of Random House, Inc., 1993) the experiences of newspapers torn by racial controversies.

Two Cases ▶

How sensitive should the media be to individuals and groups? In Minneapolis, several readers protested when the *Star Tribune* quoted a woman who was concerned that her brother's tombstone in a Catholic cemetery had been vandalized. She told a reporter, "It had to be a group of people, atheists or something. I think it's skinheads or people who are against God or something."

The reference to atheists, wrote one reader, was "a slanderous, bigoted remark. There is no evidence of atheists ever behaving vindictively against a religious group." He wrote that if the woman had complained that "Muslims or Jews were responsible, the paper would not have printed it."

Lou Gelfand, the Reader Representative for the *Star Tribune,* presented in his column two points of view on the matter:

1. **The reporter's side:** It is appropriate to state who the vandals might be in the woman's view. "We as reporters ought not to censor people's thoughts, and if someone says something offensive in a passionate moment, so be it. It was her statement at that time and I am, as a reporter, a relayer of directly spoken thoughts and language." The reporter added that the remark was the woman's "gut-level thought" and not based on any malice.

2. **Gelfand's observation:** The story should not have included the reference to "atheists." He suggested an analogy. "Substitute in place of 'atheists'

the word for any minority group, and the woman's statement would have been excised in the editing process. What she said about 'atheists' deserved the same."

In Sioux Falls, S.D., the *Argus Leader* quoted a woman about a crime—she said she saw a "Mexican" leave the scene of a theft. Jack Marsh, the executive editor of the *Argus Leader,* defended the use of the word *Mexican* in the news story. "Our job is to state exactly what people think and say," Marsh said. "If they do not want diversity, we say so." (The newspaper has been actively supporting a more diverse community.)

John Dewey said that "the striving to make stability of meaning prevail over the instability of events is the main task of intelligent human effort." These meanings are the patterns that establish relationships among facts and events. The great journalist of the muckraking period, Lincoln Steffens, said that his thinking about reporting was transformed by a prosecuting attorney during his investigation into municipal corruption in St. Louis.

◀ **Patterns and Relationships**

"He was sweeping all his cases of bribery together to form a truth out of his facts," Steffens wrote later. "He was generalizing . . . he was thinking about them all together and seeing what they meant all together." Steffens said that this thinking led the prosecutor to conclude that the corruption was systemic.

Or, as the poet Robert Frost put it, thinking "is just putting this and that together."

The causal relationship is one of the most common patterns we form. We see a situation (a child cries) and we look for the cause (he is hungry). Journalists are told not to be satisfied with the event alone but to seek its causes and possible consequences.

The first state-by-state comparison of how public schoolchildren do on national tests showed that only one in seven is proficient in mathematics among eighth graders at the eighth grade level. Why? Authorities said the data showed:

> The states whose students had the best performances are also states with the lowest proportion of families headed by single parents.
> Students with the worst performances came from southeastern states where poverty is high and from states with large, disadvantaged urban areas.
> The top 10 states in student performance were also the 10 lowest-ranked states in the percentage of students who reported watching more than six hours of television a night.

Cause and Effect. In a traffic fatality roundup in a San Francisco newspaper, the reporter made clear the causal relationship:

Ten lives in 10 hours. Such was the appalling toll yesterday of two head-on crashes that chalked up the grimmest period in Bay Area traffic history.

Not one person in the four cars involved survived. An entire family of five was snuffed out. That family, and a sixth individual, were innocent victims.

Speed was the killer. And liquor a confederate.

Three died in an explosive, flaming smashup on the Bay Bridge at 11:40 p.m. yesterday. The killer car was going 90 miles an hour.

Just 10 hours earlier, at 1:40 p.m., seven met death in a jarring smackup. . . .

Here we have to be careful. Just because a situation occurs before or in tandem with an event does not qualify the situation as the cause of the event. Scientists worry about ozone depletion in the atmosphere, but they don't think beer consumption is the cause although it has been shown that ozone's decrease parallels the increase in beer drinking.

Causal relationships are less certain in human affairs than they are in the world of mechanics and dynamics, where physical forces have visible consequences.

However, when a reporter has enough facts to indicate a relationship exists, he or she should be willing to make an inference on his or her own. The reporter will be cautious, for he or she knows that ultimate truths are rarely available to a reporter. Nevertheless, risks can be taken. Reporters for the *Minneapolis Tribune* came up with proof that the milk producers' lobby had channeled hundreds of thousands of dollars into the Republican Party treasury through dummy committees. Following these contributions, the reporters wrote, the White House decided to increase milk support prices.

There was no absolute proof that the contributions had caused the policy decision. But the reporters decided that the suggestion of a causal relationship was legitimate.

In the obituaries of Joe Pyne, a television and radio talk show host, and Hal March, a master of ceremonies on television quiz shows, *The New York Times* reported the men died of lung cancer. Then the stories noted that Pyne had been a "heavy smoker" and that "Mr. March had smoked two packs of cigarettes a day for many years." There was no proof their cigarette smoking had caused their cancer, but the data collected by the surgeon general's office had indicated a high probability of such a relationship, and the newspaper was willing to suggest the cause-and-effect relationship for its readers.

Making causal relationships in print or on the air represents a certain risk to the reporter, but experienced reporters know when to take risks. In fact, risk taking may be one of the marks of a successful journalist. The British mathematician G.B. Hardy remarked that high intelligence is not important to the success of most people. No one, he said, can make the most of his or her talents without constant application and without taking frequent risks.

Polar Alternatives ▶

Another potentially dangerous line of thinking common among harried reporters is the polar alternative. For instance, the reporter may think, "Either the Black Parents Association is right or it is wrong in its stand on school books." This either-or thinking can save the reporter time and energy, but it can lead to superficial journalism.

Causes and consequences are complex, combinations of many factors. The reporter who looks only for the black and white of situations will be limiting observations to the most obvious elements of the event. The world is hardly bilateral and the reporter should resist what is called *bilateral consciousness* by being aware of the infinite colors and shades between black and white.

Linking Facts ▶

Confronting this multitude of facets, faces and facts is half the task. The reporter's most difficult job is to put them into some meaningful pattern, to synthesize them in a story. But that is what journalism is about—linking facts to make stories.

Look back at the work of the reporter we watched as he tried to figure out the reason state GOP party leaders were meeting secretly. He was trying to link facts. But he had to provide the concepts to link his facts.

This kind of reporting takes us into the mainstream of contemporary journalism. It would have been Layer I journalism to have written that the governor had taken a vacation. Because of the reporter's hunch that there was more to the official's absence than a desire to try a Royal Coachman fly on a trout stream, the reader was taken closer to the truth. In other words, by digging for the significant relationship between the absence and the current political situation, the reporter moved into Layer II journalism.

As we have seen, these leaps to significant relationships are launched from solid ground. They are based on experience and the logical thinking of the kind described by the philosopher Isaiah Berlin: "To comprehend and contrast and classify and arrange, to see in patterns of lesser or greater complexity is not a peculiar kind of thinking, it is thinking itself."

This ability to arrange and rearrange, to categorize and recategorize, to pattern and to organize is recognized by scientists and poets as well as by philosophers. Israel Rosenfeld wrote, "We do not simply store images or bits but become more richly endowed with the *capacity to categorize* in connected ways. . . . Human intelligence is not just knowing more, but reworking, recategorizing, and thus generalizing information in new and surprising ways."

The technique of patterning is described by T.S. Eliot, the poet, this way: "The poet's mind is a receptacle for seizing and storing up numberless feelings, phrases, images, which remain there until all the particles which can unite to form a new compound are present together." In describing the emotion in a poem, he says it "is a concentration and a new thing resulting from the concentration, of a very great number of experiences which to the practical and active person would not seem to be experiences at all; it is a concentration which does not happen consciously or of deliberation."

There is not much difference in the ways poets and journalists think, indeed in the ways all creative people think. The ability to pattern observations and feelings is the mark of the thinking person, whether we look at a reporter covering a story or a composer at her piano.

The good reporter has what the philosopher Alfred North Whitehead describes as an "eye for the whole chessboard, for the bearing of one set of ideas on another." In his book *The Powers That Be,* David Halberstam describes "the great reporter's gifts" as "limitless energy, a fine mind, total recall and an ability to synthesize material."

◀ Finding the Links

Reporters are always looking for facts that relate to each other. The obituary writer wants to know the cause of death, especially if the death is sudden, unexpected.

A reporter covering such a death was given the explanation—accidental gunshot wound. But the reporter wonders. The death seems staged. Could it have been a suicide? That's playing games, he says to himself. Still, the death looks like that of a character in a novel. Thinking of this sort led the reporter to report that Ernest Hemingway had killed himself, contrary to the explanation put out by the authorities, who had agreed to cover up the truth to save the family from embarrassment.

A reporter assigned to write a year-end summary of traffic fatalities begins with the data the police department has supplied. As she scans the figures of deaths and injuries on city streets, she notices that pedestrian deaths and injuries are up 16 percent, whereas the overall increase over the previous year is 8 percent. She decides to concentrate on pedestrian accidents.

Further examination indicates that most of those killed and injured were 14 years old and under. The reporter recalls that some months ago a parents organization petitioned the city council to provide more play streets for the warm-weather months in areas where there is a heavy concentration of low-income families and few open spaces. She wonders whether the number of children who were killed and hurt in traffic accidents was high in the summer. She also checks the location of the accidents. A pattern is beginning to take shape. Now she must determine whether the facts support her ideas.

As she moves through the data, she notices the traffic department lists the times at which deaths and injuries occurred. She is surprised at the number of children who were killed or hurt in the evening. Well, she reasons, perhaps that is logical. Where else can kids play on hot summer evenings, especially youngsters from homes without air conditioning? She looks at her newspaper's clip file to check her recollections of the city council meeting. All this takes less than an hour. Next, she makes several telephone calls to gather additional information.

A reporter's approach to the story is as important as the fact gathering. She could have settled for Layer I reporting. Had she done so, her story might have begun this way:

Pedestrian deaths and injuries in the city last year were 16 percent higher than the previous year, a year-end summary of traffic accidents disclosed today.

Instead, after her first hour of thinking and checking the clips and another 45 minutes of calls, she is ready to write a story that she begins this way:

For 10 of the city's children the streets they played on last summer became a death trap.

She then gives the total figures for all deaths and injuries to children under 14 and the total traffic deaths for the city. Then she works into her story the petition the parents had presented to the city council. Her finding that the evening hours were particularly dangerous for youngsters had not been discovered by the parents, who had asked for daytime restrictions on traffic. Before writing, the reporter calls the head of the parents group and tells her about the evening accident rate. The reporter is told that the group probably will renew its petitioning, this time with the request that in the summer some streets be permanently blocked off to traffic. This new material—the concept of 24-hour play streets—goes into the story also.

The reporter not only turns out a meaningful story by linking certain facts but performs a public service for her community as well.

Born Reporter. Four youngsters on a children's program were shown pictures of a dog, a rooster, a cow and a monkey. The children were asked to find something that at least two of the animals had in common. One youngster pointed out that the monkey and the rooster walked on two legs and that the dog and cow used four legs. Another pointed to the long tails of the dog, cow and monkey. The hand of another youngster suddenly shot up and her eyes shone with excitement.

"The rooster and the cow," she announced triumphantly. The host was perplexed and asked her to explain.

"Those pink, soft things," the child said. The quiz master looked even more puzzled. Slowly, enlightenment spread over his face, and he, too, joined in the youngster's glee. Wordlessly, he pointed to the rooster's comb and the cow's udder.

Famous Forecasts

No matter how brilliant his or her insights and intuition, the reporter avoids making predictions. Forecasts have a way of turning sour. Witness these predictions from people in the know:

- Sensible and responsible women do not want to vote.—Grover Cleveland, 1905
- Heavier than air flying machines are impossible.—Lord Kelvin, president of the Royal Society, 1895
- Who the hell wants to hear actors talk?—Harry M. Warner, Warner Bros. Pictures, 1927
- There is no likelihood man can ever tap the power of the atom.—Robert Millikan, Nobel Prize for physics, 1923
- Everything that can be invented has been invented.—Charles H. Duell, director, U.S. Patent Office, 1899
- Ruth made a big mistake when he gave up pitching.—Tris Speaker, outfielder, Cleveland Indians, 1921
- Of what use is such an invention?—*The New York Tribune* on learning of Alexander Graham Bell's first communication on the telephone, 1876

◀ **Summing Up**

Journalists use their intuition and feelings to provide new insights into events and situations. Hunches and emotions are valuable but must be checked to see whether they are legitimate—verifiable and not injurious to individuals or groups. Particularly sensitive are the sentiments we carry with us from childhood—some positive, some negative. Some of these stereotypes stigmatize people.

The reporters who constantly replenish their storehouses with relevant material are able to make creative breakthroughs. They can match the deviations from the norm that they encounter in their reporting with material in their storehouse to come up with worthwhile insights.

◀ **Further Reading**

Hayakawa, S.I. *Language in Thought and Action*. New York: Harcourt Brace Jovanovich, 1978.
Lippmann, Walter. *Public Opinion*. New York: The Free Press, 1965.
Ochse, R.A. *Before the Gates of Excellence: The Determinants of Creative Genius*. New York: Cambridge University Press, 1990.

PART FIVE: From Accidents to Education

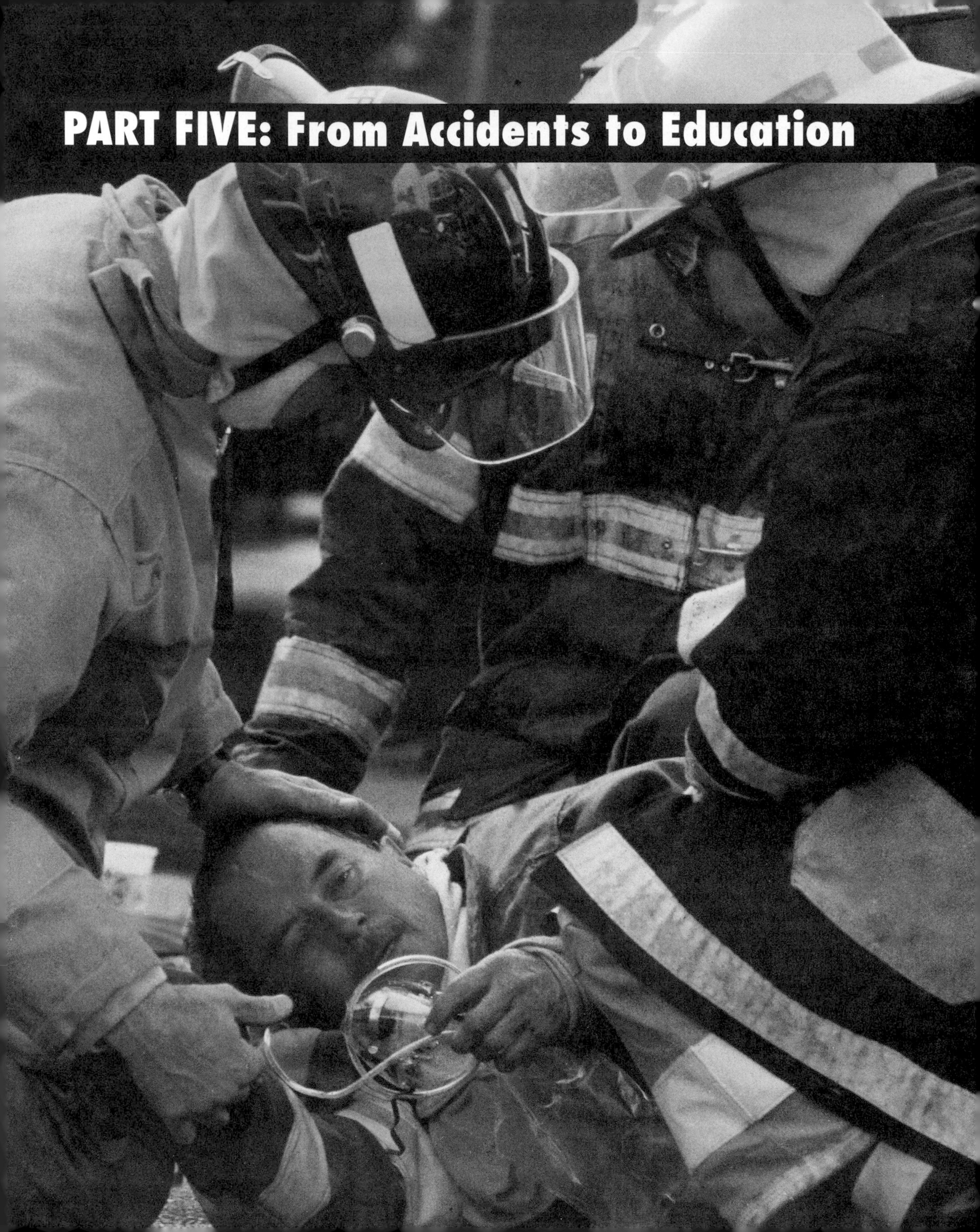

Part Five: Introduction

The preceding chapters have described the processes that underlie reporting and writing. Now we are ready to move to specific areas of coverage, beats. To help the new reporter handle these, we can devise a checklist of the necessary elements for any type of story.

For example: An obituary requires the name and identification of the deceased; the cause, time, place and location of death; the survivors; funeral and burial plans and some background about the deceased. We can make similar lists of necessities for other story types.

When a reporter goes out on an assignment, the aim should be to gather information on the checklist, the essentials of the story. The checklist is only a starting point, a takeoff point for imagination and enterprise. No rote learning of what to look for and how to structure a particular kind of story can substitute for creative journalism, just as no memorization of writing techniques can transmute slaglike prose into soaring sentences.

The elements on the checklist are not in the order they should appear in the story. Any one of the elements could be made into a lead, depending upon the circumstances. Reporters must use their judgment to determine what constitutes the news angle or theme of the event. Also, not all of the elements will appear in every story, but most will.

Students should not regard the checklist as a cook approaches a recipe for flapjacks—a cup of pancake mix, one large egg, a cup of milk, a tablespoon of liquid shortening; stir until fairly smooth and then pour on a preheated, lightly greased griddle. That may make for a satisfying short stack, but this is a textbook, not a cookbook. Creative cooks always depart from recipes anyway. The reporter's task is to put his or her personal stamp on copy. The checklist is designed to help point the reporter in the right direction.

There are two kinds of beats—topical and geographical. Some of the topical beats are education, politics, business—beats that take reporters over a wide physical area in pursuit of stories. Some of the geographical beats are the courthouse, city hall, police—beats that require the reporter to report from a specific location.

In recent years, new types of beats have emerged in the belief that the media have to reach out to the "citizen consumer." Thus, beats have been built around investing and saving, personal relationships, parents and children, health and medicine.

The beats listed in the next seven chapters cover areas of reporting that beginning reporters are most likely to be assigned to handle.

◀ **Using the Checklist**

◀ **Types of Beats**

Covering a Beat ▶

The reporter starting on a beat tries to meet everyone—clerks, secretaries, typists, assistants as well as those in charge of the offices and agencies on the beat. A sound idea is to give sources a business card or a note with your name, address and phone number.

"Shoot the breeze," says an experienced beat reporter. "That's the way to develop sources and how you find good stories. People usually are happy to chat with a reporter.

"You need to establish a relationship of trust with sources. But you make no promises you cannot fulfill or that interfere with your responsibilities as a reporter."

The editor of *The Charlotte* (N.C.) *Observer,* Rich Oppel, distributed to his staff eight tips for managing a beat. Here, in summarized form, are his suggestions:

1. **Get started fast** and get out of the office. Don't waste time. Not many stories are found in newsrooms.
2. **Set daily goals.**
3. **Build sources.** There is no substitute for regular, perhaps daily, contact.
4. **Do favors.** Where appropriate, do a favor for a source. The council member's daughter needs a copy of a month-old edition for a class project. Why not?
5. **Ask the sweeping questions;** ask the dumb questions. What's taking most of your time these days? What's the biggest problem you face in your job?
6. **Listen carefully, watch carefully.**
7. **Look at the record.** In managing a beat, go for original source material.
8. **Set up calls.** Make phone checks. Phone calls are a supplement, not a substitute, for direct contact.

Juan Carlos,
Ventura County (Calif.) *Star.*

Flood aftermath.

Preview

Local stories about accidents and disasters must include:

• Names and addresses of dead and injured.
• Extent and cost of property damage.
• Time, location and cause of accident.
• Comments from eyewitnesses and authorities when possible.

Since these stories tend to read alike, an attempt is made to find an aspect of the event that sets it apart from others like it. Eyewitness accounts can provide a unique perspective of the event. Usually, the number of dead and injured provides the theme.

For natural disasters, rescue and relief operations are highlighted.

◀ Motor Vehicle Accidents

M otor vehicles kill, injure and maim an enormous number of people each year. News of collisions, of trucks and cars careening into trees and smashing into each other on fog-bound freeways is given good play in newspapers and on local radio and television news programs. Only the routine "fender benders," as reporters describe minor accidents, are ignored or summarized. Rare is the reporter who has never written a *fatal,* a story about an accident in which at least one person died. Newsrooms frequently check so that they have the latest accident reports right up to deadline.

One accident story tends to read like another. But the enterprising reporter finds an aspect of the event that sets his or her story apart. In this story from *The News-Gazette* in Champaign-Urbana, Ill., the location of the fatality was newsworthy:

DANVILLE—A 55-year-old Martinsville, Ind., man was killed Wednesday night as he was walking across the highway in the 2500 block of Georgetown Road.

Harold Owens was killed when he was struck by a car and a pickup truck while walking across Illinois 1 in the Hegler area south of Danville at 9:40 p.m.

That dark stretch of the road has been the scene of numerous fatal pedestrian accidents, according to Vermilion County Coroner Lyle Irvin.

Mr. Owens was with a logging crew that is working in the county. He was staying at a motel in the area and was walking across the road to a tavern, Irvin said.

Ricardo Ferro,
St. Petersburg Times.

Highway Pileup

Eyewitness accounts of accidents can provide detail and drama. Here, motorists extricate a driver as a vehicle burns dangerously close.

The "dark stretch of road" has an ominous sound to it. We all know dangerous places like that. The story would have been more effective had those words in the third paragraph been worked into the lead.

We look for good quotes that set this particular accident apart from other accident stories:

CADIZ, Ky., Dec. 16 (AP)—Seven teen-age boys who had squeezed into a compact car were killed in a head-on collision on Wednesday, plunging this small town into mourning.

None of the boys was wearing a seatbelt when their car crossed the center line and collided with a four-wheel-drive vehicle outside this town of 1,600 in southwest Kentucky.

"No community this size can take seven at one time," David Goodcase, administrator of Trigg County Hospital, said as the hospital filled with friends and relatives. Boys and girls sat in clusters and wept.

Sometimes the remarks of the coroner or an official can provide material for the lead, as in this story from the *Herald-Dispatch* in Huntington, W. Va.:

ELK CREEK, W. Va.—Two brothers died early yesterday when their car went off W. Va. 65 and struck a tree, a county official said.

The deaths were the second and third traffic fatalities in Mingo County in two days, said interim County Coroner Larry Wood.

He identified the victims as Jimmy Nichols, 16, of Varney, and Clyde R. Nichols, 18, of Columbus.

He said their car left the highway about 12:15 a.m., wrapped around a tree and "practically disintegrated."

Although wreckage was scattered over a wide area, evidence at the scene indicated that Jimmy Nichols was driving, the coroner said.

"From the appearance of the car and where it left the road, excessive speed probably caused the accident," said Deputy Bill Webb of the Mingo County Sheriff's Department.

There were no witnesses to the crash, he said. . . .

That partial quote in the fourth paragraph is too good to be buried. Try your hand at including it in the lead.

The accident story's importance is determined by the number of people killed and injured and their prominence, the proximity of the accident to local readers or listeners and the circumstances of the accident.

Checklist: Motor ▶
Vehicle Accidents

___ Victims: Names, identification of dead and injured.
___ Type of vehicles involved.
___ Location.
___ Time.
___ Cause (from official source).
___ Names and identification of other drivers and passengers.
___ Cause of death, injuries.
___ Where dead taken.
___ Where injured taken and how.

___ Extent of injuries.
___ Heroism, rescues.
___ Latest condition of critically injured.
___ Funeral arrangements if available.
___ Damage to vehicles.
___ Arrests or citations by police.
___ Unusual weather or highway conditions.
___ Accounts by eyewitnesses and investigating officers.
     Speed, origin and destination of vehicles.

State highway patrol; local, suburban police; sheriff's office; hospital; am-   ◀ **Sources**
bulance service; mortuary; coroner.

Art Carey of *The Philadelphia Inquirer* says that one of the first warnings   ◀ **Cautions**
he received about covering accidents was to be careful of inadvertently attributing blame when writing about the cause. Unless one of the drivers has been cited
or arrested, it is best to avoid a detailed description of the cause. The reporter
must be especially careful about saying which vehicle struck the other since such
statements may imply responsibility. Also, be wary of eyewitness accounts and
verify addresses and the spelling of names in police reports.

Airplane accidents make headlines. A motor vehicle collision in which   ◀ **Airplane**
two are killed will not receive the attention given the crash of an airplane with   **Accidents**
the same number of fatalities. Airline crashes are big news. Local newspapers
and stations will scan the casualty list carried on the wires for the names of local
residents.

___ Number of dead and injured.   ◀ **Checklist:**
___ Time, location and official cause of crash.   **Airplane Accidents**
___ Origin and destination of plane.
___ Airline and flight number.
___ Type of plane: manufacturer, number of engines.
___ Victims: names and identification (including hometown).
___ Survivors by name.
___ Condition of injured.
___ Where dead and injured taken.
___ Cause of death: impact, fire, exposure.
___ Altitude at time of trouble.
___ Weather and flying conditions.
___ Last words of pilot.
___ Police, fire, rescue units at scene.
___ Unusual incidents; heroism.
___ Eyewitness accounts of survivors.
___ Eyewitness accounts of people on ground.
___ Comments by air controllers, officials, airline company.
___ Cost of aircraft.

Careful. Resist the temptation to write that airplanes
collided in midair, a word
that has no meaning. Just
write that they collided, says
the AP. If they collide on the
ground, say so in the lead.
  Resist pressure to give
the cause. The National
Transportation Safety Board
usually takes a year or more
to find the reason. The Avia-
tion/Space Writers Association advises, "Don't jump to
conclusions. Avoid oversim-
plifications. Attribute statements and conclusions."

___ Prominent people aboard.
___ Fire and other destruction as result of crash.
___ Direction aircraft heading before crash.
___ Flight recorder recovered?
___ If aircraft was missing, who found wreckage and how.
___ Funeral arrangements, if available.
___ Survivors of deceased, if available.
___ Official inquiry.
___ Previous crashes in area.
___ Previous crashes of same type of plane or same airline.

Sources ▶

Airline; police, fire, and other rescue units; Federal Aviation Administration (which in many large cities has a special telephone number for accident information); air traffic controllers; airport officials; National Transportation Safety Board; hospital; mortuary; coroner; morgue.

Cautions ▶

Eyewitnesses on the ground are notoriously inaccurate about aircraft crashes. Early reports of casualties tend to be exaggerated. Passenger flight lists can be erroneous; verify if possible.

Disasters ▶

The line between accidents and disasters is difficult to draw. If the difference is the number of lives lost, the amount of property destroyed or damaged, then who would set down the numbers that distinguish the two? The fatal plunge of a school bus into a river that takes the lives of six children is a tragic accident in a metropolis, but to the residents of a town of 25,000 it is a disaster and much of the news staff will be mobilized.

Perhaps one definition of a disaster is that it is a situation that draws maximum coverage. Some define a disaster as massive, widespread death and destruction of the kind usually associated with the vagaries of nature—floods, earthquakes, hurricanes, storms and drought. It might be a famine in Ethiopia, an earthquake in Mexico, a volcanic eruption in Colombia that takes 22,000 lives in one hellish night. Generally, the word *disaster* covers large loss of life:

OKLAHOMA CITY (AP)—A car bomb ripped deep into America's heartland Wednesday, killing at least 31 people and leaving 200 missing in a blast that gouged a nine-story hole in a federal office building.

This was one of the early bulletins from the bombing that took 169 lives and made Americans wonder what could have provoked those responsible to commit such a depraved act.

The National Guard is sometimes mobilized for disasters, and the Red Cross may dispatch units to help. Civil defense agencies may be present. State and federal agencies are often called upon to arrange access to the scene or to engage in rescue operations:

OKLAHOMA CITY (AP)—Choking through dusty smoke and the overpowering stench of the decaying dead buried around them, they

Accidents, storms and floods often knock down power and telephone lines, and service can be out for days. The extent of the damage and the work being done to restore service are part of the story.

© Joel Strasser.

push on. At times forced to inch along on their backs through foot-high crawl spaces, they push on.

Haunted by creaks, groans and cracks, they eye small chunks of rubble that shower them sporadically and stay alert for the scream of "Get out!," the signal that the collapse of tons of debris may be imminent.

As in the accident story, the human toll is more important than the loss of property.

◀ Checklist: Disasters

____ Dead.
____ Injured.
____ Total affected or in danger.
____ Cause of death.

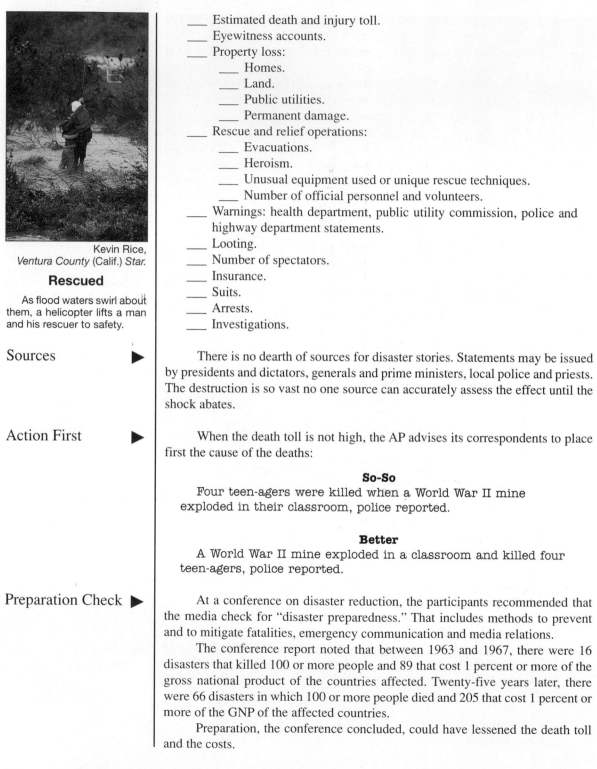

Kevin Rice,
Ventura County (Calif.) *Star.*

Rescued

As flood waters swirl about them, a helicopter lifts a man and his rescuer to safety.

___ Estimated death and injury toll.
___ Eyewitness accounts.
___ Property loss:
    ___ Homes.
    ___ Land.
    ___ Public utilities.
    ___ Permanent damage.
___ Rescue and relief operations:
    ___ Evacuations.
    ___ Heroism.
    ___ Unusual equipment used or unique rescue techniques.
    ___ Number of official personnel and volunteers.
___ Warnings: health department, public utility commission, police and highway department statements.
___ Looting.
___ Number of spectators.
___ Insurance.
___ Suits.
___ Arrests.
___ Investigations.

Sources ▶

There is no dearth of sources for disaster stories. Statements may be issued by presidents and dictators, generals and prime ministers, local police and priests. The destruction is so vast no one source can accurately assess the effect until the shock abates.

Action First ▶

When the death toll is not high, the AP advises its correspondents to place first the cause of the deaths:

So-So
Four teen-agers were killed when a World War II mine exploded in their classroom, police reported.

Better
A World War II mine exploded in a classroom and killed four teen-agers, police reported.

Preparation Check ▶

At a conference on disaster reduction, the participants recommended that the media check for "disaster preparedness." That includes methods to prevent and to mitigate fatalities, emergency communication and media relations.

The conference report noted that between 1963 and 1967, there were 16 disasters that killed 100 or more people and 89 that cost 1 percent or more of the gross national product of the countries affected. Twenty-five years later, there were 66 disasters in which 100 or more people died and 205 that cost 1 percent or more of the GNP of the affected countries.

Preparation, the conference concluded, could have lessened the death toll and the costs.

Many accident and disaster stories lack human interest because they focus on numbers of dead and injured, causes and costs. When a cold wave swept through the East over Christmas, it left seven dead in New Jersey. For his story of the disaster, Jim Dwyer chose five of the dead and began his story with vignettes: One man had in his pocket a 16-year-old newspaper clipping about his son's death; another was found dead in the front seat of a truck from which he had been ejected in a collision but to which he had returned for shelter.

A homeless man had dozed off under the Atlantic City boardwalk. "The temperature was basically warm when John went to sleep," said a friend, "but then it dropped rather drastically. In that drastic drop was when he died."

Caution: Eyewitness accounts should be treated with care, especially if they are of events that unfold rapidly and particularly if the witness to the event is emotionally involved. Studies of eyewitnesses of crimes have shown that their reports are incomplete, sometimes unreliable and often incorrect.

R. Edward Geiselman of the psychology department at the University of California at Los Angeles and Ronald P. Fisher of the psychology department at Florida International University have studied police interviews and have made recommendations that could be useful to reporters:

1. Ask the eyewitness to reconstruct the incident "in general." Ask the witness to describe the scene. This will stimulate recall.

2. Tell the witness not to hold back just because he or she thinks the detail isn't important. Report everything.

3. Tell the eyewitness to recall the event in different order. "Now that you have told it from the beginning, start with the most impressive incident, or start at the end."

4. Have the witness change perspectives. "Think about the event from the view of others who were there."

Restructuring the event in these ways aids recall, the authors say.

With stories of the dimension of a disaster, the reporter is tempted to pull out every writing device he or she knows. Resist. If resisting is difficult, pause and reflect on the story—part fact, part fiction—told of the reporter from a Philadelphia newspaper sent to cover a mine disaster in Donora, Pa., where hundreds of miners were entombed dead or facing imminent death from mine gas. The mine was surrounded by weeping relatives, and when it was opened 200 bodies were taken out.

The reporter looked at this scene of death and grief and wired his newspaper the lead: "God sits tonight on a little hill overlooking the scene of disaster. . . ."

As these words came over the telegraph machine in the newsroom in Philadelphia, an editor shouted out, "Stop," and he handed the telegraph editor a message to send back to the reporter in Donora: "Never mind disaster—interview God."

◀ Human Interest

Saved

"There's a body in the river," someone shouted as the Ventura River raged past firefighters engaged in rescuing people stranded by the floodwaters. Photographer Victoria Sayer Pearson of the *Ventura County Star* recognized BeBop, a homeless man she'd talked to the day before in the early stages of the flood. She snapped this photo moments before BeBop was pulled from the swollen river.

◀ Writing the Disaster Story

19 Obituaries

Toby Gardner.

A story lies behind every death.

Preview

Obituaries are among the most frequently read stories in the newspaper. The obituary sums up the background and outstanding qualities of the individual and includes:

- Name, age, occupation and address of deceased.
  - Time, place and cause of death.
  - Survivors.
  - Funeral and burial plans.

The obituary usually centers on the person's most noteworthy accomplishment or activity. Useful information can be obtained from the newspaper library and from friends and relatives of the deceased. The obituary can be enlivened with anecdotes about the person.

Here are two views of the obituary:

1. "The obituary is a routine story that no reporter enjoys writing."
2. "On the obituary page may be found the summing up of the glories, the achievements, the mediocrities, and the failures of a life which the rest of the paper chronicled day by day."

The first description is taken from a journalism textbook, the second from a veteran journalist's article about writing obituaries. Strangely, both summaries are accurate. Most obituaries in most newspapers are indeed routine, written by reporters who rigorously follow a formula so that only names, addresses, ages and the other vital statistics differentiate one obituary from another. However, the newspapers that ask their reporters to use their reportorial and writing skills on obituaries develop interesting stories and devoted subscribers. Obituaries are among the best-read staples in the newspaper.

No reporter should approach any story with the intention of writing routinely. Of course, some stories are difficult to make interesting, but the obituary hardly falls into this category, for the reporter has a wide panorama from which to select material—a person's entire life. No life lacks drama, if the reporter has the intelligence and the time and the desire to look for it.

William Buchanan of *The Boston Globe* was guided in writing obituaries by the thought "that what I wrote would probably be the last words ever printed about the person. That's why I always worked hard to include something in that person's life of which he or she would have been most proud."

I recall one woman who worked for years in the office of a candy factory. The part of her life she loved most was playing the violin at special Masses at St. Peter's and St. Paul's Churches in Dorchester. Or, for another example, there was a man who started as a busboy in a restaurant and later became the owner; after he became the owner, no job was too menial for him to handle. That clearly showed his character.

Even when the life is brief, the obituary can be interesting or moving. Here is an obituary of a 12-year-old boy written by a young reporter, James Eggensperger, for the *Sanders County Ledger* in Thompson Falls, Mont.

Goodbye, Ron

Ronald Laws, a rising star in Thompson Falls athletic competition, died Friday night doing one of the things he liked best, playing baseball. He was 12 years old.

Ron, as his friends and teachers and coaches called him, was batting in a Little League baseball game when he was hit in the chest by a pitched ball.

Then, according to one witness, he started running. After about 20 feet, he turned to the call of his coach, fell to the ground and never rose.

Spectators at the game rushed Ron to the Clark Fork Valley Hospital at Plains where the game was being played, but efforts there to start his heart failed.

His funeral was Monday in Thompson Falls. The Rev. Bruce Kline performed the service with special feeling because he had known Ron through Sunday school and liked him greatly. The Rev. Kline also performed graveside services at the Whitepine cemetery.

In fact, everyone who knew Ronnie liked him, teachers, classmates and teammates. He was a good sportsman and student and took pleasure in anything he undertook.

He left behind his parents, Mr. and Mrs. Larry Laws, and two brothers, Larry Lee and Timothy, and a sister, Lori.

Fittingly, the Thompson Falls and Plains All Star baseball teams are planning a two-game fund-raising baseball marathon for the 8th and 9th of July. Proceeds from the games will go to a memorial fund in Ron's name, a fund which will be used to support sports activities in both towns.

Other memorials for the fund may be sent to his parents.

Eggensperger recalls the day he took the call about the accident:

I remember feeling sick that such a thing should happen to such a good kid. But even more, that he had not had a chance to bloom into his potential and to enjoy all the things in life there are to enjoy. I put myself in his shoes and thought of all the memories, good and bad times, people and places I would have missed if I had not lived past 12, and the impact was overwhelming.

And in the back of my head was something I had been taught, which ran something like this: "An obit may be the only time a guy gets into the paper, and it's his last chance."

So I talked to some people and wrote what I felt.

Able and Willing. She had applied for a job with *The Miami Herald* after working for a small Florida newspaper but had heard nothing. Finally, she sent a one-word note: "Obits?" The city editor called Edna Buchanan the next day and put her to work.

Double Check. "The worst mistake I ever made in an obit was identifying the deceased as the same person who was shot and paralyzed in a holdup a few years earlier. I made that mistake because I didn't double check information that had been volunteered by a colleague with a reputation for accuracy."—Edna Buchanan

Obituaries Can Enlighten Us ▶

The obituary can tell us something about our past along with details of the life of the deceased. In the obituary of S.I. Hayakawa, a noted scholar on language usage who also served as a U.S. senator from California, it was reported that in 1937, while teaching at the University of Wisconsin, he married one of his students. "At the time, marriages between whites and Asians were not recognized in some states, including California, and the couple lived for nearly two decades in Chicago," the obituary reported.

Emma Bugbee was a pioneer woman reporter in New York. When she died, her obituary stressed the unique niche she had filled in the days when women were a rarity on newspaper reporting staffs:

> A founder of the Newspaper Women's Club of New York, Miss Bugbee was one of a handful of prominent female reporters who sought to expand the role of the women in what was the largely all-male world of journalism when she entered it in 1911.

Bugbee worked for *The New York Herald Tribune* for 56 years. For many of those years, she was one of only two women reporters at the newspaper. They were not allowed to sit in the city room, the obituary recalled, "but had to work down the hall."

The causes of death inform us of some of our personal and social problems:

• The obituary of Eddie Kendricks, the former lead singer of the Temptations, who died of lung cancer at the age of 52, stated, "He said the disease was caused by 30 years of smoking."

Tales from the Past

Churches and synagogues and their cemeteries are rich repositories of material. Their records and their tombstones tell stories of past and present. Walk around the cemetery. Notice that the oldest stones carry the names of children and young women. Before modern medicine, childhood diseases killed many, and in frontier states the toll was considerable. Many women died in childbirth. The older stones were sometimes handcrafted, and as families prospered their tombstones became larger, more ornate.

© Joel Strasser.

• The deadly combination of cold weather and alcohol—a too-frequent cause of death among Native Americans—was Jerry Reynolds' theme for this obituary in the newspaper *Indian Country Today:*

MARTIN S.D.—The icy claw of winter claimed another young life in Indian Country last week.

Twenty-year-old Sidney Brown Bear of Allen was found dead in the back seat of a car in Martin the morning of March 5. Companions said he had been drinking at a bar in nearby Swett, S.D., the night before and fell down twice before leaving.

A preliminary autopsy report placed his blood alcohol content at almost four times the legal limit. . . .

The preliminary report indicated that exposure appeared to be the cause of death. . . .

Deborah Howell, managing editor of the *St. Paul Pioneer Press,* says that "too many big-city dailies report just the deaths of important people—captains of industry and political leaders. That's a mistake. These newspapers ignore the woman who always feeds the ducks in the late afternoon at the city lake, the tireless youth worker at the neighborhood park, the druggist dispensing sage advice along with medicine for 50 years."

Howell recalled the obituary of a woman who died of cancer and who had asked for a party after her funeral. She was memorialized this way in the *Pioneer Press:*

The ladies sat in a circle of lawn chairs in the neatly clipped backyard, between the pea patch on the right and the tomatoes and cucumbers on the left, sipping their gentle scotches and bourbons and beers, while the mosquitoes buzzed around their ears, and the evening slowly faded without pain into the night.

Of Tom Flaherty, Howell said, "To most folks, Tom might have seemed quite ordinary. He worked his whole life as a laborer on the Great Northern Railroad, as did many of the Irish immigrants in St. Paul. At first, I worried how I was going to make an obit on Tom interesting. Then I decided that his life represented so much that is so Irish, so Catholic, so railroad, so St. Paul. When any Irish railroadman died, Tom was at the wake. At the St. Patrick's Day parade, Tom led the Flaherty section.

"I explained the kind of obit I wanted to one of our better writers. His obit began:

Tom Flaherty was an Irishman's Irishman, a John Henry of a man who for 50 years matched his mighty muscle against the hardest work the railroad had to offer.

"The trick is to make the dead person come alive again in an obituary, to remind family and friends and co-workers why someone was important," Howell said.

"Too often reporters come away with just the basic facts about birth, education, marriage, vocation and perhaps a few war medals. Obituaries can be

◀ The Druggist and the Laborer

Thurgood Marshall

The theme of Justice Marshall's obituary was obvious: He was the first black to sit on the U.S. Supreme Court. In the sidebar features in which his career was described, the theme of most of the stories was Marshall's impact on the court at the time the court was expanding its view of human rights.

examples of the paper's best writing, meaning reporters must search for the kind of detail—the unusual facts—that makes any news story interesting to read."

Richard G. West, whose comments on the obituary are quoted as No. 2 at the start of this chapter, says of the obituary, "Preparing an obituary is a delicate and exacting task, demanding the utmost diligence, insight and imagination. His obituary should be, as far as human judgment and ability may create it in the limits of a newspaper's space, a man's monument."

Monuments take time to carve, and the newspapers that attempt to carry obituaries for most of those who die within their circulation area cannot possibly devote much time or space to each. Still, some should be thoroughly reported and carefully written.

Beginning reporters often are broken in by a stint of obituary writing, because it tests the journalist's accuracy in reporting names and dates and his or her ability to work under pressure—people are always dying on deadline.

Most reporters consider obituary writing a dull assignment of little importance. "What nonsense. What an opportunity," says Joseph L. Galloway, who wrote his share of obituaries when he broke into newspaper work on a small Texas daily:

> The obits are probably read by more people with greater attention to detail than any other section of a newspaper. Nowhere else is error or omission more likely to be noticed.
>
> A good reporter gives each obit careful and accurate handling. He or she searches in the stack for the one or two that can be brought to life.
>
> Veteran of World War II, the funeral home sheet says. Did he make the D-Day landing on the beaches of Normandy? Taught junior high school English for 43 years? Find some former pupils who can still quote entire pages of Longfellow because somehow she made it live and sing for them.

Checklist: Obituaries ▶

The following items are required in all obituaries:

____ Name, age, occupation and address of deceased.
____ Time, place and cause of death.
____ Birthdate, birthplace.
____ Survivors. (Only immediate family.)
____ Memberships, military service.
____ Funeral and burial arrangements.

Many obituaries also will include:

____ Outstanding or interesting activities and achievements.
____ Memberships in fraternal, religious or civic organizations.
____ Service in armed forces.
____ Anecdotes and recollections of friends and relatives.

First news of deaths can come from different sources. Many newspapers rely on the death notices mortuaries send newspapers to be placed in the classified advertising section. The news department is given a copy. Some mortuaries will call in the death of a prominent person, and on some newspapers reporters regularly make the rounds of mortuaries by telephone.

The police and the coroner's offices will have news of deaths caused by accidents. Reporters scan wire service stories for the names of local people who may have been involved in disasters or accidents out of town.

Background material for the obituary is gathered from many sources. The starting point is the newspaper library. Friends and relatives can provide information, some of it human interest material that makes an obituary interesting, and they can clarify questionable or vague information. Here are the various sources:

◄ **Sources**

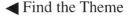

• Mortuary.
• Relatives, friends.
• Newspaper clippings.
• References such as *Who's Who.*
• Police, coroner and other officials.
• Hospital.
• Attending physician.

Starting Point

Obituaries fall into two categories, depending on the circumstances of the death. When the death is accidental—as in a traffic accident, disaster or airplane crash—the lead emphasizes the cause of death. When death is anticipated—as it is for the elderly and persons who are seriously ill—the obituary concentrates on the person's background and achievements. In both cases, of course, the obituary will list the vital facts from the checklist.

Here are examples of the two types:

◄ **Writing the Obit**

Accidental	**Anticipated**
DE KALB, Tex.—Ricky Nelson, the singing idol who grew up on television in "The Adventures of Ozzie and Harriet," died in a plane crash yesterday that killed six other people, including his fiancee and his band members, authorities said.	Walter Lippmann, the retired columnist and author and the elder statesman of American journalism, died today in New York City at the age of 85.

As with any story, the obituary should concentrate on a major point or theme. The reporter must find the aspect of the person's life that is most noteworthy.

◄ Find the Theme

When William H. Jones, managing editor of the *Chicago Tribune,* died at the age of 43 of leukemia, his professional accomplishments as an investigative reporter and an eminent editor were emphasized. The obituary noted his "tireless work, creative thinking and total integrity."

The obituary writer found in the newspaper files a story about a talk Jones gave to a graduating class at the Medill School of Journalism at Northwestern

◄ A Crusader

University. The reporter quoted from that talk in order to show Jones' philosophy of journalism. Jones had spoken about journalism as a career:

> It's a commitment to use your skills to improve your community, to speak loudly for the victims of injustice and to speak out against those who perpetuate it. Some of the best reporting begins with a single, voiceless citizen who seeks help from a newspaper that is willing to listen, and to dig out the facts.

The obituary quoted an investigator with the city's Better Government Association who worked with Jones on a series of stories that exposed widespread corruption in Chicago's private ambulance companies, which won Jones a Pulitzer Prize when he was 31. The investigator said, "Bill hated to see people abused, especially the helpless."

A Humorist ▶

Henry Morgan was a radio and television performer years before the days of talk shows. Admired for his quick wit—he usually worked without a script—he was derisive about the media and his sponsors. It was natural, then, for his obituary to dwell on some of Morgan's caustic comments and their consequences.

Richard Severo's obituary in *The New York Times* recalled that one of Morgan's sponsors was the candy bar Oh! Henry. The sponsors thought that the similarity of names would incline Morgan to sheathe his rapier wit. Hardly.

"Yes, Oh! Henry is a meal in itself," the obituary quoted a Morgan monologue, "but you eat three meals of Oh! Henrys and your teeth will fall out."

"On another broadcast," the obituary continued, "Mr. Morgan said that if children were fed enough of such candy bars they would 'get sick and die.' The makers of Oh! Henry withdrew."

When he was working for WCAU in Philadelphia as an announcer, Morgan broadcast a list of missing persons, and he included in the list the names of station executives. "It was days before they discovered it," Morgan recalled. WCAU let him go.

Then a serious note that recalled the Communist scare of the 1950s when self-appointed Communist-hunters snared entertainers as well as politicians and foreign service personnel in their nets:

> His mordant humor did not sit well with certain people, and some of them concluded that he must be either a Communist or friendly to Communists. Mr. Morgan was amazed to find himself named in the book "Red Channels," which was issued in the 1950s and listed television entertainers thought to be either Communists or friendly to Communists.

He was blacklisted and "despite a proven ability to attract audiences, had a hard time finding work."

Serious stuff. But the obituary ended on a humorous note: Morgan said little about his origin, contending that he was of "mixed parentage"—one parent was a man, the other a woman.

◀ Use Human Interest

Too many obituaries read like the label on a bottle. The major ingredients are listed, but the reader has no idea of the actual flavor. Details, human details, help the obituary writer move readers close to the person being written about. Few lives lack interest, even drama, if the reporter digs deeply enough to find it.

In an obituary of Helen Childs Boyden, who taught science and mathematics at Deerfield Academy, the reporter used several incidents from her life. When Mrs. Boyden had applied for work, the obituary reported, the principal was "not at all enthusiastic about the young applicant. But the school was too poor to insist on someone more experienced. He hired her on a temporary basis." She taught there for 63 years. The obituary continues:

> . . . In a highly personal style she cajoled thousands of students through the intricacies of mathematics and chemistry.
>
> Even in a large class she taught the individual, not the group. Her tongue was quick but never cutting. One boy, later a college president, recalls her telling him:
>
> "Victor! When will you stop trying to remember and start trying to think?"

The Boy Is a Man. Some alert students at Syracuse University point out that the writer of the Boyden obituary has a "boy" doing the recalling in the second paragraph when obviously it is a man recalling something Boyden told him when he was a boy.

Here are some paragraphs from obituaries of the well-known and the not-so-well-known:

◀ Writing with a Flair

Hyman G. Rickover—Washington (AP)—Adm. Hyman G. Rickover, the salty engineer who refused to go by the book and goaded the Navy into the nuclear era, died today. He was 86. . . . Rickover was a tiny, tidy man who was as demanding of himself as he was of others, suffering neither fools nor superiors—indeed, he often pronounced them one and the same.

Bill Stern, a radio and television sports announcer—While some radio and television critics and sportswriters contended that Mr. Stern's stories were sometimes taller than the highest infield fly, millions of listeners looked forward to his Sports Newsreel commentaries and anecdotes.

Martin Gershen, a journeyman reporter—An intense, tenacious man, he made his search for news a personal quest and treated any withholding of information as a personal affront. As a result, his life and the news often ran together.

A wealthy retired business executive who lived on an estate—He knew the butcher, the baker, the news dealer and it was significant that he died in a moving-picture theater surrounded by a fireman, a policeman and the head usherette.

Duke Ellington, composer and musician—"Duke, he went all over the world after that, but nobody ever loved him better than we did," said an old-time tap dancer who goes by the name of Kid Chocolate.

Homer Bigart, much-honored reporter—His articles remained taut, witty and astringently understated, even when created under deadline pressure and the appalling working conditions imposed by war and famine; even when they concerned mundane events that lesser reporters regarded as routine, Mr. Bigart knew that what counted was not the place but the poetry and that a reporter could create memorable prose from even the most unremarkable happening.

Paul Santangelo, Norristown, Pa., politician—The funeral drew about 100 people, which struck many as not enough

Susan Kirkman,
The (Akron) *Beacon Journal.*

Source Material

Eulogies and sermons can provide human interest details for obituaries and stories about memorial services.

of a turnout for a man said to have devoted his life to helping his constituents in every aspect of life—getting them jobs, helping them vote, performing political favors. "I guess when you live that long (94), many people are already gone," said Borough Manager Anthony Biondi, a longtime family friend.

Jerry Garcia, lead guitarist, Grateful Dead—His gentle voice and gleaming, chiming guitar lines embodied the psychedelic optimism of the Grateful Dead for three decades.

Marguerite Higgins, Pulitzer Prize reporter—Marguerite Higgins got stories other reporters didn't get. . . . Miss Higgins won her job at The Herald Tribune in a characteristic way. . . . She heard that Mrs. Chiang Kai-Shek was a patient at the Columbia-Presbyterian Hospital and had refused to grant interviews. Miss Higgins got to Mrs. Chiang's room, got her story—and her job.

The widow of a politician—She avoided the spotlight that focused on her husband through his long political career, but among teachers in local schools she was well-known as a tireless and cheerful volunteer who could be counted on to dry the tears of a newcomer to the first grade or to hand out graham crackers and milk at recess.

John McCormally, editor and publisher of The Hawk Eye, Burlington, Iowa—McCormally was born Oct. 8, 1922, in Chapman, Kan. His parents, Patrick H. and Anna Nicholson McCormally, were farmers who were broken by the Great Depression. He was 13 in 1936 when he

watched his family's friends and neighbors bid on his father's last team of mules. He watched his father cry over his lost independence. The experience helped shape McCormally's belief in fighting for the underdog, a characteristic he would carry throughout his life.

Ralph Abernathy, one of the cofounders of the civil rights movement—The flower-laden coffin was taken away on a wagon drawn by mules. Mr. Abernathy, who died Tuesday, had once requested the arrangements. He also asked, as an epitaph, two words—"I tried."

Andrew Guanche, an infant who died after a hurricane struck Miami—Baby Andrew was 9 days old when he died. He slipped away, not in a home surrounded by toys and pets, but in the coldness and loneliness of a Red Cross shelter, in a donated crib that suffocated him. (AP)

Peter Kihss, 49 years a star reporter—On the night of Nov. 9, 1965, moments after a huge power failure plunged the northeast into darkness, an assistant metropolitan editor of *The New York Times*—candle in hand—groped his way through the newspaper's darkened newsroom. "Peter," he called. "Peter." In the face of crisis, it seemed only right for the editor to call on Peter Kihss, his best reporter, to do the story.

Milton Bracker, a reporter for *The New York Times*—A restless, high-strung, energetic man whose unceasing productivity carried his work into just about every editorial corner of the *Times,* Mr. Bracker had a compulsion to write and his typewriter raced to appease his appetite for words.

Who Is Chosen ▶

Most small newspapers run at least a short item on every death in town. In large cities, where 50 or more people die daily, newspapers will run an obituary on a handful. Alden Whitman, for years the chief obituary writer for *The New York Times,* said for a person to rate an obituary in a metropolitan newspaper, a person has to be "either unassailably famous or utterly infamous."

Most of those selected are men. This is the consequence of the emphasis society places on certain kinds of occupations and achievements. Traditionally, women have been housewives, clerks, school teachers, typists and secretaries, not considered newsworthy occupations. But the perceptive reporter knows how important such tasks can be. There is as much drama—perhaps more—in the life of a woman who has reared three children or struggled to educate herself as there is in a man whose obituary is justified by the fact that he headed a local concern for 25 years.

Here is the beginning of an obituary in a Maine newspaper:

> Mrs. Verena C. Hornberger, 92, died
> Tuesday at a Waldoboro nursing home. She
> was the widow of Hiester Hornberger.
>   She was born at Bremen, daughter of
> Franklin and Emma (Hilton) Chaney. . . .

Not only is the obituary routinely written, it finds Mrs. Hornberger's prominence to be in her relationship to her husband, which might be newsworthy if he is shown to be prominent. He is not. But the obituary does contain some clues that, if followed up, might have made a fascinating story:

> . . . She graduated in 1910 from Colby
> College where she was a member of Chi
> Omega sorority.
>   She was a teacher, first working in local
> schools. She also taught in Essex, Conn.,
> and Verona, N.J., following graduate work
> in Germany at the University of Jena and
> Columbia's Teachers College.

Was she the last surviving member of the class of 1910? Does the college have any information about her? Do some students recall her? It was unusual for women in those days to finish high school, much less to graduate from college, and graduate work abroad was rare. Can someone cast light on this? Obviously, the writer simply took the mortuary form and rewrote the data. No one was interviewed. Contrast this obituary with the work of Nicolaas Van Rijn of *The Toronto Star:*

Ann Shilton didn't become the first woman principal of an academic secondary school by being a pussycat.

The principal of Jarvis Collegiate Institute from 1975 to 1983, Miss Shilton "was a very strong single woman, with strong opinions and the will to make them known," her brother Paul said yesterday.

Miss Shilton, 69, died Thursday of abdominal cancer in Princess Margaret Hospital. . . .

Here are answers to some questions about writing obituaries.

◀ **Frequently Asked Questions**

Q. Does it make sense to prepare advance obituaries?

A. Yes, even before a prominent person is ill. The AP keeps some 700 "biographical sketches" on hand, frequently brought up-to-date. A newspaper, depending on its size, may have a score or a handful. When a well-known person dies, the background, or B Matter, is ready so that all the reporter need write is a lead and the funeral arrangements.

◀ Second-Day Leads

Q. Must all second-day leads begin with the funeral or burial arrangements?

A. Not necessarily. An enterprising reporter can turn up interesting and significant material. Although many newspapers do require the standard second-day lead, nothing is as likely to discourage a reader from a story as the lead that begins: Services for (name) of (address)

will be held at (time) tomorrow at the (church or funeral home). (She/he) died at (her/his) home (date).

Verification ▶

Q. Do I verify obituaries?

A. Always. Do so by telephoning relatives, the funeral home or mortuary, the police or hospital. Strange as it may seem, there are people who call in reports of deaths for revenge or because of some neurotic compulsion.

Embarrassing
Material ▶

Q. Should I omit material from a person's life that might offend some readers or embarrass survivors or friends?

A. Follow the policy of the newspaper or station. Generally, newspapers have become more frank since the 1930s when a new reporter for *The New York Herald Tribune* would be told by City Editor Stanley Walker that there were two rules for writing obits: "First, make sure he's dead. Second, if he's a rich drunk, call him a clubman and philanthropist."

We follow Walker's first rule by verifying reports of deaths. The second rule may be applied to a local businessman everyone in town knows was a heavy and habitual drinker in the last years of his life and lost most of his business because of his drinking. But when the novelist Jack Kerouac died in 1970, *The New York Times* said he had "increasingly eased his loneliness in drink." And a former member of the Federal Communications Commission who died in a rooming house in Miami was described by physicians in an obituary as a "chronic alcoholic." We are also frank about the subject's legal entanglements, personal beliefs and even his or her sexual preference.

Unsavory activities from the person's past may be used. In the obituary of the FCC member, the lead described him as having been charged with plotting to fix the award of a television license. One obituary of Joseph P. Kennedy, the father of President Kennedy, reported that during the elder Kennedy's life there had been "whispers that Mr. Kennedy was anti-Semitic."

Jerry Garcia's obituaries all stated that he died in a California residential drug treatment center, and *The New York Times* said in the third paragraph of its page-one obituary, "In the 1960s, he was known as Captain Trips, referring to his frequent use of LSD, and he struggled through the years with a heroin addiction."

On smaller newspapers, the tendency is to look at the brighter side. However, incidents well known to the public cannot be disregarded. On the other hand, when a man or woman had led a useful life after making a mistake years past, no harm to truth is done by passing over the incident. The obituary of the former city treasurer who was sentenced to the penitentiary for graft 30 years before his death will be handled differently by different newspapers. Some will include his crime; others will not, on the ground that he paid for his mistakes and thereafter led a blameless life.

Q. When people request no flowers, what do I write?

A. Ask the caller if the family prefers that donations be made to an organization, scholarship or charity and name it: The family requests that remembrances be sent to the Douglas County Heart Association.

◀ Please Omit Flowers

Q. Do I press grieving survivors to speak to me even though they may not want to?

A. Editors usually want background about the deceased that only people close to the person can provide. An obituary celebrates the person's life, and an interview with relatives can help capture that life. Few subjects have ample material in the clip file.

Still, reporters must be sensitive to grief. If the source is unwilling to talk, do not press. But give reasons for needing the information, and try to conduct a personal interview if there is no deadline problem.

◀ Interviewing Survivors

Q. Do I always use the cause of death?

A. The cause is given, unless policy is otherwise. For years, cancer—the country's second leading cause of death—was replaced in many obituaries by the euphemisms "long illness" or "lingering illness." For some reason, many people regarded cancer as a disease too horrible to name. Under the educational program of the American Cancer Society, newspapers were encouraged to mention the disease. The cause of death should be reported whenever possible so that the public becomes aware of the major causes of death.

When lung cancer is the cause of death, reporters ask whether the deceased was a heavy smoker. For a time, newspapers ignored the deceased's smoking habit. But in recent years—after considerable criticism of this reluctance to list this possible cause of death—smoking is included, if not played up, as in this AP story:

◀ Cause of Death

COSTA MESA, Calif. (AP)—Wayne McLaren, who portrayed the rugged "Marlboro Man" in cigarette ads but became an anti-smoking crusader after developing lung cancer, has died. He was 51.

McLaren, who smoked for about 25 years and was diagnosed with the disease about two years ago, died Wednesday.

"He fought a hard battle," his mother, Louise McLaren, said. "Some of his last words were: 'Take care of the children. Tobacco will kill you, and I am living proof of it.' "

Elvis' Autopsy. The official report said Elvis Presley died of "Hypertensive Heart Disease with Coronary Artery Heart Disease as a contributing factor." And that's what the obituaries said on his death. But investigative reporters heard stories about Presley's reliance on drugs in his later years, and they found a secret autopsy report that attributed death to "multiple drug ingestion." His private physician was prescribing "immense quantities of drugs to Elvis," the reporters wrote, including codeine, quaaludes, Placidyl, Valium and Valmid.

On the other hand, when Sammy Davis Jr. died, the cover story in *People* did not mention that he died of cancer presumably caused by his two-pack-a-day cigarette habit.

AIDS ▶ **Q. What about AIDS? Do I include it as a cause of death?**

A. Yes, if it is newspaper policy to do so. More and more papers are listing AIDS as the cause of death. The taboo has lessened with the growing acceptance of the illness as a major killer. "Reporting AIDS deaths reflects the world as it is," *The Washington Post* reported in an article that said the newspaper would include AIDS as "the cause of death in its news obituaries whenever possible."

Here is how *The New York Times* reported the death of Arthur Ashe:

> Arthur Ashe, the only black man to win Wimbledon, the United States and Australian Opens and a longtime human-rights activist, died yesterday. He was 49.
> A New York Hospital administrator, Judith Lilavois, said Ashe died at 3:13 P.M. of pneumonia, a complication of AIDS.

Some newspapers will honor family requests if they insist cause of death be left out of the obituary, but fewer and fewer are making such requests.

Suicide ▶ **Q. How do I handle suicides?**

A. Follow the newspaper's policy. Most are frank; some avoid the word. The *Bangor* (Maine) *Daily News* uses the term "died unexpectedly," and the *Eagle-Tribune* in Lawrence, Mass., uses the words "short illness" for suicides. *The Morning Record and Journal* in Meriden, Conn., describes the cause of death in the final paragraph of the obituary, which allows the family to cut off the paragraph before preserving the story or sending it to others. Be careful to attribute suicide to an authority, the medical examiner or the coroner. Without such attribution, do not state suicide was the cause of death. Avoid details about the method of death.

Localizing Obituaries ▶ **Q. Should I try to localize obituaries whenever possible?**

A. Yes, if the person is a resident of your community and died elsewhere or was a former well-known resident. For example:

> John A. Nylic, 68, a retired maintenance worker at General Electric Co., died Friday night after suffering an apparent heart attack while visiting in Lebanon Springs, N.Y.
> Mr. Nylic, who lived at 78 W. Housatonic St. . . .
> —*The Berkshire Eagle* (Pittsfield, Mass.)

Q. Must the obituary always be solemn?

    A. Most are and should be. Now and then the subject lends himself or herself to lighter treatment. When the screenwriter Al Boasberg died, the lead to his obituary shocked some readers. Others found it appropriate. Boasberg had written many of the gags that were used in the Marx Brothers' movies. Some of his most famous sequences involved death, such as the one of Groucho Marx posing as a doctor taking a patient's pulse and intoning: "Either this man is dead or my watch has stopped."

    For the lead on Boasberg's obituary, Douglas Gilbert wrote:

> The joke's on Al Boasberg. He's dead.

A few newspapers assign specialists to write obituaries. Alden Whitman, for years the master obituary writer for *The New York Times,* was allowed to comment on the personal habits and the accomplishments of his subjects. When he wrote the obituary of Mies van der Rohe, the prophet of an austere modern architectural style, Whitman noted that the architect chose to live on the third floor of an old-fashioned apartment house on Chicago's north side.

In his obituary of André Malraux, the French writer, Whitman wrote that he was "a chain smoker of cheap cigarettes." In his lengthy obituary of the American socialist, Norman Thomas, Whitman said Thomas' socialism "was to Marxism what Musak is to Mozart."

Mitford, Jessica. *The American Way of Death.* New York: Fawcett Crest, 1978.

Whitman, Alden. *Come to Judgment.* New York: Viking Press, 1980.

Whitman, Alden. *The Obituary Book.* New York: Stein and Day, 1971.

◀ Humorous Obituaries

◀ **The Specialist**

◀ **Further Reading**

20 The Police Beat

Randy Piland, *The Macon* (Ga.) *Telegraph.*

Drama at every turn on the beat.

Preview

Police reporters cover a vast array of news. Their beat calls upon them to handle:

• **Breaking stories:** Accidents, crimes, arrests, fires.
• **Features:** Profiles of police personnel, criminals; stories about police investigations.
• **Interpretative articles:** Law enforcement policies, changes in personnel and procedures.
• **Investigative reporting:** Examination of false arrests, corruption, lax enforcement.

Police news is given prominent play in most newspapers because of its dramatic nature and the fact that so many people are affected. Almost 44 million Americans are victims of crimes each year, only a third of which are reported.

The Beat with Everything. "The police beat is about people and what makes them tick, what turns them into homicidal maniacs, what brings out the best in them, what drives them berserk. It has it all: greed, sex, violence, comedy and tragedy. You learn more about people than you would on any other newspaper job."—Edna Buchanan, *The Miami Herald* police reporter

F ew beats produce as much news as the police beat, and few reporters are called upon to do as much as quickly as the police reporter. Each day, a dozen or more potential stories develop on the beat. The police reporter covers:

• **Crime:** Reports of crime, investigation, arrest, booking, arraignment.
• **Accidents:** Traffic, airplane, drowning, rescue.
• **Fires:** Reports and on-the-scene coverage.
• **Departmental Activity:** Coverage of police department personnel, policies, efficiency and accountability.
• **Departmental Integrity:** Standards, policies and procedures for dealing with internal and external allegations, assumptions and attitudes about corruption that is systemic or sporadic.
• **Other Law Enforcement Agencies:** Sheriff's office, state highway patrol, suburban police departments, federal marshals.

The Range and Cost of Crime ▶

Crime affects everyone, and news of crime interests most of us. One of four households is hit by crime every year, mostly by burglary and theft. One in 20 households is struck by a violent crime—murder, rape, robbery, assault. A rape is committed every five minutes, a murder every 21 minutes. We all know someone who has been the victim of some kind of crime.

The number of crime victims is approaching 44 million, reports the U.S. Department of Justice. Of these, one-fourth are the victims of violent crimes. In its study of crime victims, the agency found 10.9 million people were the victims of murder, rape, robbery or assault last year.

Prison officials report that the number of inmates in state and federal prisons grew from 300,000 in the mid-1970s to more than 1 million 20 years later. Another 500,000 are in local jails. And 3.5 million are on probation or parole.

The crowded jails and prisons are the result of several converging forces: the public demand for longer and tougher sentences, the belief that taking criminals off the streets will lower violent crime rates and the imprisonment of drug offenders. In 25 years, the number of inmates in prison for drug offenses went from one in 16 inmates to one in five.

Two-thirds of those arrested were arrested previously, with a third of those charged having at least five prior arrest charges. Of those charged with a felony, seven of 10 were sentenced to jail or prison. Average sentences ranged from five years for robbery or assault, six years for rape and 16 years for murder. A drug-trafficking conviction resulted in an average four-year sentence.

The U.S. incarceration rate is 455 people per 100,000 population, five to eight times those of most European countries and 10 times greater than those of Japan and Sweden.

Large cities are particularly vulnerable to violent crime. In New Haven, Conn., for example, in 1960 there were six murders, four rapes and 16 robberies. Thirty years later, with a population down almost 15 percent, there were 31 murders, 168 rapes and 1,784 robberies. In Milwaukee, in 1965 there were 27 murders, 33 rapes and 214 robberies; 25 years later, again with a smaller population, there were 165 murders, 598 rapes and 4,472 robberies.

The financial cost is considerable. More than $75 billion is spent each year on the police, courts, prisons and jails and the parole and probation systems by cities, states and the federal government. This amounts to $300 a person a year.

It costs $16,000 to $25,000 a year to confine an inmate, much more in large cities; New York's cost is $58,000 a year. Costs spiral upward with the public's demand for fewer releases and longer prison and jail terms. Much of the space is being occupied by drug offenders, again because of public demands. Drug arrests in the mid-1990s were 60 percent greater than 10 years before.

Juvenile detention has also increased, at considerable cost. More than 750,000 juveniles are sent to juvenile facilities each year. The arrest rate among juveniles ages 10 to 17 jumped 100 percent from 1983 to the mid-1990s. The number of homicides among juveniles that involved handguns increased fivefold. More juveniles are being locked up, fewer placed on probation.

The amount of crime is proportionate to the size of the city. (See Table 20.1, page 425.) In recent years, however, serious crime has been rising at a faster rate in small-town America than in large cities. Over the past decade, the violent crime rate in rural counties rose 35 percent, a considerably steeper increase than that in large cities, although the highest rates remain in metropolitan areas.

Some Rates. The prison population grew almost 130 percent from the mid-1980s to the mid-1990s. The states with the highest rates of growth were Colorado (232 percent), Texas (230 percent), California (191 percent), Connecticut (180 percent) and Michigan (179 percent).

Two-thirds of all sentenced prison inmates were black, Asian, Native American or Hispanic. Hispanics make up the fastest growing minority group among those incarcerated, increasing from 7.7 percent of all federal and state prison inmates in 1980 to 14.3 percent in the mid-1990s.

The number of female inmates is increasing at a faster rate, 11 percent, than the number of male inmates, 8 percent. Washington, D.C., has by far the highest female incarceration rate (159 per 100,000 female residents); Oklahoma is next (96), then Texas (94), Nevada (61) and Arizona (57).

Of all people serving sentences in state prisons, 22 percent were imprisoned for drug offenses, 14 percent for robbery, 12 percent for burglary, 11 percent for murder and 10 percent for rape and other sexual assault.

◀ **Crime Rates**

Juvenile Crime On the Rise

Juvenile crime is at record highs. Girls and young women make up the fastest-growing group of juvenile offenders, their crime incidence increasing 35.9 percent in the past decade as against 15.2 percent for young men. Here, an officer on the San Antonio police force questions a juvenile after she and two other girls were caught driving a stolen car.

Rodolfo Gonzales, *San Antonio Light.*

Crime falls heaviest on the poor, the elderly and members of minority groups. Rape and robbery victims are twice as likely to be black as white. Among those aged 65 to 74, the violent crime victimization rate among whites is 4.2 and among blacks 13.9 per 100,000 households.

Violent crime rates declined in the 1990s in metropolitan areas, the result, say authorities, of longer sentences for frequent offenders. But they worry about the large population of juveniles who will be adults in the next decade. Many of these young men and women make up the rapidly growing group of juvenile offenders.

Table 20.1 Crime Rate

	Metropolitan Areas	Other Cities	Rural	National Average
Murder	10.6	5.3	5.4	9.5
Forcible rape	43.2	39.1	24.9	40.6
Robbery	312.0	71.3	16.6	255.8
Aggravated assault	486.4	388.8	175.3	440.1
Burglary	1,182.3	992.8	633.4	1,099.2
Larceny-theft	3,289.3	3,581.7	1,005.7	3,032.4
Motor vehicle theft	721.4	224.5	109.9	605.3

Rates per 100,000 inhabitants.
From *Crime in the United States.*

Note: The data in the tables in this chapter reflect reported crimes. But not all victims report crimes. A recent survey by the Bureau of Justice shows that 48.6 percent of violent crimes, 28.5 percent of thefts and 41.2 percent of household crimes are reported.

Crime data are available from a variety of sources. Local police departments keep records of reported crimes, arrests and disposition of cases. The departments file their figures each year with the FBI, which issues an annual report, *Crime in the United States, Uniform Crime Reports.* It is available from the Superintendent of Documents, U.S. Government Printing Office, Washington, D.C., 20402. Your local FBI office can order it for you.

Reporters can use the FBI report to compare the figures from their city and state with data from other cities and states and with national averages.

The Bureau of Justice Statistics makes available free copies of its reports that cover a wide range: national crime surveys, domestic violence, parole and probation, ages of rape victims, sentencing patterns, juvenile crime.

To be placed on the Bureau's mailing list, call toll-free 1-800-732-3277 or write: Justice Statistics Clearinghouse, National Criminal Justice Reference Service, Box 6000, Rockville, MD 20850.

Single copies are free. Public-use tapes of Bureau data sets are available from the Criminal Justice Archive and Information Network, P.O. Box 1248, Ann Arbor, MI 48106, telephone (313) 763-5010.

The Bureau also makes crime and justice data and a wide range of its publications available on CD-ROM, which can be purchased for $15 a CD. Order through the Rockville address.

To cope with this tide of criminal activity, there are 560,000 officers on state and local police forces. This works out to one police officer for every 3.5 violent crimes committed. In the 1960s, the ratio was reversed. Then, there were 3.3 officers for every violent crime reported.

In effect, this means that the police have a tenth the power they had 30 years ago to deal with crime. One response has been the employment of private police guards, who now number about 1.5 million. They guard office buildings, apartment complexes, shopping malls, gated communities, even the streets of some residential communities.

Those that can afford private protection do so. The commercial and residential areas that cannot pay must rely on police forces spread thin.

◀ **Police Power**

High Interest in Crime News ▶

You might think that over the years of intense crime coverage the public's appetite would reach the saturation point. Not so. Crime news remains high on the media agenda.

Perhaps it is the increasingly bizarre nature of crimes:

• The perfect neighbor who stabbed his next-door neighbor 13 times after she resisted his sexual advances.

• The Mormon church leader who had an entire family executed to protect his standing in the church.

• The teen-ager who persuaded his college classmates to kill his step-father.

• The lawyer who had his buddies on the police force shoot his wife and dump her and her car into a Chicago canal.

• The widow who rid herself of a series of husbands by feeding them arsenic.

Crime's Victims ▶

Perhaps it is the widening array of crime victims. Daily, we read about and watch coverage in evening newscasts of the deaths of innocent people caught in drive-by shootings, children shot as they cowered in their apartments during drug wars. We read of seemingly senseless stabbings and shootings during holdups:

When the two men demanded his leather jacket and her shearling coat, the couple did not resist.

Alexander Ortiz, 22, took off his jacket. Arlyn Gonzales, 23, terrified, fumbled over a buckle at the collar of her coat. One of the men roughly tugged at her coat.

"Don't do it," Ortiz said. "Don't hurt her. She's pregnant."

In response, one of the men shot Ortiz, once in the throat and once in the left chest.

"C'mon, c'mon, Get her jacket," Ms. Gonzales said the gunman told his associate.

Though fatally wounded, Ortiz spoke to his girlfriend. "I don't want to die. I'm afraid. Take care of the baby for me. Take care of my baby, please." He died two hours later at Jamaica Hospital.

School Fears ▶

Perhaps it is the fear parents live with when they send their children to school. The Bureau of Justice reports 9 percent of students aged 12 to 19 were crime victims in or near their schools over a six-month period; 15 percent said their schools had gangs; 16 percent said a student had attacked or threatened a teacher; 30 percent said marijuana was easy to obtain at school; 9 percent said crack and 11 percent said cocaine were easy to obtain in school; 31 percent said alcohol was easy to obtain.

Among black students in the central cities, 24 percent said they were afraid of being attacked while going to and from school. Three percent of students in central cities reported taking some kind of weapon to school to protect themselves.

Even in cities in which violent crime is rare, newspapers and stations cover the police beat thoroughly. *The Times Argus* in Barre-Montpelier, Vt., reports items such as "juveniles throwing snowballs in front of the City Center, hindering pedestrians" and "moose on highway."

The Quincy Herald-Whig tells its western Illinois readers about the kidnapping of a scarecrow, "value $15." To newcomers who wonder why the newspaper prints such material, the editor, Joseph I. Conover, replies, "Because people read it. This sort of thing is extremely well-read. People are just interested in what their neighbors are doing."

Mary Van Beusekom, the police reporter for the *Argus Leader* in Sioux Falls, S.D., does not have to report every fire call and every one of the hundred or so police items on the list of incoming 911 calls that are filed daily. But she skims each call for two purposes: to track down important stories and to gather material for her quota of at least five briefs for the daily police log.

Her eyes run down the long list. She notes the code numbers that designate the type of crime committed and whether anyone was arrested and she checks the addresses of those arrested and the location of the incident. She also looks at the number of officers who responded to the call. "If there are several, there could be a story," she says.

Next, she obtains details of the stories in which she is interested by interviewing the officer in charge. South Dakota, like several states and cities, does not permit reporters to examine the reports of investigating officers.

The captain of detectives tells Van Beusekom about three youngsters who pointed what appeared to be an automatic pistol at two boys. The pistol turned out to be a squirt gun.

◀ Small-Town Crime News

◀ **Medium-City Police Reporter**

POLICE LOG

■ **VANDALISM:** Vandals spray-painted a pentagon, a pitchfork and assorted other graffiti on the Knights of Columbus hall at 315 N. Summit Ave. on Monday, police said. The graffiti, which was found on the back wall of the hall, caused $50 damage.

■ **VANDALISM:** Vandals uprooted a fence post and threw display items such as wooden geese into the Laurel Oaks Pool at 3401 E. 49th St. on Saturday or Sunday, police said. The damage amounted to $100.

■ **VANDALISM:** A 57-year-old Sioux Falls man told police someone broke the windshield on his 1970 Ford Galaxy with rocks while it was parked at 1021 W. Bailey Ave. on Saturday, police said. Jerome K. Salwei, 521 S. Ebenezer Ave., said the damage amounted to $250, police said.

■ **VANDALISM:** Someone broke the left headlight, removed the hood ornament and scratched and dented the driver's side of a 1984 Cadillac El Dorado, causing $725 damage, on Friday or Saturday, police said. The car's owner, Alvin R. Clausen, 69, 816 W. 15th St., said he wasn't sure where the vandalism occurred.

■ **AGGRAVATED ASSAULT:** A 15-year-old boy and his 14-year-old friend told police three boys pulled what resembled a black automatic handgun on them as they rode their bikes on Westview Road from their homes to a convenience store and back Friday, police said. The "handgun" turned out to be a squirt gun.

■ **AGGRAVATED ASSAULT:** A 16-year-old Sioux Falls girl told police that her ex-boyfriend slapped and punched her on the back of her head and then struck her with a green garden hose May 31, police said. The girl said the assault occurred at her ex-boyfriend's residence in the 3300 block of South Holly Avenue and was not the first time he had struck her, police said. No arrest was made.

Backgrounding A Police Call

Mary Van Beusekom, the *Argus Leader* police reporter, takes notes for her story as a police detective reads from the arresting officer's report.

She asks about a report of domestic abuse. ("There's so much of it nowadays," she remarks.) She asks about the few items she has selected for her daily log; she needs more information about some graffiti and a fence that was pulled down and tossed into a swimming pool.

One report, about the theft of sacred items from a sweat lodge, is worth a story, and Van Beusekom asks for details.

Van Beusekom, a graduate of the University of Minnesota, is an experienced reporter. She went to Sioux Falls from Florida where she also covered the police.

Editors like to assign their younger reporters to the police beat in the belief there is no faster way to test a reporter's ability and to teach him or her about the city. The new police reporter immediately becomes acquainted with the organization of the police department and sets about making contacts with key officers. Survival depends on establishing a routine and developing good sources. Otherwise the police beat can become an impenetrable maze, and the reporter may be given only the information that the department deigns to hand out.

Types of Felonies ▶

There are seven types of felonies, which fall into two general categories, not including the so-called possessory felonies involving weapons and drugs.

- **Violent crime:** murder, rape, robbery, aggravated assault.
- **Property crime:** burglary, larceny-theft, motor-vehicle theft.

The FBI keeps crime data in these categories, as do local police. Ten percent of all felonies are violent and 90 percent are crimes against property.

Table 20.2 The Most Dangerous Cities in the United States

Violent Crime Rate		Property Crime Rate	
1. Washington	2,921.8	1. Miami	11,364.2
2. Miami	2,136.2	2. Tallahassee	9,210.3
3. New York	1,865.5	3. Washington	8,839.3
4. Alexandria, Va.	1,833.0	4. Gainesville, Fla.	8,802.7
5. Los Angeles	1,682.4	5. Tucson	8,465.7
6. Tallahassee	1,546.0	6. Myrtle Beach, S.C.	7,963.3
7. Baton Rouge	1,510.7	7. Lakeland, Fla.	7,836.5
8. Little Rock	1,453.1	8. San Antonio	7,821.3
9. Jacksonville	1,419.9	9. Corpus Christi	7,685.0
10. Pueblo, Colo.	1,403.9	10. Atlantic City	7,661.8
Average	**852.2**	**Average**	**5,192.9**

Rates per 100,000 inhabitants.
From *Crime in the United States.*

The police department is organized around the three police functions—(1) enforcement of laws, (2) prevention of crime and (3) finding and arresting criminals.

The department is headed by a chief or commissioner who is responsible to the mayor, director of public safety or city manager. The chief or commissioner is appointed and although he or she makes departmental policy, broad policy decisions affecting law enforcement come from a superior and are often made in a political context. The chief's second in command may be an assistant chief or inspector. Commissioners have deputy commissioners under them.

The rest of the organizational chart depends upon the size of the city. In large cities, deputy inspectors are put in charge of various divisions or bureaus—homicide, detective, robbery, juvenile, rape, arson, traffic. The larger the city, the more bureaus. As the patterns of criminal activity change, organizational changes are made. These changes make good stories.

The next in command in large cities are captains, who are assigned to run precincts and are assisted by lieutenants. Sergeants are placed in charge of shifts or squads at the precinct house. The private in the organization is the police officer.

The beat reporter's day-to-day contacts are for the most part with sergeants and lieutenants. Reporters, trained to be suspicious of authority, are sometimes irritated by the paramilitary structure, secretiveness and implicit authoritarianism of the police department.

Reporters new to the police beat soon learn that the police are, at best, suspicious of them. Diana K. Sugg, a police reporter for *The Sacramento Bee,* circulation 250,000, is blunt: "In most cities around the country, big or small, the cops don't like reporters." Often the reporter and the police work at cross purposes. "We want the information they can't or won't release."

Let's watch Sugg at work on a typical day to see how she manages to get along with the police, "no matter how strongly officers say they hate your paper."

It's 9 a.m. and Sugg is in the police station with her portable police scanner, pager, map and notepad. Some days she takes the sheriff's office first and then the police station.

She flips through the watch summaries of the significant events of the previous day and night. With her scanner buzzing in the background, she carefully reads every page, every notation. "I'm looking for anything strange, anything particularly cruel.

"Once a woman managed to catch a rapist by running into her bathroom with a portable telephone and calling 911. Another time a man tied up three children and then raped their mother in front of them. Or you may find material for a short feature story—like the man named the 'inept robber' by the police because he made four robbery attempts at markets—and made off with only one beer."

She also reads the arrest reports, sometimes as many as 200 a day. For the detailed reports and the watch summaries, her eyes go automatically to the name, age and, she says, "particularly the occupation. A 45-year-old unemployed man arrested for theft isn't much of a story. But a 45-year-old teacher? Why would he need to steal? When you contact him, will he tell you the arrest was a mistake?"

◀ **Police Department Organization**

◀ **Making Her Rounds**

Diana K. Sugg

She looks at the section marked "Comments" at the bottom of the arrest sheets for unusual circumstances the officers may note. "Once a man threw a rock through a window and waited for the police to come because he wanted to be arrested—he was homeless and he had AIDS. He figured the jail officers would at least take care of him."

Sugg occasionally consults a small handbook, the penal code, as crimes sometimes are listed only by the code number. "That's done to keep reporters from noticing certain arrests," she says.

She makes a point of looking in on the sergeant in charge that day. "Even if things are slow and I don't have anything to ask the sergeant, I always make a point to talk with him, sometimes sharing the hard parts of my job so he could understand why some stories were shorter, or why we weren't interested in covering some.

"During all this checking, the scanner is babbling and my pager is ringing as I am talking with a secretary. It can get nerve-wracking, because I am afraid I might miss something." Her ear is tuned to the code numbers for kidnappings, shootings, homicides, and she knows the police codes, too, those they use when they report they are going to eat, taking a bathroom break or going off duty.

Her morning checks completed, Sugg drives to the newsroom with a couple of items to run by her editor to see whether they are worth pursuing. She has to return a phone call to someone who read one of her stories and had something to add to it.

It's noon and she takes a break, her second Mounds bar, a diet Coke, maybe a giant chocolate chip cookie. The *Bee* is a morning paper, and Sugg has the afternoon to continue to gather information, to look deeper into some items, to call people on continuing stories.

Then she's off in the paper's Ford Bronco with her pager, scanner, portable radio, map and notebook. On the way to the scene, she's listening to officers talk to their supervisors. She moves fast. One day while working the night police shift—the newspaper covers the beat 'round the clock—she heard on her scanner a report of a shooting. She was off. On the way to the crime scene she heard officers report that one shooting was fatal, and then a second . . . and then a third. "Within half an hour I was dictating the story of a triple shooting over the portable radio," Sugg says. She made the deadline.

On the Scene ▶

"Neighbors are incredible sources," Sugg says. "Especially if you find the one busybody who watches the street like a hawk and knows everything about the neighbors. People like this know where someone works, the hours he or she keeps, the age of his children, when he was divorced. All this information has to be checked out, but it's a starting point."

Many crimes do not have eyewitnesses, but Sugg looks for the neighbor who heard a shot, a scream. "Once I interviewed a 7-year-old boy who watched a shooting through his apartment window."

She always tries to interview the victims. "Often, when they discover your sincerity they open up and give you unbelievable details." She makes sure to absorb the scene—the ambulance door slamming shut, the smell of the burned house, the cold fog over the scene of the triple shooting.

The police reporter knows arrest procedures, and because on some smaller newspapers and on many radio and television stations the same reporter who covers an arrest might stay with the case through the trial, a knowledge of the criminal court process is necessary, too. Here, we will discuss the arrest process. In the next chapter, criminal court procedures are outlined.

A person may be arrested on sight or upon issuance of a warrant. Let us follow a case in which a merchant spots in his store a man he believes robbed him the previous week.

The store owner calls a police officer who arrests the man. The suspect is searched on the scene and taken to the station house. The suspect is then searched again in front of the booking desk. His property is recorded and placed in a "property" envelope. The suspect's name and other identification and the alleged crime are recorded in a book known to old-time reporters as a *blotter*. (The blotter supposedly takes its name from the work of turn-of-the-century police sergeants who spilled considerable ink in their laborious efforts to transcribe information and then had to sop up the splotches with a blotter.)

The police are required to tell a suspect at the time of arrest that he has the right to remain silent and to refuse to answer questions. (This is called the Miranda warning.) He also has the right to consult an attorney at any time and is told that if he cannot afford a lawyer one will be provided. Unless the suspect waives these rights, his statements cannot be used against him at his trial.

The signed waiver permits the police immediately to interrogate the suspect about his actions, background and whereabouts in connection with the crime. If it is a homicide case, the practice is to call in an assistant prosecutor to ensure the admissibility of any admission or confession.

The officer then prepares an arrest report, which is written in the presence of the suspect who also supplies "pedigree information"—age, height, weight, date and place of birth and other details. (See "Arrest Report: An Assault," page 437.)

The suspect may then be photographed and fingerprinted and he'll be permitted to make a telephone call. A record is made of the number and person called and the suspect is returned to a detention cell to await arraignment. The arresting officer goes to the complaint room to confer with the victim and an assistant district attorney so that a complaint can be drawn up. The police officer may ask the complainant to identify the suspect again in a lineup.

The assistant district attorney has to decide whether the case is strong enough, the witness reliable, the offense worth prosecuting before a complaint is drawn. The prosecutor must also decide whether to reduce a felony charge to a lesser felony or to a misdemeanor. He may reduce the charge if he feels the reduction would lead to a guilty plea.

The police officer may have to file additional reports. If he fired his weapon, he must file an "unusual incident report," as it is described in some jurisdictions, and if he shot someone, he files an "inspector's report."

The fingerprints are checked in a central state agency to determine whether the suspect has a record, and the suspect's file is sent to the courts, which require the information before arraignment. The presiding judge decides whether bail should be set and the amount. A suspect with no record who is arrested for a

◀ The Arrest Process

Rodger Mallison,
Fort Worth Star-Telegram.

User

Officer Gabe Medrano of the Fort Worth police force has been watching an apartment where he suspects drugs are sold. When this man gets into his Oldsmobile with an expired inspection sticker, Medrano pulls it over. The man has a spot of blood on his sleeve. In the car, Medrano finds four small bags of powder.

Drugs. FBI records show that 2,570 drug arrests are made daily. Also, 50 to 75 percent of those arrested for serious crimes test positive for drugs, most often for cocaine. The percentage of men arrested who test positive for cocaine after arrest:

New York	83
Philadelphia	70
Miami	64
Washington, D.C.	59
Chicago	59
Los Angeles	55
Houston	54
New Orleans	53
Dallas	52
Cleveland	52
San Diego	51
Birmingham	51

Nearly half (47.6 percent) of juveniles arrested reported they were under the influence of either drugs or alcohol at the time of arrest.

minor crime may be released on his own recognizance—that is, without putting up bail.

Most large cities have overcrowded detention facilities and a backlog of untried cases. To cope, they may release suspects on low bail or none at all. Later, plea bargaining may be arranged in which the defendant agrees to plead guilty to a lesser charge so that the case can be disposed of at arraignment (see Chapter 21).

Effect on Police ▶

Plea bargaining may be the only way the judicial system can cope with many criminals and few judges and few cells, but it can lead to a disillusioned police force. A suspect whose arrest may have involved investigative work and some risk becomes the subject of plea bargaining and is out on the street the next day with a suspended sentence for petty theft. Eventually, police officers spend less time on the crimes they know will lead to plea bargaining and light punishment. Worse, citizens sometimes engage in vigilante activities or take the law into their own hands.

In some large cities, some nonviolent crimes have been, in effect, decriminalized. Minor drug violations are ignored. Few small burglaries are investigated. Car theft is infrequently investigated and rarely prosecuted in metropolitan areas. In New York City during a recent year, 115,000 automobiles were stolen. The police arrested 9,000 people on a charge of grand larceny motor vehicle theft. Nine were sent to prison. In many large cities, 80 percent of all felony arrests are either dismissed or plea bargained to misdemeanors or low-level felonies.

In some cities, the district attorney's office has set up what are known as early case assessment bureaus or career criminal tracking systems. They enable prosecutors to single out the defendants they consider the most likely to commit further crimes. These cases are not plea bargained.

Not Me, Officer

Photographer O. Gordon Williamson Jr. of *The Orlando Sentinel* chanced to see a bearded man make a getaway from a bank he had just robbed. Williamson followed the man to a barber shop, and while the identifying beard was being removed, Williamson called the police . . . and then took this picture.

Crime Report of a Robbery

This report describes the armed robbery of a grocery. The investigating officer who filed the report noted the weapon, physical characteristics of the holdup man and the fact that the clerk was tied up and locked in a storage area.

◀ **Arrest Stories**

Most crimes are committed by young men, and a growing number involve teen-agers. Juveniles who are arrested are turned over to the juvenile court and their names are not released. In some states, in response to the rise in violent crime by youngsters, serious offenses by youths, particularly murder, are handled by the regular court system and their names can be used, as an upstate New York newspaper did in the following crime.

The battered body of a 77-year-old man was discovered in his home at 11 p.m. by a neighbor who called the police. The neighbor said she saw two youths running from the scene. Police conducted an investigation and within five hours arrested a 16-year-old and a 14-year-old. The two were charged with second-degree murder and at their arraignment entered pleas of not guilty.

The reporter for the local afternoon newspaper learns all this on his 7 a.m. check. He calls the coroner to obtain information about the cause of death, and he questions the police about the murder weapon and the motivation. He also asks where the youths are being held and the time they were arrested. With the information on hand, he calls his desk to report what he has and the city editor tells him to give the story 150 to 200 words. The dead man was not prominent.

The editor asks about the neighbor: Did she identify the youngsters, and if not, how did the police learn their identities? The reporter says the police will not comment about the neighbor. Nor will the neighbor talk. The story will have to be a straight murder-and-arrest piece. Here is how the reporter wrote it:

Two Saratoga youths were arrested early today and charged with the murder of 77-year-old Anthony Hay, a local fuel oil and coal dealer, whose battered body was found last night in his home.

Police identified the youths as Arthur Traynor, 16, of 61 Joshua Ave., and John Martinez, 14, of 15 Doten Ave. Police said a neighbor saw two youths fleeing from Hay's residence at 342 Nelson Ave. The arrests were made within five hours of the slaying.

The youths entered pleas of not guilty at their arraignment this morning on charges of second-degree murder and were being held in the county jail pending a preliminary hearing.

Hay's body was found at 11 p.m. in the business office of his home. He was "badly beaten about the head and face and had a fractured skull," Coroner Clark Donaldson reported. Police said they recovered the death weapon, a three-foot wooden club. They declined to give any motive for the slaying.

Caution: Be careful about identifying the arrested. A libel suit resulted when a newspaper identified a crime suspect who had stolen a wallet from which police took the name. "Use special care in reporting the arrest of a public figure," advises the AP. "It is not uncommon for crime suspects to give police false names, and frequently those they provide are from sports figures, politicians, etc." Press authorities for authentication of the identification and on your own try to reach the suspect.

Victims ▶

A combination of circumstances has led to a greater interest in crime victims. Radio and television offer the public crime news quickly. Newspapers that are read at 8 a.m. over coffee cannot offer stale news, the crimes and arrests that were on last night's broadcast news.

Police reporters now dig, probe and investigate, and much of their work turns to the victims of crime. But coverage of victims is difficult, and it can pose problems. How far into a family's grief can a journalist intrude? Is it appropriate to identify the victims of sex crimes?

The Des Moines Register did so when a rape victim permitted the newspaper to name her, and some women said such identification would lessen the stigma of sex crimes. But others felt disclosure would be regressive, as many women would not report sex crimes for fear of being named in news stories.

No newspaper has a policy of naming rape victims. When the Marshall University (Huntington, W. Va.) student newspaper, *The Parthenon,* printed the name of a rape victim and adopted a policy to continue to do so, students, faculty members and others on the campus threatened to boycott the newspaper and its advertisers. The policy was dropped.

Edna Buchanan, the prizewinning police reporter for *The Miami Herald,* says:

Sometimes, we are all the victim has got.
Sometimes you feel like Wonder Woman, or Superman, going to the rescue. Reporters can find missing kids, lost grandmothers, and

misplaced corpses. We fish out people who fall through the cracks. Publicity rescues people tangled in the hopeless mazes of government and bureaucracy. We recover stolen cars and priceless family heirlooms. A story in the newspaper can secure donations of blood, money, and public support—and occasionally that rarest gift of all: justice.

Police reporters depend on inside sources. Without them—given the guarded nature of the police—the reporter has a hard time covering the beat. This is why big-city media keep at least one reporter on the police beat for years. It takes time to cultivate the police.

◀ **Sources Are Essential**

Buchanan is a veteran of the beat. "I talk to cops a lot," she says. "Talking to cops is the only way to get a lot of the stories I do. Of course, a lot of policemen don't recognize a good story, so you just have to keep talking to them so it'll come up in conversation."

Many police departments have gone to computerized reports which, Buchanan says, require that the officers only fill in blanks. The old reports, handwritten by arresting officers, had color and the officers' comments. What this means, Buchanan says, is that reporters have to go to "hands-on, person-to-person human contacts." She recalls learning about a robbery where "a guy got robbed and knocked down. No big deal." But she learned from a contact that the victim had artificial legs and was pushed off his legs "for something like a dollar and forty cents."

Readers and TV viewers also call reporters with tips. It was a tip about the death of a black motorcyclist that led to Buchanan's stories about police brutality. When an all-white jury in Tampa acquitted the police officers, a riot ensued.

◀ **Readers' Tips**

It was a "nightmare," Buchanan said, "seeing the city burning. As I have looked back, there is nothing else I could have done. And I know I did the right thing. But what happened because of it afterward was terrible."

Buchanan told her experiences to Karen Rothmyer, who collected the comments of Pulitzer Prize winners in her book, *Winning Pulitzers,* (Columbia University Press).

After the bodies of O.J. Simpson's ex-wife and her friend were discovered, police went about the investigation without releasing much information. Inside sources paid off for the *Los Angeles Times:*

◀ **O.J. Simpson**

> Mounting evidence links former football star O.J. Simpson to the brutal slayings of his former wife and a man she knew, and the famous athlete could be arrested within days, Los Angeles police sources said Tuesday.

As the murder investigation continued, more tips found their way into the *Times:*

◀ **Blood Samples**

> The blood type of samples recovered at the scene of a brutal double slaying matches that of O.J. Simpson's blood, a potentially important piece of evidence in the

investigation of the killings of his ex-wife and a man she knew, Los Angeles police sources said Wednesday.

Manhunt ▶

The police issued a warrant for Simpson's arrest and a manhunt was on:

> O.J. Simpson, the football great who rose from the mean streets of San Francisco to international celebrity, became the subject of a massive police manhunt Friday, after a warrant was issued for his arrest in connection with the murders of his ex-wife and a male friend.

Arrest ▶

And then the arrest:

> O.J. Simpson was arrested Friday for the murders of his ex-wife and a male friend after leading police on a gripping, two-hour chase through the rush-hour freeways of Southern California.

The Arrest Process

The police reporter covers all aspects of the arrest process, from the report of the arrest through the arraignment of the suspect. Most arrests receive bare mention, but the high-profile crimes are covered fully. Reporters rely for information on the police, the district attorney and the suspect's lawyer. The reporter is aware that the original charge often is reduced by the prosecutor because either the original charge cannot be sustained or the prosecutor believes the suspect is more likely to plead guilty to a lessened charge than he or she would to the original charge.

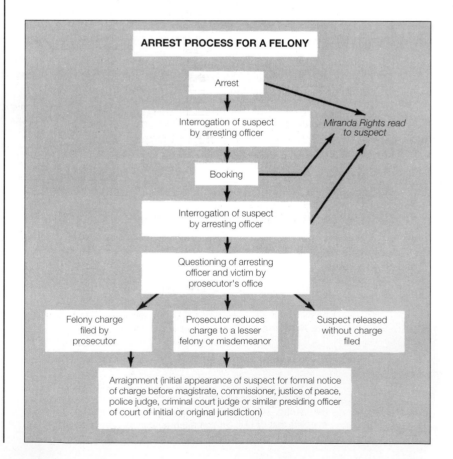

FIGURE 20.1

The police reporter stays with the story as the suspect is jailed and writes:

> A day after being captured outside his 5,700-square-foot Brentwood estate, football legend O.J. Simpson spent Saturday under suicide watch in a 7-by-9 foot jail cell, where he is being held without bail as prosecutors prepare to seek murder indictments from the county grand jury.

Notice the play on the size of Simpson's accommodations.

Once the grand jury issued the indictment, Simpson would be arraigned and the story went to the court reporters. We will pick up the Simpson saga in the next chapter where we cover the courts. Here, we will move on to reporting specific crimes.

◀ **In Jail**

The Story of an Assault

A 41 year-old unemployed plumber, described by police as a heroin addict, was arrested today in the predawn stabbing of a 22-year-old man apparently lured to an empty apartment on Manhattan's west side.

The victim, Haywood Clarke was stabbed in the back, face and side and was in serious condition at Logan Hospital. Police were questioning Roosevelt B. Thomson and a companion to try to establish a motive. . . .

On deadline, the reporter is able to find one additional piece of information, that Clarke was lured to the empty apartment. The story is on the right:

Arrest Report: An Assault

This form is typical of those used in many jurisdictions. In this arrest, the suspect is Roosevelt B. Thomson, a white male born in 1955 and residing at 1870 Columbus Ave. Thomson was arrested for assaulting a 22-year-old male, Haywood Clarke, with a knife in an empty apartment at 159 W. 105th St. The time was 3:30 a.m.

Clarke was taken to Logan Hospital where he was treated for serious stab wounds to the back, face and side. Thomson was arrested with "one other," about which the report says nothing more.

Why the men were in an empty apartment was not clarified. These details will have to be filled in by follow-up investigation. The abbreviations used in the report:

n/a—not available

a/o—arresting officer

A/C—according to complainant

T/P/O—time and place of occurrence

Murder

▶ In some areas, murder is rare—Vermont may have two homicides a year. When one is reported, coverage is intense. In metropolitan areas, where one to five murders are reported each day, only the prominence of the victim or the suspect merit full-scale coverage. There are exceptions, of course, such as the senseless shooting of the young man in a holdup that we described a few pages back.

Prominence clearly was the news value that motivated the minute coverage of the death of O.J. Simpson's ex-wife—not her fame, of course, but his. Look at how the AP wrote the first lead on the discovery of the bodies:

> LOS ANGELES, (AP)—Hall of Fame football player O.J. Simpson's ex-wife and a man were found dead early Monday outside the woman's condominium, and Simpson was being interviewed by police.

This began what some critics described as a "media circus" or a "media feeding frenzy." Journalists countered by pointing to the near-insatiable public appetite for the story.

Checklist: Homicide

Crime

▶
____ Victim, identification.
____ Time, date, place of death.
____ Weapon used.
____ Official cause of death or authoritative comment.
____ Who discovered body.
____ Clues. Any identification of slayer.
____ Police comments. Motivation for crime.
____ Comments from neighbors, friends.
____ Any police record for victim; any connection with criminal activity.
____ Consequences to victim's family, others.

Arrest

____ Name, identification of person arrested.
____ Victim's name; time, date, place of crime.
____ Exact charge.
____ Circumstances of arrest.
____ Motive.
____ Result of tip, investigation.
____ Officers involved in investigation, arrest.
____ Booking.
____ Arraignment. Bail, if any.
____ Suspect's police record (in states where it is not illegal to publish such information).

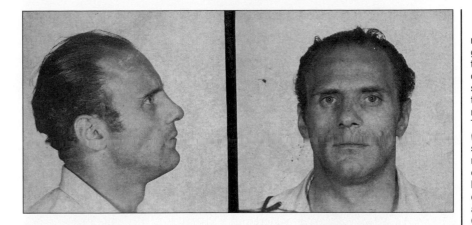

Murder strikes disproportionately among blacks, particularly among young black males. The murder victim rate per 100,000 population is 36.9 for blacks and 5.3 for whites, a ratio of almost seven to one. Blacks, who constitute 22 percent of the population, account for almost half of all murder victims.

Among black males, the murder victim rate is extraordinarily high:

Age	White	Black
12–24	11.7	114.9
25 and older	7.8	67.5

◀ Young Blacks Major Victims

The lifetime chance of being a murder victim is one in 131 for white males, one in 21 for black males. In St. Louis, one of every 13 black males will be murdered by age 45.

Two-thirds of murder victims are killed by firearms, most by handguns.

Table 20.3 Murder and Nonnegligent Manslaughter Rates

Metropolitan Areas		States	
1. Washington, D.C.	78.5	1. Louisiana	20.3
2. New Orleans	37.7	2. Mississippi	13.5
3. Shreveport, La.	25.8	3. New York	13.3
4. Jackson, Miss.	25.2	4. California	13.1
5. Jackson, Tenn.	23.3	5. Maryland	12.7
6. New York	23.2	6. Texas	11.9
7. Memphis	21.9	7. Alabama	11.6
8. Fayetteville, N.C.	21.7	8. Illinois	11.4
9. Los Angeles	21.3	8. Georgia	11.4
10. Gary-Hammond, Ind.	20.2	10. North Carolina	11.3
		10. Missouri	11.3
Average	**10.6**	**Average**	**9.5**

Rates per 100,000 inhabitants.
From *Crime in the United States.*

A Child's Nightmare

When 10-year-old Chantay came home from school, she found her mother lying naked and bleeding on the living room floor. "My momma's been hurt," Chantay screamed as she ran from the house. Neighbors called an ambulance. Taken to a hospital with two bullet wounds in her chest, the 29-year-old woman died. Police arrested a boyfriend. He was sentenced to 50 years in prison on his guilty plea to second-degree murder. The judge ordered him to serve 45 percent of his sentence before he would be eligible for parole.

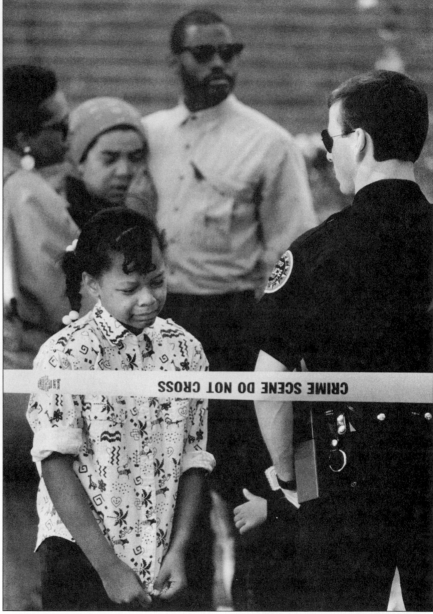

Freeman Ramsey, *The Tennessean.*

Burglary (B) is a crime against property, usually involving a home, office, or store break-in. Robbery (R) is a crime against a person, involving the removal of the person's goods or money with force or threat of force and is categorized as a violent crime.

◀ **Burglary, Robbery**

Crime

___ Victim, identification.
___ Goods or money taken. Value of goods.
___ Date, time, location of crime.
___ (R) Weapon used.
___ (B) How entry made.
___ (R) Injuries and how caused.
___ Clues.
___ Unusual circumstances. (Overlooked valuables, frequency of crime in area or to victim, etc.)
___ Statements from victim, witness.

◀ Checklist: Burglary, Robbery

Arrest

___ Name, identification of person arrested.
___ Details of crime.
___ Circumstances of arrest.

Note: Half or more of those arrested are not formally charged with the crime for which they were arrested. The names of those arrested but not charged can be used without worrying about legal action. The question is one of fairness.

About 2.5 million women are the victims of violent crime each year. The most frequent crime committed against them is assault, often domestic assault. Studies by the Bureau of Justice found that the women "most vulnerable as the victims of violence are black, Hispanic, in younger age groups, never married, with lower family income and lower education levels and in central cities."

◀ **Violence Against Women**

More than two-thirds of the women victims knew their attackers. Almost one-third of the attackers were husbands, boyfriends, or relatives; a third were acquaintances. Women victimized by strangers were six times more likely to report their attack to police as were those women attacked by relatives or friends. These women said they feared reprisals from their attackers.

While the violent crime victimization rate for males has declined, the rate for females has not.

"In general," states the Bureau, "violent crime against women was primarily intra-racial. Eight of 10 violent crimes against white women were perpetrated by white offenders. Similarly, nine of 10 violent victimizations sustained by black women were committed by black offenders."

> **Child Abuse.** The Justice Department reported child abuse and neglect reports tripled over the past decade, rising from 1 million to 3 million. The department said studies link child abuse and neglect to future delinquency and adult criminality. It predicts twice as many juvenile arrests for violent crime by 2010.

Close to half of all incidents of domestic violence against women are not reported to police. Of married women not reporting their husbands, 41 percent were subsequently assaulted by them within six months. Of those who did report their husbands, 15 percent were reassaulted.

◀ Domestic Violence

A third of all domestic violence against women consists of rape, robbery or aggravated assault.

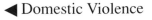

Rape ▶

More than 140,000 rapes are reported a year. Nine of 10 rape victims are women, but only about half the women report their victimizations to the police. The Bureau of Justice found about half of all rapes were perpetrated by someone known to the victim and that, in one-fifth of the cases, the offender was armed.

"Of female rape victims who took some self-protective action such as fighting back and yelling and screaming, most reported that it helped the situation rather than made it worse," the Bureau reported.

The Bureau estimates that one in six rape victims are under the age of 12. Of the 14 states that reported the age of the victim, Florida reported a total of 7,280 rapes, 14 percent of them of girls under age 11; Michigan, 4,731 rapes, 28 percent under age 11; Pennsylvania, 2,996 rapes, 14 percent under age 13; North Carolina, 2,397 rapes, 20 percent under age 16; South Carolina, 2,193 rapes, 16 percent under age 13. (States reported differently on age data.)

Of the states reporting, one in three rape victims were under age 13 in Delaware, Michigan and North Dakota; under 16 in Nebraska, Pennsylvania and Wisconsin; under 17 in Alabama; under 18 in Idaho and Washington, D.C.

Table 20.4 Forcible Rape Rates

Metropolitan Areas		States	
1. Rapid City, S.D.	99.0	1. Alaska	83.8
2. Killeen-Temple, Texas	95.8	2. Delaware	77.0
3. Ocala, Fla.	90.5	3. Michigan	71.1
4. Gainesville, Fla.	90.0	4. Washington	64.4
5. Tallahassee	88.0	5. Nevada	60.9
6. Waco, Texas	86.0	6. Texas	55.0
7. Memphis	85.8	7. Florida	53.8
8. Jacksonville	85.3	8. South Carolina	52.3
9. Anchorage	84.6	9. New Mexico	52.1
10. Yakima, Wash.	84.0	10. Oregon	51.3
Average	**43.2**	**Average**	**48.6**

Rates per 100,000 inhabitants.
From *Crime in the United States*, 1993.

Police Effectiveness ▶

Crime	Cleared by arrest
Murder	72%
Aggravated assault	58
Forcible rape	48
Robbery	24
Larceny-theft	19
Burglary	14
Motor vehicle theft	14

One measure of the effectiveness of a police force is the percentage of cases the prosecutor drops because of insufficient evidence or poor witness support. In Washington, D.C., the prosecutor drops about half of all arrests. Brian E. Forst, director of research for the Institute for Law and Social Research in Washington, says a major factor in these decisions is inadequate police work.

In Washington, a tenth of the police force accounted for half the convictions that followed arrests. "Clearly," Forst says, "some officers reveal a special skill in obtaining supportive witnesses, recovering evidence useful to the prosecutor, and in general making arrests with an eye to conviction. Most officers have no incentive for doing so, since police officers are not typically evaluated on the basis of what happens after arrest."

Another check of departmental activity can be made by examining the response to calls made to the police. A study of 2,000 calls to the St. Louis Police Department found that 25 percent of the calls were ignored. Of the 75 percent to which the police responded, arrests were made 50 percent of the time. Ten percent of those arrested went to trial, and 4 percent of those arrested were convicted.

Because of highly publicized inquiries into endemic police corruption in such cities as Albany, Boston, New York, Indianapolis and Miami, police reporters know that their editors and their readers expect them to dig into departmental integrity.

◀ Departmental Integrity

A reporter may be required to learn a new vocabulary to understand the underworld of deals, bribes and corruption. Some police officers have an "organized pad," by which they mean a secret list of underworld figures who pay them for protection. Most often, a pad contains the names of drug dealers and suppliers, vice operators and gambling operators.

The "grass eaters" are police officers who take small gratuities in connection with minor infractions, such as traffic violations, or who coerce merchants into giving them gifts and free meals. The "meat eaters" are the corrupt police who take payoffs to release suspects or who deal in drugs or perjure themselves on the witness stand.

◀ Targeting Blacks

Her story began with a hunch, says Carolyn Tuft. For years, Tuft says, blacks had been going to the *Belleville* (Ill.) *News-Democrat* newsroom to complain they had been abused by local police and wrongly arrested. "We noticed lots of blacks were being pulled over in west Belleville, taken out of their cars and handcuffed for what appeared to be routine traffic stops."

Tuft felt there was a pattern to what seemed to be harassment of black motorists in the small city of 42,000 near St. Louis. Belleville's west end is affluent and white. Its neighbor, East St. Louis, is poor and 98 percent black.

The year before, Tuft had written a series of stories about conflict of interest by the Belleville police chief and low morale in the department. Officers liked Tuft's reporting, and one of them provided the tip that cemented Tuft's hunch that the police department was engaged in an attempt to keep blacks out of Belleville.

A former officer said that the department had set up a special unit to discourage blacks from driving into west Belleville by ticketing them whenever possible.

"I then met several officers at odd hours of the night in dark bars to get the inside story on the unit," Tuft says. "Everyone backed up the account." But they worried about a story. One officer met me in a greasy spoon and tried to convince me that this story could begin a race riot in the town."

Tuft's major problem was that there was nothing in writing about the unit, no physical evidence of what it had been doing, nothing to prove what she had been told: A unit of four officers—the blue team—had been set up with the express purpose of harassing black motorists.

Carolyn Tuft

"I was determined to get the story, and determined is what you have to be," Tuft says. She knew that the proof would be in the traffic tickets. And that is where she looked.

"I spent three months in a stuffy old parking garage storage room sorting through dusty, musty old traffic tickets in banana boxes almost too heavy for me to pick up. They weighed 50 pounds each, and I weigh about 100."

Tuft looked through more than 175,000 tickets. And she interviewed many of those who were ticketed for their personal experiences. She organized her ledger entries by computer.

Finally, she was ready to write. When she finished, the story went to her city editor, Gary Dotson, who had encouraged her despite the possibility of a strong reader reaction. Then it went to the newspaper's attorneys for a libel check. Here is how the first piece begins:

Blacks receive a disproportionately higher percentage of traffic tickets in west Belleville than elsewhere in the city, an investigation by the Belleville News-Democrat shows, and former and current officers say police operated a special unit to target blacks.

The four-month investigation into 18,681 traffic tickets written by Belleville police from 1987–89 found that blacks received 42 percent of the tickets issued in west Belleville, compared with 8 percent in the rest of the city.

And a separate survey of 390 traffic tickets written this year shows the trend continues, with blacks six times more likely to be ticketed in west Belleville than in other parts of the city.

Police Chief Robert Hurst formed the special patrol shortly after he became chief in 1985, and it operated . . .

The Reaction ▶

Readers and advertisers reacted, most with anger at Tuft and the *News-Democrat*. A dozen businesses pulled their advertising, and almost 1,200 readers cancelled subscriptions.

"I received about 300 angry calls, many telling me and the newspaper to leave town," Tuft says. Some callers accused her of sleeping with a black man, and most of the those furious with the newspaper for the stories used the word *nigger* in their calls.

"I received at least half a dozen death threats. One hoped I'd be raped by a 'group of AIDS-infected wilding niggers.' "

One of Tuft's stories disclosed the city's hiring practices: Not one of the city's 384 employees was black, and in the city's 175-year history it had never hired a black, although the city has a 7 percent black population.

This revelation, she says, "caused the most hatred against me."

The Results ▶

After her series, the city hired a black sanitation worker and a black fireman and initiated an affirmative action program to hire minorities and to promote women in a manner that reflects the makeup of Belleville. Programs were set up to educate the public in racial and ethnic diversity.

Tuft's work was recognized. She won 13 local, regional and national awards, and her stories were used on the television program "60 Minutes." The *St. Louis Post-Dispatch* offered her a job, which she accepted.

Increasingly, college journalists are reporting crime on the campus as more information has become available. Crime handled by local police has always been a matter of public record. But criminal matters handled by campus security officers were covered by the Family Educational Rights and Privacy Act—the so-called Buckley Amendment—which defined campus criminal matter as "education records." And "education records" were closed to the public.

In 1992, Congress amended FERPA. It removed campus law enforcement records from the umbrella of "education records." But on some campuses, school officials still channeled criminal matters to campus disciplinary groups and did not report them to local police or the campus security office. Disciplinary hearings were usually closed.

Students in states with open-meeting laws have sought to open these hearings, some successfully, and in a few states the courts have ruled that, under the 1992 congressional amendment, disciplinary records must be open.

Local police file with the FBI each year all felonies reported to them, and these figures are available. Here are three tables listing some of these figures:

Table 20.5 Crimes on the Campus

Violent Crimes		Forcible Rape	
1. Univ. Medicine and Dentistry, Newark	85	1. Univ. Alaska, Fairbanks	8
2. Univ. Calif., Berkeley	54	2. Florida State Univ., Tallahassee	6
3. Arizona State Univ.	47	2. Boston College	6
4. Univ. Maryland	46	2. Indiana Univ., Bloomington	6
5. North Carolina State Univ., Raleigh	42	2. Jackson State Univ., Miss.	6
6. Univ. S. Florida, Tampa	40	2. Mary Washington College, Va.	6
7. Purdue	38	2. Washington State Univ.	6
7. Univ. Calif., Los Angeles	38	3. N. Arizona Univ.	5
8. Contra Costa Community College	36	3. Univ. Arizona	5
8. Texas College of Osteopathic Med.	36	3. Ball State Univ.	5
8. Texas Southern	36	3. Univ. Colorado, Boulder	5

Number of offenses reported to police.
From *Crime in the United States*.

Table 20.6 Car Theft on Campus

1.	San Diego State Univ.	135
2.	Univ. Calif., San Diego	131
3.	Univ. Calif., Los Angeles	112
4.	Calif. State Univ., Long Beach	100
5.	San Francisco State Univ.	96
6.	Calif. State Univ., Northridge	92
7.	Univ. Medicine and Dentistry, Newark	91
8.	Univ. Florida	77
9.	Florida State Univ., Tallahassee	74
10.	Univ. S. Florida, Tampa	67

Number of motor vehicles reported stolen to police.
From *Crime in the United States.*

Table 20.7 Property Crimes on Campus

1.	University of Michigan	1,845
2.	Ohio State Univ.	1,699
3.	Univ. Calif., Davis	1,602
4.	Univ. Calif., Berkeley	1,540
5.	Michigan State Univ.	1,467
6.	Arizona State Univ.	1,286
7.	University of Minnesota	1,275
8.	University of Maryland, College Park	1,214
9.	University of Arizona	1,212
10.	Indiana University	1,152

Number of crimes reported to police.
From *Crime in the United States.*

What the Beat Does to Reporters ▶

Police reporters say cynicism comes with the job. Things are seldom what they seem. A heartbroken father tells police a hitchhiker he picked up forced him out of his car at gunpoint and drove off with his 2-year-old daughter in the back seat. A distraught mother reports her 4-year-old daughter and 2-year-old son disappeared in a department store on Christmas Eve. Newspapers and television carry the woman's prayer for the safe return of her children.

Two days after the hitchhiker story is played up by Canadian newspapers and television, the child's body is found in a garbage bin in an Ontario city. The father is charged with second-degree murder; authorities say he left the child in the car on a hot day and she was asphyxiated.

Two days after a mother's tearful prayer on TV, this lead appears on a story in a New York newspaper:

> Two small Queens children whose
> mother had reported losing them in a

crowded Flushing department store on Christmas Eve were found dead in a rubblestrewn lot in East Harlem last night, and the mother and a man with whom she lives were charged with the murders.

Reporters say it is hard not to become calloused by the endless array of senseless, vicious crimes. Elinor J. Brecher of *The Courier-Journal* in Louisville, Ky., moved to features after five years on the police beat. She decided to move after she covered the murder of an elderly shopkeeper. The behavior of onlookers bothered her.

"If the senseless death of an innocent human being means no more to people than the fantasy television deaths they gorge on daily, I wanted no further part of it."

Edna Buchanan has covered 5,000 murders, and many affect her: A young father had spent six months at the bedside of his 2-year-old, who had gone into a coma after strangling herself in a recliner chair. He finally could endure no more and shot the child to death as he rocked her in his arms. The man was sent to prison with a mandatory 25-year sentence. Buchanan remains on the beat.

Newspapers report increasing complaints about crime coverage. The ombudsman for *The Fresno Bee* recommended three changes:

◀ **Crime Coverage Suggestions**

1. Stop running homicide stories in digest or shortened form. The victims deserve better.
2. Cut down on the so-called soft stories, the pieces that seem more sympathetic to the suspects than to their victims and the stories that are "overly soft on victims whose own criminal activities fostered their plight."
3. Name juvenile offenders. Readers want the "law and the media to stop protecting the identity of criminals because of their age."

"Crime in this country has been for the last 100 years one of the great evocative dramas in society," says David Simon, crime reporter for *The Baltimore Sun*. "America has always been a violent place; the reporting reflects that.

◀ **In Defense of Crime News**

"For some people who've seen enough violence on TV, they tend to turn away from the issue. But I think that's a mistake. I think that violence—violent crime, drugs, the war on drugs, the notion of a violent America—is the issue for the next decade, and the issue for the next century."

Simon wants crime reporting to cover substantive issues—the effectiveness of drug legislation, the crime bills introduced in Congress and state legislatures. And race:

The bottom line is that we come from two separate societies and the reality is that crime is affecting the black community more and more to a profound degree and that is important and that's what we should be writing about.

So I would make the argument that there's not too much crime coverage; it's just that it's misplaced. We're not telling the truth about where violence really is; we're writing about white fears of violence. . . .

Simon was critical of the media for making crime reporting an entry-level beat. "Once you get good at it you're promoted to something more dignified." The result: "You never learn anything particularly useful about crime because by the time anybody's mastered the beat, they're gone."

Cautions ▶

Garish details of rapes, homicides, suicides and assaults are considered unnecessary. Details essential to an investigation are not used, although there is no legal prohibition against using information obtained legally. Usually, police will not give reporters confessions, statements, admissions, or alibis by suspects; names of suspects or witnesses; details of sex crimes against women. (Publication of a confession or statement can jeopardize a defendant's rights.)

All names, addresses, occupations should be double-checked against the city directory, telephone book and any other available source.

Beware of sudden cleanup drives for vice, gambling. Usually, they are designed for public consumption.

When the police arrest a suspect, reporters ask for his or her arrest record or rap sheet. In many cities and states, the record may be denied or only a portion of it released. Sometimes the refusal is the result of state law. There has been a growing sensitivity among officials concerning the need to guarantee the accused a fair trial. Revelations about past crimes might compromise the defendant's rights.

Conviction data—information about a guilty plea, a conviction, or a plea of *nolo contendere*—usually can be used. Half the states make it illegal to use non-conviction data. Nonconviction material covers:

- Acquittals and dismissals.
- Information that a matter was not referred for prosecution or that proceedings have been indefinitely postponed.
- Records of arrests unaccompanied by dispositions that are more than a year old and in which no prosecution is actively pending.

State laws that seal arrest records take precedence over sunshine laws. Where there are no explicit prohibitions against the use of such records, it is permissible to use them, whatever the disposition of the arrests. Reporters can use nonconviction information that they find in public documents that are traditionally open to the press: court records of judicial proceedings, police blotters, published court opinions, wanted announcements, traffic records.

Juvenile records usually are sealed, and family court rules almost always prohibit press coverage. But there are few state laws that make it illegal to identify a juvenile as a suspect or that prohibit stories about a juvenile's conviction. Generally, the press has gone along with the contention that such publicity could make rehabilitation of the young offender more difficult.

When a 9-year-old boy turned himself in to the FBI as a bank robbery suspect, newspapers and television stations gave the story huge play. The youngster, who took $118 from a teller, held what looked like a pistol.

The newspapers and stations were unhappy about using the story but said they had no recourse. It was "pointless" not to publish a picture of the youngster,

Arrest Does Not Mean Prosecution or Prison

Typical outcome of 100 felony arrests made by police.

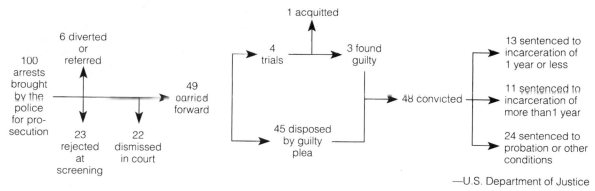

—U.S. Department of Justice

said the metropolitan editor of *The New York Times*, that was already "on television all over town."

Remember: An arrest is just that. It does not mean that the person has been charged with a crime. Charges are brought by the district attorney and indictments are made by a grand jury. When a person is arrested, the reporter can write that Jones was "arrested in connection with the robbery of a drugstore at 165 Massachusetts Ave." Or: "Jones was arrested in an investigation of the embezzlement of $45,000 from the First National Bank of Freeport."

The U.S. Department of Justice has found that half of the arrests are disposed of prior to indictment.

The police reporter monitors the police radio for reports of fires. If a fire is serious or involves a well-known building or downtown area, the reporter will go to the scene. Importance can be determined by the number of units dispatched, usually expressed in terms of the number of alarms.

◀ **Fire Coverage**

When a fire broke out in a downtown tire store at noon, it was too late for the staff of *The Anniston* (Ala.) *Star* to cover it for that day's newspaper. The presses had already started to roll. Because of the intensive radio coverage of the fire, the reporter assigned to the story knew that her piece for the next day's newspaper would have to feature some aspect other than the basic facts. Pam Newell Sohn found a feature angle and put a delayed lead on her story.

On the jump page, Sohn wrapped up the details of the fire under this lead:

> Virgil Coker Tire Service officials said today they are considering whether to rebuild a downtown Anniston warehouse blitzed by a spectacular fire Thursday.

Here are the beginnings of two fire stories that appeared in *The Tennessean* of Nashville:

A resident of an East Nashville rooming house suffered massive burns early today before fellow residents braved flames and yanked him to safety through a second-floor window.

The house at 256 Strouse Ave. was gutted by the blaze, which Metro fire officials have labeled "suspicious."

A 3-month-old Nashville girl asleep on a sofa-bed perished last night as her house went up in flames and relatives clawed in vain at an outside wall to rescue her.

The victim is the daughter of Janice Holt, who shares her 1925 16th Ave. N. home with several relatives, police said.

Firefighters arrived at the one-story dwelling off Clay Street shortly after the 6:45 p.m. call, and found the house consumed by flames, said Metro District Fire Chief Jordan Beasley.

If a fire is serious enough to merit a follow-up story, possible themes are the progress of the investigation into the cause of the fire and the conditions of the injured. Another may be the cost of replacing the destroyed structure.

Checklist: Fires ▶

Dave Kline,
Eagle-Gazette, Lancaster.

Tire Fire

The Lancaster, Ohio, fire department tries to extinguish this fire in a tire dump.

___ Deaths, injuries.
___ Location.
___ Cause.
___ When, where started.
___ How spread.
___ When brought under control.
___ Property loss: How much of structure damaged.
___ Estimated cost of damage.
___ Type of structure.
___ Measures taken to protect public safety.
___ If rescue involved, how carried out.
___ Who discovered fire.
___ Number of fire companies, firefighters assigned. (How much water used.)
___ Exact cause of deaths, injuries.
___ Where dead, injured taken.
___ Quotes from those burned out. Effect on their lives.
___ Comments of neighbors, eyewitnesses.
___ Insurance coverage.
___ Arson suspected?
___ Any arrests.
___ Unusual aspects.

Sources ▶

• Fire chief, marshal, inspector.
• Police department.
• Hospital.
• Morgue, mortuary.
• Welfare agencies, rescue groups (Red Cross).
• City building, fire inspection reports.

Entire block endangered by disabled

butane truck too near flaming building

Heroes

By PAM NEWELL SOHN
Star Staff Writer

They talked like it was all in a day's work.

. . . like anyone would work on a disabled, half-filled butane truck a few feet from a building burning out of control.

. . . like the expectation that the truck might explode and level the entire block was of no more consequence than answering a ringing phone.

Their apparent attitude: It had to be done. And the handful of men did it.

WHILE POLICE were evacuating about 100 spectators from the scene of a savage fire Thursday at Virgil Coker Tire Service on Noble Street, and while firemen were trying to tame the flames, four men ignored warnings and made fast, makeshift repairs on the tank truck. Then they half-drove, half-dragged it out of immediate danger.

The four men were Anniston Police Sgt. Mike Fincher, wrecker driver Kenneth Garrett and brothers Lamar Crosson and Buford Crosson, both employees of Virgil Coker Tire Service.

The Southern Butane Co. truck, carrying about 400 gallons of highly flammable gas, was parked for repairs near the rear of the building when a fire broke out there at about 11:20 a.m.

The front-end of the truck was near a telephone pole and could not be moved forward. Two rear wheels and the drive axle

had been removed from the truck. The empty wheel space was on the side of the burning building. Coker employees said work on the truck had reached a standstill waiting for the delivery of a new wheel hub.

WHEN IT BECAME apparent that the fire could not be extinguished quickly, some firemen and the four men began contemplating how to move the disabled truck.

Lamar Crosson said he heard mention of pulling the truck away from the blaze just as it stood. "But the (gas) valve was right there on the bottom and it could have broke and burned," said Crosson.

Crosson said that at about that time, the new hub was delivered and he and his brother began to reassemble the wheel hub and mount the tire, working between the truck and the burning building. They were assisted by fireman Jimmy Crossley, fincher and Garrett.

The men said they had to work "on and off" because of the intense smoke from the fire. And at times, according to Garrett, flames were as close as 10 feet away. When the smoke wasn't blinding and choking them, they were being doused with water from a fire pumper truck spraying cooling water on the butane tank, they said.

FINALLY, the men were able to secure one

(See Truck, Page 12A)

Cautions ▶

A New Jersey newspaper sent a young reporter to cover a fire in the business section. The fire had started in a hardware store, and the reporter asked one of the firefighters about the cause. "Looks like he had naphtha in the place," he replied, and the reporter wrote that. After the newspaper appeared, the store owner called the editor to complain that he never kept naphtha in the store. Statements about causes should be carefully handled. Only the chief, a marshal, or the fire inspector should be quoted about the cause.

Further Reading ▶

Benedict, Helen. *Virgin or Vamp, How the Press Covers Sex Crimes*. New York: Oxford University Press, 1992.

Buchanan, Edna. *Never Let Them See You Cry: More from Miami, America's Heart Beat*. New York: Random House, 1992.

Capote, Truman. *In Cold Blood*. New York: Signet, 1967.

Reiss, Albert. *The Police and the Public*. New Haven, Conn.: Yale University Press, 1971.

Reuss-Ianni, Elizabeth. *Street Cops and Management Cops*. New Brunswick, N.J.: Transaction Publishers, 1993.

21 The Courts

Files background the trial.

Preview

Coverage of state and federal courts involves:

• **Civil law:** Actions initiated by an individual, usually a person suing another individual or an organization for damages. Many actions are settled out of court.

• **Criminal law:** Actions initiated by the government for violation of criminal statutes. The legal process that begins with the arraignment of the accused and concludes with dismissal or a not-guilty verdict or sentencing after a conviction. The reporter is alert to the strategy and tactics of lawyers.

Stories about aspects of the legal system interest readers:

• Plea bargaining.
• Sentencing patterns.
• Pretrial detention, probation, judges' efficiency.
• Politics and the courts.

By the mid-1990s the number of men and women behind the bars of jails and prisons reached 1.5 million. For every one of these, five others were being processed in the criminal justice system. The number of prisoners in federal and state penitentiaries increased 80 percent in the decade since the mid-1980s.

At the same time, increasing numbers of lawsuits barraged the civil courts. People turned to these courts to claim damages for impaired health from toxic waste dumps, for what survivors claimed were cigarette-induced deaths and for injuries from automobile accidents.

The courts over the land have become overwhelmed. They are at the confluence of a swollen tide of lawmaking, crime and litigation. Watching over all this, pencil poised, is the reporter.

What a dramatic image. The truth is that the courthouse reporter constantly struggles to keep from being engulfed. The only way the reporter maintains stability in this swelling tide of words—most of which are dense and arcane—is through knowledge of the judicial system, good sources and the ability to pick out the significant and interesting stories.

There are two judicial systems, state and federal. State systems differ in detail but are similar in essentials. There are two kinds of law, criminal and civil. In criminal law, the government is the accuser. In civil law, an individual or group usually initiates the action; the government also can bring an action in the civil courts. Because crime stories make dramatic reading, the criminal courts receive

> **Terminology.** A list of officers of the court and court terms is included at the end of this chapter. When you come across a word you don't know, consult the list of Court Terms.

◄ **The Basics**

453

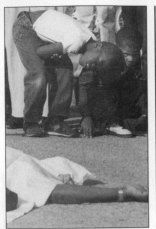

Richard Carson,
The Houston Chronicle.

Street Crime

The rising tide of violent crime has led to longer sentences for the convicted, especially for those with a record of violence.

The Federal Court System

The federal judicial system has three tiers:

District courts: Trial courts located throughout the nation.

Circuit courts: Intermediate regional appeals courts that review appeals from the district courts.

Supreme Court: Takes appeals on a discretionary basis from circuit courts.

The federal courts have power only over those matters the Constitution establishes: "controversies to which the United States shall be a party; controversies between two or more states; between a State and a citizen of another State; between citizens of different states. . . ."

the most media attention. Reporters cover the civil courts for damage suits, restraining orders and court decisions on such issues as taxes, business operations and labor conflicts.

These criminal and civil proceedings take place in state courts with a variety of titles—district, circuit, superior, supreme. The lower-level courts of original jurisdiction at the city and county levels—criminal, police, county, magistrate and the justice of the peace courts—handle misdemeanors, traffic violations and arraignments. The federal court system includes the federal district courts, the circuit courts of appeals and the Supreme Court.

The county courthouse or court reporter covers state and local courts and the office of the district attorney. The federal courthouse reporter covers the U.S. attorney, the federal magistrate and the federal courts. The magistrate arraigns those arrested and sets bail.

There are special state and local courts, such as the domestic relations or family court, sometimes called juvenile or children's court; small claims; surrogate's court (where wills are probated) and landlord-tenant court.

The court reporter's major emphasis is on the civil and criminal proceedings in the state courts of superior jurisdiction—district, superior, circuit or supreme courts—and in the federal system.

Before we go into our examination of court coverage, a note of caution: Reporting the courts has been the subject of considerable legal action. Some areas are off-limits—grand jury deliberations, certain activities of jurors—and some have been hemmed in by judicial decree. Chapter 25 surveys the continuing push-and-pull between journalists, who seek freedom to cover all aspects of the judicial system, and the courts, which have sought to limit coverage on the ground that it can compromise the defendant's right to a fair trial. Many states have press-bar guidelines.

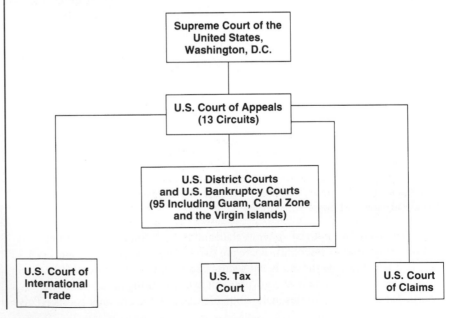

Civil law consists of two major divisions: actions at law and equity proceedings.

◀ **Civil Law**

These suits are brought for recovery of property, damages for personal injury and breach of contract. The reporter who thumbs through the daily flow of suits filed in the county courthouse singles out those in which large amounts in damages are sought and those with unusual, important or timely elements.

◀ **Actions at Law**

The following story is about a lawsuit involving unusual circumstances and a large damage claim:

OREGON CITY—A 13-year-old who broke both arms during a Little League baseball game has filed a $500,000 suit in Clackamas County Circuit Court through his guardian. It charges the Lake Oswego School District and Nordin-Schmitz, Inc., a private corporation, with negligence.

According to the suit, plaintiff Martin K. McCurdy was injured when he fell into a ditch on the boundary between the school district and Nordin-Schmitz property as he was chasing a ball during a Little League game May 16.

Caution: Lawyers often file damage suits seeking vast sums. A $1 million lawsuit is commonplace. Most damage suits are settled for far less or tossed out of court. Relatively few go to trial. The reporter examines the suit to see whether it has newsworthy elements in addition to the amount sought.

When a 26-year-old New York woman brought a $4.5 million punitive damage suit, it was news only because of the name of the defendant—Mike Tyson, then former heavyweight champion of the world—and the circumstances: The woman claimed he grabbed her breasts and buttocks and threatened her when she refused his advances in a disco. The case went to trial and the jury awarded the woman $100 in compensatory damages for his actions but declined to award any punitive damages.

Fortunate in this civil suit, Tyson had no luck later in a criminal case, as we shall soon see.

The language of the courts can be difficult, and when the reporter has mastered it, he or she must remember to define for readers all technical terms and to explain actions that appear unusual.

◀ **Explain, Explain**

Here is an example of how a reporter anticipated and then clarified a situation readers could find mystifying:

The wife of a Dallas minister was found near death from what appeared to be an attempt to strangle her. Her husband was suspected, but police said they had no evidence to charge him. The woman is in a coma.

The woman's mother sued her son-in-law in civil court and won a $16 million judgment, the money to be used for the lifetime care of the minister's wife.

Whoa, the reader says. How can a man be ordered to pay for a crime the police say they cannot charge him with? The reporter answered the question with this sentence:

> Unlike the criminal system, which requires proof beyond a reasonable doubt to convict a defendant, a civil suit requires only a preponderance of credible evidence.

Equity Proceedings ▶

The courts have the power to compel individuals and organizations to do something or to refrain from action. When such an order is requested, the complainant is said to seek equitable relief. Reporters come across these legal actions in the form of injunctions and restraining orders. Here is a story about a restraining order from the radio news wire of the UPI:

> PROVIDENCE, R.I.—A federal judge has issued a temporary order stopping efforts to put a reservist on active army duty because he refused to shave off his beard.
> District Judge Edward Day in Providence, R.I., yesterday gave the army 10 days to answer a suit filed Friday by the American Civil Liberties Union. . . .

Temporary injunctions, also known as preliminary injunctions, are issued to freeze the status quo until a court hearing can be scheduled. Thus, it makes no sense to write that the petitioner has "won" an injunction in such a preliminary proceeding (which is also called an "*ex parte* proceeding") since a permanent injunction cannot be issued until an adversary hearing is held in which both sides are heard. The respondent is ordered to show cause at the hearing—usually set for a week or two later—for why the temporary injunction should not be made final or permanent.

In this equity proceeding, a party asked the court to compel another party to take an action:

> The developers of a proposed shopping center and office complex at the intersection of Route 13 and West Trenton Avenue have asked Bucks County Court to order Falls Township to issue a building permit.
> —*Bucks County Courier Times*

Documents filed in the clerk's office usually are privileged as soon as the clerk stamps the material received. The reporter is free to use privileged material without fear of libel because it has been given official status. Statements in court also are privileged.

Pretrial and Trial ▶

A complaint lists the cause of action, the parties to the action, and the relief sought. The defendant has several alternatives. He or she may file a motion seeking to delay, alter or halt the action. He or she can ask for a change of venue or a bill of particulars or can file other motions. When the defendant is ready to contest the action, or if motions to stop the action have not been granted, he or she files an answer.

The case may then move to trial. Although there are more civil trials than criminal trials, few civil trials are covered. Reporters rely on records, lawyers and court personnel for information. Civil court stories are written on filing of the action and at the completion of the trial or at settlement.

◀ Checklist: Civil Actions

___ Identification of person or organization filing action.
___ Background of plaintiff or petitioner.
___ Defendant; respondent.
___ Type of damage alleged
___ Remedy sought.
___ Date of filing; court of jurisdiction.
___ Special motivation behind action, if any.
___ History of the conflict, disagreement.
___ Similar cases decided by courts.
___ Could suit lead to landmark decision? Is it a precedent?
___ Possibility of an out-of-court settlement.
___ Significance of action; effect on others.
___ Lawyers for both sides; types of firms they are associated with.
___ Date and presiding judge for trial, hearing.
___ Judge's reputation with similar cases.

Should the reporter cover the trial, key points for reporting are selection of the jury; relevant evidence; identification and expertise of witnesses; demeanor of witnesses on the stand; judge's rulings; pertinent material from opening and closing statements of attorneys; the damages, if any are assessed; whether the losing party intends to appeal.

Here are the essentials of verdict stories for civil actions:

◀ Checklist: Verdict Stories

___ Verdict. Damages, if awarded. (Same, less, greater than those sought.)
___ Parties involved.
___ Judge's statement, if any. Deviations by judge from jury's findings.
___ Summary of allegations by plaintiff.
___ Key testimony and attorneys' points.
___ Length of jury deliberations.
___ Comment by jurors on deliberations, verdict.
___ Any appeals or motions.

◀ Sources

Private attorneys representing plaintiff and defendant; judges and their law clerks and clerks of the court; court stenographers; county courthouse clerk or assistant who is in charge of filing such actions. The clerk is usually the best source for tips on important cases.

◀ Cautions

Negotiations between the sides often will continue even after a trial begins, and the reporter should be aware of the possibility of a sudden settlement. In many damage suits, the plaintiff threatens to go to court to support his or her demand for a certain sum or other remedy. In turn, the defendant appears to be unconcerned about the possibility of a court battle. In reality, neither side welcomes

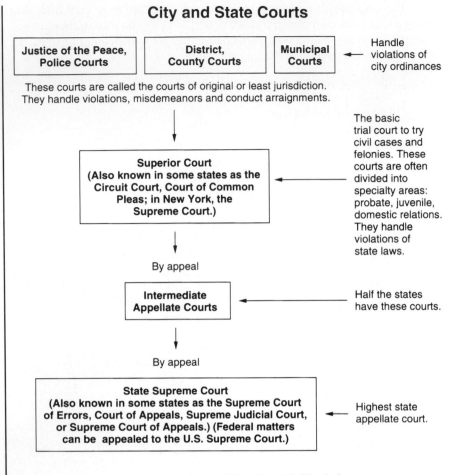

City and State Courts

Justice of the Peace, Police Courts	District, County Courts	Municipal Courts

→ Handle violations of city ordinances

These courts are called the courts of original or least jurisdiction. They handle violations, misdemeanors and conduct arraignments.

Superior Court
(Also known in some states as the Circuit Court, Court of Common Pleas; in New York, the Supreme Court.)

← The basic trial court to try civil cases and felonies. These courts are often divided into specialty areas: probate, juvenile, domestic relations. They handle violations of state laws.

By appeal

Intermediate Appellate Courts

← Half the states have these courts.

By appeal

State Supreme Court
(Also known in some states as the Supreme Court of Errors, Court of Appeals, Supreme Judicial Court, or Supreme Court of Appeals.) (Federal matters can be appealed to the U.S. Supreme Court.)

← Highest state appellate court.

the inconvenience, cost and unpredictability of a trial. The judge, too, wants a settlement. The civil courts are overwhelmed.

Attorneys for the losing side usually indicate an appeal will be filed. Do not overplay these assertions, but when an appeal is filed it can be a good story.

In civil cases, the defendant may ask the judge to dismiss the plaintiff's complaint or cause of action. Make sure to use the word *dismiss,* not *acquit,* which is a criminal term and refers to a verdict, after a full trial, by either a judge or a jury. In either a civil or criminal case, after the matter is finally decided, the judge usually orders a *judgment* to be entered in favor of the party prevailing in the action.

Criminal Law ▶

Whether it is night court where the sweepings of the city streets are gathered for misdemeanor charges, or a high-panelled district courtroom where a woman is on trial for the murder-for-hire of her wealthy husband, the criminal courts offer endless opportunities for coverage.

The assumption that underlies the criminal justice system is that an injury to the individual affects the general public. Crimes are therefore prosecuted in the name of the state as the representative of the people.

The public prosecutor, an elected official, is usually known as the district attorney, state's attorney, county attorney or people's attorney. In the federal system, the prosecutor, a presidential appointee, is called the United States attorney.

The criminal court system goes into operation shortly after the arrest and consists of pretrial and trial periods.

The pretrial period can be divided into four phases: arraignment, preliminary hearing, grand jury action and jury selection. Usually, these are accomplished in line with the constitutional provision: "In all criminal prosecutions, the accused shall enjoy the right to a speedy and public trial. . . ."

◀ Criminal Court Process

At arraignment, the defendant is told of the charges and is apprised of his or her right to an attorney and can enter a plea to the charge. If the defendant cannot afford a lawyer, the court assigns one. Arraignments are held in courts of original or least jurisdiction. These courts are empowered to try only misdemeanors and violations, such as gambling, prostitution, loitering and minor traffic offenses. In a felony case, the court will determine bail. The prosecutor is present at arraignment, and he or she may decide to dismiss or lower the charge. If a felony charge is lowered to a misdemeanor, the case can be disposed of then and there.

◀ Arraignment

The arraignment court, often called the criminal or city police court, acts like a fine-necked funnel, allowing only those felonies to pass through that the district attorney considers serious. Others are reduced to violations and misdemeanors and handled forthwith.

If the defendant pleads guilty to a misdemeanor, the court can sentence immediately. If the defendant pleads guilty to a felony charge, the case is referred to a higher court.

If a plea of not guilty is entered to a misdemeanor, the judge can then conduct a trial or preliminary hearing. For felony not-guilty pleas, the case is referred to the appropriate court for a preliminary hearing. If the preliminary hearing is waived, the defendant is then bound over to the grand jury for action. Felonies are handled by courts which are variously called district, superior or circuit courts, depending on the state.

> **O.J. Arraigned.**
> LOS ANGELES—O.J. Simpson, looking dazed and haggard, pleaded not guilty at his arraignment Monday to charges that he murdered his ex-wife and a friend of hers.
> For most of the brief session, Simpson—who was dressed in a dark suit but without tie, belt or shoelaces—stood with his head cocked to one side. He sighed deeply several times as he looked around the courtroom.

____ Formal charge.
____ Plea.
____ Bail. (Higher, lower than requested; conditional release.)
____ Behavior, statements of defendant.
____ Presentation, remarks of prosecutor, defense lawyer, judge.
____ Summary of crime.

◀ Checklist: Arraignments

Determination is made whether there are reasonable grounds, or probable cause, to believe the accused committed the offense and whether there is sufficient evidence for the case to be bound over to the grand jury. If the presiding judge considers the evidence insufficient, he or she can dismiss the charge. Also, bail can be increased, eliminated or reduced at the hearing.

◀ Preliminary Hearing

Grand Jury Action ▶

The defendant has another opportunity to seek to have the charge lowered through plea bargaining at this point in the process. Some attorneys handling criminal cases prefer to have their clients plead guilty and receive probation or a light sentence rather than risk a trial and a lengthy sentence.

The prosecutor usually goes along with plea bargaining, but if the crime is serious, the defendant has a long record or the presiding judge is convinced there is reason to believe a serious crime was committed, the case will be sent to a grand jury to decide whether the defendant should be indicted.

Here is the beginning of a story of a preliminary hearing in the federal system:

BOSTON, Dec. 24—A Harvard Law School student, who allegedly enrolled under separate identities twice in the last seven years, was ordered yesterday bound over to a United States grand jury on charges that he had falsified a federal student loan application. . . .

United States Magistrate Peter Princi found probable cause yesterday that the student falsified applications for $6,000 in federally insured loans, which helped to see him through 2½ years of law school. . . .

Criminal defendants can be brought to trial in three ways, depending on the state. In half the states, a grand jury indicts. A jury of citizens, usually 23 (of which 16 make a quorum), decides whether the evidence is sufficient for a trial on the charges brought. If 12 jurors so decide, an indictment, known as a *true bill,* is voted. If not, dismissal, known as a *no bill,* is voted. Only the state's evidence is presented to the jury.

In 20 states, the prosecutor files a charge called an *information* and a judge decides at a preliminary hearing at which witnesses testify whether there is cause for a trial. In a few states, the prosecutor files affidavits to support the charge and the judge decides whether to move to trial.

What Happens to the Defendant After Indictment

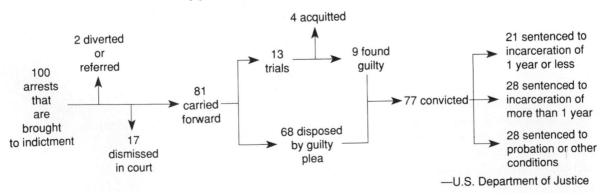

—U.S. Department of Justice

Here are leads to grand jury indictments, the first by an Indiana state grand jury, the other by a federal grand jury:

INDIANAPOLIS—Former heavyweight champion Mike Tyson was indicted here today on a charge of raping an 18-year-old Miss Black America beauty pageant contestant and on three other criminal counts.

OKLAHOMA CITY—Timothy J. McVeigh and Terry L. Nichols, former army buddies who shared a hatred for the government, were indicted by a federal grand jury today on charges of blowing up a federal building here in April with a rented truck packed with 4,800 pounds of homemade explosives.

Court Process for a Felony

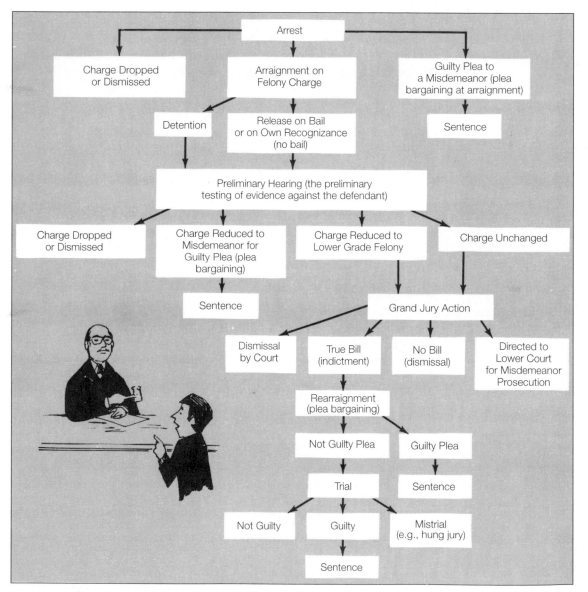

Rearraignment ▶

After the indictment, the defendant is again arraigned, this time before a judge empowered to try felony cases. If the defendant pleads not guilty, a date for trial is set and bail is set.

For example:

INDIANAPOLIS—Mike Tyson pleaded not guilty to charges he raped a beauty pageant contestant and was released on $30,000 bail.

In a 10-minute court appearance, Marion Superior Court Judge Patricia Gifford read Tyson the rape, criminal deviate conduct and confinement charges against him. If found guilty on all those charges, Tyson could face up to 63 years in prison. A trial date of Jan. 27 was set.

Plea bargaining continues at the rearraignment following grand jury indictment. Felonies, which usually are classified by degree—Class A, B, C, D and E—can be adjusted downward, a Class A felony moving down to a C or D, a Class C or D being negotiated down to a Class E felony or a misdemeanor.

Plea Bargaining ▶

Plea Bargain.

LOS ANGELES—The father of singer Marvin Gaye pleaded no contest today to voluntary manslaughter in the shooting death of his son during an argument on April 1.

The charge was reduced from first-degree murder on a plea bargain. The father could be sentenced to up to 13 years in prison, but his lawyer said he hopes to persuade the judge not to send his client to prison.

If every arrest were to be followed by a plea of not guilty and the accused granted the speedy trial promised by the Bill of Rights, the court system in every large city would collapse. The only way the courts can cope with the crush is to permit or to encourage arrangements whereby the defendant and the prosecutor agree that, in return for a lowered charge, the defendant will plead guilty. The nature of the sentence is often explicitly promised by the judge as a condition to the defendant's agreement to plead guilty.

Even serious crimes such as murder and rape are the subject of plea bargaining. In New York City, three-fourths of all murder arrests are plea bargained, and in Philadelphia three-fifths are plea bargained. Prosecutors defend the practice by saying that plea bargaining is necessary to cut down the backlog of cases in the courts. In Philadelphia, the backlog was cut from 20,000 to 13,000 through plea bargaining.

When the Bronx district attorney announced he would no longer allow plea bargaining in felony cases, legal experts said the move "could cripple the borough's criminal-justice system by overburdening judges, crowding jails and allowing some suspects to go free," *The New York Times* reported. The newspaper described the system as "a necessary evil in an overwhelmed court system," and said it is the "leading way criminal cases are decided in New York City and around the nation." Almost 85 percent of all city cases are plea bargained.

Plea bargaining continues even as the criminal trial is underway. Here is the beginning of a court story that involves plea bargaining. It was written by Joseph P. Fried of *The New York Times:*

The last defendant in the St. John's University sexual-assault case interrupted his trial yesterday to plead guilty to sharply reduced charges, then admitted he had done virtually everything he had originally been accused of.

The wrenching case came to an end in an emotional scene in a Queens courtroom in which a female spectator yelled out that the 22-year-old defendant was a "rapist" and his mother responded with screaming vituperation.

The plea bargain allowed the defendant, a student at the largest Roman Catholic university in the country who was accused with five others of what is known as acquaintance rape, to be given three years' probation. They were accused of sodomizing the victim and sexually abusing her in other ways.

After the defendant has been formally accused, several kinds of motions can be filed:

• **Motion to quash the indictment:** The defendant can challenge the legality of the indictment. If the motion to dismiss is granted, the indictment is quashed. The prosecutor can appeal the quashing. He or she also can draw up another indictment if the grand jury again hands up a true bill, even if the first has been quashed, because the constitutional protection against double jeopardy does not apply.

• **Motion for a bill of particulars:** When the defense attorney wants more details about the allegations against the accused, such a motion is filed.

• **Motion to suppress the evidence:** Evidence shown to be seized or obtained illegally may not be used in the trial if the court grants such a motion.

• **Motion for a change of venue:** A defendant who believes he or she cannot receive a fair trial in the city or judicial area where the crime took place may ask that it be transferred elsewhere. Such motions also are filed to avoid trials presided over by particular judges.

During the pretrial stage of the Tyson case, the boxer's defense team made a motion to exclude a videotape on which Tyson was supposed to have made a disparaging remark about his accuser at a news conference following his arraignment. The defense motion was upheld when the judge later ruled the tape inadmissible at the trial.

When a case emerges from the pretrial process and has been set for trial, a jury is usually empanelled. (The accused may waive the right to jury trial, in which case the judge hears the evidence in what is called a *bench trial*.)

Jurors' names are drawn from a wheel or jury box in which the names of all jurors on a jury list were placed. The list is made up of names drawn from the tax rolls, voting lists, driver's license files and so on.

Twelve jurors and several alternates are selected in a procedure during which the defense attorney and prosecutor are permitted to challenge the seating of jurors. There are two types of challenges: *peremptory,* when no reason need be given for wanting a person off the jury, and *for cause,* when a specific disqualification must be demonstrated. The number of peremptory challenges allotted each side is usually set by statute, usually 10 per side. A judge can set any number of challenges for cause.

In the Tyson case, prosecutors tried to exclude a potential juror for cause because he supposedly was biased against Tyson's accuser. The judge refused. Then the prosecution switched to a peremptory challenge, and the defense countered by

◀ **Pretrial Motions**

Motions Prepared.

LOS ANGELES—Attorneys for O.J. Simpson are laying out a battery of motions to try to undermine the case against the former football star, Simpson's lead attorney said in an interview today.

Motion Denied.

LOS ANGELES—The judge in the O.J. Simpson murder trial today denied the football great's attorneys the right to review a police detective's military records.

Simpson's lawyers are seeking to show that the detective, who found key evidence, is a racist. Judge Lance A. Ito said he found nothing in the records relevant to the case.

◀ **Jury Selection**

Alternates Chosen.

LOS ANGELES—Nine women and three men were selected yesterday as alternate jurors for the O.J. Simpson murder trial.

Immediately after the alternate panel of seven blacks, four whites and one Hispanic was sworn in, Superior Court Judge Lance Ito went into closed session with the lawyers to discuss allegations of misconduct by two members of the regular jury that was selected last month.

contending that the challenge was based solely on the defendant's race. (The U.S. Supreme Court has ruled that peremptory challenges cannot be used to exclude blacks from juries.)

"Most trials are won or lost in jury selection," says Larry Scalise, a trial lawyer who served as attorney general of Iowa. The attentive reporter can spot the strategy of the prosecution and the defense during the questioning of potential jurors. Jury selection is so important it has spawned an industry—jury consultancy. Behavioral consultants advise attorneys how to select sympathetic jurors and how to use psychological techniques to persuade juries.

Jury Consultants ▶

Jo-Ellan Dimitrius, one of about 250 jury consultants in the country, says that, in assessing prospective jurors, she seeks clues from what they take to court—their reading matter, their body language and their responses to the questions lawyers ask.

Robert B. Hirschhorn, a consultant, advised lawyers defending a young man accused of murdering a 16-year-old girl to ask potential jurors, "Can you look Kevin in the eye and say, 'Kevin, I can give you a fair trial'?"

Those who replied, "I think I can" were dismissed by the defense. Those who said yes and then "looked at their shoes, we got rid of," Hirschhorn said. Those who gave an unequivocal "yes" were accepted by the defense.

The jury acquitted Kevin.

No to Professionals ▶

Cornelius Pitts, considered one of Michigan's most effective criminal defense attorneys, says selection of "an appropriate jury" is vital. "I don't particularly care for schoolteachers or other professionals on my juries. Crimes are generally emotionally based incidents, and I want some understanding. Professionals often hold people to a higher standard."

In many of his cases, Pitts, whose law offices are in Detroit, says he is primarily trying to keep anyone with a racial bias off the jury. To detect bias in jurors, he engages in gentle questioning at first, but, he says, he will "go as far as possible trying to get responses." If someone claims no racial bias but he suspects there is, he says, "I'll ask, 'Bottom line, would you let your daughter marry a black man?'"

Potential jurors in the Tyson case were asked by defense attorneys whether they would hold a celebrity to a higher standard of conduct than they would apply to others.

The Right to Say No ▶

The Tyson prosecution asked the jurors whether they believed a woman had the right to say no: "No means no. Do you agree with that proposition?" The prosecutor then added, "If a woman says no and a man forces her against her will, that means rape."

One of those on the jury panel, a 42-year-old radio repairman, said he had trouble with that assertion because, he countered, it depended on "when did she say no and how did she say it." Suppose, he continued, a woman waited "until they're right down into doing it, that would be a little too late, wouldn't it?" The lead prosecutor used the man's question to drive home his point that a woman is in control of her body and has the right to say no at any time. The man did not serve on the jury.

A reporter cannot attend all the trials conducted in the courthouse that he or she covers. A reporter may sit through opening and closing statements and key testimony, but only the most celebrated cases are covered from opening statement to verdict and sentence. Reporters cover most trials by checking with the court clerk, the prosecutor and the defense attorney.

◀ The Trial

Nancy Stone, *The Plain Dealer.*

Witness to His Mother's Murder

Here is the beginning of the story by Katherine L. Siemon and Eric Stringfellow of *The Plain Dealer* that accompanied this dramatic photograph by Nancy Stone:

Five-year-old DeVon Stapleton vividly remembers the night last spring when a stranger bludgeoned his mother to death while he watched from the back of a van.

Yesterday he spent about an hour trying to recount for a three-judge panel in Common Pleas Court what happened that night in April, how he and his mother tried to escape, and how he was left standing alone on a dark street corner after his mother was killed.

Barely tall enough to see over the witness stand and with a voice barely loud enough to be heard without a micro-

phone, DeVon pointed to the man who is on trial for the death of Ruby Stapleton.

"There, he's right there," DeVon said, shaking his finger at Reginald Jells when Assistant County Prosecutor Carmen Marino asked the boy if he saw the stranger in the courtroom.

Jells, 21, faces the death penalty for Stapleton's killing last April 18. He also is charged with kidnapping and aggravated robbery. During opening arguments yesterday, Marino said Stapleton's blood was found inside Jells' van and a footprint matching Jells' was found near the body.

Jells has denied the killing.

Jells was convicted and sentenced to death.

Trial coverage can be tricky. Testimony may move too quickly for accurate note taking, and the reporter cannot interrupt to ask for clarification of unclear questions or answers.

Because the reporter is dependent on sources who often have a stake in the trial, court transcripts are used in important trials if they can be obtained in time for publication. A friendly court stenographer can quickly run off key testimony in an emergency.

The trial procedure follows this pattern:

1. Opening statements by prosecuting attorney and the defense attorney outline the state's case and the defense or alibi of the defendant and give a general preview of the evidence.

"The opening statement is the single most important part of the trial," says Joseph W. Cotchett, a Burlingame, Calif., lawyer. "This is the time you win your case. It's the rule of primacy; the jurors hear the details of the case for the first time. You give them the critical facts you're going to prove."

2. The prosecution presents its case through testimony of witnesses and evidence. At the end of the presentation, a judge can direct a verdict of acquittal if he or she finds that the state has not established what is called a *prima facie* case, failing to present sufficient proof of the crime that is charged. The questioning by the prosecutor of his or her witness is called *direct examination.*

In direct examination of the woman who accused Tyson of raping her, the prosecutor led her to describe the event after her introductory statement: "If I was a quitter I wouldn't be here. I start what I finish," she told the jury. Then she described in three and a half hours of testimony what had happened. She said, "I was terrified. I was begging him, trying anything that would work. It just felt like someone was ripping me apart."

The story in the *Daily News* began:

INDIANAPOLIS—Mike Tyson's 18-year-old accuser testified yesterday that the former champ laughed while she wept in agony as he raped her in his hotel suite here last July.

"Don't fight me," Tyson growled menacingly during the attack as he grabbed her, pulled her clothing off and pinned her while she feebly punched his heavyweight arms and back, she testified.

"I was telling him, 'Get off me, please stop.' I didn't know what to do," the woman said, her almost childlike voice captivating the hushed courtroom as she recounted the incident.

The prosecution calls other witnesses to support the contention of its major witnesses. In the Tyson case, the prosecutor drew from Tyson's chauffeur the statement that, when the woman left the hotel and returned to the limousine, "she looked like she may have been in a state of shock. Dazed. Disoriented. She seemed scared."

3. The defense attorney may cross-examine the state's witnesses.

In a criminal defense trial, says Pitts, the Detroit defense lawyer, "relentless cross-examination is necessary. The objective is to prevent the prosecution from winning and to do what you have to attack the complainant

Graphic Photos OK.

LOS ANGELES—The judge in the O.J. Simpson case ruled yesterday that the jury will see a series of "horrible" and "disturbing" autopsy photographs of Nicole Brown Simpson and Ronald Goldman because they provide important evidence in the prosecution's case.

"The prosecution, in order to achieve the sought-after verdicts of first-degree murder, must prove deliberate and premeditated killings with malice aforethought," Superior Court Judge Lance Ito wrote. "The prosecution is proceeding on the theory that one physically superior assailant was able to overpower and slay both victims with the same sharp and pointed cutting weapon in a very short period of time."

and the complainant's witnesses to the extent their testimony is no longer credible to the jury."

Tyson's attorney spent three hours cross-examining the boxer's accuser: "Do you recall telling Tanya St. Clair that (Tyson) has the money and the build that you like? . . . Do you recall saying you like men with 'something you can hold on to?' "

In cross-examining the chauffeur, the defense attorney's questions sought to suggest that the driver was exhausted from overwork and could not have seen the woman clearly.

INDIANAPOLIS—The attorney defending Mike Tyson failed to shake his accuser from her story in more than three hours of cross-examination yesterday, but he did set the stage for other witnesses to discredit her account of what happened that night in Tyson's hotel suite.

In a rapid-fire series of questions, attorney Vincent Fuller questioned the accuser about statements she allegedly made to other contestants in the Miss Black America Pageant and to pageant participants in the days immediately preceding and following the July 19 incident in which she says she was raped by the former heavyweight boxing champion.

—*New York Post*

4. Redirect examination is permitted the prosecutor should he or she want to re-establish the credibility of evidence or testimony that the defense's cross-examination has threatened.

5. The defense may make a motion for a directed verdict of acquittal or of dismissal based on its contention the state did not prove its case.

6. The defense may call witnesses to rebut the state's case. The defendant may or may not be called, depending on the defense attorney's strategy. The prosecutor is not permitted to comment on the defendant's failure to take the stand.

Tyson's attorneys called beauty pageant contestants to testify that his accuser had flirted with him and repeatedly talked about his money. Tyson did take the stand and under questioning by his attorney said he and his accuser had engaged in consensual sex. "No, she never told me to stop. She never said I was hurting her. She never said no. Nothing."

7. The prosecutor may cross-examine the defense witnesses.

In cross-examination of the contestants, the prosecution elicited testimony that the plaintiff was naive and "not streetwise" about a date with Tyson. Tyson also was cross-examined:

INDIANAPOLIS—A visibly rattled and slightly peevish Mike Tyson, after an hour of intense cross-examination, left the stand yesterday having had some inconsistencies in his testimony highlighted but with his basic story intact.

Attacking less with a sledgehammer than with a chisel, special prosecutor J. Gregory Garrison chipped away at Tyson's testimony but refrained from grilling Tyson about precisely what went on in Room 606 of the Canterbury Hotel on the morning of July 19, when an 18-year-old beauty pageant contestant says she was raped.

—*New York Post*

In the Simpson trial, the defense introduced an expert witness who said that the killings took too long for Simpson to have committed them. On cross-examination by the prosecutor, the witness stood fast:

> LOS ANGELES—The prosecution today attacked the theory of an expert witness for O.J. Simpson that the two victims fought long and hard for their lives. But the expert, the former chief medical examiner for New York, fended off the attack and cited his long experience with murder cases.

8.   Should the state seem to weaken the defense's case through its cross-examination, the defense may engage in redirect examination of its witnesses.

9.   Rebuttals are offered on both sides. Witnesses may be recalled. New rebuttal witnesses may be called, but new witnesses ordinarily cannot be presented without the judge's permission after a side has rested its case.

Note: At any time during the trial, the defense may move for a *mistrial,* usually on the basis that some irregularity has made a fair verdict by the jury impossible. If the judge grants the motion, the jury is discharged and the trial is stopped. Since double jeopardy does not apply in such situations, the defendant can be tried again.

10.   The defense and the state offer closing arguments in which they summarize the case for the jurors. These presentations, known as *summations,* provide reporters with considerable news. Attorneys sometimes make dramatic summations before the jury.

11.   The judge charges or instructs jurors before they retire for deliberations. The judge may review the evidence, explain the law that should be applied to the facts of the case and explain the verdicts that can be reached. The jury must accept the judge's explanation of the law but is the sole judge of the facts in the case.

12.   Jury deliberations may be short or extended. In important trials, the reporter may want to stay with the jury until deadline because verdicts make headlines. A jury may ask for further instructions on the law, or it may wish to review certain material from the trial. Stories can be written speculating on the meaning of lengthy deliberations or the questions the jury asks the judge.

13.   The verdict in criminal trials must be unanimous. After being discharged, jurors may report their discussions in the jury room to the press unless the judge gags the jurors. (In most states, the judge does not have the right to gag jurors, and the First Amendment would seem to forbid such power anywhere.) A jury may return a verdict of guilty or not guilty. If the jury reports it is hopelessly deadlocked, the judge declares a mistrial because of the *hung jury.* After a verdict of guilty, the defense may file to set aside the verdict, or it may make a motion for a new trial. The motion usually is denied but the decision can be appealed.

Ventura County Star.

Simpson Verdict

Many newspapers gave over much of their front pages to the jury's decision that O.J. Simpson was not guilty.

The time the jury deliberated, the counts on which the jury convicted and the possible length of the sentence(s) must be included in the verdict story.

INDIANAPOLIS, Feb. 10—Mike Tyson, the former heavyweight champion and one of the world's most recognized figures in and out of boxing, was found guilty tonight of raping an 18-year-old beauty pageant contestant last July.

In a verdict handed down almost 10 hours after it went to the jury, Mr. Tyson was found guilty on one count of rape and two counts of criminal deviate conduct.

Sentencing is set for March 6. Each of the counts carries a maximum sentence of six to 20 years. Under Indiana law, Mr. Tyson will likely receive an eight to 12 year sentence as a first-time offender with a juvenile record, Reuters reported.

—*The New York Times*

In the case of an acquittal, the time of deliberation, the charge and the length of the trial usually go into the lead. In some cases, the makeup of the jury is considered relevant, as in this lead:

LOS ANGELES—O.J. Simpson was found not guilty of the murders of his ex-wife and her friend after a year-long trial that attracted world-wide attention.

The jury of eight blacks, two whites and one Hispanic reached their verdict yesterday after less than four hours of deliberation. The verdict was announced today in Superior Court by Judge Lance Ito.

14. The sentence may be pronounced immediately after the verdict or later, pending a probation report. State laws usually set ranges—minimum and maximum sentences—that may be imposed.

◀ Sentencing

INDIANAPOLIS, March 26—Mike Tyson, the former heavyweight champion who was convicted of rape last month, was sentenced to 10 years in prison today. But the judge suspended the last four years, meaning he will spend no more than six years behind bars.

In a rape case that has attracted worldwide attention and prompted debate about sexual roles and racial attitudes in the criminal justice system, Mr. Tyson is likely to be freed in three years with time off for good behavior.

—*The New York Times*

Convictions on more than one count can lead to concurrent or consecutive sentences. A judge also may issue a suspended sentence, place the defendant on probation or levy a fine.

A majority of offenders in all states are placed under community supervision of some kind rather than incarcerated.

In some states, in trials involving the possibility of a death sentence, the jury decides the sentence following conviction, or a new jury is empanelled to decide.

> **The Full Story.** It's not enough to give the sentence in the story. Tell the reader when the convicted person could be paroled. Except for sentences that specify no parole is possible, most criminals are let out of jail long before their full sentences, even for murder. For example:
>
> He will be sentenced Feb. 6 to a mandatory life term with a possibility of parole after 9½ years.

Tougher Sentences ▶

An increasing number of states are turning from the indefinite sentence to definite or determinate sentences which are fixed by law with no judicial latitude and no parole. This is a response to the public demand that the justice system be tougher with those committing violent crimes.

Studies indicate that only 15 percent of those arrested are first-time offenders, that 60 percent are recidivists—criminals who already have served prison terms—and 25 percent have been convicted but were given probation. These findings have led to the "three strikes and you're out" laws—life sentences for three-time offenders.

Checklist:
Criminal Trials ▶

A story written at any one of the 14 stages outlined should include the current developments and the following basic information:

____ Formal charge.
____ Full identification of defendant.
____ Circumstances surrounding criminal act.
____ Summary of preceding developments.
____ Likely next stage.

Sources ▶

Private attorneys; prosecutor's office, which includes assistant prosecutors, investigators and bureau heads; legal aid attorneys; law clerks of the judges; clerks of the court; court stenographers; bailiffs and security guards; police officers; probation department; state parole office; trial judges, many of whom like to chat with reporters. Clerks also can tip off reporters to important motions, hearings and trial dates.

Look for Color,
Strategy, Tactics ▶

Material that gives the trial individuality may include the behavior of the defendant or of the defense attorney, unusual testimony. Drama is enhanced by describing the setting, the reactions of spectators and the reactions of jurors.

Stories about testimony can be dramatized by using the question-and-answer technique for crucial testimony:

Q: Can you identify the man you say attacked you?

A: Yes, I can. He is sitting there, to your right at the other table where I'm pointing.

Material for the Q and A usually is taken from the court transcript to ensure accuracy.

Reporters understand the necessity of finding patterns of strategy and tactics during a trial. Every prosecutor has a plan, and every defense attorney keys his or her presentation to a theme. Each witness, every bit of evidence is presented with a purpose. The reporter's job is to discover the design of each side in this adversary proceeding. Strategy and tactics shift with the evidence, requiring the reporter to be alert during each day's testimony. The reporter asks himself or herself: What is the purpose of this line of questioning, this witness, this piece of evidence?

This kind of coverage gives the reader, listener or viewer a sense of the movement and direction of the trial. All other coverage is episodic.

Convictions may be appealed to a higher court. In criminal cases, the appeal usually concerns errors or improper actions by the presiding judge. Sometimes, jury selection is appealed. Here is how the *Chicago Tribune* handled Mike Tyson's appeal:

Court reporters scan these decisions and then write interpretative pieces, as Mike Shaw did for *USA Today:*

Boxer Mike Tyson's rape conviction and six-year sentence was upheld Friday by a state appeals court, which rejected arguments that a judge improperly limited defense testimony.

In a 2-1 decision, the Indiana Court of Appeals ruled that the trial court acted within its authority in blocking the testimony of three witnesses who would have contradicted the woman who accused the former world heavyweight boxing champion of raping her in a hotel room in 1991.

Despite Friday's Indiana Appellate Court victory against ex-heavyweight boxing champion Mike Tyson, the reaction of his conquerors was a subdued one.

That's because the narrow decision signals danger ahead as Tyson's lawyers continue the appellate process.

Shaw quotes the dissenting opinion that stated, "my review . . . leads me to the inescapable decision that Tyson did not receive the requisite fairness that is essential to our system of criminal justice."

USA Today interviewed a friend of Tyson for his reaction to the appeals court decision and began its story this way:

Ex-heavyweight champion Mike Tyson was not shocked, but was upset when an Indiana appeals court KO'd his request for a new rape trial.

"He wasn't expecting too much from these people" longtime friend Jay Bright said Sunday. "But the day it happened he was disappointed. There was some tension in his voice. He was edgy."

The magazine *Sports Illustrated,* which came out a week after the appeals court decision, used Tyson's reaction and his lawyer's performance at his trial for its lead:

Mike Tyson was reportedly "angry and disappointed" last Friday after an Indiana court of appeals ruled 2-1 to uphold his March 1992 rape conviction. Tyson, who has served 17 months of a six-year prison sentence, would do well to consider his lawyer's role in last week's decision.

Danger: Reporter in the Courtroom

When I sat on the bench I always wondered about any reporter I saw in my courtroom. Often I knew that the reporter had no idea what I was doing, what the judicial system was about, what the language being used in the courtroom meant, and what rights were being protected and advanced through the legal system. Rarely do reporters have any expertise in the law; the vast majority come from journalism or liberal arts schools, not law schools. Covering "cops and courts" is usually an entry-level position at newspapers and is subject to general-assignment reporting at television stations. Trained court reporters are a dying breed. Turnover is high.

As a result of this ignorance of the system, the public usually gets superficial and inaccurate reporting on the judicial process. Reporters often portray the judiciary merely as an extension of the prosecutors and police, and commonly overemphasize the day-to-day proceedings of the court without looking at the entirety of the judicial system. Court reporting is therefore often inaccurate, sensational, oversimplified, distorted, and routine.

—Thomas S. Hodson

Stories About the System ▶

Court Records. With the docket number, records may be obtained, such as the police complaint, the affidavit filed by the complainant, the felony complaint, the disposition if a plea was made at the arraignment or preliminary hearing, the amount of bail. If a trial has been held, the trial record may be kept in another file, again by docket number.

Profiles ▶

Courthouse reporters are increasingly being asked to take an overview of their beats. Editors want stories about trends in the handling of criminal cases, how Supreme Court decisions affect the local judicial system, plea bargaining, new investigative techniques by the prosecutor's office, politics and the courts. Some editors want their reporters to do accountability pieces: Does the system work; are some judges giving unusually light sentences to mobsters or drug pushers; are judges efficient in clearing caseloads; are white-collar criminals being treated leniently?

Some of the most sensitive issues in setting crime control policy are bail and pretrial detention. Denial of bail resulting in detention deprives the defendant, presumed not guilty, of freedom, limits his or her participation in preparing a defense and deprives the person of earnings. Pretrial release, however, makes it possible for the defendant to commit crimes or to flee.

The court reporter can write profiles of prosecutors and defense attorneys. Diane M. Goldie began her portrait of a 41-year-old prosecutor this way in the *Sun-Sentinel* of Ft. Lauderdale, Fla.:

> Before the sun has even considered rousing itself and before most of us get our motors running each morning, Palm Beach County Assistant State Attorney Michael Gersten is setting the wheels of justice in motion.
>
> At 5 a.m., on many weekday mornings, Gersten can be found telephoning police officers to alert them that the deadline for filing a case is that day.

Bonnie Britt of the *Asbury* (N.J.) *Park Press* found that some parents—most of them fathers—were avoiding child support ordered by the courts. More than $650 million was owed in the state, but law enforcement officers did nothing to require a penny in collections. Some mothers who were owed child support, she wrote, were evicted from their homes when they could not pay rent.

 **◀ Deadbeat Dads**

Monica Rohr of the *Sun-Sentinel*'s Miami bureau described a new factor in child-custody cases. Fathers are becoming more aggressive:

◀ Aggressive Dads

In the child custody war, the stakes are high, the strategies sometimes ruthless. Everything can become a weapon—child support, visitation, accusations of child molestation.

Now, something new is happening: Dads are fighting back. They're forming support groups and lobbying for legal reform.

They say child custody procedures often push fathers out of the family picture, leaving them to pay excessive child support while being isolated from their children.

These dads say the family court system is skewed against non-custodial parents—who in 90 percent of cases are men, legal experts say.

Inequities in family court do exist, with many older judges unwilling to give fathers the same rights as mothers, says Nancy Palmer, an Orlando lawyer who is chairman of The Florida Bar's legislative committee on family law. . . .

Elizabeth Hayes, who covered the courts for *The Montgomery* (Ala.) *Advertiser,* says she is always on the lookout for features and explanatory stories about the judicial system. One piece explored the Montgomery Municipal Court, "the lowest tier of trial courts in the state system," she writes, where about 300 cases a week are heard, "including dozens of quirky disputes," such as the dog-chicken dispute. A man was arrested for shooting a gun in the city, and in the trial it transpired that the man tried to fend off a dog attacking his chicken. In the melee, the man shot his chicken.

◀ Lower Court

Hayes also described how a Supreme Court opinion forbidding prosecutors from excluding blacks from juries on the basis of race has affected local courts. Another piece examined the cost of providing indigents with defense lawyers. The underfunding, she found, has led some lawyers to contend poor defendants are not being adequately represented.

How tough are the courts on those convicted of violent crimes? A national survey found these results when it asked whether the court system dealt too harshly or not harshly enough with defendants:

◀ Getting Tough

Too harshly	3%
Not harshly enough	79
About right	12
Don't know	6

A computer check of sentences by crime committed has turned up sentencing stories for a number of newspapers and stations.

Behave or Face the Consequences

One of the techniques prison authorities are using to discipline their young prisoners is the adoption of army training procedures. Youthful offenders are given the equivalent of a basic training course, and those who refuse to abide by rules and regulations pay the consequences.

John Davenport, *The Houston Chronicle.*

Underage Drinkers ▶

Tom Puleo of *The Hartford Courant* examined the practice of arresting and trying the owners of bars for serving underage drinkers but not prosecuting the customers who had used forged and faked drivers' licenses. He found 95 percent of the underage drinkers were not arrested. After two months of stories, the state liquor control division issued a new set of guidelines calling for the arrest of the underage customers.

Sentencing Blacks ▶

The state prison population is mostly male, young and minority. Data show that almost half (48 percent) of all prison inmates are black, though the black population is 12 percent of the total. The Sentencing Project in Washington, D.C., reports that "on any given day one in four black men between the ages of 20 and 29 is in prison or on probation or parole."

In some cities, the figures are staggering: 42 percent of the black men in Washington, D.C., aged 18 to 35 are in prison; for Baltimore, the figure is 57 percent.

Does this mean that the law enforcement and judicial systems have a bias that makes for these results?

Donna Wasiczko of the *Contra Costa Times* tried to answer this question. She looked at the local situation, and while she found no definitive answers she did find some troubling indicators.

She quotes lawyers for minority defendants who do say there is bias. For example, there is a greater tendency to deny bail to black defendants, who are therefore confined while awaiting trial. All but one of the local judges (the exception is a Hispanic woman judge) are white. Most of the juries are all white.

In the county, 9 percent of the population is black. Of inmates in the state prison from Contra Costa County, 51 percent are black.

Few reporters bother with life behind bars. Once the man or woman is sentenced, coverage concludes. The work of David Ward, professor of sociology at the University of Minnesota and a four-decade student of prisoners and prisons, points the way to a trove of stories about prison life. From his research in maximum security prisons he has concluded:

◀ **Doing Time**

- Most prisoners advocate harsh measures to deter crime. "They are as concerned about what's happening in our society as everybody else. They are disgusted by child molesters and rapists and drive-by shooters. If anything, their remedies for crime are harsher than the general public's."
- Maximum security prisons, which some civil libertarians condemn, provide protection for inmates who, Ward says, told him that they "are concerned about personal safety. They're willing to give up some of the freedoms of a more open environment to feel safer."
- The general prison population is treated too leniently. "As far as I'm concerned inmates are living in hotels with amenities and people to wait on them. The staff takes care of their every need. There is not enough time for reflection."

Ward supports mandatory sentences and has little confidence in psychological counseling. He finds "not a shred of evidence that psychological treatments work."

State law closes the doors of juvenile hearings to the public. The theory is that rehabilitation is enhanced without publicity. But changes are being made in the system:

◀ **Juvenile Defendants**

- More juveniles are being tried as adults, and the hearings and trials are open.
- Because of the heinous nature of some crimes, the media are using names of juveniles.
- In states where laws are stringent, the media are seeking access to the judicial process.

When a teen-ager was accused of murder in Sioux Falls, S.D., the *Argus Leader* asked for public hearings for the defendant. By law, juvenile proceedings are closed in South Dakota unless a judge decides there are compelling reasons to open them. In response to the paper's request, the judge proposed a contract with the newspaper in which the newspaper would agree not to publish certain material such as names, photographs and addresses of witnesses or those involved in the slaying.

The *Argus Leader* declined to compromise. The newspaper and other newspapers and broadcast stations had used the juvenile's name and address and run photos of him, which the teen-ager's lawyer said violated state law.

Note: The prohibition against disclosing the names of juvenile offenders usually applies to officials, not the media, which means that if a reporter obtains a name, he or she is not prohibited from using it.

In reply to the judge's request that the newspaper limit coverage, Jack Marsh, executive editor of the *Argus Leader,* said, "Our request is that this court case be conducted in the public's full view. It would not be appropriate, nor practical, for us to be admitted to the courtroom and then be restricted in the information we publish. As the public's eyes and ears, the *Argus Leader* needs to be free to report fully what we observe."

In response, the judge said the teen-ager's right to privacy outweighs the public's right to know.

Politics and the Courts ▶

Elected or appointed, the judiciary has a deep involvement in politics. Mayors, governors, senators and the president reward party members and campaign supporters, despite their campaign promises of appointments to the bench on the basis of merit.

Picking Judges. Eight states select all of their judges in partisan elections: Alabama, Arkansas, Illinois, Mississippi, North Carolina, Pennsylvania, Texas and West Virginia.

In many areas, the path to the bench begins with a political apprenticeship, either in a campaign or in a party post. Or it may be paved with contributions to a campaign. A vacancy on the Sixth Circuit, which includes Kentucky, Ohio, Michigan and Tennessee, was considered a Tennessee seat and priority was given to Sen. James Sasser of that state. He favored Gilbert Merritt, a contributor to Sasser's campaigns. (Three contributions of $1,000 each were made to Sasser by three of Merritt's children, the oldest 12 years of age.) Merritt was given the appointment as a federal judge.

When President John Kennedy wanted congressional action on key legislation he found it bogged down in the Senate, blocked by Sen. Robert Kerr. A Kennedy aide called Kerr and asked why, and Kerr answered, "Tell him to get his dumb (expletive) brother to quit opposing my friend Ross Bohannon for a federal judgeship in Oklahoma." (Kennedy's brother, Robert, was attorney general.) Kennedy thereupon called up his brother, Bohannon was confirmed as a federal judge and Kennedy soon had Senate action on his bill.

Appointees Screened ▶

During the Reagan and Bush administrations, court appointees were screened for their attitudes toward abortion, affirmative action and First Amendment rights.

The approach that the Reagan-Bush presidencies took to the Supreme Court could be seen in George Bush's appointment of Clarence Thomas to the so-called black seat on the Court, which had been held by Thurgood Marshall. Thomas passed Bush's tests on abortion rights (against) and affirmative action (against). Marshall supported both in cases before the Court.

One of the results of the Reagan and Bush screening were nominees who were male, white and rich:

- **Reagan:** 97 percent Republican, 93 percent white, 91 percent male, more than 20 percent millionaires.
- **Bush:** 93 percent white, 89 percent male, 64 percent reporting a net worth of more than $500,000.

The Clinton administration's judicial appointees were consistent with Clinton's campaign promise to diversify the Supreme Court. His first appointee was a Jewish woman. Clinton also was sensitive to the growing conservatism of the electorate, and as a result of his appointments the Supreme Court moved closer to a centrist position on many issues.

Judicial campaigns can be so costly that some candidates have to seek campaign contributions from lawyers and others who may appear before them in the courts. Some qualified candidates refuse to consider running because of the costs of a campaign. The Fund for Modern Courts has found that among elected—as opposed to appointed—judges there are fewer women and minorities.

Good judges have come out of the political system. Some of the great justices on the Supreme Court of the United States owed their appointments to political considerations. The reporter who examines the system of election and appointment to the bench must be careful not to predict performance.

The grand jury may initiate investigations as well as act on charges brought by a prosecutor. It can look into the administration of public institutions and the conduct of local and state officials and investigate crime. In some states, grand juries must be empanelled to make periodic examinations of specific state institutions and official bodies.

◀ The Grand Jury

Special grand juries can be appointed to look into matters such as mistreatment of patients in a state hospital or a tie-in between the police vice squad and organized crime. The district attorney or the attorney general's office directs the inquiry, although the governor may appoint a special prosecutor to direct the investigation.

When a grand jury initiates action on its own and hands up a report on offenses, the report is known as a *presentment*. A presentment may be a statement of the jury's findings or it can charge a person with a crime.

Grand jury deliberations are secret and any publication of the discussions is treated severely by the courts. However, reporters are free to write about the area of investigation, and witnesses can talk to the press about their testimony in most states. Reporters often will try to learn who is testifying by stationing themselves near the jury room. Knowing the identity of witnesses, reporters are free to speculate. But the morality of publishing the names of witnesses is questionable, since the grand jury may question witnesses not directly involved in wrongdoing, and even those under suspicion are not to be considered guilty.

One way reporters have learned about witnesses is by watching for motions to dismiss subpoenas issued to require witnesses to appear before the grand jury.

Such motions are usually part of the public record and thereby provide the reporter with a document that can be reported.

In covering grand jury matters, as any pretrial proceeding, the danger is that publicity may harm innocent people or impair a defendant's right to a fair trial. Several verdicts have been reversed because of newspaper and broadcast coverage. The reporter must balance the right of the individual with the public's need to know what its official bodies are doing. Once the grand jury takes formal action, the report can be publicized.

Trouble Areas ▶

Some reporters knowingly violate or skirt the laws in obtaining information about grand jury investigations. They act in the belief that there will be no prosecution of their deeds. Sometimes they are mistaken, as the managing editor, city editor and two reporters for *The Fresno Bee* learned after their newspaper published material from a sealed grand jury transcript. They refused to reveal their source and were charged with contempt of court.

The reporter should check local and state laws, particularly when assigned to the police or court beats. Here are some actions that violate the laws of many states:

• Publishing confidential grand jury information leaked by someone in the prosecutor's office. (It is legal to use information provided by a witness about what he or she told the grand jury.)
• Using documents or property stolen from the police or an individual.
• Using confidential records transmitted or sold by the police.

In these instances, the reporter becomes an accomplice to a criminal act and can be prosecuted.

Time out for a Good Laugh ▶

Court coverage can be an unrelieved series of serious, sometimes high-tension stories. But courtrooms sometimes ring with laughter. Attorneys do crack jokes, judges deign to comment sarcastically on cases and witnesses unwittingly provide laughs:

• A reporter heard this aside in a South Dakota federal district court from a man charged with theft of livestock when the jury returned a not-guilty verdict: "Does this mean I get to keep the cows?"
• In his summation before a state district court in the Midwest, the lawyer for a man charged with armed robbery pleaded, "I ask you, ladies and gentlemen of the jury, to give the defendant your best shot."
• When a Minnesota county court judge was asked to perform a marriage for two men, the judge turned to one of them and asked, "Which one of you has the menstrual cycle?"
"Not me," said one of the men. "I got a Harley-Davidson."
• The judge in a New York case looked at the divorcing couple and announced, "I am going to give Mrs. Sheldon $3,000 a month."
"Great," her husband said. "And I'll toss in a few bucks myself."

The judicial system has a language of its own that lawyers, judges and clerks use with exactitude. The beginning reporter should learn these terms and add to them through reading and experience.

◄ Court Language

Officers of the Court

attorneys Prosecutors and defense lawyers whose duties are to represent their clients; the attorney's role is partisan, he or she is an advocate; It Is not unusual, therefore, for an attorney to try to sell his or her case to the press. The press should be skeptical of statements outside the courtroom.

bailiff Keeps order in courtroom; takes charge of the jury; sees to it no one talks to the jury.

court clerk Calls the court to order before each stage of the proceedings and administers the oath to witnesses. The clerk's office contains records of all judicial proceedings. This office is an excellent source of news.

court reporter Records the courtroom proceedings. Unless records are sealed, transcripts can be purchased; the price varies from court to court and state to state.

judge Presides over a trial, rules on points of law dealing with trial procedure, evidence and law. The jury determines the facts.

Court Terms

acquit A verdict of not guilty; the legal and formal certification of innocence of a person charged with a crime.

adjudicate To make a final determination through legal action.

adversary proceeding An action that is contested by opposing parties.

alibi Used in criminal law: to be elsewhere, in another place.

allegation The assertion, declaration or statement of a party to an action; an assertion of what is expected to be proved.

amicus curiae A friend of the court; one who interposes and volunteers information about some matter of law.

answer A pleading by which the defendant tries to dispute the plaintiff's right to recover by disproving the facts alleged by the plaintiff or the principle of law relied on by him or her, or both.

appearance The formal proceeding by which a defendant submits himself or herself to the jurisdiction of the court.

appellant The party appealing a decision or judgment to a higher court.

appellate court A court that hears appeals and reviews lower court decisions, generally on the lower court record only.

appellee The successful party in the lower court against whom an appeal is taken.

arraign In criminal practice, the formal calling of a prisoner to the bar of the court to answer charges in the indictment or to give information as to whether he or she is guilty or not guilty. The suspect is acquainted with the charge against him or her following arrest; bail is set at arraignment.

arrest The deprivation of a person's liberty by authority of the law.

autopsy The inspection and dissection of a body to learn the cause of death.

bail The security given for the release of a prisoner. Cash or a bond is placed in the court to guarantee that the person held in legal custody will appear at the time and the place the court sets. Defendants are usually entitled to be set at liberty on bail unless charged with an offense punishable by death and even sometimes in these instances. The judge or magistrate sets bail. The Constitution prohibits excessive bail.

bench warrant An order issued by the court ("from the bench") for the attachment or arrest of a person.

beneficiary One for whose benefit a trust is created.

bind over To hold on bail for trial.

booking The process whereby a suspect's name, address and purported crime are entered into a book in the police precinct or police headquarters.

bribery The receiving, offering or soliciting by or to any person whose profession or business involves the administration of public justice or who has other official status in order to influence behavior. Giving or taking a reward in connection with voting also constitutes bribery.

brief A written document prepared by counsel to serve as the basis for argument. It embodies the points of law that the counsel desires to establish.

burglary Breaking and entering the house or other property of another with intention of committing a felony, whether the felony is committed or not. Burglary does not involve a crime against a person, which is **robbery.**

certiorari An order commanding judges or officers of a lower court to certify the record of a case for judicial review by an appellate court.

challenge for cause An objection to the qualifications of a juror for which a reason is given; usually on the grounds of personal acquaintance with one of the parties or the existence of a bias that may affect the verdict.

chambers The private room or office of a judge.

change of venue The removal for trial of a suit begun in one county or district to another or from one court to another in the same county or district.

charge In criminal law, an accusation.

circumstantial evidence All evidence of indirect nature; the process of decision by which the court or jury may reason from circumstances known or proved to establish by inference the principal fact.

code A collection, compendium or revision of laws.

common law Law that derives its authority solely from usages and customs of immemorial antiquity or from the judgment and decrees of courts.

commutation The change of a punishment from a greater degree to a lesser degree, as from death to life imprisonment.

complainant A person who brings a criminal or civil action.

complaint The first or initiatory pleading on the part of the complainant, or plaintiff, in a civil action.

concurrent In a prison sentence, terms that are to be served together (not in succession). In the judge's action or opinion, an agreement.

conspiracy In criminal law, an agreement between two or more people for the purpose of committing some unlawful act.

contempt of court Any act calculated to embarrass, hinder or obstruct a court in the administration of justice or calculated to lessen its authority or dignity. Contempts are of two kinds: direct or indirect. Direct contempts are those committed in the immediate presence of the court; indirect is the term chiefly used with reference to the failure or refusal to obey a lawful order.

contract A promissory agreement between two or more persons that creates, modifies or destroys a legal relation.

cross-examination The practice whereby an opposing lawyer questions a witness at a hearing or trial.

cumulative sentence Sentences for two or more crimes to run successively rather than concurrently.

declaratory judgment One that declares the rights of the parties or expresses the opinion of the court on a question of law, without necessarily ordering anything to be done.

decree A decision or order of the court. A final decree is one that fully and finally disposes of the litigation; an interlocutory decree is a provisional or preliminary decree that is not final.

de facto In fact or actually. Usually refers to a situation or an action that has the appearance of legality and is generally accepted as such but is actually illegal.

default In an action of law, occurs when a defendant fails to plead within the time allowed or fails to appear at the trial.

defendant A person in a criminal or civil action who defends or denies the allegations.

de jure Rightful, legitimate, legal.

deposition The testimony of a witness not taken in open court in pursuance of authority given by statute or rule of court to take testimony elsewhere.

discovery A proceeding whereby one party to an action may be informed about facts known by other parties or witnesses.

dissent The explicit disagreement of one or more judges with the decision passed by the majority in a case before them.

eminent domain The power to take private property for public use by paying for it.

entrapment The act of officers or agents of a government in inducing a person to commit a crime not contemplated by him or her, for the purpose of instituting a criminal prosecution against him or her.

evidence Concrete objects presented at trial through witnesses, records and documents for the purpose of inducing belief in the minds of the trial judge or jury.

exculpatory Clearing or tending to clear from alleged guilt.

ex parte By or for one party; done for in behalf of or on the application of one party only, without notice to the other.

extradition When one state (or nation) surrenders to another state an individual accused or convicted of a crime outside its territory.

felony A crime of a graver or more atrocious nature than one designated as a misdemeanor. Usually punishable by more than one year in a penitentiary.

grand jury A jury of inquiry whose duty is to receive complaints and accusations in criminal cases, to hear the evidence presented by the state and to find bills of indictment when the jury is satisfied a trial ought to be held.

habeas corpus "You have the body." The name given a variety of writs whose object is to bring a person before a court or judge. In most common usage, it commands the official or person detaining another to produce the prisoner or person detained so the court may determine if such person has been denied liberty under due process of the law.

hearsay Evidence not proceeding from the personal knowledge of the witness.

homicide The killing of a human being.

in camera In chambers; in private.

indeterminate sentence An indefinite sentence of "not less than" and "not more than" so many years, the exact term to be served being afterwards determined by parole authorities within the minimum and maximum limits set by the court or by statute.

indictment An accusation handed up to the court by a grand jury.

indigent A poor person. In court, an indigent is usually defended by legal aid or an attorney in the public defender's office.

information A formal accusation of crime by the appropriate public official such as the prosecuting attorney. In some states, accused persons may be brought to trial by an information—a sworn, written accusation that leads to an indictment without a grand jury investigation.

injunction A mandatory or prohibitive writ issued by a court.

instruction A direction given by the judge to the jury concerning the law of the case.

jury The court-approved individuals—twelve for criminal cases and six or eight for civil cases depending on the attorneys' stipulations—who decide the guilt or innocence of defendant(s) in a trial; their verdict in a criminal case must be unanimous. (Referred to as petit juries in criminal and civil cases.)

manslaughter The unlawful killing without malice of another human being.

misdemeanor Offenses lower than felonies and generally punishable by fine or imprisonment in other than a penitentiary.

mistrial An erroneous or invalid trial; a trial that cannot stand in law because of lack of jurisdiction, wrong drawing of jurors or disregard of some other fundamental requisite.

no bill This phrase, endorsed by a grand jury on the indictment, is equivalent to "not found" or "not a true bill." It means that, in the opinion of the jury, evidence was insufficient to warrant the return of a formal charge.

nolo contendere "I will not contest it." The defendant's announcement that he or she does not contest the facts. The plea has the same legal effect as a plea of guilty, but it cannot be used as an admission of guilt elsewhere, as in a civil suit.

parole The conditional release of a prisoner from confinement. The condition usually is that if the prisoner meets the terms of the parole, he or she will be given an absolute discharge from the remainder of the sentence. If not, the prisoner is returned to serve the unexpired term.

peremptory challenge The right of parties in criminal and civil cases to dismiss a prospective juror without giving any reason. The number of such challenges is limited by statute.

plea A response to the court made by the defendant or a representative either answering the charges or showing why the defendant should not be required to answer.

plea bargaining The arrangement between prosecutor and defendant whereby the state offers to reduce the charges against the defendant in return for a guilty plea.

pleading The process by which the parties in a suit or action alternately present written statements, each responding to the other and each narrowing the controversy until one or a few points—called "the issue"—become the basis of the trial.

preliminary hearing Follows arraignment; evidence is heard to determine if a crime has been committed and whether the matter should proceed to trial. The judge may dismiss the case if he or she feels the evidence against the suspect is insufficient or was illegally obtained. If the evidence is sufficient, he or she will bind the case over to the grand jury for possible indictment. If an indictment ensues, the case is transferred to a higher court.

presentment The written action by a grand jury without an indictment; a presentment usually seeks to change the nature or operation of a particular institution that permitted offenses against the public.

probation A suspension of sentence allowing a person convicted of a criminal offense to stay out of jail during good behavior and generally under the supervision or guardianship of a probation officer.

search warrant A court order authorizing an officer or a citizen to search a specified house or other premises for evidence, stolen property or unlawful goods.

stay An action that stops or arrests a judicial proceeding by order of the court.

subpoena A process to cause a witness to appear and give testimony before a court or magistrate.

summons A notification to the named person that an action has been commenced against him or her in court and that he or she is required to appear, on the day named, and answer the complaint in such action.

suspended sentence A sentence withheld or postponed by the judge. In most cases, the suspension is indefinite and depends upon satisfactory probation reports.

term Used in some jurisdictions to denote the ordinary session of court.

tort An injury or wrong committed, either with or without force, to another person or the property of another.

unconstitutional An action or law that is contrary to the Constitution or to state constitutions. (Do not confuse with **illegal**.)

venire Technically, a writ summoning people to court to act as jurors; popularly used for the body of names thus summoned.

venue The place or county in which an injury or crime is said to have been committed.

voir dire The preliminary examination that the court or lawyers may make of a prospective juror to determine whether he or she is acceptable to decide a case as a juror.

waiver of immunity A means authorized by statutes by which a witness, in advance of giving testimony or producing evidence, may renounce the fundamental right guaranteed by the Constitution that no person shall be compelled to be a witness against himself or herself.

warrant of arrest A writ issued by a magistrate, justice or other competent authority to a sheriff or other officer requiring him or her to arrest a person therein named and bring him or her before the magistrate or court to answer to a specified charge.

writ An order issuing from a court of justice and requiring the performance of a specified act or giving authority and commission to have it done.

Further Reading ▶

Media Studies Journal. *Crime Story.* New York: The Freedom Forum Media Studies Center, 1992. This is an excellent selection of articles about police and courts by a variety of authors including judges and reporters. It is available from Media Studies, Freedom Forum New York Conference Center & Display Case Newseum, 580 Madison Avenue, New York, NY 10022. Ask for the Winter 1992 issue.

22 Sports

Dave Kline, *Eagle-Gazette,* (Lancaster, Ohio).

"Get in there . . . and jam them."

Preview

The most heavily read section of the newspaper after local news is sports news. Television coverage draws millions of viewers. The nation is made up of fans, many of them experts on the sports they follow.

The sports reporter handles:

• **Game stories:** Coverage requires the score, key plays and players, effect of the game on standings, turning point of the game and post-game interviews.

• **Profiles:** Personality stories on new players, athletes having outstanding seasons, game stars, coaches. Profiles require background, plenty of quotations, the individual in action.

• **Illegal and improper activities:** Payoffs to college players, drug use, racism, academic violations by coaches and schools, penalties to colleges.

When Susan V. Hands went to her first job to cover sports for *The Charlotte Observer,* she was anxious to investigate the growth of participant sports and to promote the development of women's athletics. Hands, the *Observer*'s first woman sportswriter, quickly shifted gears.

"I learned that people buy the morning paper to find out what happened in last night's football or basketball game. And our readers would be angry if, instead of finding the highlights and statistics of yesterday's North Carolina State basketball game, there was an investigative piece on the lack of athletic training available to girls in Charlotte high schools," she says.

Readers want to read about the game. They want to savor the important plays again, despite having seen them twice—once as they unfolded and once again, courtesy of instant replay. But the assumption that readers have seen the game on television may no longer be valid, says Frank Barrows, managing editor of the *Observer.* With so many games available to television viewers, the reporter cannot presume that the reader saw any particular game.

"Game results sell newspapers," says Hands.

Fans also want to know what goes on off the court and the field. "We take you behind the scenes," says Mark Mulvoy, the publisher of *Sports Illustrated,* whose circulation of 3 million is said to reach 16 million men and 5 million women for each issue. And that is with a subscription cost of $70 a year, one of the highest among magazines.

Insatiable Demand ▶

The appetite for sports is voracious. The Super Bowl draws 150 million viewers, and advertisers line up to spend a million dollars for a brief commercial during the game. The Associated Press assigns 100 writers to cover sports, and these writers send out more than 150,000 words a day plus statistics—enough to fill 20 pages of an eight-column newspaper. And that doesn't include the outpouring of the local sports staffs.

Then there are the sports briefs every 15 minutes on all-news radio stations. And the all-sports radio stations and television channels that broadcast everything from midget car racing to table tennis tournaments.

It wasn't always this way, of course, though the interest in sports is longstanding. Hearst and Pulitzer recognized the appeal of sports news as they waged their battle for the pennies of the emerging working class. But the plunge into sports mania, some historians say, came with a boxing match in 1926.

The Fight That Did It ▶

When the Manassa Mauler, Jack Dempsey, met the erudite Gene Tunney for the heavyweight championship, the nation—and parts of the world—stood still. Publishers who had paid sports scant attention now found that "it is impossible to print too much," reported Will Owen Jones, the editor of the *Nebraska State Journal*. Jones had been asked by the American Society of Newspaper Editors to look into the "national obsession for sporting intelligence" because the serious editors were alarmed by the interest in what they considered entertainment.

Seven hundred reporters covered the fight. They dispatched 2 million words to an enthralled public, says Bruce J. Evensen of DePaul University in his article in the *Journalism Quarterly,* " 'Cave Man' Meets 'Student Champion': Sports Page Storytelling for a Nervous Generation During America's Jazz Age." Evensen writes, "Press coverage of the Dempsey-Tunney 1926 title fight signaled the arrival of the modern sports page as a major player in the struggle for circulation."

By the way, Tunney won that match, dethroning the mighty Dempsey who had reigned as champion for seven years. The rematch the following year generated even more print, and it is still discussed on the sports pages. In the seventh round, Dempsey knocked Tunney down. But the referee did not begin to count over the downed new champ because, so it's said, Dempsey failed to go to his corner. Tunney went on to win the rematch.

To test prospective hires, some sports editors ask the applicants, "What's the 'long count'?" Those who answer, "Dempsey-Tunney, 1927," get the job.

Expanded Coverage ▶

Today's sports reporters do much more than offer a blow-by-blow account of athletic events. New areas of coverage have opened up: labor negotiations, increasing women's competition, the use of drugs by athletes, the commercialization and sometimes the corruption of college sports, high school recruiting.

Considerable man- and woman-power is devoted to this coverage. A fifth of the country's reporters are assigned to sports, more than to any other beat. And sports makes up about 20 percent of the editorial content of a metropolitan newspaper.

Participant sports have grown enormously. Hunting and fishing columns are regular features in many newspapers. Local tennis and golf tournaments attract coverage. A young journalist who fancies a sportswriting career would be wise to learn about these sports.

Fans want details. They turn to the sports pages to find out why the UCLA coach pulled his quarterback in the second half, the strategy by which Missouri managed to hold Kansas State to three baskets in the last six minutes of play. Game stories must tell the fan what happened and also how and why.

◀ Personal Lives

At one time, what athletes did off the field was their business, even if it affected their play. For example, no one tried to find out why Hank Thompson played third base so strangely for the New York Giants. "I had always supposed it was simply Thompson's way to scoop up a grounder along with the bag and whatever bits of grass and gravel were in the area and hurl the entire package across the diamond, leaving the first baseman to sort it out as best he could," said Peter Andrews of the days he covered the team.

Today, he would find out and probably report that Thompson often played third base drunk.

Alan Robinson, an AP sportswriter, says, "We're people writing about people instead of people writing about heroes. That's healthy."

◀ A Dream Realized

Jerry Tipton of the *Herald-Leader* in Lexington, Ky., wrote a moving profile of George Adams, a University of Kentucky tailback, from interviews with the football player and his friends and family. Tipton begins:

> When Ruth Adams, mother of nine, sits in the living room of her Lexington home, she can look at nine photographs of her children. Five of them are of her younger son, George.
>
> "The others get on me for having so much about George," she said. "I love them all, the grandchildren, too. But George has a special place."

Tipton develops his story slowly, and the picture that emerges is of a family with many difficulties. Adams' father drank. A brother and a sister have served time in jail. Another son, the mother said, is "in trouble."

"George never gave me no kind of trouble," she said, breaking a long pause. "He always brought good things home from school. He made me happy."

When others caused so much trouble, why didn't George?

"He saw so much pain in his mother's eyes," said Donnie Harville, who coached Adams in basketball at Lafayette High. "And he decided he wouldn't make his mother suffer more."

Tipton delves into the family's problems:

> Adams can remember seeing his father walking unsteadily down a street. The son would cross to the other side to avoid a face-to-face meeting. . . .

Yo Nagaya.
On the Mat

The so-called minor sports such as wrestling, fencing, soccer, gymnastics, swimming and track and field have fans as avid as the followers of basketball, baseball and football.

> "When I was young, it hurt a lot,"
> Adams said. "I mean a whole lot. I told
> myself I'm not going to be like that."

Adams had a dream. "If I can play pro football, the first thing I want to do with my first contract is buy my mother a house," he told Tipton.

Adams was selected in the first round of the professional football draft. He signed a four-year contract for $1.5 million, and he did buy a house for his mother.

A Career Discarded ▶

There is darkness as well as sunshine in sports, and Bill Zack's story of Eddie J. took readers into the shadowy world of drugs and crime. Eddie Johnson was an all-star guard in the National Basketball Association. At 32, he had spent eight years with the Atlanta Hawks, one in Cleveland.

A star at Auburn, he was drafted by the Hawks in 1977 on the third round. The first thing he did was buy a 924 Porsche. He had the salary to match, ranging from $300,000 to $491,000 a year in his career.

His play at Auburn was erratic, as it was in the pro ranks. No one knew he was on cocaine. Gradually, drugs took their toll and Johnson reached the end of the line. An undercover agent said he gave Johnson $20 for crack. Johnson was arrested and jailed in Florida, his home state.

At this point, Zack talked his paper, the *Gwinnett* (Ga.) *Daily News,* into letting him report what the headline writer described as "The sad saga of Eddie J."

Here is how Zack's story begins:

Morris Berman,
Pittsburgh Post-Gazette.

A Career Ended

Dazed and bloodied after being tackled in his end zone, New York Giants quarterback Y.A. Title realized his playing days were over.

TAVARES, Fla.—The man shuffled through the unlocked barred door, the chain binding his feet clinking against the floor as he eased slowly onto a wooden bench. His shirt and pants were dark blue and loose-fitting, his unsocked feet pressed into a pair of beach sandals. A small, aqua colored cross dangled from around his neck. He looked tired, older than his 32 years, his hair cropped close, a wisp of a moustache outlined above his lip.

Eddie Johnson has returned home, not in triumph, but in chains.

Zack went back as far as he could to try to understand why Johnson had destroyed himself. "I talked to as many people as I could find who knew Eddie, had grown up with him, taught him, coached him. I felt the more I knew about Eddie Johnson the easier it would be to write the in-depth piece I wanted."

He knew that he could not possibly use all the information he was gathering, but the material was important in helping him, he said, to "form and draw into focus the background you need to write effectively."

When he finally sat down, the piece "gushed forth like some kind of underground geyser. Fiction writers call this 'stepping through the window.' It's a special feeling you get in writing when the words come effortlessly and everything fits together."

Sports: The
Great Teacher ▶

Scholars as well as students, philosophers and accountants and plumbers, lawyers and laborers—all share a fascination for sports. "Most of what Americans know about the humanistic traditions—about excellence in act, about discipline, about community, about unity of body and will and spirit—they learn first-hand from their experience in sport," says Michael Novak, a writer and theologian.

In addition to covering games, the sports reporter attends sports banquets, drops by the pro shops at the golf and tennis courts, chats with the unsung athletes on the high school swimming, soccer, wrestling and track teams. The high school and college athletes who may go through a season never playing before more than a handful of spectators make for good stories. Not many readers understand why a youngster will run 10 to 20 miles a day to prepare for a cross-country meet, what it is like to engage in a noncontact sport in which the only adversary is the athlete's own mind and body. The runners, the javelin throwers, the swimmers, the gymnasts, the fencers and the wrestlers should not be overwhelmed by the glut of basketball and football coverage.

On most newspapers, a reporter will cover several sports and has a list of key contacts who can supply background quickly and accurately. Usually, the first name on the reporter's list is the athletic director or the publicity director. For high school sports, the coach is the major source.

Fans, especially the armchair expert who has made a vocation of following one of the local teams, can be excellent sources. The "sports nut," as some reporters call this person, has at his or her fingertips records, statistics and standings going back years.

◀ **The Beat**

> **Tough Beat.** Professional basketball writers say theirs is the most grueling of all sports beats. Covering games in 27 cities requires frequent travel, sometimes coast to coast twice in a week. "I take care of my body as if I were a player," says David DuPree of *USA Today.* "I don't drink or smoke." Jackie MacMullan of *The Boston Globe* says she works out daily on road trips.

◀ Enterprise

Editors count on their sports reporters to enterprise stories. In such a competitive field, the reporters who go far are those with imagination as well as talent.

When Columbia University's new football coach arrived at a New York airport, he spotted a man holding a sign with the new coach's name, "Ray Teller." Presuming the sign holder was a driver who would take him to the university, the coach walked over. "Yes, I'm Ray Teller."

But the sign holder was a reporter who was after, and was given, an exclusive interview with the new coach.

◀ Close and
Too Close

Ron Rapoport, sports columnist for the *Los Angeles Daily News,* sees two major differences between sports reporting and other coverage. One is that sports reporters are generally closer to the people they write about, often traveling with them and being around them on a regular basis. The other is that sports reporters are generally allowed more latitude in expressing their opinions. There is almost always room in the game story for why the reporter thinks the winner won and the loser lost as well as who, what, when and where. These two factors can have both a good and bad effect, says Rapoport.

"If you are around a group of people a lot, you are going to learn a great deal about them and this can only help your reporting," Rapoport says. "The flip side of this, of course, is that familiarity breeds both admiration and contempt. Some sports personalities are delightful human beings; others are selfish creeps. Yet you cannot—must not—play favorites in your coverage even while you are expressing your opinion. Likewise, the team must not become 'we.' You must guard against letting your prejudices show."

Sports reporters are fans but not team loyalists. Their loyalty is to the sport, not to any team or to the athletes they cover. The reporter has to avoid trying to please athletes who, says former pitcher Jim Bouton, expect serious coverage of some of their activities. But when "the media want to show some perspective about sports, or get behind something more important than who won or who lost, the athletes generally dislike them. . . . Generally speaking, athletes dislike the media in direct proportion to the extent that reporters exercise their journalistic responsibilities."

Wanted: Writers ▶

Sportswriting, which used to be considered hyperactive and cliché ridden, now is one of the newspaper's brightest showcases. Talented writers display their prose in news stories and columns. Truth is that sports has always brought out some of the best in writers. Consider this gem by John Updike about the last at-bat of the great Boston Red Sox outfielder Ted Williams. Williams had done the unbelievable—he hit a home run.

Though we thumped, wept, and chanted "We want Ted" for minutes after he hid in the dugout, he did not come back. Our noise for some seconds passed beyond excitement into a kind of immense open anguish, a wailing, a cry to be saved. But immortality is not transferable. The papers said that other players, and even the umpires on the field, begged him to come out and acknowledge us in some way, but he never had and did not now. God does not answer letters.

When the New York Yankees were winning pennant after pennant and Mickey Mantle was the home run king, Jim Murray of the *Los Angeles Times* wrote, "Rooting for the New York Yankees is like rooting for U.S. Steel."

Good writing means retaining the colorful language of sports, not falling into the homogeneous prose that infects too much of newspaper and television writing. Russell Baker, a columnist on *The New York Times* editorial page and a die-hard sports fan, bemoaned the decline of baseball talk that, he wrote, once "crackled with terseness, vibrancy and metaphor."

Baker had heard a television sportscaster say, "Ryan has good velocity and excellent location." He meant, Baker wrote, that "Ryan is throwing very fast and putting the ball where he wants to."

The stilted writing of some reporters makes a sports fan long for Dizzy Dean, the St. Louis Cardinals pitcher and later a sports announcer who was known for his picturesque language. Once he was struck on the toe while pitching and a doctor examined him on the mound. "This toe is fractured," the doctor said. To which Dean replied, "Fractured hell. The damn thing's broken."

Sportswriters carry stories such as the Dizzy Dean incident in their hip pockets. They also have a collection of Yogi Berra's comments handy for use when appropriate:

- It's not over 'til it's over.
- It gets late early at Yankee Stadium.
- You can see a lot just by observing.
- That place is too crowded; nobody goes there anymore.
- Ninety percent of baseball is half-mental.
- It's déjà vu all over again.

Joel Sartore,
The Wichita Eagle-Beacon.

Turning Point

The end-zone catch, the successful goal-line stand, the last-second missed three-point attempt, the ninth-inning double play—these turning points in the game usually are the ingredients of the game story lead.

Did Berra, former catcher for the New York Yankees and manager of a couple of major league teams, really say all that, or are they creations of baseball writers who needed to brighten their copy? No one is talking.

Sportswriters have written some memorable lines, such as this one about a midwestern quarterback who was a wizard on the field, a dunce in the classroom: "He could do anything with a football but autograph it." (The line came back to some sportswriters when they wrote about a football player at UCLA who was arrested for killing his drug dealer. The player, it turned out, could not read—the product of the win-at-any-price philosophy of big-time sports.)

Red Smith was a master writer. Of a notorious spitball pitcher, he wrote that "papers needed three columns for his pitching record: won, lost and relative humidity." Look at this lead he wrote about Buck Leonard, a black first baseman whose career ended before baseball was integrated:

> Wearing a store suit, horn-rimmed glasses, and a smile that could light up Yankee Stadium, a sunny gentleman of 64 revisited his past yesterday and recalled what it was like to be the black Lou Gehrig on a food allowance of 60 cents a day.

The last few words chill an otherwise warm recollection. They sum up a period of American life in a phrase.

Sportswriters are insatiable collectors of anecdotes they tuck away for use at the appropriate moment.

When an imaginative boxing promoter was trying to schedule a match between Muhammad Ali, who had made a friendly visit to Arab countries, and Mike Rossman, who carried the nicknames the Jewish Bomber and the Kosher Butcher, James Tuite of *The New York Times* recalled in his story a similar ethnic promotion. Years before, Irish Eddy Kelly and Benny Leonard, a Jewish fighter, were in the ring. Leonard was battering Kelly. Finally, in a clinch, Kelly whispered to Leonard, "Hub rachmones. [Yiddish for "take pity."] I'm really Bernie Schwartz."

Rossman, Tuite pointed out, was born Mike DePuano and took to wearing the Star of David on his trunks along with his new name to help sell tickets. The Ali-Rossman match was laughed out of the ring by pieces such as Tuite's.

When Reggie Jackson was elected to the Baseball Hall of Fame, sportswriters trundled out a battery of anecdotes about Jackson, who once referred to "the magnitude of me."

Jackson, who played with the Oakland Athletics, California Angels and New York Yankees, was a massive presence on the field: He hit 563 home runs in his 12 seasons, the sixth highest total in the history of the game, and led his teams to 11 division championships. He struck out more often (2,597) than any other player. And he was as large a force off the field as on, bragging, "I'm the straw that stirs the drink," to one reporter and to another, "I help intimidate the opposition just because I'm here."

Details. "Always look for something to make your story more colorful. Don't just say someone made a diving catch. Describe the dive. Describe the winning hit. Did it hit the wall? Did it roll into the left-field corner? Did that line drive knock off the shortstop's glove?"—AP

◄ Anecdotes

He bragged to fellow players that he had an IQ of 160, to which Mickey Rivers, a Yankee teammate, replied, "You don't even know how to spell IQ."

Rivers was a man of plain talk and said to Jackson one day as Jackson— whose full name is Reginald Martinez Jackson—was rattling on about his greatness: "You got a white man's first name, a Puerto Rican's middle name and a black man's last name. No wonder you're so screwed up."

Let 'em Talk ▶

The reporter's technique of letting the source talk works well for sports coverage. In a piece about Billy Williams, a Chicago Cubs outfielder for many years and later its batting coach, Frederick C. Klein of *The Wall Street Journal* quotes him on hitting:

> "You hear fans saying that this star or that one was a 'natural,' but 99 percent of the time they're wrong. Sure, you gotta have ability, but you also gotta work, and every good hitter I knew worked hard to get that way. You have to practice your swing all the time, just like a golf pro. And if you think golf's hard, try it sometime with a guy throwing the ball at you."

One of the best places to listen to athletes, and to ask talk-inducing questions, is the locker room.

"Right after a game when you're talking with athletes . . . that's when they're at their most vulnerable, and that's when you get the most out of a player," says Suzyn Waldman of radio station WFAN in New York, whose beat includes the New York Yankees and the Knicks. She says, "Sports is flesh and blood, people and stories, and so much humanity."

Reporting Is the Key ▶

The game trophy may seem to go to the writers of the trade. But that's a superficial assessment. Roger Angell, who covers baseball for *The New Yorker* and is called the laureate of the sport because of the high quality of his writing, calls himself a journalist, a working reporter.

He says that his reporting, his insistence on using carefully observed details in his writing, gives his work authenticity. He also knows his trade. He knows, for example, whom to interview.

Pick the wrong player, Angell says, and you get clichés.

The reporters who spend time on their beats know who the right players are, and they realize that, no matter how much they think they know about the sports they cover, there is always an insightful athlete who can add to their understanding. They seek out these players.

Starting Out ▶

Many sports reporters learn the basics covering high school sports. Cathy Henkel, sports editor of *The Seattle Times,* began her career covering high school football games for *The Register-Guard* in Eugene, Ore.

"It was the best start I could have gotten," she says.

Some aspiring sportswriters begin in high school as stringers for local and regional newspapers and stations. Then they go on to cover college sports. Sam

Smith, who covers the Chicago Bulls for the *Chicago Tribune,* was an accounting major at Pace College in New York. He liked sports and decided to cover it for the college weekly newspaper, the *Pace Press.*

The newspaper adviser spotted Smith's talent and suggested he add journalism to his studies. He did, found it a close fit with his interests and abilities and sold his accounting textbooks.

To the young reporter who can quote the pass completion records of the quarterbacks in the National Football League, being assigned to cover a high school football game may seem a letdown, if not a putdown.

Richard H. Growald, the UPI's national reporter, noted that "despite the growth in popularity of such attractions as professional football, local high school sports remains a dominant civic factor. An American may not be too familiar with the workings of his city hall, but he knows his high school football team lineup."

High school sports are the major sports entertainment in most towns and cities because they are the only local spectator sports available to these fans. For every Ohio State enthusiast, there are a dozen high school fans in the state.

"It's not uncommon in North and South Carolina for 10,000 people to watch a regular season high school football game," says *The Charlotte Observer*'s Susan Hands. "And every one of those 10,000 is a potential reader of the sports page, if his or her hometown high school hero's name is in the paper."

In fact, Hands says, the most widely read stories in the *Observer* are high school sports. Hands was responsible for covering 116 high school teams in the Carolinas. She handled most of the coverage by telephone and covered one game a week.

In Danville, Ill., the *Commercial-News* covers two local high schools and 30 area high schools as well as a local junior college and Big Ten sports at the University of Illinois and Purdue. Fowler Connell, the sports editor, says that during the school year, "football and basketball on the local scene are king, although the other sports are covered also.

"We feel we are obligated to do more for our readers than any big-city paper can possibly do. Danville and our area towns belong to 'us' and, conversely, we like to think they want us in their homes," he says.

The paper covers all home and away games of the local teams and each of the other 30 high schools at least once. If an area team is in contention for the state playoffs, the newspaper will cover it several times.

Young sportswriters sometimes try too hard. They push the language, reach too hard for words and phrases. When this happens, the result is sawdust and shavings.

Direct, slender, purposive prose flows naturally from the event. Sports has the built-in essentials of drama—conflict, leading characters, dramatic resolution. There are enough incidents and examples to highlight the event; anecdotes that illustrate the situation; high-quality quotations that reveal the nature of the individual and the event.

Good sportswriting is not confined to the big newspapers covering major teams. Jack Schlottman of *The Globe-Times* of Bethlehem, Pa., learned just

Quiz. Which sports events require the largest sportswriting team the AP sends out? The Olympics. But for annual events, it is the Indianapolis 500. The wire service stations men and women in the infield hospital, garages, the crow's nest, the pits and in the stands.

◀ Don't Push

before game time that the coach of a high school football team had benched 22 of his players for the season-ending traditional game with an intracity rival. The players had been told to go directly to their homeroom, not to stop for breakfast the morning of the game. Instead, they stopped off at a restaurant and started a food fight that led to a disturbance.

After the game that night, which the team with the benched players lost 43-0, Schlottman interviewed the coach, whose comment ended the piece:

"I'm still in the boy business and I hurt some boys tonight," the coach said. "Hopefully, I made some men."

Checklist: Games ▶

___ Result: final score, names of teams, type of sport (if necessary, explain that it is high school, college, professional). League (NFL, AFC, Big Eight, Ivy League, Adams Division).
___ Where and when game took place.
___ Turning point of game; winning play; key strategy.
___ Outstanding players.
___ Effect on standings, rankings, individual records.
___ Scoring. Details of important baskets, goals, runs, etc.; summaries of others.
___ Streaks, records involved, by team or player.
___ Postgame comments.
___ External factors: weather; spectators.
___ Size of crowd.
___ Injuries and subsequent condition of athletes.
___ Statistics.
___ Duration of game when relevant.

Leads ▶

The game story can begin with a key play or player and the score:

> BUFFALO—Bill Brooks, filling in for the injured Andre Reed, caught six passes for 109 yards and two touchdowns and lifted the Buffalo Bills to a 27-21 victory over Seattle.

If the game involves a record, this goes into the lead. In this case, the record is a negative one.

> AUBURN, Ala.—Florida's Gators had their work cut out for them this afternoon: The Auburn Tigers had not lost a home game in their coach's tenure. But a 28-point scoring spree by Florida ended the streak despite a capacity home crowd roaring and pleading for a comeback.
> The 49-38 Florida victory included four touchdown passes. . . .

Advice From a Pro: Try Again, and Again

Red Smith was always helpful to young writers. When a college student sent Smith columns he had written for his school newspaper, Smith replied:

> When I was a cub in Milwaukee I had a city editor who'd stroll over and read across a guy's shoulder when he was writing a lead. Sometimes he would approve and sometimes say gently, "Try again," and walk away.
>
> My best advice is, try again. And then again. If you're for this racket, and not many really are, then you've got an eternity of sweat and tears ahead. I don't mean just you; I mean anybody.

Charles McCabe of the San Francisco *Chronicle* wrote a column shortly after Smith's death in which he said:

> Red was nearly always the last man to leave the press room. Like Westbrook Pegler, he was a bleeder. I well remember him at the Olympic Games in Squaw Valley. When everyone else left and was up at the bar, Red sat sweating, piles of rejected leads surrounding him. He hadn't really even started his story yet. But when the lead came he wrote fluently and always met his deadline.

Smith once remarked, "The English language, if handled with respect, scarcely ever poisoned the user."

Notice that the lead does not have to include the score. With radio and television broadcasts the night before presenting the score, the print journalist can put the score in the second, sometimes even the third, paragraph:

EAST RUTHERFORD, N.J.—The Kentucky Wildcats, favored by as many as 14 points, were supposed to breeze past the Syracuse Orangemen tonight in the NCAA championship final.

But Syracuse kept coming back, once moving to within two points of the much deeper Kentucky team.

Finally, the Orangemen ran out of steam with four minutes to play and Kentucky took a hard-earned 76–67 victory.

Since many fans are experts in the sports they follow, the sports reporter has to know more than his or her readers or viewers do. When Andrea Sachs, a journalism student, was assigned to interview a jockey at a horse track, she was worried. Sachs had never been to a track and, as she put it, "I did not know the difference between a horse and a goat:

> That night, I bought a copy of *The Daily Racing Form* and two track magazines at a newsstand. I asked the man behind the counter if he knew anything about racing. He suggested that I talk to the customer standing next to me.
>
> The customer was able to give me the names of the top jockeys at the track, and he explained a little about racing.

 **◀ Quick Learning**

Track Talk

Jockey Robbie Davis, one of the country's leading riders, describes his rise from county fair tracks in Idaho to the New York–Callifornia–Florida circuit. The reporter, who had never been to a horse race, prepared for the interview by reading racing newspapers and interviewing race-goers. Sources respond to reporters who ask questions based on a knowledge of their sport.

New York Racing Authority.

Before I went to the track, I read the racing section of the newspaper. I discovered that a race was being televised that Saturday and bought another *Racing Form* and watched the race. That provided me with background knowledge and some conversation openers for my interviews.

Sachs left early for the track to watch the horses being exercised. She wandered around the track, chatting with jockeys and trainers. At the coffee stand, she asked a man to explain the betting system. Finally, it was time to interview her jockey, Robbie Davis, a youngster from Pocatello, Idaho, who had just won his first race at the track.

"He was amazingly open and willing to answer any questions. I spoke to him several times during the afternoon."

Her article for her class assignment began:

Robbie Davis' first race at Belmont was a young jockey's dream.

The shy 21-year-old apprentice jockey from Pocatello, Idaho, had driven to New York a week earlier from Louisiana Downs, where he had been riding since May. After exercising horses for a few days at Aqueduct, Davis went to Belmont in early September for the first time.

He was to ride Comanche Brave in a mile-and-an-eighth claiming race with experienced jockeys such as Angel Cordero and George Martens.

Davis recalls his feelings: "I didn't know the track at all . . . it was the biggest track I'd ever seen."

Comanche Brave went off at 20-1 odds, on a muddy track. Davis, who was used to shorter tracks, said that he watched "real close, trying to save as much horse as I could, because I knew it was a long straightaway."

The strategy worked. The next thing he knew, Davis was sitting in the winner's circle. "I couldn't believe it."

Encouraged by her instructor, Sachs sold the article to Davis' hometown newspaper, *The Idaho Journal*.

Game stories can be difficult to handle because of the pressure to meet a deadline and because of the essential similarity of the stories—one team wins, the other loses. The reporter copes with deadlines with careful preparations. This may mean arriving at a high school gym well ahead of the game to find a telephone that will be available late in the evening so that the story can be called in to the sports desk.

"With starting times constantly being pushed back—all World Series games are now played at night, for example—and deadlines always being moved forward, you simply can't have too much in your notebook too soon," says Rapoport.

"As for post-game interviews in the locker room," says Rapoport, "the two worst things a reporter can do are (a) not have a line of inquiry or some questions prepared, and (b) not deviate from this preplanning when circumstances dictate. This may sound easy but sometimes the hardest thing to do is to abandon the idea you worked so hard to formulate when something better suddenly comes along."

When she covered high school games out of town, Hands would trade information with local reporters. The exchange turned up nicknames, personal information about the players and the detail that gives a game story an individual touch.

One way to avoid trouble about game facts is to keep statistics of the event. Let us watch Hands cover a high school football game.

When she arrives at the field, she checks the program to make sure the numbers on the players' jerseys are the same as those on the program. Then she sets up her scoring sheet.

"Every sportswriter has developed his or her own method of keeping a play-by-play and statistics, and of course, each sport lends itself to a different method," she says. "It's a good idea for a beginner to check with his or her editors or other sportswriters and to try a few out on radio or TV games before trying the first one at a game. It's necessary because you can't count on being able to remember the sequence of plays, and you'd better not count on anybody else keeping statistics.

"You have to keep all the statistics you can because you can never tell what's going to be important. The game may be decided by punting. It may be decided by return yardage (which is not included in total offense). The key to the game may be one player's ability to set up tackles.

"If you can bring along a friend to spot tackles while you keep offense, that's great. Sometimes you can trade off with another sportswriter in the press box. I've never seen anybody who can keep offense and defense at the same time, but I'm told there are a couple.

◀ **Coverage Preparation**

◀ **Keeping Statistics**

"Use halftime to tally up. Sometimes it is surprising to see what the statistics reveal. They don't always match the appearances."

Hands says she does not mind doing most press box chores herself. "That way, I'm never at the mercy of PR men. I'm glad to have them help me, but I don't have to count on it," she says.

Reporters hang on to these statistics, their recollections and their score cards. Nothing beats having that one vital encounter, that one vital number close at hand. When Ben Johnson's use of steroids cost him the Olympic gold medal in the 100-meter dash at the 1988 Olympics in Seoul, it was important to remember that Johnson's chief rival, Carl Lewis, had implied Johnson used the illicit drug after losing to him a year earlier at a race in Rome. Johnson had set the world record at that meet and Lewis' remarks had been widely ridiculed as sour grapes. Johnson's time, his victory over Lewis and Lewis' vindication were all important parts of the Johnson-steroid story.

From the Players' Perspective

To see the game the right way, look at it the way the players do. The advice is given by Thomas Boswell, a sportswriter for *The Washington Post,* in his book *Why Time Begins on Opening Day* (New York: Doubleday, 1984). Boswell writes about baseball, but his suggestions apply to most sports that reporters cover:

Judge slowly. "Never judge a player over a unit of time shorter than a month . . . you must see a player hot, cold, and in between before you can put the whole package together."

Assume everybody is trying reasonably hard. ". . . giving 110 percent . . . would be counterproductive for most players. . . . Usually something on the order of 80 percent effort is about right."

Forgive even the most grotesque physical errors. "It's assumed that every player is physically capable of performing every task asked of him. If he doesn't it's never his fault. His mistake is simply regarded as part of a professional's natural margin of error."

Judge mental errors harshly. "The distinction as to whether a mistake has been made 'from the neck up or the neck down' is always drawn."

Pay more attention to the mundane than to the spectacular. "The necessity for consistency usually outweighs the need for the inspired."

Pay more attention to the theory of the game than to the outcome of the game. Don't let your evaluations be swayed too greatly by the final score. "If a team loses a game but has used its resources properly . . . then that team is often able to ignore defeat utterly. Players say, 'We did everything right but win.' "

Keep in mind that players always know best how they're playing. "At the technical level, they seldom fool themselves—the stakes are too high."

Stay ahead of the action, not behind it or even neck and neck with it. "Remember that the immediate past is almost always prelude."

Unless a game is exciting or important, Rapoport says he tends not to include much detail.

"Usually a couple of paragraphs are enough to sum up the key plays. I prefer to use the space to concentrate on one or two or three of the most interesting things that happened and to tell what the players involved or the manager thought about them.

"Often, a game story will be built around somebody who had a large effect—positive or negative—on the outcome," Rapoport says. "It is almost mandatory that we hear from this key player and, though there are some spontaneous talkers who begin at the sight of a notebook, it is almost always better to have a question in mind. This sounds simple enough, but often takes some thought. The right question will often do wonders.

"I also like to listen to what's being said by the players—not to reporters—but to each other. They often have funny conversations when they've won, sympathetic ones when they've lost. Good dialogue can dress up a story."

Listen to Edd Roush, who played for the Cincinnati Reds from 1916 to 1931 and had a lifetime .323 average. He is talking about today's ballplayers: "Don't ask me about these modern players. If they had come out to the park when I was playing we'd have run them out of town. These fellers bat .265 and think they're hitters. Their gloves are as big as two of ours and they still can't catch the ball. And they're millionaires." (From "A Visit to Edd Roush," by William Zinsser, *The American Scholar,* Winter 1989.)

Actions sometimes are as revealing as words. The small moves, the slight shift in the linebacker's position, a change in the way a guard plays his man—these details that the observant reporter picks up often mean the difference between victory and defeat. Watch a center fielder play each batter differently. Keep an eye on the way a forward moves to the basket in the second period after all his shots missed or were blocked in the first period.

"Sportswriting has survived because of the guys who don't cheer," said Jimmy Cannon, a gifted New York sports columnist. He was friendly with some of the players whose teams he covered but was never a cheerleader. In broadcasting, the premier announcer in radio's palmiest days was Red Barber, and his credo was nonpartisanship. In a warm southern drawl, he described the Brooklyn Dodgers with no greater affection than the visiting Giants or Cubs. His love was the game, not the team. His ability to call the shots impartially may have cost Barber his job when local sports coverage on television turned to the gee-whiz crowd and the rooters.

The partisanship of broadcasters has become so obvious that it has given rise to the word "homer" to describe the hometown bias of the sportscasters. The exceptions are rare. Ed Westfall, a former hockey player who does the color for New York Islanders games, saw an Islander defenseman cross-check an opponent and called it that way. But the referee gave both men two-minute penalties. Westfall showed the incident on replay and commented, "I might offend some people if I say something. But really, look at this. You see? Oh well, they each get two minutes, Morrow for giving, Franceschetti for receiving."

◀ **Game Details**

◀ **Partisanship**

Reporters do cover local teams from the point of view of the hometown fans. This is fair. But the good journalist crosses the line between reporter and rooter.

Distance Is Best ▶

The unwavering support for athletes and athletic programs despite NCAA violations, the mockery of university standards and criminal acts stem in part from reporters identifying with the teams they cover. Young reporters have to decide whether to handle sports as news or entertainment and how to treat the athletes and their coaches. Stanley Woodward, sports editor of *The New York Herald Tribune,* would shake his head at the veneration of athletes that would seep through copy. "Will you please stop godding up these ball players," he would tell his reporters.

The sports reporter who becomes too deeply involved with his or her sources might chat with the political reporter, who can provide ample evidence of what partisanship can do to a working journalist.

A certain distance—from the sports, the players and the fans—is essential.

Boosterism in Seattle ▶

Sometimes the reporter's employer is too close, as occurred in Seattle at KIRO-TV when the station president killed a story about the nationally ranked University of Washington football team. The station's special assignment team had found that the university did not pay much attention to the education or behavior of its student athletes.

In the first part of the series, reporters revealed the university's poor record for graduating players. The second part was to report that five players had ignored warrants ordering them to appear in court for offenses ranging from assault to driving without a license.

The second story was killed by the station president who said, "All it was was a great big embarrassment to a proud institution and a great football team at a point in time when we should be cheering them on." The special assignment team leader, Mark Sauter, quit. After the censorship became a big story in Seattle and staffers and the public protested, the station ran a version of the piece.

And in Nebraska ▶

At the University of Nebraska, football coach Tom Osborne succeeded in watering down a tough story about the antics of his players that was to appear in the *Omaha World-Herald.* Osborne learned that the paper was readying a page-one Sunday story that found football players had twice as many misdemeanors and alcohol-related offenses as the run of male students at the university.

Osborne called editors and complained. He was worried about the timing of the story, that if it appeared before he had completed his recruiting of high school students for the university, some might not want to attend.

The result: The story was delayed until after the recruiting deadline; it ran on a Saturday on the sports page instead of on Sunday's page one; the lead about the behavior of the players was moved down to the 15th paragraph. (The story of the newspaper's cave-in is told by Allan Wolper in *Editor & Publisher,* Oct. 28, 1995.)

At the University of Nebraska, a running back on the successful 1995–96 football team who was found guilty of misdemeanor assault charges was reinstated on the team. The player had thrown his former girlfriend to the floor and dragged her down three flights of stairs. As punishment, the university required that he attend counselling sessions, do community service and attend his classes. The director of the university women's center wondered, "Since when is going to class at a university punishment? They want him for the bowl game." He played, and Nebraska won.

The *Lexington Herald-Leader* published a series of articles describing cash payments by boosters to basketball players at the University of Kentucky. The players also received up to $1,000 each for their complimentary tickets. A player said he made $8,400 selling tickets to a lawyer. Another player said he made eight to a dozen talks at $150 each, and some said they were paid as much as $500 for a talk.

All this, the newspaper said, took place during the period Joe B. Hall coached the team. The reporters, Jeffrey Marx and Michael York, interviewed 33 players, 31 of whom said they knew of violations of the rules of the National Collegiate Athletic Association; 26 admitted receiving cash or some other kind of improper benefit during their playing careers at Kentucky.

The reaction was swift and angry. Kentucky has, in York's words, "the winningest of all college basketball programs, and basketball has been called the most widely practiced religion in the Bluegrass state."

Fans cancelled subscriptions. The newspaper received bomb threats. York was offered a bulletproof vest by a member of the police department. What was especially galling was the reaction of some radio and television journalists, most of whom lined up behind the university. An ABC affiliate said the stories were evidence of the newspaper's "self-serving sensationalism."

The reporters were awarded the Pulitzer Prize for investigative reporting.

After editorials in Oklahoma newspapers called for the resignation of Barry Switzer, the Oklahoma University football coach, fans rose up in anger. Never mind that the NCAA put the school on three years' probation for underhanded activity and accused Switzer of failing to "exercise supervisory control," and disregarding the arrest of five of his football players within two months of the suspension—three for rape, one for selling cocaine and the fifth for shooting his roommate. What counted to the fans—whose calls to a newspaper and television station were three to one against Switzer's removal—was that Switzer was a winner. Nonetheless, Switzer resigned.

Phil Dessauer, former managing editor of *The Tulsa World* who teaches journalism at the University of Tulsa, says winning "created a Sooner subculture, if not a religion, and the more than 70,000 seats in the stadium only begin to tell the extent of the fervor."

A president of the university years ago noted the football team's prowess and remarked sardonically that he hoped the state would "have a university the football team can be proud of."

◀ Hoopla in Kentucky

Bob Thayer, *The Journal Bulletin.*

Fans Cheer Reporters Observe

◀ Fervor in Oklahoma

Anger in Arizona ▶

When William J. Woestendiek was running *The Arizona Daily Star* in Phoenix, he suggested his reporters check the university football program. Clark Hallas and Bob Lowe discovered some unusual hotel bills and learned they were not for the stays of football recruits but for women. "We ran the story and the roof fell in," Woestendiek recalls. "As our reporters began an intensive investigation of every aspect of the football program, I became the target of a vicious campaign by the community.

"In more than 35 years in the business, I have never been vilified or threatened more." The threats, he said, were from "business leaders, wealthy alumni, the president of the university and other prominent citizens." Automobile dealers boycotted the newspaper. Letters threatened his family. Woestendiek bent backwards. After the first story, he held off additional pieces so that the school could respond and the team could play in the Fiesta Bowl untarnished.

When the coach failed to meet with the newspaper to answer the charges, the pieces were printed and the *Star* won a Pulitzer Prize for the investigation.

For many fans, what counts is winning, and they will tolerate such abuses as the University of Iowa's allowing some athletes to remain eligible while taking for

Chris Dawson, *The Press Democrat.*

Sore Losers

To some fans, games are serious matters, life and death struggles between powerful adversaries. And when the calls go against their team, they voice disapproval of the officiating. Some go further and stalk their prey. After a game between Drake and Petaluma high schools in California, angry Petaluma fans and players attacked a referee.

college credit such courses as karate, billiards, tennis, advanced bowling, advanced slow-pitch softball and jogging—part of the college transcript of an Iowa defensive back. The athlete's sophomore grades were three F's, one D and one C. He did have an A—for playing football. But the university kept him eligible.

A Michigan State football player was arrested for theft as a freshman and a couple of years later was arrested for breaking and entering. He served 30 days in jail for the break-in. The university did not revoke his athletic scholarship. Not serious enough, said a spokesman.

In 26 states, the football coach at the largest public university is paid more than the governor, and in 17 states the basketball coach makes more than the governor. The basketball coach at Georgetown, John Thompson, was paid $362,575, second only to the head of surgery at the university's medical school. When Thompson was being wooed by Oklahoma University, Georgetown bought a house in Washington for $350,000, which tax records show Thompson owns.

As we've seen, objective, nonpartisan coverage sometimes doesn't sit well with fans, players or their coaches. One coach got even. Norm Van Brocklin, whose long career included coaching professional football teams, remarked after being criticized for a losing season, "If I get a brain transplant, I want a sportswriter's brain. That way I'll get one that's never been used." ◀ **The Last Word**

Sports are big business. The 100 major sports universities have revenues of more than $1 billion, and No. 1 on this list is Notre Dame. Just the products the university licenses bring in $1 million a year. ◀ **Money: Illusion and Reality**

But because expenses are so high, few of the universities make a profit. Murray Sperber of Indiana University has examined sports revenues and says only 10 to 20 athletic programs consistently make money. The others, more than 2,300, lose up to a million dollars a year. The University of Michigan, for example, projected a $5.3 million annual deficit for the 1990s, despite selling out the football stadium and trips to the Rose Bowl. Deficits, says Sperber, are made up from the general education fund.

The National Association of College and University Business Officers investigated the money scene and found that seven out of 10 Division I teams lose money, and that the average profit of Division I-A programs is $39,000. All other divisions average deficits ranging from $145,000 to $782,000.

Despite the probability "that their institutions may never realize profits from intercollegiate athletics, many choose to build up their programs or selected teams for the visibility they believe major athletic programs will provide," the group reported. Some schools think high-profile programs will help them raise money, foster favor with state legislators at budget time, instill local or regional pride.

As the schools rely more on alumni contributions and booster donations, there are "opportunities for groups entirely outside of the institution to exercise financial leverage over athletics, perhaps reducing institutional control," the report stated. ◀ **Outside Control**

A similar loss of control is seen in "allowing the networks to dictate the terms and conditions for televising college sports. . . ." The report pointed to the effect on student athletes of TV's requiring away games at 9 o'clock or later on weekday nights when classes are held early the next morning.

Booster groups' paying some or all of the salaries of coaches "has led to salaries that are well above those paid to professors and senior administrators."

Dunning Students ▶ And Taxpayers

For Division I-A schools, ticket sales make up more than a third of all revenues. In all other divisions, student activity fees and student assessments unrelated to admissions to games make up the largest share of revenues.

The business officers group worried about student fees being used to support athletic programs. The fees increase the cost of education to students. This inflated cost is used by the schools and the government in determining how much student aid to make available. Taxpayers may resent devoting scarce revenues to high-visibility sports programs. The report urged university presidents to "understand how they are using tax monies as an indirect subsidy of athletics. . . ."

The area of financing intercollegiate athletics, never before a concern for sports reporters, is becoming the subject of coverage as universities cut back on academic programs and slice student aid.

Win at Any Cost ▶

The drive to build winning teams has led to lying, cheating and hypocrisy. In commenting on college sports, *The New York Times* stated that "some schools care more about winning than educating." The newspaper reported the following graduation rates for Division I-A basketball scholarship athletes who entered school from 1985 through 1988. The accounting was made after six years, to allow for those dropping out and returning:

> Arizona Univ., 20 percent; Univ. Georgia, 19; Georgia Tech, 33; Univ. Illinois, 13; Univ. Kentucky, 21; Louisville, 27; Univ. Minnesota, 19; Seton Hall, 36; Syracuse, 21.

The graduation rate for Division I-A athletes who entered school in 1988–89 was 56 percent for football players, 42 percent for male and 65 percent for female basketball players.

The *Times* pointed out that recruiting semiliterate basketball players with little chance of graduating is not the policy of all Division I-A schools. Some basketball powers do have academically qualified students on the court. Here are some of their graduation rates:

> Duke, 69 percent; Georgetown, 86; North Carolina, 82; Providence, 91; Stanford, 86; Villanova and Virginia, 83.

Some other items dug up by sports reporters:

• A three-month investigation by the Associated Press of scholarship athletes who enrolled in 1990 at the University of Florida, Florida State and Miami University showed that 27 of the 56 athletes received degrees, a graduation rate of 48 percent.

• At the Nike Camps where 120 of the best high school basketball players in the country demonstrate their athletic ability for college coaches, a test

The Most Penalized

The National Collegiate Athletic Association enforces the rules and regulations of intercollegiate athletics. Institutions that violate these agreements are subjected to penalties for their infractions that range from reducing the number of athletic grants to prohibition of postseason games.

Infractions include academic fraud and improper activities in employment of athletes, financial aid, recruiting contacts and recruiting transportation.

Here are the institutions with the largest number of public penalties levied by the NCAA:

Seven Cases
Southern Methodist University
Wichita State University
Six Cases
Arizona State University
Five Cases
Arizona, University of
Florida State University
Illinois, University of, Champaign
Kansas, University of
Kentucky, University of
Memphis State University
Minnesota, University of, Twin Cities
North Carolina State University
Oklahoma, University of
Texas A&M University
West Texas State University
Four Cases
Auburn University
California, University of, Berkeley
California, University of, Los Angeles
Cincinnati, University of
Florida, University of
Georgia, University of
Houston, University of
Southern California, University of
Western Kentucky University
Wisconsin, University of, Madison

Game Prayers. Many teams hold prayer meetings before and after games, but public displays of religion violate the First Amendment. The federal courts have ruled against a Dallas high school basketball team that paused for prayer at center court after each game and against a Florida high school football team. But some schools still engage in the practice.

showed that one-fourth read below a sixth grade level and 10 were functionally illiterate. The chancellor of Louisiana State University said that the competition for high school athletes is so intense that some of those recruited "read at the fourth-, fifth- or sixth-grade level." A North Carolina State basketball recruit was admitted with a total SAT score of 470. For signing your name and answering a single question, you can achieve a score of 400.

• The University of New Mexico basketball coach was paid $99,000 a year plus $15,000 extra if his players maintained a cumulative 2.0 grade-point average. There was no payment one year; his players averaged 1.88 on a scale of 4.0. An average of 2.0 is required for graduation.

• Over a 10-year period, the University of Louisville, a basketball power, graduated 16 percent of its scholarship players.

• Indiana University, a perennial basketball power, graduated 75 percent of its white players and no blacks from the freshman classes of 1983–87.

• Jerry Tarkanian, longtime coach of the University of Nevada at Las Vegas basketball team and frequent target of NCAA investigations, finally quit after the *Las Vegas Review-Journal* published photos of three UNLV players in a hot tub with a man convicted of fixing sports events. He now coaches at Fresno State.

• When an SMU head football coach spotted a bulletin board in a Texas high school with cards from other recruiters, he took a $100 bill and tacked it over the rival recruiters' cards and announced to prospects nearby, "That is our business card."

• Steve Courson, an offensive lineman with the Pittsburgh Steelers and the Tampa Bay Bucaneers, said he was told to take steroids as a 19-year-old sophomore on the University of South Carolina team. The team physician wrote out a prescription. In his book *False Glory,* he says steroid use was widespread among linemen, and amphetamines were pushed by coaches to get players "up" for games.

• From 1985 through 1991, not one North Carolina State basketball player earned a degree. To tighten its academic standards for athletes, the university now requires freshmen to maintain a 1.5 grade average, which is the equivalent of D+.

• Dexter Manley, a professional football player, testified before Congress that he was illiterate during the four years he played football at Oklahoma State.

• An Australian basketball player enrolled at Seton Hall University in New Jersey in October, stayed long enough to help the team make the NCAA finals and left the following April. While he was at the university, his courses included First Aid, Youth Activities, Creative Movement and Ethics.

• At Texas Christian University, a high school prospect was taken to a motel and entertained with meals and prostitutes. He signed a letter of intent. During his four seasons with TCU, he was paid $27,100 to play.

• An SMU football player told Dallas TV station WFAA, "I received $25,000 to attend SMU."

• At the University of Oklahoma, a football player was charged with shooting a teammate, and three other players were arrested and charged with gang rape. Two were sentenced to 10 years in prison. The quarterback on the same team was sentenced to two years in prison for selling cocaine.

Sports for Sale

"America is a society obsessed with winning." This is the beginning of Howard Weinberg's outline for a Bill Moyers documentary on the state of intercollegiate athletics. Weinberg had hoped to describe how the obsession corrupts sports from elementary school through high school and college. But he had to narrow his focus to college sports because there was so much to cover. Weinberg, who produced and directed the documentary, begins with a clip of Dexter Manley, who played football for four years at Oklahoma State University and then many years of professional football. Manley is testifying before Congress: "Three years ago, I just began learning to—learn how to read and write."

© Howard Weinberg.

• A community college instructor in Nevada said she was going to give a star basketball player an incomplete in a summer English correspondence course, but the grade form handed her by a college official had a C already written in. The incomplete would have made him ineligible to play for the University of Nevada at Las Vegas. The student, the nation's second highest scorer, ran into trouble at UNLV anyway when it was revealed that his tutor had written a paper for him after the player had "verbalized" his thoughts to the instructor. He was suspended from postseason play.

Tell the Story ▶

For too long, sportswriters failed to tell the story of abuses by the schools they covered. Tates Locke, a former Clemson basketball coach, says sports reporters must have known of the corruption and sleaziness in collegiate sports: "You guys are in the locker room. And when I say, 'What's going on?' and you reply, 'I don't know. I didn't see anything' that's a lie. You see what kind of clothes he wears, you see his car, you've been to his room. And he comes from the Pulpwood city limits—you gotta be kidding."

As we have seen, for those who do tell truths about the system, there can be retaliation. A story about ticket scalping by football players led to death threats to Oklahoma City reporters, and when Texas A&M football players were shown to be receiving secret payments, bricks were thrown through a Dallas editor's windows.

When Tom Witosky and a fellow reporter on the staff of *The Des Moines Register* revealed that three members of the University of Iowa basketball team had undergone substance abuse treatment during the summer at a cost to the university of $16,000, a colleague in the newsroom told him, "You have destroyed my son's faith in his hero (one of the players)." Witosky received letters and calls telling him he was a troublemaker and a racist (the players are black). A month later, two Iowa State athletes attempted an armed robbery of a Burger King and engaged in a shootout with police while trying to escape. Iowa State fans complained that the *Register's* coverage was too thorough.

When *The Montgomery Advertiser* published secretly taped conversations between a former Auburn football player and his coaches about payoffs, the football coach suggested that Auburn fans begin a subscription and advertiser boycott.

The Consequences ▶

One of the results of the continuing scandals was the appointment of the Knight Foundation Commission on Intercollegiate Athletics. After several years of looking into abuses in college sports, the commission found:

• Athletes are routinely admitted to college even though they do not come close to meeting minimal admission standards. (Jerry Tarkanian said when he was coach of the University of Nevada at Las Vegas basketball team he saw nothing wrong with admitting illiterate athletes who had no expectation of graduating.)
• Athletes often do not graduate.
• Slush funds abound.

• Almost half the big-time football programs have been punished for breaking NCAA rules.

• Athletic programs spend money so recklessly they put the health of college athletics at risk.

The commission recommended that presidents take control of their athletic departments and the money they generate, that colleges adopt a no-pass-no-play rule and that booster clubs loosen their grip on the schools' athletics and their funds. Also recommended: No more money to coaches from equipment companies for endorsements.

Schools with big-time football and basketball programs, the commission reported, are 10 times as likely as other schools to admit underqualified students who play these sports.

The commission report was greeted with skepticism by many who felt it did not go far enough. It was, said Barbara Bergmann, an economics professor at American University and a former president of the American Association of University Professors, "essentially a cheerleader for the whole regime.

"What we have to deal with and what wasn't dealt with by the commission was fake students taking fake courses. We have professional athletes on college campuses, and everything flows from that."

In his comment on the commission's four-year study, columnist Ira Berkow of *The New York Times* said nothing will change until it is left to the athletes to choose whether they will be treated as students or paid as professionals on campus. Otherwise, he wrote, "return athletics to its original intent, a basic recreation."

Attempts to tighten eligibility and to cut the number of athletic scholarships have run into vigorous opposition. Because many of the borderline athletes are black, the cry of racism has greeted attempts at reform.

◀ **Tougher Rules Rebuffed**

An example: NCAA school presidents and athletic directors, worried about the rising costs of their athletic programs, wanted to make a 10 percent cut in scholarships for men's sports. This would have reduced the number of basketball scholarships from 15 to 13.

The coaches' response was that 330 students—two-thirds of them black—would be denied a chance at a good education and the future a college education opens. *The New York Times* took editorial notice of the complaints:

Understanding this struggle requires an ear for hypocrisy and an appreciation for power plays masquerading as benign and virtuous gestures. . . . If the coaches were truly concerned about the education of minorities, why then did 44 large universities fail to graduate a *single* black basketball player who started his freshman year between 1983 and 1987? . . .

This is a reasonable request that terrifies coaches who have been allowed, for much too long, to operate in a universe of their own making.

Sports Isn't the Way out of the Ghetto

And the question arises: Can sports in fact help change the despair, and rebuild the community?

It hasn't. Once many more of us believed that sports and sports figures as models could lead us to the promised land. . . .

But today's life in the inner cities demonstrates that sports as a vehicle for change is not nearly as vital as it once was, or as we had once hoped, or expected.

It was Arthur Ashe who said, rightly, that minority kids spend too much time on the playing fields and not enough time in the libraries. There has simply been too much exploitation and offerings of false or miniscule hope in regard to minority youths in athletics. . . .

—Ira Berkow, *The New York Times* columnist

Recruiting High Schoolers ▶

The demand for winning teams by boosters, fans and television is intense, so much so that many colleges accept high school athletes with grade-school-level academic scores. They even take criminals.

Seton Hall University in New Jersey grabbed one of the country's leading high school basketball players although he could not earn more than a combined score of 700 on his SAT test. The university kept its offer open to the youth even after he pleaded guilty to sexual abuse in a plea bargain. He had sodomized a young woman on the high school stairway.

When journalists wrote about the incident, the university grudgingly rescinded its scholarship offer. Two weeks later, a major basketball power in Utah made the student an offer.

A leading schoolboy basketball player in Hampton, Va., was convicted on three felony counts of malicious wounding by mob. Would that affect his chances to play college ball? "Every school in the country wants him," Bob Gibbons, a top scout of high school basketball players, told *USA Today*. "If he was John Dillinger, they'd take him."

Why stop with recruiting high school players for college? High school sports is, as we've seen, a major attraction in hundreds of cities. High schools are recruiting. "Now the college fan is wanting to follow the kids," says Mike Lardner of Sports Channel. "Teen-agers are part of a $10 billion market."

A Case Study ▶

In a two-part series, Sam Roe of *The Blade* described how some Toledo high schools were violating state high school athletic association rules by recruiting athletes from other high schools and from junior high schools. More than half the players on one nationally ranked basketball team were transfers. Roe quoted the mother of one transfer as saying that the coach had pressured her to lie about her residence. At another basketball powerhouse, a player's mother said the coach and his aides found an apartment for her family within the school district and paid the security deposit and two months rent.

Some parents transferred "legal custody of their children to relatives in other school districts so the students can be eligible to play for the best teams," Roe wrote.

The reaction to the series was immediate. The state high school athletic association announced an inquiry, and a coalition of ministers held a rally at which Roe was denounced. More than 500 people at the rally condemned Roe, chanting, "In the South, they had Jim Crow. In Toledo, we have Sam Roe."

The group demanded a front-page retraction of the series and Roe's dismissal.

Six months later, the high school athletic association completed its investigation and placed the two high schools Roe wrote about on probation for two years and fined them $1,000 each for recruiting violations for their basketball teams.

Youngsters are lured to sports-minded high schools in ways similar to the way high school students are recruited by colleges. The same promises of a glittering future are made.

◀ Promises, Promises

Today's school basketball player is told—fairly accurately, sportswriters say—that should he make the professional ranks he will be playing for $50,000 a game. He is not told that the odds against that happening are several thousand to one.

Of the 5.4 million high school students who play varsity or junior varsity sports, one in 50 makes a college team. And of the college players, one in a thousand plays some form of professional sports.

> **10,000 to 1.** "You have a better chance of being a brain surgeon that you do of being an NBA player. Only one of every 10,000 high school players will make the pros."—Bob Minnix, NCAA director of enforcement

"In high schools, kids pursue the dream, not aware that the chance of becoming a doctor or a lawyer is much greater than that of becoming a National Basketball Association player," says Richard Lapchick, director of the Institute for Sports in Society at Northeastern University. (The Society conducts studies of sports, which are made available to journalists on request.)

Two major changes have swept through sports in the past four decades: The increasingly important role of money in amateur as well as professional sports and the inclusion of blacks and women in activities that had been closed to them.

◀ **Changes**

Twenty years ago, the average salary for a major league baseball player was $35,000 a year. Today, it is $1.1 million. Eighteen players make more than $6 million a year; 40 make more than $5 million annually. Players with .220 batting averages make more than $1 million a year, and a Pittsburgh Pirates outfielder refused to play for his team because he considered his salary of $5.2 million a year too low. He signed with the San Francisco Giants for $7.3 million a year. Cecil Fielder is paid $9,237,500 by the Detroit Tigers, $14,433 every time he bats.

◀ Money

In the old days, players stayed with one team for their entire careers. Now, they move to the call of the highest bidder, and teams are likely to trade away athletes with high salaries. Owners desert cities and move teams to what they believe are greener pastures. Historian Henry Steele Commager commented about player and team mobility, "We have nothing to be loyal to."

New Players ▶

On April 15, 1947, Jackie Robinson ran out of the Brooklyn Dodgers dugout and broke the color line in baseball. That year, recalls one of his team-mates, every opposing pitcher threw at Robinson, and opposing players baited him mercilessly. The St. Louis Cardinals were especially vituperative. In one game with the Dodgers, Enos Slaughter was an easy out but went out of his way to spike Robinson across the calf.

Robinson quietly endured the taunts and the spikings and the beanballs. But as he settled in, he became more aggressive. In 1949, as Slaughter was coming into second on what would have been a routine double play, Robinson took the throw from the shortstop and instead of relaying it to first, he planted the ball in the mouth of the sliding Slaughter. Slaughter got to his feet slowly, his mouth bloodied, teeth broken. He turned and slowly walked to the Cardinal dugout.

But the Cardinals changed, as did most other National League teams. David Halberstam recalls in his book *October 1964* that the Cardinals owner Gussie Busch visited spring training one year and noticed no black players.

"Where are our black players?" he asked a coach. He was told there were none. "How can it be the great American game if blacks can't play? Hell, we sell beer to everyone." (Busch owned the St. Louis brewery Budweiser.)

The 1964 season ended with the Cardinals, heavily dependent on black players, defeating the white New York Yankees in the World Series. The Cardinals ace pitcher in the Series, Bob Gibson, was noted for being outspoken. When told by his catcher Tim McCarver that "a colored guy is waiting for you," Gibson asked, "What color is he?"

Since Robinson's day, blacks have been the dominant figures in many sports. In baseball, over a recent dozen years, 22 of the 24 National and American League stolen-base leaders were black, as were most of the batting champions. Every rushing leader in the National Football League since 1963 has been black, and in the National Basketball Association only a few white players have led the league in scoring since 1960 and only two in rebounding since 1957.

Today, blacks make up 25 percent of baseball rosters, 40 percent of the players in the National Football League and 80 percent of the players in the National Basketball Association.

Although they make up only 6 percent of the college population, they account for more than 20 percent of all college athletes, more than 40 percent of the football players and about 60 percent of the basketball players.

At some colleges, a survey by *The Chronicle of Higher Education* found, more than half the black men on campus were athletic scholarship students.

The consequences, according to Harry Edwards, a sociologist at the University of California at Berkeley, is that a stereotype of blacks is reinforced:

> By not recruiting representative numbers of African-American students while simultaneously increasing the number of African-American athletes who are almost uniformly less qualified than the black students who are turned down, the impression is created that blacks do better in athletics because they are either disinclined or incompetent to perform academically.

Fans, Too. As Hank Aaron approached Babe Ruth's record 714 home runs, he was subjected to treatment similar to that given Roger Maris 14 years before, in 1961, when Maris' 61 home runs topped Ruth's 60 homers in a season: Anger and fury. The beloved Babe would no longer top the list. In Aaron's case, the anger had an extra dimension: "Vitriolic racial prejudice," wrote *The New York Times.* The Atlanta police provided Aaron with an armed bodyguard.

© Joel Strasser.

No Longer Insulated

Professional sports has a spotty record on diversifying its administrative offices. After years of resistance, baseball owners finally agreed to a far-reaching program. But it came only after pressure from civil rights leaders, members of Congress and the players' union. Also, it followed an incident in which Cincinnati Reds baseball owner, Marge Schott, was suspended from baseball for a year for making remarks that insulted blacks and Jews.

Even the insulated world of golf was shaken in the 1990s by revelations that many of the courses on the Professional Golfers' Association tour are associated with all-white clubs. The founder of the Shoal Creek Country Club near Birmingham said that "we don't discriminate in every other area except the blacks." The club was the site of the 1990 PGA Championship. A PGA official estimated that three out of four of the country's private clubs have restrictive membership practices.

◀ Women:
Players, Reporters

Long relegated to the sidelines of playing fields, women athletes have come into their own. Not that colleges and universities initiated the change. It took federal action requiring schools to equalize expenditures on male and female athletic programs.

Today, women engage in many intercollegiate sports, and women's basketball is a big TV draw.

Women also have stepped into the press boxes. The transition here, too, was not easy.

"I think women belong in the kitchen," said the owner of the San Francisco 49ers football team, Edward DeBartolo Jr. He was commenting after a federal judge ruled that the National Football League team had to grant equal access to its locker room to a female sports reporter for *The Sacramento Bee.* Many athletes wanted no women in locker rooms either.

That's part of history. There are now more than 200 women reporting sports. "The battle is over. Equal access is the law," says Ron Rapoport, whose book, *A Kind of Grace,* contains 73 articles by women sportswriters.

Women Now in the Running in the Sports Scene

For generations, women's participation in sports lacked the intense competition that marked men's sports. Women athletes were supposed to be "ladylike." But with the changes in gender roles and the passage of Title IX (which prohibits educational institutions from discriminating on the basis of sex), women were encouraged to take part in all sports. The number of women in intercollegiate athletics grew from 16,000 in 1966 to more than 10 times that total today. From high school through college, women take part in most sports. Here Montana high school students compete in the 400-meter relay at a state meet.

Bob Zellar, *The Billings Gazette.*

Women Sports Reporters

The distance women reporters have traveled is revealed by an incident Rapoport describes involving Lesley Visser, a television sports reporter. When Visser graduated from Boston College in 1976, the *Boston Globe* assigned her to cover the New England Patriots professional football team. She was the first female beat writer in the National Football League.

After a Patriots game with the Pittsburgh Steelers, Visser waited outside the Steelers locker room to interview quarterback Terry Bradshaw. When Bradshaw spotted her with her notebook, he automatically took it from her and signed his name.

Now, the Associated Press sports editor is a woman, as are the editors of half a dozen newspaper sports departments. Women are assigned to cover all the major sports on a regular basis. Some players still pick on the women assigned to their teams, but the women usually give as much, or more, than they get. Suzyn Waldman, says baseball players are among the worst, basketball players the best.

After a baseball game, Waldman was bothered by a baseball player. "I told him, 'Brad, if you spent less time hassling women and more on baseball you wouldn't have done eight years in the minors.'"

Tracy Dodds, assistant sports editor of *The Orange County Register* and national president of the Association of Women in Sports Media, was confronted in a locker-room interview by a naked athlete who, she said, "presented his pride and joy" to her and asked, "Do you know what this is?" Her reply: "It looks like a penis, only smaller."

Most athletes no longer care whether they are interviewed by a male or a female sportswriter. The story is told about a female sportswriter in the San Diego basketball team's locker room following a game. As Randy Smith started to pull off his uniform, a fellow player cautioned him, "Randy, there's a lady in the room." Smith replied, "That's no lady. That's only a writer."

Roger Kahn—who wrote a fine book about baseball, *The Boys of Summer*— has a basic approach to his reporting. Most good sportswriters do. Here, from one of Kahn's columns in *Esquire,* is how he describes his approach to his beat:

Sports tells anyone who watches intelligently about the times in which we live: about managed news and corporate policies, about race and terror and what the process of aging does to strong men. If that sounds grim, there is courage and high humor, too. . . .

. . . I find sport a better area than most to look for truth. A great hockey goalie, describing his life on ice, once said, "That puck comes so hard, it could take an eye.

I've had 250 stitches and I don't like pain. I get so nervous before every game, I lose my lunch."

"Some football players," I said to the goalie, whose name is Glenn Hall, "say that when they're badly scared, they pray."

Hall looked disgusted, "If there is a God," he said, "let's hope he's doing something more important than watching hockey games." Offhand I can't recall a better sermon.

Red Smith, who was writing his sports column for *The New York Times* until a few days before he died in 1982, said of sports:

Sports is not really a play world. I think it's the real world. The people we're writing about in professional sports, they're suffering and living and dying and loving and trying to make their way through life just as the bricklayers and politicians are.

This may sound defensive—I don't think it is—but I'm aware that games are a part of every culture we know anything about. And often taken seriously. It's no accident that of all the monuments left of the Greco-Roman culture, the biggest is the ball park, the Colosseum, the Yankee Stadium of ancient times. The man who reports on these games contributes his small bit to the history of his times.

Rapoport takes what he calls a practical view of sports coverage. "If you can't find something light or something that will make the reader smile or laugh, at least remember and try to show, in style or substance, that these are games these people are involved in, not foreign policy discussions," he says.

However, says Rapoport, "intensely dramatic and emotional things do happen, and when they do the reporter should not be afraid to haul out the heavy artillery.

"Just remember that in such cases the facts are usually enough."

They were for Rapoport on a November day in 1991 when he received a phone call telling him to be at the Los Angeles Forum in two hours for an important announcement by Magic Johnson. Rapoport described the event in a column:

Earvin Johnson is the only man I know who could smile while announcing he had contracted the virus that causes AIDS.

Perhaps I shouldn't have been surprised at this, because over the years Johnson has

done so many things no one else could ever do. But on Thursday afternoon, he outdid even himself.

Wearing his sharpest suit and smiling his nice smile, Johnson strode into the

Forum Club as if he were about to be handed another Most Valuable Player Award, or announce one more lucrative commercial endorsement.

Instead, he said he had contracted HIV, the human immunodeficiency virus, and was quitting basketball as part of the treatment doctors hope will keep him from dying.

Further Reading ▶

Anderson, David, ed. *The Red Smith Reader.* New York: Random House, 1983.

Berkow, Ira. *Red: A Biography of Red Smith.* New York: Times Books, 1986.

Halberstam, David. *October 1964.* New York: Villard Books, 1994.

Kahn, Roger. *The Boys of Summer.* New York: New American Library, 1973.

Klatell, David A., and Norman Marcus. *Sports for Sale: Television, Money, and the Fans.* New York: Oxford University Press, 1988.

Mantle, Mickey, and Phil Pepe. *My Favorite Summer 1956.* New York: Doubleday, 1991.

Miller, Marvin. *A Whole Different Ball Game: The Sport and Business of Baseball.* Secaucus, N.J.: Birch Lane Press, 1991.

Rapoport, Ron. *A Kind of Grace.* Berkeley, Calif.: Zenobia Press, 1994.

Robinson, Ray. *The Home Run Heard 'Round the World: The Dramatic Story of the 1951 Giants-Dodgers Pennant Race.* New York: HarperCollins, 1991.

Smith, Red. *Strawberries in the Wintertime.* New York: Quadrangle Times Books, 1974.

Whittingham, Richard. *The Meat Market: The Inside Story of the N.F.L. Draft.* New York: Macmillan, 1992. (Whittingham says that every year of the 4,500 college players, 336 are drafted, 130 survive their team's final cuts and 30 become starters.)

23 Business Reporting

GT Capital Management.
Bond trader at work.

Preview

Business and economic activity affects the cost and quality of the goods we buy; whether people buy or rent a home; the kind of car a person buys; even the college a high school graduate attends.

The business reporter handles:

• **Local spot news stories:** Store openings and closings, company personnel changes, new construction, changes in the business climate, annual reports of local companies.

• **Features:** New products developed by local enterprises, profiles of company officials and workers.

• **Interpretative stories:** Effects of national and international economic activity on local business, the influence of local business leaders on municipal policies and the budget.

N ews about business and economics has become everybody's personal business. People want to know about the cost of living, job possibilities, how high or low interest rates may go, whether layoffs are imminent in local industries and the value of a bond or stock that they own.

Our food, clothing and shelter are produced by business enterprises, and their quality and the prices we pay for them are largely a result of business decisions. Even the quality of the air we breathe and the water we drink is affected by decisions made by the business community. We have a large stake in those decisions, and we want to be informed of them and to know how they are made.

News about commerce is as old as the newspaper itself. The gazettes and newsletters of the 17th century were established in the business centers of Europe for the emerging commercial class. Though it seems obvious that everyone would have a great interest in pocketbook news—news of the economy—editors came late to the realization and, until recently, business news was a minor part of the newspaper.

One cause of the awakening was the consumer movement in the 1970s that resulted in a new kind of coverage for television and for many newspapers—consumer journalism. Reacting to what appeared to be an attitude of *caveat emptor* (let the buyer beware) among U.S. businesses, newspapers and broadcast stations went into the marketplace to find out why the quality of goods and services was declining while prices were steadily rising.

> **Good Writing.** Business stories need not be dull:
>
> BURBANK, Calif.—After a year and a half of courtship, Mickey Mouse left Miss Piggy at the altar.
>
> This *Wall Street Journal* lead began a story of the breakdown in plans by Walt Disney Co. to acquire the Muppet characters.

Curiosity, if not skepticism, about business was strong. Consumers were irritated by products that fell apart too soon and too often, and they were infuriated by the indifference of manufacturers, sellers, repairmen and mechanics.

The environmental movement also turned public attention, and then media attention, to the boardrooms of corporations. Journalists decided that their job was to make corporate power accountable. Tom Johnson, publisher of the *Los Angeles Times,* said, "Business news has become page one news because of the emergence of highly controversial issues in which there is an obvious potential for conflict between the corporate and the public interest." In 1968, the *Times* business staff had eight reporters. Today, there are 10 times as many.

Business and economic reporting on television has exploded. From the boring nightly reading of the Dow Jones industrial average and a few other statistics, it has grown to an imaginative and innovative branch of television journalism.

The Scope of Business News ▶

On Friday night, Tom and Ann Ryan sit down after dinner to make a decision. The birth of their second child means they will need another bedroom. They must decide whether to rent a larger apartment or buy a house.

Tom Ryan spreads out a page of the local newspaper on the dining room table. He points to an article with a headline, "Mortgage Shopping." It begins:

> New York (AP)—Attention mortgage shoppers: Today's specials are 30-year conventional loans—just a 7.5 percent rate and no points if you buy your home now.

The story says that "at no time have there been so many loan options available for those looking to buy or refinance a home. Not since nearly 20 years ago have rates been so low and home prices so stable."

That clinches it for the Ryans. They decide to buy a new home.

Interest rates also are a concern of the Goldensohn family. Robert, a high school senior, wants to attend a private college. The tuition is high and he must have a student loan. The family income meets the necessities and little more. Robert may have to borrow at least $5,000 a year.

If they cannot handle the loan, Robert will have to attend a community college. Their newspaper carries a story on the latest information about student loans and interest rates. The Goldensohns decide they can afford a loan. Robert will go to a private college.

In homes in every part of the city, people look to business stories for information. Workers whose contracts are tied to the cost of living watch the papers and television to see how their paychecks will be affected by the latest figures from Washington. Farmers follow the livestock and commodity markets. Vacationers search through the list of foreign exchange rates to see what the dollar is worth abroad before deciding where to spend their vacations. Residents north of the city hear that a new shopping center will be built there; they look through the business pages to find out more about it.

When the interest rates on savings accounts and certificates of deposit sank below 3 percent in the early 1990s, people began to look for higher-interest

Bob Thayer, *The Journal-Bulletin.*

From New Cafes to Credit Cards

investments and were lured by advertisements: "Good News for C.D. Holders." What the ads did not point out is that unlike the certificates of deposit, whose principal is guaranteed by the Federal Deposit Insurance Corporation, the touted new investments had high risk.

Business reporters warned their readers of the risk, as they did when investment firms pushed closed-end government bond funds. Investing in such funds, wrote a *Wall Street Journal* reporter, was like paying $1.10 for a roll of 100 pennies.

A business reporter for *The New York Times* watched a recruiter lecturing potential insurance sales personnel for Primerica Financial Services and heard what he later wrote was "a mix of fact and half-truths." Then the reporter, Michael Quint, widened his scope to describe "a companywide pattern of exaggerations in the recruitment of agents and the selling of policies to hundreds of thousands of Americans."

He pointed out that the company has 110,000 agents, "more than 90 percent of them part-timers with little training but a need for extra income." The sales tactics, Quint found by firsthand reporting, "are often misleading and sometimes dangerous to a customer's financial security."

The business reporter ranges widely. In the morning, she interviews local service station dealers about their price war, and that afternoon she localizes a story about the new prime rate and the failure of the coffee crop in Brazil.

Local stories include:

- Store openings, expansions and closings.
- Real estate transactions. New products from local enterprises. Construction projects planned.
- Plants opened, expanded, closed. Personnel changes, awards, retirements. Layoffs, bankruptcies.
- Annual and quarterly business reports. Annual meetings.
- Bond offerings by local government units.

If the newspaper or station has no labor reporter, the business reporter covers labor-management relations and the activities of labor unions.

In addition to these spot news stories, the business reporter is aware of trends and developments in the community and area. The business reporter knows the relationship between the prime rate and the local housing market and understands how the city's parking policies affect downtown merchants.

Here is how Bob Freund of *The Times-News* in Twin Falls, Idaho, began a roundup that blended local and national business and economic activity with area trends:

TWIN FALLS—As spring turned into summer, the brightest news for the Magic Valley economy was coming from consumers.

They climbed into new cars at an accelerated pace, and sought credit both to pay for the new wheels and for improvements at home.

Literacy. If you were to become business editor of your local newspaper and were able to make one major change in content or direction, what would it be?

I'd give my staff an economic literacy test. I'd ask them to define the difference between earnings and revenues, profits and profitability, ownership and management. If they failed the test, I'd give them the choice of taking a good course in business economics or moving on. . . . You can't write about football unless you know the difference between a fourth-down punt and a field goal. And you can't write about business unless you understand it and master its vocabulary.—Herbert Schmertz, vice president, Mobil Oil Corporation

They benefited from a vicious war of price cutting and couponing among area grocery stores.

Indicators compiled by The Times-News for the second quarter ending June 30 show some momentum in the Magic Valley economy, but also some significant drags.

Despite lower mortgage rates and a national surge in homebuying, the biggest consumer of all, the home buyer, still is not pounding down the doors at Magic Valley real estate agencies.

Agriculture, the underlying financial pump for the valley economy, remains grounded by low commodity prices.

Of course, the Magic Valley is not alone in these problems. Idaho's economy generally is weak, and with trade imbalances pressing more and more on manufacturing, the U.S. is wavering in a twilight zone between recession and growth.

Nationally, economists are calling the situation a growth recession. The economy is growing, but it is not gaining enough strength to cut unemployment substantially.

A Drugstore Opening ▶

The more the newspaper or station stresses local news, the more detailed business stories will be, and in small communities the line between news and free advertising is so narrow it approaches invisibility. A large department store opening will be reported by the biggest newspapers. But a drugstore opening will not. The smaller newspaper or station will carry the drugstore opening and might cover the enlargement of a hardware store.

Here is the beginning of an 11-paragraph story that appeared in *The Berkshire Eagle:*

For 10 years, tailor Frank Saporito plied his trade with Davis & Norton Inc. on North Street here, where he was in charge of all alterations. When that business closed last month, Saporito was out of work—but not for long.

Saporito landed on his feet and decided to go into business for himself at 251 Fenn St., just across the street from the post office. He's been open there a little more than a week.

"I wanted to try it by myself," Saporito said. "I think it's a good move. I sure hope so."

Chain Store Alert ▶

Business reporters keep an eye open for any moves into town by the major chain stores. Such moves can have a major impact on local business.

When Wal-Mart started building a store two miles outside Hudson, N.Y., local store owners took notice. The massive chain, the nation's largest retailer, has in other areas driven local businesses out because of its pricing policies. In Hudson, which marked a move into the northeast for the chain, local businesses spruced up their stores and decided that they will profit from the new shoppers who will be attracted to the area.

In other areas, the mood has been pessimistic. In Greenfield, Mass., local residents voted to bar Wal-Mart from moving into town.

Among the story possibilities: Sale of land for the new store; new employment; new tax revenues; impact on local business now, a year later, five years later.

Advertising salespeople sometimes promise an advertiser a story about a store expansion or about the cashier who has spent 25 years behind the Hamburger Heaven checkout counter. When the publisher orders a story, the piece is known as a BOM (business office must).

These stories are considered free advertising. Still, it could be argued that some of these events can make good stories. The perceptive business reporter sent to interview the hardware merchant who is enlarging his store might find that the store owner is staking his last dime on this gamble to keep from losing business to the Kmart outside town. And the Hamburger Heaven cashier could become a human interest story.

◀ **Puff Pieces**

Because business stories can be complicated, writers try to introduce human interest whenever possible in their copy. Vivian Marino—the AP business writer whose story on mortgage rates influenced the Ryans to buy a home rather than rent—says, "I try to keep my stories as interesting and memorable as possible, often by using anecdotal examples to which readers can relate."

In a story about the problems people are having in a receding economy, she began with a retired worker trying to get by on his pension:

◀ **The Human Element**

NEW YORK (AP)—After three decades laboring in the grimy steel mills around Pittsburgh, Richard L. Walters thought he earned a clean retirement.

But since taking early leave from LTV Corp., Walters, 60, and his wife Audrey, 54, have been barely getting by. His $922 monthly pension check isn't enough for the loan payments on the couple's New Brighton, Pa., Victorian, along with food bills and other escalating expenses.

So he's trying to go back to work. "Right now, it's pretty hard to get a job around here. I've been tinkering around on people's cars, making a couple of dollars here and there. I would like to just stay retired, but the way things are now I can't."

Business Writer

When Vivian Marino joined the Miami bureau of the AP, she was assigned to do a series on the labor problems of Eastern Airlines. When she had done that, she was given more business assignments.

"I decided to carve out my own niche by concentrating on business and finance." Soon she was appointed regional business writer.

Then she was transferred to New York. "I had to learn about the markets and more complicated business and financial issues. I learned from my colleagues and from many of my sources. I also read a lot."

Marino writes a column on consumer affairs and personal finance for the AP.

Marino ranges widely. She has written pieces about compulsive credit card spenders, growing numbers of auto repossessions, how to obtain a credit file and how to challenge inaccurate information. For her New Frugality series, she described what happened to Yuppies, the free-spending generation of professionals. They have now become Grumpies, she writes—Grown-up mature professionals—who skimp along on reduced incomes.

For a piece on college scholarships, her reporting turned up the availability of thousands of scholarships offering billions of dollars. In fact, she writes, nearly "$7 billion in college money goes unclaimed each year, or about $600 for every student in the United States." Her piece begins:

NEW YORK (AP)—Short of cash for college? Billions of dollars are waiting for the right students to come along.

The Two-Ten International Footwear Foundation, for instance, provides up to $2,000 for undergrads with parents in the shoe business. Post-graduate students can get $12,500 from the International Union for Vacuum Science, provided they study—you guessed it—vacuum science.

Even comedian David Letterman has gotten into the act, offering scholarships for telecommunications majors at alma mater Ball State University in Muncie, Ind. Grades aren't important.

The Reporter's Requirements ▶

The business reporter is a specialist who feels at home with numbers and is not frightened by lengthy reports and press releases, many of which contain rates, percentages, business and consumer indexes and the jargon of the business world.

Among the skills and attitudes the business reporter takes to the job is the recognition of the power business exerts. Along with this, the reporter has a healthy skepticism that keeps him or her from being awed by the muscle and money that business power generates.

The business reporter approaches the money managers and manipulators with the same objectivity and distance that any reporter takes on an assignment. In his profile of a corporate raider, Michael A. Hiltzik of the *Los Angeles Times* was able to find sources and anecdotes to get to the heart of his subject, Irwin L. Jacobs of Minneapolis. Jacobs acquires and merges companies, usually at great profit.

Jacobs usually would pledge to operate rather than to dismantle the firms "on the insight that Americans lionize industrialists and not liquidators," Hiltzik says. For his piece, Hiltzik was able to show that Jacobs dismantled one firm in 17 days, despite his promise to operate Mid American Bancorporation of Minnesota "for his children and his children's children," the story said. Jacobs' profit: an estimated $4 million.

Specialist though he or she may be, the business reporter must know much more than the world of finance. When Hiltzik was assigned to cover the tribulations of a precious metals investment firm, he had to look through court documents with the same scrupulous and knowledgeable attention a courthouse reporter gives the records. In fact, Hiltzik found in one of the documents a human interest lead to his story about the complicated activities of the firm.

He began his lengthy account of Monex International Ltd. with the story of Kathleen Ann Mahoney, a professional singer who was living in Newport Beach, Calif., when she bought $10,000 worth of silver through Monex. The price of silver went up, and Hiltzik reports, she "invested another $12,000, then another $10,000, and then her last $13,000, relying on what she says was a Monex salesman's pitch that silver prices were rising so fast they might earn $100,000 for her over a year's time." The price of silver reached $50 an ounce.

"Four days later, Mahoney was wiped out. Silver had plunged to $28, and the crash had taken most of her investment with it," Hiltzik wrote.

The business reporter has a harder job digging for information than most journalists do. Most reporters deal with public officials who live in goldfish bowls. Laws and a long tradition have made the public sector public.

The business world, however, is generally private, secretive and authoritarian. The head of a company can order his or her employees not to talk to reporters. Since businesspeople usually are in competition, secrecy is a natural part of business life. True, businesses are required to file many kinds of reports with various governmental agencies, and these are excellent sources of information. But in the day-to-day coverage of the beat, the business reporter must rely on human sources. Good sources can break the code of silence and secrecy.

◀ **Sources of Information**

Good contacts and sources can be made among the following:

◀ **Human Sources**

- Bank officers, tellers.
- Savings and loan officials.
- Chamber of Commerce secretaries.
- Union leaders and working people.
- Securities dealers.
- Financial analysts.
- Real estate brokers.
- Trade organization officials.
- Teachers of business, economics.
- Transportation company officials.
- Federal and state officials in agencies such as the Small Business Administration, Commerce Department, various regulatory agencies.

Grocery will feature ethnic twist

Comments

■ I saw a sign saying a new grocery store was coming soon. New store owners love to talk about their business. I try to make it somewhat personal or give the column that "small town/heard-over-the-fence" feel. I always ask, "Why?"

■ This is another example of watching for signs on stores that have been vacant.

■ The owner sent a press release. Another section of the paper followed this item up with a feature.

■ I knew from covering the company it is expanding fast and likely would move its outlet from an industrial location to a retail site.

■ When Matt Sapari was deciding on a name for his new specialty grocery store, he chose something that reminds him of a popular Middle Eastern dish—stuffed grape leaves.

The Grape Vine, at 1921 S. Minnesota Ave., will sell Mediterranean sweets, cheese, olives, coffees, spices, Middle Eastern breads and groceries. Sapari said the store will be similar to the Olive Branch, which was open a few years ago on East 10th Street.

He hopes to be open by the end of March. The fresh baked products, such as baklava, will be shipped in from Detroit.

"There was a demand for something like that in South Dakota," Sapari said.

Sapari, who moved here from Kuwait seven years ago, has been in the construction business the last two years. His wife and a brother will operate the store.

■ Walt and Nancy Landry open Mind Games at noon today at 2012 S. Minnesota Ave.

The store will sell board games that have been tough to find in Sioux Falls and will rent game rooms to players who want to gather a group to play at the store. Popcorn is free.

"We think we'll appeal to a crowd that goes from 10-year-olds all the way up to kids of 60," he said.

The Landrys decided to start their business after they noticed friends going to Omaha, Neb., and Minneapolis to shop for games. With a little research, they found out Sioux City, Iowa, has three game businesses.

"If Sioux City can support three stores at 75,000, surely Sioux Falls at 120,000 could support one store," he said.

Mind Games will sell strategic and tactical games such as Dungeons and Dragons, Wild West and Micro Armor, a game that uses mini tanks and recreates famous wars.

"You actually play against other people vs. playing against a computer," he said.

■ Dan Winkler of Sioux Falls has opened The Next Dimension, stand-up virtual reality games in the Dayton's wing at The Empire mall. A game is $5 for about five minutes.

Players also can join forces with other players to meet the computer challenges. Participants wear headsets, see texture mapped 3-D color graphics and hear stereo sound.

"You don't just play the game, you are the game," Winkler said.

■ Gateway 2000 opened its factory outlet this week at 3109 W. 41st St., Suite 4. The outlet is open from 9 a.m. to 9 p.m. Monday through Friday, 9 a.m. to 5 p.m. Saturday and noon to 4 p.m. Sunday.

The personal computer manufacturer's previous outlet was at 700 E. 54th St. N.

Brenda Wade Schmidt is business editor of the Argus Leader. You can write her at P.O. Box 5034, Sioux Falls, S.D. 57117–5034, or call 331–2321.

Brenda Schmidt, business editor of the *Argus Leader* in Sioux Falls, S.D., writes the "Eye on Business" column. Usually, she has four or five items about the local business scene. On the opposite page is a typical column with Schmidt's comments about her sources alongside.

Sources Are Everywhere ◄

Schmidt's co-workers pass along information. An *Argus Leader* employee saw a sign that The Keg on East 10th Street was moving. Schmidt called the owner of the neighborhood bar known for its deep-fried chicken, and he told her, "We've just kind of outgrown the place."

Friends pass along tips. One said a piece of ground in The Empire mall parking lot would be used by Burger King, making it the city's ninth outlet for the fast-food chain.

Mike Kuehl called Schmidt to tell her his Powerhouse Gym, Fitness and Rehabilitation Center would open in three weeks. Sharon Busch called to say her Toys & Treasures store would be honored at the national toy fair in New York "for sponsoring a Goetz doll signing in October."

Even her husband pitches in. He told her about a longtime downtown fixture, 3 & Co. Antiques, leaving for a nearby town. Schmidt checked and a co-owner told her parking was the problem. Customers, he said, "are not going to concentrate on a $1,000 piece of furniture if they're worried about a $3 parking ticket."

On first contact with a reporter, the business source is likely to be wary, says James L. Rowe Jr., New York financial correspondent of *The Washington Post*. "As a result, it is often difficult to gain the source's trust.

◄ Cultivating Sources

"But if the reporter does his or her homework, learns what motivates business people, is not afraid to ask the intelligent questions but doesn't have to ask the dumb one, more than enough sources will break down."

In developing these sources, the reporter will want to find people who can put events into perspective and who can clarify some of the complexities the reporter cannot. Caution is important. Not only must the sources be dependable, they must be independent of compromising connections and affiliations. Obviously, such sources are hard to find. The traditional independent source was the academician, the cloistered professor who had no financial stake in the matters he would comment about. But no more. Academicians now serve on the boards of banks, chemical companies and pesticide manufacturers. The alert reporter makes certain that background information from such sources is neither biased nor self-serving.

When quoting a source, note all of the person's business affiliations relevant to the story. In a banking story, it's not enough to say that Professor Thomas Graham teaches economics at the state university. His membership on the board of directors of the First National Bank should also be included.

The background source is rarely quoted, and so readers and viewers cannot assess the information in terms of the source's affiliations. Since background sources influence reporters by providing perspective, the independence of these sources is essential. Good background sources can be found without leaving the office. The accountants, marketing people and the legal adviser to the newspaper

◄ Background Source

or station can figure out some of the complexities of reports and documents. They also are close to the business community.

The business office has access to the local credit bureau and the facilities of Dun and Bradstreet, which can provide confidential information. These are helpful in running a check on a local business.

Chris Welles, a veteran business writer, says, "By far the most important sources on company stories are former executives. Unconstrained by the fear of being fired if word gets out that they talked to you, they can be extremely forthcoming about their former employer." Competitors are another good source, as are suppliers, the managers of investment portfolios, bankers and others who are likely to know the company's financial situation, such as the financial analysts who prepare reports on public corporations.

In interviews, Welles will share his problems in obtaining material. "Most people are predisposed to respond favorably to someone who, in a non-threatening way, asks for a little help." Welles says he listens "with great interest and sympathy." He says that "sources have a great deal of trouble terminating a conversation with someone who seems to be hanging on their every word."

Physical Sources ▶

At the local level, reporters know how to use city and county tax records. The city and county keep excellent records of real estate transfers, and the assessor's office has the valuation of real property and of the physical plant and equipment—whatever is taxed. The sales tax shows how much business a firm is doing. Many local governments issue business licenses on which the principals involved are named and other information is given.

State governments also issue business licenses. There are scores of state boards; they license barbers, engineers, cosmetologists, doctors, morticians, lawyers, accountants and others. These agencies usually keep basic information about the businesses they oversee.

The state corporation commission or the secretary of state will have the names, addresses and sometimes the stock held by directors of corporations incorporated in the state and of firms that do a large amount of business in the state. The company's articles of incorporation and bylaws are also on file.

Federal Records ▶

For companies with $1 million in assets and at least 500 stockholders, the Securities and Exchange Commission requires regular reports. Some 10,000 companies file such reports, listed in the annual Directory of Companies Required to File Annual Reports. To obtain the directory and other reports write: Public Reference Section, Securities and Exchange Commission, 450 Fifth St. N.W., Washington, D.C. 20549. For general information, call (202) 272-2650.

Among the SEC reports available is the 10-K, an annual report that many reporters use because it includes the company's finances, ownership, major contracts, management history, salaries and other compensation paid the major officers.

Welles, who has been writing about business and economics for 30 years, says that when he is to write about a company, the first step he takes is to obtain three basic documents: the 10-K, the annual report and the proxy statement. Like

Scenes from a Troubled Past

Unemployment benefits, union shops, welfare payments, social security . . . These aids for working people were accomplished during the turbulence of the Great Depression that struck the United States with the stock market crash in 1929 and continued for a decade. About one-fourth of the work force was unemployed, and in large cities, soup kitchens like this one in Chicago and bread lines fed the poor. Men who could find work were paid $1 a day, women half that.

President Franklin D. Roosevelt supported organized labor but industry refused to go along. In 1934, automobile workers struck, a nationwide textile strike was called and in San Francisco workers staged a general strike. All were unsuccessful, and the San Francisco strike and the textile strike were broken by the militia and self-constituted vigilante groups.

The National Archives.

the 10-K, the other two are available from the SEC. Welles describes the annual report as "a kind of public relations version of the 10-K."

He says that "no single body of information is more crucial to the understanding of a corporation than its financial statements." We will be looking at the annual report in detail later in this chapter.

The proxy statement, an SEC-mandated document, is sent to all stockholders before an annual meeting. It contains the salaries and bonuses of the five top company officers and stockholdings of most senior executives. The statement also lists any deals between the firm and its management or directors. Proxy statements also include biographies of the directors. Some of these directors are from outside the company and are good sources.

Other useful documents are the 8-K, which is filed monthly for important company activities such as mergers, and the 10-Q, a quarterly report with information like that in the annual 10-K.

Nonprofit organizations must file Form 990 with the Internal Revenue Service. The report includes information on the income and expenses of officials of the organizations. The expenses can be illuminating. Often, a small part of the money raised by the organization is used for the purpose the organization says it is seeking donations.

SEC material can be obtained from regional SEC offices. Companies will send on request their 10-Ks, proxy statements and annual reports.

The Bureau of the Census issues many economic reports, some of them covering city and county business activity. Major economic censuses are taken every five years, for the years ending in 2 and 7. Also, there are annual surveys. The Bureau has a vast publications program. For a general guide to what the Bureau does and what data it makes available, write to the U.S. Department of Commerce, Bureau of the Census, Washington, D.C. 20233, and ask for the Guide to Economic Censuses and Related Statistics for the current year.

Reading ▶

Daily reading of *The Wall Street Journal* is necessary for the business reporter. Written for businesspeople and those with some involvement in financial matters, the stories nevertheless are written in layman's language. The newspaper is both record keeper for the business community and its watchdog. Its investigative reporting is among the best in the country.

Business Week, a weekly business newsmagazine, is staffed by journalists with a good command of business, finance and economics. The magazine concentrates on the major industries and companies. Its long articles are aimed at the men and women who are in executive posts in business, people who will be interested in these business topics.

Forbes is addressed to investors, people who own stock in companies. The *Journal, Business Week,* and *Forbes* are pro-business. Though they do go after the bad apples in the barrel, they never question the barrel, the system itself, as former *Journal* staffer Kent MacDougall puts it. The most pro-business publication is *Nation's Business,* which is published by the U.S. Chamber of Commerce and the National Association of Manufacturers.

A good source of story ideas and general information is the *FDA Consumer,* a monthly publication of the Food and Drug Administration. One issue listed prescription drugs that are dangerous for pregnant women and described the dangers of sunbathing. Another issue contained material about electrical muscle stimulators that some health spas and figure salons use for weight control, bust development, wrinkle removal and nonsurgical face-lifts. The stimulator, the FDA warned, should be used only by people with expertise to treat specific medical problems.

The publication costs $12 a year and is available from the Superintendent of Documents, Washington, D.C. 20402-9371.

There are 5,000 trade publications, magazines and newspapers that cover businesses and trades. The reporter who specializes will be a regular reader of the trade publications in his or her field.

A good local library or any business school library at a college or university will have the following references that business reporters find useful: ◀ **References**

- **Dun and Bradstreet directories:** One covers companies with capital under $1 million; another is for those whose capital exceeds $1 million. (Address, corporate officers, sales, number of employees.)
- **Who Owns Whom:** To find the parent company of a firm you are checking.
- **Standard & Poor's Register of Corporations, Directors and Executives.**
- **Moody's Manuals.**
- **Standard & Poor's Corporation Record:** Seven volumes of basic information on almost every publicly traded stock.

The conscientious business reporter can look forward to a good salary. *Quill* magazine reported that three business journalists earn more than $1 million a year: Louis Rukeyser, host of public television's "Wall Street Week"; Marshall Loeb, editor of *Fortune;* Lou Dobbs, lead anchor of CNN's business news. ◀ **The Payoff**

The journalism magazine listed six more who make more than $500,000 a year: Jane Bryant Quinn, *Newsweek;* Frank Lalli, *Money* magazine; Stuart Varney, CNN; James W. Michaels, *Forbes;* Dan Dorfman, *Money;* and Irving R. Levine, NBC.

All levels of government regulate business. Local laws prescribe health, fire and safety regulations to which businesses must adhere. The city grants franchises and checks to see that the provisions are followed, such as those requiring public access to the local cable television company. Regional and county governments set standards for factory emissions. ◀ **Regulatory Agencies**

The state regulates some banks, savings and loan institutions, insurance companies and public utilities. State agencies handle rate applications and oversee operational procedures of utilities. Basic information about these businesses is available to the journalist.

State licensing boards also regulate the trades and professions they license. Usually, they have the power to investigate complaints and to hold hearings. Although most of these boards are creatures of the businesses and professions they regulate, occasionally a board will act decisively. Failure to take action is an even better story, as one reporter learned when the board regulating veterinarians failed to hold a hearing for a veterinarian who was the subject of a number of complaints by pet owners whose dogs and cats had died in his care.

Although most federal regulatory agencies are in Washington and too distant for personal checking, a local business reporter can ask the newspaper's Washington bureau or the AP or UPI to run something down. Federal agencies compile considerable material about companies and individuals seeking permission to operate interstate. Some agencies:

- **Federal Communications Commission (FCC):** Regulates radio and television stations. Ownership and stock information are available.
- **National Labor Relations Board (NLRB):** Concerned with labor disputes.

Enterprise ▶

Don Moffitt, a *Wall Street Journal* editor, says that business reporters "should consider that they have a license to inquire into the nuts and bolts of how people make a living and secure their well-being.

"For a local paper, the fortunes of the community's barbers, auto mechanics, bankers and public servants are business stories. Business is how people survive.

"If people are falling behind in their mortgage payments, show how and why they are falling behind, how they feel about it and what they're trying to do about it," he says.

When the Business Base Disappears

Treece had been a thriving Kansas mining town until the lead ore ran out and people left. There are no jobs, no schools, no stores and lots of enmity and feuding, as Joe Smith's sign and shotgun indicate.

THIS HOUSE IS GUARDED BY A 12" GAUGE SHOTGUN THREE NIGHTS A WEEK YOU PICK WHICH NIGHTS!

Joel Sartore, *The Wichita Eagle-Beacon.*

"Local government financing and spending is, in part, a business story. Who's making money off the local bond issues, and why? Is the bank keeping the county's low-interest deposits and using the cash to buy the county's high-yielding paper? Who suffers when the township cuts the budget, or can't increase it? Show how they suffer."

Always go beyond the press release, business reporters say. When a $69 million reconstruction job at a shopping center was announced, the developers sent out stacks of press releases. By asking why so much money was being spent on releases, a reporter learned that sales at the center had sharply declined recently—a fact not mentioned in any of the releases.

Steve Lipson, business news writer for *The Times-News,* develops ideas for stories by a simple technique—keeping his eyes open. "I read ads, I notice changes in the businesses where I shop. I count the number of cars in a car dealer's lot, and I look at what people wear, eat and drink," Lipson says.

"I look for unique stories," he says. He did one on the growing popularity of potato-skin appetizers. "This big boost to potato consumption would land someone in the Idaho Hall of Fame if anyone knew who was responsible. Alas, my story found no one really knows."

The school system and the city and the county often decide on major construction projects. To finance them, large amounts of money have to be raised by selling bonds. ◀ Municipal Bonds

The bond story involves interest rates, the financial standing or rating of the local government and related matters that may seem complex for readers but that can be simplified with good reporting. First, check the rating of the governmental unit.

If the local government is not rated financially healthy, the bonds might not be seen as a good investment. To attract buyers of the bonds, the interest rate then might have to be set high, and just half of 1 percent more in interest could mean millions of dollars more that the taxpayers will have to pay in interest over the life of the bonds.

Reporters can learn about the health of the local government by examining two kinds of documents, the bond prospectus and the analysis by the rating agencies:

Prospectus: This document is required by law for the information of potential investors. It contains considerable information about the government entity offering the bonds.

Rating: The government entity's debt (which is what a bond is) is rated by organizations such as Moody's or Standard & Poor's. The lower the rating, the higher the interest rate on the bonds and the greater the cost to taxpayers. Reporters can obtain these ratings.

University Bonds ▶

Almost all governments issue bonds and so do many private entities. Your university probably has issued bonds for a dormitory or classroom construction, possibly for a stadium. All of these bond-issuing entities are rated. Here is the beginning of a story from the *Spectator* at Columbia University:

Executives from Moody's Investment Service and Standard & Poor's, the two major companies that handle Columbia University's debt, are planning to visit the University in two weeks to evaluate its credit.

The review process, which takes one to two weeks, will be carried out by the companies' higher education rating group.

Standard & Poor's now gives Columbia's bonds a rating of AA+, the second-highest rating; Moody's rates Columbia AAA, its highest rating. Of the 3,000 educational institutions that Moody's evaluates, only 10 to 15 percent have the top rating.

The higher Columbia's rating, the lower the interest rate the University has to pay on its bonds. . . .

Skepticism and Doubt ▶

"The business page is singularly marked by credulity," says Bernard Nossiter, a veteran business reporter for *The Washington Post* and other newspapers. "Corporate and even Treasury pronouncements are treated as holy writ. Corporate officials are likely to be regarded with awe, at least until they are indicted."

One reason, he says, is that "reporters are literate rather than numerate," more at home with words than with figures.

One of the stories business interests find reporters eager to write is the new business or development piece. Anything that promises new jobs or an expanding economy in town is snapped up, even when the venture is speculative. In Alexandria, Va., a developer put up a huge sign announcing an 800,000-square-foot

---

Handout Watchout

Here are the beginnings of three press releases. What do they have in common?

United States Steel Corp. today announced a series of moves designed to insure that its steel sector will continue as a major force in world steel markets for the balance of the century and beyond. . . .

Greenbelt Cooperative Inc.'s Board of Directors unanimously approved a plan to strengthen the organization's financial position and continue expansion. . . .

W & J Sloane, the retail furniture company long noted for its reputation for quality, style and trend-setting furniture, is once again taking the lead in the furniture industry. . . .

If you found the companies are about to report high earnings or an expansion, go to the rear of the class. The firms were all announcing bad news. U.S. Steel cut 15,600 jobs and closed plants in several cities. Greenbelt closed its cooperative supermarkets and gas stations. And W & J Sloane closed a store and sharply reduced its range of furniture in other stores. All this was in the releases—buried.

---

office building, and *The Washington Post* ran a picture and story. No tenant was ever signed up. Reporters need to dig deeper:

- **Questions for new ventures:** What evidence is there of secure financing? Who are the lenders?
- **Questions for developers:** What tenants have signed leases? Are they being given free rent? Have building permits been issued?

Morton Mintz, for many years a digging reporter at *The Washington Post* who exposed corporate greed that resulted in danger and death to the public, says that the press has failed to audit "impersonal crime committed by the large corporation." He recalls the response of Alfred P. Sloan Jr., head of General Motors, when GM was urged to use safety glass for windshields, as Ford had been doing for years.

GM was using ordinary flat glass, which, Mintz says, "breaks into shards, disfiguring, slashing, killing." Sloan's response:

> Accidents or no accidents, my concern on this matter is a matter of profit and loss. . . . I am trying to protect the stockholders of General Motors and the Corporation's operating position—it is not my responsibility to sell safety glass. . . . You can say, perhaps, that I am selfish, but business is selfish. We are not a charitable institution—we are trying to make a profit for our stockholders.

Many students are attracted to journalism because they like to write and because journalism is concerned with how people get along with each other. These students are interested in the qualitative aspect of life. Journalism, with its feature stories and its emphasis on human interest, can use the talents these students take to the job. But much of what we know about the world—and people—is derived from quantitative studies.

◀ **Numbers Count**

The student who is thinking about a career in business journalism—and this is one area of journalism that never seems to have enough reporters and editors—cannot manage without an ability to deal with numbers. If business is the bottom line on a balance sheet, then the student thinking of becoming a business reporter has to know what to make of the numbers on the line.

Pauline Tai, former director of the Knight-Bagehot Fellowship Program in business journalism at Columbia University, says business reporters must be able to "analyze numbers. You can't just accept what a CEO tells you. You should be able to calculate. You have to know how the CEO came to a figure and what it means. You just don't take what you are being told as the truth. You have to look into it, and sometimes you have to stick your neck out and make judgments."

◀ Checking on Numbers

Note: More than a third of business executives polled by the Freedom Forum First Amendment Center said they regularly lie to the media. See *The Headline vs. The Bottom Line* by Mike Haggerty and Wallace Rasmussen, available from the Center at Vanderbilt University, 1207 18th Avenue, Nashville, TN 37212, (615) 321-9588.

The ability to blend the qualitative and the quantitative is essential to the business journalist. Numbers alone do say a lot, but when these barometers are matched with human beings, they take on dramatic significance. When home loan applications go down (quantitative), the reporter finds a family like the Ryans we met a while back and shows why this family decided to buy rather than to rent (qualitative).

Let's look at an example of a story the business reporter handles that is concerned primarily with figures. In our list of stories the business reporter deals with, we mentioned annual reports, the yearly accounting of publicly owned companies.

Annual Reports ▶

Newspapers usually run a summary of the annual reports of industries and businesses in their readership area. Readers want to know the economic health of the companies that employ local people, and some may own stock in these firms. Many readers also want to know about the status of the firms that have large numbers of shares of stock distributed nationwide—IBM, Kodak, General Motors, Polaroid, AT&T, Ford, General Electric. These readers may be shareholders— more than half the adult population owns stock—or they may be planning to invest in stocks. The business reporter must be able to swim through a sea of figures toward the few pieces of essential information in the report.

What to Look For ▶

First, read the auditor's report, which is usually at the back. "Generally, if the Auditor's Report is two paragraphs long, the financial statements have been given a clean bill of health," says the American Institute of Certified Public Accountants. "Anything longer—an extra paragraph or so—and normally that's a red flag alerting you to look further."

Jane Bryant Quinn, CBS business commentator, says the words "subject to" in the auditor's report are a warning signal.

"They mean the financial report is clean *only* if you take the company's word about a particular piece of business, and the accountant isn't sure you should," she says.

The CPA Institute has a general caution about the auditor's report: "All it means is that the financial statements are fairly presented in conformity with generally accepted accounting principles." It doesn't mean that the company is in great financial shape, or even in adequate condition. All it means is that the books are kept properly.

A number of suits have been filed against major auditing firms for failing to catch slippery entries in the books. The SEC has tightened up its requirements for auditors as a result of a number of businesses failing despite approval from the auditors.

Next, skim through the footnotes, says Quinn. Sometimes they explain the figures that seem surprising, even alarming. Earnings might be down. But the footnote may explain that the company has applied a policy of accelerated depreciation on plants and other equipment. "This," says the CPA Institute, "could reduce earnings, while a slower depreciation rate could boost earnings."

Next, look at the letter from the chairman or the president's report in front of the annual report. It usually is frank—if it adheres to the standards set by the CPA Institute. Usually, the statement is a candid summary of the past year and of prospects.

The figure in which most people are interested is *earnings per share,* also called *net income per common share.* (See Table 23.1.) This is the bottom line, a sign of the company's health. It is, in effect, the profit the company has made. It is computed by dividing the total earnings by the number of shares outstanding. The CPA Institute says that slight year-to-year changes can be ignored. Look for the trend in the five- and ten-year summaries. "If the EPS either remains unchanged or drops off, this may pinpoint trouble ahead," it says.

Look at the record of dividends as well as the current dividend. Is there a trend? Here is a five-year period of dividends of NRW Enterprises:

Dividends per	1995	1994	1993	1992	1991
common share	$1.14	$1.03	$1.00	$0.99	$0.91

This firm shows a steady climb in dividends over the past five years. However, the business reporter will note that although the 1995 dividend is larger than the previous year's dividend, the company's net income per share on continuing operations is down—from $3.18 to $2.62. (See Table 23.1.) In other words, the company plowed less of its earnings back into the firm in 1995 than it did in 1994 in order to keep the dividends on an upward course.

◀ The Figures

Key Figure. Net income per common share, the sixth item from the top in Table 23.1, is an indicator of the company's health. Also called *earnings per share,* it can be tracked over several years to determine how the company is doing.

Table 23.1 Net Income per Common Share: NRW Enterprises

	1995	1994	% Change
Net sales from continuing operations	$671,227,000	$601,960,000	+11.5
Income from continuing operations	$36,031,000	$43,685,000	−17.5
Income from discontinued operations	—	$1,112,000	—
Gain on sale of discontinued operations	$5,300,000	—	—
Net income	$41,331,000	$44,797,000	−7.7
Net income per common share	$2.62	$3.18	−17.6
Discontinued operations	—	$.08	—
Gain on sale of discontinued operations	$.39	—	—
Net income per common share	$3.01	$3.26	−7.7
Dividends per common share	$1.14	$1.03	+10.7
Cash dividends paid	$15,251,225	$13,736,454	+11.0
Capital expenditures	$27,535,000	$20,722,000	+32.9
Stockholders' equity	$259,668,000	$233,529,000	+11.2
Equity per common share at year end	$18.91	$17.02	+11.1
Outstanding common shares at year end	13,730,288	13,720,186	—

Be careful about earnings per share. A sudden increase can come from selling a plant or cutting advertising or research, says Quinn. The footnotes will explain unusual increases if they have unusual causes. A sudden decrease can come from a change in the number of shares, a stock split or a new issue—which is also noted in the report.

Next, look for the figures on working capital. "This is regarded as an important index of a company's condition because it reports whether operations generate enough cash to meet payroll, buy raw materials and conduct all the other essential day-to-day operations of the company," says the CPA Institute.

After all the expenses have been met, the company uses part of its net income to pay dividends. These are paid from net working capital, and if this figure (net working capital) shrinks consistently from year to year, even quarter to quarter, it is a sign the company may "not be able to keep dividends growing rapidly," says Quinn.

For further information about how to read an annual report, write the CPA Institute, 1211 Avenue of the Americas, New York City, NY, 10036, and ask for the booklet "What Else Can Financial Statements Tell You?"

Stories About Earnings ▶

Companies issue quarterly earnings reports as well as their annual reports, and reporters also write up these quarterly reports. The AP says that the most widely written business news story is the earnings report. And the most important part of the earnings story, says *The Wall Street Journal,* is "net income because that gives us a consistent gauge from company to company and quarter to quarter."

Here is a quarterly report from McDonald's Corp. for the period July 1 to Sept. 31 of this year compared with the same period of the preceding year.

	Current	**Preceding Year**	**% Change**
Sales	$6,964,000,000	$6,145,700,000	+13.3
Revenue	2,270,100,000	1,931,900,000	+17.5
Net. inc.	308,900,000	264,500,000	+16.9
Sh. earn	.43	.36	

Here is a story based on these figures:

> The McDonald's Corporation said yesterday that earnings rose 17 percent in the third quarter on continued robust sales from the company's expansion abroad.
> The company earned $308.9 million, or 43 cents a share, up from $264.5 million, or 36 cents a share, in the corresponding quarter a year ago.

Note: The word *revenue* sometimes is mistaken for the key figure. Revenue includes several cost items. *Net income* is what people want to know about, how much profit the company is making.

Here is a checklist that the AP provides its reporters for quarterly earnings stories:

◀ Checklist: Quarterly Earnings

___ Percentage of increase or decrease in earnings for quarter.
___ Reasons for increase or decrease.
___ Net income for quarter and income per share, compared with net income and income per share for same quarter previous year.
___ Brief description of company's business, products, etc.
___ Total revenue for quarter and total revenue for quarter previous year.
___ Net income for year to date, net income per share and total revenue for year to date compared with same figures for previous year.
___ If quarterly dividend is increased or decreased, amount of the increase or decrease, when the new dividend will be paid and shareholders eligible.

This checklist is also appropriate for stories based on annual reports.

◀ Local Folos

If you work in Topeka or Birmingham, chances are you will not be handling the McDonald's quarterly report data. But what about checking the local McDonald's outlets? How did they fare in the same period?

When Anheuser-Busch reports a 2.2 percent gain in total sales, you might find that the local distributor contributed a significant increase—or decrease—to the total sales picture. This, in turn, could lead to another story about the changing habits of local beer and soft drink imbibers. Beer and soft drinks are among the most hotly contested retail commodities.

By following the annual and quarterly reports of the parent firms, the reporter can initiate local stories of considerable reader interest.

◀ **Depth Reporting**

The Founding Fathers were concerned about the dangers of a strong central government. They could not have imagined the power that business would acquire. International banks and the conglomerates exercise enormous influence over the lives of people everywhere, and this power is worthy of scrutiny by the press in its role as watchdog.

Such examination starts at the local level. How much power do local realtors have over planning and zoning decisions? What role does money play in elections? Does local government really have to give businesses and developers tax write-offs and abatements as an incentive? Is the tax structure equitable or does it fall too heavily on families, working people, home owners? In states with natural resources, is the severance tax properly balanced with other taxes, or are the extractive industries penalized or given preferential treatment?

As the 1990s drew to a close, local and state governments found themselves in deep financial straits. Revenues were not meeting the demands the public was placing on government. The business community demanded an end to regulations, taxes and fees that, it said, caused high prices and was an erosion of the tax base.

Many cities and states listened. But to cut taxes, these governmental units had to cut services, especially those to the poor, and this led to tensions with serious political consequences.

Better Stories. Paul Hemp of *The Boston Globe* makes these suggestions for improving business and economic stories:

• Avoid economic jargon.
• Define economic terms.
• Use statistics sparingly.
• Humanize business news.
• Go beyond the press release.
• Get both sides.
• Show the significance of statistics.

Stock Tables ▶

The New York Stock Exchange.

New York Stock Exchange

Behind these pillars hundreds of millions of shares of stocks and bonds are sold and bought daily. These transactions affect world finance.

Caution. Be wary of press releases about new products or plans. These may be planted to drive up the price of a stock. Avoid advising readers or listeners to buy or sell a stock. This is called *touting;* to offer such advice you must be registered with the SEC. Reporters who offer such advice have been fined.

The business reporter sometimes needs to check the current price or the dividend of a stock listed on one of the exchanges. Here are a few stocks listed on the New York Stock Exchange and a guide to understanding the symbols:

High	Low	Stock	Div.	Yld %	P-E Ratio	Sales 100s	High	Low	Close	Net Chg.
59⅛	[1] **40⅛**	[2] **ATT**	[3] **1.32**	2.3	20	10740	57⅜	56⅝	57⅜	+⅜
55⅜	41¼	Gannett	1.28	[4] **2.5**	[5] **21**	1833	52⅛	51¼	51½	–⅝
44½	35⅛	GMot **pf** [6]	3.31	7.9	. . .	[7] **700**	42½	41⅞	42⅛	–¼
49¼	31⅝	Goodyr	1.00	2.33	10.7	1190	[8] 43½	42⅞	43	–1
39⅝	25⅞	McDonalds	.27	.73	20.5	55547	37½	36⅝	[9] 37⅛	**–1**

1. The highest and the lowest price the stock has sold for in the past 52 weeks.

2. Abbreviated name of the corporation that lists the stock. Stocks are common stocks unless an entry after the name indicates otherwise.

3. The annual dividend. When a letter follows the dividend, consult a box at the bottom of the stock table for reference.

4. Yield, the dividend paid by the company expressed as a percentage of the current price of the stock. A stock that sells for $50 at the current market value and that is paying a dividend at the rate of $2 a year is said to return or to have a yield of 4 percent. In the example of Gannett, the dividend of $1.28 divided by the price of 51½ results in the yield percentage of 2.5.

5. The price-earnings ratio. The price of a share of stock is divided by the earnings per share over a 12-month period. A stock selling for $50 a share with annual earnings of $5 a share is selling at the price-earnings ratio of 10 to 1. The P-E ratio is 10. In the table, Gannett's P-E ratio of 21 is calculated by dividing the closing price of 51½ by Gannett's annual earnings of $2.45: 51½ ÷ 2.45 = 21.

6. A preferred stock. Usually, preferred stock entitles stockholders to a specified rate of dividends, here $3.31 a year. Holders of preferred stock are entitled to a claim on the company's earnings before dividends may be paid to holders of common stock.

7. The number of shares traded this day for the stock, listed in 100s. Here, 70,000 shares of General Motors preferred stock were sold.

8. The highest price paid for this stock during the day's trading (43½. The lowest price paid was 42⅞).

9. The closing price, or the price of the stock on the last sale of the trading day. Here, the closing price was 37⅛, or $37.13 a share. The closing price was down $1 from the closing price of the previous day.

Business Terms

This material was prepared by Jim O'Shea for *The Des Moines Register.*

assets These are anything of value the company owns or has an interest in. Assets usually are expressed in dollar value.

balance sheet A financial statement that lists the company's assets, liabilities and stockholder's equity. It usually includes an *Earnings* or *Income Statement* that details the company's source of income and its expenses.

calendar or **fiscal year** Some companies report their income or do business on the regular calendar year. Others do it on a fiscal year that could run from any one month to the same month a year later. Always ask if the companies do business on a fiscal or calendar year. If the answer is fiscal, ask the dates and why. You might find out something unusual about the company.

capital expenditures This is the amount of money a company spends on major projects, such as plant expansions or capacity additions. It is important to the company and the community as well. If the company is expanding, include it in the story. Frequently, such plans are disclosed in stock prospectuses and other SEC reports long before the local paper gets its press release.

earnings Used synonymously with *profit*. Earnings can be expressed in dollar terms (XYZ earned $40) or on a per-share basis (XYZ earned $1 per share for each of its 40 shares of stock). When used as an earnings figure, always compare it to the earnings for the same period in the prior year. For example, if you want to say XYZ earned $1 a share during the first quarter, half or nine months of 1993, compare that with the 50 cents per share the company earned in the first quarter, half or nine months of 1992. That would be a 100 percent increase in profit.

liabilities These are any debts of any kind. There are two types of liabilities: short term and long term. Companies consider anything that has to be paid off within a year a short-term liability and anything over a year a long-term liability.

sales or **revenues** These terms are used synonymously in many companies. A bank, for example, doesn't have sales. It has revenues. A manufacturer's sales and revenues frequently are the same thing, unless the company has some income from investments it made. Always include the company's sales in a story with its earnings. If you say a company earned $40 in 1993 compared to $30 in 1992, you also should tell the reader that the profit was the result of a 100 percent increase in the company's sales, from $100 in 1992 to $200 in 1993. Use both sales and earnings figures. Don't use one and not the other.

stockholder's equity This is the financial interest the stockholders have in the company once all of its debts are paid. For example, say XYZ company has assets of $1,000 and total debts of $600. The company's stockholder's equity is $400. If that figure is expressed on a per-share basis, it is called *book value.* (If XYZ had issued 40 shares of stock, each share would have a book value of $10.)

Deficit: The difference between expenditures and revenues.

Debt: The total of all deficits. It is covered by debt obligations such as Treasury bonds and bills.

Daniells, Lorna. *Business Information Sources,* 2d ed. Berkeley, Calif.: University of California Press, 1985.

Galbraith, J. Kenneth. *The Affluent Society.* Boston: Houghton Mifflin, 1958.

Kluge, Pamela Hollie. *Guide to Business and Economics Journalism.* New York: Columbia University Press, 1991.

◀ **Further Reading**

Mintz, Morton. *At Any Cost*. New York: Pantheon Books, 1985.

Moffitt, Donald, ed. *Swindled: Classic Business Frauds of the Seventies*. Princeton, N.J.: Dow Jones Books, 1976.

Silk, Leonard. *Economics in the Real World*. New York: Simon & Schuster, 1985.

Smith, Adam. *The Money Game*. New York: Random House, 1976.

24 Local Government and Education

Frank Woodruff, *The Sun-Bulletin* (Binghamton, N.Y.).

Homeless youth, an urban problem.

Preview

Local government reporters cover the actions of agencies and departments and the interplay of interest groups and government. Some areas of coverage are:

- **Budgets, taxes and bond issues.**
- **Politics:** The activities of candidates and elected officials.
- **City planning and zoning.**

The local government reporter covers government as a process. He or she covers the daily interaction of the public, pressure groups and city government and reports how the consequences affect residents of the community.

Education reporters cover the financing of the school system, curriculum decisions and the quality of education offered students.

Newspaper readers, television viewers and radio listeners are more interested in local events than in any other kind of news. They want to know what the ambulance was doing around the corner, why the principal of the Walt Whitman High School was dismissed and how the new city manager tamed the city council.

Newspapers and stations respond to this interest by assigning their best reporters to key local beats, and usually the best of the best is assigned to city hall, the nerve center of local government. From city hall, elected and appointed officials direct the affairs of the community—from the preparation of absentee ballots to the adoption of zoning regulations. They supervise street maintenance and construction, issue birth and death certificates, conduct restaurant inspections, collect waste and dispose of it and collect parking meter coins.

The city hall reporter is expected to cover all these activities. To do this, the reporter must know how local government works—the processes and procedures of agencies and departments, the relationship of the mayor's office to the city council, how the city auditor or comptroller checks on the financial activities of city offices.

The city government engages in many essential activities that the reporter scrutinizes:

◀ **City Government Activities**

1. Authorization of public improvements, such as streets, new buildings, bridges, viaducts.
2. Submission to the public of bond issues to finance these improvements.

3. Adoption of various codes, such as building, sanitation, zoning.

4. Issuance of regulations affecting public health, welfare and safety. Traffic regulations come under this category.

5. Consideration of appeals from planning and zoning bodies.

6. Appointment and removal of city officials.

7. Authorization of land purchases and sales.

8. Awarding of franchises.

9. Adoption of the expense and capital budgets.

The city is a major buyer of goods and services and usually one of the city's largest employers. Its decisions can enrich some businesses, as indicated in the beginning of this story by Josh Getlin of the *Los Angeles Times:*

During the last year, Los Angeles Councilman Howard Finn and his wife enjoyed a free weekend in Newport Beach and Councilwoman Peggy Stevenson was wined and dined at some of New York's finer restaurants.

In both cases, Group W Cable TV officials were wooing council members to round up votes for the East San Fernando Valley franchise that could be worth $75 million.

Lavish entertaining is just part of a multimillion dollar campaign by six firms to win the city's last major cable franchise. . . .

The city is the creature of the state. The state assigns certain of its powers to the city, enabling the city to govern itself. The city has the three traditional branches of government—a judicial system and executive and legislative arms. In some cities, the executive is a powerful mayor who has control over much of the municipal machinery. In others, the mayor's job is largely ceremonial and the mayor may not even have a vote on the city council.

Legislative branches differ, too. But for the most part, the city council or commission has the power to act in the nine areas outlined.

The council or commission takes action in the form of ordinances and resolutions. An *ordinance* is a law. A *resolution* is a declaration or an advisory that indicates the intention or opinion of the legislative branch.

An ordinance is *enacted:* The city council last night enacted an ordinance requiring dog owners to have their pets innoculated against rabies.

A resolution is *adopted:* City commission members last night adopted a resolution to make June 18 Frances Osmond Day in honor of the longtime city clerk who died last Tuesday.

Forms of Local Government ▶

The city council-mayor system is the most common form of local government. In large cities, the mayor is usually a powerful figure in city government, the centerpiece of what is called the strong mayor system. In this system, the mayor appoints the heads of departments and all other officials not directly elected. This system enables the mayor to select the people he or she wants to carry out executive policies.

Governing the City

Mayor-Manager Form

(A strong mayor system)

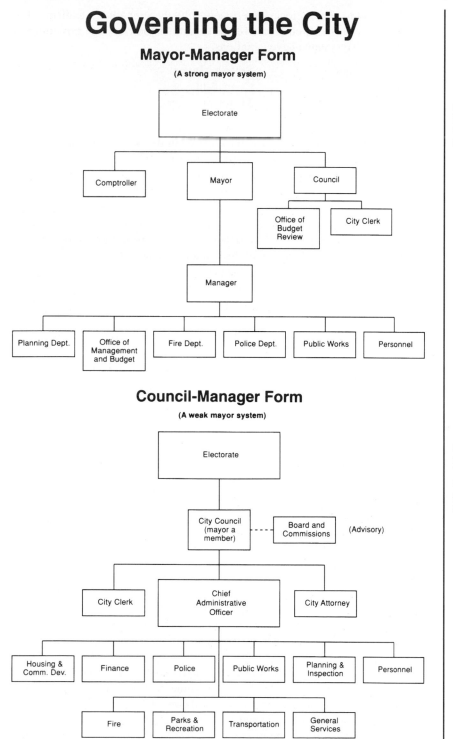

The mayor appoints most department and agency heads and the city manager, who is responsible for day-to-day operations.

Council-Manager Form

(A weak mayor system)

The mayor, who is separately elected, serves as a member of the city council. The mayor's powers are mostly ceremonial. Major appointments are made by the council.

One way to classify local government is by the strength of the office of the mayor, the power the chief executive has to initiate and carry out programs and policies. The two systems have variations:

Weak Mayor	Strong Mayor
Commission	Council-mayor
Commission-manager	Mayor-manager
Council-manager	

The weak mayor systems and the creation of the post of city manager were reactions to the misuse of power by strong mayors and their inability to manage the bureaucracy. To be elected and to hold office, the mayor must be an astute politician, not necessarily an able administrator. The wheelings and dealings of the strong mayors—exposed by such muckrakers as Lincoln Steffens—led people to reject a system that some critics said encouraged corruption. A movement toward less-politicized and more efficient local government developed early in the 20th century. It took the form of the council-manager system.

The manager, who is hired by the council, is a professionally trained public administrator who attends to the technical tasks of running the city government—preparing the budget, hiring, administering departments and agencies. While the manager does increase the managerial efficiency of local government, the system has been criticized as insulating government from the electorate by dispersing responsibility and accountability. Several cities have returned to the strong mayor system in an effort to place responsibility in the hands of an identifiable, elected official.

An offshoot of the council-manager system is the mayor-manager plan. This combines the strong mayor, politically responsive to the electorate, with the trained technician who carries out executive policies and handles day-to-day governmental activities.

In weak mayor systems, elected commissioners serve as the legislative branch and the executive branch. The commissioners are legislators and also head various municipal departments—finance, public works, public safety, planning, personnel. Often, the commissioner of public safety also serves as mayor, a largely ceremonial post in this system.

The commission form has been criticized for blurring the separation of powers between the legislative and executive branches. In the commission system, there is no single official that the electorate can hold responsible for the conduct of local affairs.

The council-manager and the mayor-manager systems are the most prevalent. The commission system, once strong in cities of less than 500,000 population, appears to be giving way to the commission-manager.

The Public Interest ▶

As we saw, the city manager plan was initiated during a period of reform as a means of taking politics out of local government. Other means have been advanced: the nonpartisan ballot, extension of the merit system and career services to protect city jobs from being used for patronage, the payment of low salaries to mayors and council or commission members to take the profit out of public service. Many cities have been the battlegrounds between the good government groups and their opponents, who disdainfully describe the good government people as the "goo-goos." Some contend that the result of taking power from party leaders and elected officials is its transfer to nongovernmental groups and bureaucracies.

There are few identifiable public interests that most people agree upon. There can be a public consensus on such matters as public safety and national defense. But the great majority of issues resolve into a contest among differing special interests. The political process involves much more than the nomination and election of candidates. We can define the political process as the daily interaction of government, interest groups and the citizenry.

Professors Wallace S. Sayre of Columbia University and Herbert Kaufman of Yale put the political process in terms useful to the government reporter. They describe the participants as actors in a contest for a variety of goals, stakes, rewards and prizes. The police officer on the beat whose union is seeking to fend off reductions in the police force is an actor in the contest, as is the mother of three who is urging her school's Parents Association to speak out for more crossing guards at the elementary school. They are as much a part of the political process as the mayor who journeys to the state capital to seek a larger slice of state funds for welfare and health or who decides to seek re-election and lines up backing from unions and ethnic groups.

◀ Participants in the Political Process

We can group the participants in the city's political process as follows:

- **The political party leaders:** The leaders and their organizations have a strong hand in the nominating process, but the other participants have increased their power and influence as the political party has declined in importance. Insurgents sometimes capture nominations, and the leaders must compromise their choices for the highest offices in the interest of finding candidates who can win.

- **Elected and appointed officials:** The mayor, members of the city council or commission and their administrators occupy key roles in governing the city. As the party's power has waned, the mayor and the visible elected and appointed officials have become independent decision makers.

- **Interest (pressure) groups:** Every aspect of city policy making is monitored by one or more of the political interest groups. Business groups are especially interested in the budget process: Real estate interests will want a low property tax rate, larger and more efficient police and fire departments; the banks scrutinize the debt policies since they are the buyers of bonds and notes; contractors urge public improvements. The bar associations watch the law enforcement agencies and the legal department as well as the judiciary.

Religious groups and educational organizations keep track of school policies. Medical and health professions examine the activities of the health department. The nominating process and the election campaigns attract ethnic and labor groups as well as the good government groups.

Interest groups compete with each other to influence the city leadership and its bureaucracy, and this limits their influence. Sometimes, however, an interest group may control the decision making of a department or agency, as when, for example, the real estate interests take over the planning and zoning department or the banks and bond market control decisions about the sale of bonds.

• **Organized and professional bureaucracies:** City employees have become independent of the party organization as the merit system, unionization and the professionalization of city services have increased. Police, firefighters and teachers have been among the most active in influencing the political process.

• **Other governments:** The city government is in daily contact with a variety of other governmental units: the county, the state, the federal government, public authorities and special assessment districts. These governments are linked by a complex web of legal and financial involvements. State approval is often necessary for certain actions by the city. State and federal governments appropriate funds for such city services as education, health and welfare. City officials are almost always bargaining with other governmental units.

• **The press:** "The communication media provide the larger stage upon which the other participants in the city's political contest play their parts with the general public as an audience," says Kaufman. But, he continues, the media "do more than merely provide the public stage." They also take a direct part in the process. Having its own values, emphasis, stereotypes and preoccupations, the press is not an exact mirror or reporter, he says. The media highlight personalities, are fond of exposés, are prone to fall for stories about new public works, are too zealous in looking for stories about patronage crumbs—and are too skeptical of officials and party leaders, he says.

Lewis W. Wolfson, a professor of journalism at American University, says that the press too often depicts government "not as a process, but as a succession of events, many of them in fact staged for the media." He suggests that the press "tell people more about how government works, how it affects them, and how they can influence it."

Auditing the Community ▶

Along with covering the nine governmental activities listed at the beginning of this chapter, the local government reporter keeps tabs on the city's economic and social conditions.

The Economy ▶

Much of the community's health depends on its economy—the availability of jobs, the ability of the city to meet its bonded indebtedness and to support first-rate schools and services. Reporters use several measuring sticks to gauge the local economy:

• Employment and unemployment rates.
• Housing starts.
• Telephone and utility connections.
• Automobile sales.

- Hotel and motel occupancy rates.
- Sales tax revenues.

These factors also are considered by the agencies that rate the city's credit. A high rating means the city will be able to sell bonds at a low interest rate. A low rating means the city is in poor financial condition and will have to offer high interest rates as an inducement to buy its bonds, which furthers the city's tight financial condition. The local reporter regularly checks the city's credit rating.

◀ **The Schools**

Good schools help to make the city financially secure since industry and business are attracted to communities with an educated work force. Some measures of the quality of education include dropout rate; high school graduation rate; percentage of graduates going on to college; SAT and ACT scores; pupil-teacher ratio; average teacher salary.

We will look in greater detail at education later in this chapter.

◀ **Other Indicators**

Other measures of a community's well-being include:

- **Health data:** Children's immunization rate; infant mortality and maternal death rates; suicide rate; availability of child health clinics;
- **Social conditions:** Percentage of children in single-parent homes, in poverty, born to teen-agers; divorce rate; crime rates.

Robin Graubard,
The New York Post.
City Tensions

One of the most important indicators of a community's health is its social harmony. Is diversity a community goal? Here, the reporter relies on sources among the community's religious, political and economic leaders; teachers and students; working people.

The larger the city, the more pressing the problems of race. But race is entwined with class—that is, minority groups are poor: 46 percent of black and 40 percent of Hispanic children live in poverty. Despite a steady rise in the economic condition of many, the poor have become poorer.

◀ Inner-City Problems

Increasing attention is being paid to what one writer described as "dreadful enclosures," the areas marked by drugs, crime and poverty. For decades, any examination of the problems of minority groups was attacked with the charge of racism, the response that befell a study in 1965 by Daniel Patrick Moynihan who warned that the growing numbers of children being born to single black mothers was likely to result in serious social problems.

At the time Moynihan published his study, the illegitimacy rate among blacks was 26 percent. Today it is 68 percent. The white rate of out-of-wedlock births, 23 percent, is growing at an even more accelerated rate.

The consequence can be seen in some data sociologists find disturbing: More than two-thirds of juveniles confined for violent offenses grew up in single-parent homes. Violent crime is being committed by younger and younger men, most the product of fatherless homes.

From Idyllic Village to Urban Nightmare

". . . Not only are the streets dominated by the criminal element, but the schools and the housing projects as well. One's life is up for grabs, one's children will either be victimized by the criminal element or recruited into criminal enterprise. Almost nothing can be done to help the law-abiding majority of the ghetto unless and until crime and the drug trade are brought under control. . . ."—Irving Kristol, *The Wall Street Journal.* Right, Mel Finkelstein, © *New York Daily News,* Inc. Above right, Larry C. Price, *The Philadelphia Inquirer Magazine.* Above left, The Plumas County Museum.

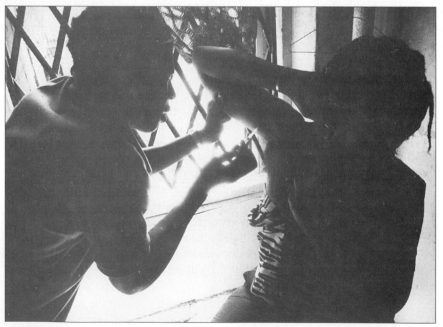

Debbie Noda, *The Modesto Bee*

Homelessness: A Growing City Problem

For increasing numbers of men and women, poverty means calling a park bench or a cot in a shelter home. With his morning haul of bottles and cans, this homeless man is on his way to lunch at the Salvation Army center. Later, he will cash in his collection for a few dollars. Many of the homeless pose massive social problems—alcoholism, drug addiction, mental instability—that city governments are unable to handle because of dwindling resources and public apathy.

The murder victimization rate for white males is 9.0, for white females 2.8. For black males, it is 69.2, and for black females 13.5. The Department of Justice estimates that one of every 21 black men can expect to be murdered.

Some sociologists forecast an epidemic of violent crime as youngsters born to teen-age mothers in an environment of drugs and poverty reach their teens. John DeIulio of Princeton predicts 35,000 to 40,000 homicides a year by the turn of the century, an increase of 75 to 100 percent.

As the figures reveal, minorities are the victims of crime disproportionately to their numbers, and this has led many in minority communities to speak out. Rep. John Lewis, a Georgia Democrat, said:

> All across the nation black communities are under an assault of crime and violence that is without precedent in our history. Under the savage assault, it is not too much to say that the low-income black community is disintegrating and violence and crime are the order of the day.

He went on to cite homicide data and illegitimacy rates, and he said that when "schools dare to record the truth, the dropout rates are a continuing disaster."

Black children, he said, "are the principal victims of child abuse and neglect. The leading cause of death for black children aged one to four is fire."

He said, "Increasingly over the past 30 years, crime and violence have been allowed to run virtually unchecked through poor black communities . . . more and more the most conspicuous models of success were the racketeer, the pimp and the insidious drug dealer. . . . It is not only poverty that has caused crime. In a very real sense it is crime that has caused poverty, and is the most powerful cause of poverty today."

By the mid-1990s, the conspiracy of silence was broken. The media began to describe the tragedies and triumphs of daily life in the ghetto.

The New York Times ran a series, called "Children of the Shadows." One story tells of Ladeeta, an 18-year-old high school senior, who has "survived almost every plague of adolescence in neighborhoods defined by hopeless girls with babies and angry boys with guns." Her father drank himself to death. Her mother, a crack addict, died of AIDS. Ladeeta ran with a gang of girls that beat and robbed other girls. "Her first job was holding drugs and cash for a major neighborhood crack dealer," the story states.

Her grandmother plucked Ladeeta from the street life and sent her to a school where teachers took an interest in her. They are struggling to convince her she can have a future. She wonders: "Sometimes I think, how far am I going to be able to go being female and black—two things against me."

Disparities. Increasingly, journalism is concerned with the growing differences in economic status by race.

Median Income

Black	$21,548
Hispanic	$23,912
White	$39,308

Families Below the Poverty Line

Black	31.3%
Hispanic	26.2%
White	9.4%

An African proverb states, "It takes a whole village to raise a child." With that in mind, an organization called Zero Population Growth combed through dozens of studies and reports to derive a "Children's Environmental Index," a rating of more than 200 U.S. cities in terms of air and water quality, crime, education, social and economic factors, toxics in the environment. Here are its winners and losers, the top and bottom 20 cities:

Rank	Top Rated	Rank	Bottom Rated
1	Madison, Wis.	207	San Bernardino, Calif.
2	Burlington, Vt.	206	Newark, N.J.
3	Stamford, Ct.	205	Long Beach, Calif.
4	Fargo, N.D.	204	El Monte, Calif.
5	Lincoln, Neb.	203	Inglewood, Calif.

6	Overland Park, Kan.	202	Los Angeles, Calif.
7	Sioux Falls, S.D.	201	Pomona, Calif.
8	Livonia, Mich.	200	Atlanta, Ga.
9	Green Bay, Wis.	199	Riverside, Calif.
10	Virginia Beach, Va.	198	St. Louis, Mo.
11	Cedar Rapids, Iowa	197	Detroit, Mich.
12	Sterling Heights, Mich.	196	Ontario, Calif.
13	Billings, Mont.	195	Fresno, Calif.
14	Lubbock, Texas	194	Moreno Valley, Calif.
15	Sunnyvale, Calif.	193	Stockton, Calif.
16	Des Moines, Iowa	192	Miami, Fla.
17	Raleigh, N.C.	191	Oxnard, Calif.
18	Hampton, Va.	190	Gary, Ind.
19	Boise City, Idaho	189	Tampa, Fla.
20	Plano, Texas	188	Baton Rouge, La.

The study, with its detailed ratings of 207 cities in more than 50 categories, is available from ZPG, 1400 16th St., NW, Suite 320, Washington, DC 20036.

Many issues are settled by elections. The task of the reporter covering politics is to make clear to readers and viewers the issues that define and differentiate the candidates so that an informed choice may be made.

Despite appearances to the contrary, campaigns are carefully planned. Ralph Whitehead at the University of Massachusetts says, "It is possible to read a campaign. Assume every decision is made for a reason. Hence, a campaign can be decoded. A reporter's job is to do this decoding," he says.

David Broder, who covers politics for *The Washington Post,* says the reporter's job is to cull from campaign rhetoric "those few words, incidents and impressions that convey the flavor, the mood and the significance of what occurred." This means selectivity, Broder says, "the essence of all contemporary journalism. And selectivity implies criteria. Criteria depend on value judgments, which is a fancy term for opinions, preconceptions and prejudices. There is no neutral journalism."

One of the journalist's values is that officials and candidates for public office are accountable. This means that reporters consider themselves obligated to push candidates on issues that the reporters consider important. When a reporter reads a candidate's campaign as one in which relevant issues are skirted or covered over with generalities, the reporter presses the questions that will force out the issues.

If it's a congressional race, the public is entitled to know the candidates' positions on the federal budget, aid to the states, tax rates, welfare, prayer in school, abortion. If it's a city council election, the reporter should ask about the property tax rate, needed long-range improvements to be financed by bonds, ways to attract business and industry. If it's a school board election, ways to improve academic performance, sex education, AIDS instruction, prayer in school, the voucher system, teaching students values and school financing.

◄ **Politics**

Politics Defined. Ambrose Bierce defined politics as "a strife of interests masquerading as a contest of principles." John Kenneth Galbraith said, "Politics is not the art of the possible. It consists in choosing between the disastrous and the unpalatable."

Key Elements. David Yepsen of *The Des Moines Register* says there are four elements to a political campaign—the candidate, the money, the issues and the organization. Coverage of each involves:
Candidate: profile, interviews with friends, associates.
Money: political fundraisers, campaign disclosure reports, advertising program.
Issues: candidate's platform, public's input.
Organization: key figures, campaign plans.

This kind of substantive coverage is more informative than what is known as "horse race" reporting, which consists of using polls to indicate who is ahead at various stages of the campaign.

Some Tips on
Campaign Coverage ▶

Candidates go where the votes are. This is a useful guide for covering candidates for local and state offices, less so for candidates for the major national offices since television takes their campaigns into homes everywhere. The reporter covering a mayoral or gubernatorial campaign who watches the candidates' schedules for the week can make some informed conclusions, says Whitehead.

Where does the candidate go, how often and on what terms? When a Jewish candidate spends most of his time in the Catholic areas of town, one conclusion may be drawn. If he gives a large part of his time to appearances at synagogues and Jewish organizations, another conclusion may be drawn.

Another tip: Watch the media purchases. If the candidate is buying television spots near daytime soap operas, he or she is looking for the homemaker's vote.

Follow the Buck ▶

Go to the People. David Broder of *The Washington Post* advises journalists, "The campaign is really the property of the voters. We should be spending a lot of time with voters. Literally, spending time with voters—walking precincts, knocking on doors, talking to people in their living rooms. What I am talking about is a serious, conscientious reporting effort to determine what the voters' concerns are—and then letting that agenda drive our coverage."

Whose money fuels the candidates' campaigns? It's easy to find out since all states require financial disclosure in state and federal races. Some states demand reports as often as every two weeks before the election. Political action committees are large donors. PACs favor incumbents. A study showed they donate 10 times as much to House incumbents as to their challengers.

PACs and other large donors are not giving from the goodness of their hearts. They want favorable legislation. In the Nebraska legislature, for example, the PAC of the state's 4,000 liquor retailers wanted a no vote on a bill that would require bars to post signs warning that drinking during pregnancy could cause birth defects. On the legislative committee considering the bill, legislators who opposed it had received an average of 53 percent more in PAC contributions than did the legislators who voted for the bill.

Thomas Winship, former editor of the *Boston Globe,* suggests that it should be a matter "of routine coverage for all newspapers to print an updated financial profile of each member of their congressional delegation before they go to Washington for an upcoming session." He says such an accounting can be had from the Federal Elections Commission and the Center for Responsive Politics, both in Washington, D.C. The Center publishes a handbook, *Follow the Money,* by Larry Makinson that is designed to help reporters set up databases to relate campaign donations to a politician's votes.

Most candidates run to win, but sometimes a candidate runs to raise an issue, or is being used as a strawman or stalking horse for other interests. If an Irish candidate is running against a candidate of Polish descent, the Irishman may field another candidate of Polish descent to split the Polish vote. The subsidized candidate is known as a stalking horse.

Reporting the
Issues ▶

The political reporter has a sense of what the public considers important, and this becomes the substance of questions directed to the candidates. Their answers can provide the voters with more information than can the source-originated handout, speech or television commercial.

Too many reporters have more interest in the politics of government than in its substance. "The *what* is missing because most reporters still lack either the interest or the confidence to judge the substance of government as acutely as they judge politics," says James Fallows, a veteran journalist.

◀ Cutting Through the Rhetoric

The banner across the window of campaign headquarters reads, "Your congressman is there when you need him." The theme is repeated in the congressman's campaign for re-election. No one bothers to ask what it means. Emboldened by the acceptance of slogans and generalities, politicians and office seekers generate empty catchphrases by the bushel.

The political reporter should see through these substitutes for the specific, calculated devices by which the candidate or official avoids taking a position. It is impossible to hold a public official accountable for the rebounding promise, "I pledge to work for you." Nor is the public a whit more informed after being told the candidate intends to "listen to you."

Pretense and sham pervade politics. Candidates blur issues and try to appear as cozy as the television advertising pitchman. And reporters sometimes fall for this. "Our great democracies," said the philosopher Bertrand Russell, "still tend to think that a stupid man is more likely to be honest than a clever man, and our politicians take advantage of this prejudice by pretending to be even more stupid than nature made them."

◀ New Players

Time was when it was legal for a man to beat his wife, as long as the stick he used was no wider that the width of his thumb. Times have changed. But progress has been slow for women in politics. In the United States, they gained the right to vote in 1920, but by the mid-1990s, they held only about one-tenth of the 535 seats in the Senate and the House. They have fared better in cities and in state legislatures. They hold the mayor's office in 150 large cities and have one-fifth of the seats in state legislatures.

Women have become a powerful voting bloc. Studies show they tend to vote on issues more than men do. In recent elections, they have made decisions on the basis of the candidates' positions on abortion, day care, education, care for the poor and the elderly and health care.

To the Point. "I think it's about time we voted for senators with breasts. After all, we've been voting for boobs long enough."—Claire Sargent, Arizona senatorial candidate, 1992. (She lost.)

◀ Cynicism and Stenography

Reporters who cover government are so trained to find the malfunctions and the excesses and failures that they become cynical about government. They forget that the tasks of government often reflect the demands citizens make on it. They join a skeptical public in what Felix Frankfurter, a distinguished justice of the Supreme Court of the United States, described as "the paradox of both distrusting and burdening government." He said that this state of mind "reveals the lack of a conscious philosophy of politics."

A reporter needs to define for himself or herself some approach to the job of covering the interaction between those who govern and those who are governed. Cynicism disables the reporter in the task of helping the public to articulate its demands of its officials. The cynic believes that the process is futile or the actors in it are hopelessly corrupt or so inefficient that nothing can work.

The Electorate. "Half of the American people never read a newspaper. Half never vote for president. One hopes it is the same half."—Gore Vidal

The reporter who acts as stenographer to officialdom is equally useless since by failing to use his or her knowledge and experience, essential issues may not become part of the agenda for public debate.

The Budget ▶

Covering local government—indeed, covering all levels of government—requires a knowledge of how money is raised and how it is spent. Money fuels the system. The relationship between money and the workings of government can be seen in the budget process.

"I've had to learn how to cover five governmental units, and I find the single best way to learn what they are doing is to attend budget hearings," says David Yepsen, political reporter for *The Des Moines Register.* "They let you know the current situation, what the problems are, the proposed solutions and where government is headed."

"Follow the buck," says the experienced reporter. The city hall reporter follows the path of the parking-meter dime and the property tax dollar as they make their way through government. The path of these dimes and dollars is set by the budget.

The budget is a forecast or estimate of expenditures that a government will make during the year and the revenues needed to meet those expenses. It is, in short, a balance sheet. Budgets are made for the fiscal year, which may be the calendar year or may run from July 1 through June 30 or other dates. The budget is made by the executive branch (mayor, governor, president, school superintendent) and then submitted to the legislative body (city council, state legislature, Congress, board of education) for adoption.

The budget is the final resolution of the conflicting claims of individuals and groups to public monies. This means that the conscientious reporter watches the budgeting process as carefully as he or she examines the finished document. Aaron Wildavsky of the University of California at Berkeley describes the budget as "a series of goals with price tags attached." If it is followed, he says, things happen, certain policy objectives are accomplished.

The budget is a sociological and political document. As Prime Minister William Ewart Gladstone of Britain remarked more than 100 years ago, the budget "in a thousand ways goes to the root of the prosperity of the individuals and relation of classes and the strength of kingdoms."

The budget can determine how long a pregnant woman waits to see a doctor in a well-baby clinic, how many children are in a grade school class, whether city workers will seek to defeat the mayor in the next election.

Here is the beginning of a budget story by Paul Rilling of *The Anniston* (Ala.) *Star:*

A city budget may look like a gray mass of dull and incomprehensible statistics, but it is the best guide there is to the plans and priorities of city government.

Rhetoric and promises aside, how the city council decides to spend available money says what it really sees as the city's top priorities.

Tuesday, the Anniston City Council will consider for formal adoption the proposed city budget for fiscal . . .

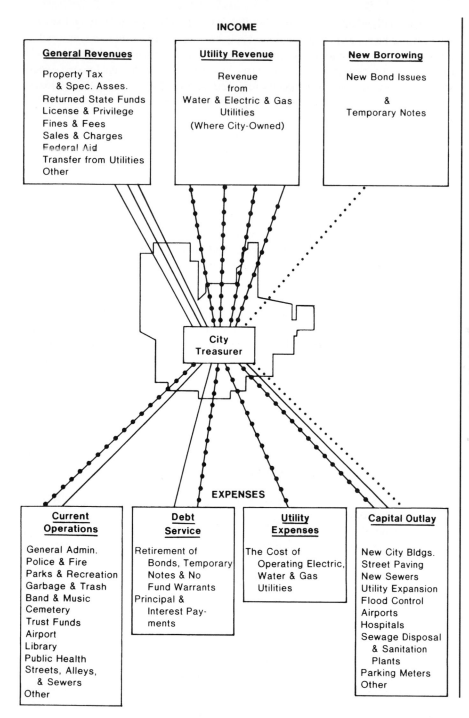

INCOME

General Revenues

Property Tax
& Spec. Asses.
Returned State Funds
License & Privilege
Fines & Fees
Sales & Charges
Federal Aid
Transfer from Utilities
Other

Utility Revenue

Revenue
from
Water & Electric & Gas
Utilities
(Where City-Owned)

New Borrowing

New Bond Issues

&

Temporary Notes

City
Treasurer

EXPENSES

**Current
Operations**

General Admin.
Police & Fire
Parks & Recreation
Garbage & Trash
Band & Music
Cemetery
Trust Funds
Airport
Library
Public Health
Streets, Alleys,
& Sewers
Other

**Debt
Service**

Retirement of
Bonds, Temporary
Notes & No
Fund Warrants
Principal &
Interest Pay-
ments

**Utility
Expenses**

The Cost of
Operating Electric,
Water & Gas
Utilities

Capital Outlay

New City Bldgs.
Street Paving
New Sewers
Utility Expansion
Flood Control
Airports
Hospitals
Sewage Disposal
& Sanitation
Plants
Parking Meters
Other

A City's Money Flow

This chart describes the major sources of revenue and the major areas of expenditures in an average city. Note the specific uses to which income may be put by following the different types of lines to and from the city treasurer.

Cover the Whole Process ▶

City hall, education, county and legislative reporters handle budget stories on a regular basis. Reporters on these beats begin to write stories several months before the budget is adopted so that the public can be informed of the give-and-take of the process and participate early in the decision making. In a six-week span, Bill Mertens, city hall reporter for *The Hawk Eye,* wrote more than a dozen stories. Here are the beginning paragraphs of two of them:

> School crossing guards may be one of the programs lost if Burlington city councilmen intend to hold the new budget close to the existing one.

> The city council has asked Burlington fire department heads to cut $30,000 from their budget request.

Most of the dozen-plus stories were enterprised by Mertens. Knowing the budget process and having good sources, Mertens was able to keep a steady flow of interesting and important copy moving to the city desk. In his stories, Mertens was always conscious of the human consequences of the belt tightening. By writing about possible cuts in such areas as school crossing guards and the fire department, Mertens alerted the public. Residents could, if they wished, inform their council members of their opposition to the cuts.

Types of Budgets ▶

Two types of governmental expenditures are budgeted—funds for daily expenses and funds for long-range projects. At the local governmental level, these spending decisions are included in two kinds of budgets: expense budgets and capital budgets.

Expense Budgets ▶

The expense or executive budget covers costs of daily expenses, which include salaries, debt service and the purchase of goods and services. Expense budget revenues are gathered from three major sources:

- Taxes on real estate—the property tax—usually the single largest source of income.
- General fund receipts, which include revenues from fines, permits, licenses, and taxes such as income, corporation, sales and luxury taxes. (States must give cities permission to levy taxes.)
- Grants-in-aid from the federal and state governments.

Capital Budgets ▶

The capital or construction budget lists the costs of capital projects to be built and major equipment and products to be purchased. Capital budget funds are raised by borrowing, usually through the sale of bonds pledged against the assessed valuation of real estate in the governmental unit. Bonds are approved by the voters and then sold to security firms through bidding. The firms then offer them for public sale. The loan is paid back much like a home owner's payments on a mortgage over an extended period, 10, 20 or 30 years. Principal and interest are paid out of current revenues and are listed in the expenditures column of the expense budget as "debt service," which should run under 10 percent of the total budget for the city to be on safe economic footing.

Most budgets are adopted in this series of steps:

◀ Making the Budget

1. Budget request forms go out to all department heads, who must decide on priorities for the coming year and submit them to the budget officer, mayor or school superintendent.
2. Meetings are held between the budget officer and department heads to adjust requests and formulate a single balanced program.
3. The budget is submitted to the city council or commission, the board of education or other legislative arm of the governmental unit. The budget is sometimes accompanied by a narrative explaining the requests.
4. The legislative body examines budget items for each department and agrees on allocations for each.
5. Public hearings are held.
6. The budget is adopted.

The reporter can cover each stage of this process, the behind-the-scenes bickering, dickering and politicking as well as the formal activities of the various department heads, executives and legislators. All sorts of pressures are brought to bear on the budget makers. Property owners and real estate interests want the budget held down, for increased expenditures usually mean higher property taxes. The businessmen and -women who rely on selling goods and services to the city seek hefty budgets for the departments and agencies they serve. Employees want salary increases, generous fringe benefits and more lines in the budget for promotions. Politicians seek to reward constituencies and to fulfill campaign promises.

Adoption

◀ Checklist: Budgets

___ Amount to be spent.
___ New or increased taxes, higher license and permit fees and other income that will be necessary to meet expenditures.
___ Cuts, if any, to be made in such taxes, fees or fines.
___ Comparison with preceding year(s).
___ Justification for increases sought, cuts made.
___ Rate of current spending, under or over budget of previous year.
___ Patterns behind submission and subsequent adjustments, such as political motives, pressure groups, history.
___ Consequences of budget for agencies, departments, businesses, public.

Follow-Up

___ Per-person comparison of costs for specific services with other cities or school districts of same size.
___ Check of one or more departments to see how funds are used, whether all funds were necessary.

Sources ▶

There are five major interest groups that seek to influence budget making and so constitute the reporter's sources:

1. **Government:** Chief executive, who submits the budget; mayor, governor, school superintendent, president; city manager; head of budget bureau or budget director; department heads; finance and taxation committees of the city council or commission; council members. (Party leaders outside government are sometimes helpful.)

2. **Money-providing constituencies:** Local real estate association; property owners association; chamber of commerce; taxpayer organizations; merchant and business groups; banks; savings and loan associations.

3. **Service-demanding groups:** Lobbyists for education, health, welfare and other services.

4. **Organized bureaucracies:** Public employees; municipal unions; civil service associations; the public employees' retirement fund manager.

5. **Independent groups:** League of Women Voters; National Municipal League; National League of Cities; U.S. Conference of Mayors; Advisory Commission on Intergovernmental Relations.

Cautions ▶

Taxes are the source of great passion in the political marketplace. Politicians seek to impress the public with promises of parsimony to avoid angering the money-providing constituencies.

The truth is that many items in the budget are mandated costs that cannot be shifted or eliminated without massive political changes. The mandated funds include salaries, debt service, pensions and matching funds that localities must produce to meet state and federal grants, particularly for such services as health, welfare and education. When the city accepts grants from the state or federal government, it must abide by rules and regulations that often require local expenditures.

The actual maneuvering room in most budgets is not great, especially since salaries, which represent the largest single expense item, are set by contract in many cities. Because of mandated costs, less than 10 percent of the budgets for most large cities is discretionary.

Costs can be reduced if commitments to the poor, the elderly and the ill are cut back. This, however, would antagonize the service-demanding constituencies. Maneuvering room could be created by changing earmarked funds, such as those for education, to general funds. Again, groups that benefit from the status quo would object. In tight times, city employees are pressed to forego wage increases.

The competition for free-floating general funds is always intense, and the perceptive reporter will examine this contest during the budgetary process. In this competition, the administrator finds it necessary to trade off the demands of various groups. The trade-offs make good stories.

Departments and agencies usually exaggerate their needs, and pressure groups seek deeper cuts than are feasible. Budget making is a give-and-take process. Despite the agonized pleas or the dire warnings of the participants, the city, state or nation usually survives.

Some aspects of the process are hidden from view. The reporter must dig them out and learn which constituencies are involved, the motives of the participants. Are political debts being paid by building a school in one section of the city or by increasing salaries in a particular agency? Have cuts been made in the department of a critical or independent administrator?

During a legislative session, the Republican governor of New York proposed a new formula for the distribution of state aid to local school districts that reflected the demands of big-city school officials. A few days later, a group of Republican state senators and assembly members from Long Island met with the governor, who was facing re-election. Following the meeting, the governor's aid formula was changed to give more aid to suburban school districts.

"What happened at the gathering," reported *The New York Times,* "was summed up later by Joseph M. Margiotta of Uniondale, the powerful Nassau County Republican leader, who related that the Long Island delegation had simply delivered to the governor the stern message that without more state education aid, Long Island property taxes would skyrocket in September and the governor's campaign would sink in October."

When Mayor John Lindsay of New York "dropped the broom and picked up the nightstick"—the graphic phrase the *Daily News* used to describe the shift in budget priorities from clean streets to public safety—it was widely interpreted as Lindsay's recognition that law and order would make a more attractive national issue than sanitation. Lindsay had presidential ambitions.

The 1990s were marked at the state and local level by unbalanced budgets. When governments did act, the political consequences were often dramatic: student protests against tuition increases at tax-supported colleges and universities, homeless people sleeping in welfare offices, oversized classes and school closings leading to parent protests.

The property tax is the largest single source of income for municipalities, counties, special districts and school systems. It affects more people than any other local tax but the sales tax. Considerable local, county and school coverage centers on the action of the council, commission or board in setting the property tax.

The tax is formally known as the *mill levy.* A mill is .1 cent (1/10¢), and the property tax technically is expressed in terms of mills levied for each dollar of assessed valuation of property. One-tenth of a mill per dollar works out to 10 cents per $100 in assessed valuation, or $1 per $1,000 in valuation.

Here is the formula for figuring the property tax or mill levy:

Mill levy = Taxes to be collected ÷ Assessed valuation

Let us assume budget officials estimate that $1 million will have to be collected from the property tax and that the assessed valuation of real estate in the city or school district is $80 million. Here is how the tax is figured:

Mill levy = $1 million ÷ $80 million

Mill levy = $1 ÷ $80 = $.0125

Mill levy = 1.25 cents on each $1 of assessed valuation

◀ Budget Politics

Suburban Growth. Almost half the country's population lives in suburbs; 14 states have a majority suburban population. Some effects: political strength (majority Republican) shifting to the suburbs; a hostility to central-city government; greater concern for security and privacy; less concern for inner-city problems of race and class.

◀ **Property Tax**

Since mill levies are usually expressed against $100 or $1,000 in assessed valuation, the levy in this community would be $1.25 for each $100 in valuation, or $12.50 for each $1,000 in valuation.

Note that the mill levy is applied to assessed valuations, not to actual value as determined in the marketplace. Assessed value is usually a percentage of market value.

Here is the beginning of a story about the adoption of the city budget:

The Mt. Pleasant City Council adopted a $217 million budget last night and set a tax rate of $108.50 for each $1,000 in assessed valuation.

The rate represents a $6 increase in the tax rate for property owners for next year.

Those owning homes assessed at $50,000, which is the average Mt. Pleasant assessment, will pay $5,425 a year in city property taxes. The current bill for a $50,000 home is $5,125.

Remember that the property tax is a major source of revenue for several governmental units—city, county, school, special assessment districts. When covering the action of one unit in setting a tax rate, it is necessary to inform the reader that this particular property tax is not the only one the property owner will pay.

Property taxes levied by special assessment districts can add a large chunk to the tax bill. The special districts construct and maintain services such as power and water lines, hospitals, sewage systems and community development projects. Each district has the power to levy taxes on property within the district.

Property valuations are made by the tax assessor and are public record. The tax rate is set each year, but valuations on individual pieces of property are not changed often. Total assessed valuation does change each year because of new construction and shutdowns that add to or subtract from the tax rolls. The taxing district must establish the total assessed valuation each year before a new tax rate can be set.

Reassessments ▶

When the assessor does make new valuations, the intensity of feeling is considerable, as revealed in this story:

SPRING VALLEY, N.Y., Dec. 12—Listening to people here, a visitor would almost think that someone was stalking the streets, sowing horror and destruction.

But it is only the tax assessor, equipped with a collapsible 10-foot measuring stick, a set of appraisal cards, a practiced eye that

can tell the difference between a toilet and a water closet and experience that tells him which adds more value to a house.

This village of 22,450 persons, 2,219 dwellings and 109 commercial properties is nearing the end of a year-long reappraisal. . . .

The purpose of reassessments is not to increase the city's property tax income but to redistribute the tax burden. With reassessment, some pay less, and some pay more. People on fixed incomes whose property is valued higher than it was in previous years often have trouble, especially the elderly. Some states have what is known as "circuit breaker" regulations that limit tax hikes for certain groups.

When their assessments were increased, 2,000 Greenwich, Conn., property owners complained, including a multimillionaire developer and the singer Diana

Ross. In his story, Christopher Keating of *The Hartford Courant* quoted the chairman of the Board of Tax Review: "If we knock down everybody, the mill rate will have to go up."

Keating was pointing out that when a community decides to increase revenues through the property tax, it has two choices: raise assessed valuations or raise the property tax rate. A reassessment generally is more equitable.

The assessor sometimes is politically motivated in establishing assessments. In some cities, residential properties are consistently underassessed in order to placate home owners. In Philadelphia, tax officials assessed residences at 40 percent of market value, whereas commercial property was assessed at 54 percent and industrial property at 59 percent. In Chicago, the political machine of Mayor Richard J. Daley underassessed large corporations and industries. At election time, these beneficiaries of the assessor could be counted on for large campaign contributions.

Most cities need seasonal funds to tide them over while waiting for income from taxes or grants to arrive. They also need money to finance major construction projects. ◀ **Borrowing**

For seasonal borrowing or for emergencies when small amounts are needed, the city may issue and sell to banks anticipation notes. Future tax collections and anticipated grants-in-aid are pledged as security. Usually, the state must approve. Most borrowing for large projects is done through the sale of bonds.

The idea behind the sale of bonds is that the costs of such long-range projects as schools, hospitals, streets, sewage plants and mass transit should be borne by those who use them over the anticipated lives of the projects. ◀ **Bonds**

There are three major types of bonds. They differ as to the type of security pledged to repay them:

• **General Obligation:** Most frequently issued. Security is the general taxing power of the city. Bonds are retired by taxes on all property in the city.

• **Special Improvement:** For construction of sidewalks, sewers and similar public works. Taxes are levied on the property owners who will benefit from the construction. Charges levied on the property are called *special assessments*. Special assessment districts are set up to levy and collect the taxes.

• **Revenue Bonds:** To pay for the acquisition, construction and improvement of such properties as college dormitories and public utilities. The pledge is a lien on earnings, which are used to redeem the bonds. These earnings come from room charges in dormitories; water, gas and electric collections from utility customers; toll charges on bridges and highways.

Bonds are paid off in two ways:

• **Term Bond:** The securities are retired at the end of the specified term, 10, 15, 20 years. Meanwhile, money is set aside regularly in a sinking fund and invested to be used to retire the bonds at the end of the term.

• **Serial Bond:** Most common. A portion is retired each year.

In writing bond stories, the reporter should make sure to include the cost of the bonds to taxpayers. Some readers will be astonished to learn how much a seemingly small rate of interest can add to the principal.

When Nassau County in New York sold $103 million in bonds for roads, land purchases and new sewers, officials estimated that interest would cost about $50 million over the life of the bonds. One reason for the high cost of debt was the downgrading of the county by bond-rating agencies as a result of the county's financial problems. The downgrading resulted in the county having to offer higher interest rates to attract investors worried about the lowered rating of the bonds.

Here is the beginning of a story about a credit downgrading:

> TROY, N.Y. (AP)—The City of Troy, which continues to struggle with a four-year-old financial crisis, had its credit rating reduced below investment grade Friday by Moody's Investors Service.
>
> Moody's said it had cut Troy's credit rating from B-aa to B-a, one step below investment grade. . . .

Anticipation Notes ▶

Short-term low-interest borrowing consists of three types of anticipation notes—revenue, tax and bond. All notes must be repaid in a year.

Grants-in-aid are an important part of the governmental unit's income or revenue. But these federal and state payments for such items as education, welfare, health and other services usually do not arrive in time to meet the payroll or the demands of vendors to be paid for their goods and services. The city, county or school district may have to borrow money for a short time and then pay it back when the grants arrive. This borrowing is in the form of revenue anticipation notes (RANS) sold to banks.

Some local taxes are not collected until late in the year, and the anticipated income has to be made up for by short-term loans, which are made by issuing tax anticipation notes (TANS). Bond anticipation notes (BANS) are sold in anticipation of revenue from the sale of bonds.

Checking Up ▶

Wherever public money is involved, there is an overseeing agency that checks to see that the money is spent properly. Most governmental units undergo internal checks made by agency auditors, and these make good stories. Here is the beginning of a story by Jayne Garrison of the *San Francisco Examiner:*

> OAKLAND—A Social Services Department audit says mismanagement and internal squabbling are so severe that clients would be better off if the agency were dismantled.

In addition, checks are made by an independent government agency or office. Cities, states and the federal government have a department or office independent of the executive that checks the financial activities of all agencies within government. At the federal level, the Government Accounting Office does this work. At the state level, the state auditor or comptroller is the watchdog, and at the city level an elected official, also known as the auditor or comptroller, examines the financial records of city offices.

A regular or pre-audit examination is made of purchase orders and vouchers. This audit determines whether there is money to pay for the goods, whether there are certified receipts for the delivered goods, whether there has been competitive bidding when required by law, whether the prices are reasonable.

Increasingly, auditors and comptrollers are conducting performance audits, which check the efficiency of the services, the quality of the goods and the necessity for purchasing them.

Pre-audit example: A state official claims travel reimbursement for an official trip between Boulder and Denver. The auditor will determine whether the 39 miles claimed on the official's expense account attached to a pay order is the actual distance and will see whether the 29 cents a mile claimed is the standard state payment.

Performance audit example: The comptroller has decided to make a check of welfare rolls to see whether money is going out to ineligible people. The office makes a computer check of the welfare rolls against (a) death lists; (b) marriage certificates (if a person receiving aid to dependent children has married, the working spouse is obligated to support the children); (c) children in foster care homes still listed as at the residence; (d) city and state payrolls to determine if any employed people are receiving welfare.

Journalists make their own checks also. They regularly look through vouchers and pay orders in the auditor's office, and they look at the cancelled checks in the treasurer's office.

When a governmental unit wants to buy something, it sends a purchase order to the comptroller's or auditor's office, which makes a pre-audit. Records are kept by the number of the purchase order, by the agency involved and often by the name of the vendor.

On delivery of the goods or services, a voucher is made up with the accompanying bill, and this starts the payment to the vendor. The payment is made in the form of a check, a warrant.

When Christopher Scanlan of *The Providence Journal* was examining vouchers of the Providence Housing Authority, he came upon payments of $3,319.59 made to restaurants in Providence and Warwick for "authority meetings." On checking, he learned that members of the authority had been meeting over meals for years. "The restaurant tabs were paid from authority funds, the majority of which are derived from rents paid by low income tenants at the city's 14 public housing projects and from federal subsidies," Scanlan wrote. After the story ran, the authority members agreed to hold meetings in the housing projects it manages.

An examination of vouchers and warrants enabled George Thiem, a reporter for *The Chicago Daily News,* to expose a multimillion-dollar corruption scheme by the Illinois state treasurer. Thiem could see that a number of checks were endorsed by typewriter. Interviewing some of those who supposedly were paid by these checks for work done for the state, he learned that the people listed on the checks had never done state work; nor had they received the checks. The treasurer went to prison as a result of Thiem's investigation.

Investigating Government ▶

Official misconduct is the subject of most investigative projects. Reporters have a keen sense of their obligation to check on public officials who are entrusted by their constituents to spend money wisely and to make policy decisions with the public welfare in mind. It doesn't always work that way, and often someone who knows what is going on tips a reporter.

Reporters describe such sources as being "inside the factory." Not all tips are useful and some are extremely difficult to verify. All must be handled with caution. Bill Marimow of *The Philadelphia Inquirer* says he does the following after receiving allegations of misconduct from a source:

1. Asks the source whether he or she knows of anything in writing: an audit by an official agency or a report by a private accounting firm; a deposition in a civil suit or any other documents that support the allegations.

2. Finds out whether anyone else knows about the misconduct and is willing to talk about it—"preferably, on-the-record, but, if not, on a not-for-attribution basis." Would this person know of anything on the public record?

"At all times, in the initial phase of research, the emphasis should be on finding out if there is anything whatsoever—however small—on the public record to document the allegations," Marimow says.

3. Tries to assure the source that while the allegations sound plausible, he still needs to prove it "through documentable and attributable information" to write a story. "If you were me," Marimow suggests telling the source, "how would you go about documenting these allegations?" Does the source know of any official inquiry—by the FBI, district attorney, auditor, comptroller?

The Shoebox Papers ▶

While she was gathering material for an article about the effects of federal budget cuts on the poor, Carol Matlack of the *Arkansas Gazette* spoke to a church worker who told her about an elderly man and his wife who had lost their home through foreclosure.

"She told me there was something suspicious about it," Matlack says.

"She gave me a bundle of the man's papers—he had recently died—that had been stored in a shoebox in his house.

"The documents proved the key to the story."

With the papers and from records in the county courthouse and through interviews, Matlack was able to piece together the story of an interlocking relationship between a private investment firm and a special assessment district in a poor neighborhood that cost residents their homes through foreclosures.

Her series begins this way:

> Hosie and Clover Mae Willis were stunned when they got a letter ordering them to move out of their home. It was their first notice that their modest frame house on College Station's Frazier Pike had been sold for nonpayment of $62 in special improvement taxes several years earlier.

After describing the couple's improvements to the property, in which they had reared three children, Matlack disclosed that Southern Investment Co. of Little Rock had purchased the property from Water Improvement District 74 for $124.71 in taxes and penalties.

Had the Willises inquired further, they would have learned that the commissioners of Water Improvement District 74 who sold their property—W.J. White, Jack Barger and Marcelite Cook—all were affiliated with Southern Investment.

They would also have learned that at least two dozen College Station residents have lost their property in similar fashion because of a failure to pay taxes—sometimes as little as $20—to one of five water improvement districts in the predominantly poor, black community south of Little Rock Airport.

Residents said they had never been told their taxes were delinquent. Nor were they notified their land was being sold.

Why all the activity in a poor, black neighborhood? Matlack answers the question in her third article that begins:

> "Little nuggets of gold." That's how Pratt Remmel Sr., a Little Rock businessman, describes a string of weedchoked lots he owns along a potholed road in College Station.

Matlack points out that a highway would soon go by the area, carrying "one of the heaviest traffic volumes in Arkansas." An interchange was to be built north of College Station, and the area would have hotels, restaurants, motels and an industrial park.

Follow the buck. The paper trail Matlack followed led from the simple homes of poor folk to the offices of wheelers and dealers.

Postscript: In its next session, the General Assembly of Arkansas reformed procedures for delinquent tax notification.

For centuries, the mentally ill were locked up. The reasons seemed logical: Isolated, the mentally ill could be healed more rapidly; free in society, their conditions worsened; they were a danger to others and to themselves. Gradually, the truth seeped out. Journalists showed that institutions for the mentally ill were snake pits where the patients were treated inhumanely. Few were cured, and many were made worse. With the development of tranquilizing drugs and other treatment, it became possible to offer outpatient care. But there had to be a transition, a halfway house to help the patient adjust after institutionalization.

◀ **Zoning and Planning**

Neighborhood Stories ▶

Covering the Schools ▶

In New Jersey, the Catholic Diocese of Trenton decided to administer several such houses. The state intended to deinstitutionalize its mental patients, and the diocese sought to help. The diocese found a structure in Willingboro that fit its needs. But permission was required from the zoning board since the building was in a residential area.

The Willingboro zoning board, like thousands of other such boards, carries out the community's planning goals, which are usually set by the planning commission. The zoning boards divide an area into zones or districts and designate them residential, commercial or industrial. The boards then grant building and construction permits consistent with these designations.

The boards also regulate the use of land and buildings within these zones. They regulate the height of buildings, lot size, yard dimensions and other aspects of construction. City councils enact the ordinances that the zoning boards enforce.

Zoning can be restrictive, a way of keeping certain people out of an area. By requiring that new construction be of single-residence homes on one-acre lots, a zoning regulation will effectively keep out of the area all but the well-to-do. When Laura King, who covered Willingboro on her suburban beat, attended the zoning board meeting at which the diocese requested a variance for its halfway house, she was struck by the hostility of the spectators. King decided that the opposition to the house was the story.

City hall reporters spend too much of their time in city hall, says a veteran municipal government reporter. He recommends that they make regular trips out of the protected environs of the municipal building and into the neighborhoods of the community to see what is on the minds of people, to check how city programs and policies have been carried out. Here is the beginning of a neighborhood story by Jayne Garrison of the *San Francisco Examiner:*

OAKLAND—In the heart of the Oakland flatlands, the moms and pops of small business are plotting to sweep out the rubble: dope, litter and boarded buildings.

About 35 merchants meeting in churches and stores the last few weeks have organized a voice they hope will boom across town to City Hall—the Central East Oakland Merchants Association.

This is the first time in more than a decade that merchants along central East 14th Street have tried to wield clout together. The odds against them are steep.

They have little political pull and even less money. They face absentee landlords who own some boarded storefronts, and youths who have no work outside the drug trade.

But they do have determination.

"You see that red church down there?" said Al Parham, nodding toward a tall brick steeple half a block past Seminary Avenue on East 14th Street. "They just built that. So people are coming back into the community. And they're going to church. They care."

Communities spend more money on public education than on any other single tax-supported activity. Free public education has a long history in the United States. In 1642, the Massachusetts Bay Colony made education compulsory in the primary grades and required towns to establish public schools. The cost is borne by all in the community, whether the individual has children in the public school or not. The reason was given succinctly by Thaddeus Stevens to the

James Woodcock, *The Billings Gazette.*

Ms. Olson's Crowded First Grade Classroom

Tight financing has caused overcrowding in classrooms. Here, in the Meadowlark Elementary School in Billings, Mont., Bonnie Olson tries to cope with her 26 students. The state set 20 as the classroom limit, but Meadowlark had to request an exemption because of the school's severe financial straits. The school district also had to ask for a waiver on the requirements for a librarian in each school and a guidance counselor for each 400 students.

Pennsylvania state legislature in 1835 when some legislators objected to the general financing of the schools.

"Many complain of the school tax," Stevens said, "not so much on account of its amount, as because it is for the benefit of others and not themselves. This is a mistake. It is for their own benefit, inasmuch as it perpetuates the government and ensures the due administration of the laws under which they live, and by which their lives and property are protected."

The faith in education as the underpinning of democracy is a constant theme in American life, along with the belief that it paves the way to a good job, if not to the good life. Education pervades the life of most families because they have children in school.

The interest in schools—which really means a concern for the community's children—led *The Fincastle Herald* in Virginia to run a banner across page one

The Process. The school budget is drafted by the city school superintendent and presented to the school board for approval. In many cities, the voters then must approve the budget.

Usually, the schools seek as much as possible and the board attempts to cut back in order to lower the mill levy. The board members have mixed motives: While sensitive to the needs of schoolchildren, members reflect property owners' desires to keep taxes down.

when the Scholastic Aptitude Test (SAT) scores for the county were made public. "Low SAT scores surprise school officials," read the headline. The story was accompanied by a large box comparing county scores with those in Virginia, southern states and the nation. The story by Edwin McCoy begins:

> Botetourt County students scored at least 20 points below the state and national averages on both parts of the Scholastic Aptitude Test (SAT), according to figures provided by the county school system this week.

McCoy described education as the "focal point in the community" in an editorial accompanying the news story. "The quality of education is important to industrial or commercial development because developers are interested in the quality of life in any area they choose to expand in or move to."

Structure of the System ▶

The school system is based in school districts. The schools are independent of municipal government and are subject to state regulations through a state board of education. School boards, usually with five to seven members, are elected in nonpartisan elections, though in some cities board members are appointed by the mayor. The board hires a superintendent of schools who is responsible to the board.

Stories from the board and the superintendent's office involve such subjects as changes in the curriculum and personnel, teacher contracts, the purchase of new equipment, aid to education, teacher certification, school dates for opening, closing and holidays and the vast area of school financing that includes budgeting and the issuance of bonds.

The school administration can provide material for assessing the performance of the system and its schools. Dropout and truancy records are kept, as are the results of standardized tests. Reporters can compare the scores in their communities with those of other cities. Comparisons also can be made of schools within the system. Do the students in the low-scoring schools come from economically depressed areas with serious social and economic problems? Is there a correlation between income and achievement?

A check of high school graduates would indicate what percentage is going to college from each school. Interviews with the students may uncover information just as revealing as the students' test scores. This takes us to the primary responsibility of the education reporter.

In the Classroom ▶

The education reporter's responsibility is to hold the school system accountable to parents and to the community. The United States has committed itself to an educational system that will turn out large numbers of people educated beyond the level that the country demanded only of its educated elite a century ago. How well is it doing this?

The best way to begin to find out is to visit the classroom, to look at what is happening day after day and to check your observations against test scores and the assessments of parents and educators. When Bob Frazier of the *Register-Guard* in

Eugene, Ore., covered education, he would scrunch all 6′ 4″ into a grade schooler's chair and sit in class. The stories he wrote were much more significant than any release from the superintendent's office.

School visits will tell the reporter whether the principal has a sense of mission and exerts strong leadership. They will reveal the professional level of teachers, whether they are given respect and whether they, in turn, give students respect and attention. The school environment is checked: Is the school safe? Is there a strong code of behavior, and are violators punished? Is truancy increasing or declining? Records can be examined for the frequency, number and type of discipline problems and vandalism.

Does the high school have various tracks for its students, such as academic, vocational and general, and, if so, what percentage of students is in each? In the early 1960s, one of 10 students nationally was in the general track; by 1990, almost half were. (The general track usually gives credit for physical and health education, work experience outside school, remedial English and mathematics and developmental courses such as training for adulthood and marriage.)

How much homework is given? A national survey of eighth graders found youngsters spent 5½ hours a week on homework, 21 hours a week watching television. *The Raleigh Times* put at the top of page one its education reporter's story that half the state's students in the sixth and ninth grades do less than three hours of homework a week.

The education writer, who can be considered a consumer reporter since coverage is devoted to determining the quality of the product, also can play the role of book reviewer. Textbooks should be examined every so often, especially during the adoption period.

The reality of the textbook industry is that it is no different from any other market-driven business. When a small-town couple in Texas succeeded in forcing the Texas textbook adoption board to downplay evolution and to make Charles Darwin a nonperson in biology textbooks, the entire textbook industry was affected. Because Texas adopts few textbooks in each subject, it orders huge numbers of the books it selects. To meet the demands of the Texas adopters, publishers caved in to the religious right.

The publishers, for example, made their authors include "creation science" in general science and biology textbooks. This is a religious tenet that states that a divine being created all life several thousand years ago. Although federal courts have overturned state laws requiring the teaching of creationism in the public schools because of its religious nature, pressure groups continue to push for its inclusion in textbooks.

Despite some improvement in textbook adoption procedure in Texas, publishers were still having problems with the adoption board in the mid-1990s. Several groups attacked high school health textbooks submitted for adoption, demanding more than a thousand changes in the books. Among the changes demanded were the deletion of self-examination techniques for breast and testicular cancer, information about the transmission of HIV and, of course, sex.

Depressing Data. Studies have shown:
- Fewer than a fifth of 11th graders can write a note applying for a summer job at a swimming pool.
- Of 21 to 25-year-olds, only 38 percent could figure their change from $3 if they had a 60-cent cup of soup and a $1.95 sandwich. One of five young adults can read a schedule well enough to tell when a bus will reach a terminal.
- Among college seniors, 58 percent could not identify Plato as the author of *The Republic;* 60 percent could not recognize the definition of Reconstruction; 58 percent knew that the Civil War was fought between 1850 and 1900; 25 percent did not know that Columbus landed in the New World before 1500.

◀ **Textbook Adoptions**

◀ **Creation Science**

Alabama Persists. The Alabama Board of Education requires a sticker on all biology textbooks used in public schools that says evolution is "a controversial theory some scientists present as a scientific explanation for the origin of living things . . . any statement about life's origins should be considered as theory, not fact. . . ."

The textbook board reduced the demands to 300, but one publisher, Holt, Rinehart and Winston Inc., pulled its textbook out of the competition. "We simply cannot produce a product that does not provide children with adequate instruction on life-threatening issues," the publisher stated. Other publishers made the changes.

An official of the Association of American Publishers said that the requested changes urged by the board were made for "political reasons. This was another case in which factions of the religious right are getting more involved in boards of education all over the country."

Dumbed Down ▶

A study of textbooks by the U.S. Department of Education found that many have decreased in difficulty by two grade levels since the mid-1970s. Few, if any, publishers aim their books at above-average students, the federal study found.

In one Massachusetts school district, the board dropped books by Mark Twain, John Steinbeck, Charles Dickens and others because they feared the authors' books might bore students. Among the books tossed out: *Tom Sawyer* and *A Tale of Two Cities*.

Key Issues ▶

Like all beat reporters, education reporters make periodic checks of certain specific topics. Here are some suggestions for the education beat checklist:

Teacher preparation: Every system admits to a shortage of quality instructors. Some systems want to use merit pay to stimulate good teaching. About 20 states give teachers examinations to test their competence. Some states found that many graduates of schools of education failed the tests.

Curriculum: Responding to criticism that history and related courses are dominated by white males, school systems have attempted to include women, Native Americans, blacks and others in these courses. But some substitutes, sometimes described as a "Curriculum of Inclusion," have stirred angry debate. Critics say these changes encourage separateness and divisiveness.

Misconduct: Administrators report an increasing number of charges against teachers, including sexual advances. Some reporters have shown a reluctance by administrators to press charges. Teachers simply are transferred to other schools.

Required courses: Test scores indicate many high school students have minimal competence in mathematics. At a meeting of a Connecticut school board, Christopher Keating of *The Hartford Courant* reported an incredulous board member saying, "Kids can get out of high school without ever having cracked an algebra book, and still get their three credits in math." To which another board member replied, "All youngsters don't have the capability of taking algebra."

Reporters do not have to wait for board meetings to find out what is and what is not required for high school graduation. Such an investigation will help the community understand whether its tax dollars are being used to prepare students for a technological society or for "a job with Burger King," as one of Keating's sources said.

Segregation: Because of housing patterns, black and Hispanic students make up the majorities of students in many urban schools. In Hartford, for example, more than 90 percent of the students were in these two groups, whereas in the nearby community of Farmington, the schools had a 90 percent white student body. The differences in achievement were marked:

	Percentage above remedial level	
	Hartford	Farmington
Reading	39.3	93.4
Writing	71.5	96.8
Math	58.9	97.0

Thirty-one percent of the Hartford high school students went on to four-year colleges, compared with 76.4 percent of the Farmington students.

The result: A suit by civil-rights lawyers to integrate the city's schools with those in the suburbs.

School year: What's the best way to schedule the school year? Some systems are going to the "year-'round" plan, three or four terms separated by short vacation periods.

Vouchers: Bills have been introduced in a number of states that would direct tax money to parents who could then use the funds for schools of their selection. Advocates say that this would give parents choice and result in a better education for all children.

Opponents of the voucher system say that the result would be the destruction of the public school system. Also, they say, the voucher system would allow tax monies to be used for religious schools, a breach of the First Amendment.

Among the states in which the voucher plan has considerable support: Arizona, Connecticut, Florida, Indiana, New Jersey, New York, North Carolina, Ohio, Pennsylvania, Texas, Wisconsin.

Library books: Periodic attempts are made to purge books from school libraries, especially the books that deal with sex, race and sensitive contemporary subjects. Sometimes even the librarian is purged. The West Valley School Board of Kalispell, Mont., fired its grade school librarian after she had helped two seventh grade students with their research for a class report on witchcraft in the middle ages.

Ethnic sensitivities: In Southampton, Long Island, school administrators refused to allow a student production of "Peter Pan" on the ground that the well-known song "Ugg-a-Wugg" demeans Native Americans.

Values: Some parents and some special-interest groups want schools to offer "moral training." They also do not want sexual issues discussed. The failure of a New York City school chancellor to heed parents' objections to condom distribution in high school and the discussion of homosexuality in grade school led to the city school board's vote to oust him.

Most Often Banned. *Of Mice and Men,* John Steinbeck; *The Catcher in the Rye,* J.D. Salinger; *The Adventures of Huckleberry Finn,* Mark Twain; *I Know Why the Caged Bird Sings,* Maya Angelou; *The Color Purple,* Alice Walker.

Values is one of the key words in the reform vocabulary of the so-called religious right. Its agenda is to use religious values to teach students morality.

As the religious right strengthened in the 1990s, its influence was felt in the nation's public schools. In a special report, the Anti-Defamation League stated, "Religion is currently entering the public school system through a variety of means, including school prayer, graduation prayer, religious clubs, religion in the curriculum, creationism, censorship, distribution of religious materials and voucher plans."

The so-called wall of separation between church and state in effect keeps government out of religion and religion out of government. The Supreme Court has ruled unconstitutional such practices as ceremonial readings from the Bible in the classroom and organized prayer at student assemblies, athletic activities and special events.

Yet such practices exist and are stoutly defended in a number of communities. They continue until someone goes to court to challenge the breach in the wall of separation.

Conservative Christian candidates have been winning school board elections in many states. "Right now the religious right movement has a lot of muscle," reports People for the American Way. On its agenda are the removal of certain books from school libraries, the introduction of school prayer, an emphasis on abstinence in sex education classes and the teaching of creationism.

Crumbling Buildings: By 1996, the nation's school buildings were falling apart, and new construction was needed to alleviate severe overcrowding. The total bill, estimated by the General Accounting Office, amounted to $112 billion. Less than $3.5 billion a year is being spent to repair and replace buildings, some of them a century old. In 1997, enrollment in elementary and secondary schools surpassed the 1971 peak of 51 million, and indications are that the school-age population will reach 56 million in 2004.

Local taxpayers, the source of most of the funds for schools, are unwilling to shoulder the cost. And the national anti-tax mood makes state and federal assistance unlikely. Taxpayers are also being asked to finance an improvement in student performance, which, educators contend, requires smaller classes, better-paid teachers and technological and other educational additions to classrooms.

Whether the public schools will be able to attract increased financing depends on decisions made in a political context. Though many candidates for office pledge to improve the schools, once in office they usually allocate funds grudgingly, say educators.

Affirmative Action: Racial preference programs have produced what David K. Shipler, a former *New York Times* reporter describes as "a legacy of tangible successes and poisonous resentments." Proposed as a temporary remedy for decades of racism and sexism in education and employment, affirmative action gradually became politically unpopular with the white

Divisive. Disturbed by the strongly religious repertoire and the frequent church appearances of her Salt Lake City public school choir, a 16-year-old West High School choir member and her parents filed suit when the school refused to acknowledge their objections. The student was called a "dirty Jew" and a "Jew bitch," and when she ran for school office, swastikas were drawn on her campaign posters.

A federal appellate court ordered the choir to refrain from performing two religious songs at the school graduation, but during the ceremony a student leaped on the stage and urged people to sing one of the songs. They did so, with enthusiasm.

In Okaloosa County, Fla., the practice of praying before football games went to court and the prayer was eliminated. In a Texas case, *Doe v. Duncanville,* the court held that the girls' basketball coach could not lead the team in the Lord's Prayer.

The legal issue today is whether students may, on their own initiative, lead prayer at graduation ceremonies, pep rallies, athletic events and the like.

middle class. In 1995, for example, the regents of the University of California system abolished the program for admission to the university.

Some educators maintain that it is possible to select good candidates for college admission even if their paper qualifications do not match those of whites. At the University of Texas Law School, using grades and test scores would have resulted in a class with nine blacks and 18 Mexican Americans. Under the affirmative action guidelines of the school, 41 blacks and 55 Mexican Americans were admitted. Four rejected white applicants sued, and a federal judge ruled, "Until society sufficiently overcomes the effects of pervasive racism, affirmative action is necessary."

Affirmative action, like the voucher plan, has become politicized, which takes us to a reality that education reporters must contend with.

The conventional wisdom is that education is "above politics." The proof: The administration of the schools is separated from city government and placed in an independent board whose members are chosen without regard to party affiliation, usually in elections set apart from the partisan campaigning of the regular local election.

◀ Politics and Education

The truth is that education is inextricably bound up with politics. Politics enters the scene because, to put it simply, people differ in their notions of how youth should be trained, who should pay for it, who should control it. These differences are resolved in a political context. The conflict and its resolution should be at the heart of much of the reporter's coverage. The political debate runs from the White House to the local school board that meets in the little red schoolhouse.

Surveys have shown that a majority of parents are pleased with their children's education. Yet every measure of school achievement contains alarming material about students in many states.

◀ Pleased Parents, Disturbing Data

The education reporter who consults the National Assessment of Educational Progress conducted by the U.S. Department of Education has available an unbiased insight into his or her state's schools. A recent NAEP survey found that fourth graders in 13 states could not read at the "basic" level, defined as "partial mastery" of the knowledge and skills in reading that are expected of a fourth grader.

Parents Matter. "If every parent in America made it their patriotic duty to find an extra 30 minutes to help their children learn more each and every day, it would literally revolutionize American education."—Richard Riley, Secretary of Education.

These states are Alabama, Arizona, Arkansas, California, Delaware, Florida, Georgia, Hawaii, Louisiana, Maryland, Mississippi, New Mexico and South Carolina.

Nationally, 42 percent of fourth graders score below the basic level. If we divide this overall figure into ethnic and racial groups, we find these percentages of low-scoring students:

White	32 percent
Black	72
Hispanic	67
Asian	23

The 10 states with the highest scoring fourth graders in the NAEP test were Connecticut, Indiana, Iowa, Maine, Massachusetts, Montana, Nebraska, New Hampshire, North Dakota and Wisconsin.

The enterprising reporter will try to find causes for these figures. Among the factors that educators consider to affect academic performance are class size and pupil-teacher ratio. The better performing states showed a much higher over-all percentage of classes with fewer than 25 students than did the states with poorly performing students. Also, the highest pupil-teacher ratio in the better states was 15.8 whereas the lowest ratio in the poor-performing states was 16.6. The median class size for the high-scoring states was 15.3; the median class size for the low-scoring states was 17.3.

Maine's class size averaged 14.1, California's 24.1.

The NAEP describes itself as "the only nationally representative and con-tinuous assessment of what America's students know and can do in various sub-ject areas." It issues "Report Cards" frequently. They are available to the public at this address: National Library of Education, Office of Educational Research and Improvement, U.S. Department of Education, 555 New Jersey Avenue, NW, Washington, DC 20208-5641, (202) 219-1651.

The Other Half ▶

While much attention is focused on the students whose grades and scores indicate severe academic problems, many of them stemming from social causes, little attention is being paid to the deterioration in the academic achievement of college-bound high school students. Studies show that since the mid-1970s, these students have been performing below their abilities.

One of the first to state the problem was the National Commission on Ex-cellence in Education, which in its study "A Nation at Risk," published in 1983, stated, "Each generation of Americans has outstripped its parents in education, in literacy, and in economic attainment. For the first time in the history of our coun-try, the educational skills of one generation will not surpass, will not equal, will not even approach, those of their parents."

Test scores among students in the lowest quarter have been going up, espe-cially among black student test takers. But there has been a considerable drop among the middle- and the top-ranking students.

In 1972, 11.4 percent of the students taking the SAT had verbal scores over 600. In 1983, the number dropped to 6.9 percent, and it is still in the low digits. Even the elite colleges show a 50- to 60-point drop in verbal scores of those ad-mitted. College faculty members state in several studies that they are spending too much time and their institutions are spending too much money on material their students should have mastered in high school.

Writing seems to be a major casualty among college students. Given the high school emphasis on first-person narratives, students enter college lacking the ability to analyze material and to marshal evidence to support a logical argu-ment. The NAEP reported in 1984 that its analysis of writing tests led to the con-clusion that "Analytic writing was difficult for students in all grades," and that they had "less difficulty with tasks requiring short responses based on personal experience."

The state of the smartest students in the classroom is even more perilous, a federal study found. Many of the country's most talented children, particularly talented poor and minority students, are never identified as gifted, and when they are they are not encouraged to work hard or to master rigorous and complex material. Most of these schoolchildren spend time in classes that require little effort.

Only 2 cents out of every $100 spent on K–12 education is devoted to talented children, most of whom have mastered a third to a half of the curriculum of their classes before they attend. In high school, high-achieving students are asked to do less than an hour's homework a day.

One of the results, the federal report stated, is that there is such a shortage of mathematics and science students that many large companies must go abroad to recruit employees.

Any number of ideas are suggested in the name of school reform. How can a journalist judge the effectiveness of some of the changes that have been instituted? The bottom line is performance, and usually that is assessed by test scores.

Albert Shanker, president of the American Federation of Teachers, says that for years when he spoke to principals and superintendents in large urban school districts where students were not doing well, they "would tell me that they had a new plan or policy or initiative that was making a tremendous difference.

"You couldn't see any difference in the test scores, they'd say. But that was not the whole story. If I would only go into the schools, I'd see kids smiling, and I'd feel the warmth in the classroom. That would tell me a whole lot more than test scores."

Shanker did not buy the reassurances. "The whole point of school reform," he says, "is to have students learn more. If this doesn't happen, the experiment is a failure, no matter how happy the children, the parents and teachers—and the reformers—are."

Schools rely for a good part of their revenue on the local property tax, and revenues depend on the valuations in the school district. Thus, one well-to-do district in Texas spent $56,791 a year for each student, and the poorest school district spent $2,337 per student. In Montana, spending per pupil ranged from $2,650 to $9,750.

The disparity in Montana led a judge to strike down the state school financing formula, and in Texas attempts to alter the system have been in the courts since the 1960s. Since 1990, lawsuits have been filed in 28 states in an attempt to increase revenues for impoverished school districts and to equalize the expenditures over the state.

Michigan experimented with a different set of taxes to finance the schools. Instead of relying on the property tax, the state uses sales and other taxes to fund its 3,286 schools. State officials said the new plan would equalize expenditures in rich and poor school districts. It also would cut property taxes, a popular political move.

◀ **The Top 5 Percent**

Cream of the Crop. The country's best mathematics students were tested against the best math students of other nations. The U.S. students finished 17th, a hairline ahead of students from Zimbabwe.

◀ **Assessing Reforms**

Americanization. Immigrant children do better in school than their American-born classmates. But the longer they are in the United States, the worse they perform. Foreign-born children spend more time on homework, studies show, with Vietnamese children spending an average of three hours a day on homework. Among immigrant children, Vietnamese score highest.

◀ **Funding Schools**

Like other governmental issues, school finances can be complex. Reporters resist the temptation to pass on the complexities and the jargon. Look at how Ramon Renteria handled the Texas school funding issue, which he describes as "a complicated, extremely boring topic." He said he decided to "personalize the issue. I used two little girls and their aspirations to illuminate the issue." Here's how his story begins:

Veronica Marin and Kelli Freeman—two bright and vibrant 8-year-olds—share the same dream. They want to go to college and become teachers.

But these two laughing little Texas girls live 600 miles and a world apart. And that could make all the difference. One's dream is endangered.

In Texas, poor school districts like Veronica's have far less to spend on education than rich district's like Kelli's. And that, according to a lawsuit moving through Texas courts, means the quality of education often depends on the wealth of the districts.

"Bienvenido a Nuestra Escuela Welcome to Our School" reads the sign at the door of San Elizario Elementary School.

Her dark hair swaying, her backpack heavy with books, Veronica Marin walks down a dusty caliche road to school. Like a gentle princess in blue jeans, she hardly notices the harshness along the way: the outhouses and open irrigation ditches; the neighbors living in rusty school buses, cardboard-covered shacks and feeble homes of tar paper, railroad ties and cinder blocks. . . .

Across most of Texas, just north of Dallas, cheerful, red-headed Kelli Freeman, with her freckles and ponytail and hot pink jogging suit, hops into the family car in suburban Richardson.

Her dad drives her one block to school. And like Veronica, she hardly notices the familiar neighborhood: the crewcut lawns and neat brick homes of doctors, professors, engineers.

Renteria takes the reader inside the schools to show the differences. "Most school districts probably spend more on extracurricular activities than we do in our basic (educational) program," Renteria quotes Veronica's school superintendent. The high school to which Veronica will go has an apalling academic record: one of seven go on to college. A table sets out the record of minimum skills testing in stark terms. These are the percentages of students working at grade level:

	Grade	San Elizario	Richardson
Math	5	47.0	97
	11	21.6	98
Reading	5	25.7	96
	11	63.4	95
Writing	5	22.2	92
	9	23.3	93

Of the many factors affecting the contrasting academic accomplishments of the children, Renteria focuses on the unequal financing of the schools, which is the result of differences in assessed valuations in the two school districts. Richardson has a healthy tax base, and the property tax nets sufficient funds for the schools. With $11.6 billion in taxable property, Richardson has $411,000 of property wealth per student. San Elizario has $31 million in its tax base, or $28,300 a student.

Sam Roe of *The Blade* of Toledo used a similar comparison of two school-girls to show that the Toledo public school system has two school districts offering unequal education. The two-district arrangement, he writes, "didn't happen by chance." Powerful political leaders "maneuvered around state laws to keep the districts separate."

◀ Separate— on Purpose

One contains the city's poorest areas, many of them "solidly black," he writes. The other is "predominantly white." Washington Local has smaller classes than Toledo Public, a 19:1 pupil: teacher ratio compared with 23:1. Washington has better financing, ending the year with a $670,000 surplus, compared with Toledo Public's $7 million deficit. Violence, dropout and attendance rates and courses offered—all were compared, to Toledo Public's disadvantage. At Washington, one of 10 students is from a welfare home; at Toledo Public, it is four of 10.

Roe's story begins:

Joanna Hammer and Anne Marie Meiers both live on 288th Street in Toledo. Joanna lives on the east side, Anne Marie on the west. Joanna is in the fifth grade. So is Anne Marie.

Each weekday, they walk down their street to go to school. For Joanna, that means Toledo Public Schools, a district beset by mounting deficits, violent crime, and an uncertain future.

But Anne Marie doesn't go to Joanna's school. Because she lives on the opposite side of the street, she boards a bus that takes her to an entirely different public school system: Washington Local. It is richer, safer, and, according to many key statistics, simply better than Toledo Public Schools.

This scenario is nothing new. It has been common in Toledo for years.

But it bewilders and outrages people today the same way it has for a quarter-century.

"I've never understood this," says Fred Hammer, Joanna's father. "What is the ratio-nale for Toledo having two separate school districts? I'd much rather have my daughter go to Washington Local, but she can't. I see that as a form of discrimination."

One city. Two districts. Scores of split neighborhoods.

Nowhere else in Ohio is there a situation like it: two large, independent school systems almost wholly within the same city boundaries.

It is an arrangement that few local officials like to talk about but one that affects tens of thousands of students and parents each year.

It is also an arrangement that didn't happen by chance.

Since the 1950s, some of the area's most powerful leaders, men like the late Ned Skeldon, struck deals and maneuvered around laws to keep the districts separate.

The result: a school boundary line splitting the city in two, much like it splits Anne Marie's and Joanna's street right down the middle.

◀ Comparing SAT Scores

Beginning in 1995, what had for decades been the average, 500 on the 200 to 800 scale, changed: On the verbal, a score of 424 would become 500; and on the mathematics section, a score of 478 would become a 500. That is, lower scores under the old system would henceforth be made higher. This means that without the help of a table of comparisons, scores from 1995 on cannot be compared with those of previous years.

The College Board, which administers the SAT tests, stated that the old average had been made with only 10,000 test takers, and now more than a million students take the tests. The larger pool is less selective, the Board said. Robert J.

Samuelson, a columnist for *Newsweek,* criticized the change. He contended that the college track in high school was being "mediocritized." He continued:

Grades were inflated. Courses became less demanding. Less homework was required. Fewer term papers were assigned. The effects cannot be washed away by raising SAT scores. But they can be disguised. High schools do not want to be seen producing poor students; colleges do not want to be seen misspending on the ill-prepared. This is the real reason—conscious or otherwise—for "recentering." It is to make "educators" look better.

Covering a School ▶ Board Election

Increasingly, school board elections have become the focus of community tensions. As special-interest groups with a conservative agenda put candidates on the ballot, the lines dividing residents grow sharper.

In Sioux Falls, S.D., in a recent school board election, two conservative candidates challenged two incumbents seeking re-election. The incumbents were

Mike Roemer, *Argus Leader.*

A Candidate Calls for Fiscal Austerity

Candidates in a school board election in Sioux Falls, S.D., faced questions about how the school system would cope with declining income. Candidate Lora Hubbell, viewed as a conservative candidate, is saying that she would target administrative positions for cuts to protect teaching positions. She also calls for an emphasis on "the basics" and on "values" and less spending on programs that she says led to the current financial problems.

part of a 3-2 liberal majority, and the local newspaper made it clear that much was at stake in the election: What values shall the community's children be taught, and how would the school board respond to property-tax concerns?

Early in the campaign, the *Argus Leader* asked the candidates about these two issues, and it ran their replies along with biographical information about the four candidates. The newspaper was stating what it felt were key issues the candidates should speak about so that voters would have relevant material on which to base their votes.

One of the candidates said that to save money he would eliminate sex education and "social agenda items not academic." As for teaching of values, this candidate stated, "We need Bible reading back in the school, not interpretation, but reading."

In her coverage of the election campaign, Corrine Olson, explored the candidates' approaches to the teaching of values. The challengers were quoted as emphasizing "values in the instruction and discipline of children." The incumbents contended that the schools in Sioux Falls have been teaching values and stressed the importance of "tolerance" as "one of the values that should be embraced." One challenger said that Christian teachers should be able to practice their faith in their instruction in the schools.

Paralleling the news coverage, the editorial page set the issues out early. Rob Swenson, the editorial page editor, wrote a month before the election, "Voters will determine whether the board stays the present course or turns further to the right." In a final editorial before the vote, Swenson wrote that voters faced a choice between "ideologues of the radical, religious-tinged right" and the incumbents, described as "moderates" who would join with a liberal member to form a majority of three on the five-member board. The other two incumbents were described as having "reactionary views on issues such as patriotism and sex."

Olson's story of the election results begins:

> Sioux Falls voters decided Tuesday to stick with incumbents just one year after they supported a new direction for the school board.
> The incumbents won by a vote of almost two to one.

School board meetings are often political battlegrounds on which important issues are fought out. The well-prepared reporter is able to provide depth coverage of these issues. The reporter not only knows the names of the top administrators in the school system and the names of board members, but also is aware of their positions on some of the important matters that have come before the board. Here is a guide to covering board meetings.

___ Actions taken.
___ How each member voted. If no formal vote but an informal consensus, get nods of heads or any other signs of approval or disapproval. Ask if uncertain.

Conservative Agenda. In Merrimack, N.H., a conservative majority took control of the school board and adopted silent prayer for the schools, removed the schools' health curriculum and banned Planned Parenthood literature. When two conservative members supported the teaching of creationism, 200 parents crowded a school board meeting to protest. A parent was quoted as saying, "They cut money for computers and yet they're considering creationism." One of the creationism backers on the board stated, "If you're only going to teach evolution, then your God is King Kong. I'm sorry—my children and grandchildren did not come from apes."

The actions of the majority brought a record turnout for the next school board election for two seats. The so-called liberal candidates defeated the conservative pair 2,800 to 1,300.

◀ Board of Education Meetings

◀ Checklist

___ Size and makeup of audience.
___ Reaction of audience to proposal(s).
___ Position of groups or organizations with a position on issue. (Obtain beforehand, if possible.)
___ Arguments on all sides.
___ Statements from those for and against proposal on what decision of board means.

New Educational Programs ▶

Many meetings of school boards are concerned with new programs. Here is a checklist of items for the reporter:

Checklist ▶

___ Source of idea.
___ Superiority to present program as claimed by sponsors.
___ Cost and source of funding program.
___ Basic philosophy or idea of program.
___ Other places it has been tried and results there. (Make independent check of this, if possible. How well is it working there? What is cost?)
___ Whether it has been tried before and discarded.
___ How does it fit in with what system is doing now? How it fits with trends in area, state, nation.
___ If someone is suggested to head it, who?
___ Arguments pro and con, naming those involved.

Information Available ▶

> **Complaints.** School superintendents complain:
> • Reporters emphasize events rather than trends, thus failing to give the public a rounded view of the system.
> • Writers do not go into schools and classrooms enough. They give too much attention to the views of administrators, not enough to those of teachers.
> • Reporters overlook the impact on education of changes in children such as their defiance of authority, sexual precocity, expectation of constant entertainment and frequent shifts in subject matter—changes, officials say, that have been brought about by television.

How well do states educate their students for college? One measure is student performance on the American College Testing program (ACT) and the Scholastic Aptitude Test (SAT).

The average ACT score hovers between 18.5 and 19 (maximum is 35). Of the 28 states whose students take the test, these states have had lower-than-average scores: Alabama, Alaska, Arkansas, Kentucky, Louisiana, Mississippi, New Mexico, North Dakota, Oklahoma, Tennessee and West Virginia.

The average SAT score among students in the 22 states whose schools offer the test has averaged 422 to 424 in the verbal test, 474 to 479 in the mathematical test under the pre-1995 scoring system. Scores among minority groups are significantly lower, especially among black students. However, black students made the most gains in scores, increasing their verbal scores 20 points since 1976 and their mathematics scores 34 points in the same period. For this period, verbal test scores for whites declined seven points and mathematics scores went up one point.

Among the states scoring lower than the SAT averages are California, Delaware, Florida, Georgia, Hawaii, Indiana, Maine, New Jersey, New York, North Carolina, Pennsylvania, Rhode Island, South Carolina, Vermont and Texas. Midwestern states scored well above the average.

SAT material is available from the College Entrance Examination Board, Box 886, New York, NY 10101-0886.

Adrian, C.R., and C. Press. *Governing Urban America,* 5th ed. New York: McGraw-Hill, 1977.

Cremin, Lawrence A. *Transformation of the School: Progressivism in American Education.* New York: Random House, 1964.

French, Thomas. *South of Heaven: Welcome to High School at the End of the Twentieth Century.* New York: Doubleday, 1993.

Hewlett, Sylvia Ann. *When the Bough Breaks: The Cost of Neglecting Our Children.* New York: Basic Books, 1991.

Kidder, Tracy. *Among Schoolchildren.* Boston: Houghton Mifflin, 1989.

Sayre, Wallace S., and Herbert Kaufman. *Governing New York City.* New York: Norton, 1965.

Shefter, Martin. *Political Crisis/Fiscal Crisis: The Collapse and Revival of New York City.* New York: Basic Books, 1985.

Wildavsky, Aaron. *The Politics of the Budgetary Process,* 2d ed. Boston: Little, Brown, 1974.

◀ **Further Reading**

PART SIX: Laws, Taste and Taboos, Codes and Ethics

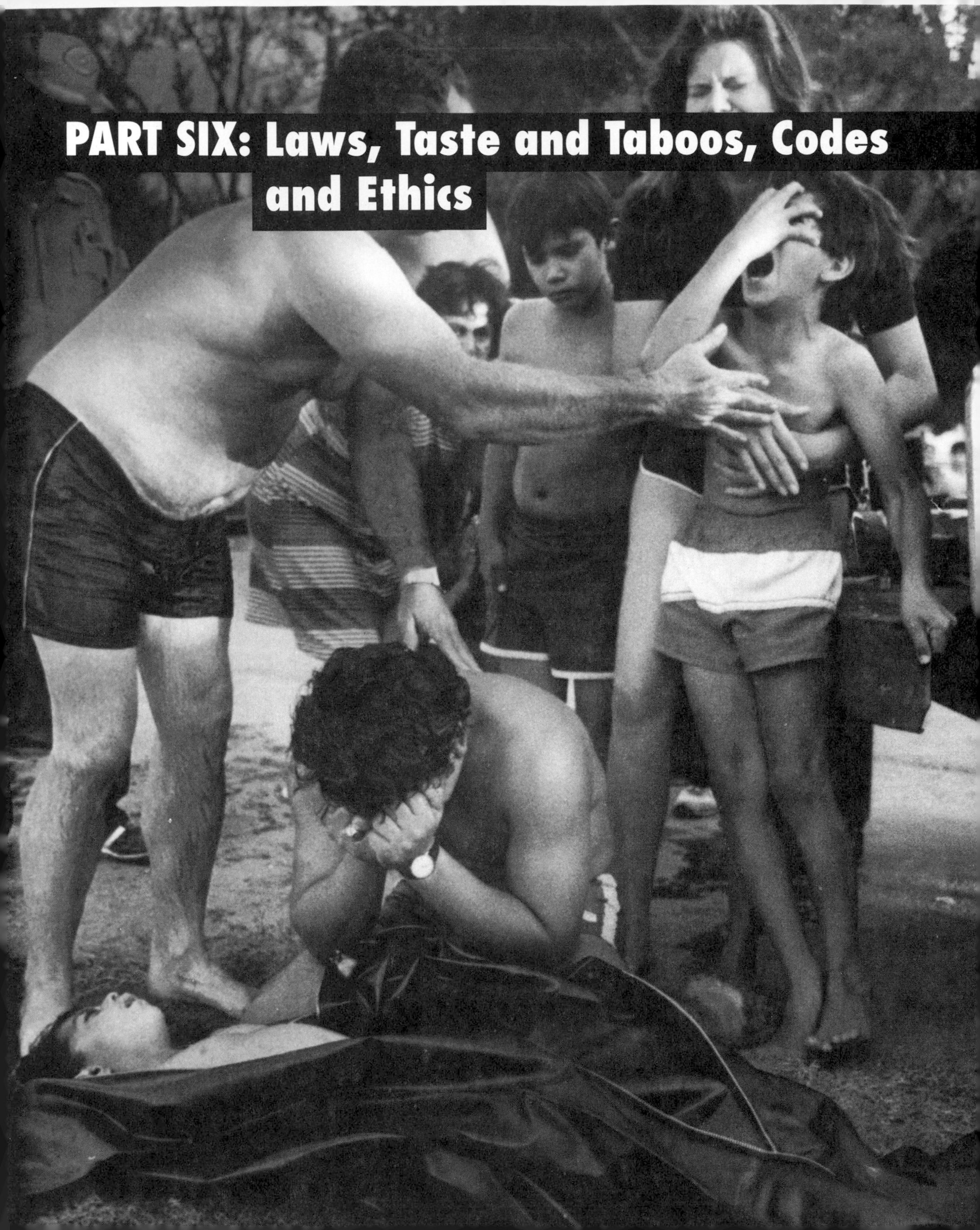

Part Six: Introduction

The final three chapters concern general guidelines for the journalist. As in most of journalism, there are few absolutes in these areas, and even those we tend to think of as unchanging do shift in time. Take libel law, for example: Before 1964, libel was state law and wire service journalists had to exercise special care, for what was acceptable in one state could be the basis of a lawsuit in another. But with the Supreme Court decision in *The New York Times v. Sullivan* everything changed. In Chapter 25, we will examine the wide latitude this decision has given journalists.

Perhaps the greatest changes have occurred in the area of taste, where once journalists were hemmed in by a long list of taboos and agreed-upon prohibitions. In this Age of Candor, little seems off-limits, as we shall see in Chapter 26.

The last chapter, 27, takes us to the area of ethics, and here, too, journalism has changed. Once-acceptable practices are now considered unethical, such as racial and religious identifications.

The areas overlap, as the photo of a family's grief that opens this section illustrates. It was legal for the photographer to snap this public scene at a California beach. But is it so wrenching that it approaches bad taste to spread the photo across a newspaper's pages? Another question: Is it an invasion of this family's privacy to show them grieving moments after the child's body was recovered? This is a matter of ethics, the morality of journalism. The newspaper apologized later, but the photographer said use of the photo was a public service in that it shows what can happen when water safety rules are not observed.

25 Reporters and the Law

Preview

The laws of libel and privacy limit what reporters may write. Stories that damage a person's reputation can be libelous, unless the material is privileged or can be proved to be true. Stories about an individual's personal life can invade the person's right to privacy.

• **Libel:** Most libelous stories are the result of careless reporting. Material that might injure someone is double-checked. The courts have made it more difficult for public figures or public officials to prove libel; but recent court decisions have limited these exceptions.

• **Privacy:** The right to privacy is protected by law. The personal activities of an individual can be reported if the material is about a newsworthy person and is not highly offensive.

O ne of the most dangerous areas for the journalist is libel. To the beginner, the region of libel is a land of mystery in which all the guideposts read, "Don't." To the experienced reporter, danger of libel is a cautionary presence in the newsroom.

Libel is published defamation of character. It is writing or pictures that:

• Expose a person to hatred, shame, disgrace, contempt or ridicule.
• Injure a person's reputation or cause the person to be shunned or avoided.
• Injure the person in his or her occupation.

Of course, many articles and pictures do libel individuals. In most cases, the defamatory material may be safe for publication if it is *privileged*. By privileged, we mean that the article is a fair and accurate report of a judicial, legislative or other public official proceeding or of anything said in the course of such sessions, trials or proceedings. The contents of most public records are privileged. Those who made our laws recognized that open debate of serious issues would be impeded unless the public had full access to official actions.

Another defense against libel is *truth*. No matter how serious the defamation may be, if the statement can be proved to be true and to have been made without malice, the defamed individual cannot successfully bring legal action.

A third defense, *fair comment and criticism,* most often involves editorial writers and reviewers. As long as the comment or criticism is directed at the work and not at the individual, the writing is safe.

In summary, the libel laws hold that a reporter is not in danger if the material is from a privileged proceeding (public *and* official) or if the material is substantially accurate or constitutes fair comment.

For broadcast journalists, defamatory statements made from a prepared script fall under libel, whereas extemporaneous defamatory remarks are treated as *slander,* which can be defined as oral or uttered defamation.

Matter that might be held libelous by a court would have to:

1. Imply commission of a crime.
2. Tend to injure a person in his or her profession or job.
3. Imply a person has a disease, usually a loathsome disease that might lead to the individual's ostracism.
4. Damage a person's credit.
5. Imply unchaste behavior.
6. Indicate a lack of mental capacity.
7. Incite public ridicule or contempt.

For years, libel was a great weight on the shoulders of the press, particularly for newspapers that handled controversy and emphasized investigative reporting. The press associations had special concerns, for libel law was state law and was beyond the protection of the Constitution. What was legal in one state might have been libelous in another.

In effect, libel laws restrained the press, as the Supreme Court recognized in an epochal decision in 1964 that was to lighten the burden on the press. The court ruled that defamatory statements could have First Amendment protection. Our seven danger points are still to be watched, but the press now has much stronger defenses, thanks to the Supreme Court. To understand that decision—and to understand the organic nature of the law—we must travel back in time to Montgomery, Ala.

When Rosa Parks boarded the Cleveland Avenue bus in December 1955, she spotted an empty seat just behind the section reserved for whites. Tired from a day's work in a downtown department store, she eased into the space, only to be ordered to move. Seats were saved for white passengers.

Mrs. Parks, a quiet, reserved woman, refused to give up her seat. She was taken off the bus and arrested. That weekend, plans were made by the black community to boycott Montgomery's buses.

Martin Luther King Jr., a black minister who helped plan the boycott, recalled how he awoke early Monday morning to see whether Montgomery's black residents would heed the word that it was better to walk in dignity than to ride in shame. The bus line that passed by the King home carried more blacks than any other line in the city. The first bus went by at 6 a.m. It was empty. Another, 15 minutes later, was empty, too.

That was the beginning of the boycott. Some 42,000 Montgomery blacks said they would walk to and from work or use volunteer vehicles and

◀ **Grounds for Libel Suits**

Expensive. The threat of a libel suit can be intimidating because of the cost involved in fighting such a suit. The *St. Petersburg Times* spent $500,000 defending itself against a suit by a former sheriff and his deputy. The jury took less than three hours to find the articles were true and thus not libelous.

Jury awards for libel in the 1980s averaged under $500,000. A decade later, they averaged $9 million. Most of the huge awards were reduced on appeal, a costly process itself.

◀ **An Incident on a Bus**

black-owned taxis until the bus system altered its seating arrangements and hired black drivers for buses along the predominantly black routes.

For 381 days, they stayed off the buses rather than be told to move to the back. Many people went to jail for violating the state's anti-boycott laws, including Mrs. Parks and Dr. King. Finally, the Supreme Court ruled bus segregation illegal.

Tension Mounts ▶

To some blacks, the action of Mrs. Parks and others was more significant than the decision of the Supreme Court the year before that prohibited the segregation of public schools. In Montgomery, blacks had brought about change by themselves. This effort accelerated the mass movement of nonviolent resistance to discrimination among blacks. It was to develop slowly in the 1950s and to spread in the early 1960s in marches, lunchroom sit-ins, Freedom Rides and picketing throughout the South.

Tensions mounted. In 1963, Medgar Evers, a black civil rights worker, was murdered in the doorway of his home in Jackson, Miss. The following year, three young civil rights workers were murdered in Philadelphia, Miss.

Newspapers and television stations sent waves of reporters to the South to report the conflict. Viewers saw fire hoses, police dogs and cattle prods used on blacks in Birmingham, and they saw the clubs of state troopers in Selma. The press reported the cry of blacks for an end to humiliation, economic exploitation, segregation in schools and discrimination at the polls.

It was also obvious the South was hardly budging. The border areas, portions of Tennessee and Kentucky and metropolitan communities such as Atlanta and Richmond accommodated. But not the towns and parishes of the Black Belt—Selma, Plaquemines, Yazoo City. Here, nonviolence met intractable resistance. Blacks might wait patiently outside the courthouse in Selma to register to vote. But the doors would stay closed to them, unless they were broken down by the federal government and the courts.

Press Coverage Increases ▶

Because of the intensive coverage in the press, a consensus was developing outside the Black Belt. Most of the nation saw the anguish of the blacks who were hurling themselves against the wall of segregation, and some believed the nation was heading toward a race war.

In 1963, President Kennedy, aware of the developing conflict, declared that the struggle of blacks for civil rights was a "moral issue." Then four girls attending Sunday school in the black Sixteenth Street Baptist Church in Birmingham died in a bomb blast at the church.

The press stepped up its coverage. In some northern newspapers and on network television, the South was presented as a forbidding region of racism, its law officers openly defiant of the law, its white citizens unwilling to adjust to the changing times. Southerners were dismayed by the coverage, and some whites assaulted reporters covering civil rights demonstrations. The retaliation also took the form of suits against the press and television.

Millions of dollars in damages were claimed by officials, who asserted they had been defamed by press and television. By 1964, libel suits seeking $300 million in damages were pending against news organizations covering the racial story. One of the largest suits was brought against *The New York Times* by five officials in Alabama who contended that they had been inferentially damaged in an advertisement in the *Times* in 1960 that sought to raise funds for the civil rights movement. The advertisement, headlined "Heed Their Rising Voices," described the treatment of black schoolchildren by the Alabama police. The five officials brought suit for a total of $3 million.

The first case to be tried involved L.B. Sullivan, a Montgomery city commissioner responsible for the police department. The judge ordered segregated seating in the courtroom, and after he praised the "white man's justice" that had been brought to the country by the "Anglo-Saxon race," the all-white jury heard testimony. The jurors, whose names and photographs were printed in the local press, were told that although Sullivan's name had not been mentioned in the advertisement, his reputation had been damaged by the erroneous statements about the police.

During the trial, it was evident that the advertisement contained errors. It stated that Montgomery students had been expelled from school after singing "My Country 'Tis of Thee" on the steps of the state capitol. Actually, they were expelled for a sit-in in the courthouse grill. The advertisement also said students had been locked out of their lunchroom to "starve them into submission," which was false.

The jury agreed that Sullivan had been libeled and awarded him $500,000 in compensatory and punitive damages from the *Times*.

In a headline over the story about the suits against the *Times,* a Montgomery newspaper seemed to reveal the motives behind the libel suits: "State Finds Formidable Legal Club to Swing at Out-of-State Press."

◀ A Legal Club

It was in this atmosphere that the Supreme Court considered the appeal of the *Times* from the state court decision. The case of *The New York Times v. Sullivan* (376 US 254) in 1964 was to mark a major change in the libel laws. But more important, by granting the press wider latitude in covering and commenting on the actions of public officials, the decision gave the press greater freedom to present issues of public concern, like the racial conflict that was tearing the country apart.

◀ **The Court Acts**

The Supreme Court understood the unique nature of the appeal. The Court commented, "We are required for the first time in this case to determine the extent to which the Constitutional protections for speech and press limit a state's power to award damages in a libel action brought by a public official against the critics of his official conduct."

In its decision, the Supreme Court took from the states their power to award damages for libel "in actions brought by public officials against critics of their official conduct." The Constitutional protections for free speech and free press would be seriously limited by state actions of the kind the Alabama court took, the Court said.

Justice William J. Brennan wrote, "The Constitutional guarantees require, we think, a federal rule that prohibits a public official from recovering damages for a defamatory falsehood relating to his official conduct unless he proves that the statement was made with 'actual malice'—that is, with knowledge that it was false or with reckless disregard to whether it was false or not."

The Court apparently agreed with the argument of Herbert F. Wechsler, who wrote in a brief for the *Times,* "This is not a time—there never was a time—when it would serve the values enshrined in the Constitution to force the press to curtail its attention to the tensest issues that confront the country or to forego the dissemination of its publications in the areas where tension is extreme."

Justice Brennan noted in his opinion that the Supreme Court had seen in the use of such legal concepts as "insurrection," "contempt," "breach of the peace," "obscenity" and "solicitation of legal business" attempts to suppress the open discussion of public issues. Now it was libel.

In the Sullivan libel case, the Court extended the First Amendment in order to accomplish a social-political purpose—the protection of dissident voices in a repressive atmosphere.

The decision, establishing what became known as the Times Doctrine, noted that the "Constitutional safeguard was fashioned to assure unfettered interchange of ideas for the bringing about of political and social changes desired by the people." To accomplish this, there must be "maintenance of the opportunity for free political discussion to the end that government may be responsive to the will of the people and that changes may be obtained by lawful means, an opportunity essential to the security of the Republic. . . .

"Erroneous statement is inevitable in free debate," Brennan said. Running through the decision is the belief that free discussion will lead to a peaceful settlement of issues. Free expression, he was saying, has social utility. The Court seemed to be addressing itself to the millions of Americans in trauma because of the racial conflict.

In summary, the decision in the case makes it clear that, under the Constitution, no public official can recover damages for defamation in a newspaper article or "editorial advertisement" concerning his or her official conduct unless he or she can prove the article is defamatory and false and also show that:

1. The publication was made with the knowledge that it was false; or
2. The statement was made with reckless disregard of whether or not it was false.

Items 1 and 2 constitute the Court's concept of "actual malice."

The decision is the law in every state and takes precedence over federal and state laws, state constitutions and all previous state and federal court decisions.

Extension and ► Contraction of Times Doctrine

In the decade following the enunciation of the Times Doctrine, the Court went beyond applying it to public officials and included public figures and then private individuals involved in matters of public concern.

In a significant case, a businessman lost a libel suit that involved a clear case of error by a radio station. A distributor of nudist magazines was arrested while delivering magazines to a newsstand. The Philadelphia, Pa., police reported the incident to a local radio station, which broadcast an item about the distributor's arrest on a charge of selling obscene materials. Further, the station stated that the magazines were obscene. In a subsequent trial, the distributor was acquitted. The distributor said he had been defamed by the radio station and sued. A jury awarded him general and punitive damages.

The radio newsman had violated one of the first rules a beginner learns: Never state as fact what is only charged and therefore subject to determination in the courts.

The reporter and his station were fortunate, however. The Court of Appeals reversed the lower court verdict, and in 1971 the Supreme Court upheld the reversal on the distributor's appeal (*Rosenbloom v. Metromedia, Inc.,* 403 US 29). The Court ruled:

> We thus hold that a libel action, as here by a private individual against a licensed radio station for a defamatory falsehood in a newscast relating to his involvement in an event of public or general concern may be sustained only upon clear and convincing proof that the defamatory falsehood was published with knowledge that it was false or with reckless disregard of whether it was false or not.
>
> Calculated falsehood, of course, falls outside the "fruitful exercise of the right of free speech."

Rosenbloom was neither a public official nor a public figure. But he was involved in an event of "public or general concern," and ordinary citizens so involved can successfully bring a libel action only by a showing of actual malice, the Court stated.

Rosenbloom might have been luckier had his troubles occurred later, for the Supreme Court in 1974 reversed directions and did so again in 1976 and 1979. These rulings made it possible for many more libel plaintiffs to collect damages for defamatory falsehoods, since for private citizens the proof of defamation may be negligence or carelessness, not the actual malice public figures are required to prove.

In the 1974 case of *Gertz v. Robert Welch, Inc.* (418 US 323), the Supreme Court suddenly ceased the steady expansion of First Amendment protection to publications in libel actions. Elmer Gertz, a civil rights lawyer in Chicago, had been defamed by *American Opinion,* a monthly magazine published by the John Birch Society. The magazine described Gertz as a "Communist-fronter" and said he had designed a national campaign to discredit the police. Although the trial judge had found no evidence the magazine had published recklessly, a jury awarded Gertz $50,000. The magazine appealed.

The Supreme Court ruled that as a private citizen Gertz did not have to show "actual malice" but was entitled to damages if he could prove the material was false and defamatory and that it had been the result of negligence or carelessness by the publication. The Court returned to an emphasis on the plaintiff's status rather than the subject matter.

◀ **A Change in Directions**

In 1976, the Court altered slightly the definition of "public figure" in a case involving *Time* magazine, which had appealed a Florida court decision awarding $100,000 in damages in a libel suit brought by Mary Alice Firestone. *Time* had incorrectly reported the grounds on which Mrs. Firestone's husband had been granted a divorce. *Time* contended Mrs. Firestone was a public figure, which would have required her to submit proof of "actual malice" by *Time*. Mrs. Firestone had not submitted such proof. But the Court ruled that although Mrs. Firestone was a well-known socialite, she "didn't assume any role of especial prominence in the affairs of society . . ." (409 US 875).

In 1979, the Court further constricted the definition of "public figure." The cases, decided eight to one, were *Hutchinson v. Proxmire* (443 US 111) and *Wolston v. Reader's Digest Assn., Inc.* (443 US 157). The Court said there are two kinds of public figures: "A small group of individuals" who occupy positions of "persuasive power and influence" and people who have "thrust themselves to the forefront of particular public controversies in order to influence the resolution of the issues involved" and have, therefore, become public figures for the limited purpose of comment on their connection with these controversies.

In *Hutchinson,* the Court ruled against Sen. William Proxmire, who, in bestowing one of his Golden Fleece awards, had belittled a project by Ronald R. Hutchinson, a scientist who had used monkeys in an effort to find an objective measure of aggression. Several of the federal agencies that had granted Hutchinson $500,000 to fund his research were cited by Proxmire as wasting public money. Hutchinson brought a libel action against Proxmire, seeking $8 million for mental anguish and loss of income. A lower federal court ruled against Hutchinson in two areas. It said that by soliciting and receiving federal grants, Hutchinson had become a public figure and that Proxmire had legislative immunity.

The Supreme Court rejected the defense contention that Hutchinson was a public figure. The Court said that the scientist "did not have the regular and continuing access to the media that is one of the accoutrements of having become a public figure." As for Proxmire's immunity, the Court said that the Golden Fleece award was made known by the senator's newsletter and press releases, and these do not enjoy the same protection as words on the Senate floor. The court rejected the assertions of House and Senate leaders that Proxmire's public relations activities were part of the "informing function" of Congress. Proxmire settled out of court with a payment of $10,000 to Hutchinson.

In the other 1979 case, Ilya Wolston contended he was libeled by *Reader's Digest* when it falsely listed him in a book as a Soviet agent. The book used an erroneous FBI document as its source. In 1958, Wolston had failed to appear before a grand jury investigating a spy ring. He later pleaded guilty to contempt and was given a suspended sentence. The Wolston situation attracted considerable attention, but the Court ruled that Wolston did not "voluntarily thrust" or inject himself into the controversy over the inquiry. "It would be more accurate to say that Wolston was dragged unwillingly into the controversy," Justice William H. Rehnquist wrote.

"A private individual is not automatically transformed into a public figure just by becoming involved in or associated with a matter that attracts attention," the justice wrote. A person who engages in criminal conduct does not automatically become a public figure. "To hold otherwise would create an 'open season' for all who sought to defame persons convicted of a crime," Rehnquist said.

Bruce W. Sanford, a libel lawyer, described Rehnquist's remarks as "unbelievable language. Reporters and editors don't go hunting for people (least of all criminals) to defame." The Court, he said, had made a "startling" ruling by rejecting—here Sanford quotes the Court—the "contention that any person who engages in criminal conduct automatically becomes a public figure for purposes of comment on a limited range of issues relating to his conviction." This is a significant shift in the Court's views since *Rosenbloom.* Sanford states the decision means the criminal suspect or defendant "now will probably not be classifiable as a public figure."

◀ Courts Differ

Just where is the line that divides a public figure from a private figure? The Supreme Court has not clarified the point. Lower courts have differed.

The Washington Post escaped a libel judgment when a federal district court ruled a police informant was a public figure and had to prove actual malice. The *Post* had incorrectly stated the informant was a drug user. But three months later, a federal judge in Maryland ruled that a police informant was a private individual and thus need only prove that a Baltimore newspaper was careless in mistakenly stating he had broken into a lawyer's office to steal documents for the police.

In state courts, a Kansas judge ruled that a lawyer appointed to defend a penniless criminal defendant was a public official. Two months later, a Michigan judge said that an attorney appointed to represent an impoverished defendant was neither public figure nor public official.

In Virginia, a circuit court ruled that a high school English teacher was a public figure. The teacher had sued the *Richmond Times-Dispatch* for a story that criticized her teaching. She appealed and the state Supreme Court concluded she was not a public figure because she was in no position to influence or control "any public affairs or school policy." The newspaper appealed to the U.S. Supreme Court and lost. The teacher was awarded $100,000.

The Supreme Court may have clarified the status of police officers. In 1989, it ruled that an officer *The Danville* (Ill.) *Commercial News* had linked to a suspected burglary ring was a public official and would have to prove actual malice. A student newspaper at Cleveland State University profited from this decision when a suit in which a campus police officer sought $300,000 in damages was dismissed. The newspaper had stated in an editorial that the officer had a reputation for "excessive force, brutality and discrimination."

Caution: Events that are the subject of gossip or public curiosity and have no significant relation to public affairs usually do not confer on the persons involved in them the status of public figures. This means that no matter how public a person's marriage rift may be, that person is not necessarily a public figure.

If the reporter can prove that an event relates to public affairs or an important social issue, then the persons involved may be classified as public figures. For example, if a physician or a lawyer injects himself or herself into a controversy over a local bond issue, then the person has become a public figure for news about the bonds but not about his or her personal life.

Repeating a Libel ▶

In a story about neighborhood politics, a student newspaper printed this paragraph:

> A member of Board 9, who asked not to be identified, charged that Lawrence and Fine were involved in a kickback scheme in which the district manager, who is the board's paid administrator, pushed along projects beneficial to Chevra in return for an unspecified kickback.

Asked if he knew that the allegation about kickbacks is clearly libelous since accepting a kickback is a crime, the student reporter replied, "But I attributed it." His instructor could only shrug in exasperation. A reporter can be held liable if he or she repeats a libelous statement or quotes someone making such a statement unless the original material is privileged.

If the assertion had been made in court or at an official meeting, the statement—even if untrue—would be privileged and the privilege would be a defense against claims for damages, provided the report was fair and accurate.

Conditional and Absolute Privilege ▶

The privilege to those participating in court cases and legislative sessions is an "absolute privilege," meaning the participants—the judge, lawyers, witnesses—cannot be held legally accountable even for malicious and deliberately false statements that are made within the scope of their participation in the proceedings. A newspaper or station, however, cannot use absolute privilege as a defense in libel suits. Their protection is known as "conditional" or "qualified privilege." The newspaper must present full, fair and accurate reports that are free of actual malice in order to be granted privilege.

A candidate for re-election to Congress who says of his opponent, "That man is a swindler" on the floor of the House of Representatives can make the statement with impunity, and a reporter can publish the accusation. (Obviously, the reporter would also carry the accused's reply.) But should the congressman make the charge in a political rally and the reporter's newspaper print the allegation, both are in trouble, unless the reporter can prove the man is indeed a swindler, and this would require proof of the man's conviction on that charge.

Warning: These protections do not cover proceedings, meetings, or activities that are private in nature. They also do not cover records that are sealed by law or court order.

Some federal courts have adopted the concept of "neutral reporting," which allows a newspaper to report a defamatory charge—in effect to repeat it—if the charge is made by a responsible organization and is accurately reported. The concept emerged in *Edwards v. National Audubon Society* [556F. 2d 113 (1977)] in which *The New York Times* was sued by three scientists whom a Society spokesman accused of misusing bird counts to suggest that DDT did not harm birds. The Second Circuit Court of Appeals ruled unanimously that the "First Amendment protects the accurate and disinterested reporting" of charges "regardless of the reporter's private views of their validity." The Supreme Court refused to review the case.

◀ Neutral Reporting

The concept of a neutral reporting privilege was given a significant boost in a 1989 California state court decision. The *Stockton Record* had said that a murder suspect charged a police sergeant with extracting a false confession. The suspect's claim was false and the officer sued. The paper's request for a summary judgment against the plaintiff was denied and the paper appealed.

The appellate court said that state law and the First Amendment make the newspaper "privileged to print a fair report, attributed to a third party, of a claim of official misconduct denied by the official, and is under no duty to resolve conflicting claims of what happened." The court noted that the story also included the officer's denial. **Caution:** Some states have rejected the neutral reporting privilege.

The Supreme Court has been generous to reporters who make mistakes under pressure of deadline. But reporters who have time to check material may not fare so well under the Court's distinction between "hot news" and "time copy." The differences were spelled out in two companion cases decided in 1967, *Curtis Publishing Co. v. Butts* and *Associated Press v. Walker* (both 388 US 130), involving public figures.

◀ Time Copy

Edwin Walker was a former Army general who had become involved in the civil rights disputes in the South and had taken a position against desegregation. He was on the campus of the University of Mississippi in September 1962 when it erupted over the enrollment of James Meredith, a black student.

The AP moved a story that Walker had taken command of a violent crowd and had personally led a charge against federal marshals on the campus. The AP said Walker had encouraged rioters to use violence and had instructed white students how to combat the effects of tear gas. He sued for $800,000 in damages. Walker testified that he had counseled restraint and peaceful protest and had not charged the marshals. The jury believed his account and awarded him the sum he sought. The trial judge cut out the $300,000 in punitive damages because he found no actual malice in the AP account.

Wally Butts was the athletic director of the University of Georgia in 1962. He was employed by the Georgia Athletic Association, a private corporation, and so, like Walker, he was a private citizen when, according to *The Saturday Evening Post,* he conspired to fix a football game between Georgia and Alabama in 1962. An article in the magazine said an Atlanta insurance salesman had overheard a conversation between Butts and Bear Bryant, coach of the Alabama football team, in which Butts outlined Georgia's offensive strategy in the coming game and advised Bryant about defending against the plays.

Butts sued for $5 million in compensatory damages and $5 million in punitive damages. The jury awarded him $60,000 on the first charge and $3 million on the second, which was subsequently reduced to $460,000.

The Curtis Publishing Co., publishers of *The Saturday Evening Post,* and the AP appealed to the Supreme Court. Butts won his appeal, but Walker lost. The Court ruled that the evidence showed that the Butts story was not "hot news," but that the Walker story was. The *Post*'s editors, the Court stated, "recognized the need for a thorough investigation of the serious charges" but failed to make the investigation.

In the Walker case, the Court noted, "In contrast to the Butts article, the dispatch which concerns us in *Walker* was news which required immediate dissemination. . . . Considering the necessity for rapid dissemination, nothing in this series of events gives the slightest hint of a severe departure from publishing standards. We therefore conclude that Walker should not be entitled to damages from the Associated Press."

All Speech Not Equal ▶

In a decision that worried some journalists, the Supreme Court in 1985 ruled that punitive damages can be awarded without the plaintiff's proving actual malice if the libelous material is not a matter of "public concern." The case, decided in 1985 by a vote of five to four, arose from an erroneous credit report by Dun & Bradstreet about a firm, Greenmoss Builders. The court let stand a $300,000 award for punitive damages.

"We have long recognized that not all speech is of equal First Amendment importance," wrote Justice Lewis E. Powell in his opinion. "It is speech on 'matters of public concern' that is 'at the heart of the First Amendment's protection.' . . . Speech on matters of purely private concern is of less First Amendment concern."

The court did not define "public concern," and this worried journalists and their lawyers, who were also concerned by the Court's decision not to apply what is known as the Gertz rule, which prohibits the award of punitive damages when there is no showing of actual malice. The court said the Gertz rule does not apply on matters of nonpublic concern.

Punitive Damages. "Money a court awards to an individual who has been harmed in a malicious or willful way. The amount is not related to the actual cost of the injury or harm suffered. Its purpose is to keep that sort of act from happening again. Punitive damages serve as a deterrent."

Privacy ▶

While truth is the strongest defense against libel, it is the basis of invasion of privacy suits. Invasion of privacy is said to occur when an individual is exposed to public view and suffers mental distress as a consequence of the publicity. Unlike defamation, which has deep roots in the common law, the right to privacy is a fairly new legal development and one in which there is even less certainty for the reporter than in the area of libel.

The balance must be struck by the courts between the public's right to know—a right commonly accepted though not in the Constitution—and the individual's right to privacy.

Three categories of privacy concern the reporter:

1. Publicity that places a person in a false light in the public eye. The Times Doctrine applies, provided the matter is of public interest.

2. Public disclosure of embarrassing private facts about an individual. If the facts are in an official document, they can be published but not if they are private acts of no legitimate concern to the public.

3. Intrusion by the journalist into a private area for a story or a picture without permission—eavesdropping or trespassing. The use of electronic devices to invade a home or office is illegal. Newsworthiness is not a defense.

Except for intrusion, the newsworthiness of the event is a defense against invasion of privacy suits. A public event cannot have privacy grafted on it at the behest of the participants. However, the reporter cannot invade a person's home or office to seek out news and make public what is private. Nor can he or she misrepresent the purpose of reporting to gain access to home or office. There is no prohibition against following and watching a person in a public place, but the reporter cannot harass an individual.

Although the law of libel and the right of privacy are closely related, they involve distinctive legal principles and are fundamentally different. Libel law is designed to protect a person's character and reputation. The right of privacy protects a person's peace of mind, feelings, spirits and sensibilities. Generally, privacy guarantees an individual freedom from the unwarranted and unauthorized public exposure of the person or his or her affairs in which the public has no legitimate interest.

The right of privacy is the right of a person to be let alone unless he or she waives or relinquishes that right, the UPI tells its reporters. Certain people, defined by the federal courts as "newsworthy," lose their right to privacy, but the material published about them cannot be "highly offensive."

In making rulings on the claim of invasion of privacy, the Supreme Court has applied the Times Doctrine. That is, even if the claimant could prove that the report was false, if it were a matter of public interest, the person bringing the action would have to show the error was made "with knowledge of its falsity or in reckless disregard of the truth."

In one case, decided in 1974 by the Supreme Court, such disregard of the truth was proved by a claimant. The Court in *Cantrell v. Forest City Publishing Co.* (419 US 245) upheld an award against *The Plain Dealer* in Cleveland on the ground that a reporter's story about a visit to the home of the claimant "contained significant misrepresentations." Although the woman was not at home when the reporter visited, the article said she "will talk neither about what happened nor about how they were doing. . . ." He wrote that the widow "wears the same mask of nonexpression she wore at the funeral." A lower court jury awarded her

Pro & Con. *USA Today* revealed that Arthur Ashe had AIDS, despite Ashe's request that his condition be kept confidential. Ashe had been a world-class tennis champion and was clearly a public figure.

Pro: Peter Prichard, editor of *USA Today*—"When the press has kept secrets . . . that conspiracy of silence has not served the public. . . . Journalists serve the public by reporting news, not hiding it."

Con: Jonathon Yardley, *The Washington Post*— "Arthur Ashe was absolutely right to insist on his privacy and *USA Today* was absolutely wrong to violate it. No public issues were at stake. No journalistic 'rights' were threatened."

A similar controversy arose when Colin Powell was suggested as a candidate for the presidency. *The Philadelphia Inquirer* and *Newsweek* reported that Mrs. Powell was taking medication for depression. Publication was defended as relevant to Powell's possible candidacy. But A.M. Rosenthal, former managing editor of *The New York Times,* said the information "was not news, not pertinent and not our business . . . an invasion of privacy." Powell said he had no complaints about the story.

◀ "Calculated Falsehoods"

$60,000 to compensate for the mental distress and shame the article caused. An appeals court reversed the verdict, and the woman appealed to the Supreme Court, which found the reporter's statements implying that the woman had been interviewed were "calculated falsehoods."

The decision was eight to one. Some months later in another eight to one decision, the Supreme Court ruled on the second category involving privacy—the rights of private individuals to keep their personal affairs from public disclosure. In this case, the Court nullified a Georgia law that made it a misdemeanor to print or broadcast the name of a rape victim. The case involved the father of a young woman who had been raped and killed by a gang of teen-age boys. An Atlanta television station had used the victim's name, and the state court had ruled in favor of the father under the state law. The station appealed.

In setting aside the Georgia law, the Supreme Court stated that "once true information is disclosed in public court documents open to public inspection, the press cannot be sanctioned for publishing it." The Court stated (in *Cox Broadcasting Corp. v. Martin Cohn,* 420 US 469):

> The commission of crimes, prosecutions resulting therefrom, and judicial proceedings arising from the prosecutions are events of legitimate concern to the public and consequently fall within the press' responsibility to report the operations of government.

In both cases, the Supreme Court cautioned against broad interpretations of its rulings. Nevertheless, the first case clearly indicates that the press must take care in publishing material about individuals that is false, and the second indicates the Court will not extend the right of privacy to private persons involved in actions described in official documents.

A quick guideline in matters of privacy is provided by a case involving a surfer who was interviewed by *Sports Illustrated* and then sued because the published report contained unflattering material about his personal life along with information about his surfing activities. A federal appeals court ruled that the public had a legitimate interest in him and that the facts reported were not so offensive as "to lose newsworthiness protection." The guideline:

> A reporter or publication that gives publicity to the private life of a person is not subject to liability for unreasonable invasion of privacy if the material (1) is about a newsworthy person—who need not be an elected official or a celebrity—and (2) is not "highly offensive to a reasonable person, one of ordinary sensibilities and is of legitimate public concern."

Secret Taping ▶

The use of hidden electronic mechanisms for newsgathering may result in trouble if stories are based on the material gathered by hidden cameras and microphones. A federal court in California ruled in 1972 (*Dietemann v. Time, Inc.,* 449 F. 2d 245) that a man who was healing people with herbs, clay and minerals could sue for invasion of privacy because of the tactics used by employees of *Life* magazine in gathering information. The reporter, who posed as someone needing help, had a radio transmitter in her pocketbook. The transmitter relayed to other reporters the healer's conversation as he examined her in his home. Also, a picture was taken with a hidden camera; the picture was later published in the magazine.

The ground rules of journalism require reporters usually to tell sources when they are being photographed, taped or quoted. The television journalist, for example, should inform his or her source when the camera is on, unless it is made clear beforehand that anything and everything may be filmed and recorded. But such full disclosure usually is impossible in investigative reporting, said the attorneys for *Life* in their defense. However, the appeals court ruled that intrusion had occurred. The court stated:

> We agree that newsgathering is an integral part of news dissemination. We strongly disagree, however, that the hidden mechanical contrivances are "indispensable tools" of newsgathering. Investigative reporting is an ancient art; its successful practice long antecedes the invention of miniature cameras and electronic devices. The First Amendment has never been construed to accord newsmen immunity from torts or crimes committed during the course of newsgathering. The First Amendment is not a license to trespass, to steal, or to intrude by electronic means into the precincts of another's home or office. . . .

Note: There is an ethical as well as a legal aspect to privacy. Some journalists and many readers question the moral right of reporters to pry into the personal affairs of individuals, even when they are public figures or hold public office.

The guide in libel and invasion of privacy suits seems fairly clear. Caution is necessary when the following are *not* involved—public officials, public figures, public events. When a private individual is drawn into the news, the news report must be full, fair and accurate. Of course, no journalist relies upon the law for loopholes. He or she is always fair and accurate in coverage.

◀ **Avoiding the Dangers**

Libel suits usually result from:

- Carelessness.
- Exaggerated or enthusiastic writing.
- Opinions not based on facts.
- Statements of officials or informants made outside a privileged situation.
- Inadequate verification.
- Failure to check with the subject of the defamation.

When a libel has been committed, a retraction should be published. Although a retraction is not a defense, it serves to lessen damages and may deprive the plaintiff of punitive damages.

Most libel suits result from a reporter's rush to publish or broadcast the story. The usual care is not exercised in the speed-up. When the *New York Post* reported that Whitney Houston had been hospitalized in Miami after overdosing on diet pills, a $60 million libel suit was filed. The reporters handling the story would have learned it was a hoax had they called the hospital, which had no

◀ Rush + Inference = Libel Troubles

record of the singer's admission or treatment. The newspaper retracted the story the next day.

Libel suits also result from one of our old enemies—the inference, or jumping from the known to the unknown. A copy editor for an Indiana newspaper wrote this headline over the story of the closing of a restaurant: "Health board shuts doors at Bandido's; Investigators find rats, bugs at north-side eatery." The restaurant owner sued, contending the investigators did not find rats in his eatery. The copy editor testified in the trial: "When I saw the word 'rodent' or 'rodent droppings,' that said rats to me."

The jury awarded the restaurant owner $985,000.

The Reporter's ▶ Rights

The press carries a heavy burden. It has taken on the task of gathering and publishing the news, interpreting and commenting on the news and acting as watchdog in the public interest over wide areas of public concern. The burden of the press has been lightened by the foresight of the Founding Fathers through the guarantee in the First Amendment of the Constitution that Congress shall make no law abridging freedom of speech or of the press. This meant that the press has the right to publish what it finds without prior restraint.

To journalists, it also came to mean that they had the freedom to gather and prepare news and that the processes involved in these activities were shielded from a prying government and others. Also, journalists understood that their sources, their notes, their thoughts and their discussions with sources and their editors were protected.

They had good reason to believe all this. State legislatures and the courts had interpreted the concept of press freedom to cover these wide areas of news-gathering and publication. In 1896, for example, the state of Maryland passed a law allowing reporters to conceal their sources from the courts and from other officials. The concern of the public traditionally has been that the press be free and strong enough to counterpose a powerful executive. This sensitivity to central government began with the revolution against the British Crown. It was reinforced by the generations of immigrants who fled czars, kings, dictators and tyrants.

Old as the story of the abuse of power may be, and as frequent as the exposures of its ruinous consequences have been by the press, the dangers implicit in centralized government are always present, as the Watergate revelations taught U.S. citizens. This tendency of government to excessive use of its power was foreseen by the American revolutionaries who sought to make in the press a Fourth Estate outside government control and free to check on government.

There is, however, no clear-cut constitutional statement giving the press the privileges it came to consider immutable. Absolute freedom of the press has never been endorsed by a majority of the Supreme Court, but the federal courts usually have been sympathetic to the rights of the press. However, in the 1970s following Watergate, as the press started to dig and check with growing tenacity, a former ally in its battles with governmental power—the judiciary—began to render decisions the press found to be increasingly restricting. Many of these decisions—particularly those of the Supreme Court—convinced the press that its assumptions about its privileges were false. The press, the courts ruled, has no greater rights than any citizen of the land.

In its balancing of the public right to know against individual rights to privacy and the accused's rights to a fair trial, the courts denied the confidentiality of sources, the protection of unpublished material and the privacy of the editorial process. The courts gradually limited the press' access to information, and some newsgathering was specifically prohibited.

There are, of course, still wide areas of newsgathering open to the press. Generally, the actions of official bodies are accessible to journalists. Judicial, legislative and executive activities can be freely covered—with exceptions. A reporter has the right to cover a city council meeting, except for executive sessions. But the reporter has no legal right to sit in on a meeting of the board of the American Telephone & Telegraph Co., a private company.

Journalists have rights—along with all citizens—to vast areas of official activities. The Supreme Court has ruled (*Branzburg v. Hayes*) that the press has protection in some of its newsgathering activities. The Court stated that "without some protection for seeking out the news, freedom of the press would be eviscerated."

But the Court ruled in *Branzburg* that a reporter cannot protect information a grand jury seeks, and grand jury proceedings are closed to the press. When *The Fresno Bee* published material from a grand jury inquiry and its staff members refused to tell the court how they had obtained the information, they were sent to jail for contempt of court.

Executive sessions of public bodies may be closed to the press, but the reason for holding closed-door sessions must not be trivial. Usually, state laws define what constitutes an executive session. Reporters are free to dig up material discussed at these meetings.

Material of a confidential and personal nature held by such agencies as health and welfare departments is not available to the press. A reporter has no legal right to learn whether a certain high school student was treated for gonorrhea by a public health clinic. But the reporter is entitled to data on how many were treated last month or last year and at what cost, how many people the clinic has on its staff and so on. Nor are there prohibitions against a reporter interviewing a clinic user who is willing to talk about his or her treatment, just as a person who appears before a grand jury may tell reporters about the testimony he or she gave to the jury.

Judges contend that some news can prejudice jurors and thus compromise a defendant's Sixth Amendment "right to an impartial jury," making a fair trial impossible. Criminal convictions in lower courts have been set aside because of such publicity.

Pretrial hearings involve material that is potentially prejudicial. At these hearings, decisions are made about whether a confession is voluntary, whether a wiretap violates constitutional safeguards, whether the defendant is competent to stand trial, whether a search leading to physical evidence was conducted with constitutional protections.

◀ Newsgathering

Constitutional Guarantees

First Amendment: Congress shall make no law . . . abridging the freedom of speech or the press.

Sixth Amendment: In all criminal prosecutions, the accused shall enjoy the right to a speedy and public trial, by an impartial jury of the State and District wherein the crime shall have been committed . . . and to have the assistance of counsel for his defense.

Fourteenth Amendment: . . . nor shall any State deprive a person of life, liberty, or property without due process of law, nor deny to any person within its jurisdiction the equal protection of the laws.

◀ Free Press— Fair Trial

A judge may toss out a confession. He or she may rule that certain evidence cannot be admitted. News reports of the matters before the court at the pretrial hearing might be heard or read by jurors who would not have been allowed to hear such information at the trial.

There seems to be little question that pretrial publicity does influence jurors. Studies of actual and simulated jury trials have indicated that when jurors have been given pretrial publicity about prior criminal records and information about confessions, the jurors are prone to find guilt. Jurors not exposed to such pretrial material are less likely to find the defendant guilty. Nevertheless, the traditional position of the judiciary had been, in the words of an opinion of the Third Circuit Court of Appeals, that "secret hearings—though they be scrupulously fair in reality—are suspect by nature. Public confidence cannot long be maintained where important legal decisions are made behind closed doors and then announced in conclusive terms to the public, with the record supporting the court's decision sealed from view."

Judges do have ways to protect the defendant from damaging publicity that would compromise the defendant's right to a fair trial. In *Nebraska Press Association v. Stuart* (427 US 539), the Supreme Court discussed changing the location of the trial, adjourning the trial until pretrial publicity that may be prejudicial has dissipated, careful questioning of jurors during the voir dire (jury empanelling), sequestering the jury and other strategies.

In 1979, in a ruling that stunned the press and many court observers, the Supreme Court voted five to four that the Sixth Amendment does not create the right of access to pretrial proceedings for the public and the press. In immediate response, 239 motions were introduced in various courts to bar the press from criminal justice proceedings. At least 37 were motions to close actual trials and court proceedings. More than half the attempts at closure were successful. Aware that it had made a mistake, the next year, 1980, the Court took up the issue of whether criminal trials must be open to the public.

Pretrials Open ▶

In *Richmond Newspapers, Inc. v. Virginia* (448 US 555), the Court decided seven to one that "openness" is essential to the criminal trial and that media representatives should enjoy the same right of access as does the public. In his opinion, Chief Justice Burger wrote:

> People in an open society do not demand infallibility from their institutions, but it is difficult for them to accept what they are prohibited from observing. . . .
>
> Plainly it would be difficult to single out any aspect of government of higher concern and importance to the people than the manner in which criminal trials are conducted. . . .
>
> What this means in the context of trials is that the First Amendment guarantees of speech and press, standing alone, prohibit government from summarily closing courtroom doors which had long been open to the public at the time that amendment was adopted. . . .
>
> Absent an overriding interest articulated in findings, the trial of a criminal case must be open to the public.

But what of pretrial hearings? Although the press at first welcomed *Richmond* as opening these hearings, a close examination of the decision led to despair. Pretrial hearings in criminal cases could, it appeared, still be closed.

In 1982, the Court did allow a California court to bar the press from jury selection in a criminal trial. But two years later, the Court in *Press-Enterprise v. Superior Court of California* (104 S. Ct. 819) unanimously overturned a California court order barring the press from jury selection. The Court appeared to imply that jury selection is part of the trial rather than a pretrial proceeding. The Court did suggest that such proceedings can be closed if it is made clear that the defendant's right to a fair trial cannot be protected any other way and if the privacy of potential jurors and those not party to the suit cannot be protected otherwise.

The *Press-Enterprise* of Riverside, Calif., then became involved in another significant Supreme Court decision affecting access to pretrial proceedings. The newspaper had been barred from covering the 40-day preliminary hearing for a nurse who was charged with murdering 12 people. The county court judge ruled that press coverage would endanger the nurse's Sixth Amendment right to a fair trial, and two state appellate courts agreed. They ruled that no constitutional right of access to preliminary hearings exists.

The Supreme Court disagreed. It ruled seven to two in 1986 that the press has a qualified right to attend such hearings, even over the objection of the defendant. It said the First Amendment bars closing preliminary hearings in criminal cases unless the action is "essential" and no "reasonable alternatives to closure" are available.

Chief Justice Burger noted that in California most defendants plead guilty after their preliminary hearings, so these hearings are the only chance for the press and public to hear the detailed evidence in the case. Openness of pretrial proceedings, he wrote, plays a "positive role in the actual functioning of the process."

The press hailed the decision, *Press-Enterprise Company v. Superior Court of California* (106 S. Ct. 2735), which is known as Press-Enterprise II to distinguish it from the 1984 case, known as Press-Enterprise I. Press-Enterprise II was seen by the press as a great victory for access to criminal proceedings.

> **Campus Freedom.** Student journalists at tax-supported colleges and universities have the same First Amendment rights as professional journalists. A series of federal court rulings over the past 35 years have solidified the basic freedom. Campus journalists have access to such information as campus crime records.

◀ Congress Acts

A campus press freedom case resulted in a major press victory. The case involved a police search of files in the offices of the Stanford campus newspaper. Police had obtained a search warrant after a campus demonstration was covered by the newspaper. The student newspaper said a search warrant was inappropriate if no one was suspected of a crime, that a subpoena was the appropriate device. Subpoenas are issued after adversarial court hearings; search warrants are issued by judges in *ex-parte* proceedings, hearings at which only one side is represented.

Two lower courts agreed with the newspaper, but the Supreme Court in 1978 ruled for the police in *Zurcher v. Stanford Daily.*

Congress then stepped in and passed the Privacy Protection Act. Overwhelmingly, it voted that federal, state and local law enforcement officers could not, except under limited circumstances, use search warrants for notes, films, tapes or other materials used by those involved in broadcasting and publishing. The authorities would have to obtain subpoenas, which would give news organizations the chance to oppose the requests in court.

Confidentiality Requires Protection ▶

Many attacks on the press in the courts have concerned confidentiality. The courts have been determined to seek out the sources of information in order, it has been said, to assist law enforcement officers and defendants. The press has been equally determined to honor its promise of confidentiality to sources.

A Boston television reporter was sentenced to three months in jail for contempt of court for refusing to identify a source who told her he saw police officers loot a pharmacy. A grand jury was looking into the matter and a prosecutor told the judge his office was stymied without the testimony of the witness.

Journalists traditionally have honored the request for confidentiality, sometimes at a heavy price. In 17th-century England, a printer, John Twyn, refused to give the Star Chamber the name of the author of a pamphlet about justice that Twyn had published. The Chamber called the pamphlet treasonous, and when Twyn would not speak, it passed the following sentence:

> (You will be) . . . drawn upon an hurdle to the place of execution; and there you shall be hanged by the neck, and being alive, shall be cut down, and your privy members shall be cut off, your entrails shall be taken out of your body, the same to be burnt before your eyes; your head to be cut off, your body to be divided into four quarters, and your head and quarters to be disposed of at the pleasure of the King's Majesty.

Shield Laws ▶

One effect of the attack on confidentiality was the enactment of state shield laws, in effect in most states. These laws provide varying degrees of confidentiality for sources and materials.

Reporters contend that their notes—which may include the names of confidential sources as well as the reporters' own investigative work—should be treated as confidential. State shield laws grant the reporter this protection unless in a criminal case the defense can prove that the notes are relevant and that alternative sources of information have been exhausted.

Shield laws are important. When the highest state court rules on matters covered by the state constitution, the issue cannot be reviewed by the U.S. Supreme Court because the state court is the final authority on the meaning of the state's constitutional guarantees. Some state constitutions have even broader protections than the U.S. Constitution.

The shield law is a helpful successor to the sunshine law, which requires public bodies to meet in public unless there is a compelling reason for privacy.

Newspapers and broadcast stations contend that confidentiality is essential to freedom of the press. The press points out that the power of the government to punish people involved in unpopular causes led the courts to safeguard anonymity in many areas. The courts recognize the doctor-patient and lawyer-client relationship as generally beyond legal inquiry. Journalists have sought the same protection for their sources.

If the press is to be the watchdog of government, as the press believes the framers of the Constitution intended, then the press must be free to discover what public officials are doing, not limited to print what officials say they are doing. In order to ferret out the activities of public officials, insiders and informants are necessary. These informants usually must be promised anonymity. The courts, however, have not been sympathetic to reporters who seek to honor confidentiality in the face of court demands for disclosure.

Once a reporter promises confidentiality, he or she must honor that pledge, ◀ **Keep the Promise**
the Supreme Court ruled in *Cohen v. Cowles Media* in a 1991 decision. St. Paul and Minneapolis newspapers promised a source that damaging information he gave them about a candidate would not carry his name.

After the newspapers decided to use the source's name, he was fired from his job. The source sued, and the court ruled that First Amendment protections do not prevent a newspaper from being held liable for violating a promise of confidentiality. The state law on an implied contract was violated, the court ruled.

Here is some useful advice taken from court decisions, laws and the expe- ◀ **Tips and Tidbits**
rience of journalists:

Jurors are free to talk about their experiences once a trial ends. But contact ◀ **Interviewing Jurors**
with jurors while they are deliberating can lead to contempt-of-court charges.

The same general rule applies to those serving on grand juries. The laws affecting witnesses appearing before grand juries vary from state to state. Some allow witnesses to talk about their testimony, but others forbid it until the grand jury inquiry is over.

The courts have ruled that it is illegal to use a tape recorder secretly while ◀ **Taping**
posing as someone else. This is invasion of privacy through *intrusion.*

Don R. Pember of the University of Washington, author of a mass media law textbook, advises his students to turn on the tape recorder and to ask permission. Then the consent is recorded. Generally, he says, be "up-front with recorders."

Recording a telephone conversation is illegal in 10 states unless both par- ◀ **Telephone Talk**
ties consent to the taping: California, Florida, Illinois, Maryland, Massachusetts, Montana, New Hampshire, Oregon, Pennsylvania and Washington. Other states and federal law allow recording with only one party's knowledge.

Newspapers that publish wire service stories with libelous material have ◀ **Wire Service Defense**
been protected by the "wire service defense." This legal concept holds that if the   **Valid**
newspaper was not aware of the defamatory material in the story, could not reasonably have been expected to detect such material and reprinted the material without substantial changes, then the publication will not be held liable, whether private or public figures are defamed by the article.

Altering Quotes ▶

The U.S. Supreme Court has ruled that changing a quote does not necessarily constitute libel unless the change gives a different meaning than the source intended. The Court stated:

> If every alteration constituted the falsity required to prove actual malice, the practice of journalism, which the First Amendment standard is designed to protect, would require a radical change, one inconsistent with our precedents and First Amendment principles.

Causes and Consequences ▶

The press considers itself a critic not only of sacred cows but of sacred institutions. This disturbs those who want and need ideals and heroes, men and women to look up to, to be loyal to. Few individuals or institutions can stand up under the scrutiny to which the press subjects them.

The public reaction has been to resort to the ancient technique of blaming the messenger.

Tyrone Brown, a law clerk to Chief Justice Earl Warren in the 1960s, then general counsel for Post-Newsweek Broadcasting and later a member of the Federal Communications Commission, said the Court's rulings reflect attitudes toward the press.

"All those so-called absolute principles like the First Amendment are functions of the time when they're decided," Brown says. "The Justices' role is a process role—making accommodations between various power groups in the country at various times."

In several decisions affecting the press, some justices have suggested that the Times Doctrine be re-examined. They have asserted that subsequent rulings for the press have permitted the press to abuse privacy and to be held exempt from responsibility for its articles.

Local, state and federal courts have been more willing to close judicial proceedings and to gag those involved in civil and criminal trials. And countless officials are more reluctant to allow reporters access to public records and entrance to meetings.

"There is an attitude of too many public officials that the material they are caretakers for belongs to them and not to the public," said Paul K. McMasters, the deputy editorial director of *USA Today.*

Although every state and the District of Columbia have open records and open meetings laws, "many newspapers ranging in size from the smallest to the largest national dailies find themselves almost continually snarled in disputes over one of our most basic democratic rights: To find out what branches of the government and its agencies are doing," reported the American Society of Newspaper Editors.

Summing Up ▶

- The police cannot arbitrarily deny a press pass to a reporter.
- Except for placing reasonable restrictions on access to events behind police lines, the police cannot interfere with a reporter engaged in news-gathering activities in public places.
- Reporters cannot be denied access to open meetings of legislative or executive bodies.

- The reporter can try to use state law to open certain hearings of public bodies that have been closed as "executive sessions." But there is no constitutional right to attend. Several states have adopted "sunshine laws" that require public agencies to have open meetings and open records.
- Reporters do not have a constitutional right to documents and reports not available to the general public. (The Supreme Court has equated the press's right to access with the right of access of the public.)

Reporters:

- Have no special right of access to news.
- Should be careful about what they print about the records of criminal defendants.
- May be asked to divulge the thoughts they had before they wrote a story.
- Can have their files examined by police.
- Cannot guarantee a source confidentiality.
- May be required to give testimony or documents to a grand jury.
- Should be careful about telling sources the press and the source are protected by a state shield law.

◀ **Further Reading**

Cater, Douglass. *The Fourth Branch of Government*. New York: Vintage, 1959.

Chaffee, Zechariah Jr. *Free Speech in the United States*. Cambridge, Mass.: Harvard, 1948.

Denniston, Lyle. *The Reporter and the Law*. New York: Hastings House, 1980.

Hand, Learned. *Liberty*. Stamford, Conn.: Overbrook Press, 1941.

Lewis, Anthony. *Make No Law: The Sullivan Case and the First Amendment*. New York: Random House, 1992.

Oran, Daniel. *Law Dictionary for Non-Lawyers*. St. Paul, Minn.: West Publishing Co., 1975.

Pember, Don R. *Mass Media Law,* 6th ed. Dubuque, Iowa: Wm. C. Brown, 1993.

Sanford, Bruce W. *Synopsis of the Law of Libel and the Right of Privacy*. New York: World Almanac Publications, 1984.

26 Taste—Defining the Appropriate

Preview

Material that is obscene, vulgar or profane can offend readers and listeners. But it also can be informative, and sometimes the reporter risks offending to move closer to the truth.

Decisions to use such material depend on:

• **Context:** If the event is significant and the material is essential to describing the event, offensive material may be used.

• **Nature of the audience:** A publication for adults or a special-interest group will contain material that a mass medium might not.

• **Prominence of those involved:** Public officials and public figures lead public lives. What would constitute prying into the life of a private individual may be necessary reporting of the activities of those in public life.

Durall Hall Jr., *The Courier-Journal.*

Photos cause most complaints.

Two Cornell University astronomers had an idea for the Pioneer 10 spacecraft flight. For its journey beyond our solar system it would carry a drawing of a man and a woman as well as information about the planet Earth. Should the spacecraft then nuzzle down on some distant civilization the inhabitants could visualize what Earth man and woman look like.

The National Aeronautics and Space Administration accepted the suggestion, and when Pioneer 10 was launched, a gold-plated aluminum plaque engraved with a sketch of the Earth and its solar system and a drawing of a naked man and woman standing next to each other was aboard. NASA released the drawing to newspapers, thereupon confronting many editors with a dilemma. The picture was newsworthy, but would its publication be in bad taste?

The *Chicago Sun-Times* published the drawing in an early edition after an artist had removed the man's testicles. In a later edition, the rest of the genitals were erased. *The Philadelphia Inquirer* did even more brushwork: The male had no genitals and the nipples had been removed from the woman's breasts. The *Los Angeles Times* ran the drawing untouched. "Filth," a reader wrote in protest.

Now, some 30 years later, the assertions of bad taste and the editors' anxieties seem as obsolete as the embarrassment that pregnant women once were made to feel in male-oriented society. (The word *confinement* to describe the term of pregnancy goes back to this period because pregnant women were kept at

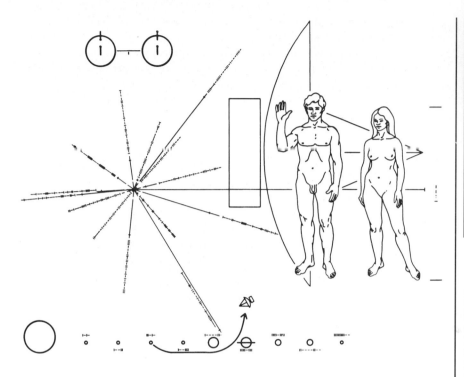

Changing Times

When this drawing, which was carried on the first human-made object to leave the solar system, was reproduced in the *Los Angeles Times,* a reader complained that it was "filth," and many newspapers removed various parts of the bodies of the man and woman before running it. Twenty years later, newspapers were carrying stories about AIDS and condoms and running advertisements about birth control.

home to hide their supposed shame.) But no matter how liberated we may think ourselves, matters of taste still concern the reporter.

How, for example, do the media cover a Senate hearing that is concerned with what some groups insist is record-album pornography?

The committee is considering whether the First Amendment gives free-speech rights to rap groups that sing about rape, suicide, murder, sadomasochism and sex. The hearing attracts hundreds of spectators and a large complement of reporters. Four-letter words and sexually explicit lines explode.

The reporters quote Sen. Ernest Hollings: "It is outrageous filth and we must do something about it." And they quote those who oppose censorship.

But they do not use the words or lines of the music in their stories.

Editors admit they are trying to navigate through muddy waters. The news is filled with unspeakable brutalities—Serbs raping thousands of women in ethnic cleansing, crimes that even years-hardened police officers cannot describe calmly. These are reported. Yet when the lyrics of 2 Live Crew became a news item, the words that recommend the tearing or damaging of girls' vaginas were glossed over by all but 11 of 108 newspapers that carried the story.

No one wants to offend readers or viewers. Nor—in the case of broadcast journalists—is there sense in offending the Federal Communications Commission, which has rules about obscenity, indecency and profanity. But how does a reporter or an editor decide when to risk giving offense in order to provide essential information? Just what is the "good taste" that journalists are supposed to exercise?

Taste is usually defined as a set of value judgments in behavior, manners, or the arts held in common by a group or class of people. Generally, these values help to keep society stable, to insulate it from sudden and possibly destructive change. Those who advocate strict controls on pornography, for example, argue that such material stimulates anti-social behavior.

The values that determine decisions about taste are not absolute. They change with time, place and context.

Time ▶

The Washington Post tells its reporters that "society's concepts of taste and decency are constantly changing. A word offensive to the last generation can be part of the next generation's common vocabulary."

In 1939, the public was scandalized when in the movie *Gone with the Wind*, Rhett Butler turned to Scarlett O'Hara and said, "Frankly, my dear, I don't give a damn." The word *rape* was taboo in many newspapers until the 1950s.

By the 1990s, movies, theater, books and magazines left little to the imagination. For those with exotic tastes, a $7 billion a year pornography industry catered to every conceivable fantasy, with not much legal interference. In time, journalism dropped many of its taboos, too.

AIDS ▶

Much of the shift toward explicitness stems from the AIDS epidemic.

At first reluctant to use direct language and graphic descriptions, television, radio and newspapers finally faced the reality of AIDS reporting. They dropped the euphemism *safe sex* and spoke and wrote about *condoms*. They replaced vague allusions to *sexual practices* and used *anal* and *oral intercourse* in describing how the disease can be transmitted.

The New York Times, hardly an innovator among newspapers, ran a story in 1987 headlined, "Among Women, the Talk Is of Condoms." Here is an excerpt from the piece:

"I keep them with me," said Rebecca Pailes, a 25-year-old fashion designer. "I have them in my house. I won't have sex without them."

She uses a diaphragm also for birth control. "I use condoms," she said, "just to prevent disease."

"I don't trust anybody," said Judith, the 37-year-old owner of a small employment agency, who asked that her last name not be used. "I'm cynical about men. Nobody's worth the risk. Who knows who the people they've been with have been with? But I'm not going to give up sex."

Judith, who described herself as alternating between celibacy and promiscuity, keeps a drawerful of condoms in her kitchen.

"I give them to my friends who are celibate and say 'Here, now you can have sex,' " she said.

By 1989, the three major television networks had agreed to broadcast a public-service advertising campaign that promoted the use of condoms to prevent the spread of AIDS. Surgeon General C. Everett Koop welcomed the change and pointed out that "those in the communications field have a responsibility to repeat this message again and again until the use of a condom becomes a habitually conditioned reflex."

Even the soap operas took on AIDS. In "Another World," Dawn Rollo was the first soap victim of the disease.

This was quite a change from the guarded coverage of the death from AIDS of the movie star Rock Hudson in 1985. Although many publications used the death to illustrate the danger of unsafe sex, only *Time* used the word *condom*.

Taste changes according to place. Behavior appropriate in a football stadium would be boorish in an opera house. Language inoffensive to most residents of San Francisco would be tasteless, if not worse, to residents of Salt Lake City.

◄ Place and Context

Taste also is a function of the context in which the material is used. A story in *Rolling Stone* would contain language and references abhorrent to a reader of *The Christian Science Monitor*. Here is a sidebar to an article by Karen Rothmyer in the *Columbia Journalism Review:*

Meeting Mr. Scaife

Richard Scaife rarely speaks to the press. After several unsuccessful efforts to obtain an interview, this reporter decided to make one last attempt in Boston, where Scaife was scheduled to attend the annual meeting of the First Boston Corporation.

Scaife, a company director, did not show up while the meeting was in progress. Reached eventually by telephone as he dined with the other directors at the exclusive Union Club, he hung up the moment he heard the caller's name. A few minutes later he appeared at the top of the Club steps. At the bottom of the stairs, the following exchange occurred:

"Mr. Scaife, could you explain why you give so much money to the New Right?"

"You fucking Communist cunt, get out of here."

Well. The rest of the five-minute interview was conducted at a rapid trot down Park Street, during which Scaife tried to hail a taxi. Scaife volunteered two statements of opinion regarding his questioner's personal appearance—he said she was ugly and that her teeth were "terrible"—and also the comment that she was engaged in "hatchet journalism." His questioner thanked Scaife for his time.

"Don't look behind you." Scaife offered by way of a goodbye.

Not quite sure what this remark meant, the reporter suggested that if someone were approaching it was probably her mother, whom she had arranged to meet nearby. "She's ugly, too," Scaife said, and strode off.

Freud on Language. "Anyone who considers sex as something mortifying and humiliating to human nature is at liberty to make use of the more genteel expressions 'Eros' and 'erotic.' I might have done so myself from the first and spared myself much opposition. But I did not want to, for I like to avoid concessions to faintheartedness. One can never tell where that road may lead; one gives way first in words, and then little by little in substance too. I cannot see any merit in being ashamed of sex . . . ."—Sigmund Freud, *Group Psychology and the Analysis of the Ego* (1921)

The *Review*'s editors wanted to show its readers the full dimension of Scaife's personality. Since most of the readers are journalists, the editors knew this brief exchange would enlighten rather than offend them.

A vulgarity uttered by the president may be essential to the story, whereas an offhand obscene remark by an athlete may be unnecessary. During the negotiations with steel companies about price increases, President Kennedy said, "My father always told me businessmen were sons-of-bitches." *The New York Times* printed the president's remarks as made. But almost 20 years later, the *Times* in-house bulletin, *Winners & Sinners,* was unhappy about a sports story that quoted Reggie Jackson, then with the New York Yankees, saying, "I can say this because George can do nothing to me. He can do nothing because I can hit the baseball over the wall. But when I can't hit, they'll screw me too. I know they'll screw me the same way they screwed Rosen."

Winners & Sinners criticized the Jackson quotation, saying that such language can be used "only when the printing of the objectionable word or words will give the reader an insight into matters of great moment—an insight that cannot be otherwise conveyed."

A Guideline ▶

The most important guide to the use of questionable subject matter and explicit language is that the event must be significant and the questionable material essential to the story to justify its use. *The Washington Post* advises reporters to "avoid profanities and obscenities unless their use is so essential to a story of significance that its meaning is lost without them."

We must qualify this guideline in two ways. There are legitimate differences of opinion about what constitutes significance or importance, and place must be considered in the application of the guideline. When Charles Alexander, the editor of *The Journal Herald* in Dayton, Ohio, decided his readers should have the fullest possible account of a quarrel between two agents with the Treasury Department, he approved the following quotation:

> "Gibson God damn it, you are fucking
> with my family. You are fucking with my
> future. I am not going to let you do it. I'll
> kill you first."

The paper was quoting agent Casper Carroll Gibson's account of the quarrel. Gibson said the other agent then started to pull a gun out of his pocket. Gibson grabbed the gun, it went off and his colleague fell dead.

Alexander's bosses found the use of the words indefensible for Dayton readers. When Alexander would not back down and apologize, he was fired.

"It's a matter of truth," Alexander said. "To me, the telling of that message from an incident in real life, including in one instance the raw vulgarity used by a man blind with rage, is a lesson that every man, woman and child should perceive in all its dimensions. It is shocking—it surely should be. . . ."

Alexander lost his job in 1975. Four years before, *The Record* in Bergen County, N.J., across the Hudson River from New York City, carried a story about a Democratic party official's reaction to being told she could not attend a party meeting at the home of the state chairman. She went anyway. When she arrived, the chairman told her she would have been welcome but for the language the men used in their discussions. To which she replied, "I don't give a shit what kind of language you use."

The Record quoted her as saying just that. (The men then told her she could attend.)

Offensive Detail. A *New York Times* column about the death of a Justice Department official who was killed in an airliner crash began:

A week after he went down with Pan American flight 103, Michael Bernstein, or what they could collect of him, was still in Lockerbie, Scotland.

The lead was defended as showing the devastation and the horror of the crash. But to many the description of the condition of the body added nothing essential and was unnecessarily offensive.

Changing Standards ▶

Standards in taste traditionally were set by the upper class and the elders of the community. This worked, more or less, until the Depression of the 1930s and then World War II in the following decade.

With economic collapse came a questioning of the old ways, an unwillingness to accept edicts from on high and a willingness to experiment with new, daring and different ideas. People were on the move, and long-standing community structures were disrupted.

World War II thrust an isolationst nation into a maelstrom. Not only did the shrinking of the protective oceans force the country to change its geopolitical assumptions, the war caused massive social disruption: Millions of young men were uprooted, hundreds of thousands of women were enlisted in the work force, blacks migrated from the agrarian south to the industrialized midwest and northeast. Classes, sexes and races mixed and mingled.

At the same time, events occurred—some unbearably sad, some unspeakably vicious and indecent—that were so monumental they had to be reported. The Depression gave the country malnourished children, uprooted families, forced proud but jobless men and women to seek handouts.

◀ Events Required Truth Telling

The Nazi brutalities, at first disbelieved as too vile to be true, were verified. Murder of the young, the handicapped and the "different" had become German state policy, and a nation that had given the world Beethoven and Goethe acquiesced in the state's slaughter.

The civil rights struggles of the 1950s and the liberation movements of the 1960s involved actions and language the old rules of taste would have deemed improper. But journalists knew that they had to be reported. The profanities and obscene acts that accompanied the country's crises were symbols of the collapse of the old order. The battles and the new balances—the young, for example, were exerting greater social and political power—had to be reported.

Although some of the more conservative members of the community considered the young to be the modern counterparts of the barbarians at the gates, the young unquestionably were causing significant changes in society. But to report the full dimensions of these activities—the language and slogans—the press would risk censure by the upholders of order in the community, the very people upon whom the newspaper depends for its survival. Radio and television station managers had less leeway. The FCC, they said, required them to conform to contemporary community standards.

The country was in flux. Years of racial strife and urban crises, the consequences of the women's movement, the disenchantment with political and business leaders as a result of Vietnam, Watergate and business scandals had made the standard-setters suspect. Had not the best and the brightest of them led us into the Vietnam quagmire?

Shocking. The cover of the Aug. 15, 1993, *New York Times Magazine* brought gasps from its 1.8 million readers—and shock, anger and applause. The cover was a full-page color photograph of a woman in a white dress displaying her scarred chest, the result of her mastectomy that removed a breast. It was used to illustrate an article about breast cancer, "You Can't Look Away Any More."

The photograph drew 500 letters, about two-thirds favorable. The woman in the photograph, the model Matuschka, who took the photo herself, said she has tried to use her own experience to make people confront the growing problem of breast cancer. She said the magazine editor accepted her photo "without a lot of hemming and hawing . . . it took a lot of guts."

Awareness that journalists themselves could define taste was inevitable. Events had made it imperative that the press describe social and political changes, and to describe them accurately a new sense of the appropriate in language and subject matter was necessary.

◀ The Turning Point

In 1960, during a school integration demonstration in New Orleans, the AP quoted some of the women who were shouting at the leader of the school sit-ins: "Jew bastard, nigger lover." In answer to many protests that the use of such words was in bad taste, the AP said it "judged them essential to establishing the temper and the mood of the demonstrators."

Gradually, pertinence or significance was becoming the guideline in determining whether an obscenity or profanity should be included in news accounts.

A major turning point was reached during Watergate when the tapes of the White House conversations revealed a profusion of vulgarities and profanities. As a West Coast journalism review, *feed/back,* put it, the "Nixon administration made inoperative the detente that existed in the daily press against words once excised by editors."

The words *shit* and *fuck,* used in the White House, appeared in such papers as *The Washington Post,* the *St. Paul Dispatch* and *Pioneer Press,* the Atlanta *Journal,* the *Kansas City Star* and *The Seattle Times.*

It would have been impossible, many editors felt, to have changed the emphatic language of a statement by President Nixon from the key tape of March 22, 1973:

> I don't give a shit what happens. I want you all to stonewall it, let them plead the Fifth Amendment, cover up or anything else if it'll save the plan. That's the whole point.

The AP made a survey of newspapers using the Watergate material and found nearly 30 percent of them printed all or nearly all of the obscenities without alteration. Slightly more than half sanitized the word *shit* or other words, and 15 percent of the papers completely edited out the vulgarities and profanities by paraphrase or deletion.

One of the newspapers that did not use Nixon's language was the Huntington (W. Va.) *Herald-Dispatch* and *Advertiser,* whose executive editor said, "In this very Fundamentalist market, we came to the conclusion that there was no reason to offend unnecessarily."

Turning away from some kinds of reality while daily parading humanity's most obscene acts—murder, torture, terrorism—seems an act of hypocrisy to some editors. Another kind of hypocrisy—the discrepancy between private and public morality—is revealed by an incident involving television station WGBH in Boston. The station decided to do a program a few days after the 1968 student demonstrations on the Harvard campus. It invited people from the community to have their say. One of those who showed up took the microphone at the beginning of the program and shouted, "What I have to say is fuck Harvard and fuck Pusey [Harvard's president] and fuck everybody." David Ives, the president of the public TV station recalled, "I was upstairs, and you have never seen so many telephone calls. The most interesting thing about them was the quality of what they said."

"One woman said, 'I just want you to know that no language like that has ever been permitted in this house.' And in the background you could hear a man saying, 'You know God damn well it has.' Another protest came from a man who called and said, 'I'm just not going to have any of that kind of shit in my living room.' "

Public Outrage, Private Delight. When it was discovered that Miss America was being displayed in the nude in *Penthouse* magazine (the photos had been taken before she won the title), the public was outraged and the pageant took away her crown. The issue with the photos sold 6 million copies, twice the magazine's normal circulation.

Reactions ▶

The steady lifting of taboos has not gone unnoticed by those in society who describe themselves as having traditional values. They are convinced that a liberal approach to matters of taste is really a corruption of our value system, and their organizations pepper broadcast stations and publications with complaints.

Ignored at first as the grousing of a small segment of the public, the protests found widening support in the mid-1990s. So much support, that politicians—

whose sensitivities to public sentiment are finely tuned—made "values" a political issue. They could tell a mood change was in the air. Violence in films, mayhem on television, rap lyrics that glorified killing the police and described women as whores . . . many people were beginning to wonder whether the media were going too far.

Here are some reactions to the reaction.

◀ Censorship or Bad Taste?

The *Los Angeles Times,* no capitulator to the conservative elements on taste, nevertheless forced a youth newspaper to kill part of a story on AIDS prevention. As a public service, the *Times* prints *LA Youth,* a tabloid written by and for teen-agers. But it objected to part of a story about "Club Prophylactive" in which teen-agers learn about safe sex.

Unless the material was killed, the *Times* declared, it would not print that issue of *LA Youth.* The offending material quoted a flyer that described in detail how to assure protection from AIDS while having oral sex and quoted a student referring to a video presentation: "They actually showed some guy putting a condom on his erect penis. Gross! They showed people having sex."

The newspaper, which is distributed to 300 schools in the Los Angeles area, reluctantly agreed to the cuts, alleging censorship. A *Times* spokeswoman said, "This is a taste issue . . . we are held accountable by parents, teachers and other people."

◀ Condom Ads

After the surgeon general had advocated the use of condoms to prevent the spread of AIDS and other sexually transmitted diseases, the television networks accepted commercials for prophylactics. But stations were flooded with protests, and CBS, ABC and NBC decided to accept only public service announcements concerning the use of condoms for disease prevention, not for pregnancy prevention. The FOX network will accept paid condom advertising but only for disease prevention.

Sometimes, the public service announcements that are aired are followed by a disclaimer that urges abstinence.

Newspapers generally accept paid advertising urging condom use for prevention of unwanted pregnancy.

Contraception and abortion are explosive subjects, and the other equally volatile public issue may be homosexuality. The media have treated the subject gingerly.

◀ Gay Weddings

Slowly, and despite many complaints from the community, gay and lesbian couples are having their relationships acknowledged by newspapers. In 1993, *The Salina Journal* published the first gay or lesbian wedding announcement ever published in a Kansas daily newspaper. The announcement was carried in a full-page story in the Lifestyles section under the headline "Out of the Closet."

The reaction: A handful wrote to support the newspaper. Most wrote that they were shocked and appalled, and 116 readers cancelled subscriptions. But for the first time in anyone's recollection at the paper, the Sunday issue sold out.

The *Journal*'s editor, George Pyle, said, "Our editorial policy has always been in favor of equal rights. It would be kind of hypocritical to say that on the editorial page and then to say on the lifestyle pages that 'We're not going to include you.' "

In an editorial follow-up, Pyle recommended that Kansas legalize gay and lesbian marriages: "It's time for America to get out of this massive state of denial. They're queer. They're here. Get used to it."

Rape ▶

Almost as incendiary in the area of taste is the subject of rape. Is it offensive to name the victim? Generally, newspapers do not print the names of women who allege that they have been raped, even when they testify at trials. Some reasons:

- The victim risks being blamed. Some people believe the victims want to be raped.
- Publication would stigmatize the woman.

When she was editor of *The Des Moines Register,* Geneva Overholser said that although her newspaper did not run the names of rape victims she favored their publication because it would help erase the stigma and focus attention on the crime which is one of "brutal violence" rather than a "crime of sex."

Rape, she said, is "an American shame. Our society needs to see that and to attend to it, not hide it or hush it up. As long as rape is deemed unspeakable—and is therefore not fully and honestly spoken of—the public outrage will be muted as well."

Parental Rape ▶

When a Spokane man was arrested for raping his four daughters, ages 4 to 8, *The Spokesman-Review* did not publish his name to spare embarrassment to the children, whose identity would be clear. But the policy bothered Chris Peck, the managing editor, and he asked readers what they thought about naming parental rapists.

The response was two to one in favor of naming the man, and the paper did so when he was sentenced. The man's wife, who videotaped the rapes and was convicted of failing to report the crime to authorities, was also named.

For their frankly written series on sexual abuse of children, Rebecca Mabry and Mike Howie were explicit. One story in their series in *The News-Gazette* of Champaign-Urbana, Ill., began:

> As a teen-ager, Jan tried three times to get help in stopping her father.
> The first time was when she was 13, and although her father had been molesting Jan since she was about 5, he had never before attempted intercourse with her.
> Jan recalls he held a knife to her throat and told her that if she ever told anyone what he had done, she would never speak again.

Obscenity and the Law ▶

On matters of obscenity, indecency and profanity, *Miller v. California* in 1973 (413 US 15) is the standard for determining whether a printed work is obscene. The Court for the first time set state rather than national standards. It asserted, "Diversity is not to be strangled by the absolutism of imposed uniformity."

The test is whether the work, taken as a whole, (a) appeals to the prurient interest as decided by "an average person applying contemporary community standards," (b) depicts or describes in a patently offensive way sexual conduct specifically defined by the applicable state law, and (c) lacks to a reasonable person any serious literary, artistic, political or scientific value.

For the work to be ruled obscene, all three elements must be present.

Although the courts have ruled that obscenity is not constitutionally protected, they have been reluctant to rule against printed material, even the pornographic publications that are sold at newsstands.

The taboos against explicit reference to intercourse and other sexual activities have been eased at a much slower pace than other prohibitions. Still, there have been changes, hardly surprising in view of the vast alterations in society over the past three decades. If journalism is the mirror held to life, then a journalism that is prohibited from chronicling changes in how we live offers a distorted image.

◀ Sexual Matters

The press has followed the arts, which journey wherever the imagination soars. Fiction, the movies and magazines flung off the fig leaf and discarded the asterisk and dash years ago. The press lagged, and this failure to keep up, some press critics say, led to a public uninformed on such issues as sex education, venereal disease and how sex influences our behavior.

But some publications became aware of the necessity to report these matters and their consequences. They began to report fully such issues as family planning, abortion, birth control, homosexuality, sex education, teen-age sex, family relationships, venereal disease and laws affecting sexual behavior.

The pioneering work on human sexual behavior, Alfred C. Kinsey's *Sexual Behavior in the Human Male,* had been treated gingerly by the mass media when it was published in 1948. In 1966, another important work on sexual activity, *Human Sexual Response,* by Dr. William H. Masters and Virginia E. Johnson, was published. The result of a detailed 11-year study of sexual physiology, the work was too important to be ignored. The question was not whether to run a news story—times had changed—but how the story was to be written. The study was based on the direct observation of sexual intercourse and masturbation and it was published to give information to those treating problems of sexual inadequacy.

The story that appeared in the April 18, 1966, issue of *The New York Times* about the Masters-Johnson study used sexually explicit words such as *vagina, vaginal lubrication, intravaginal diaphragms* and *orgasm.* As the story was being edited, a problem came up on the copy desk.

◀ Offensive Words

As the event is recounted by a *Times* copy editor, the desk noticed the frequent and explicit references to the female sex organ (six) and only euphemistic references (two) to the male organ—"genital organ" and "the organ." The question was referred to an assistant managing editor who served as the arbiter of language and taste at the *Times.* He decreed *vagina* for the woman and *organ* for the man as proper.

Two years later, the *Times* was more forthcoming in its use of explicit language. Reporting the changes *The Washington Post* and *Chicago Tribune* had made in a review appearing in their Sunday book review supplement. "Book World," the *Times* reported that the newspapers had called back a press run of the supplement to delete a section that "consisted of a paragraph containing reference to the penis in a discussion of the sexual behavior of primates."

Here is the paragraph that so offended the sensibilities of decision makers at the *Post* and *Tribune* that they called back a million copies of the press run at a cost of $100,000:

> Many a cocktail party this winter will be kept in motion by this provocative chit chat; man is the sexiest primate alive; the human male and not the gorilla possesses the largest penis of all primates. . . .

The *Post* and *Tribune* were clinging to the concept of the newspaper as family reading, though *Life* and *Newsweek* had used the word in their stories about the book, *The Naked Ape* by Desmond Morris, and though it was commonplace among millions of nursery school children who had been told to call a penis a penis.

Limits on Broadcasting ▶

The FCC is empowered to enforce federal statutes and the decisions of the courts in the areas of obscenity, indecency and profanity. The FCC can fine a station or revoke its license if it finds that it violated section 1464 of the federal Criminal Code, which provides for penalties for uttering "any obscene, indecent or profane language by means of radio communication." ("Radio" includes television.)

But even broadcasters and the FCC have changed with the times. In 1960, NBC censored the use of the initials *W.C.* on a nightly televised network talk program. *W.C.* stands for *water closet,* which in Britain means *toilet.* A dozen years later, the Public Broadcasting Service showed an "education entertainment" called the "V.D. Blues." There were no protests about the initials, and there were surprisingly few objections to some of the language in such songs as "Don't Give a Dose to the One You Love Most" and "Even Dr. Pepper Won't Help You," which was about the futility of douching as a contraceptive practice.

Although some stations made cuts, and stations in Arkansas and Mississippi did not carry the program, the majority of public broadcast stations decided that the program was a public service. When "V.D. Blues" was followed by a 2 ½ hour hotline on a New York City station, 15,000 people called with questions about venereal disease. One of the city's V.D. clinics reported the next day that the number of persons seeking blood tests went up by a third.

The program obviously was aimed at teen-agers, whose venereal disease rate is epidemic. But stations must be aware of children in the audience, as the FCC and Congress have indicated.

In 1973, in a broadcast in the early afternoon over station WBAI (FM) in New York City, George Carlin gave a comedy monologue entitled "The Seven Words You Can't Say on Radio and Television." Carlin said his intent was to show that the language of ordinary people is not threatening or obscene. The station later said in its defense that the broadcast was in the tradition of satire. In the broadcasts Carlin had said:

◀ **The Case of the "Filthy Words"**

> I was thinking one night about the words you couldn't say on the public airwaves . . . and it came down to seven but the list is open to amendment and in fact has been changed. . . . The original seven words were shit, piss, fuck, cunt, cocksucker, motherfucker and tits. . . .

He repeated the tabooed words several times in what he said later was a purposeful "verbal shock treatment."

There was one complaint, and the FCC investigated. In 1975, it issued a declaratory order finding that the words were "patently offensive by contemporary community standards for the broadcast medium and are accordingly 'indecent' when broadcast by radio or television. These words were broadcast at a time when children were undoubtedly in the audience."

The station was not prosecuted. The finding, however, was made part of the station's file. In effect, the station was put on probation.

The station appealed to the federal courts, and many stations and civil rights advocates joined the appeal against what was seen as a threat to freedom of expression. The case—which became known as the "Filthy Words Case"— reached the United States Supreme Court, and in 1978 in *FCC v. Pacifica,* the Court ruled five to four that radio and television stations do not have the constitutional right to broadcast indecent words. It said that the government has the right to forbid such words because of the broadcast medium's "uniquely pervasive presence in the lives of all Americans." The Court stated that "of all forms of communication, it is broadcasting that has received the most limited First Amendment protection."

The Supreme Court emphasized the limits of its ruling:

> It is appropriate, in conclusion, to emphasize the narrowness of our ruling. . . . The Commission's (FCC) decision rested entirely on a nuisance rationale under which context is all important. . . . The time of day was emphasized by the Commission. . . .

Since the court ruling, the FCC and Congress have tried to find the fine line between First Amendment freedom for broadcasters and regulation of what it considers indecent material. In 1987 it established a "safe harbor," the six hours between midnight and 6 a.m. when children ostensibly would be asleep and stations could broadcast so-called indecent programming.

Two years later, Congress imposed a 'round-the-clock ban on such material, but a federal Court of Appeals found the law unconstitutionally broad. In

1992, as a warning to commercial broadcasters, the FCC fined a New York talk show host, Howard Stern, $600,000 for broadcasting indecent material.

Note: The new communications technologies—interactive cable television, home satellite services and computer bulletin board networks—are not subject to FCC rules. In return for their freedom, cable stations, which routinely run material that contains foul language, nudity and R-rated sex scenes, must offer their subscribers lockout devices to enable them to control what their children view.

Pictures ▶

Some editors say that pictures arouse greater reader response than a story that may be offensive. Readers, says the Reader Representative of *The Hartford Courant,* may be "appalled at a news story, but they are shocked and outraged at a news photo."

The Flint (Mich.) *Journal* ran an AP photo of a Somali mother mourning the death of her young son before taking him in a wheelchair for burial. The emaciated body of the child was clearly visible in the photo, and a reader called to complain that the photo offended her. An editorial responded:

Good. It should.

It should offend all of us.

We should be outraged and incensed—not that newspapers would publish such a graphic and tragic image, but that the world would allow such suffering, such violence to continue.

Yes, the picture was horrifying. It made people uncomfortable. That was the point in publishing it. It was to open people's eyes to the catastrophe that continues to unfold there.

Three years later, the genocidal slaughter in Rwanda was documented with gruesome photographs of the dead and dying. There was no public outcry about the pictures.

A Child's Drowning ▶

The day was hot and humid, and in the newsroom of the *Mercury-Register* in Oroville, Calif., David C. Neilsen II, the newspaper's head photographer, was monitoring his police scanner. The quiet was broken by a call: A car had tumbled into a 30-foot-deep pond. A child was trapped inside.

Neilsen raced to the scene and found volunteer and full-time firefighters desperately searching the murky waters for a 3-year-old boy. The car's driver looked on from the bank.

When one of the rescuers surfaced with the limp child in his arms, Neilsen was there with his camera. His photos show the anguish and the desperate concern of the men as they emerged with the child.

Clearly, the story would be a major part of Saturday's morning newspaper. But the photos presented a problem to the city desk: Here was an identifiable picture of the child, who died shortly after his discovery in the pond. The desk called John Fenrich, publisher of the 10,000 circulation newspaper, a newspaper Fenrich describes as "family-oriented." What should they do?

Fenrich rushed to the newsroom, and for 45 minutes he and his staff looked at the photos and talked over their use.

"My feeling was that the story was in the anguish in the faces of the men," Fenrich said. He rejected the photo that showed the child's face and selected one

Conviction. The driver of the car with the trapped child was later convicted of drunk driving and manslaughter.

David C. Neilsen II, *Mercury-Register,* Oroville, Calif.

that was less revealing. "We didn't feel this one was an intrusion of the privacy of the family."

The newspaper has an advisory board made up of a cross section of the community, from high school students to blue and white collar workers. He asked the board members if anyone had heard objections to the photograph. No one had.

Claude Cookman, who worked as a picture editor for newspapers, had to make decisions about the use of photographs that might offend readers.

◀ Photo Guidelines

Cookman says that these questions must be resolved:

1. What do the pictures really show?
2. What are the readers likely to add to or read into their interpretation of the photos' content?
3. What are the circumstances under which the photographs were obtained?
4. How compelling is the news situation out of which the photos arose?
5. How compelling or significant are the photos in terms of what they teach us about the human experience?
6. Do the positive reasons for publishing the photos outweigh the almost certain negative reaction they will elicit from a sizable portion of the readership?

You might apply Cookman's guidelines to some of the photographs in the textbook. The photo of a family crying over the body of the drowned child that opens Part Six became one of the most disputed photographs of the 1980s. Many readers protested its use in *The Bakersfield Californian* as an invasion of the family's privacy. The managing editor apologized: "We make mistakes—and this clearly was a big one."

The photographer, John Harte, did not apologize for taking it or for his newspaper's using it:

> Our area is plagued by an unusually high number of drownings annually. During the week this photo was taken, there were four drownings, two that day, in our area's public waters. . . . We hoped that by running this one our readers would have gotten the message that we felt it was important they witness the horror that can result when water safety is taken lightly.

Harte was applying No. 6 in Cookman's list. Is this sufficient to defend the use of the photograph?

Christopher Meyers, a member of the philosophy department at the California State University at Bakersfield, wrote that the basic defense for use of the photograph was its journalistic merit: "It was timely; the 'story' was relevant to *Californian* readers; the photograph is both artistically compelling and emotionally gripping. . . ."

But he finds its use morally indefensible. It was an invasion of the family's privacy and it reduced the family to objects of our interest, denying them their status as "part of the human family." As for the argument the photographer presents, Meyers says that it would be impossible to determine that the photograph did indeed save any lives. This use of utilitarian ethics as a defense might "justify some use of the photo," he said, but not the way it was used.

There was in this case, he says, "too much emphasis on journalistic values and not enough on moral values."

In brief, what seems a matter of taste is actually a question of morals. This is true in many matters that involve taste.

Death ▶

Photographs of bodies are infrequently used because editors know that they arouse intense reactions among readers.

Nora Ephron, a media critic, says of pictures of death: "I recognize that printing pictures of corpses raises all sorts of problems about taste and titillation and sensationalism; the fact is, however, that people die. Death happens to be one of life's main events. And it is irresponsible—and more than that, inaccurate—for newspapers to fail to show it."

A sensitivity to personal feelings is essential to the journalist, not because invasions of privacy are illegal but because compassion is a compelling moral demand on the journalist. The photograph can be as callously intrusive as the television crew at the scene of a disaster poking camera and microphone in the faces of the bereaved. Yet death is part of reality, and it is possible to be overly sensitive to it.

Death has provided the press with almost as many problems as has sexual material. We cringe at confrontation with our mortality. Morticians try to make death resemble life. Wakes are no longer fashionable. Black for the bereaved is a past practice. Children are kept from funerals by solicitous relatives. Death is said to be our last taboo.

Young reporters sometimes go to the other extreme. Carried away by the drama of violence, they may chronicle the details of death—the conditions of bodies strewn alongside the airliner, the mutilated homicide victim, the precise plans of the youngster who committed suicide in the garage.

This enthusiasm is as tasteless as prurient sexual interest, for it uses the tabooed subject as the means to shock readers, to call attention to the reporting rather than to the subject. Death can be terrible and horrifying. But its terror and horror are best made known through understatement. In sensitive areas, the whisper speaks louder than the shout.

<aside>
Angry Readers. When the *New York Post* ran a photograph showing the side of the face of a rock guitarist's 4-year-old son who had fallen from a 49-story window, readers were furious. The next day, the newspaper apologized to those who were offended but said the photo illustrated the need for window guards. The competing *Daily News* used a photo with the child's body covered by a blanket.
</aside>

◄ **General Guidelines**

Reporters are often told that in matters of taste the decision about what will be used will be made by an editor or the copy desk. Nevertheless, reporters should set criteria for themselves. Obviously, what and how a reporter sees are influenced by his or her attitudes and values. A censurious reporter may block out relevant material. A prurient reporter may overindulge his or her fantasies. An open attitude toward these issues is a corrective to the natural propensity to be guided, and consequently victimized, by impulse and sentiment.

By their nature, editors are conservative. Like libel lawyers, when they are in doubt they tend to throw out questionable material. Reporters learn early in their careers to fight for stories. The reporter who has a set of standards from which to argue his or her story past the desk will be better able to do a good job of presenting to readers and listeners the world of reality.

The self-appointed guardians of good taste no longer have the power to issue dicta. Now, it's the journalist who decides what is essential and what is offensive and unnecessary. Guidelines are essential for responsible use of this power. Here are some:

1. Is the questionable material essential to a story of significance? If so, there is compelling reason to use it.

2. Use depends on the nature of the publication's readers and the station's listeners. But care should be taken to see to it that all are considered, not just those who are most vociferous.

3. The tradition of the publication or station is a consideration.

4. The private as well as the public actions of public officials and public figures are the subject of journalism if they bear on matters of public concern.

The Morality of Journalism

27

Bob Thayer, *The Journal-Bulletin.*

Diversity is part of the beat.

Preview

Journalism ethics has developed in two directions.

1. News organizations have adopted codes of ethics and guidelines that:

• Prohibit journalists from accepting anything of value from sources.

• Limit activities that may pose conflicts of interest.

• Stress the journalist's responsibility to society and the obligation to be accurate, impartial and independent.

2. Reporters have adopted a personal code that stresses:

• Compassion for the poor, the handicapped, the different.

• Moral indignation when the powerless are victimized.

• Willingness to place responsibility for the failures of policies on those who made them.

• Commitment to the improvement of their skills.

I don't mean to seem unfriendly," the fragile old man said, "but I just don't want people to see any stories about me." He looked down for a moment and then back to his visitor, Kevin Krajick, a reporter for *Corrections* magazine. Krajick was on assignment to interview elderly prisoners, and during his stop at the Fishkill, N.Y., state penitentiary, he had been told about one of the oldest, Paul Geidel, 84 years old and in his 68th year behind bars for murder.

Geidel offered to make toast and tea for Krajick, and he accepted. Geidel had turned away many reporters before, but a guard had suggested Krajick try anyway, and he had led the young reporter to Geidel's 10 × 10 room in the prison infirmary.

With the gentleness of his age, Geidel said he understood that Krajick's job was "to get a story." He respected that calling, he said, but he really didn't want to talk about himself.

"I began slipping in questions about his past, his feelings about his life," Krajick recalled, "He answered several of them, but he said several times, he did not want 'any story.' "

620

"He had tried to live in solitude and repentance, he said, and any notoriety upset him. He wanted to die in obscurity," Krajick said. A reporter had visited Geidel a few years before and had promised that no story would come out of their conversation, Geidel told Krajick.

"I thought they would leave me alone, but then one day I pick up the paper, and oh, there's my name and my picture splattered all over the front page."

Geidel, the son of an alcoholic saloon keeper, was put in an orphanage at seven. At 14, he quit school and worked at menial jobs. When he was 17, he broke into a hotel room in New York, stuffed a chloroformed gag in a guest's mouth, grabbed a few dollars and fled in a panic. The victim suffocated. Geidel was sentenced to life in prison for second-degree murder.

It was all in the newspaper, again, 60 years later.

"It was terrible, just terrible," Geidel said.

◀ **The Dilemma**

"I had decided at that point that I would not put him through the pain of printing a story about him," Krajick said. "I told him that I would not. I figured there were plenty of interesting elderly prisoners who wouldn't mind being written about."

The two chatted about an hour and parted good friends.

"Then I learned that Mr. Geidel had served the longest prison term in U.S. history. I started to waver. I checked the files and found that several magazines and television stations had run stories on him when he refused parole at the age of 81. I then called the state corrections and parole authorities to find out how Geidel had been held for such an incredible term—a point that had not been made clear in the previous articles.

"It turned out that he had been classified as criminally insane on what turned out to be a pretty flimsy basis and then totally forgotten about. He had not stood up for himself during all those years and had no one on the outside to do it for him."

◀ No Story . . .

"This obviously was a story of more significance than I had first thought. It was the most dramatic demonstration possible of the abuse of power under the boundless mental commitment statutes that most states have. What could be more moving than the story of the man who had spent the longest term ever, whom everyone acknowledged as meek and repentant and who, under other circumstances, would have been released before he reached the age of 40?

"The public clearly had reason to know about this man's life. It would be difficult to justify leaving him out since I was writing what was supposed to be a definitive article on elderly prisoners for the definitive publication on prisons."

Krajick faced a moral dilemma. Were the reasons for publishing his story sufficiently compelling to outweigh his promise to Geidel and the pain that the article would certainly inflict on the old man?

"I was anxious not to hurt a man who had, as prison records and he himself said, spent his life in mental anguish. I was sympathetic with his wish to remain obscure."

◀ . . . Or a Story of Significance?

Critical. Surveys show that among the major complaints against reporters is their supposed lack of concern about whether their stories hurt people. The other major criticisms are sensationalism and invasion of personal privacy.

In his work, Krajick had faced situations in which people had been imprudently frank with him and had asked to be spared publicity. Those decisions had not been hard to make. He had reasoned that those who are hurt or embarrassed by the truth usually deserve to be. But Geidel deserved neither society's curiosity nor its condemnation. He had paid his debt to society.

In the balance Krajick was striking—a balance of conflicting values—were two other factors: Articles had already been written about Geidel and he had become a statistic in the *Guinness Book of World Records,* which would soon draw other reporters whose articles, Krajick felt, would be more flamboyant and less accurate than his.

"On this basis, I decided to print the article, though not without misgivings," Krajick said. "I realized that if Mr. Geidel were to see the article he would be distressed, and he would feel betrayed by the young man who was nice to him but ended up lying. I only hope those around him have the sense not to show him the article. That would be the only escape for my conscience."

The piece appeared in the magazine under the title, "The Longest Term Ever Served: 'Forget Me.' " The concluding paragraph of the article reads:

> As his visitor left, he offered to write to Geidel. "Oh, no, please," he said. "Please. I don't mean to seem unfriendly. But please don't write. Forget me. Forget all about me." A distressed look crossed his face and he turned and hobbled down the hall to clean the teapot.

Solicitude for people is fairly new to journalism. For many years, outsiders had urged on the press a sense of responsibility, a caution that the First Amendment was not a license for unconscionable money making and sensation mongering. In the 1970s, the press began to heed these criticisms, and the scrutiny included an examination of ethical problems.

This self-examination led to the adoption of codes and standards that call for accuracy, impartiality and avoidance of conflicts of interest and that proscribe certain activities, such as the acceptance of gifts from sources.

Journalists realized that without some kind of moral framework, the practice of journalism is reduced to a repetitive chase after disconnected stories, and this becomes for the journalist a life empty of meaning and dignity.

Causes for Concern ▶

Some journalistic practices became embarrassing to a craft increasingly concerned with becoming a profession. Reporters accepted gifts, free travel and assorted favors. In 1972, *The Detroit News* estimated that the Christmas hams, watches and junkets added up to $56,000 a year.

A study that year showed that four out of five newspapers accepted free travel for staffers. The situation called for changes, and one direction seemed the adoption of rules, codes of acceptable conduct. In 1974, one of 10 newspapers had such codes. In a decade, three of four had codes.

Balancing Values ▶

Giving In. After considerable thought, *The Washington Post* and *The New York Times* acceded to the demand of the "Unabomber" and published his 35,000-word manifesto. It cost the papers around $40,000. The rambling essay had no journalistic value, the *Post*'s publisher said, but this was balanced against the promise of the killer to stop his campaign if the material was printed.

"We thought there was an obvious public safety issue involved," said Donald E. Graham, publisher of the *Post.* "The best advice available from the FBI and others, is that the Unabomber may well not bomb again," said *Times* publisher Arthur Sulzberger Jr.

A similarity of the Manifesto's writing style to material found in a Chicago home led to the arrest of the Unabomber.

The codes forbid specific practices and urge caution in other areas. They prohibit the acceptance of gifts, and they warn against conflicts of interest. For example, a political reporter who accepted theater tickets or worked part-time as a speechwriter for a candidate would compromise his or her position as a journalist.

These newspaper codes were modeled on general codes of ethics such as the one adopted in 1923 by Sigma Delta Chi, a journalism fraternity. The codes not only prohibited specific practices, they sought to establish ethical norms for a craft with aspirations to professional status. They were a reaction to an outlook and to practices that had tainted journalism with a grubbiness inconsistent with the standards of professional conduct.

The renewed interest in establishing journalism as a profession found a base on which to build in the report of the Commission on Freedom of the Press. The study, issued in 1947, was a response to extensive criticism of the U.S. press as insular, often sensational and sometimes irresponsible. The members of the Commission—most of them prestigious faculty members at leading universities—concluded that the press had not been "adequate to the needs of society."

One finding was particularly pertinent—that the press had failed to give "a representative picture of the constituent groups in the society." Vast segments of society had been ignored by the press, particularly the young and the aged, racial minorities, the poor and women.

Gradually, the press became more responsive to external criticism. Journalists themselves became outspoken, and their criticisms began to appear in the various press reviews that sprang up around the country. Journalists began to take their trade more seriously—possibly because of the steady infusion of college-trained reporters who were questioning some of the assumptions of the craft. The climate was established for journalists to codify good practices, to set lines between the acceptable and the morally indefensible.

Although the codes establish boundaries and describe acceptable practices, they are only a beginning. They cannot assist the journalist in resolving some of the most difficult problems. These involve dilemmas in which the choice is between conflicting moral or ethical actions.

Krajick had to choose between what he saw as two positive ends. To print the story would reveal some truths about a system that crushed one prisoner and might still be affecting others. It would be morally right to use Geidel to illustrate the inadequacy of the mental competency process, he believed. Not writing about Geidel would also be a moral action because then Geidel would be spared the further agony of the public exposure. Surely, a man who has spent 68 years behind bars deserves our compassion. Moreover, there was Krajick's promise not to use the material. Can a public need justify the reporter's going back on his or her word?

Looking to codes for guidance, we find in one of them, that of the Society of Professional Journalists, that the journalist should "serve the general welfare." Krajick would serve the general welfare with publication. The same code stresses "respect for the dignity, privacy, rights and well-being of people encountered in

◀ **Codes of Conduct**

Conflict. When several reporters marched in support of abortion rights at a Washington, D.C., rally, newspaper editors were forced to set a line between the duties and responsibilities of a citizen and the conflict-of-interest policies of their newspapers. Two approaches emerged:

1. No newsroom personnel should take part in demonstrations with political overtones: *The Washington Post, The Philadelphia Inquirer,* ABC News, AP and the *Chicago Tribune* asserted this policy.

2. A less restrictive policy was enunciated by *The New York Times,* the *Los Angeles Times,* NBC News and *The Baltimore Sun,* which said that only reporters covering partisan issues were prohibited from such participation.

◀ Limitations of the Codes

the course of gathering and presenting the news." Clearly, respect for Geidel would mean heeding his plea not to write about him. The codes are no help here beyond identifying the clear moral choices.

No code can make a journalist a person of good conscience. Only a personal commitment to a journalistic morality can do so. Unfortunately, the codes tend to emphasize prohibitions, understandably so since much of the criticism of the press is addressed to what is printed or broadcast. The press does overemphasize the pseudo-events orchestrated by people in power, and it does play up disconnected tidbits of news and entertainment.

But the great failure of the press, as the Commission on Freedom of the Press sought to get across, is not its sins of commission, but rather its sins of omission, its failure to look into the significant actions of the powerful and the travails and the longings of the powerless.

Sins of Omission ▶

No code led *The Charlotte Observer* to point out that North Carolina's leading income producer, its tobacco crop, is the single greatest cause of lung cancer, which is responsible, health authorities say, for 1,000 deaths a day. It was the conscience of the *Observer*'s management and editors that led the newspaper to examine the issue in detail in a special section.

Nor did any code stimulate the Atlanta *Journal and Constitution* to investigate racial discrimination practiced by lending institutions in Atlanta. Bill Dedman took on the task of proving that banks and other lenders were systematically denying loans to blacks. His reporting led to significant reforms. (Dedman won the Pulitzer Prize for investigative reporting.)

These newspapers and their staff members understood the necessity to act in the public interest, just as did Donna Halvorsen and Allen Short of the *Star Tribune* in Minneapolis. Their extensive examination of the careers of 767 sex criminals revealed the state's courts and prisons were ineffective in dealing with child molesters and rapists.

Repeat offenses, they found, were far greater than the state had admitted, and those who had been sent to a psychological treatment center were more likely to commit new sex crimes than those who were not treated.

The newspaper allowed the reporters ample time to make the computer-assisted study—it took nine months. And it devoted considerable space to the series, which ran to 30,000 words.

Sins of omission occur when the journalist refuses to act in situations in which revelation is required. The philosopher Jeremy Bentham described this immoral act as "Keeping at rest; that is, forebearing."

Theory of Responsibility. In its report, the Commission included five requirements for the media:

1. The press must give a truthful, comprehensive and intelligent account of the day's events in a context that gives them some meaning.

2. The press must provide a forum for the exchange of comment and criticism.

3. The press must project a representative picture of the constituent groups in the society.

4. The press must present and clarify the goals and values of the society.

5. The press must provide full access to the day's intelligence.

Morality Underlies Journalism ▶

Morality is basic to the theory and practice of journalism. The press justifies its freedom in terms of moral imperatives; it rationalizes much of its behavior with moral declarations.

If public consent freely given is essential to the proper functioning of a democracy, then for the consent to be meaningful the public must be adequately informed by a press free of government or any other control. Thomas Jefferson expressed this simply: "Where the press is free and every man able to read, all is safe." The First Amendment makes this consensual system possible. Although neither the Constitution nor any laws require that the press carry out its essential role in the system, the press takes on the responsibility for setting before the public the issues it considers important so that they can be openly discussed. The cultural historian Christopher Lasch says, "The job of the press is to encourage debate," and he cites the philosopher John Dewey's contention that communities need the knowledge that emerges from "dialogue," from "direct give and take."

Journalists differ in their interpretation of their role as suppliers of information. Some contend that it is sufficient for journalism to create a record, to report the deeds and declarations of those in power. Others go further. They would initiate coverage, make searching examinations of power, practice what some of them describe as an "activist journalism."

◀ Recorders vs. Activists

The first group believes that journalists are called upon to present matters that readers are interested in, and some of these editors conduct focus groups and have reader-advisory panels to inform them of their readers' concerns.

The second group prefers to lead from its own conception of community needs, its own insight into what constitutes community misdeeds. Thomas Winship, former editor of *The Boston Globe,* was labeled an "activist editor" by colleagues, a label he bore proudly, he says. He learned about this kind of journalism when he was breaking in as a reporter at *The Washington Post.* The publisher, Philip L. Graham, "burned into my young, impressionistic head the idea that the license to print carried with it the obligation to give something back to the community," Winship says.

Activist journalists subscribe to Bentham's moral injunction: They must speak up when injustice exists, whatever the majority opinion in the community, however much those in power prefer to keep things as is. Journalists can look to a long history of such journalism, deep antecedents that motivate current practitioners of journalism.

Schomburg Center for Research in Black Culture, The New York Public Library, Astor, Lenox, and Tilden Foundation.

Ida B. Wells

◀ **Past and Present**

During the American colonial period, journalists in the 13 colonies vigorously opposed what they termed "onerous taxes" and the lack of representation in decision making. These journalists became a major force in the struggle for independence. The colonial journalist had a point of view and expressed it.

Before the Civil War, an outspoken and active abolitionist press called for the emancipation of the slaves. And after the abolition of slavery, as Jim Crow laws and practices became commonplace in some parts of the country, journalists spoke out. Ida B. Wells, for example, exposed lynch law and mob rule at great personal risk.

Murdered. In 1837, Elijah P. Lovejoy, an anti-slavery editor, was slain by a mob in Alton, Ill., as he tried to defend his press.

As people moved to the cities and the country grew from an agrarian economy to become an industrial behemoth, exploitation and abuses proliferated. Industrialists—some described as "robber barons" because of their ruthless practices—took control of major industries. Workers were overworked, underpaid and prevented from forming unions, sometimes at the point of a gun. Crooked politicians ran many large cities. In response, a group of journalists began to tell the story.

The Muckrakers ▶

At first derisively described as *muckrakers,* this group of brilliant men and women took on the robber barons, the labor exploiters and the political hacks. They became known as the nation's voices of conscience. Some wrote books and others magazine articles, several took photographs and some worked for the daily press.

As the 20th century began, four-fifths of the people in the United States lived in poverty. People were commodities. The mines and mills exploited child labor. Blacks were treated as chattel.

Racism ▶

The Library of Congress

Major Muckraker

Lincoln Steffens provided theory for and demonstrated the practice of muckraking. In articles published in *The Shame of the Cities* (1904), he exposed municipal corruption and provided a theoretical approach to investigative reporting.

Ray Stannard Baker in 1908 described racism in Southern courts.

> One thing impressed me especially, not only in this court but in all others I have visited: a Negro brought in for drunkenness, for example, was punished much more severely than a white man arrested for the same offense. . . . The white man sometimes escaped with a reprimand, he was sometimes fined three dollars and costs, but the Negro, especially if he had no white man to intercede for him, was usually punished with a ten or fifteen dollar fine, which often meant he had to go to the chain-gang.

Baker points out that one reason for the large number of arrests is the profit to the counties and state in hiring out convicts to private contractors. "Last year the net profit to Georgia from chain-gangs, to which the commission refers with pride, reached the great sum of $354,853.55. . . . The natural tendency is to convict as many men as possible—it furnishes steady, cheap labour to the contractors and profit to the state. . . ."

These journalists did not condemn some vague system. They named names and held individuals responsible for their actions. Baker wrote that "some of the large fortunes in Atlanta have come chiefly from the labour of chain-gangs of convicts leased from the state." He described a banker who was also a member of the city police board and the owner of brickyards where many convicts were used on lease from the state at cheap rates.

Like the other muckrakers, Baker was adept at using files and records:

> From the records I find that in 1906, one boy 6-years-old, seven of 7 years, 33 of 8 years, 69 of 9 years, 107 of 10 years, 142 of 11 years, and 219 of 12 years were arrested and brought into court, 578 boys and girls, mostly Negroes, under 12 years of age.

Pulitzer's Journalism ▶

One of the major practitioners of muckraking journalism was Joseph Pulitzer, the owner of the *St. Louis Post-Dispatch* and the New York *World.* Pulitzer's Editors conducted crusades, newspaper campaigns to expose and remedy practices they considered wrong, unfair, unjust. They took their cue from Pulitzer's edict that the newspapers should never be content with "merely printing the news."

Instead, he said, his newspapers should be concerned "with the things that ought to happen tomorrow, or the next month, or the next year," and that they "will seek to make what ought to be come to pass." The "highest mission of the press," he said, "is to render public service."

His legacy continued under editors who were committed to using the press as an instrument of justice, reform and change. One Pulitzer reporter, Paul Y. Anderson, doggedly followed a paper trail that led to the exposure of the collusion of two of President Harding's cabinet members with oil interests that corruptly leased federal oil field reserves. The Pulitzer newspapers defended Eugene V. Debs, a leading socialist who was jailed under the Espionage Act, a law passed during the Red Scare following World War I.

Pulitzer's edict to his editors to seek out issues, to make news of injustice and wrongdoing could be described as an instruction to journalists to establish agendas for their communities. This is an approach to journalism that has no borders.

◀ Recent Activism

Harold Evans, editor of London's *Sunday Times,* said the "real power" of the press consists of its ability "to create an agenda for society."

◀ Deformed Children

Fair play was on Evans' mind when he heard that the manufacturers of the drug thalidomide had pressured parents of children deformed by the drug to accept a pittance in damages. Through its coverage of the issue, Evans said, the *Times* forced the crippled children "into the conscience of the country." The stories led to settlements 50 times greater than the original stipend.

When Argentina was in the grip of a murderous military dictatorship in the 1970s and into the 1980s, few dared protest the arrests of thousands of men and women, many of them college students, who opposed the tyranny. People were snatched from their homes, grabbed on the streets. Tortured, never given a trial, some tossed out of military planes over the ocean, most simply disappeared.

◀ Terror in Argentina

The political journalist Rodolfo Walsh could not remain silent. He wrote a public indictment of "the most savage reign of terror Argentina has ever known"; that its rulers had created "virtual concentration camps in all the principal military bases"; that the torturers felt a "need to utterly destroy their victims, depriving them of all human dignity. . . ."

Walsh knew he was signing his own death warrant through his reporting. He closed his indictment by saying that he had to speak out to be "faithful to the commitment I made a long time ago to be a witness in difficult times." The day after his statement was released, he was abducted. His body was never found.

In the United States, racial justice has been a constant theme of activist journalists. Courageous editors and publishers have bucked community traditions—and advertisers—to support equal treatment of the races and to expose racism.

◀ Speaking out on Race

Hazel Brannon Smith, the editor of two weekly newspapers in the Mississippi Delta country, spoke up. In 1946, she was found guilty of contempt of court for interviewing the widow of a black man who was whipped to death.

In an editorial she wrote in 1954, she accused the sheriff who had shot a young black man in the back of "violating every concept of justice, decency and right." The sheriff sued for libel and was awarded $10,000. The state supreme court overturned the ruling.

An Invitation Declined ▶

That year, Smith was invited to join "something called a 'Citizens' Council," she said, by "a local prominent man" who called on her. The idea was to maintain segregation in the schools. Legal, nonviolent tactics would be used, she was told. "If a Nigra won't go along with our thinking on what's best for the community as a whole," Smith said the man told her, "he'll simply have his credit cut off." The idea was to use fear, he told her. Smith refused to go along. Her refusal cost her dearly.

She said the community became a battleground with intimidation the weapon, not only against blacks but against those who opposed the Council. "It finally got to the point where bank presidents and leading physicians were afraid to speak their honest opinions because of the monster among us," she said. "The idea was that 'we' would present a solid, united stand.

"I dissented by presuming to say that the truth had to be printed."

She was one of the few who dissented, and the pressure grew.

"My newspapers were boycotted, bombed and burned, a new newspaper was organized in Lexington to put me out of business, my life was threatened, and my husband lost his job as county hospital administrator—all because of pressure brought by this professional hate-peddling organization," she said.

She and her husband managed to keep one of the papers going, but the income was never enough and she had to mortgage her home to pay her bills. Finally, in 1985, she gave up the remaining newspaper. The bank took her home. Soon thereafter she died, penniless.

> **Truth.** "The smallest atom of truth represents someone's bitter toil and agony; for every ponderable chunk of it there is a brave truth-seeker's grave upon some lonely ash dump. . . ."—H.L. Mencken

Talking Back ▶

Another small-town editor, Hodding Carter, took on the bigots and racists in his newspaper, the *Delta Democrat-Times* in Greenville, Miss. When white townspeople objected to listing black veterans on the town's World War II honor roll, he wrote an editorial, "Our Honor Roll Is a Monument to Intolerance and Timidity." It and others he wrote won the 1946 Pulitzer Prize.

When the White Citizens' Councils resisted the Supreme Court's school desegregation decision, Carter spoke out against them. In response to his criticism, the Mississippi House of Representatives formally denounced Carter. Whereupon Carter responded in an editorial:

By a vote of 89 to 19 the Mississippi House of Representatives has resolved the editor of this newspaper into a liar because of an article I wrote. . . . If this charge were true it would make me well qualified to serve with that body. It is not true. So . . . I herewith resolve by a vote of 1 to 0 that there are 89 liars in the State Legislature, beginning with Speaker Silvers and working way on down to Rep. Eck Windham of Prentiss whose name is fittingly made up of the words 'wind' and 'ham.' . . . Meanwhile, those 89 character mobbers can go to hell collectively or singly and wait there until I back down. They needn't plan on returning.

Racial discrimination continues to be a concern of the activist press, which has taken seriously the warning that the United States cannot continue to remain two distinct societies, white and black, without serious consequences. Some recent newspaper campaigns include:

◀ **Current Examples**

- *The Daily Progress,* **Charlottesville, Va.:** A two-year study revealed racial disparity in sentencing local criminal defendants.
- *Leader-Telegram,* **Eau Claire, Wis.:** A staff project exposed racial discrimination in housing rentals.
- *The Dallas Morning News:* Reporters showed how a development plan would crowd thousands more blacks into one of the city's poorest and most dangerous neighborhoods.

Here are some other examples of public service journalism:

◀ Drunks Driving, Wastes Polluting

- *The Philadelphia Inquirer:* Showed that city police dogs had attacked 350 innocent people.
- *The Albuquerque Tribune:* Showed that drunk drivers are allowed to keep driving despite many convictions. Uncovered extensive dumping of dangerous wastes in New Mexico.
- *The Ledger,* **Lakeland, Fla.:** Revealed that a fungicide caused crop and nursery damage and that the manufacturer, DuPont Co., knew that the fungicide had the potential to cause harm but was silent.
- *Star Tribune,* **Minneapolis:** Revealed that the state's foster-care system allowed known criminals and sex offenders to become foster parents.
- *The Muskegon* **(Mich.)** *Chronicle:* Showed that the founder of a chemical plant made huge profits while knowingly exposing his workers to a cancer-causing chemical.
- *Fort Worth Star-Telegram:* Reported that 250 U.S. servicemen had lost their lives as a result of a design problem in helicopters.

An activist journalism calls on the community to act: To see that city officials rid the local water supply of carcinogens (*The Washington* (N.C.) *Daily News*); to make the government regulate the American blood industry (*The Philadelphia Inquirer*); to force the Federal Aviation Administration to do a better job of the medical screening of airline pilots (*The Pittsburgh Press*); to require the county child-welfare agency to protect neglected and abused children (*The Blade*).

Let's watch one of these activist reporters, Sam Roe of *The Blade* in Toledo, Ohio, answer the obligation not to forebear, to go beyond "merely printing the news."

◀ 'Abused by The System'

For several years, Roe says he had heard complaints about the Lucas County Children Services. Too often, abused youngsters were returned to homes where they were battered, molested or neglected again. Some children were placed with relatives, friends and previously absent fathers, although some of these people were drug users, sex offenders and child abusers. Children Services often waited months, sometimes years, before removing children from such homes.

To do the story properly, Roe needed records, documents that proved—or disproved—the rumors. But children's records are confidential.

Roe was helped by two of the traditional aids of the reporter—a source and Roe's knowledge of the system. The source had in a downtown basement copies of complete files of Children Services' records. But the records were voluminous, and it would take months to pour through them for a representative group.

Roe decided to use only cases of children currently in foster care, most of whom had been in the system many years. But the names of foster children are confidential.

"Then I discovered a useful bit of information," Roe says. "Foster parents receive monthly checks for caring for abused children." He knew that the county auditor issued the checks, which are public. By obtaining names from the list of those issued checks, he was able to find what he needed in the files in the basement.

The Files ▶

Roe said he found a "wealth of information that included police reports, social histories, psychiatrists' reports and school records." Some of the files were a foot thick, and they were all up-to-date.

"At first, I wasn't sure what I would find," Roe said. "But after reading through the first few cases I knew I was on to something.

"One of the first cases involved a mother who had abused and neglected her children for years. Twice officials took them away, and twice they were returned to her.

"They even gave the kids back after her infant son died of pneumonia on a night she left him home alone so she could go cruising with friends. Officials never arrested her, though they could have several times."

As he read through the cases, patterns became apparent:

• Abused children were returned home, where they were again battered, molested, neglected.
• Cocaine babies received little or no care.
• Bad parents were sent to counseling classes, not jail.

These groupings became the basis of the organization of Roe's story. "If the file indicated the child was a cocaine baby, I put a circled C on the page. If officials had to remove the child more than once, I wrote down '2X' or '3X.' "

The Writing ▶

By organizing his notes by themes, Roe was able to structure his articles. Then he went back to the files and took detailed notes on the cases that supported these themes. (His source would not allow Roe to make copies of the files.)

"By now, I realized that my story was more than an exposé of Children Services. The entire system, including doctors, lawyers, judges and social workers, was often to blame when kids fell through the cracks."

Roe did not want his story to read like a records-search story. "So I tracked down parents, children and officials in several key cases. Their quotes and anecdotes help bring the stories to life."

Here are two pages from Roe's notepad. The first describes a mother whose three children were born addicted to cocaine and were returned to the mother and then taken away. The second involves children who were molested and sexually abused and then returned to the abusive home several times. (Last names are blocked out.)

His work led to a lengthy four-part series, which begins:

Marquell Scott was tired of living this way. Tired of living in a foul, filthy home with no heat, lights, water, and refrigerator.

When he wanted to wash, he had to borrow water from neighbors. When he wanted to see at night, he had to feel around with candles. When his mother's monthly welfare check came in, she blew it on Wild Irish Rose wine.

For six months, the 14-year-old and his four younger brothers and sisters lived like this.

And for six months, child-protection officials did nothing.

So one night, just after midnight, Marquell called the police on his mother himself.

When officers arrived at the Old West End home, they surveyed the squalor. Exposed electrical wires. A toilet that wouldn't flush. An unbearable stench.

The mother was nowhere in sight, and Marquell told the officers the children generally fended for themselves.

Convinced this was no way for children to live, the officers removed them all, including the youngest, who had never been enrolled in school, even though she was 7.

Yet all of this could have been prevented. Lucas County Children Services knew about the conditions but did not act.

Plus, the agency had previously taken custody of the children because of years of neglect, but instead of finding a proper home for them, officials placed them back with their mother.

This case is not unusual. Time and time again, children in the Toledo area have been returned to wretched homes and abusive parents—then battered, molested, or neglected again.

In each case, the children were returned with the blessings of Children Services, the local government agency legally responsible for the welfare of abused children.

Some children have been so severely abused after being reunited with their parents that they had to be hospitalized.

Others have wound up homeless and living in the streets.

Still others have ended up living in crack houses.

These cases are detailed in thousands of confidential government records reviewed by The Blade. Most of the documents are from Children Services, a 399-employee agency that has been virtually immune to public scrutiny because of laws limiting disclosure of its records and decisions.

But over the last four months, The Blade has reviewed the records of 700 children who have had extensive contact with the agency.

The picture that emerges is a child-protection system, led by Children Services, intensely committed to keeping children with their parents.

This "family preservation" philosophy—trying to mend troubled families rather than removing children from the home—has been adopted by child-protection agencies nationwide but is now facing mounting criticism.

The Reaction ▶

The Lucas county commissioners called for a special meeting with Children Services immediately after the fourth in Roe's series ran. There were a total of 17 front-page follow-up stories, one of which, Roe said, "broke the agency's back."

"A few days after the series, with pressure mounting, a 5-year-old boy was found bound, beaten and bloodied in his home. Police took him to the hospital, then to Children Services for safekeeping. But officials there returned him home just hours later. Only after the police complained did the agency go back and remove the child."

Two days after Roe wrote about this, the agency announced it would overhaul the system. Within days, it made several changes. A month later, Roe wrote:

Lucas County Children Services became involved in more child abuse cases last month than in any month in three years.

It is also removing children from their homes for safekeeping at a skyrocketing rate.

Children Services attributed the increases, in part, to a series of Blade stories that have detailed problems in the child-welfare system.

"There is a heightened awareness in the community," John Hollingsworth, a Children Services program administrator, said yesterday. "There is a heightened awareness even in the agency."

Guiding Values ▶

In their reporting and editing, journalists are always making choices: what to report, whom to interview, what to put in the story, what to leave out. Selection, the heart of journalistic practice, is guided by values that reflect prevailing concerns and the value system of society and the individual.

These values guide us when the choice is between alternative actions, each of which has some claim to principle. This is no different from the decision making most of us face in our daily lives. "The world that we encounter in ordinary experience," says the philosopher Isaiah Berlin, "is one in which we are faced with choices between ends equally ultimate and claims equally absolute, the realization of some of which must inevitably involve the sacrifice of others. . . . If, as I believe, the ends of men are many, and not all of them are in principle compatible with each other, then the possibility of conflict—and of tragedy—can never be wholly eliminated from human life, either personal or social. The necessity of choosing between absolute claims is then an inescapable characteristic of the human condition."

Can the journalist refer to some universal values as guides to choice, or is decision subject to particular circumstances—what the philosophers call a *situational ethic?* Traditionally—perhaps instinctively—people have sought absolutes as guides. And as often as the priest or the guru has supplied them, they have been found to be impractical. Or they have been discovered to be a way of keeping a religious, political, economic or social system in power.

Even so, we may find in these searches for an ethic to live by some suggestions for a useful journalistic morality. The concern for the good life, the properly led life, is almost as powerful as the need for sustenance. We may find some guides from religion and philosophy, from the Prophets and Plato, from the guru who traces his ethic to the Bhagavad-Gita and from contemporary philosophers.

"Life is the referent of value," says Allen Wheelis, a psychiatrist, who writes about ethics. "What enlarges and enriches life is good; what diminishes and endangers life is evil." If we start our search for an ethic by first defining life as physical survival and apply Wheelis' referent to one of the immediate problems of industrial societies, we can conclude that what poisons the air, water and earth is bad. To preserve an atmosphere we can breathe is good. Industries that endanger the lives of their workers or nearby residents are bad. Safety procedures—or plant closures if this cannot be accomplished—are good.

But some factory owners and some automobile manufacturers have opposed strict environmental protection standards. To clean up a plant, to make a car that does not emit pollutants, to make a process safe in the factory would increase the price of the car or make operating the plant so expensive it might have to be shut down, owners have said. This means unemployment, a loss of taxes to the local community, a decline in business where the plant or factory is located. No wonder that workers and politicians often join industrialists to oppose proposals for safety, clean air and clean water.

Is it the responsibility of the journalist to continue to point out that the factory is poisoning the air? Or does the reporter turn away? If he or she does, jobs may be saved, the profits of the company assured and taxes kept low.

The dilemma is not new. The playwright Henrik Ibsen describes it in "An Enemy of the People." Dr. Thomas Stockman, medical officer of the municipal baths, a considerable tourist attraction, discovers that the baths—the source of the town's economic resurgence—are being poisoned by the nearby tanneries. He wants to close them as a menace to public health.

But the community leaders and the local newspaper editor point out that any revelation about the pollution will lead people to shun the baths, and this will cause economic problems, among them unemployment and higher tax rates for property owners. Dr. Stockman is reviled as an enemy of the people.

The practical concerns of a money-based society have occupied many writers. Dickens' novels cry out against the "cash-nexus" as the "only bond between man and man," as one literary critic put it.

"Breathe the polluted air," Dickens says in *Dombey and Son.* "And then, calling up some ghastly child, with stunted form and wicked face, hold forth on its unnatural sinfulness, and lament its being, so early, far away from Heaven— but think a little of its being conceived, and born, and bred, in Hell!"

◀ Life as Referent

Vern Herschberger, *Tobacco Free Youth Reporter.*

You Decide

Would you run this cartoon with a story about a proposed city ordinance that would penalize store owners who sell cigarettes to minors?

If "life is the referent of value," what other choice has the professional whose reason for being is service to the public than to see and to speak out so that others may see and understand? In the calculus of values, life means more than the bottom line on a ledger sheet. Joseph Conrad said, "My task which I am trying to achieve is, by the power of the written word, to make you hear, make you feel—it is, before all, to make you see. That—and no more, and it is everything."

Harold Fruchtbaum, a Columbia University social scientist, describes as "one of the intellectual's primary functions" the task of placing "responsibility for the failures of our society on the people and the institutions that control the society." Translated into a moral concern for the journalist, this is the task of holding power accountable, whether the power be held by a nation's president or a school superintendent.

Communal Life ▶

In holding the powerful accountable to the people, the journalist takes to his or her job a sense of communal life. That is, the reporter has a set of values that reveal when power is being abused to the point that the quality of life in the community suffers. Philosophers through the ages have talked about the "good life," which has its starting point in a communal life whose underpinnings are freedom, tolerance and fairness. In such a society, individuals have basic rights that neither the state nor other individuals may violate, and the individual has, in turn, obligations to the community.

In writing about the American philosopher John Dewey, Sidney Hook said that Dewey believed

> . . . the logic of democracy requires the elimination of economic, ethnic, religious and educational injustices if the freedom of choice presupposed by the ethos of democracy is to be realized.
>
> One man, one vote is not enough—if one man can arbitrarily determine the livelihood of many others, determine where and under what conditions they can live, determine what they can read in the press or hear on the air.

Dewey believed that the community has the responsibility for eliminating hunger and poverty, that political power must be harnessed to solve the problems of group and individual welfare. Economic conditions must be such, he wrote, that the equal right of all to free choice and free action is achieved.

Communal life is an unfolding process in which the experienced past and the desired and anticipated future are considered in making the present. The journalist plays a key role in this process. The reporter describes the immediate and more distant past while showing the possible future in his or her work every day.

When moral philosophers speak of the good life they mean a life in which people can read, speak and choose freely; that they need not live in fear of want; that they can count on shared values such as the desirability of equal opportunity and the undesirability of crime.

◀ **The Good Life**

Journalists enrich and promote these activities through the values and assumptions that they take to the job. For example, a journalist is told that at the local university the political science department is promoting Marxism, that instructors are doing more than describing the ideology; they are endorsing it. To check on the charge, the reporter disguises herself as a student and attends classes. In her story, she describes her experiences, quoting class lectures and discussions, using the names of students and instructors. The charge is found to be groundless.

We do know that posing and using disguises are generally not acceptable in society. Let us strike a balance in deciding whether the use of a disguise by the reporter was ethical:

- **The benefits:** An irresponsible allegation was proved false. The reporter was able to do firsthand reporting, which is more persuasive and closer to truth than transcribing the instructors' denials.
- **The costs:** Deception was used as a journalistic method. Privacy was violated.

We can say that the costs of some of these actions—no matter how well intended—outweigh the benefits if we keep in mind that the good life is the healthy communal life. What kind of campus community will we have if we cannot speak freely and openly to one another in class because we fear our words may be broadcast or published? What kind of community will we have when we fear peering eyes so much that we must shred our garbage?

There may well be exceptions to the shared value of the right to privacy, of the abhorrence most of us feel at the use of disguises, of our belief that the classroom should be a forum where everyone can discuss ideas without fear of being quoted in a news story. We will look at some of these exceptions later.

Actions that hurt people or disrupt the community are immoral, unless justified by powerful moral considerations, we all agree. A story about a convicted rapist will hurt the rapist; but we justify the story because punishment of those who commit crimes shows the community that society does not tolerate and will punish crimes. Crime unpunished can lead to the breakdown of the community.

Survival and the good communal life—are there additional guidelines, more specific guidelines that we can find that are of use to the journalist in helping him or her to make choices? Through an examination of a few of the practical problems reporters face, we may find some.

To Print or Not to Print ▶

The news shocked the people of Missoula. The 21-year-old daughter of a well-known couple had been stabbed to death outside her Washington, D.C., apartment house. She had been a high school honor student and an accomplished musician and had won a scholarship to Radcliffe.

Less than a week later, Rod Deckert, the managing editor of *The Missoulian,* a 32,500 circulation daily in the city, had an even more shocking story on his desk: The young woman had been a streetwalker in Washington, "a $50-a-trick prostitute" who "used to talk freely about her work and bragged about being 'a pro,' " according to a story *The Washington Post* planned to run the next day under the headline, "A Life of Promise That Took a Strange and Fatal Turn." The *Post* had learned she had returned to Missoula after dropping out of Radcliffe and one night in a bar she had been approached by a man who asked her to return with him to the East. He was a pimp who recruited young women around the country.

Deckert was confronted with a difficult decision. If he ran the story, the family would suffer new anguish. If he did not, he would be suppressing news that was bound to be known since papers distributed in Missoula and nearby might carry the dramatic story of a small-town girl who came to a sordid end in the East. It was, Deckert said, "the most painful day in my 11 years of life in the newsroom."

Deckert reasoned that the young woman's experience could be a warning to other young women in the university community. However, he had to weigh this against the pain it would cause the family and friends.

Deckert decided to run an edited version of *The Washington Post* story with some locally-gathered inserts. Deckert played the story on page 12 with no art under an eight-column headline.

You Make the Call ▶

1. A local police officer secretly videotaped himself having consensual sex with two women friends. At a public disciplinary hearing for the officer, the women's lawyer asked that their names be withheld and they were not revealed in their testimony.

• **Use the names:** Real names make a story real. The women openly testified. The officer was identified.

> **Public or Private?** A city councilwoman has AIDS. A candidate for governor is known as a womanizer. Newsworthy?
>
> Some guidelines provided by Carl Sessions Stepp of the University of Maryland:
>
> • Verify the report.
> • Does it affect the person's public performance?
> • If the fact is well known, no good is served by keeping it out of print.
> • If a competing station or paper uses it, the fact is now public. Use it.
>
> Leonard Downie, managing editor of *The Washington Post,* says to use information "when the private conduct of a public figure is symptomatic of a societal problem."

- **Don't use the names:** The women are entitled to their privacy. They could be likened to rape victims. Publishing their names added nothing to the story.

2. Shortly after a rape charge was filed against a young member of the Kennedy family, a London newspaper and then a U.S. supermarket tabloid published the victim's name.

- **Use her name:** It has already been revealed. The name of the accused is used; so should the accuser's name be used.
- **Don't use her name:** The standard policy of most of the media is to grant the accuser or victim anonymity.

3. A businessman prominent in the community has died. It is learned that 30 years before as a county official, he was sentenced to probation when a shortage was discovered in his office funds. Since then, he has led an exemplary life.

- **Use the incident in the obituary:** It's part of his past and is on record.
- **Don't use it:** The man has more than atoned for a crime committed so long ago no one will recall it.

4. One of the questions raised during the early stage of the trial of O.J. Simpson for murder was whether the prosecution would ask for the death penalty. A poll would take the public's pulse.

- **Take the poll:** The public is fascinated by the trial. The issue is significant.
- **Don't take the poll:** The actual trial with its sordid details is enough.

5. You can digitally alter these photos. Which, if any, do you alter?

- A photo you want to use shows a boy with his fly unzipped.
- The sky is drained of color in otherwise excellent shots.
- You need a super shot for the cover of a photography book but cannot find one.
- An athlete's genital area is slightly visible.

1. *The Patriot Ledger* in Quincy, Mass., used the names of the women. The city editor said the newspaper's policy is "to print names, unless there is a compelling reason not to. . . . printing the names served to dispel rumors about just who was involved in the videotaping."

2. NBC and *The New York Times* used her name on the ground that it had already been revealed. (The Kennedy relative was found not guilty.)

3. The newspaper published the man's crime and then apologized for doing so after readers complained.

4. "America Tonight," a CBS program, held a call-in poll introduced by Deborah Norville: "We'd like you to make a life or death decision."

Media Frenzy? The minute-by-minute coverage of the O.J. Simpson murder trial led some media critics to condemn TV and newspapers for what they contended was pandering to morbid curiosity. But others said the trial was a legitimate news event.

◀ The Decisions

Howard Kurtz media critic of *The Washington Post* called this a "lowlight" of trial coverage.

5. All of the photos were digitally doctored:

- *The Orange County Register* zipped up the boy's fly.
- The *Register* also changed the color of the sky, making it bluer.
- The editors of *A Day in the Life of America* took a photo of a cowboy on horseback, put him on a hillside and enlarged the moon. "I don't know if it's right or wrong," said one of the book's editors. "All I know is it sells the book better."
- *The National Geographic* extended a towel around the athlete to cover the genital area.

A Few Conclusions ▶

It is difficult to say with certainty whether the decisions in these situations were moral or immoral. We can, however, make some headway in reaching a defensible decision if we establish some bases from which to launch our assessments.

In balancing a special interest against the general interest, the latter should prevail. Defining the general interest is not easy, for, as some maintain, there is no general public interest but a melange of special interests. Still, access to information is one of the essential underpinnings for the full functioning of a democracy.

The journalist with an overly acute sense of responsibility can be as dangerous to the community as the recklessly irresponsible reporter. When the newspaper published the conviction of the deceased former county official, it did disregard a personal interest (his family's) for the general interest. Yet what general interest was served?

Disclosure of a minor crime committed 30 years before by a person who is dead seems to serve no end but the purpose—often sound enough—of full disclosure. If truth is served by presenting all the facts, then certainly we are on sound moral ground if we include this unsavory but factual detail in the obituary. But the journalist knows that he or she is forced to select for use from a limited stockpile of information the few facts that can be fitted into the restricted time and space allocations. In this selection process, the journalist applies to the material the tests of utility, relevance and significance within a value system. (Several days after the obituary appeared, the editor apologized to the family.)

Had the crime been well known at the time of the man's death, the journalist could not ignore it. What the public knows the press cannot skip over without risking charges of covering up information.

The Missoula Disclosure ▶

This guideline applies to the Missoula case. There was no way the community would remain ignorant of the death of the young woman. Had the newspaper failed to run some story, accusations could have been made that the newspaper showed partiality to a middle-class family while day after day it chronicles the troubles of others less affluent and influential. The newspaper could have handled the story with an editor's note admitting its dilemma, which might have alleviated the violent reaction to publication—the newspaper's editorial writer condemned the story and scores of people protested with calls and cancellations. (Krajick's dilemma might have been less intense had he considered such an editor's note. Although readers usually need not be told the reporter's problems, situations such as these can be less troublesome with full disclosure.)

Suppose the Missoula newspaper alone had learned that the young woman died a prostitute. Should it have included the fact in its story? If her work had been an inextricable part of the crime, there would have been no way to avoid it. But she had been found dead near her apartment house, the victim of an unknown assailant. No newspaper dredges up every aspect of an individual's past, whether for an obituary or a straight news story.

However, as it turned out later, her work was part of her death, for the man charged with her murder was her pimp. The sordid affair would have to have been told when her murderer was arrested and charged.

Postscript: Eight months after the *Missoulian* published the story of the young woman's murder, a late model Chrysler New Yorker rolled into Missoula and the four occupants went to work. Two cruised bars, and two went to the high schools. Within hours, the police were informed by an alerted public. The four men were arrested and convicted of criminal trespass and soliciting for prostitution.

The Missoula incident posed an ethical problem for me. In the first draft of this section, I used the young woman's name, following the instinctive reaction of a journalist to supply basic information. Surely, in a book that seeks to examine a subject in detail, the name would seem to be relevant. But is it? What does it add to the information necessary to understand the situation? Nothing. It would appear to be information for the sake of information, which has some merit. Balance this against the damage revelation could cause.

This textbook is used at the University of Montana and it could cause grief to the family. Still, there is a principle no journalist can turn from: What the public knows or will learn, the journalist cannot ignore. Surely, after the newspaper ran the story, most people in town knew the identity of the young woman. But the story is now several years old.

The argument can continue indefinitely. Unlike the philosopher, who may spin out syllogisms for a lifetime, the journalist must act quickly. The decision in this case was against disclosure. What would you have done?

◀ **The Author's Dilemma**

The reporter who writes straightforward accounts of events may feed the fires of bigotry and violence and occasionally it might seem responsible not to use what some people would consider derogatory material. But such decisions corrode the journalist's moral injunction to be the carrier of information, bad as well as good. In the area of racial news, much has changed since newspapers gingerly approached news about racial and ethnic groups.

In a roundup on the ways the press was handling racial news in the 1970s, *The Wall Street Journal* summarized the journalist's dilemma:

◀ **Racial Issues**

> If the press hews to its ideals and holds
> a mirror up to society, reflecting all its evils,
> cankers and tensions as well as its virtues, it
> runs the risk of stirring dangerous passions.

> But if it deliberately distorts the image or blots out the parts that might inflame, it casts itself in the dubious role of censor and judge.

Some newspapers and stations, the *Journal* reported, had taken on self-censorship. Some agreed to arrangements whereby news of racial disturbances would be delayed. Most said they strove to be careful in handling sensitive racial news but would not limit coverage. "It is the public, not the press, that must in the end find a way out of racial crisis—and the public can't be expected to do that unless the press gives it an accurate picture of society, warts and all," the *Journal* stated.

The black poet Langston Hughes remarked that he would know television—and society—had matured when TV shows could portray a black as a liar, a cheat or a criminal.

Resolution ▶

Now, 20 years after the *Journal* presented the dilemma and 35 years after Hughes called for honest portrayal, the issue has been resolved. When journalism turned away from reality, society suffered. In fact, the very people who were thought to be protected by this distorted view of events were victimized by the journalism of half truth.

By ignoring the fact that minorities are the major victims of violent crime, journalists did little to help society cope with a lawlessness whose victims include children caught in drug-war shootouts. When attention was not paid to the fact that HIV and AIDS strike disproportionately in the black and Hispanic communities, preventive efforts lagged.

Because it has been taboo to examine what some sociologists described as the culture of poverty, fourth- and fifth-generation fatherless families on welfare pose widening problems for these families and for society. The media, usually ahead of the public, learned that the public was concerned when, in a mid-term congressional election, voters sent to Congress legislators who pledged to amend the welfare system drastically.

The accusations that negative racial news is racist have grown fainter, though it is clear that the subject remains sensitive and what the majority journalist may consider racially neutral may appear to the minority journalist as racism. One of the ways journalism has sought to cope with this tension is through the employment of black, Hispanic, Native American and Asian journalists who can provide insights denied whites.

The Pose and the Disguise ▶

Deception has had a long and, until recently, an honorable journalistic history. In 1886, a young and ambitious reporter who called herself Nellie Bly feigned insanity to enter a mental hospital. This enabled her to expose inhuman conditions in the hospital. A century later, a reporter from *The Washington Post* gained admission to St. Elizabeth's, a federal hospital in Washington D.C., with the same ruse.

Early in this textbook, we saw how a reporter posed as a pregnant woman in order to expose an abortion mill. One of the most revealing and dramatic books

A Journalist's Moral Framework

• **Loyalty to the facts.** "You inevitably develop an intense sense of revulsion or a mild attachment for one candidate or the other," said Joseph Alsop Jr., a political writer. "But you have to be loyal to the facts or lose your reputation." John Dewey put it this way: "Devotion to fact, to truth, is a necessary moral demand."

• **An involvement in the affairs of men and women** that requires experiencing or witnessing directly the lives of human beings. Involvement generates com passion, accuracy and fairness, which are the foundations of an ethical journalism.

• **The ability to distance one's self from experience** to generate understanding. Antonio Gramsci, an Italian writer imprisoned by Mussolini for his commitment to freedom, said he had to learn the necessity of being "above the surroundings within which one lives, but without despising them or believing one's self superior to them."

• **A detached curiosity,** an exploratory attitude toward events and ideas. Detachment requires the journalist to be bound by evidence and reasonable deductions. Detachment is not indifference, which develops when, as Northrop Frye puts it, the person "ceases to think of himself as participating in the life of society. . . ."

• **A reverence for shared values, rules, codes, laws and arrangements** that give a sense of community. Such concern causes the journalist to keep careful watch for any action that can divide people by groups, classes or races.

• **Faith in experience** when intelligently used as a means of disclosing some truths.

• **An avoidance of a valueless objectivity.** This kind of objectivity can lead to what philosopher Stuart Hampshire describes as an "ice age of not caring." He writes that such an attitude can mean the end of civilization "not in a flurry of egotism and appetite leading to conflict . . . but in passivity and non-attachment, in a general spreading coldness. . . ."

• **A willingness "to hold belief in suspense,"** to doubt until evidence is obtained, to go where the evidence points instead of putting first a personally preferred conclusion; "to hold ideas in solution and use them as hypotheses instead of dogmas to be asserted; and (possibly the most distinctive of all) enjoyment of new fields for inquiry and of new problems." (John Dewey.)

• **An awareness of our limitations and responsibilities.** The story can never equal the whole truth. A concern for the consequences, the impact of what we write. A firm understanding of the line between fact and fiction.

• **Belief in the methods of journalism**—the conviction that this method will lead to some kind of truth worth sharing.

• **A moral vision of the future.** "If you don't have that vision," says the Indian writer Ved Mehta, "sooner or later the system will collapse." Without a moral vision, the journalist's compulsion may be power, profit and place in society.

• **An understanding that our words have consequences** and that we have some responsibility for the consequences.

• **To be active rather than reactive.** Walter Karp, a contributing editor of *Harper's Magazine,* writes: "The first fact of American journalism is its overwhelming dependence on sources, mostly official, usually powerful." The reporter who develops his or her own agenda for coverage is not source driven. This reporter goes into the community to help define the issues.

The Journalist. "A journalist, in any effort to render truth, has three responsibilities: to his reader, to his conscience and to his human subjects."—John Hersey, *New Yorker* writer

The reporter's obligation is to "serve the public—not the profession of journalism, not a particular newspaper, not the government, but the public. . . ."—Clifton Daniel, former managing editor of *The New York Times*

about life for blacks in the South, *Black Like Me,* was written by a white man who darkened his skin to pass as a black.

Reporters have disguised themselves as priests and police officers, as doctors and distraught relatives to get stories. Some of the great coups in journalism have come through deception. Although many of the questionable methods are used for laudable ends—usually the exposure of corruption—questions have been raised about their use.

Is there a dividing line we can locate between permissible deception and irresponsible impersonation? Is the line located where an adversary press checks power to serve the legitimate public interest?

If we use life as the referent for testing the moral validity of actions, then posing to gain access to health clinics is morally defensible since lives are involved. But the adoption of poses for routine stories would appear unjustified. The reporter who disguises himself as a health seeker to gain access to the tent of a faith healer may have greater claim to moral justification than does the reporter who poses as a customer to expose a garage that overcharges.

A Philosopher's Guidelines ▶

One of the time-tested guides to behavior is Immanuel Kant's categorical imperative: "Act as if the maxim from which you act were to become through your will a universal law of nature."

Kant had another imperative: "So act as to treat humanity, whether in your own person or that of another, in every case as an end in itself, never as a means."The imperatives of Kant, a major figure in the history of philosophy, may appear old-fashioned at first glance, but his prescriptions can help to resolve some of the sticky moral questions journalists face.

In a sense, people are always means to the journalist's end, which is the news story. Even when deception is not used, the reporter maneuvers and manipulates sources to his or her end. The reporter justifies this on the ground that such actions serve useful purposes, even for the source, since the individual is a member of the society that is being served by the reporter.

Dishonesty ▶

Impostors come in different guises. The reporter who poses as a priest to reach a grieving widow is one. The reporter who claims the work of a colleague as his or her own or who invents material is another.

Plagiarism ▶

Incidents of plagiarism are increasing. Some reporters have used the work of syndicated columnists as their own. A reporter for a California newspaper wrote a column that was almost a word-for-word copy of a column by Art Buchwald.

A *Sacramento Bee* television critic was forced to resign when his column was found to contain material from a column in *The Orlando Sentinel* as was the *Chicago Sun-Times* editorial page editor who plagiarized material from *The Washington Post*.

Databases have made it much easier for reporters to locate material they need for their work, and databases have increased the temptation to borrow. The seduction may begin in journalism school. A student, assigned to write a profile, chose to write about a theatrical producer. He used a database to dig for pieces

Getting Ahead. High school seniors were asked how far they would bend their ethical standards to get ahead in business. A third said they would plagiarize to pass a certification test.

about his subject and located a profile about his man, which he copied. Unfortunately for him, the student stopped his search too quickly. His subject had died two years after the newspaper profile had appeared. The student was dismissed from the program.

Invention is tempting. A reporter for a Chicago newspaper invented a bar in Texas and quoted characters he devised. A reporter for *The Washington Post* invented an 8-year-old heroin addict and wrote a harrowing tale that won the author a Pulitzer Prize. She lost the Prize and her job when the ruse was discovered.

◀ Fabrication

In their defense, some of these inventive reporters contend that their work should be judged like any creative writing—imaginative in detail but true in ultimate meaning. They say they have poetic license. Unfortunately for them, journalism issues no such licenses.

Everyone who tries to capture meaning—whether on paper, on film, on canvas or in spoken words—inevitably is attracted to the means of conveying ideas. Thus, the writer works on writing skills, the television journalist sharpens techniques of picture taking. Without skill, without a highly honed technique, the reporter may not convey a message with the desired impact.

◀ The Seduction of Technique

But style and technique can be fatally attractive. Too often, the means overwhelm the ends. "In television, coverage—the ability to converge on an event and transmit pictures of the scene itself—has largely replaced reporting—the attempt to reconstruct, interpret, and understand what is happening," says Lawrence K. Grossman, former president of NBC News.

For print journalists, the message from seminars, institutes and publications over the past few years is clear: Improve your writing.

Writing and related techniques are important, but they are not what journalism is about. Journalism uses style to develop content; substance is the center of our work.

The possible conflict between style and truth was understood by Leo Tolstoy, the Russian writer:

> The aesthetic and the ethical are two arms of one lever; to the extent to which one side becomes longer and heavier, the other side becomes shorter and lighter. As soon as a man loses his moral sense, he becomes particularly responsive to the aesthetic.

When journalists talk about what they do, they call it *reporting;* and when they describe themselves, they use the word *reporters.* The journalist's moral responsibility is to report, and it is in this sphere that his or her major efforts are directed. The journalist cannot see the world clearly without constant replenishment of his or her knowledge of that world, and it is in this area that major work is to be done. Content and substance, not style and technique, are the focus.

Fact and Fiction. A longtime *New Yorker* writer told students at Yale that he fabricated people, sometimes invented scenes and created conversations for some of his pieces. These embellishments, he said, made his articles more accurate.

John Hersey, another longtime *New Yorker* writer, said there is one sacred rule in journalism: "The writer must not invent. The legend on the license must read: None of this was made up. The ethics of journalism, if we can be allowed such a boon, must be based on the simple truth that every journalist knows the difference between the distortion that comes from subtracting observed data and the distortion that comes from adding invented data."

Knowledge as a Value ▶

The journalist cannot in conscience be complicitous in any attempt to counter public awareness. "If you are among brigands and you are silent, you are a brigand yourself," a Hungarian poem tells us. The brigands come in all shapes and sizes. Some are treated leniently by the press because they appear innocently misguided, censoring books and movies for what they believe is the public welfare. Others play on that part of us that fears knowing too much. Some are in our own newsrooms—timid, fretful journalists.

The journalist must recognize these people as threats to an immanent value, the necessity of knowing, of having information that will liberate us from ignorance, prejudice and the limitations of time and place. Information becomes memory, and memory, says the Polish writer Czeslaw Milosz, "provides a foundation for values" by which a society lives.

This does not mean that journalists use everything they can find. All facts are not equal, and other values come into play in the selection of what is to be published and broadcast.

The open society can be perilous. When all the winds of doctrine are set loose, the turbulence can be overwhelming. The journalist hardly contributes to order, for the journalist's task is to broadcast competing ideas and doctrines. It is the journalist's task, some journalists believe, to maintain an adversary relationship to centers of power, which also can be upsetting.

Adversary Journalism ▶

Governments seek the cooperation, even the compliance, of the press. When the head of the Central Intelligence Agency told editors he reserves the right to enlist journalists in secret missions, the editors protested that reporters need to be what they represent themselves as, independent seekers after information for the public. In response to the charge that the editors' position is unpatriotic, *The New York Times* stated in an editorial:

> There is no higher service for a free press than to operate openly and independently to inform all Americans, including the intelligence agencies. That, too, is serving the nation. As Justice Hugo Black once observed, the press is "one of the very agencies the Framers of our Constitution thoughtfully and deliberately selected to improve our society and keep it free. That worthy ideal cannot be pursued if the line between the American press and the American government is so dangerously blurred."

The choice between adversary journalism and compliance with power may seem trivialized by a comment by the Italian journalist Oriana Fallaci, but it does go to the heart of the matter. She said, "Almost every time I have tried to absolve even partially some famous son-of-a-bitch, I have been bitterly sorry."

But journalists also realize that leadership is important, that people need to have faith in their leaders, and they fear feeding the stereotype that politicians are crooked, corrupt or stupid.

And so journalists worry about their traditional role as adversaries to power. But they are more concerned about the uses of power by the state and its functionaries. The powerful state, says Milosz, "like a crab, has eaten up all the substance of society." The society versus the state, he says, "is the basic issue of the twentieth century."

The last word on adversary journalism comes from Richard Nixon, who once described the press as delighting in giving him a "going over." Ten years out of office, Nixon said, "There has to be an adversarial relationship between the press and whoever is in office."

◀ The Democratic Commitment

The journalist who is committed to the open society, to democratic values, has a moral structure from which to work, an alertness to institutions and their activities that threaten the right of anyone to take part justly, equally and freely in a meaningful community life. Any word or deed that denies this way of life to people because of their sex, age, race, sexual preference, origin, religion or position in society must be revealed by the journalist.

When *Times* columnist Anthony Lewis learned that the Nixon administration had made a deal with Vice President Spiro Agnew for his resignation in return for the promise of a nonprison sentence on his plea of "no contest" to a felony, he wrote that this was the correct action. It was right, Lewis said, on "political grounds: the need to investigate the president's wrongdoing without having as his potential successor someone who was himself under indictment."

But Lewis then had second thoughts following the sentencing to prison of two businessmen whose confession of corrupt payments had led to Agnew's resignation from the vice presidency. "So they go to prison," Lewis wrote, "while the sleazy felon who soiled our politics earns $100,000 in his new career as 'business broker.' " Instead of trusting the democratic institutions of law and politics to work, Lewis wrote, the attorney general had made personal policy.

"That unhappy precedent was carried further in the pardon of Richard Nixon," he wrote. "Of course, Watergate is not alone in examples of law applied unequally. It is commonplace, and terribly damaging to our system of criminal justice, for the powerful to go free while the little wrongdoers go to prison."

◀ Publishers' Responsibility

William Dean Singleton, the publisher of newspapers in Houston, Dallas and Denver, has a simple journalistic philosophy: Give readers what they want. After he conducts market research, he orients his newspaper in the direction readers indicate. If it means spending half his editorial budget on sports and entertainment, he says, he will do so.

"The newspaper of tomorrow is going to have to give readers what they want and not what they need," he said. "Who are we to say what they need?"

He described the newspaper as being "like a candy bar. You have to package it to be attractive to the reader. You have to put in the ingredients they want. You have to market it properly."

Compare these remarks with those of Bernard Stein, publisher of *The Riverdale Press*, a weekly newspaper in New York: "We're committed to the idea that people have to band together to shape their own lives and that of their communities. We give them an instrument to do that by telling them about issues."

The *Press* was firebombed in 1989 after it defended an author whose novel had offended Iran's rulers. The newspaper then repeated its contention that Iran's death threat to the author violated civilized behavior.

Double Standard. When the editor and publisher of the *Reno Gazette-Journal* joined the board of the firm that runs one of Nevada's biggest gambling casinos, staffers and other editors and publishers in the state were disturbed at what they saw as a potential for conflict of interest. In reply, the publisher said, "Many publishers serve on bank boards, chambers of commerce and United Way. What's the difference?"

The publisher or station owner who does not carry out his or her obligations to the staff—a decent salary, adequate staffing of reportorial and editing positions, full support for penetrating journalism, intelligent and independent leadership—cannot demand the loyalty of the staff. When he was dean of the School of Journalism at Columbia University, Edward W. Barrett advised students to establish a "go-to-hell fund" on the job, a few dollars squirreled away that would enable them to quit should they find their newspapers or stations irresponsible.

A Personal Credo ▶

For every story a reporter covers, there are two the reporter never sees because he or she has not developed a moral sensitivity. Young journalists might consider adopting personal values as guidelines in their work. From a variety of sources—from the Greek philosophers to police reporters—the following emerge as suggestions for consideration:

- A belief in and a commitment to a political culture in which the cornerstone is restraint in the use of power.
- Moderation in life and behavior.
- A secular, scientific attitude toward the work at hand. Knowledge is allowed to speak for itself. The professional does not believe on the basis of hope but of evidence.
- An openmindedness that seeks out and tries to comprehend various points of view, including those in conflict with those the reporter holds.
- Responsibility to one's abilities and talent. To leave them fallow, to fail to labor to develop them through indolence or want of seriousness of purpose demeans the self and punishes the society whose betterment depends on new ideas vigorously pursued. For Homer, the good was the fulfillment of function. For Aristotle, the good was living up to one's potential, and for Kant the development of one's talents was a duty, and adherence to "duties" constituted the moral life. The reporter who fails to report and write to his or her potential is immoral.
- An understanding of and a tolerance for the ambiguities involved in most important issues and the ability to act despite these uncertainties and doubts. The willingness to take responsibility for these actions.
- The willingness to admit errors.
- A capacity to endure solitude and criticism, the price of independence.
- A reluctance to create heroes and villains to the rhythm of the deadline.
- A knowledge of the pathfinders in fields of knowledge, including journalism.
- A commitment to work.
- A sense of the past. W.H. Auden said, "Let us remember that though great artists of the past could not change the course of history, it is only through their work that we are able to break bread with the dead, and without communion with the dead, a fully human life is impossible."
- Resistance to praise. Humility. "You have to fight against the praise of people who like you," says I.F. Stone, the crusading journalist. "Because you know darn well it wasn't good enough." He tells the story of the great

Eye of Conscience. During the Depression, a group of photographers set out to show the dire results of poverty. The most noted was Dorothea Lange, who said of herself, "All my life I tried very hard to make a place where what I did would count." Her photos of migrant workers and their children were reproduced in newspapers, magazines and books.

Pare Lorentz, the great producer of film documentaries, said of Lange that she did "more for these tragic nomads than all the politicians of the country." *The New York Times* said, "She functioned as our national eye of conscience. Her constant concerns—the survival of human dignity under impossible conditions, the confrontation of the system by the individual, and the helpless ignorance of children—were perfectly suited to the subject."

conductor Arturo Toscanini who was engulfed by admirers after a concert. "Maestro, you were wonderful," one said. Toscanini knew the oboe had not come in at the right point and that the violins were off. And Toscanini burst into tears because he knew it had not been good enough.

• Duty. John Dewey said, "If a man is burdened with an idea, he not only desires to express it; he ought to express it. He owes it to his conscience and the common good. The indispensable function of expressing ideas is one of obligation—to the community and also to something beyond the community, let us say to truth."

• Avoidance of the desire to please. Self-censorship is a greater enemy than outside censorship. Pleasing an editor, the publisher or the source is commonplace. Setting one's values to the "pragmatic level of the newsroom group," as Warren Breed puts it, can lead to timid, status-quo journalism.

• A wariness about the making words an end in themselves. André Maurois, the French writer and political activist, writes:

> Power, Glory and Money are only secondary objects for the writer. No man can be a great writer without having a great philosophy, though it may often be unexpressed. A great writer has respect for *values*. His essential function is to raise life to the dignity of thought, and he does this by giving it a shape. If he refuses to perform this function he can be a clever juggler and play tricks with words such as his fellow writers may admire, but his books will be of little interest to anybody else. If, on the contrary, he fulfills it, he will be happy in his writing. Borne aloft by the world as reflected in himself, and producing a sound echo in his times, he helps to shape it by showing to men an image of themselves which is at once true and disciplined.

Reporters should seek to give voice to all groups in society, not to report solely those who hold power.

The public's need to know is an immanent value.

In determining what shall be reported and what shall be included in a news story, the reporter should consider the relevance of the material to the real needs of the audience.

If the reporter cannot disclose in the story the tactics and techniques used to gather information for the story, such tactics should not be used.

The reporter should:

• Be wary of treating people as a means.

• Believe on the basis of facts, not hope.

• Be committed to a value system but be free from ideologies and commitments that limit thought.

• Be wary of promising to help a source in return for material.

◀ **Summing Up**

In balancing moral alternatives, the choice can be made on the basis of:

- The importance of the possible actions to life. (Life is the referent of value.)
- The public interest as against the private interest.
- The extent of knowledge of the event. If it is public knowledge or is likely to become so and the material is significant and relevant, the information should be used.
- Serving the needs of society. If the material assists people in participating justly, equally and freely in a meaningful community life, then it should be used.

The code of the Society of Professional Journalists is in Appendix D.

Further Reading ▶

The Adversary Press. St. Petersburg, Fla.: The Poynter Institute for Media Studies, 1983. A discussion of ethics by 19 editors, publishers and scholars at an Institute seminar.

Bagdikian, Ben H. *The Effete Conspiracy and Other Crimes by the Press*. New York: Harper & Row, 1972.

Benjamin, Burton. *Fair Play*. New York: Harper & Row, 1988.

Black, Max, ed. *The Morality of Scholarship*. Ithaca, N.Y.: Cornell University Press, 1967.

Fallows, James. *Breaking the News: How the Media Undermine American Democracy*. New York: Pantheon Books, 1996.

Gerald, J. Edward. *The Social Responsibility of the Press*. Minneapolis: University of Minnesota Press, 1963.

Hulteng, John. *Playing It Straight*. Chester, Conn.: The Globe Pequot Press, 1981.

Ibsen, Henrik. *An Enemy of the People*. 1882. Available in many anthologies and collections.

McCulloch, Frank, ed. *Drawing the Line*. St. Petersburg, Fla.: The Poynter Institute for Media Studies, 1984.

Pierce, Robert N. *A Sacred Trust. Nelson Poynter and the St. Petersburg Times*. Gainesville, Fla.: University Press of Florida, 1994.

Reston, James. *The Artillery of the Press*. New York: Harper & Row, 1960.

Smith, Z.N., and Pamela Zekman. *The Mirage*. New York: Random House, 1979.

Swados, Harvey. *Years of Conscience: The Muckrakers*. New York: The World Publishing Co., 1962.

Waldron, Ann. *Hodding Carter: The Reconstruction of a Racist*. Chapel Hill, N.C.: Algonquin Books of Chapel Hill, 1993.

Stylebook

addresses Abbreviate *Avenue, Boulevard, Street* with specific address: *1314 Kentucky St.* Spell out without specific address: *construction on Fifth Avenue.*

Use figures for the address number: *3 Third Ave.; 45 Main St.* Spell out numbers under 10 as street names: *21 Fourth Ave.; 450 11th St.*

age Use figures. To express age as an adjective, use hyphens: *a 3-year-old girl.* Also use hyphens when age is expressed as a noun as in: *a 10-year-old.* Unless otherwise stated, the figure is presumed to indicate years: *a boy, 4, and his sister, 6 months.*

Infant: under one year of age; *child:* someone in the period between infancy and youth, ages 1 to 13; *girl, boy:* under 18; *youth:* 13–18; *man, woman:* over 18; *adult:* over 18, unless used in specific legal context for crimes such as drinking; *middle-aged:* 35–55; *elderly:* over 65. Avoid *elderly* when describing individuals.

a.m., p.m. Lowercase with periods.

amendment Capitalize when referring to specific amendments to the U.S. Constitution. Spell out for the first through ninth; use figures for 10th and above: *First Amendment, 10th Amendment.*

anti- Hyphenate all but words that have their own meanings: *antibiotic, antibody, anticlimax, antidote, antifreeze, antihistamine, antiknock, antimatter, antiparticle, antipasto, antiperspirant, antiseptic, antiserum, antithesis, antitoxin, antitrust.*

bi, semi When used with periods of time, the prefix *bi* means every other; *semi* means twice. A biannual conference meets every other year. A semiweekly newspaper comes out twice a week. No hyphens.

brand name A nonlegal term for a trademark. Do not use them as generic terms or as verbs: *soft drink* instead of *Coke* or *coke; photocopy* instead of *Xerox.*

capitalization Generally, follow a down style.

Proper nouns: Use capitals for names of persons, places, trademarks; titles when used with names; nicknames of people, states, teams; titles of books, plays, movies.

century Lowercase, spelling out numbers less than 10, except when used in proper nouns—*the fifth century, 18th century,* but *20th Century-Fox* and *Nineteenth Century Society*—following the organization's practice.

chairman, chairwoman Use *chairman* or *chairwoman* instead of *chair* or *chairperson; spokesman* or *spokeswoman* instead of *spokesperson* and similar constructions unless the *-person* construction is a formal title.

Use *chairman* or *spokesman* when referring to the office in general. A neutral word such as *representative* often may be the best choice.

co- Use a hyphen when forming nouns, adjectives and verbs that indicate occupation or status: *co-star, co-written.* No hyphen for other constructions: *coeducation, coexist.*

Congress Capitalize when referring to the U.S. Senate and House of Representatives. The term is correctly used only in reference to the two legislative branches together. Capitalize also when referring to foreign governments that use the term or its equivalent.

Do not capitalize *congressional* unless it is part of a proper name.

Constitution, constitutional Capitalize when referring to the U.S. Constitution, with or without the *U.S.* modifier. When referring to other constitutions, capitalize only when preceded by the name of a nation or state. Lowercase *constitutional.*

court names Capitalize the full proper names of courts at all levels. Retain capitalization if *U.S.* or a state name is dropped.

dates *July 6, 1957,* was her birth date. (Use commas.) *She was born in July 1957.* (No comma between the month and year.)

Abbreviate the month with a specific date: *Feb. 19.* Spell out all months when standing alone. With dates, use abbreviations: *Jan., Feb., Aug., Sept., Oct., Nov., Dec.* Spell out *March, April, May, June, July.*

directions and regions Lowercase *north, south, northeast,* etc. when they indicate compass direction: *Police followed the car south on Route 22.*

Capitalize when they refer to regions: *Southern accent; Northeastern industry.*

With names of nations, lowercase except when they are part of a proper name or are used to designate a politically divided nation: *tourism in southern France,* but *South Korea* and *Northern Ireland.*

Lowercase compass points when they describe a section of a state or city except when they are part of a proper name (*South Dakota*) or when they refer to a widely known region (*Southern California; the East Side of New York*).

Capitalize them when combining them with a common noun to form a proper noun: *the Eastern Hemisphere; the North Woods.*

entitled Does not mean *titled. Citizens 18 and older are entitled to vote,* but *the book is titled "News Reporting and Writing."*

ex- No hyphen for words that use *ex* in the sense of *out of: excommunicate, expropriate.* Hyphenate when using in the sense of *former: ex-husband, ex-convict. Former* is preferred with titles: *Former President Gerald R. Ford.*

fireman Use *firefighter* since some women hold this job.

fractions Spell out amounts less than 1, using hyphens: *one-half, two-thirds.* Use figures for amounts larger than 1, converting to decimals whenever possible: *3.5* instead of *three and one-half* or *3½.*
     Figures are preferred in tabular material and in stories about stocks.

gay Acceptable as a popular synonym for *homosexual.* May be used as a noun and an adjective.

historical periods and events Capitalize widely recognized periods and events in anthropology, archeology, geology and history: *the Bronze Age, the Ice Age, the Renaissance.*
     Capitalize widely recognized popular names for eras and events: *the Glorious Revolution, the Roaring '20s.*

holidays and holy days Capitalize them. In federal law, the legal holidays are New Year's, Martin Luther King's Birthday, President's Day, Memorial Day, Independence Day, Labor Day, Columbus Day, Veterans Day, Thanksgiving and Christmas.
     States are not required to follow the federal lead in designating holidays, except that federal employees must receive the day off or must be paid overtime if they work.
     Jewish holy days: Hanukkah, Passover, Purim, Rosh Hashana, Shavuot, Sukkot and Yom Kippur.

in- No hyphen when it means *not: invalid; inaccurate.* Mostly used without the hyphen in other combinations, but there are a few exceptions: *in-house; in-depth.* Consult a dictionary when in doubt.

-in Always precede with a hyphen: *break-in; sit-in; write-in.*

initials Use periods and no space: *H.L. Mencken; C.S. Lewis.* This practice has been adopted to ensure that initials will be set on the same line.

like- Follow with a hyphen when used to mean *similar to: like-minded; like-natured.*

-like No hyphen unless the *l* would be tripled: *lifelike,* but *shell-like.*

mailman Use the term *letter carrier* or *mail carrier* since many women work for the Postal Service.

man, mankind *Humanity* is preferred for the plural form. Use *a person* or *an individual* in the singular. A phrase or sentence usually can be reconstructed to eliminate any awkwardness.

nationalities and races Capitalize the proper names of nationalities, peoples, races, tribes, etc. Lowercase *black* and *white*. Lowercase derogatory terms such as *honky* and *nigger*. Use them only in direct quotations.

See *race* for guidelines on when racial identification is pertinent in a story.

National Organization for Women. Not *National Organization of Women.*

nobility Capitalize *king, queen, duke* and other titles when they precede the individual's name. Lowercase when standing alone: *King Juan Carlos,* but *the king of Spain.*

non- In general, do not hyphenate if *not* could be used before the root word. Hyphenate before proper nouns or in awkward combinations: *non-nuclear.*

numerals Spell out *one* through *nine,* except when used to indicate age or in dates. Use figures for *10* and above.

Spell out a number when it begins a sentence: *Fifteen members voted against the bill.* Use figures when a year begins a sentence: *1990 began auspiciously.*

Use figures for percentages, percents, and money: *$5* but *a dollar.*

For amounts of $1 million and more, use the *$* sign and figures up to two decimal places with the *million, billion, trillion* spelled out: *$1.65 million.* Exact amounts are given in figures: *$1,650,398.*

When spelling out large numbers, separate numbers ending in *y* from the next number with a hyphen: *seventy-nine; one hundred seventy-nine.*

people, persons Use *person* when referring to an individual. *People* is preferred to *persons* in all plural uses.

People also is a collective noun that takes a plural verb when used to refer to a single race or nation: *The Philippine people are awaiting the president's decision on the offer of aid.* In this sense, *peoples* is the plural form: *The peoples of Western Europe do not always agree on East-West issues.*

percentages Use figures—decimals, not fractions—and the word *percent,* not the symbol: *2.5 percent; 10 percent.* For amounts less than 1 percent, place a zero before the decimal: *0.6 percent.*

When presenting a range, repeat *percent* after each figure: *2 percent to 5 percent.*

policeman Use *police officer* instead.

political parties and philosophies Capitalize the name of the party and the word *party* when it is used as part of the organization's proper name: *the Democratic Party.*

Capitalize *Communist, Conservative, Democrat, Liberal,* etc., when they refer to the activities of a specific party or to individual members.

Lowercase the name of a philosophy in noun and adjective forms unless it is derived from a proper name: *communism; fascist,* but *Marxism; Nazi.*

In general, avoid the terms *conservative, radical, leftist* and *rightist.* In casual and popular usage, the meanings of these terms vary, depending on the user and the situation being discussed. A more precise description of an individual's or a group's political views is preferred.

post office Should not be capitalized. The agency is the U.S. Postal Service.

prefixes See entries for specific prefixes. Generally, do not hyphenate when using a prefix with a word starting with a consonant.

Except for *cooperate* and *coordinate,* use a hyphen if the prefix ends in the same vowel that begins the following word: *re-elect,* not *reelect.*

Use a hyphen if the word that follows is capitalized: *pan-American, anti-Catholic.*

Use a hyphen to join doubled prefixes: *sub-subclause.*

presidency Always lowercase.

president Capitalized only as a title before an individual's name: *President Bill Clinton,* but *the president said he would spend New Year's in Houston.*

presidential Lowercase unless part of a proper name: *presidential approval,* but *Presidential Medal of Freedom.*

race Race, religion and national origin are sometimes essential to a story but too often are injected when they are not pertinent. When in doubt about relevance, substitute descriptions such as *white, Baptist, French.* If one of these descriptions would be pertinent, use the original term.

religious references

DEITIES: Capitalize the proper names of monotheistic deities, pagan and mythological gods and goddesses: *Allah, the Father, Zeus.* Lowercase pronouns that refer to the deity: *he, him, thee, who,* etc.

Lowercase *gods* when referring to the deities of polytheistic religions. Lowercase such words as *god-awful, godlike, godsend.*

LIFE OF JESUS CHRIST: Capitalize the names of major events in the life of Jesus Christ in references that do not use his name: *the Last Supper; the Resurrection.* Lowercase when the words are used with his name: *the ascension of Christ.* Apply the same principle to events in the life of his mother, Mary.

RITES: Capitalize proper names for rites that commemorate the Last Supper or signify a belief in Jesus Christ's presence: *the Lord's Supper; Holy Eucharist.* Lowercase the names of other sacraments.

HOLY DAYS: Capitalize the names of holy days: *Hanukkah.*

OTHER WORDS: Lowercase *heaven, hell, devil, angel, cherub, apostle, priest,* etc.

rock 'n' roll Not *rock and roll.*

room numbers Use figures and capitalize *room:* The faculty met in Room 516. Capitalize the names of specially designated rooms: *Oval Office; Blue Room.*

saint Abbreviate as *St.* in the names of saints, cities and other places except *Saint John* (New Brunswick), to distinguish it from St. John's, Newfoundland, and *Sault Ste. Marie.*

seasons Lowercase *spring, summer, fall, winter* and their derivatives. Capitalize when part of a formal name: *St. Paul Winter Carnival; Summer Olympics.*

self- Always hyphenate: *self-motivated; self-taught.*

senate, senatorial Capitalize all references to specific legislative bodies, regardless of whether the name of the nation or state is used: *U.S. Senate; the state Senate.*

Lowercase plural uses: *the Iowa and Kansas state senates.* Lowercase references to nongovernmental bodies: *the student-faculty senate.*

Always lowercase *senatorial.*

sexism Avoid stereotyping women or men. Be conscious of equality in treatment of both sexes.

When writing of careers and jobs, avoid presuming that the wage earner is a man and that the woman is a homemaker: *the average family of five* instead of *the average worker with a wife and three children.*

Avoid physical descriptions of women or men when not absolutely relevant to the story.

Use parallel references to both sexes: *the men and the women,* not *the men and the ladies; husband and wife,* not *man and wife.*

Do not use nouns and pronouns to indicate sex unless the sex difference is basic to understanding or there is no suitable substitute. One way to avoid such subtle sexism is to change the noun to the plural, eliminating the masculine pronoun: *Drivers should carry their licenses,* not *Every driver should carry his license.*

Personal appearance and marital and family relationships should be used only when relevant to the story.

state names Spell out names of the 50 U.S. states when they stand alone in textual matter.

The names of eight states are never abbreviated: *Alaska, Hawaii, Idaho, Iowa, Maine, Ohio, Texas, Utah.*

Abbreviate other state names when used with a city, in a dateline or with party affiliation. Do not use Postal Service abbreviations.

Ala.	*Fla.*	*Md.*	*Neb.*	*N.D.*	*Tenn.*
Ariz.	*Ga.*	*Mass.*	*Nev.*	*Okla.*	*Vt.*
Ark.	*Ill.*	*Mich.*	*N.H.*	*Ore.*	*Va.*
Calif.	*Ind.*	*Minn.*	*N.J.*	*Pa.*	*Wash.*
Colo.	*Kan.*	*Miss.*	*N.M.*	*R.I.*	*W.Va.*
Conn.	*Ky.*	*Mo.*	*N.Y.*	*S.C.*	*Wis.*
Del.	*La.*	*Mont.*	*N.C.*	*S.D.*	*Wyo.*

statehouse Capitalize all references to a specific statehouse, with or without the state name. But lowercase in all plural uses: *the New Mexico Statehouse; the Arizona and New Mexico statehouses.*

suspensive hyphenation Use as follows: *The 19- and 20-year-olds were not served alcoholic beverages.* Use in all similar cases.

Although the form looks somewhat awkward, it guides readers, who may otherwise expect a noun to follow the first figure.

syllabus, syllabuses Also: *memorandum, memorandums.*

teen, teen-ager (noun), **teen-age** (adjective) Do not use *teen-aged.*

telecast (noun), **televise** (verb)

temperatures Use figures for all except *zero.* Use the word *minus,* not a minus sign, to indicate temperatures below zero. *The day's high was 9; the day's low was minus 9.*

Temperatures are higher and lower and they rise and fall but they do not become warmer or cooler.

Third World The economically developing nations of Africa, Asia and Latin America.

time Exact times often are unnecessary. *Last night* and *this morning* are acceptable substitutes for *yesterday* and *today.* Use exact time when pertinent but avoid redundancies: *8 a.m. this morning* should be *8 a.m. today* or *8 o'clock this morning.*

Use figures except for *noon* and *midnight: 12 noon* is redundant.

Separate hours from minutes with a colon: *3:15 p.m.*

titles

ACADEMIC TITLES: Capitalize and spell out formal titles such as *professor, dean, president, chancellor and chairman* when they precede a name. Lowercase elsewhere. Do not abbreviate *Professor* as *Prof.*

Lowercase modifiers such as *journalism* in *journalism Professor John Rist* or *department* in *department chairwoman Kim Power,* unless the modifier is a proper name: *French Professor Jeannette Spear.*

COURTESY TITLES: Do not use the courtesy titles *Miss, Mr., Mrs.* or *Ms.* on first reference. Instead, use the person's first and last names. Do not use *Mr.* unless it is combined with *Mrs.: Kyle Scott Hotsenpiller; Mr. and Mrs. Kyle Scott Hotsenpiller.*

Courtesy titles may be used on second reference for women, according to the woman's preference and these guidelines:

- Married women: On first reference, identify a woman by her own first name and her husband's last name, if she uses it: *Betty Phillips.* Use *Mrs.* on first reference only if a woman requests that her husband's first name be used or her own first name cannot be determined: *Mrs. Steven A. Phillips.*

  On second reference, use *Mrs.* unless a woman initially identified by her own first name prefers *Ms.: Rachel Finch; Mrs. Finch; Ms. Finch.* Or use no title: *Finch; Rachel Finch.*

  If a married woman is known by her maiden name, precede it by *Miss* on second reference unless she prefers *Ms.: Sarah Wilson; Miss Wilson* or *Ms. Wilson.*

- Unmarried women: Use *Miss, Ms.* or no title on second reference, according to the woman's preference.

For divorced and widowed women, the normal practice is to use *Mrs.* or no title on second reference, according to the woman's preference. Use *Miss, Ms.* or no title, according to the woman's preference, if the woman returns to her maiden name.

If a woman prefers *Ms.* or no title, do not include her marital status in a story unless it is pertinent.

GOVERNMENTAL TITLES: Capitalize when used as a formal title in front of a person's name. It is not necessary to use a title on second reference: *Gov. Fred Florence; Florence.* For women who hold official positions, use the courtesy title on second reference, according to the guidelines for courtesy titles: *Gov. Ruth Arnold; Miss Arnold, Mrs. Arnold, Ms. Arnold, Arnold.* (Some newspapers do not use the courtesy title on second reference.)

Abbreviate *Governor* as *Gov., Lieutenant Governor* as *Lt. Gov.* when used as a formal title before a name.

Congressional titles: Before names, abbreviate *Senator* as *Sen.* and *Representative* as *Rep.* Add *U.S.* or *state* if necessary to avoid confusion.

Short form punctuation for party affiliation: Use abbreviations listed under **state names** and set them off from the person's name with commas: *Sen. Nancy Landon Kassebaum, R-Kan., and Rep. Charles Hatcher, D-Ga., attended the ceremony.*

Capitalize and spell out other formal government titles before a person's name. Do not use titles on second reference: *Attorney General Jay Craven spoke. Craven said . . .*

Capitalize and spell out formal titles instead of abbreviating before the person's name in direct quotations only. Lowercase in all uses not mentioned already.

OCCUPATIONAL TITLES: They are always lowercase: *senior vice president Nancy Harden.* Avoid false titles: *bridge champion Helen P. George* should be: *Helen P. George, Sioux Falls bridge tourney winner.*

RELIGIOUS TITLES: The first reference to a clergyman, clergywoman or nun should include a capitalized title before the person's name.

On second reference: for men, use only a last name if he uses a surname. If a man is known only by a religious name, repeat the title: *Pope Paul VI* or *Pope Paul* on first reference; *the pope* or *the pontiff* on second reference. For women, use *Miss, Mrs., Ms.* or no title, according to the woman's preference.

Cardinals, archbishops, bishops: On first reference, use the title before the person's first and last name. On second reference, use the last name only or the title.

Ministers and priests: Use *the Rev.* before a name on first reference. Substitute *Monsignor* before the name of a Roman Catholic priest who has received this honor.

Rabbis: Use *Rabbi* before a name on first reference. On second reference, use only the last name of a man; use *Miss, Mrs., Ms.* or no title before a woman's last name, according to her preference.

Nuns: Always use *Sister* or *Mother: Sister Agnes Mary* in all references if the nun uses only a religious name; *Sister Ann Marie Graham* on first reference if she uses a surname, *Sister Graham* on second.

TITLES OF WORKS: For titles of books, movies, operas, plays, poems, songs, television programs and lectures, speeches and works of art, apply the following guidelines:

Capitalize the principal words, including prepositions and conjunctions of four or more letters.

Capitalize an article or word of fewer than four letters if it is the first or last word in a title.

Place quotation marks around the names of all such works except the Bible and books that are primarily catalogs of reference material, including almanacs, directories, dictionaries, encyclopedias, handbooks and similar publications.

Translate a foreign title into English unless a work is known to the American public by its foreign name.

Do not use quotation marks or italics with the names of newspapers and magazines.

TV Acceptable as an adjective but should not be used as a noun.

upstate, downstate Always lowercase.

venereal disease *VD* is acceptable on second reference.

versus Abbreviate as *vs.* in all uses.

vice Use two words, no hyphen.

vice president Follow the guidelines for **president.**

war Capitalize when part of the name for a particular conflict: *World War II; the Cold War.*

well- Hyphenate as part of a compound modifier: *a well-dressed man.*

wide- Usually hyphenated: *wide-eyed.* Exception: *widespread.*

words as words When italics are available, italicize them. Otherwise, place in quotation marks: *Rep. Ellen Jacobson asked journalists to address her as "congresswoman."*

years Use figures. Use an *s* without the apostrophe to indicate spans of centuries: *the 1800s.* Use an apostrophe to indicate omitted numerals and an *s* to indicate decades: the *'80s.*

Years are the only figures that may be placed at the start of a sentence: *1959 was a year of rapid city growth.*

◀ **Punctuation**

Keep a good grammar book handy. No stylebook can adequately cover the complexities of the 13 punctuation marks: apostrophe, bracket, colon, comma, dash, ellipsis, exclamation point, hyphen, parenthesis, period, question mark, quotation mark, semicolon. The following is a guide to frequent problems and usages:

Apostrophe Use (1) for possessives, (2) to indicate omitted figures or letters and (3) to form some plurals.

1. **Possessives.** Add apostrophe and *s* ('s) to the end of singular and plural nouns or the indefinite pronoun unless it has an *s* or *z* sound.
   The woman's coat. The women's coats.
   The child's toy. The children's toys.
   Someone's pistol. One's hopes.
   If the word is plural and ends in an *s* or *z* sound, add an apostrophe only:
   Boys' books. Joneses' farm.
   For singular common nouns ending in *s,* add an apostrophe and *s* ('s) unless the next word begins with s:
   The hostess's gown. The hostess' seat.
   For singular proper nouns, add only an apostrophe:
   Dickens' novels. James' hat.
2. **Omitted figures or letters.** Use in contractions: *Don't, can't.* Put in place of omitted figures: *Class of '88.*
3. **To form some plurals.** When figures, letters, symbols and words are referred to as words, use the apostrophe and *s.*
   a. Figures: *She skated perfect 8's.*
   b. Letters: *He received all A's in his finals.*
   c. Symbols: *Journalists never use &'s to substitute for the ands in their copy.*

Caution: The pronouns *ours, yours, theirs, his, hers, whose* do not take the apostrophe. *Its* is the possessive pronoun. *It's* is the contraction of *it is.*

Note: Compound words and nouns in joint possession use the possessive in the last word:

- Everybody else's homes.
- His sister-in-law's book.
- Clinton and Kennedy's party.

If there is separate possession, each noun takes the possessive form: *Clinton's and Kennedy's opinions differ.*

Brackets Check whether the newspaper can set them. Use to enclose a word or words within a quote that the writer inserts: *"Happiness [his note read] is a state of mind."* Try to avoid the need for such an insertion. Use for paragraphs within a story that refer to an event separate from the datelined material.

Colon The colon is usually used at the end of a sentence to call attention to what follows. It introduces lists, tabulations, texts and quotations of more than one sentence.

It also can be used to mark a full stop before a dramatic word or statement: *She had only one goal in life: work.* The colon is used in the time of day: *7:45 p.m.;* elapsed time of an event: *4:01.1;* in dialogue in question and answer, as from a trial.

Comma The best general guide for the use of the comma is the human voice as it pauses, stops and varies in tone. The comma marks the pause, the short stop:

1. He looked into the hospital room, but he was unable to find the patient.
2. Although he continued his search on the floor for another 20 minutes, he was unable to find anyone to help him.

3. He decided that he would go downstairs, ask at the desk and then telephone the police.
4. If that also failed, he thought to himself, he would have to give up the search.

Note that when reading these sentences aloud, the commas are natural resting points for pauses. The four sentences also illustrate the four principles governing the use of commas:

1. The comma is used to separate main clauses when they are joined by a coordinating conjunction. (The coordinating conjunctions are *for, nor, and, but, or.*) The comma can be eliminated if the main clauses are short: *He looked into the room and he froze.*
2. Use the comma after an introductory element: a clause, long phrase, transitional expression or interjection.
3. Use the comma to separate words, phrases or clauses in a series. Also, use it in a series of coordinate adjectives: *He was wearing a long, full cape.*
4. Set off nonessential material in a sentence with comma(s). When the parenthetical or interrupting nonrestrictive clauses and phrases are in the middle of a sentence, two commas are needed: *The country, he was told, needed his assistance.*

Other uses of the comma:

• With full sentence quotes, not with partial quotes: *He asked, "Where are you going?" The man replied that he was "blindly groping" his way home.*
• To separate city and county, city and state. In place of the word *of* between a name and city: *Jimmy Carter, Plains, Ga.*
• To set off a person's age: *Orville Sterb, 19, of Fullerton, Calif.*
• In dates: *March 19, 1940, was the date he entered the army.*
• In party affiliations: *Bill Bradley, D-N.J., spoke.*

Caution: The comma is frequently misused by placing it instead of the period or semicolon between two main clauses. This is called *comma splice:*

> WRONG: The typewriter was jammed, he could not type his theme.
> RIGHT: The typewriter was jammed. He could not type his theme.
>   The typewriter was jammed; he could not type his theme.

Dash Use a dash (1) to indicate a sudden or dramatic shift in thought within a sentence, (2) to set off a series of words that contains commas and (3) to introduce sections of a list or a summary.

The dash is a call for a short pause, just as are the comma and the parenthesis. The comma is the most often used and is the least dramatic of the separators. The parenthesis sets off unimportant elements. The dash tends to emphasize material. It has this quality because it is used sparingly.

1. He stared at the picture—and he was startled to find himself thinking of her face. The man stood up—painfully and awkwardly—and extended his hand in greeting.
2. There were three people watching them—an elderly woman, a youth with a crutch at his side and a young woman in jeans holding a paperback—and he pulled her aside out of their view.

3. He gave her his reasons for being there:
    —He wanted to apologize;
    —He needed to give her some material;
    —He was leaving on a long trip.
    Note: This third form should be used infrequently, usually when the listing will be followed by an elaboration.

The dash is also used in datelines.

Ellipsis Use the ellipsis to indicate material omitted from a quoted passage from a text, transcript, play, etc.: *The minutes stated that Breen had asked, "How many gallons of paint . . . were used in the project?"* Put one space before and one space after each of the three periods. If the omission ends with a period, use four periods, one to mark the end of the sentence (without space, as a regular period), three more for the ellipsis.

The ellipsis is also used by some columnists to separate short items in a paragraph.

Do not use to mark pauses or shifts in thought or for emphasis.

Exclamation point Much overused. There are reporters who have gone through a lifetime of writing and have never used the exclamation point, except when copying material in which it is used. The exclamation point is used to indicate powerful feelings, surprise, wonder. Most good writers prefer to let the material move the reader to provide his or her own exclamation.

When using, do not place a comma or period after the exclamation point. Place inside quotation marks if it is part of the quoted material.

Hyphen The hyphen is used (1) to join words to express a single idea or (2) to avoid confusion or ambiguity.

1. Use the hyphen to join two or more words that serve as a single adjective before a noun: *A well-known movie is on television tonight. He had a know-it-all expression.*
    Caution: Do not use the hyphen when the first word of the compound ends in *-ly* or when the words follow the noun: *He is an easily recognized person. Her hair was blond black.*
2. Avoid (a) ambiguity or (b) an awkward joining of letters or syllables by putting a hyphen between prefixes or suffixes and the root word.
    a. He recovered the chair. He re-covered the chair.
    b. Re-enter, macro-economics, shell-like.

Parenthesis Generally, avoid. It may be necessary for the insertion of background or to set off supplementary or illustrative material.

Use a period inside a closing parenthesis if the matter begins with a capital letter.

Period Use the period at the end of declarative sentences, indirect questions, most imperative sentences and most abbreviations. Place the period inside quotation marks.

Question mark The question mark is used for direct questions, not indirect questions.

DIRECT: Where are you going?
INDIRECT: He asked where she was going.

The question mark goes inside quotation marks if it applies to the quoted material: *He asked, "Have you seen the movie?"* Put it outside if it applies to the entire sentence: *Have you seen "Guys and Dolls"?*

Quotation marks Quotation marks set off (1) direct quotations, (2) some titles and nicknames and (3) words used in a special way.

1. Set off the exact words of the speaker: *"He walked like a duck," she said. He replied that he walked "more like an alley cat on the prowl."*
2. Use for titles of books, movies, short stories, poems, songs, articles from magazines and plays. Some nicknames take quotation marks. Do not use for nicknames of sports figures.
3. For words used in a special sense: *"Indian giver" and similar phrases are considered to be ethnic slurs.*

Punctuation with quotation marks:

The comma: Use it outside the quotation marks when setting off the speaker at the beginning of a sentence: *He said, "You care too much for money."* Use inside the quotation marks when the speaker ends the sentence: *"I just want to be safe," she replied.*

The colon and semicolon: Always place outside the quotation marks: *He mentioned her "incredible desire for work"; he meant her "insatiable desire for work."*

The dash, question mark and exclamation point: Place them inside when they apply to quoted matter only; outside when they refer to the whole sentence: *She asked, "How do you know so much?" Did she really wonder why he knew "so much"?*

For quotes within quotes, use a single quote mark (the apostrophe on a typewriter) for the inner quotation: *"Have you read 'War and Peace'?" he asked.* Note, no comma is used after the question mark.

Semicolon Usually overused by beginning reporters. Unless there is a special reason to use the semicolon, use the period.

Use the semicolon to separate a series of equal elements when the individual segments contain material that is set off by commas. This makes for clarity in the series: *He suggested that she spend her allowance on the new series at the opera, "Operas of the Present"; books of plays by Shaw, Ibsen and Aristophanes; and novels by Tolstoy, Dickens and F. Scott Fitzgerald.*

Grammar

In our grandparents' day, students spent hours diagramming sentences, breaking them down into nouns, verbs, pronouns and the dozens of other segments that describe sentence parts. Today, grammar is not given as much attention in schools, and for journalists, whose living depends on mastery of the language, this is inadequate training.

One way journalists cope with this inadequacy is to invest in a handbook of grammar. It not only solves grammatical problems quickly, but it expands the journalist's writing range.

Think of the humiliation a *New York Times* reporter experienced when he saw in print this sentence he had written:

> While urging parents to remain loving,
> the program, which is controversial in that
> it's techniques are considered questionable
> by a good number of experts, advises them
> to stop being intimidated and manipulated
> by their misbehaving children.

Contorted as this sentence is, the one error that shouts for attention is the misuse of *it's*.

The following guide will help you to avoid grammatical errors that frequently turn up in student copy.

Agreement ▶

A verb must agree in number with its subject. Writers encounter trouble when they are unsure of the subject or when they cannot decide whether the subject is singular or plural.

Uncertainty often arises when there are words between the subject and the verb:

WRONG: John, as well as several others in the class, were unhappy with the instructor.

RIGHT: John, as well as several others in the class, was unhappy with the instructor.

The subject is *John*, singular.

WRONG: The barrage of traffic noises, telephone calls and similar interruptions make it difficult to study.

RIGHT: The barrage of traffic noises, telephone calls and similar interruptions makes it difficult to study.

The subject is *barrage*, singular.

A collective noun takes a singular verb when the group is considered a unit and a plural verb when the individuals are thought of separately.

RIGHT: The committee usually votes unanimously.

RIGHT: The family lives around the corner.

RIGHT: The family were gathered around the fire, some reading, some napping.

The pronouns *anybody, anyone, each, either, everyone, everybody, neither, no one, nobody, someone* and *somebody* take the singular verb.

A pronoun must agree in number with its antecedent.

WRONG: The team has added two players to their squad.

RIGHT: The team has added two players to its squad.

WRONG: Everyone does their best.

RIGHT: Everyone does his or her best.

WRONG: Each of the companies reported their profits had declined.

RIGHT: Each of the companies reported its profits had declined.

Another trouble spot is the dangling modifier—the word, phrase or clause that does not refer logically or clearly to some word in the sentence. We all know what these look like: *Walking through the woods,* the trees loomed up.

◀ **Dangling Modifier**

The italicized phrase is a dangling participle, the most common of these errors.

There are also dangling infinitive phrases: *To learn to shoot well,* courses in markmanship were offered.

The way to correct the dangling modifier is to add words that make the meaning clear or to rearrange the words in the sentence to make the modifier refer to the correct word. We can easily fix the two sentences:

- Walking through the woods, *the runaway boy* felt the trees loom up at him.
- To learn to shoot well, *the police* were offered courses in markmanship.

Related parts of the sentence should not be separated. When they are separated, the sentence loses clarity.

◀ **Misplaced Words**

Adverbs such as *almost, even, hardly, just, merely, scarcely, ever* and *nearly* should be placed immediately before the words they modify:

VAGUE: He only wanted three keys.

CLEAR: He wanted only three keys.

VAGUE: She nearly ate the whole meal.
CLEAR: She ate nearly the whole meal.

Avoid splitting the subject and verb:

AWKWARD: She, to make her point, shouted at the bartender.
BETTER: To make her point, she shouted at the bartender.

Do not separate parts of verb phrases:

AWKWARD: The governor said he had last year seen the document.
BETTER: The governor said he had seen the document last year.

Avoid split infinitives:

AWKWARD: She offered to personally give him the note.
BETTER: She offered to give him the note personally.

Note: Watch long sentences. Misplaced clauses and phrases can muddy the intended meaning. Read the sentence aloud if you are unsure about the placement of certain words. Generally, the problem can be solved by placing the subject and verb of the main clause together.

Parallel Construction ►

The parts of a sentence that express parallel thoughts should be balanced in grammatical form:

UNBALANCED: The people started to shove and crowding each other.
BALANCED: The people started to shove and crowd each other.
UNBALANCED: The typewriter can be used for writing and to do finger exercises.
BALANCED: The typewriter can be used for writing and for doing finger exercises.

Pronouns ►

A pronoun should agree with its antecedent in number, person and gender. The most common errors are shifts in number and shifts in person.

WRONG: The organization added basketball and hockey to their winter program.
RIGHT: The organization added basketball and hockey to its winter program.

The pronoun *its* agrees in number with its antecedent, *the organization.*

WRONG: When one wants to ski, you have to buy good equipment.
RIGHT: When one wants to ski, he or she has to buy good equipment.

The pronouns *he* and *she* agree in person with the antecedent, *one.*
A common error is to give teams, groups and organizations the plural pronoun:

WRONG: The team played their best shortstop.
RIGHT: The team played its best shortstop.

WRONG: The Police Department wants recruits. They need 1,500 applicants.
RIGHT: The Police Department wants recruits. It needs 1,500 applicants.

A phrase or a subordinate clause should not be used as a complete sentence:

◀ Sentence Fragments

FRAGMENT: The book was long. And dull.
CORRECT: The book was long and dull.
FRAGMENT: The score was tied. With only a minute left to play.
CORRECT: The score was tied with only a minute left to play.
FRAGMENT: He worked all night on the story. And then collapsed in a heap.
CORRECT: He worked all night on the story and then collapsed in a heap.

Note: Sometimes writers use a sentence fragment for a specific writing purpose, usually for emphasis: *When in doubt, always use the dictionary. Always.*

One of the most troublesome grammatical areas for the beginning journalist is the use of tenses. Improper and inconsistent tense changes are frequent. Since the newspaper story is almost always told in the past tense, this is the anchoring tense from which changes are made.

◀ Sequence of Tenses

WRONG: He *looked* into the briefcase and *finds* a small parcel.
RIGHT: He *looked* into the briefcase and *found* a small parcel.

Not all changes from past to present are incorrect. The present tense can be used to describe universal truths and situations that are permanently true:

The Court *said* the Constitution *requires* due process.

When two actions are being described and one was completed before the other occurred, a tense change from the past to the past perfect is best for reader comprehension:

The patrolman *testified* that he *had placed* his revolver on the table.

Broadcast writers, who tell most of their stories in the present tense, can handle similar situations with a change from the present tense to the present perfect:

The company *denies* it *has paid* women less than men for comparable work.

In the course of the story, the tense should not make needless shifts from sentence to sentence. The reader is directed by the verb, and if the verb is incorrect, the reader is likely to be confused:

CONFUSING: Moore said he *shot* the animal in the back. It *escaped* from the pen in which it was kept.

The reader wonders: Did the animal escape after it was shot, or did it escape and then it was shot? If the former, inserting the word *then* at the start of the second sentence or before the verb would help make it clear. If the animal escaped and then was shot, the second sentence should use the past perfect tense to indicate this:

CLEAR: It *had escaped* from the pen in which it was kept.

Spelling ▶

Good spellers use the dictionary. Poor spellers do not. Every editor knows that some writers cannot spell well. Editors accept this, but they do not accept excuses for misspelled words. They expect all their reporters to use the dictionary.

The first step in improving spelling is to diagnose the particular spelling problem. One frequent cause of misspellings is mispronunciation. We usually spell as we pronounce, and if we say *goverment, sophmore, Febuary, athalete* and *hinderance,* this is how we will spell these words—incorrectly.

Sometimes we are fooled by words that sound alike or nearly alike but have different meanings:

accent, ascent, assent	formally, formerly
accept, except	irrelevant, irreverent
advice, advise	later, latter
affect, effect	loose, lose
allusive, elusive, illusive	moral, morale
altar, alter	precede, proceed
capital, capitol	prophecy, prophesy
choose, chose	respectfully, respectively
complement, compliment	stationary, stationery
decent, descent, dissent	who's, whose

One way to overcome a spelling problem is to keep a list of words you often misspell. Poor spellers usually assume they are spelling correctly, which is one reason poor spellers give for not using the dictionary. To start your list, here is a compilation of commonly misspelled words. Look them over. If any surprise you, jot them down.

Basic Reference

A dictionary is kept at hand on the desk. Many reporters carry pocket dictionaries with them on assignments.

accommodate	exaggerate	parallel
a lot	exhilarate	possess
already	exorbitant	precede
altogether	February	prejudice
arctic	finally	privilege
athlete	forty	restaurant
calendar	governor	seize
career	grammar	separate
cemetery	harass	siege
commitment	hindrance	sophomore
competent	immediately	strictly
consensus	indispensable	tragedy
dependent	judgment	truly

descendant	lightning	undoubtedly
ecstasy	mathematics	vacuum
eighth	nickel	villain
embarrass	nuclear	weird
environment	occurrence	

◄ Usage

The dictionary is a guide to meaning as well as to spelling. Use it to distinguish between words of similar sound and spelling such as the following words that are frequently confused. They are not synonyms.

anticipate, expect	lay, lie
because, since	lighted, lit
boycott, embargo	like, as
compose, comprise, constitute	majority, plurality
convince, persuade	misdemeanor, felony
due to, because of	pretense, pretext
fewer, less	rack, wrack
flaunt, flout	ravage, ravish
imply, infer	rebut, refute
last, latest	rifle, riffle

◄ Jargon

Avoid using the specialized terminology of the sciences, arts and academic disciplines. Jargon is unintelligible to lay people, and when it comes into common usage, as has much computer terminology, it is pretentious.

JARGON: As a caterer, she interfaces with many of the city's most prominent business people.
BETTER: As a caterer, she meets many of the city's most prominent business people.
JARGON: Many people have been losing money in the bear market.
BETTER: Many people have been losing money as prices on the stock market have been declined.

◄ Clichés

Many once brilliant metaphors and figures of speech are now so commonplace that they are bankrupt of meaning. Don't rely on clichés such as these to describe a situation or to present an image: *an eye for an eye, a far cry, nose to the grindstone, beast of burden, high time, water under the bridge, when the chickens come home to roost.*

Because these sentences and phrases are heard everywhere, all the time, writers have them imprinted in their memory banks, and in the writer's struggle to find an apt expression they pop out. Shove them back in again.

George Orwell advised writers to be wary of using any phrase they are accustomed to seeing in print.

Wordiness ►

Good writing is crisp and clear. Each word contributes to the meaning of the sentence. Flabby writing can be improved by trimming useless words. Usually this means letting nouns and verbs do the work.

One way to tighten a sentence is to use the positive form for assertions. The positive form not only shortens the sentence, but also can replace adjectives or verb phrases with active verbs.

WORDY: Mrs. Jones said she would not buy the company's products because the company advertises on television programs that portray violence.

BETTER: Mrs. Jones said she would boycott the company's products because the company advertises on television programs that portray violence.

WORDY: In a campus poll, 35 percent of freshmen said they do not trust politicians.

BETTER: In a campus poll, 35 percent of freshmen said they distrust politicians.

A change from the negative to the positive form emphasizes the meanings of subject complements:

WEAK: Three of the six council members were not present at last night's meeting.

STRONGER: Three of the six council members were absent from last night's meeting.

WEAK: Professor Smith does not care about his students' complaints about homework.

STRONGER: Professor Smith is indifferent to his students' complaints about homework.

Writers who make each word count avoid the use of qualifying adjectives and adverbs such as *very, rather, quite, kind of, sort of* and *somewhat.* A play that is very good is simply good—unless it is excellent. A man who is rather tall is tall—or he towers. Someone who is rather tired is either tired or exhausted.

The use of modifiers also leads to another symptom of muddy writing: redundancies.

Editor & Publisher carried this cutline:

The Associated Press staff in Santiago, Chile, goes back to work after armed gunmen from the Manuel Rodriguez Patriotic Front raided the office.

If the raiders were gunmen, obviously they were armed.
The use of adjectives and adverbs leads to these absurdities:

totally destroyed	successfully docked
first annual	fatally killed
serious crisis	

Here is a list of the most common redundancies seen in newspaper copy. It was compiled by the Minnesota Newspaper Association:

absolutely necessary	important essentials
advance planning	necessary requirements
ask the question	open up
assemble together	other alternative
at a later day	patently obvious
attached hereto	plain and simple
at the present time	postpone until later
canceled out	reasonable and fair
carbon copy	redo again
city of Chicago	refer back
close proximity	refuse and decline
consensus of opinion	revert back
continue on	right and proper
cooperate together	rise up
each and every	rules and regulations
enclosed you will find	send in
exactly identical	small in size
fair and just	still remain
fall down	temporarily suspended
first and foremost	totally unnecessary
friend of mine	true facts
gathered together	various and sundry
honest truth	

Sometimes redundancies and other useless words come in the form of prepositions added to verbs:

call up	pay out
drop off	send off, send over
end up	shout out
go out	start up

WORDY: She immediately called up her doctor.
BETTER: She immediately called her doctor.
WORDY: The couple paid out $30,000 in back taxes.
BETTER: The couple paid $30,000 in back taxes.
WORDY: Doc's Diner's sales have dropped off 15 percent since the campus grill opened up in October.
BETTER: Doc's Diner's sales have dropped 15 percent since the campus grill opened in October.

Another way to tighten your writing is to combine sentences:

WORDY: Mitch Ellington is the youngest player to make a hole-in-one on the course. He is 13.
BETTER: Thirteen-year-old Mitch Ellington is the youngest player to make a hole-in-one on the course.

Public Opinion Polling Checklist

The Necessities ▶

Reporters should satisfy themselves on each of the following points before making extensive use of any poll:

- **Date:** When was the poll taken? Later polls are more accurate than earlier ones in political races as people have less time to change their minds.

- **Interviews:** How many were made? How were they conducted? Face-to-face interviews at home are best; telephone polls are quicker and cheaper. Mail surveys achieve small returns and those answering may be nonrepresentative.

- **Methods:** Does the pollster divulge the methods used and allow reporters to see computer breakdowns that are the basis of the pollster's conclusions? How have those who "don't know" been handled in adding up the final percentages? What was the technique used to estimate those who are eligible to vote and those likely or unlikely to vote? How big is the subsample of groups that is being broken out for specific analysis?

- **Disclosure:** What part of the data is disclosed and what part is not? If the data are released by sources other than the pollster, does the material have the approval of the pollster? Is the material self-serving?

- **Sample:** Who was interviewed and how were interviewees selected? Was a probability sample used? (Did everyone eligible have an equal likelihood of being interviewed?) If a probability sample was used, how was the list compiled from which the sample was drawn? The population sampled should be made clear. Make sure the poll claims no more than the people in the sample are qualified to say.

- **Questions:** Is the exact wording of all questions provided? Questions can be slanted to favor a predetermined result. (A national mail survey asking who voters favored for the Republican nomination for president offered only the names of conservative candidates.) The questions may be unclear. Are the questions of the generally accepted type for the purpose? If not, were they pretested?

• **Interviewers:** Who are they? Survey interviewers are supposed to be trained for the task. Campaign workers and reporters often are not. (Most reputable newspaper and television polls are conducted by professional organizations.)

• **Sponsor:** Is it clear who paid for the poll and who made it? Polls made by businesses, trade groups, candidates and political parties should be scrupulously examined.

• **Accuracy:** Does the information include the error allowance or margin of error that will allow the results to be set within the actual limits of reliability? All polls should include this information, and the reporter should include it in the story. A pollster or a politician cannot claim that a 51 to 49 result is conclusive if the margin of error is the usual 3 percentage points in a national poll. Readers and listeners should know this. (See "Margin of Error.")

Early Polls

Polls taken some time—a month or more—before an election say more about the state of the campaign at that precise moment than about the possible outcome. The closer to election day, the less time for voters to change their minds. But voters are often undecided even as they enter the voting booth.

The release of early polls by a candidate may be intended to influence the election. The press itself may accomplish the same result with its own early polling, although there is no clear evidence that the "bandwagon influence" is any more real than the "underdog influence." The victory the newspapers and everyone else forecast for Thomas E. Dewey in 1948 turned out to be almost as sour a prediction as the Landon victory in 1936. One newspaper, the *Chicago Tribune*, went so far as to banner Dewey's victory across page one in an early edition. One of the most famous political photographs shows a beaming Harry Truman holding the *Tribune* the day after the election.

There is no question that a strong start helps a candidate and that early polls showing strength can affect donations and press coverage. Cash tends to follow success. A potential donor may divert a contribution from what appears to be a losing cause. The press also takes cues from early polls. A third or fourth finisher in a preprimary poll will not be given as much coverage as the leaders. Thus, a self-fulfilling prophecy is brought about: The polls say Bettinger is trailing; we will not spend much time covering his primary campaign, which guarantees the public will know little of Bettinger. Without adequate press coverage, Bettinger cannot compete equally, and he loses.

Margin of Error

If a poll were to be made of everyone in a group that we want to learn something about, our conclusions would be completely reliable. But because of such practical considerations as time and cost, population samples must be used, and they lead to sampling error—the difference between what we would have learned from the entire group (called the *universe* in polling parlance) and what we found out from the sample.

The more people interviewed, the smaller the margin of error. At a 95 percent confidence level—which means that in 95 of 100 surveys the data will be within the limits of the margin of error stated—the error will be:

Number Interviewed	Margin of Error
50	± 14 percent
200	± 7
600	± 4
1,500	± 3
9,600	± 1

If we wanted the maximum confidence (99 percent) and the minimum margin of error (plus or minus 1 percent), we would have to interview 16,590 people. In national polls, a 95 percent confidence level with a 3 percentage point margin of error is usually accepted as meaningful.

By the time a national pollster has conducted a number of polls on the same question, his or her cumulative totals sometimes approach the numbers that give maximum confidence and minimum margin of error.

The margin of error should be applied to all polling results so that they do not seem to be more exact than they are. Here is how the margin of error is applied:

With a 3 percent margin of error, a candidate's percentage can move up or down 3 points, which is a 6 percent range or spread. Thus, polling results that are close cannot be said to favor one or the other of the candidates. With a 3 percent margin of error, any results that are separated by 6 percentage points or fewer are too close to call.

A poll that shows Jackson leading Torrance 53 to 47 could actually be a nip-and-tuck race, 50 to 50 (subtracting 3 percent from Jackson; adding 3 percent to Torrance). Or it could be decisively for Jackson, 56 to 44 (adding 3 percent to Jackson and subtracting 3 percent from Torrance).

If the poll showed Jackson leading Torrance 52 to 48 with a 3 percent margin of error, the actual result might be Torrance ahead 51 to 49 (subtracting 3 percent from Jackson and adding 3 percent to Torrance).

Even these margins do not tell the full story. Five times out of 100 (the confidence level) our poll can be off target. Also, these are the lower limits of possible error. There are problems that exist beyond the statistical area, such as the human errors made during polling and the mistakes made in interpreting the results.

Stories about polls should include the margin of error. Predictions about the results must be measured against the limits set by these statistical necessities. The reporter should tell the whole story, including what he or she does not know.

Subgroups

Pollsters make groupings on the basis of religion, occupation, sex, region, race and income. The generalized assumption of the pollster is that people with particular characteristics will vote in ways that differ significantly from the voting patterns usually evident among persons with other characteristics.

This has led to such generalities as Jewish areas vote more Democratic than the overall average; Lutherans vote more Republican; factory workers vote more Democratic; farmers vote more Republican. When such groups behave differently, change their normal voting proportions, there is a story in the shift.

However, journalists should be cautious about drawing conclusions from such data. The way a person votes is a reflection of a variety of influences. Also, patterns change as old ethnic neighborhoods break up or as workers become more affluent. As the culture becomes more diverse, it is increasingly difficult to establish a cause-and-effect relationship. Beware of single-cause explanations.

• **Saliency:** Do opinions reflect subject matters of importance to respondents? Do respondents have enough information to understand the question?

• **Interpretation:** What does the pollster or source distributing the results claim? Has the poll been fragmented in the interpretation so that only favorable results are used? Does the pollster or source claim more than the results indicate? Sometimes a segment of a poll will be used to assert that a certain part of the population favors a candidate when the actual sample of that part of the population is too small for the claims. The smaller the sample, the larger the margin of error.

Polls and surveys are useful additions to the standard reporting techniques. There is nothing magical, nothing fraudulent about polls. Used within the limits of their capabilities by discerning journalists, they extend the reporter's eyes and ears beyond the traditional interviewing process.

◀ **Summing Up**

Newspapers should describe how they conduct their polls. One way to do this is to run a short piece next to the main story explaining the polling methods used. Here is a piece that could serve as a model:

This poll is based on telephone interviews November 18 through 23 with 600 adults who live in the city.

The telephone numbers were chosen in such a way that all sections of the city were represented in proportion to population. Numbers were formed by random digits, thus permitting access to unlisted and listed numbers.

The results have been weighted to take account of household size and to adjust for variations in the sample relating to race, sex, age and education.

In theory, it can be said that in 95 cases out of 100 the results based on this sample differ by no more than four percentage points in either direction than from what would have been obtained by interviewing all adults in the city.

The theoretical errors do not take into account a margin of additional error that could result from the several practical difficulties in taking any survey of public opinion.

How to Use the FOIA—
Freedom of Information Act

**Who Can Make
a Request?** ▶

The FOIA permits "any person" to request access to agency records.

In practice, this includes U.S. citizens, permanent resident aliens and foreign nationals, as well as corporations, unincorporated associations, universities, state and local governments and members of Congress.

**How Quickly
Will an Agency
Respond?** ▶

The FOIA requires an agency to respond to an initial request within 10 working days and to an administrative appeal within 20 working days.

An agency may take an additional 10 days to respond to either the initial request or the administrative appeal in "unusual circumstances" involving the agency's need to obtain records from field facilities, process separate and distinct records or consult with another agency or two or more of its own components having a substantial interest in the request.

If the agency fails to comply with the applicable time limit requirements, the requester is deemed to have exhausted his or her administrative remedies and may seek satisfaction in court. In such a case, however, if the agency can show that "exceptional circumstances" exist and that it is exercising due diligence in responding to the request, the court may retain jurisdiction and allow the agency additional time to complete its review of the records.

Otherwise, upon any determination by an agency to comply with a request, the FOIA requires that the records "shall be made promptly available" to the requester.

Where to Write ▶

The first order of business in making an FOIA request is to determine which agency should receive it.

If you are uncertain about which agency may have the information you seek, go to the library and check records you want and find out the specific mailing address for its FOIA office.

Sample Request Letter

Tel. No. (business hours)
Return Address
Date

Name of Public Body
Address

To the FOI Officer:

This request is made under the federal Freedom of Information Act, 5 U.S.C. 552.

Please send me copies of [*Clearly describe what you want. Include identifying material, such as names, places and the period of time about which you are inquiring. If you wish, attach news clips, reports and other documents describing the subject of your research.*]

As you know, the FOI Act provides that if portions of a document are exempt from release, the remainder must be segregated and disclosed. Therefore, I will expect you to send me all nonexempt portions of the records that I have requested and ask that you justify any deletions by reference to specific exemptions of the FOI Act. I reserve the right to appeal your decision to withhold any materials.

I promise to pay reasonable search and duplication fees in connection with this request. However, if you estimate that the total fees will exceed $ _____, please notify me so that I may authorize expenditure of a greater amount.

[Optional] I am prepared to pay reasonable search and duplication fees in connection with this request. However, the FOI Act provides for waiver or reduction of fees if disclosure could be considered as "primarily benefiting the general public." I am a journalist employed by [*name of news organization*] and intend to use the information I am requesting as the basis for a planned article [*broadcast*]. [*Add arguments here in support of fee waiver.*] Therefore, I ask that you waive all search and duplication fees. If you deny this request, however, and the fees will exceed $ _____, please notify me of the charges before you fill my request so that I may decide whether to pay the fees or appeal your denial of my request for a waiver.

As I am making this request in the capacity of a journalist and this information is of timely value, I will appreciate your communicating with me by telephone, rather than by mail, if you have any questions regarding this request. Thank you for your assistance, and I will look forward to receiving your reply within 10 business days, as required by law.

Very truly yours,

[Signature]

Describing What You Want ▶

The FOIA simply requires that a request must "reasonably describe" the records being sought. This means that the description must be sufficiently specific so that a government employee who is familiar with an agency's filing system will be able to locate the records within a reasonable amount of time. There is no requirement that you explain why you are seeking the information, but such an explanation might be necessary if you want the agency to waive its fees or comply more fully with your request. The more precise and accurate the request, the more likely you are to get a prompt and complete response, with lower search fees. If you do not give a clear description of the information that is being requested, the agency will contact you for clarification.

Plan Your Request Strategy ▶

Informal Request. The first step, suggests David H. Morrissey of Colorado State University, should be to "make a personal, informal request with the government. . . . Mention you've tried to find the information in the library, or by contacting an expert in the field. Let them know you've put some work into this. Be polite. Then ask for their help." You might at this stage, he says, get at least some of what you need. Officials like this as it avoids a lot of paperwork for them.

• Try to limit your request to what you really want. If you simply ask for "all files relating to" a particular subject (including yourself), you may give the agency an excuse to delay its response and needlessly run up search and copying costs.

• If you know that the request involves a voluminous number of records, try to state both what your request includes and what it does not include.

• Try to be specific about the "search logic" you want the agency to follow. Use *and/or* to describe the different subject matters under request. By using the word *and* between different topics (for example, "mail openings *and* surveillance"), you may receive information that falls into both categories but receive none of the documents that relate *only* to "mail openings" or *only* to "surveillance."

• If you want material released to you in an order of specific priorities, inform the agency of your needs; for example, you might want to have materials reviewed and released to you in chronological or geographical order, or you may simply not want to wait for *all* of the records to be reviewed before any are released.

• Decide whether you want to write a local or regional office of a given agency instead of (or in addition to) the headquarters. Headquarters will ordinarily have policy-making information, plus information of a more general nature than the local officials have chosen to report; the field offices ordinarily have the working files.

Identify What You Want as Clearly as Possible ▶

• If there are published accounts—newspaper clips, articles, congressional reports, etc.—of the material requested, these should be cited specifically. If they are brief, it may also be helpful to enclose copies of relevant sections.

• If you know that portions of the requested records already have been released, point this out. (It may eliminate or reduce search fees.) Give information, if possible, to identify that release (i.e., date, release number, original requester).

• If you know the title or date of a document, who wrote it, the addressee, or the division or field office of the agency in which it originated, such information should be included.

Code of Ethics

Adopted by the Society of Professional Journalists, Sigma Delta Chi, 1987.

The Society of Professional Journalists, Sigma Delta Chi, believes the duty of journalists is to serve the truth.

We believe the agencies of mass communication are carriers of public discussion and information, acting on their Constitutional mandate and freedom to learn and report the facts.

We believe in public enlightenment as the forerunner of justice, and in our Constitutional role to seek the truth as part of the public's right to know the truth.

We believe those responsibilities carry obligations that require journalists to perform with intelligence, objectivity, accuracy, and fairness.

To these ends, we declare acceptance of the standards of practice here set forth:

I. RESPONSIBILITY: The public's right to know of events of public importance and interest is the overriding mission of the mass media. The purpose of distributing news and enlightened opinion is to serve the general welfare. Journalists who use their professional status as representatives of the public for selfish or other unworthy motives violate a high trust.

II. FREEDOM OF THE PRESS: Freedom of the press is to be guarded as an inalienable right of people in a free society. It carries with it the freedom and the responsibility to discuss, question, and challenge actions and utterances of our government and of our public and private institutions. Journalists uphold the right to speak unpopular opinions and the privilege to agree with the majority.

III. ETHICS: Journalists must be free of obligation to any interest other than the public's right to know the truth.

1. Gifts, favors, free travel, special treatment or privileges can compromise the integrity of journalists and their employers. Nothing of value should be accepted.

2. Secondary employment, political involvement, holding public office, and service in community organizations should be avoided if it compromises the integrity of journalists and their employers. Journalists and their employers should conduct their personal lives in a manner that protects them from conflict of interest, real or apparent. Their responsibilities to the public are paramount. That is the nature of their profession.

3. So-called news communications from private sources should not be published or broadcast without substantiation of their claims to news value.

4. Journalists will seek news that serves the public interest, despite the obstacles. They will make constant efforts to assure that the public's business is conducted in public and that public records are open to public inspection.

5. Journalists acknowledge the newsman's ethic of protecting confidential sources of information.

6. Plagiarism is dishonest and unacceptable.

IV. ACCURACY AND OBJECTIVITY: Good faith with the public is the foundation of all worthy journalism.

1. Truth is our ultimate goal.

2. Objectivity in reporting the news is another goal, which serves as the mark of an experienced professional. It is a standard of performance toward which we strive. We honor those who achieve it.

3. There is no excuse for inaccuracies or lack of thoroughness.

4. Newspaper headlines should be fully warranted by the contents of the articles they accompany. Photographs and telecasts should give an accurate picture of an event and not highlight a minor incident out of context.

5. Sound practice makes clear distinction between news reports and expressions of opinion. News reports should be free of opinion or bias and represent all sides of an issue.

6. Partisanship in editorial comment that knowingly departs from the truth violates the spirit of American journalism.

7. Journalists recognize their responsibility for offering informed analysis, comment, and editorial opinion on public events and issues. They accept the obligation to present such material by individuals whose competence, experience, and judgment qualify them for it.

8. Special articles or presentations devoted to advocacy or the writer's own conclusions and interpretations should be labeled as such.

V. FAIR PLAY: Journalists at all times will show respect for the dignity, privacy, rights, and well-being of people encountered in the course of gathering and presenting the news.

1. The news media should not communicate unofficial charges affecting reputation or moral character without giving the accused a chance to reply.

2. The news media must guard against invading a person's right to privacy.

3. The media should not pander to morbid curiosity about details of vice and crime.

4. It is the duty of news media to make prompt and complete correction of their errors.

5. Journalists should be accountable to the public for their reports and the public should be encouraged to voice its grievances against the media. Open dialogue with our readers, viewers, and listeners should be fostered.

VI. PLEDGE: Adherence to this code is intended to preserve and strengthen the bond of mutual trust and respect between American journalists and the American people.

The Society shall—by programs of education and other means—encourage individual journalists to adhere to these tenets, and shall encourage journalistic publications and broadcasters to recognize their responsibility to frame codes of ethics in concert with their employees to serve as guidelines in furthering these goals.

Glossary

These definitions were provided by the press associations and working reporters and editors. Most of the brief entries are from the *New England Daily Newspaper Study,* an examination of 105 daily newspapers, edited by Loren Ghiglione (Southbridge, Mass.: Southbridge Evening News Inc., 1973).

Print Terms

add An addition to a story already written or in the process of being written.

assignment Instruction to a reporter to cover an event. An editor keeps an assignment book that contains notations for reporters such as the following:

Jacobs—10 a.m.: Health officials tour new sewage treatment plant.

Klaren—11 a.m.: Interview Ben Wastersen, possible Democratic congressional candidate.

Mannen—Noon: Rotary Club luncheon speaker, Horlan, the numerologist. A feature?

attribution Designation of the person being quoted. Also, the source of information in a story. Sometimes, information is given on a not-for-attribution basis.

background Material in a story that gives the circumstances surrounding or preceding the event.

banger An exclamation point. Avoid. Let the reader do the exclaiming.

banner Headline across or near the top of all or most of a newspaper page. Also called a *line, ribbon, streamer, screamer.*

B copy Bottom section of a story written ahead of an event that will occur too close to deadline for the entire story to be processed. The B copy usually consists of background material.

beat Area assigned to a reporter for regular coverage—for example, police or city hall. Also, an exclusive story.

body type Type in which most of a newspaper is set, usually 8- or 9-point type.

boldface Heavy, black typeface; type that is blacker than the text with which it is used. Abbreviated *bf.*

break When a news development becomes known and available. Also, the point of interruption in a story continued from one page to another.

bright Short, amusing story.

bulldog Early edition, usually the first of a newspaper.

byline Name of the reporter who wrote the story, placed atop the published article. An old-timer comments on the current use of bylines: "In the old days, a reporter was given a byline if he or she personally covered an important or unusual story, or the story was an exclusive. Sometimes if the writing was superior, a byline was given. Nowadays, every-

Joel Sartore,
Wichita Eagle-Beacon.

one gets a byline, even if the story is a rewrite and the reporter never saw the event described in the story."

caps Capital letters; same as *uppercase.*

caps and lower case Initial capital in a word followed by small letters. See **lowercase.**

caption See **cutline.**

clip News story clipped from a newspaper, usually for future reference.

cold type In composition, type set photographically or by pasting up letters and pictures on acetate or paper.

column The vertical division of the news page. A standard-size newspaper is divided into five to eight columns. Also, a signed article of opinion or strong personal expression, frequently by an authority or expert—a sports column, a medical column, political or social commentary.

copy Written form in which a news story or other material is prepared.

copy flow After a reporter finishes a story, it moves to the city desk where the city editor reads it for major errors or problems. If it does not need further work, the story is moved to the copy desk for final editing and a headline. It then moves to the mechanical department.

correction Errors that reach publication are retracted or corrected if they are serious or someone demands a correction. Libelous matter is always corrected immediately, often in a separate news story rather than in the standard box assigned to corrections.

correspondent Reporter who sends news from outside a newspaper office. On smaller papers, often not a regular full-time staff member.

crony journalism Reporting that ignores or treats lightly negative news about friends of a reporter. Beat reporters sometimes have a tendency to protect their informants in order to retain them as sources.

crop To cut or mask the unwanted portions, usually of a photograph.

cut Printed picture or illustration. Also, to eliminate material from a story. See **trim.**

cutline Any descriptive or explanatory material under a picture.

dateline Name of the city or town and sometimes the date at the start of a story that is not of local origin.

deadline Time at which the copy for an edition must be ready.

edition One version of a newspaper. Some papers have one edition a day, some several. Not to be confused with *issue,* which usually refers to all editions under a single date.

editorial Article of comment or opinion, usually on the editorial page.

editorial material All material in the newspaper that is not advertising.

enterprise copy Story, often initiated by a reporter, that digs deeper than the usual news story.

exclusive Story a reporter has obtained to the exclusion of the competition. Popularly known as a *scoop,* a term never used in the newsroom.

feature Story emphasizing the human or entertaining aspects of a situation. A news story or other material differentiated from straight news. As a verb, it means to give prominence to a story.

file To send a story to the office, usually by wire or telephone or to put news service stories on the wire.

filler Material used to fill space. Small items used to fill out columns where needed. Also called *column closers* and *shorts.*

flag Printed title of a newspaper on page one. Also known as *logotype* or *nameplate.*

folo Story that follows up on a theme in a news story. When a fire destroyed a parochial school in Chicago, newspapers followed up the fire coverage with stories about fire safety precautions in the Chicago schools.

free advertising Use of the names of businesses and products not essential to the story. Instead of the brand name, use the broad term *camera* for Leica or Kodak.

futures calendar Date book in which story ideas, meetings and activities scheduled for a later occurrence are listed. Also known as a *futures book.* Kept by city and assignment editors and by careful reporters.

good night An expression meaning there is nothing further for the reporter from the desk for the day. On some newspapers, the call is made for the lunch break, too. Desks need to know where their reporters are in case of breaking stories.

graf Abbreviation for *paragraph.*

Guild Newspaper Guild, an international union to which reporters and other newspaper workers belong. Newspapers that have contracts with the Guild are said to be "organized."

handout Term for written publicity or special-interest news sent to a newspaper for publication.

hard news Spot news; live and current news in contrast to **features.**

head or headline The display type over a printed news story.

head shot Picture featuring little more than the head and shoulders of the person shown.

HFR Abbreviation for "hold for release." Material that cannot be used until it is released by the source or at a designated time. Also known as *embargoed material.*

insert Material placed between copy in a story. Usually, a paragraph or more to be placed in material already sent to the desk.

investigative reporting Technique used to unearth information that sources often want hidden. This type of reporting involves examination of documents and records, the cultivation of informants, painstaking and extended research. Investigative reporting usually seeks to expose wrongdoing and has concentrated on public officials and their activities.

In recent years, industry and business have been scrutinized. Some journalists contend that the term is redundant, that all good reporting is investigative, that behind every surface fact is the real story that a resourceful, curious and persistent reporter can dig up.

italics Type in which letters and characters slant to the right.

jump Continuation of a story from one page to another. As a verb, to continue material. Also called *runover.*

kill To delete a section from copy or to discard the entire story; also, to *spike* a story.

lead (pronounced *leed*) First paragraph in a news story. In a direct or straight news lead, it summarizes the main facts. In a delayed lead, usually used on feature stories, it evokes a scene or sets a mood.

Also used to refer to the main idea of a story: An editor will ask a reporter, "What's the lead on the piece?" expecting a quick summary of the main facts.

Also, a tip on a story; an idea for a story. A source will tell a reporter, "I have a lead on a story for you."

localize To emphasize the names of persons from the local community who are involved in events outside the city or region: A local couple rescued in a Paris hotel fire; the city police chief who speaks at a national conference.

lowercase Small letters, as contrasted with capitals.

LTK Designation on copy for "lead to come." Usually placed after the **slug.** Indicates the written material will be given a lead later.

makeup Layout or design. The arrangement of body type, headlines and illustrations into pages.

masthead Formal statement of a newspaper's name, officers, place of publication and other descriptive information, usually on the editorial page. Sometimes confused with *flag* or *nameplate.*

morgue Newspaper library.

mug shot See **head shot.**

new lead See **running story.**

news hole Space in a newspaper allotted to news, illustrations and other nonadvertising material.

obituary Account of a person's death; also called *obit.*

offset Printing process in which an image is transferred from a printing plate to a rubber roller and then set off on paper.

off-the-record Describes material offered the reporter in confidence. If the reporter accepts the material with this understanding, it cannot be used except as general background in a later story. Some reporters never accept off-the-record material. Some reporters will accept the material with the provision that if they can obtain the information elsewhere, they will use it. Reporters who learn of off-the-record material from other than the original source can use it.

No public, official meeting can be off-the-record, and almost all official documents (court records, police information) are public information. Private groups can ask that their meetings be kept off-the-record, but reporters frequently ignore such requests when the meeting is public or large numbers of people are present.

op-ed page Abbreviation for the page opposite the editorial page. The page is frequently devoted to opinion columns and related illustrations.

overnight Story usually written late at night for the afternoon newspapers of the next day. Most often used by the press services. The overnight, or *overnighter,* usually has little new information in it but is cleverly written so that the reader thinks the story is new. Also known as *second-day stories.*

play Emphasis given to a news story or picture—size and place in the newspaper of the story; typeface and size of headline.

P.M. Afternoon or evening newspaper.

pool Arrangement whereby limited numbers of reporters and photographers are selected to represent all those assigned to the story. Pooling is adopted when a large number of people would overwhelm the event or alter its nature. The news and film are shared with the rest of the press corps.

precede Story written prior to an event; also, the section of a story preceding the lead, sometimes set in italic.

press release Publicity handout, or a story given to the news media for publication.

proof Reproduction of type on paper for the purpose of making corrections or alterations.

puff piece or puffery Publicity story or a story that contains unwarranted superlatives.

quotes Quotation marks; also a part of a story in which someone is directly quoted.

rewrite To write for a second time to strengthen a story or to condense it.

rewriteman Person who takes the facts of stories over the telephone and then puts them together into a story and who may rewrite reporters' stories.

roundup A story that joins two or more events with a common theme, such as traffic accidents, weather, police reports. When the events occur in different cities and are wrapped up in one story, the story is known as an *undated roundup.*

rowback A story that attempts to correct a previous story without indicating that the prior story had been in error or without taking responsibility for the error.

running story Event that develops and is covered over a period of time. For an event covered in subsequent editions of a newspaper or on a single cycle of a wire service, additional material is handled as follows:

New lead—important new information; Adds and inserts—less important information; Sub—material that replaces dated material, which is removed.

sell Presentation a reporter makes to impress the editor with the importance of his or her story; also, editors sell stories to their superiors at news conferences.

shirttail Short, related story added to the end of a longer one.

short Filler, generally of some current news value.

sidebar Story that emphasizes and elaborates on one part of another nearby story.

situationer Story that pulls together a continuing event for the reader who may not have kept track as it unfolded. The situationer is helpful with complex or technical developments or on stories with varied datelines and participants.

slant To write a story so as to influence the reader's thinking. To editorialize: to color or misrepresent.

slug Word or words placed on all copy to identify the story.

source Person, record, document or event that provides the information for the story.

sourcebook Alphabetical listing, by name and by title, of the addresses and the office and home telephone numbers of people on the reporter's beat and some general numbers—FBI agent in charge in town, police and fire department spokesperson, hospital information, weather bureau.

split page Front page of an inside section; also known as the *break page, second front page.*

stringer Correspondent, not a regular staff member, who is paid by the story or by the number of words written.

style Rules for capitalization, punctuation and spelling that standardize usage so that the material presented is uniform. Most newspapers and stations have stylebooks. The most frequently used is the common stylebook of the United Press International and the Associated Press. Some newspapers stress the "down" or "lowercase" style in their titles. Some newspapers capitalize (uppercase) frequently. Also, the unique characteristics of a reporter's writing or news delivery.

stylebook Specific listing of the conventions of spelling, abbreviation, punctuation and capitalization used by a particular newspaper or wire service. Broadcast stylebooks include pronunciations.

sub See **running story.**

subhead One-line and sometimes two-line head (usually in boldface body type) inserted in a long story at intervals for emphasis or to break up a long column of type.

text Verbatim report of a speech or public statement.

tight Refers to a paper so crowded with ads that the news space must be reduced. It is the opposite of the *wide open paper.*

tip Information passed to a reporter, often in confidence. The material usually requires further fact gathering. Occasionally, verification is impossible and the reporter must decide whether to go with the tip on the strength of the insider's knowledge. Sometimes the reporter will not want to seek confirmation for fear of alerting sources who will alter the situation or release the information to the competition. Tips often lead to exclusives.

trim To reduce or condense copy carefully.

update Story that brings the reader up-to-date on a situation or personality previously in the news. If the state legislature appropriated additional funds for five new criminal court judges to meet the increased number of cases in the courts, an update might be written some months later about how many more cases were handled after the judges went to work. An update usually has no hard news angle.

VDT Video display terminal; part of the electronic system used in news and advertising departments that eliminates typewriters. Copy is written on typewriterlike keyboards, and words appear on attached television screens rather than on paper. The story is stored on a disk or in a computer. Editing is done on the terminals.

verification Determination of the truth of the material the reporter gathers or is given. The assertions, sometimes even the actual observations, do not necessarily mean the information is accurate or true. Some of the basic tools of verification are the telephone book, for names and addresses; the city directory, for occupations; *Who's Who,* for biographical information. For verification of more complex material, the procedure of Thucydides, the Greek historian and author of the *History of the Peloponnesian War,* is good advice for the journalist:

"As to the deeds done in the war, I have not thought myself at liberty to record them on hearsay from the first informant or on arbitrary conjecture. My account rests either on personal knowledge or on the closest possible scrutiny of each statement made by others. The process of research was laborious, because the conflicting accounts were given by those who had witnessed the several events, as partiality swayed or memory served them."

wire services Synonym for *press associations,* the Associated Press and United Press International. There are foreign-owned press services to which some newspapers subscribe: Reuters, Tass, Agence France-Presse.

Broadcast Terms

actuality An on-the-scene report.

audio Sound.

close-up Shot of the face of the subject that dominates the frame so that little background is visible.

cover shot A long shot usually cut in at the beginning of a sequence to establish place or location.

cue A signal in script or by word or gesture to begin or to stop. Two types: incue and outcue.

cut Quick transition from one type of picture to another. Radio: A portion of an actuality on tape used on broadcast.

cutaway Transition shot—usually short—from one theme to another; used to avoid **jump cut.** Often, a shot of the interviewer listening.

dissolve Smooth fading of one picture for another. As the second shot becomes distinct, the first slowly disappears.

dolly Camera platform. Dolly-in: Move platform toward subject. Dolly-out: Move platform away.

dub The transfer of one videotape to another.

establishing shot Frequently a wide shot; used to give the viewer a sense of the scene of action.

FI or **fade in** A scene that begins without full brilliance and gradually assumes full brightness. **FO** or **fade out** is the opposite.

freeze frame A single frame that is frozen into position.

graphics All visual displays, such as artwork, maps, charts and still photos.

jump cut Transition from one subject to a different subject in an abrupt manner. Avoided with **cutaway** shot between the scenes.

lead-in Introductory statements to film or tape of actual event. The lead-in sets up the actuality by giving the context of the event.

lead-out Copy that comes immediately after tape or film of an actuality. The lead-out identifies the newsmaker again so listeners and viewers will know whom they just heard or saw. Used more often in radio. Also known as *tag lines.*

long shot Framing that takes in the scene of the event.

medium shot Framing of one person from head to waist or of a small group seated at a table. Known as *MS.*

mix Combining two or more sound elements into one.

montage A series of brief shots of various subjects to give a single impression or communicate one idea.

O/C On camera. A reporter delivering copy directly to the camera without covering pictures.

outtakes Scenes that are discarded for the final story.

panning or pan shot Moving the camera from left to right or right to left.

remote A taped or live broadcast from a location outside the studio; also, the unit that originates such a broadcast.

segue An uninterrupted transition from one sound to another; a sound dissolve. (Pronounced *seg-way.*)

SOF Sound on film. Recorded simultaneously with the picture.

SOT Sound on tape. Recorded simultaneously with picture on tape.

trim To eliminate material.

V/O Reporter's voice over pictures.

VTR Videotape recording.

zooming Use of a variable focus lens to take close-ups and wide angle shots from a stationary position. By using a zoom lens, a camera operator can give the impression of moving closer to or farther from the subject.

Credits

Literary

Chapter 1

pp. 1–2: Leads from the Associated Press. Used with permission. **p. 15:** Excerpt from People for the American Way. Used with permission. **p. 19:** Excerpt used with permission of *The Washington Post Deskbook on Style* edited by Robert A. Webb. New York: The McGraw-Hill Book Company. **p. 29:** Advertisement from Patrick Fagan, Keller Crescent Co.

Chapter 2

pp. 38–39: News stories from the Associated Press. Used with permission. **pp. 43–44:** Excerpts from news story from *The New York Times.* © *The New York Times.*

Chapter 3

p. 59: Front page of *Rocky Mountain News* (Shuttle Extra edition). Reprinted with permission. **p. 60:** Front page of *Amsterdam News.* Reprinted with permission. **p. 69:** Map reproduced with permission of the American Society of Newspaper Editors.

Chapter 4

pp. 102–7: Library excerpts used with permission of LEXIS®-NEXIS® a division of Reed Elsevier Inc. **pp. 107–8:** Material and map used with permission of People for the American Way.

Chapter 5

p. 120: News story from The Charlotte Observer. Used with permission. **p. 122:** News story from the Daily News. Used with permission. **p. 123:** News story from *The New York Times.* Used with permission. **p. 129:** News story from *The Charlotte Observer.* Used with permission.

Chapter 6

p. 130: Front page *New York Post.* **p. 138:** Excerpt from news story used with permission of *The Modesto Bee.* **pp. 138–39:** Excerpt from news story used with permission of the *El Paso Herald-Post.* **pp. 140–41:** News story from the *San Francisco Chronicle.* Used with permission. **pp. 141–42:** Excerpt from news story used with permission of *The Wall Street Journal.*

Chapter 7

p. 170: Excerpt from an article in *APF Reporter.* Used with permission. **p. 175:** News story from *The Miami Herald.* Used with permission. **p. 176:** Front page of the *Daily News.* Used with permission. **p. 177:** News story from *The State Journal* (Topeka, Kan.). Used with permission. **pp. 177–78:** News story from *The Fresno Bee.* Used with permission. **p. 179:** Advertisement used with permission of Keller Crescent Co.

Chapter 8

pp. 188–89: Excerpts from news story used with permission of the *Lexington* (Ky.) *Herald-Leader.* **pp. 191–92:** Excerpts from news story used with permission of the *Houston Chronicle.* **pp. 193–94:** Excerpts from news story used with permission of *The Evening Sun* (Baltimore). **pp. 198–200:** Excerpts from news story used with permission of the Associated Press. **p. 204:** News story from *The Fresno Bee.* Used with permission. **pp. 209–10, 212, 214, 216–17:** Excerpts from news stories in *The Blade* (Toledo). Used with permission.

Chapter 9

pp. 221, 222, 223, 224, 228, 229: Excerpts from Associated Press stories. Used with permission. **pp. 231–32:** Excerpts from ABC "World News Tonight" broadcast. Used with permission. **pp. 235–37:** Excerpts from WSMV-TV script. Used with permission. **pp. 237–38:** Excerpts from "The CBS Evening News." Used with permission. **p. 239:** Adapted from *Writing Broadcast News* by Mervin Block. Used with permission. (Bonus Books, 1987.)

Chapter 10

p. 249, 257–58: Excerpts from news stories in *The Philadelphia Inquirer.* Used with permission.

Chapter 11

p. 279: Excerpt from news story in the *Fort Worth Star-Telegram.* Used with permission. **p. 284:** Excerpt from story in the *Winston-Salem Journal.* Used with permission. **pp. 288–89:** By Charles M. Young. From *Rolling Stone Magazine,* June 1, 1978. By Straight Arrow Publishers, Inc., © 1978. All Rights Reserved. Reprinted by permission.

Chapter 12

p. 299: Excerpt from news story in *The New York Times.* Used with permission. **p. 304:** Excerpt from news story in *The Albuquerque* (N.M.) *Journal.* Used with permission.

Chapter 13

pp. 306–7: Excerpts from news story in *The St. Petersburg Times.* Used with permission. **p. 320:** Portion of front page of *The Wall Street Journal.* Used with permission.

Chapter 14

p. 327: Page excerpt from the *Winston-Salem Journal.* Used with permission. **pp. 333–35:** Excerpts from news stories in *The Providence Journal-Bulletin.* Used with permission.

Chapter 15

pp. 350, 351–52: Excerpts from news stories in *The Sacramento Bee.* Used with permission.

Chapter 16

pp. 370–71: Excerpt from news story in *The Brattleboro* (Vt.) *Reformer.* Used with permission. **pp. 371–72:** Excerpt from news story in *The* (Louisville) *Courier-Journal.*

Chapter 18

p. 401: News story from *The News Gazette,* Champaign-Urbana, Ill. Used with permission. **p. 402:** News stories from the *Associated Press* and the *Herald-Dispatch,* Huntington, W. Va. Used with permission.

Chapter 19

p. 409: News story from *Sanders County Ledger.* Used with permission. **p. 411:** Excerpt from *Indian Country Today.* Used with permission.

Chapter 20

p. 427: Police log from the *Argus Leader* (Sioux Falls, S.D.). Used with permission. **p. 444:** Excerpt from news story from the *Belleville* (Ill.) *News-Democrat.* Used with permission. **p. 449:** Line art from U.S. Dept. of Justice. **p. 451:** Excerpt from news story from *The Anniston* (Ala.) *Star.* Used with permission.

Chapter 21

p. 472: Excerpts from news stories from the *Sun-Sentinel,* Ft. Lauderdale, Fla.

Chapter 22

pp. 485–86: Excerpts from news story from the *Herald-Leader,* Lexington, Ky. Used with permission. **p. 505:** TV script excerpt by Howard Weinberg. Used with permission.

Chapter 23

p. 519: Excerpt from news story by Associated Press. Used with permission. **p. 522:** Column by Brend Schmidt reprinted from the *Argus Leader* with permission.

Chapter 24

p. 560: Excerpt from news story by the Associated Press. Used with permission. **p. 563:** Excerpts from news stories in the *Arkansas Gazette.* Used with permission. **p. 564:** Excerpt from news story. Used with permission. **p. 575:** Excerpt from news story from *The Blade.* Used with permission.

Chapter 26

p. 607: Excerpt from *Columbia Journalism Review.* Used with permission.

Chapter 27

pp. 631–32: Excerpt from news story from *The Blade.* Used with permission. **p. 633:** Cartoon from *Tobacco-free Youth Reporter.*

Photo

Part Openers

1: Jack Rendulich, *The Duluth News-Tribune;* **2:** Carlos Antonio Rios, *Houston Chronicle;* **3:** Greg Latza, *Argus Leader;* **4:** Bob Zellar, *The Billings* (Mont.) *Gazette;* **5:** Dave Kline, *Eagle-Gazette,* Lancaster, Ohio; **6:** John Harte, *The Bakersfield Californian.*

Chapter 1

Opener: Chris Hardy, *San Francisco Examiner;* **p. 5 (top and bottom):** Associated Press; **p. 18:** Jack Ackerman, *The Blade;* **p. 21:** © John Carl D'Annabile, *Times Union;* **p. 22:** © Capital Cities/ABC, Inc.; **p. 23 (bottom):** *Argus Leader,* Sioux Falls, S.D.

Chapter 2

Opener: Steve Apps, *The Post-Crescent,* Appleton, Wisc.; **p. 35:** Kevin Hann, *The Toronto Sun;* **p. 38:** Doug Carroll, *The Norfolk Daily News;* **p. 47:** Bart Ah You, *The Modesto Bee.*

Chapter 3

Opener: Naomi Halperin, *The Morning Call,* Allentown, Pa.; **p. 56:** The Library of Congress; **p. 62 (left):** © Joel Strasser; **p. 64:** Mark B. Sluder, *The Charlotte Observer,* courtesy of Knight Publishing Company.

Chapter 4

p. 100 (left): Charles Ruppman, *Daily News;* **p. 107:** courtesy of People For The American Way.

Chapter 5

Opener: Phil Sears, *Tallahassee Democrat;* **p. 129:** Robert Lahser, *The Charlotte Observer.*

Chapter 6

Opener: Michael Norcia, *New York Post;* **p. 136:** © Associated Press; **p. 138:** Debbie Noda, *The Modesto Bee* **p. 141:** Kerwin Plevka, *Houston Chronicle.*

Chapter 7

p. 155: © Gregg Lovett; **p. 170 (top and bottom):** Vince Heptig, courtesy of Alicia Patterson Foundation; **p. 173:** Mark Henle, *The Phoenix Gazette.*

Chapter 8

Opener: Bob Thayer, *The Journal-Bulletin,* Providence, R.I.; **p. 188:** Anita Henderson, *Beloit* (Wis.) *Daily News;* **p. 189:** Tom Woods II, *The Lexington Herald-Leader;* **p. 190:** Betty Tichich, *Houston Chronicle;* **p. 192 (left and right):** Steve Campbell, *Houston Chronicle;* **p. 195:** James J. Malloy, *The Providence Journal;* **p. 201:** Steve Ueckert, *Houston Chronicle;* **p. 210:** Tom O'Reilly, *The Blade;* **pp. 212–13:** Alan Detrich, *The Blade;* **p. 215:** David Zapotosky, *The Blade;* **p. 219:** American Heritage Center, University of Wyoming.

Chapter 9

Opener: © National Broadcasting Company, Inc.; **p. 230:** © National Broadcasting Company, Inc.; **p. 241:** © Capital Cities/ABC, Inc.

Chapter 10

Opener: Jeff McAdory, *The Commercial Appeal;* **p. 246:** Jim Urick, *The Port St. Lucie News;* **p. 250:** © Mark Avery; **p. 258:** Lena H. Sun, *Washington Post;* **p. 261:** Frank Woodruff, *Sun-Bulletin,* Binghamton, NY.

Chapter 11

Opener: Rick Mussacchio, *The Tennessean;* **p. 273:** © Greg Lovett; **p. 276:** Bob Thayer, *The Providence Journal-Bulletin.;* **p. 278:** Rodger Mallison, *Fort Worth Star-Telegram;* **p. 284:** Charles Buchanan, *Winston-Salem Journal.;* **p. 292:** Charlie Starr, *The San Diego Union-Tribune.*

Chapter 12

Opener: Todd Panagopoulos, *The Star,* Chicago Heights, IL.; **p. 297:** Joe Munson, *The Kentucky Post;* **p. 302 (top):** Plumas County Museum; **p. 302 (bottom):** National Archives, Washington, DC.

Chapter 13

Opener: John Davenport, *The Houston Chronicle.;* **p. 307:** Ken Elkins, *The Anniston Star.*

Chapter 14

Opener: © National Broadcasting Company, Inc.; **p. 335:** Andy Dickerman, *The Providence Journal-Bulletin;* **pp. 337, 345:** © Joel Strasser.

Chapter 15

p. 350: Rich Turner, *The Stockton Record;* **p. 363:** United Press International.

Chapter 16

Opener: Bob Thayer, *The Providence Journal;* **p. 368:** Robert E. Kollar, *Tennessee Valley Authority;* **p. 375:** © Joan Vitale Strong.

Chapter 17

Opener: John Walker, *The Fresno Bee;* **p. 383:** The Library of Congress; **p. 384:** John Walker, *The Fresno Bee;* **p. 386:** Bob Christy, *Daily Kent Stater;* **p. 390:** © Marc Geller.

Chapter 18

Opener: Juan Carlos, *Ventura County* (Calif.) *Star;* **p. 402:** Ricardo Ferro, *St. Petersburg Times;* **p. 405:** © Joel Strasser; **p. 406:** Kevin Rice, *Ventura County Star;* **p. 407:** Victoria Sayer Pearson, *Ventura County Star.*

Chapter 19

Opener: © Toby Gardner; **p. 410:** © Joel Strasser; **p. 416:** Susan Kirkman, *The* (Akron) *Beacon Journal.*

Chapter 20

Opener: Randy Piland, *The Macon* (Ga.) *Telegraph;* **p. 424:** Rodolfo Gonzales, *San Antonio Light;* **p. 431:** Rodger Mallison, *Forth Worth Star-Telegram;* **p. 432:** O. Gordon Williamson, Jr., *The Orlando Sentinel;* **p. 440:** Freeman Ramsey, *The Tennessean;* **p. 450:** Dave Kline, *Eagle-Gazette,* Lancaster, Ohio; **p. 451:** Jeff Widener, *Evansville Press.*

Chapter 21

p. 454: Richard Carson, *The Houston Chronicle;* **p. 465:** Nancy Stone, *The Plain Dealer;* **p. 468:** *Ventura County Star;* **p. 474:** John Davenport, *The Houston Chronicle.*

Chapter 22

Opener: Dave Kline, *Eagle-Gazette,* Lancaster, Ohio; **p. 485:** Yo Nagaya and James Madison University, Dept. of Communications; **p. 486:** Morris Berman, *Pittsburgh Post-Gazette;* **p. 488:** Joel Sartore, *The Wichita Eagle-Beacon;* **p. 494:** New York Racing Authority; **p. 499:** Bob Thayer, *The Journal-Bulletin;* **p. 500:** Chris Dawson, *The Press Democrat;* **p. 505 (top):** © Howard Weinberg; **p. 511:** © Joel Strasser; **p. 512:** Bob Zellar, *The Billings Gazette.*

Chapter 23

Opener: Courtesy of G.T. Capital Management; **p. 516:** Bob Thayer, *The Journal-Bulletin;* **p. 522:** *Argus Leader* **p. 525 (top and bottom):** The National Archives; **p. 529:** © Joel Sartore, *The Wichita Eagle-Beacon;* **p. 536:** The New York Stock Exchange.

Chapter 24

Opener: Frank Woodruff, *Sun-Bulletin,* Binghamton, NY; **p. 545:** *The New York Post,* photo by Robin Graubard; **p. 546 (top left):** The Plumas County Museum; **p. 546 (top right):** Larry C. Price, *The Philadelphia Inquirer Magazine;* **p. 546 (bottom):** Mel Finkelstein, *New York Daily News, Inc.;* **p. 547:** Debbie Noda, *The Modesto Bee;* **p. 565:** James Woodcock, *The Billings Gazette;* **p. 576:** Mike Roemer, *Argus Leader,* Sioux Falls, SD.

Chapter 26

Opener: Durall Hall, Jr., *The Courier-Journal ;* **p. 605 (right):** Planned Parenthood Federation of America, Inc.; **p. 617:** David C. Neilsen II, *Mercury-Register,* Oroville, Calif.

Chapter 27

Opener: Bob Thayer, *The Journal-Bulletin;* **p. 625:** Schomburg Center for Research in Black Culture, The New York Public Library, Astor, Lenox, and Tilden Foundation; **p. 626:** The Library of Congress.

Appendix G

p. 680: © Joel Sartore, *Wichita Eagle-Beacon.*

Name Index

B

Babel, Isaac, 165
Bagdikian, Ben, 69–70, 75, 648
Baker, Ray Stannard, 626
Baker, Russell, 251, 488
The Bakersfield Californian, 618
Ball, Lucille, 301
Baltimore, 206, 474
The Baltimore Sun, 149, 182, 356, 623
Bangor (Maine) *Daily News,* 420, 633
Barber, James David, 184
Barber, Red, 497
Barlett, Donald L., 217–18, 263–64, 314
Barrett, Edward W., 646
Barrett, Joan, 240
Barrows, Frank, 190, 483
Barry, Marion, 331–32
Bartlett's Familiar Quotations, 78
Barzun, Jacques, 116
The Beacon Journal (Akron, Ohio), 416
Beasley, David M., 277
The Beatles, 70, 356
Beck, Joan, 154
Becker, Gretchen, 370
Beethoven, Ludwig van, 50, 344, 609
Before the Gates of Excellence: The Determinants of Creative Genius, 397
Begody, Irene, 173
Behrens, John C., 270
Belasco, David, 209
Belk, Henry, 273
Bell, Alexander Graham, 397
Belleville (Ill.) *News-Democrat,* 443–44
Bellow, Saul, 181
Beloit (Wis.) *Daily News,* 188
Benedict, Helen, 344, 346, 452
Benjamin, Burton, 53, 648
Bennett, James Gordon, 56
Bensman, Joseph, 53, 254
Bentham, Jeremy, 624, 625
Berg, Thomasine, 153
Bergmann, Barbara, 507
Berke, Richard L., 277, 375, 376
Berkeley, Bill, 290
Berkow, Ira, 507, 508, 514
The Berkshire Eagle (Pittsfield, Mass.), 420, 518
Berlin, Isaiah, 187, 395, 632
Berman, Morris, 486
Bernstein, Carl, 30, 37, 307, 362
Bernstein, Michael, 608
Berra, Yogi, 488–89
Berry, Raymond, 381
Best Newspaper Writing, 185
Bettag, Tom, 22, 241
Beveridge, W.I.B., 272, 274, 276, 292
Bible, 51, 131, 163, 180, 634
Bierce, Ambrose, 118
Bigart, Homer, 35, 276–77, 415
The Billings (Mont.) *Gazette,* 512, 565

Birmingham, Ala., 584
Bitter Cry of the Children, 383
Black, Max, 648
Blackburne, Laura D., 309
Black Like Me, 282, 642
Blackwell, Sam, 156
The Blade (Toledo, Ohio), 18, 209–10, 212, 214, 215, 575, 629
Blake, William, 293
Block, Mervin, 183, 221–26, 229, 239, 241, 264
Blum, Howard, 341–42
Blumer, Herbert, 75
Bly, Nellie, 30, 640
Blyskal, Jeff, 251
Blyskal, Marie, 251
Boasberg, Al, 421
Boccardi, Louis D., 82–83
Bogart, John B., 57
Bogart, Leo, 65, 70
Bohannon, Ross, 476
Bonner, Raymond, 44, 49
Boorstin, Daniel J., 252, 270
Bosnia, 4, 240
Boston, 206, 443, 600
The Boston Globe, 146, 147, 169, 308
Boswell, Thomas, 119, 496
Bouton, Jim, 487
Bovard, O.K., 275
Boyden, Helen Childs, 415
Boyer, Peter J., 242
Boyle, Hal, 153
The Boys of Summer, 513, 514
The Boys on the Bus, 270
Bracker, Milton, 416
Bradlee, Benjamin C., 64, 68
Bradley, Bill, 298
Bradley, Joseph B., 388
Bradley-Steck, Tara, 197
Bradshaw, Terry, 512
Branzburg v. Hayes, 597
The Brattleboro (Vt.) *Reformer,* 370
Brecher, Elinor J., 447
Breed, Warren, 647
Brennan, William J., 586, 587, 588, 598
Breslin, Jimmy, 184, 197, 265, 329
Bridgeman, P.W., 160
Brink, William, 176
British Broadcasting Corporation, 66
Britt, Bonnie, 473
Broadcast Newswriting: The RTNDA Reference Guide, 241
Broder, David, 549, 550
Brody, Jane E., 123
Brontë, Emily, 180
Brown, Cailin, 21
Brown, Jerry, 332
Brown, Les, 331
Brown, Peter, 634
Brown, Tyrone, 602

Brown v. Board of Education, Topeka, 296, 586
Bryant, Paul (Bear), 592
Buchanan, Charles, 284
Buchanan, Edna, 51, 134–35, 142–43, 157, 169, 409, 422, 434–35, 447, 452
Buchanan, William, 409
Buchwald, Art, 218, 642
Bucks County Courier Times, 456
Buffalo Female Academy, 158
Bugbee, Emma, 410
Buñuel, Luis, 388
Bunyan, John, 180
Burger, Warren, 598, 599
Burroughs, William, 162
Busch, Gussie, 510
Bush, George, 253, 266, 313, 476–77
Business Information Sources, 537
Business Week, 526
Butts, Wally, 592
But We Were Born Free, 48–49

C

Caesar, Julius, 55, 57
California, 423, 571, 572, 578, 591, 594, 599, 601, 611
Calley, William, 276–77
Cambodia, 43, 44
The Camera Age: Essays on Television, 241
Campbell, Carroll A., Jr., 277
Campbell, Steve, 192
Campbell, Will, 634
Canada, 15, 300
Cannon, Jimmy, 497
Cannon, Lou, 46
The Canterbury Tales, 296
Cantrell v. Forest City Publishing Co., 593
Capital Cities/ABC, Inc., 22, 241
Capote, Truman, 346, 357, 452
Cappon, Jack, 171
Carey, Art, 206, 403
Carlin, George, 615
Carlos, Juan, 401
Caro, Robert, 182
Carroll, Doug, 38
Carroll, Lewis, 119
Carson, Richard, 454
Carson, Traci, 301
Carter, Hodding, 30, 628, 648
Carter, Jimmy, 330
Cassidy, John, 385
Castro, Fidel, 67, 238–39, 279, 280
The Catcher in the Rye, 15, 132, 569
Cater, Douglass, 602
Cather, Willa, 180
Catholic Diocese of Trenton, N.J., 564
CBS, 611, 637
CBS Evening News, 224, 237, 241

Cecil, David, 187
Center for Responsive Politics, 550
Centers for Disease Control and
   Prevention, 74, 88–89, 101
Cerf, Bennett, 358
Chaffee, Zechariah, Jr., 602
Chambers, Marcia, 298, 300, 374
Chancellor, John W., 53, 132, 133
Changing Times, 526
The Charlotte (N.C.) *Observer,* 64, 65,
   91, 120, 624
Chaucer, Geoffrey, 296
Chekhov, Anton, 159, 286
Chesterton, G.K., 416
Chicago, 525, 559
Chicago Sun-Times, 264, 604, 642
Chicago Tribune, 138, 147, 471, 614,
   623, 671
Chicago Tribune Press Service, 77
China, 9–10, 20, 55, 66, 250, 251, 258
The Chocolate War, 107
The Christian Science Monitor, 148,
   607, 633
Christy, Bob, 386
The Chronicle of Higher Education, 510
Ciardi, John, 145, 155, 183
Cicero, 175
Citizen Hearst, 187, 219
Civil War, 187, 296, 567, 625
Clark, Kenneth, 307
Clark, Mike, 71
Clark, Roy Peter, 184
Cleveland, 206
Cleveland, Grover, 397
Cleveland State University, 590
Clinton, Bill, 253–54, 304, 477
Clinton, Hillary, 253–54
Clurman, Richard, 75
Cochran, Johnnie, 470
Coffey, Raymond R., 7, 19
Cohen, Richard, 392
Cohen v. Cowles Media, 601
Coker, Matt, 67
Cole, William, 336, 366
Coles, Robert, 289
College Board, 575
College Entrance Examination
   Board, 578
Collum, Joe, 262
Colorado, 423
The Color Purple, 569
Columbia Journalism Review, 607
Columbia University, 286, 530
Columbus, Christopher, 567
Come to Judgment, 421
Coming of Age in Samoa, 289
Commager, Henry Steele, 509
The Commercial Appeal (Memphis), 245
Commission on Freedom of the Press,
   49, 53, 623, 624
Common Sense, 172

*Computer Assisted Research: A Guide to
   Tapping Online Information,* 116
Confessions of a Muckraker, 342–43
Confessions of an S.O.B., 259
Confucius, 175
Congressional Quarterly, 84
Connecticut, 423, 569, 571
Connell, Fowler, 491
Connolly, Cyril, 296
Conover, Joseph I., 427
Conrad, Joseph, 296, 634
Constitution (Atlanta), 46
Cookman, Claude, 617–18
Coolidge, Calvin, 516
Cooney, John Michael, 183
Copernicus, Nicolaus, 339
Cormier, Robert, 107
Cornell University, 604
Cotchett, Joseph W., 466
Cottell, John, 315
The Courier-Journal (Louisville),
   371, 604
Courson, Steve, 504
*Cox Broadcasting Corp. v. Martin
   Cohn,* 594
Cox Newspapers, 85
Coy, Peter, 148
CPA Institute, 532, 533, 534
Craft and Consciousness, 53
Cremin, Lawrence A., 579
*Crime in the United States, Uniform
   Crime Reports,* 425, 428, 439, 442,
   445, 446
Crime Story, 482
Cronkite, Walter, 241
Croteau, Maureen, 116
Crouse, Timothy, 270
Cuomo, Mario, 240
Current Biography, 78
Curtis Publishing Co., 592
Curtis Publishing Co. v. Butts, 591

D

Daily Kent Stater, 386
The Daily Mirror, 146
Daily News (New York), 24, 25, 26, 58,
   100, 110, 122, 131, 137, 144, 146,
   176, 368, 466, 546, 557, 619
Daily Pilot, 67
The Daily Progress (Charlottesville,
   Va.), 629
Daley, Richard, 361, 559
Dallas, 503
The Dallas Morning News, 629
D'Amato, Alfonse, 84
Dana, Charles A., 57
Daniel, Clifton, 641
Daniells, Lorna, 537
D'Annabile, John Carl, 21
The Danville (Ill.) *Commercial News,* 590

Dart, Justin, 331
Darwin, Charles, 386, 567
Data Center and Clearinghouse for
   Drugs & Crime, 90
Datatimes, 99
Davenport, John, 306, 474
Davis, Elmer, 48
Davis, Richard Harding, 178–79
Davis, Robbie, 494
Davis, Sammy, Jr., 419
Dawson, Chris, 500
Day, Benjamin H., 56
A Day in the Life of America, 638
Dayton (Ohio) *Daily News,* 84
Dean, Dizzy, 488
DeBartolo, Edward, Jr., 511
Debs, Eugene V., 627
Deciding What's News, 75
Deckert, Rod, 636
DeConcini, Dennis, 361
Dedman, Bill, 624
Deeb, Gary, 70
Deep Throat, 307, 362
Defoe, Daniel, 175
DeIulio, John, 547
Delaware, 571, 578
Delta Democrat-Times (Greenville,
   Miss.), 628
de Maupassant, Guy, 276
Dempsey, Jack, 484
Dennis, Everette, 622
Denniston, Lyle, 602
Denora, Pa., 407
Denver, 206
DePuano, Mike, 489
Desert Storm, 74
The Des Moines Register, 434, 506, 612
Dessauer, Phil, 499
Detrich, Alan, 212–13
Detroit, 206
The Detroit News, 38, 622
*Developing Understanding of Self and
   Others,* 107
Dewey, John, 298, 393, 625, 635,
   641, 647
Dewey, Thomas E., 671
Dialog, 99
Dickens, Charles, 14, 132, 157, 181,
   227, 568, 633, 661
Dickerman, Andy, 335
Dictionary of American Biography, 78
Dietemann v. Time, Inc., 594
Dillinger, John, 508
Dimitrius, Jo-Ellan, 464
Discovering the News, 75
Doar, Rheta Childe, 383
Dobbs, Lou, 527
Dodds, Tracy, 512
Doe v. Duncanville, 570
Dole, Robert, 304, 375
Dombey and Son, 633

Garrett, Robert T., 371
Garrison, Jayne, 560, 564
Gartner, Michael, 362
Gates, Daryl, 332
Gavshon, Arthur L., 307–8, 313
Gaye, Marvin, 462
Gazette (Indiana, Pa.), 163
Geidel, Paul, 620–22, 623, 624
Geiselman, R. Edward, 407
Geismar, Maxwell, 153
Gelfand, Lou, 392
Geller, Mark, 390
General Electric, 70, 532
General Motors, 531, 532, 536
George Polk award, 74, 262, 286
Georgetown University, 501
Georgia, 571, 578, 594, 626
Gerald, J. Edward, 648
Gerchas, Maryanne, 470
Gers, Irving E., 116
Gershen, Martin, 415
Gertz, Elmer, 587
Gertz v. Robert Welch, Inc., 587, 592
Getlin, Josh, 540
Ghiglione, Loren, 680
Giago, Tim, 391
Gibbons, Bob, 508
GI Bill of Rights, 267
Gibson, Bob, 510
Gibson, Casper Carroll, 608
Gide, André, 59
Gideon's Trumpet, 305
Gilbert, Douglas, 421
Gill, Brendan, 332
Gingrich, Arnold, 361
The Girls in the Balcony: Women, Men, and The New York Times, 30
Gladstone, William Ewart, 552
GLOBE, 34
Go Ask Alice, 107
Goethe, Johann Wolfgang von, 609
Goffman, Erving, 310
Golden Fleece awards, 588
Goldensohn, Robert, 516
Goldie, Diane M., 472
Goldman, Ronald, 456, 466
Gomez, David, 286
Gone with the Wind, 606
Gonzales, Rodolfo, 424
Gonzalez, J.J., 363–65
Good Housekeeping, 633
Goodman, Walter, 240
Good War: An Oral History of World War Two, 185
Gooseberries, 286
Gould, Stephen Jay, 291
Gourmet, 34
Governing New York City, 579
Governing Urban America, 579
Graff, Henry F., 116
Graham, Billy, 71

Graham, Donald E., 622
Graham, Philip L., 625
Gramm, Phil, 375
Gramsci, Antonio, 641
The Grapes of Wrath, 90
The Grateful Dead, 82, 416
Graubard, Robin, 545
Great Depression, 525, 608, 609, 646
The Great Gatsby, 159
Greeley, Horace, 187, 300
Greenbelt Cooperative Inc., 530
Greene, Bob, 263, 309, 312, 354–55
Greenfield, Mass., 518
Greenmoss Builders, 592
The Greenville (S.C.) *News,* 368
Greenwich, Conn., 558
Gretzky, Wayne, 381
Griffey, Ken, Jr., 509
Griffin, George, 14
Griffin, Howard, 282
Grimes, Sara, 173, 285
Gross, Terry, 351
Grossfeld, Stan, 169
Grossman, Lawrence K., 643
Group Psychology and the Analysis of the Ego, 607
Growald, Richard H., 491
GT Capital Management, 515
Guanche, Andrew, 416
Guatemala, 170
Guide to Business and Economics Journalism, 537
Guinness Book of World Records, 622
Gumbel, Bryant, 325
Guthrie, Patricia, 286
Guzman Reynoso, Abimael, 17, 18
Gwinnett (Ga.) *Daily News,* 486

H

Haggerty, Mike, 531
Halberstam, David, 218, 395, 510, 514
Hale, Edward Everett, 118
Hall, Durall, Jr., 604
Hall, Joe B., 499
Hallas, Clark, 260, 500
Halperin, Naomi, 55
Halvorsen, Donna, 85, 624
Hamill, Pete, 311
Hamilton, Alexander, 266
Hamilton, David, 50
Hammarskjöld, Dag, 271–72
Hampshire, Stuart, 641
Hand, Learned, 602
Hands, Susan V., 483, 491, 495
Hann, Kevin, 35
Hanover, Donna, 318–19
Hanson, Kathleen A., 322
Harding, Warren G., 182, 384, 627
Hardwick, Elizabeth, 4
Hardy, Chris, 3
Hardy, G.B., 394

Harlan, John Marshall, 614
Harmetz, Aljean, 136
Harper's Bazaar, 64
Harrison, George, 356
Harris Poll, 109
Harte, John, 618
Hartford, Conn., 569
The Hartford Courant, 616
Harvard University, 610
Harvey, John, 218
Hastings, Karen, 190
Hawaii, 571, 578
The Hawk Eye (Burlington, Iowa), 326, 554
Hawpe, David W., 72
Hawthorne, Nathaniel, 181
Hayakawa, S.I., 389, 397, 410
Hayes, Elizabeth, 473
Hayes, Harold, 182
The Headline vs. The Bottom Line, 531
Hearst, William Randolph, 57, 187, 219, 484
Heath, Jena, 128–29
Hechler, David, 202
Hecht, Ben, 219
Heider, Don, 235
Heilbroner, Robert L., 389
Hemingway, Ernest, 14, 153, 154, 158, 159, 395
Hemp, Paul, 535
Henderson, Anita, 188
Henkel, Cathy, 490
Henle, Mark, 173
Henry, Wendy, 360
Heptig, Vince, 170
Herald (New York), 56
Herald-Dispatch (Huntington, W. Va.), 402, 610
The Herald Tribune, 146
Herbert, Bob, 305
Herman, Judith Lewis, 313
Herschberger, Vern, 633
Hersey, John, 180, 270, 641, 643
Hersh, Seymour, 275, 378, 380
Herzberg, Joseph G., 50, 187
Heschel, Abraham, 634
Hess, Stephen, 270, 322
Hesse, Hermann, 322
Hewitt, Don, 241
Hewlett, Sylvia, 579
Hiassen, Carl, 195
Higgins, Marguerite, 416
Hiltzik, Michael A., 520–21
Hirschhorn, Robert B., 464
History of the Pelopennesian War, 680
Hodding Carter: The Reconstruction of a Racist, 30, 648
Hodson, Thomas S., 472
Holbrook, Hal, 15
Hollings, Ernest, 605

Kravetz, Nathan, 141
Kress, Mary, 309–10
Kristof, Nicholas D., 9–10
Kristol, Irving, 274, 298, 546
Kroeger, Brooke, 30
Kuehl, Mike, 523
Kueter, Mary, 24
Ku Klux Klan, 302, 350
Kuralt, Charles, 227
Kurtz, Howard, 391, 392, 638

L

Lahser, Robert, 129
Lakota Times, 63
Lalli, Frank, 527
Landauer, Jerry, 380
Landers, Ann, 197
Landi, Joe, 363
Landon, Alf, 112, 671
Lange, Dorothea, 646
Language in Thought and Action, 397
Language of Prejudice, 387
Lapchick, Richard, 509
Lardner, John, 493
Lardner, Mike, 508
Lardner, Ring, 162, 383
Lasch, Christopher, 625
Las Vegas Review-Journal, 504
Law Dictionary for Non-Lawyers, 603
Lawlor, Eric, 191–92, 201
LA Youth, 611
Leader-Telegram (Eau Claire, Wis.), 629
League of Women Voters, 556
Leaking: Who Does It? Who Benefits? At What Cost?, 323
Le Carré, John, 315
Lectures in America, 164
The Ledger (Lakeland, Fla.), 629
Lee, Irving, 387
Lee, Spike, 169, 175, 392
Lehr, Dick, 147
Lemann, Nicholas, 316, 328, 345
Leonard, Benny, 489
Leonard, Buck, 489
Leonard, Elmore, 344
Lester, Will, 37
Let Us Now Praise Famous Men, 289, 292
Levi, Primo, 177
Levine, Irving R., 527
Levi Strauss & Co., 114
Levitt, Leonard, 189
Levy, Howard B., 276–77
Lewin, Leonard, 146
Lewis, Anthony, 44–45, 305, 602, 645
Lewis, Carl, 496
Lewis, John, 548
Lewis, Oscar, 289, 356
Lexington Herald-Leader, 188–89, 485, 499, 590
Lexis®-Nexis®, 14, 84, 99, 101–7

Liberty, 602
Liebling, A.J., 33, 53, 336, 347, 366
Life, 594–95, 614
Lilienfield, Robert, 53, 254
Lin, Wendy, 137
Lincoln, Abraham, 180
Lindsay, John, 557
Lippmann, Walter, 268, 281, 305, 310, 388, 397, 413
Lipson, Steve, 529
Lipstadt, Deborah, 279–80, 292
Literary Digest, 112
Little, Carl Victor, 130
Locke, Tates, 506
Loeb, Marshall, 527
Loercher, Diana, 339
Loh, Jules, 188, 198–200, 365
Loizeaux, Jack, 137
Lomax, Michael, 564
Long Island, N.Y., 16
Lopez, Laura, 17
Lopez, Rosa, 470
Lorentz, Pare, 646
Los Angeles, 206
The Los Angeles Times, 19, 77, 84, 259, 331, 435, 540, 604, 605, 611, 623
Louisiana, 571, 578
Louisiana State University, 503
Lovejoy, Elijah P., 625
Lovelady, Steve, 217–18
Lovett, Greg, 155, 273
Lowe, Bob, 500
Lowe, Robert B., 260
Lubow, Arthur, 57, 178
Lunden, Joan, 34
Lyons, Louis, 156

M

Mabry, Rebecca, 612
MacArthur, Charles, 219
Macdonald, Dwight, 124
MacDougal, Kent, 526
Mack, Richard, 342–43
MacLaine, Shirley, 71
MacMasters, Paul K., 602
MacMullan, Jackie, 487
The Macon (Ga.) *Telegraph,* 422
Madison, Wis., 259
Magazine Publishers Association, 633
Magna Charta, 296
Mahoney, Kathleen Ann, 520–21
Mailer, Norman, 162
Maine, 571, 572, 578
Make No Law: The Sullivan Case and the First Amendment, 602
Makinson, Larry, 550
Mallison, Rodger, 278, 431
Malloy, James J., 195
Malraux, André, 421
Manchild in the Promised Land, 12
Manley, Dexter, 504–5

Mann, Horace, 300
Mantle, Mickey, 488, 514
March, Hal, 394
Marcus, Norman, 514
Margiotta, Joseph M., 557
Marimow, Bill, 562
Marino, Vivian, 519–20
Markham, Edwin, 383
Marsh, Jack, 23, 24, 393, 476
Marshall, Thurgood, 146–47, 275, 411, 476, 588
Marx, Groucho, 421
Marx, Jeffrey, 499
Maryland, 571, 596, 601
Maslin, Paul, 112
Massachusetts, 568, 571, 601
Massachusetts Bay Colony, 564
Mass Media Law, 603
Masters, William H., 613
Matlack, Carol, 562–63
Mattingly, Terry, 70
Matuschka, 609
Maurois, André, 674
Maxine's Tree, 15
May, Clifford D., 359
Mayer, Louis B., 264
McAdory, Jeff, 245
McCabe, Charles, 493
McCarthy, Joseph, 48, 379, 382
McCarver, Tim, 510
McCormally, John, 416
McCormick, Mona, 116
McCoy, Edwin, 566
McCulloch, Frank, 648
McDonald, Duncan, 655
McDonald's Corp., 534–35
McGill, Ralph, 163
McGinniss, Joe, 270
McGuffey's Readers, 355
McKelway, St. Clair, 131
McNamara, Joseph, 122
McNulty, Henry, 154
McPhee, John, 132, 180, 202, 204, 298
McSorley's Wonderful Saloon, 218
McVeigh, Timothy J., 461
Mead, Margaret, 289
Mears, Walter R., 53, 132, 133
The Meat Market: The Inside Story of the N.F.L. Draft, 514
Media Circus: The Trouble with America's Newspapers, 392
The Media Monopoly, 69, 75
Media Studies Journal, 482
Medline, 84
Medrano, Gabe, 431
Mehta, Ved, 641
Melville, Herman, 181, 190
Memphis, 279
Memphis Daily Appeal, 130
Mencken, H.L., 182, 294, 295, 651
Mercer, Lucy, 63

Mercury-News (San Jose), 90, 466
Mercury-Register (Oroville, Calif.), 617
Meredith, James, 591
Merrimack, N.H., 577
Merritt, Gilbert, 476
Mertens, Bill, 554
Meyer, Philip, 116
Meyers, Christopher, 618
Miami, 443
The Miami Herald, 51, 134, 142, 175, 195
Miami University, 502
Michaels, James, W., 527
Michigan, 423, 573, 589
Michigan State University, 501
Mickey Mouse, 515
Mies van der Rohe, Ludwig, 224, 421
Miller, Ed, 84
Miller, Jack, 137
Miller, Marvin, 514
Miller, Norman C., 253, 255
Miller v. California, 612
Millikan, Robert, 397
Mills, Cecil J., 460
Mills, Kay, 53
Millstein, Gilbert, 181
Milosz, Czeslaw, 644
Milton, John, 90
Milwaukee, 423
Minneapolis, 600
Minneapolis Tribune, 394
Minnesota Newspaper Association, 669
Minnix, Bob, 509
Mintz, Morton, 531, 538
Mintz, Phil, 146
Minute by Minute, 241
The Mirage, 648
Miss America, 610
Mississippi, 476, 571, 578, 614
The Missoulian (Missoula, Mont.), 636, 638–39
Miss Piggy, 515
Miss U.S.A., 361
Mitchell, Andrea, 230
Mitchell, Joseph, 194, 218, 332, 346
Mitford, Jessica, 358, 366, 421
The Modern Researcher, 116
The Modesto Bee, 47, 138, 547
Moffitt, Donald, 218, 528, 538
Molly Ivins Can't Say That, Can She?, 185
Monex International Ltd., 520–21
The Money Game, 538
Montana, 571, 573, 601
Montgomery, Ala., 583–84
The Montgomery (Ala.) Advertiser, 473, 506
Moody, Sid, 138, 346
Moody's, 527, 529
The Morality of Scholarship, 648
Morey, Pat, 259
Morgan, Henry, 414–15
Morgan, Lorrie, 344

Morgenthau, Robert, 372–73
The Morning Call (Allentown, Pa.), 55
The Morning Record and Journal (Meriden, Conn.), 420
Morris, Richard B., 129
Morrissey, David H., 381, 676
Moschandreas, Katherine, 113
Moses, Robert, 182
Mosher, Steven, 251
The Most of A.J. Liebling, 336, 366
Moyers, Bill, 18–19, 207–9, 505
Moynihan, Daniel Patrick, 545
MTV, 125
Muasacchio, Rick, 271
Muhammad, Khalid Abdul, 386
Mulligan, Arthur, 26–28
Mulvoy, Mark, 483
Munson, Joe, 297
The Murders in the Rue Morgue, 272
Murdoch, Rupert, 66
Murray, Donald, 151, 183
Murray, Jim, 488
Murrow, Edward R., 30, 49, 227, 240, 241, 242, 280
Murrow: His Life and Times, 242
The Muskegon (Mich.) Chronicle, 629
My Favorite Summer 1956, 514
My Lai, 276, 378

N

Nagaya, Yo, 485
The Naked Ape, 614
Nassau County, N.Y., 560
National Assessment of Educational Progress (NAEP), 97, 296, 571, 572
National Association of College and University Business Officers, 501
National Association of Manufacturers, 526
National Basketball Association, 510
National Collegiate Athletic Association (NCAA), 498, 499, 503, 504, 507
National Commission on Excellence in Education, 572
National Enquirer, 68
National Football League (NFL), 491, 510, 512, 514
National Geographic, 638
National Guard, 404
National League of Cities, 556
National Municipal League, 556
National Press Photographers Association, 298
National Rifle Association, 83
National Transporation Safety Board, 403, 404
The National Zip Code & Post Office Directory, 78
A Nation at Risk, 572
Nation's Business, 526
Nazario, Sonia L., 156

NBC, 70, 220, 230, 324, 611, 614, 637
NBC News, 623
Neak Luong, 43
Nebraska, 550, 571
Nebraska Press Association v. Stuart, 598
Negroponte, Nicholas, 81
Neilsen, David C., II, 616–17
Nellie Bly: Daredevil, Reporter, Feminist, 30
Nelson, Rick, 262
Nelson, Ricky, 413
Netscape, 108
Neuharth, Allen, 259
Nevada, 423
Never Let Them See You Cry: More from Miami, America's Heart Beat, 452
New Deal, 268, 296
New England Daily Newspaper Study, 680
New England Patriots, 512
New Hampshire, 571, 601
New Haven, Conn., 423
New Jersey, 569, 578
New Journalism, 174, 178
Newman, Barry, 52
Newman, John Henry, 175
Newman, Lisa, 19–20
New Mexico, 571, 578
The New Muckrakers, 323
Newport, Ky., 259
The New Republic, 360
The News & Observer (Raleigh, N.C.), 129
News-American (Baltimore), 589
Newsbreak, 223
The News Business, 53, 133
Newsday (Melville, N.Y.), 137, 145, 146, 147, 340
The News-Gazette (Champaign-Urbana, Ill.), 401, 612
Newsmaking, 75
Newswatch: How TV Decides the News, 75
Newsweek, 176, 360, 576, 593, 614
Newton (Conn.) Bee, 58
New York, 569, 578
New York, N.Y., 94, 176, 187, 206, 260, 268, 274, 296, 423, 432, 443, 462, 569, 579, 614
The New Yorker, 361
The New York Herald Tribune, 57, 131
New York Post, 24, 25, 130, 266, 385, 467, 545, 595, 619
New York Public Library, 625
New York Racing Authority, 494
New York Stock Exchange, 536
New York Sun, 56, 57
The New York Times, 9, 26, 30, 40, 42, 43, 44, 45–46, 50, 52, 84, 98, 103, 109, 123, 131, 136, 139, 141, 143,

276, 279, 322, 414, 499, 500, 624, 628, 643
Pumsy in Pursuit of Excellence, 107
The Purple Decades: A Reader, 129, 178
Pyle, Ernie, 179–80
Pyle, George, 611–12
Pyne, Joe, 394

Q

Quayle, Dan, 313, 343–44
Quill, 527
The Quincy (Ill.) *Herald-Whig,* 427
Quinn, Jane Bryant, 527, 532, 534
Quint, Michael, 141, 517

R

Rabi, I.I., 329–30
Raising Hell: How the Center for Investigative Reporting Gets the Story, 270
The Raleigh Times, 567
Ramsey, Freeman, 440
Rapoport, Ron, 487, 495, 497, 511–12, 513, 514
Rasmussen, Wallace, 531
Rather, Dan, 237, 240
Rawls, Wendell, Jr., 341
Rawson, Joel, 184
Read, Herbert, 150, 180
Reader's Digest, 262, 633
Reader's Guide to Periodical Literature, 78, 336
Reagan, Nancy, 70
Reagan, Ronald, 44, 46, 70, 90, 253, 313, 330, 476–77
Reasoning with Statistics, 116
Rebchook, John, 138
The Record (Bergen County, N.J.), 608
Red: A Biography of Red Smith, 514
Red Cross, 404
The Red Smith Reader, 514
Rehnquist, William H., 588–89
Reiss, Albert, 452
Rembrandt, 190
Reno Gazette-Journal, 645
Renteria, Ramon, 574
The Reporter and the Law, 602
Reporter's Handbook: An Investigator's Guide to Documents and Techniques, 305
Reporters and Officials, 323
The Reporter Who Would Be King, 57, 178
Reporting, 185
The Republic, 131, 386, 567
Reston, James, 648
Reuss-Ianni, Elizabeth, 452
Reuters, 683
Rewriting Network News: WordWatching Tips from 345 TV and Radio Scripts, 241

Reynolds, Jerry, 411
Reynolds, Joshua, 153
Rhode Island, 578
Rhodes, Robert E., 666
Rice, Kevin, 406
Richmond, Va., 584
Richmond Newspapers, Inc. v. Virginia, 598–99
Richmond (Va.) *Times-Dispatch,* 589
Rickover, Hyman G., 415
Rilling, Paul, 552
Ringwald, Christopher, 291
The Riverdale (N.Y.) *Press,* 645
Rivers, Mickey, 490
R.L. Polk and Company, 80
Robbins, Charles, 160
Roberts, Gail, 261
Roberts, Gene, 151, 273, 281
Robertson, Nan, 30
Robinson, Alan, 485
Robinson, Jackie, 510
Robinson, Ray, 514
Rock, Marcia, 292
Rockefeller, John D., 383
Rocky Mountain News (Denver), 59
Rodriguez Law, 267
Roe, Sam, 18, 209–12, 214–17, 258, 259, 353–54, 508–9, 575, 629–32
Roemer, Mike, 576
Rohr, Monica, 473
Rolling Stone, 107, 288, 607
Romanoff, Harry, 264
Roosevelt, Eleanor, 254
Roosevelt, Franklin D., 63, 112, 239, 254, 525
Roper Poll, 109, 113, 227
Rose, Charlie, 343–44
Rose Bowl, 501
Rosenbloom v. Metromedia, Inc., 587, 589
Rosenfeld, Harry M., 362
Rosenfeld, Israel, 395
Rosenthal, A.M., 238–39, 593
Rosenthal, Andrew, 266
Roshco, Bernard, 75
Ross, Diana, 558–59
Ross, Harold, 164, 183, 337
Ross, Lillian, 185, 357, 358
Rossman, Mike, 489
Rothchild, Barbara S., 141
Rothmyer, Karen, 435, 607
Roush, Edd, 497
Rowe, James L., 523
RTNDA Communicator, 229
Rukeyser, Louis, 527
Russell, Bertrand, 34, 551
Russell, Bill, 301
Russell, George, 17
Russell, Liz, 301
Rwanda, 11–12, 140, 616
Ryan, Ann, 516, 519

Ryan, Robert T., 71
Ryan, Tom, 516, 519

S

Sachs, Andrea, 493–94
Sacramento Bee, 642
A Sacred Trust. Nelson Poynter and the St. Petersburg Times, 648
Safer, Morley, 239
Salant, Richard, 63
The Salina (Kan.) *Journal,* 611
Salinger, J.D., 14, 15, 132, 569
Salt Lake City, 570
Samuelson, Robert J., 575–76
San Antonio Light, 424
Sandburg, Carl, 361
Sanders, Bob, 84–85
Sanders, Marlene, 292
Sanders, Ralph, 319, 321
Sanders County Ledger (Thompson Falls, Mont.), 409
The San Diego Union-Tribune, 292
San Francisco, 525
San Francisco Chronicle, 110, 140
San Francisco Examiner, 3, 560, 564
Santa Claus, 109
Santangelo, Paul, 415
Santyana, George, 279
Sargent, Claire, 551
Sartore, Joel, 488, 528, 680
Sasser, James, 476
Saturday Evening Post, 592
Sauter, Mark, 498
Sayre, Wallace S., 543, 579
Scaife, Richard, 607
Scalise, Larry, 464
Scanlan, Christopher, 129, 185, 333, 335, 561
Scary Stories to Tell in the Dark, 107
Schanberg, Sidney, 43–44, 49
Schiefelbein, Lynn, 23
Schiller, Dan, 53
Schlottman, Jack, 491–92
Schmertz, Herbert, 517
Schmidt, Brenda, 522–23
Schneider, Andrew, 85
Schoenberg, Nara, 258, 259
Scholastic Aptitude Test (SAT), 503, 508, 545, 566, 572, 575, 578
Schomburg Center for Research in Black Culture, 625
Schorr, Lisbeth, 214
Schott, Marge, 511
Schraeder, Terry, 308
Schudson, Michael, 75
Schwartz, Alvin, 107
Scott, George C., 156
Sears, Phil, 117
The Seattle Times, 610, 633
Selcraig, Bruce, 354
The Selling of the President 1968, 270

Selma, Ala., 584
Serrill, Michael S., 17, 18
Seton Hall University, 504, 508
The Seven Words You Can't Say on Radio and Television, 615
Severo, Richard, 414
Sexual Behavior in the Human Male, 613
Shakespeare, William, 14, 78, 180, 295
The Shame of the Cities, 626
Shanker, Albert, 573
Shaw, George Bernard, 295, 661
Shaw, Mike, 417
Sheean, Vincent, 30
Shefter, Martin, 579
Shelly, Mike, 301
Shining Path, 17, 18
Shipler, David K., 570
Shoal Creek Country Club, 511
Short, Allen, 85, 624
Shpunt, Loretta M., 164
Siebert, Fred S., 53
Siegenthaler, John, 68
Siemon, Katherine L., 465
Sigal, Leon V., 323
Sigma Delta Chi, 623, 677
Sigma Delta Chi Award, 44
Silberman, Laurence, 52
Silk, Leonard, 538
Silvestrini, Elaine, 35
Simon, David, 447–48
Simon & Schuster, 70
Simplesse, 114
Simpson, Nicole Brown, 456, 466
Simpson, O.J., 23–24, 435–38, 456, 459, 460, 463, 466, 467, 468, 469, 470, 637
Sims, Calvin, 309
Singleton, William Dean, 645
Sinnott, William, 363
Sixth Amendment, 597, 598, 599
60 Minutes, 238, 444
Skaggs, Joe, 311–12
Sketches, 294
Slaughter, Enos, 510
Sloan, Alfred P., Jr., 531
Sluder, Mark B., 64
Smith, Adam, 296, 538
Smith, H. Allen, 131
Smith, Hazel Brannon, 627–28
Smith, Joe, 528
Smith, Randy, 512
Smith, Red, 183, 184, 276, 281, 489, 493, 513, 514
Smith, Sally Bedell, 241
Smith, Sam, 490–91
Smith, Steven Cole, 287
Smith, Z.N., 648
Smoking and Health Review, 315–16
Snyder, Louis L., 129
The Social Responsibility of the Press, 648

The Social Work Interview, 346
Society of Professional Journalists, 623, 648, 677
Socrates, 387
Sohn, Pam Newell, 449, 451
Somalia, 75, 240, 616
Sosin, Milt, 306–7
Southampton, N.Y., 569
South Carolina, 571, 578
Southern Methodist University, 504
South of Heaven: Welcome to High School at the End of the Twentieth Century, 579
Spacek, Sissy, 308
Spargo, John, 383
Speaker, Tris, 397
Spectator (Columbia University), 530
Specter, Arlen, 375
Sperber, Ann M., 242
Sperber, Murray, 501
The Spokesman-Review (Spokane, Wash.), 612
Sports Illustrated, 471, 594
Sports for Sale: Television, Money, and the Fans, 514
Spuds McKenzie, 296
St. Louis, 206
St. Paul, Minn., 600
St. Paul Dispatch, 610
St. Paul Pioneer Press, 411, 610
The St. Petersburg (Fla.) *Times,* 306, 402, 583, 648
Standard & Poor's, 529, 560
Standard & Poor's Corporation Record, 527
Standard & Poor's Register of Corporations, Directors and Executives, 527
Stanford, Bruce W., 589, 603
Stanford University, 599
The Star (Chicago Heights, Ill.), 293
Star Chamber, 600
Starr, Charlie, 292
Starr, Ringo, 344
Star Tribune (Minneapolis), 85, 391, 392, 629
The State Journal, 177
Steel, Ronald, 305
Steele, James B., 217–18, 263–64, 314
Steffens, Lincoln, 30, 247, 383, 393, 542, 626
Stein, Bernard, 645
Stein, Gertrude, 153, 164
Steinbeck, John, 14, 15, 90, 107, 568, 569
Steinfels, Peter, 71
Stephen F. Austin State University, 504
Stepp, Carl Sessions, 636
Stepp, Laura Sessions, 173
Sterling, Peter, 382
Stern, Bill, 415

Stern, Howard, 616
Stevens, K.C., 191–92
Stevens, Thaddeus, 564–65
Stevens, Wallace, 172
Stevenson, Robert Louis, 50
Stockman, Thomas, 633
The Stockton (Calif.) *Record,* 350, 591
Stone, I.F., 646
Stone, Nancy, 465
Strasser, Joel, 62, 337, 345, 405, 410, 511
Strawberries in Wintertime, 514
Street Cops and Management Cops, 452
Street Corner Society, 283
Stringfellow, Eric, 465
Strong, Joan Vitale, 375
Strunk, William, Jr., 118
Stumbo, Bella, 155, 331–32
Sudbury, Ont., 34
Sugar Bowl, 330, 484
Sugg, Diane, 8, 350–52, 429–30
Sullivan, L.B., 585
Sullivan, Louis W., 316
Sulzberger, Arthur, Jr., 622
Sun, Lena H., 10, 189, 258
Sun-Bulletin (Binghamton, N.Y.), 261, 539
Sun Newspapers, 81
Sun-Sentinel (Fort Lauderdale, Fla.), 472, 473
Svenson, Andrew E., 131
Swados, Harvey, 648
Swanberg, W.A., 187, 219
Swenson, Rob, 577
Swindled: Classic Business Frauds of the Seventies, 538
Switzer, Barry, 499
Synopsis of the Law of Libel and the Right of Privacy, 603
Syracuse University, 415

T

Tai, Pauline, 531
A Tale of Two Cities, 132, 568
Talese, Gay, 30, 182
Tallahassee Democrat, 117
Tannenbaum, Jeffrey A., 203, 265, 319–20, 321
Tarbell, Ida, 383
Tarkanian, Jerry, 504, 506
Tass, 683
Tax Reform Act, 263, 314
Teague, Robert L., 146
Tecumseh Street (Toledo, Ohio), 211–14, 353
Teller, Ray, 487
Temple University, 259
The Tennessean (Nashville), 271, 440, 450
Tennessee, 578, 584

The Virginian-Pilot (Norfolk, Va.), 72, 135
Virgin or Vamp: How the Press Covers Sex Crimes, 452
Visser, Lesley, 512
Voboril, Mary, 283
Vonnegut, Kurt, 14
Voter News Service, 112

W

W & J Sloane, 530
Waiting for Prime Time: The Women of Television News, 292
Wakefield, Dan, 365
Waldman, Suzyn, 490, 512
Waldron, Ann, 30, 648
Walker, Alice, 569
Walker, Edwin, 591, 592
Walker, Herschel, 330
Walker, John, 378, 384
Walker, Jon, 23
Walker, Stanley, 20, 57, 418
Wallace, George C., 252
The Wall Street Journal, 44, 52, 57, 81, 83, 125, 141, 142, 156, 178, 253, 255, 320, 362, 380, 490, 515, 526, 534, 639–40
Wal-Mart, 518
Walsh, Rodolfo, 627
Walter Lippmann and the American Century, 305
War and Peace, 154
Ward, David, 475
Ward, Gene, 146
Ward, Phil, 82
Warner, Harry M., 397
Warren, Earl, 602
Warren, Jim, 188–89
Warrentown, W. Va., 268
Washington, 601
Washington, D.C., 11, 94, 339, 423, 442, 474, 623, 636
The Washington (N.C.) *Daily News,* 629
Washington Herald, 131
Washington Journalism Review, 240
The Washington Post, 10, 19, 37, 42, 44, 45, 46, 52, 84, 128, 148, 189, 255, 258, 259, 307, 329, 360, 369, 385, 420, 531, 589, 606, 608, 610, 614, 622, 623, 636, 640, 642, 643
The Washington Post & Times Herald, 130
Washington Post News Service, 77
The Washington Reporter, 270
The Washington Times, 137
Wasiczko, Donna, 475
Watergate, 37, 57, 148, 270, 280, 307, 362, 586, 596, 609, 610, 645
Watertown Daily Times, 291
Watson, Douglas, 329
WBAI (FM)(New York City), 615
WBRZ-TV (Baton Rouge), 234
WCCO-TV (Minneapolis), 234
Webb, Eugene J., 366

Wechsler, Herbert F., 586
Weinberg, Howard, 18, 207, 209, 505
Weir, David, 270
Weisberger, Bernard, 56
Welch, Amy, 81
Welles, Chris, 524
Wellington, C.G. (Pete), 158
Wells, Ida B., 625
West, Nathanael, 181
West, Richard G., 412
Westfall, Ed, 497
Westheimer, Ruth, 141
Westin, Av, 57, 75
West Valley School Board of Kalispell, Mont., 569
West Virginia, 476, 578
WGBH-TV (Boston), 610
Whalen, Elizabeth, 64–65
Wheelis, Allen, 633
When the Bough Breaks: The Cost of Neglecting Our Children, 579
White, E.B., 118, 385
Whitehead, Alfred North, 395
Whitehead, Ralph, 549, 550
Whiteside, Thurman, 342
Whitford, Ellen, 20, 262
Whitley, Keith, 344
Whitman, Alden, 416, 421
Whitman, Walt, 153
Whittingham, Richard, 514
Who Killed CBS?, 242
A Whole Different Ball Game: The Sport and Business of Baseball, 514
Who Owns Whom, 527
Who's Who in America, 78, 336, 683
Whyte, William Foote, 283, 285
Why Time Begins on Opening Day, 496
The Wichita Eagle-Beacon, 488, 528, 680
Wicker, Tom, 255, 314–15, 380
Widener, Jeff, 451
Wildavsky, Aaron, 552, 579
Wilke, John R., 141
Williams, Billy, 490
Williams, Frederick, 116
Williams, Juan, 392
Williams, Ted, 52, 488
Williamson, George, 140
Williamson, O. Gordon, 432
Willingboro, N.J., 564
Wilson, Cammy, 10–11, 29, 256
Wilson, Ellen, 129, 178
Wimpy, 174
Winkler, Kirk, 241
Winners & Sinners, 607–8
Winning Pulitzers, 435
Winship, Thomas, 550, 624
Winston-Salem Journal, 284, 327
Winternitz, Felix, 259
Wisconsin, 442, 569, 571
Witosky, Tom, 506
WKTV (Utica, N.Y.), 318
Woestendiek, William J., 500

Wolfe, Tom, 70, 157, 178, 200, 348
Wolfson, Lewis, W., 544
Wolin, Sheldon S., 109
Wolper, Allan, 498
Wolston, Ilya, 588
Wolston v. Reader's Digest Assn., Inc., 588
Womack, Jimmy, 330
Women of the World: The Great Foreign Correspondents, 53
Wong, Jan, 10, 20, 250
Woodcock, James, 565
Woodruff, Frank, 261, 539
Woods, Tom, II, 189
Woodward, Bob, 30, 37, 307, 362
Woodward, Stanley, 498
Woolf, Virginia, 181
Worcester, Wayne, 116, 371
Working: People Talk About What They Do All Day and What They Think of While They Do It, 172, 185
World (New York), 56
The World According to Breslin, 184
World News Tonight, 231
World Series, 495
World War II, 46, 48, 69, 267, 279, 296, 341, 608–9, 628, 657
World Wide Web, 81, 108
Woster, Kevin, 23, 24
Wright, Eric, 301
Writing Broadcast News—Shorter, Sharper, Stronger, 239, 241
Writing for Your Reader, 151
WSMV-TV (Nashville), 234, 235

Y

Yale Law School, 15
Yardley, Jonathan, 593
Years of Conscience: The Muckrakers, 648
Yeh, Emerald, 234
Yellow Journalism, 187
Yepsen, David, 549, 552
Yoffe, Emily, 365
Yom Kippur, 300–301, 651
York, Michael, 499
You, Bart Ah, 47
You Can Fool All of the People All the Time, 218
Young, Charles, 287–88

Z

Zack, Bill, 486
Zagoria, Sam, 46
Zapotosky, David, 215
Zekman, Pamela, 648
Zellar, Bob, 512
Zero Population Growth (ZPG), 548–49
Zerwick, Phoebe, 284, 326–27
Zimbabwe, 573
Zimmermann, Fred L., 307, 336, 345, 346
Zinsser, William, 497
Zunigha, Curtis, 391
Zurcher v. Stanford Daily, 599

Subject Index

Books, 303, 306
  censorship, 14–17, 107, 569
  recommended reading, 30, 53, 75,
    116, 129, 151, 184–85, 218–19,
    241–42, 270, 292, 305, 323, 346,
    366, 397, 421, 452, 482, 514,
    537–38, 579, 603, 648
  reference, 76, 78, 527
  textbooks, 386, 567–68
Bosnia, 4, 240
Boston, 206, 443, 600
Boycotts, 526
Brainwashing, 160
Breaking news stories, 28, 29, 130, 422
  leads, 134
Brevity, 33, 50, 51, 53
Brights, 202, 680
Broadcast reporting, 230–38
  fire stories, 8
  interviewing guidelines, 233
  vs. print reporting, 63, 139, 202, 220
Broadcast writing, 220–42
  anchoring tense, 227
  attribution, 221, 226, 228
  clarity, 228
  copy, 164, 238
  editing ethics, 238–39
  glossary of terms, 683–84
  guidelines, 239
  language, 220, 226–28
  leads, 229–30
  long stories, 234–38
  obscene/indecent/profane material,
    240, 614–16
  quotations and paraphrasing, 227
  reporting and writing to tape, 232
  rewriting news wires, 221–26
  sentence length, 148, 220, 230
  sentence structure, 226–28
  short news features, 232–33
  technical instructions, 238
  tenses, 227–28
  words, 227
  writing for the ear, 226–27
Budget stories, 539, 540, 552–57
  budget process, 555
  politics, 557
  school funding, 565, 573–75
  sources, 556
  story essentials, 555
  types of budgets, 554
Burglary stories, 441
Buried leads, 120–21
"Business office must," 519
Business reporting, 308, 515–38
  annual reports, 517, 521, 524, 532
  bond offerings, 517, 529–30
  earnings stories, 534–35
    story essentials, 535
  features, 515
  federal records, 524, 526

glossary of terms, 537
human interest, 519, 531, 535
interpretative stories, 515
local spot news, 515, 517, 518
puff pieces, 519
recommended journals and
  references, 526–27
requirements for covering the beat,
  517, 520
salaries, 527
sources, 521–24
stock tables, 536
story guidelines, 535

C

Cable television, 70, 616
Calculated falsehoods, 593–94
California, 423, 571, 572, 578, 591, 594,
  599, 601, 611
Call-in poll, 110
Cambodia, 43, 44
Cameras, hidden, 594–95, 601
Campaign stories, 539, 549–51
  key elements, 549
  tips on covering, 550
Campus crime stories, 445–46
Campus press freedom, 599–600
Canada, 15, 300
Capital budgets, 554
Capitalization 78, 649, 683
Cart, 230
Causal relationship, 393–94
Causes, 28–29, 39, 248, 266, 272,
  393–94, 402, 403, 450, 602
Cautions, 41, 113, 159, 266, 658, 659
  accident stories, 403, 404
  court stories, 454, 455, 457–58
  crime stories, 434, 448–49
  delayed leads, 142
  disaster stories, 407
  government stories, 556–57
  libel, 590, 591
  long stories, 205
CD-ROMs, 76, 81
Censorship, 14–17, 107, 498, 569,
  611, 640
Census data, 76, 83, 85, 86–87, 314
Chain newspapers, 68–70, 187
Charges, 39
Checklists, 126–27, 169, 171–77, 399
  accident stories
    airplane, 403–4
    motor vehicle, 402–3
  arraignment stories, 459
  arrest stories, 438, 441
  budget stories, 555
  burglary and robbery stories, 441
  civil action stories, 457
  criminal trial stories, 470
  disaster stories, 405–6

earnings and annual reports
  stories, 535
education stories
  new education programs, 578
  school board meetings, 577–78
fire stories, 450
leads, 147
meeting stories, 370
murder stories, 438
news conference stories, 374
obituaries, 408, 412
profile stories, 330
speech stories, 368
sports stories, 483, 491
  game stories, 492
Chicago, 525, 559
Child abuse, 441
Children's environmental index, 548–49
China, 9–10, 20, 55, 66, 250, 251, 258
Cigarettes, 64–65, 94, 315–16, 394,
  410, 419
Circulation wars, 57, 187
Cities with competing newspapers, 69
City desk, 24–25
City directories, 41, 80, 270, 683
City hall reporting, 26, 308, 539–64, 579
City planning stories, 539, 540, 563–64
Civil law stories, 453, 455–58
Civil rights, 68, 252, 255, 304,
  583–85, 609
Clarity, 50, 51, 130, 154, 158, 163, 164
  broadcast writing, 228
Clause leads, 135
Cleveland, 206
Clichés, 53, 229, 488, 490, 667
Climax, 124, 168, 186
Clippings, 41, 76, 317–18, 336, 337, 680
Closed-ended questions, 338
Close-ups, 232, 683
Codes of conduct, 623–24, 632–34, 636,
  642, 646–47, 677–79
  limitations of, 623–24
Colorado, 423
Combo leads, 142–43, 151
Commercials, 550
  Super Bowl, 484
Comparisons, 167
Compassion, 378, 384
Completeness, 45, 46
Compound sentences, 148
Computer-assisted reporting, 84–87, 100
Computer literacy, 81
Computers, 76, 77, 85, 99, 382
Conditional privilege, 590
Condoms, 605, 606, 607, 611
Confidential sources, 310, 325, 359,
  362, 369, 597, 600, 603
  guidelines, 362–63
Conflict, 55, 61, 201, 491
Conjunctions, 163
Connecticut, 423, 569, 571

Equation, reporter's, 280
Equity proceedings, 456
ERIC, 84
Errors, 30, 34, 41, 272, 300–301, 314–15, 409, 646
Ethics, 4, 240, 283, 341, 353, 478, 581, 595, 620–48
    altering photographs, 637
    codes of conduct, 623–24, 632–34, 636, 642, 646–47, 677–679
    limitations of, 623–24
    moral framework, 263, 641
    naming victims, 594, 636–37, 638–39
    plagiarism and fabrication, 642–43
    poses and disguises, 601, 635–36, 640, 642
Euphemisms, 161
Evolution, 567
Exit poll, 112
Expense budgets, 554
Experience, 380, 552
Experts, 312
Explanatory briefings, 255
Explanatory journalism, 267
Explicit language, 608, 613–14
Exploitation, 289
Exposés, 9, 255, 339, 630
Extreme close-ups, 232
Eyewitnesses, 306, 310, 319, 401, 403, 406, 407

F

Fabrication, 643
Facts, 20, 46, 49, 152, 157
Fair comment, 582
Fairness, 33, 45–46, 47, 53, 201, 328, 441, 582, 627, 677, 678
    guidelines, 45
Fair trial, 597–99
Farmington, Conn., 569
Features, 33, 56, 67, 186–202, 422, 681
    brights, 202, 680
    broadcasting, 202, 206–9
    feature-type leads, 7
    guidelines, 188, 200–202
    investigative series, 217–18
    leads, 137
    long, 202–9
    news, 140, 186, 195–96
    series, 109–18
    short, 204
    story ideas, 196–200
    tone and style, 193–94, 201, 232
Feelings, 378, 383–85, 397
    guidelines, 384–85
Felonies
    court process, 461
    types of, 428
Feminist movement, 304
Films, 306
Filtering, 35–37

"Filthy Words Case," 615
Fire stories, 6–7, 39, 63, 449–52
    broadcast, 8
    sources, 450
    story essentials, 450
First Amendment, 266, 360, 468, 476, 503, 569, 582, 583, 586, 587, 588, 591, 592, 596, 597, 599, 601, 602, 603, 605, 615, 622, 625, 649
Firsthand observation, 34–36, 245, 248, 255, 264, 325, 355
First-person stories, 202
Five W's and an H, 120, 152
Florida, 442, 503, 569, 571, 578, 588, 601
Focus, 33
Focus groups, 254
Follow-up stories, 5, 13, 340
Folo stories, 13, 257, 535, 681
    leads, 148–49
Forecasts, 397
Form 990, 526
Fourteenth Amendment, 597
France, 111, 296
Freedom of Information Act (FOIA), 90–91, 309, 381, 674–76
Freedom of speech and the press, 266, 360, 468, 476, 503, 569, 582, 583, 586, 587, 588, 591, 592, 596, 597, 599, 601, 602, 603, 605, 615, 622, 625, 649
    campus press freedom, 599–600
Front page, 23, 264
Front page journalism, 187
Futures book, 79, 681

G

Gag leads, 135
Gazettes, 55, 515
General assignment reporting, 21, 26
Geography, 303
George Polk award, 74, 262, 286
Georgia, 571, 578, 594, 626
Glossaries, 77, 479–81
    broadcast terms, 683–84
    business terms, 537
    court terms, 479–81
    print terms, 680–83
Gobbledygook, 160
Gossip, 590
Government databases, 84–85, 100
Government reporting, 26, 308, 539–64, 579
    bond stories, 539, 559–60
    budget stories, 539, 540, 552–57
        budget process, 555
        politics, 557
        school funding, 565, 573–75
        sources, 556
        story essentials, 555
        types of budgets, 554
    cautions, 556–57

city government activities, 539–40, 544
city planning and zoning stories, 539, 540, 563–64
education issues, 545, 571, 573
forms of local government, 540–42
guidelines for investigating, 562
local economy, 544–45
participants in the political process, 543–44
political campaign stories, 539, 549–51
    key elements, 549
    tips on covering, 550
property tax and reassessment stories, 539, 557–59, 573
sources, 556
Grammar, 163–64, 227, 359, 662–69
    agreement, 662–63
    clichés, 53, 229, 488, 490, 667
    dangling modifiers, 663
    jargon, 149, 160, 520, 535, 667
    misplaced words, 663–64
    parallel structure, 167, 664
    pronouns, 163, 166, 664–65
    redundancy, 53, 265, 668–69
    sentence fragments, 665
    sequence of tenses, 665–66
    spelling, 34, 78, 154, 162–63, 247, 270, 317, 666–67, 683
    usage, 667
    wordiness, 668
Grand juries, 454, 460, 477–78, 480, 600, 603
"Grass eaters," 443
Greenwich, Conn., 558
Guatemala, 170
Guidelines
    balance, 47
    beats, 400
    broadcast interviewing, 233
    broadcast writing, 239
    business reporting, 535
    confidential sources, 362–63
    fairness, 45
    features, 188, 200–202
    feelings, 384–85
    government investigations, 562
    journalistic, 44
    leads, 150–51
    leaked material, 313–14
    libel and privacy suits, 595–96, 601–2
    listening, 356
    news, 58
    photojournalism, 617–18
    political campaigns, 550
    polls, 670
    privacy, 594
    reporting, 270
    selecting relevant facts, 273

speeches, news conferences and
panel discussions, 377
taste, 608
writing, 157

H

Handbills, 57
Hard news stories, 67, 188, 681
leads, 134
pegs, 160
Hartford, Conn., 569
Hawaii, 571, 578
Headlines, 26, 67, 176, 264
Herd journalism, 272
Hidden cameras/microphones,
594–95, 601
Hierarchy of credibility, 312
History, 303
Hoaxes, 311–12, 359, 595
Homosexuality, 71, 108, 354, 389, 390,
569, 611–12, 613, 651
Honesty, 4, 45, 46
Hoohah section, 206
"Horse race" reporting, 550
Hot news, 591
How, 120, 152, 266, 268, 270, 450, 485,
550, 577, 578
Hudson, N.Y., 518
Human interest, 33, 51–52, 152, 157,
158, 169, 174–75, 281, 407, 519,
531, 535
leads, 520
in obituaries, 415
Human sources, 33, 169, 306, 307–14,
317, 318, 322, 325, 521
Humor, 196, 421, 478
Hunches, 275, 365, 378–83, 397
Hypocrisy, 610

I

Idaho, 442
Ideas, story, 28–29, 196–200, 472–76
Identification, 337, 367, 374, 399, 402,
438, 441, 457
Ideology, 67–68
Illinois, 476, 601
Illustrations, 203
Impact, 55, 59, 248
Indecency, 612
Independence, 68
Indiana, 569, 571, 578
Indianapolis, 443
Indictment, 460, 463, 480
Indirect Observation, 34
Individuality, 276–77
Infant mortality rates, 87–88, 100–101
Inference, 267, 272, 595–96
Information gathering, 145–70, 271, 308
Injuries, 275, 492
Inside pages, 24

Interest groups, 539, 543, 556
Interjections, 163
Internet, 81–83, 108
Interpretative reporting, 17, 245, 248,
266, 267–68, 422, 471
Interviewing, 16–17, 82, 203, 323,
324–65
appearance and behavior, 348–49
broadcasting, 363–65
guidelines, 233
ground rules, 328–29
guidelines, 345–46, 359, 362–63
hidden cameras/microphones,
594–95, 601
listening, 341–42, 350–53, 356–57
making sources open up, 340–41
news, 324, 329–30
"no comment," 342–43
note-taking, 357
observing, 355–56
practices, 347–65
listening, 345, 350–53, 356
role-playing, 349–53
preparation, 336, 338, 347–48, 494
principles, 324–46
profiles, 324, 330–36
questions
asking, 336–40
assumed-truth, 354
direct, 338
embarrassing, 345
open- and closed-ended, 338–39
sensitive, 353–54
talk-inducing, 490
tough, 339–40, 345, 354–55
treading water, 346
quotations, using and abusing,
359–61
role-playing, 349–50, 353
taping, 358
types of, 326
Intrusion, 593, 595, 601, 621
Intuition, 274, 378–83, 397
Inverted pyramid, 124
Investigative reporting, 10–11, 217–18,
245, 260–63, 309, 342, 354, 422, 499,
562, 583, 595, 681
Involvement, problems of, 289–91
Iowa, 571

J

Japan, 305
Jargon, 149, 160, 520, 535, 667
Joint operating agreements, 69
Journalism
activist, 625–33
adversary, 644–45
advocacy, 74
anticipatory, 304–5
computer-assisted, 84–87, 100
education, 301, 303

ethics, 4, 240, 283, 341, 353, 478,
581, 595, 620–48
altering photographs, 637
codes of conduct, 623–24,
632–34, 636, 642, 646–47,
677–79
limitations of, 623–24
moral framework, 263, 641
naming victims, 594, 636–37,
638–39
plagiarism and fabrication,
642–43
poses and disguises, 601,
635–36, 640, 642
explanatory, 267
front page journalism, 187
herd journalism, 272
interpretative, 17, 245, 248, 266,
267–68, 422, 471
minority hiring, 391
New, 174, 178
obstacles to, 280, 281
on-line, 81, 99, 101–7
pack, 272
print vs. broadcast, 63, 139, 202, 220
public service, 57, 260, 305, 396, 629
reporter's rights, 596–603
salaries for business reporters, 527
statistics, 484
tools of 76, 116
Yellow, 187
Journalistic guidelines, 44
Journalists, 3–30
attire, 348–49
beats, 26, 50, 62, 70–72, 309–10,
399, 680
characteristics, 3, 4, 19–21
equation, 280
feelings, 378, 383–85, 397
guidelines, 384–85
general assignment, 21, 26
hunches, 275, 365, 378–83, 397
intuition, 274, 378–83, 397
math skills, 76, 92–99
minorities, 391–92
rights, 596–603
as stenographers, 551–52, 625
Judges, 476–77
Judgment, 42, 45–46, 71, 123, 267,
277, 283
Jumps, 218
Juries, 597–98, 601
selection, 463
Jury consultants, 464
Juvenile crime, 424, 447, 448, 475–76,
545, 547
rates, 423

K

Kansas, 589
Kentucky, 578, 584, 590

Pressure groups, 539, 543, 556
Pretrials, 598–99
    motions, 463
Price-earnings ratio, 536
Print vs. broadcast news, 63, 139, 202, 220
Privacy, 91, 283, 476, 581, 582, 592–95,
    597, 601, 618, 621, 636, 637
    avoiding lawsuits, 595–96, 601–2
    categories of, 593
    guidelines, 594
    reporter's rights, 596–603
Privileged information, 582, 583, 590
    absolute/conditional/qualified,
        590–91
    neutral reporting, 591
Profanity, 604, 608, 609, 610, 612
    broadcasting standards, 240, 614–16
Profiles, 357, 422, 472
    interviews, 324, 326, 330–36
    story essentials, 330
Prominence, 55, 59, 402, 404, 417,
    433, 604
Pronouncers, 230
Pronouns, 163, 166, 664–65
Property tax stories, 554, 557–58, 573
Prose, purple, 160
Prospectus, 529
Proximity, 55, 60, 402
Proxy statements, 524, 526
Pseudo-events, 251–52, 255, 624
Pseudo-sources, 308
Public figures, 588
Public interest, 542–43, 596, 624
Publicity, 593, 598
Publicity handouts, 68, 245, 248, 264,
    530, 550, 681
Public journalism, 72
Public officials, 589
Public opinion, 67, 76
Public records, 35, 41, 47, 89–91, 298,
    524, 526–28, 582
Public relations, 247, 254, 255
Public service advertising, 606
Public service journalism, 57, 260, 305,
    396, 581, 629
Publishers, 645–46
Puff pieces, 519
Pulitzer Prizes, 12, 44, 84, 86, 90, 140,
    142, 166, 188, 194, 197, 260, 264,
    276, 279, 322, 414, 499, 500, 624,
    628, 643
Punctuation, 78, 163, 164, 227,
    657–61, 683
Punitive damages, 592
Purple prose, 160

Q

Qualified privilege, 590
Question and answer period, 367, 375
Questions, 347
    asking, 336–40

assumed-truth, 354
closed-ended, 338
direct, 338
embarrassing, 345
off the record, 40, 358–59, 369, 682
on the record, 39, 40
open-ended, 338
sensitive, 353–54
talk-inducing, 490
tough, 339–40, 345, 354–55
treading water, 346
Quotations, 33, 77, 152, 157, 169,
    172–74, 201, 203, 330, 344, 357, 358,
    367, 371, 372, 450, 630, 682
    altering, 602
    in broadcast writing, 227
    direct, 38, 150, 661
    exact, 361
    paraphrasing, 172–73, 201, 227,
        360, 372
    quotation marks, 661
Quote leads, 135, 369

R

Race and racism, 385–86, 390–91,
    443–44, 483, 569, 584, 626–29,
    639–40, 653
Radio, 59
Random sample, 112
Rape, 85, 258–59, 434, 441, 442, 445,
    594, 612
Rapport, 325
Rap sheet, 439
Rates, 94, 96, 520, 545
    AIDS, 89
    campus crime, 445–46
    cities, 458–59
    crime, 423–25, 428
    death, 97
    drug arrests, 431
    education, 571–72
    infant mortality, 87–88, 100–101
    juvenile crime, 423
    murder, 94, 97–98, 439, 547
    rape, 442, 445
    sentencing, 474–75
Readability, 147, 149–50, 151, 165
Readers/viewers/listeners, 66–67,
    153, 268, 271, 274, 356, 483, 539,
    605, 671
Reading, 29, 179–81, 197–98, 303, 494
    recommended books, 30, 53, 75,
        116, 129, 151, 184–85, 218–19,
        241–42, 270, 292, 305, 323, 346,
        366, 397, 421, 452, 482, 514,
        537–38, 579, 603, 648
    recommended journals for the
        business beat, 526–27
Records
    arrest, 314, 431, 433, 437
    court, 472

federal, 524, 526
public, 35, 41, 47, 89–91, 298, 524,
    526–28, 582
Redling, 85, 207–9, 564
Redundancy, 53, 265, 668–69
Reference books, 76, 78, 527
Relevance, 45, 271, 340
Religion, 385–86, 390–91, 653
    news, 70–71, 155
Reporters, 3–30
    attire, 348–49
    beats, 26, 50, 62, 70–72, 309–10,
        399, 680
    characteristics, 3, 4,19–21
    equation, 280
    feelings, 378, 383–85, 397
    general assignment, 21, 26
    hunches, 275, 365, 378–83, 397
    intuition, 274, 378–83, 397
    math skills, 76, 92–99
    minorities, 391–92
    rights, 596–603
    as stenographers, 551–52, 625
Reporting
    broadcast, 230–38
    by telephone, 68, 76, 77, 79, 265,
        318, 400, 491, 601
    computer-assisted, 84, 100
    explanatory, 267
    guidelines, 270
    interpretative, 17, 245, 248, 266,
        267–68, 422, 471
    investigative, 10–11, 245, 260–63,
        309, 342, 354, 422, 499, 562,
        583, 595, 681
    Layer I, 247–51, 257, 263, 268, 281,
        343, 394, 396
        dangers of, 254–55
    Layer II, 248, 251, 253, 256–66,
        268, 395
    Layer III, 248, 266–68
    neutral, 591
    obstacles to, 280, 281
    on-line, 81, 99, 101–7
    print vs. broadcast, 64, 139,
        202, 220
    process, 269
    reporter's rights, 596–603
Reportorial enterprise, 245, 248,
    319–22, 528–29
Resolutions, 540
Responsibility, 52, 624, 645–46, 677
Retractions, 595
Revenue, 534, 535, 537
Revenue bonds, 559
Reverse directories, 78
Rewrites, 68, 181, 221–26, 682
Rhode Island, 578
Rhythm, 166, 220
Richmond, Va., 584
Robbery stories, 441

"Rodriguez Law," 267
Role-playing, 349–53
Roundup leads, 143
Rwanda, 11–12, 140, 616

S

Said, 161–62
Salt Lake City, 570
San Francisco, 525
Satire, 615
Schedule, 24–25
Scholastic Aptitude Test (SAT), 503, 508, 545, 566, 572, 575, 578
Scripts, examples of 207–9, 222, 223, 224, 226, 231–32, 235–38, 505
Second-day leads, 417–18
Secondhand observation, 34–37, 41
Segregation, 569, 584
Selectivity, 50–51
Selma, Ala., 584
Sensationalism, 621
Sensitivity, 391–92
Sentences
    compound, 148
    fragments, 665
    length, 51, 145, 152, 165, 194
        broadcast writing, 148, 230
    structure
        broadcast writing, 226–28, 241
        parallel, 167
        S-V-O, 130, 144–46, 150, 151, 180
Sentencing, 469–70
    rates, 474–75
Serial bonds, 559
Series, 64, 186, 193, 209–18, 258, 264, 286, 384, 444, 498, 548, 612, 631
    investigative, 217–18, 499, 563
Sexism, 388–89, 417
Sexuality, 17, 108, 354, 389, 390, 567, 606, 611, 612
Shadow reality, 386–87
Shield laws, 310, 600, 603
Shopping malls, 64, 72
Short-circuited responses, 385
Shotgun leads, 135
Sidebars, 186, 203, 683
Sigma Delta Chi award, 44
Similes, 47, 229
Single-element leads, 144, 151
Single-element stories, 119–21
    structure, 121
Situational ethics, 633
Sixth Amendment, 597, 598, 599
Skepticism, 279, 349, 516, 520, 530
Slander, 583
Slug, 25, 230, 238, 365, 682, 683
Smoking, 64–65, 94, 315–16, 394, 410, 419
Somalia, 75, 240, 616
Sound bite, 238, 240

Sources, 33, 79, 152, 201, 306–23, 596, 683
    accident stories, 403, 404
    budget stories, 556
    business reporting, 521–24
    civil law stories, 457
    criminal law stories, 470
    disaster stories, 406
    fire stories, 450
    human, 33, 169, 306, 307–14, 317, 318, 322, 521
        anonymous, 40, 362, 600
        authoritative, 35, 171, 401
        confidential, 310, 325, 359, 362, 369, 597, 600, 603
    local government reporting, 556
    obituaries, 413
    physical, 33, 169, 269, 306, 314–17, 318, 322, 325, 524
        census data, 76, 83, 85, 86–87, 314
        computers, 76, 77, 85, 99, 382
        databases, 14, 76, 82, 83–89, 99, 314
    police reporting, 435
    pseudo, 308
    reliability, 310–13
    sports reporting, 487
South Carolina, 571, 578
Southampton, N.Y., 569
Speeches, 245, 248, 550
    guidelines for covering, 377
Speech stories, 171, 367–69
    story essentials, 368
Spelling, 34, 78, 154, 162–63, 247, 270, 317, 666–67, 683
Sports reporting, 309–10, 483–514
    coverage preparation, 495
    deadlines, 495
    game stories, 483
        leads, 488, 492–93
        story essentials, 492
    high school athletics, 490–92
    illegal and improper activities, 483, 498–509
    most penalized universities, 503
    objectivity, 487–88, 497–98, 501
    profiles, 483
    sources, 487
    statistics, 492, 495–96
    story essentials, 483, 491
    women, 484, 511–12
Spot news stories, 121, 186, 271
St. Louis, 206
St. Paul, Minn., 600
Stalking horse, 550
Statements, 38, 248
Statistics, 535
Stereotypes, 290, 378, 385, 386–89
    racial and religious, 390–91
Stock tables, 536

Stories
    accidents, 401–4, 407, 422
        airplanes, 403–4
        motor vehicle, 401–3
    arrest, 433–37
    breaking news, 28, 29
    business, 515–38
    campus crime, 445–46
    courts, 26, 45, 308, 453–82
        civil, 453, 455–58
        criminal, 453, 458–70
    developing ideas, 28–29, 196–98
    disasters, 20, 404–7
    enterprise, 28, 487, 528–29, 681
    features, 33, 56, 67, 186–202, 204, 681
    fire, 6–7, 39, 449–52
    first-person, 202
    follow-ups, 5, 13, 340
    folo, 13, 257
    hard news, 67, 188, 681
    limitations, 280
    local government, 26, 308, 539–64, 579
    long, 186, 202–9
    meetings, 367, 369–72
    miniprofiles, 333
    multiple-element, 122–23
    murder, 438–40
    news, 33, 186, 274
    news conferences, 367, 372–76
    obituaries, 117, 187, 308, 394, 395, 399, 408–21
    panel discussions, 376–77
    profiles, 330, 422, 472
    religion, 70–71, 155
    series, 64, 186, 193, 209–18, 258, 264, 286, 384, 444, 498, 548, 612
        investigative, 217–18, 499, 563
    single-element, 119–21
    speech, 171, 367–69
    sports, 309–10, 483–514
    spot news, 121, 186, 188, 271
    tell, 220, 221
    three-element, 123
    trial, 465–69
    two-element, 122
    types, 28
    weather, 71–72, 303
Story components, 33–53, 169
    accuracy, 3, 21, 33–37, 40, 47, 53, 116, 149, 152, 154, 158, 159–62, 201, 264, 269, 328, 365, 386, 412, 582, 677, 678
    attribution, 33, 38, 39, 41, 53, 254, 403
    balance, 33, 42, 44, 45, 46–47, 201
    brevity, 33, 50, 51, 53
    fairness, 33, 45–46, 47, 53, 201, 328, 441, 582, 627, 677, 678
    focus, 33

objectivity, 33, 49, 53, 75, 177, 201, 310, 677, 678
verification, 33, 34, 41–45, 52, 245, 248, 251, 256, 279, 403, 418, 595
Story essentials, 126–27, 169, 171–77, 399
  accidents
    airplane, 403–4
    motor vehicle, 402–3
  arraignments, 459
  arrests, 438, 441
  budgets, 555
  burglary and robbery, 441
  civil action, 457
  criminal trials, 470
  disasters, 405–6
  earnings and annual reports, 535
  education
    new education programs, 578
    school board meetings, 577–78
  fires, 450
  leads, 147
  meetings, 370
  murder, 438
  news conference, 374
  obituaries, 408, 412
  profiles, 330
  speech stories, 368
  sports, 483, 491
    game stories, 492
Story ideas, 28–29
  features, 196–200
Story rudiments, 152
Story structure, 117–29, 152, 274
  inverted pyramid, 124
  single-element, 121
Storytelling form, 125
Strawman, 550
Straw poll, 110
Stringers, 490, 683
Style, 169, 175–78, 184, 186, 281, 683
  appropriate, 159, 175–76
  features, 193–94
Stylebooks, 45, 78, 385, 649–61, 683
Suburbs, 557
Sudbury, Ont., 34
Suicide, 74, 351
Summaries, 124, 173
Summary leads, 144, 376
Sunshine laws, 90, 600
Super Bowl, 484
Surveys, 109
Survivors, 408, 412, 419
S-V-O sentence structure, 130, 144–46, 150, 151, 180
  in broadcast writing, 226, 241

T

Tabloid newspapers, 68
Talk-inducing questions, 490
Tape recorders, 76, 77, 358
  in secret, 594–95, 601

Taste, 65, 159, 169, 175–78, 340, 581, 604–19
  broadcast reporting, 240, 614–16
  censorship, 611
  context, 604, 606–9
  guidelines, 608
  nature of the audience, 604
  photojournalism, 609, 616–19
  prominence, 604
  in relation to time, 606–7
Technical instructions, 238
Tecumseh Street (Toledo, Ohio), 211–14, 353
Teenage pregnancy, 133–34
Telegraph, 56, 76
Telephone
  directories, 41, 78, 80, 270, 448, 683
  numbers, 13, 41, 99, 246
  reporting by, 68, 76, 77, 79, 265, 318, 400, 491, 601
Tell stories, 220, 221
10-Ks, 524, 526
10-Qs, 526, 534–35
Tennessee, 578, 584
Tenses, 665–66
  in broadcast writing, 227–28
Term bonds, 559
Test scores, 572, 575–76, 578
  American College Testing (ACT), 545, 578
  Scholastic Aptitude Test (SAT), 503, 508, 545, 566, 572, 575, 578
Texas, 423, 567, 569, 570, 573, 578
Textbooks, 386, 567–68
Themes, 271, 275–76
Thirdhand observation, 36–37, 41
Three-element stories, 123
Three W's, 57
Time, 147, 167, 281, 374, 399, 401, 402, 403, 408, 412, 438, 441, 655
  in relation to taste, 606–7, 608–9
Time copy 591–92
Timeliness, 55, 58
Tips, 9, 309, 425, 562, 683
Titles, 227, 655–57
Tobacco, 64–65, 94, 315–16, 394, 410, 419
Tone (in features), 193–94, 201, 232
Tools of journalism, 76–116
"Touting," 536
Transitions, 152, 165–67
Trespassing, 593
Trial balloons, 40, 254, 313
Trial stories, 465–69
Truth, 19, 33, 40, 41, 44, 280, 281, 582, 609, 628
Two-element stories, 122

U

University bonds, 530
Unobtrusive observation, 271, 282–83
Unusual, 368, 403

V

Verbs, 126, 132, 145, 148, 150, 151, 157, 163, 183, 227
Verification, 33, 34, 41–45, 52, 245, 248, 251, 256, 279, 403, 418, 595, 683
  techniques, 42
Vermont, 438, 578
Veterans, 74, 198–200
Victims, 317, 351, 402, 403, 405, 422, 423, 426, 434–35, 438, 441, 447, 594, 612
  referring to them by name, 594, 636–37, 638–39
Video press release, 240
Vietnam, 35, 49, 57, 198–99, 276–77, 315, 378, 609
Viewers/listeners/readers, 66–67, 153, 268, 271, 274, 356, 483, 539, 605, 671
Virginia, 566, 589, 598
Vital statistics, 47, 314, 408
Vocabulary, 296
Voice-over videotape, 224–25, 232
Vulgarity, 65, 604, 607, 610
  broadcasting standards, 240, 614–16

W

Warnings, 41, 113, 159, 266, 658, 659
  accident stories, 403, 404
  court stories, 454, 455, 457–58
  crime stories, 434, 448–49
  delayed leads, 142
  disaster stories, 407
  government stories, 556–57
  libel, 590, 591
  long stories, 205
Warrentown, W. Va., 268
Washington, 601
Washington, D.C., 11, 94, 339, 423, 442, 474, 623, 636
Weather news, 71–72, 303
West Virginia, 476, 578
What, 120, 132, 134, 136, 145, 152, 266, 346, 368, 377, 485, 531, 550, 551
When, 120, 152, 450, 492
Where, 120, 152, 270, 450, 492, 550
Whistle-blowers, 309, 313, 362
Who, 120, 132, 134, 136, 145, 152, 270, 368, 438, 450, 529, 531, 578
Why, 120, 152, 266, 346, 268, 365, 393, 485, 522, 529
Wire service defense, 601
Wire services, 77, 220, 581, 683
Wisconsin, 442, 569, 571
Words, 45, 47, 51, 144, 153, 160, 491, 663, 668
  broadcast, 220, 226–28, 683–84
  business, 537
  court, 479–81
  explicit/offensive, 608, 613–14
  misplaced, 663–64